The Bomb

South Africa's Nuclear Weapons Programme

Nic von Wielligh
Lydia von Wielligh-Steyn

LITERA

Published by Litera Publications
PO Box 14690
Hatfield, Pretoria, 0028
theresap@litera.co.za
www.litera.co.za
Copyright © 2015 Authors

All rights reserved. No part of this book may be reproduced or transmitted in any form or by any means, electronic or mechanical, including photocopying, recording, microfilming or any information storage or retrieval system, without permission in writing from the publisher.

Originally published in Afrikaans as *Die Bom: Suid-Afrika se kernwapenprogram* by Litera Publikasies 2014.
First English edition, first printing 2015

ISBN 978-1-920188-48-1

Cover design: Tienie du Plessis
Cover photograph: USA Operation Nougat
                      Test: Truckee, 9 June 1962
                      Area: Christmas Island
                      Air-launched, 210 kilotons of TNT
Translation: Sandra Mills

Prior to publication the publisher made every reasonable effort to obtain permission for the limited use of photographs and quotations from other sources. Correspondence in this regard can be directed to the publisher, who will place suitable acknowledgements in any subsequent reprints.

Layout and typesetting by Jigsaw Graphic Design, Pretoria
Set in 11 on 13.5 pt Minion Pro
Printed and bound by Paarl Media, Paarl

The publication of the English edition was made possible by support from the Institute for Security Studies, through a generous financial contribution from the Government of Norway.

Contents

FOREWORD	i
PREFACE	v
ACRONYMS AND ABBREVIATIONS	viii
PROLOGUE	xiv

Part 1	**1**
25 CENTURIES FROM ABDERA TO HIROSHIMA	3
THE ATOM HAS A STORY OF ITS OWN …	3
Stereotypes	3
Holy curiosity	3
A long history	4
Of apples and planets	5
Faraday, Maxwell and the Cavendish Laboratory	6
The Republic of Science	7
Joseph John Thomson	8
Ernest Rutherford	8
Exhilarating decades	11
After 2 500 years, a workable model of the atom	12
Things get more complex	13
Neutron bombardment	14
A detour to Switzerland	14
How much more damage?	16
Neutron bombardment continues	17
Multiplication	18
Isotope separation	20
Bellicose atoms	21
The spadework	21
Bat bombs	24
Behind the scenes in Britain	24
The necessary spark	26
From theory to practice	26

The momentum builds up	29
Plutonium	32
Basic nuclear weapons design	33
Criticality and critical mass	36
Dilemma	38
A physics experiment becomes a political cudgel	39
Did the nuclear bombs force Japan to surrender?	42
The death throes of the Manhattan Project	44
A time to reap	45
What did the Germans achieve?	47
Soviet moles	48
The Soviet Union catches up with the USA	51
Scaling up	53
"With the bloody Union Jack on top of it …"	56
Another consequence of the Quebec Agreement	57
France, the fourth country with the *force de frappe*	59
China, the fifth nuclear power	62

Part 2   65
ATOMS IN THE SERVICE OF PEACE (OR HOW TO TAME A MONSTER)   67

A very old story	67
Peaceful applications – a possibility?	69
"Good" and "bad" electricity	70
Heir presumptive of a remarkable family; wars and peacekeeping bodies	71
A delicate balancing act	73
The general triumphs in the talking shop	74
How altruistic were Eisenhower's plans?	77
Birth pangs	79
Pronouncements at the First Geneva Conference	80
What are safeguards?	82
Were the safeguards adequate?	84
Back to the drawing board: the design of comprehensive safeguards agreements	87
IAEA inspections	88
Smiling Buddha, and the cat is set among the pigeons	90

India's hostile neighbours	90
Chain reaction of another kind	92
How do the Zangger Committee and the Nuclear Suppliers Group operate?	93
International control over the proliferation of nuclear weapons	94

Part 3   95
THE BOMB IN THE BUSHVELD   97

EARLY BEGINNINGS	97
The home-grown product	97
Ampie Roux	98
Wally Grant	99
The father of South Africa's nuclear weapons	100
Wynand de Villiers brings a souvenir home	101
"Let's get down to work"	102
Tragedy on the farm Pelindaba	102
The heart of Pelindaba	104
The Safari-1 reactor	106
A difficult choice	110
Northern Tyres and Accessories – what the façade concealed	112
UF_6 and hydrogen	114
Separative work	116
FLEXING THEIR MUSCLES	117
John Vorster's announcement of 20 July 1970	120
ISOLATION AND RESOURCEFULNESS	123
Criticism	123
Wooing the Germans	124
The Y-plant	126
Technical aspects	126
Courage in action	128
A love-hate relationship	130
Indian breach of faith affects South Africa	131
A more aggressive approach	133
SPIED ON AND SHUNNED	134
Progress	134
Nuclear devices and nuclear weapons	135
Dirty work in the desert	136
What the spooks in the USA thought	142

How did the Soviet Union know where to look?	143
Another Trojan horse?	146
Further interference by the Americans	147
In case of need	149
MYSTERIOUS INCIDENT NO. 747 OF 22 SEPTEMBER 1979	150
Plutonium for the crocodiles	150
Vela 6911 registers a double flash	151
Double flashes and bhangmeters	152
Search for the truth	155
If it was a weapons test, who did the testing?	157
Vela postscript – a ghost from the past	160
Jonathan Jay Pollard	161
ARMSCOR STEPS UP	164
The Kentron Circle facility	166
The programme makes headway	170
Nuclear weapons	174
The Gouriqua project: materials for sophisticated devices	174
Ad hoc cabinet committee: September 1985	176
Overview of the most important UNSC resolutions	178
The RSA missile series	184
Missiles and South Africa's interest in them	184
Further reflections on Project Festival	187
The requirements of the South African Defence Force	189
Status in September 1987	190
ELSEWHERE ON THE FARM	193
Koeberg, the Z-plant and Beva	193
Koeberg nuclear power plant	196
More "sabotage" – of a kind that casts a long, dark shadow	199
The Z- and U-plants and Beva	200
Eskom's PBMR	205

Part 4 — 207
THE END OF AN ERA — 209

Butterflies and chaos	209
The butterfly in the USSR	209
The new broom	213
The "Mantel" Project	216
Nuclear weaponry command and control procedures	218

The dismantlement process	222
Chuck Norris to the rescue	223
The destruction of documentation	224
Saddam Hussein causes trouble	226
Unscom and the IAEA's action team	227
The Additional Protocol	229
Signing the NPT and the IAEA's Safeguards Agreement	230
The IAEA: organisation and legal rights	236
A game with new rules	237
The corpse with the dagger in its back	240
In search of the MUF	242
What is MUF?	242
Pale faces and furious blushes	245
Ballpoint pens to the rescue	246
Deep in the desert	247
Nuclear forensics	249
The pressure builds up	251
The 5000 building complex	255
A rough neighbourhood – and a surprise announcement	258
Putting things in perspective	261
Prelude to 23 March 1993	263
Resuscitating the CCI	267
A Russian bomb-maker takes the wheel	269
The remainder of that chaotic year: 1993	269
A magical substance	272
A spectacular affair	275
An interesting visit	275
An African bomb?	278
Jorge Risquet Valdés	281

Part 5 — 283
COOPERATION BETWEEN ISRAEL AND SOUTH AFRICA — 285

The Israeli nuclear programme	285
Christian convert/successful spy	289
Strange bedfellows – the Jewish parallel	291
Operation Tea Leaves	294
The end of the friendship	299

Part 6   303
FROM POLECAT TO MODEL CITIZEN   305
A modern Aeolus   305
Harold Macmillan and the biggest ever Western nuclear disaster   307
The last decade of the 20th century   309
South Africa in the non-proliferation arena   311
Theft and an application for membership of the NSG   314
South Africa's missile programme and the MTCR   316
Distress on the other side of the Atlantic   317
Bankrolling demolition   320
The big prize – membership of the MTCR   321
A spectacular debut in New York   322
The NAM – "a broad church"   323
A new man on the scene   334
Interlude in Iraq   337
An unworthy end to a career   339

Part 7   341
A SOUTH AFRICAN STALL IN KHAN'S ATOMIC BAZAAR   343
The UNSC   343
Gernot Zippe's legacy   344
In the land of cheese and windmills   345
Two Germans and a South African   349
Friends, butter factories and skulduggery   352
Espionage and letter bombs   352
The tide turns against Pakistan   354
An impending threat and missile systems   355
India and Israel   355
The other Khan works behind the scenes   358
Indian and Pakistani nuclear tests   358
A party with an agenda   360
Gaddafi's dream, Khan's contract   362
The nuclear smugglers fall into a snare   364
The dominoes fall   365
The second domino   367
Names mentioned in the Malaysian press release   367
Arrests in Switzerland, Germany, Turkey and the Netherlands   368

How did the Americans and the British know about the cargo on board the *BBC China*?	369
The Tinners	371
Paid for but not delivered – the focus shifts	372
A visit to Tradefin in Vanderbijlpark and further arrests	373
Fact or fiction?	380
Meyer provides the nails for the coffin	382
The case	386
Lerch's fate	388
Did A.Q. Khan do the unthinkable?	388

Part 8   391
A MURKY CRYSTAL BALL   393

Deterrent or miracle?	393
The Cuban missile crisis of 1962 and the man who saved the world	399
The faceless enemy	405
War can get dirty	408
The world has changed	410
"Global (no?) zero"	410
Nuclear weapons: states that have them and those that want them	412
Unholy curiosity	419
International treaties and disarmament	421
Black swans and nuclear power	423
The Fukushima disaster	424
Nuclear energy, green energy and the German experiment	430
And South Africa?	434

GLOSSARY   439

BIBLIOGRAPHY   451

APPENDIX   459

INDEX   515

Foreword

Nic von Wielligh and I go back a long way. We were closely associated during the dismantling of South Africa's nuclear capability in the early 1990s and subsequent accession to the Nuclear Non-Proliferation Treaty (NPT) of the United Nations. I have always found Nic to be an extremely precise and professional person who strives to uphold high ethical standards in everything he does. This is amply illustrated by the following incident:

After South Africa signed the NPT on 10 July 1991, the country was given eighteen months to enter into a comprehensive safeguards agreement with the International Atomic Energy Agency (IAEA) in Vienna. Within two months of the conclusion of this agreement a so-called Initial Report on all nuclear material and nuclear facilities which fell within the safeguards had to be submitted. This inventory is an extremely important document, since the subsequent credibility of the member country is measured by the extent of its disclosure of its nuclear activities. This was by no means a simple task for the then Atomic Energy Corporation (AEC), because the inventory had to cover far more than the billets of highly enriched uranium under safeguards in a vault at Pelindaba. There were literally hundreds of smaller quantities of uranium stored in various degrees of enrichment and various chemical forms in all the test loops and in many laboratories, even on filters and in cylinders. The mass of every quantity of uranium, its degree of enrichment, form and position had to be defined as far as possible for the purpose of subsequent verification by the IAEA inspectors.

Understandably Nic pleaded that we should use the full eighteen months' grace before signing the comprehensive safeguards agreement to give him and his team sufficient time to compile this inventory. However, South Africa was under enormous political pressure to "prove" its credibility to the international community. The country had to be able to demonstrate that it was serious in its bid to accede to the NPT and not, like North Korea and Iraq at that time, "playing games" while continuing behind the scenes with illicit nuclear activities that fell outside the provisions of the NPT. My answer was therefore: "Sorry, Nic, this is the position: State President F.W. de Klerk's orders are that South Africa must strive for maximum acceptance by the international community in its entry into the NPT. We will probably sign the IAEA's safeguards agreement shortly, in September 1991, at the General

Conference of the IAEA's member countries in Vienna." That meant South Africa's Initial Report on nuclear material and facilities had to be submitted to the IAEA before November 1991. Nic shook his head and said: "That is completely impossible!"

Nevertheless, Nic rose to the occasion. He and his team plunged in headlong and began working virtually round the clock. Towards the end of October 1991 the initial inventory was submitted to the IAEA. For many years afterwards (and quite possibly to this day) the IAEA acknowledged that "South Africa's Initial Report of Nuclear Materials to be placed under safeguards was the most professional and complete declaration within the IAEA to date".

The safeguards agreement with the IAEA was signed in Vienna on 16 September 1991 by the then South African ambassador, Cecile Schmidt, and the then Director-General of the IAEA, Dr Hans Blix – 30 minutes before the commencement of the General Conference of all the IAEA member countries. Dr Blix's opening speech began as follows: "Ladies and gentlemen, I am very pleased to announce that South Africa has signed the Comprehensive Safeguards Agreement with the IAEA this morning." There was consternation among the thousand or so delegates. South Africa was still the "polecat" of the world and its accession to the NPT was greeted with great scepticism. Understandably, on the last day of the five-day conference a special resolution was adopted to instruct the IAEA "to determine the correctness and completeness of South Africa's Initial Report of Nuclear Materials and Facilities and report back to the General Conference". This resolution was superfluous, because correctness and completeness had to be determined under the safeguards agreement in any case, but for understandable reasons South Africa was being treated as a special case. South Africa's credibility was internationally acknowledged by "the acceptance of South Africa's Initial Report of Nuclear Materials and Facilities" by the General Conference of the IAEA in September 1993 and by the UN General Assembly in November of the same year. This illustrates just how important that initial inventory was for South Africa.

While the story of South Africa's own nuclear capacity is presented in an accessible form in this book, I am certain that the text has been impeccably researched.

The first part of the story deals with the early technological stage from which humankind emerged by degrees until we acquired the knowledge to release the enormous forces that are locked up in the atom. The astonishing part about this is the way a jigsaw puzzle of knowledge was built from contributions from all over the world until an answer was found. This stage is one of diffusion of knowledge and it could not have been arrested even if we had wanted to do so. The human desire to explore and gain a better understanding of the universe which the Creator has put in our hands is simply too strong.

The next part deals with the "war-driven haste" with which the newfound technology was propelled towards full destructive maturity. One can only speculate on what would have happened to this knowledge had it not been for the Second World War. Would we have been better able to control the "genie that was let out of the bottle" and use it for the benefit of humankind?

The following stage was one of "international madness" during the Cold War, when by competing with each other the great powers built up the capacity to destroy every living creature on earth not once but ten times over! One can only shake one's head and wonder how we ever stooped so low. The authors then launch into a graphic description of the accompanying efforts to get the genie back into the bottle, first through Eisenhower's unsuccessful Atoms for Peace programme and shortly afterwards through the UN-initiated NPT, which divided the world into "haves" and "have nots". Although the NPT is one of the most divisive treaties of our time, and this division has even been entrenched in the veto in the Security Council of the UN possessed by the five "haves", the NPT is probably the most practical treaty that we, the guardians of this world, have been able to put together.

Meanwhile the diffusion of knowledge surged ahead. This story describes South Africa's troubled course, with its deep political undercurrents, in vivid but also personal detail. Would South Africa ever have gone this route had it not been for international isolation and our determination to "show them"? From my personal experience with the scientists at Pelindaba I am inclined to believe that we would not have. I base my conclusion on the strong principle embraced by the political leaders of that time that South Africa's nuclear devices would never be used as tactical weapons, even though the national security bodies of the time were inclined to move in that direction and had done the necessary spadework. The political leaders, and Mr P.W. Botha in particular, realised all too well that if South Africa made tactical use of its nuclear capability in Angola, our big cities would have been flattened within a few weeks.

The story as recorded here then moves to a stage of "drawing back from the verge of our own destruction". Mr F.W. de Klerk's opening remarks to a few ministers and officials whom he convened in September 1989, shortly after he assumed office as the new state president, were:

"In my term of office I am going to lead this country back to a position of an internationally respected member of the world community and this means two things: We are going to turn the political system round to a fully democratic system by unbanning the ANC and releasing Mr Nelson Mandela, and secondly we are going to dismantle our nuclear arsenal and accede to the NPT." From this broad vision his instructions to me were to "garner the maximum amount of international credibility from our accession to the NPT". It was a rocky road but at the end of it South Africa stood out as a model of transparency and even today our country is held up as the only example of a country that voluntarily dismantled an active nuclear capability and then joined the NPT as a non-nuclear-weapon state. The fact that the African nuclear treaty is internationally known as the "Pelindaba Treaty" is further evidence that our relationship with our neighbours on the continent, so troubled for many years, has been strengthened by South Africa's "story".

Will the world ever be able to put the destructive side to the "genie" back into the bottle and do without nuclear weapons, as the NPT envisages? This appears improbable at present, but it remains an aspiration to which everyone on this planet should look forward. Can we really continue indefinitely to pour so much of our planet's resources into something that will merely increase human misery? The enormous poverty which prevails requires us to wake up and heed the pleas of the Biblical prophets Isaiah, Joel and Micah to beat our swords into ploughshares.

If this almost monumental work by Nic von Wielligh and his daughter Lydia von Wielligh-Steyn can contribute to this vision of peace, all their hard work will be more than worthwhile. The two authors must be congratulated. This is truly the only comprehensive work so far on South Africa's share in this historic topic which has been turned into a readable account.

WALDO STUMPF
Professor of Metallurgic Engineering
University of Pretoria
26 June 2013

Preface

The Institute for Security Studies (ISS) is a leading African organisation which enhances human security to enable Africa's sustainable development and economic prosperity. Our mission is to inform a better understanding of Africa's peace and human security challenges, develop appropriate policies and strategies, and build sustainable capacity to ensure appropriate and effective responses that deliver safety and stability for Africans.

Ever since the ISS established its "Africa's Development and the Threat of Weapons of Mass Destruction Project" in May 2007, with funding from the Royal Norwegian Government, we have intended to fill the gap in the public's understanding of the development and subsequent dismantlement of South Africa's nuclear weapons programme. While a great deal has been written on this programme, in many of these accounts it is difficult to discern speculative analysis from evidential investigation.

Nic von Wielligh and his daughter Lydia von Wielligh-Steyn have now filled this gap with an "insider" account of the programme and have produced the most comprehensive and accurate account of the development and dismantlement of South Africa's nuclear weapons programme. The aim of "Africa's Development and the Threat of Weapons of Mass Destruction Project" within the broader ISS context is to enhance Africa's role in international efforts to support disarmament and non-proliferation in the context of Africa's developmental and security imperatives through the provision of primary research, policy formulation and implementation activities, by inter alia distributing information that will influence the formulation and implementation of disarmament and non-proliferation policies, activities and legislation at the national level in Africa and build African capacity to engage in relevant international forums.

As such the ISS is proud to be associated with Litera Publications and the publication of the English edition and updated version of this book. At the same time, the opinions expressed by the authors do not necessarily reflect those of the ISS, its trustees, members of the Advisory Council or donors.

From our viewpoint, *The Bomb* is important for two reasons. Firstly, it provides a South African, and indeed African, perspective on the history of the development of nuclear weapons internationally and their first use in 1945 and the current initiatives to prevent their spread and to ensure that sensitive equipment, materials and technology that could be diverted for proliferation purposes are controlled. It also provides an overview of the challenges faced in the quest for a world free of nuclear weapons, whether from non-state actors or from the continuing failure of the nuclear weapon states to negotiate nuclear disarmament.

Secondly, and crucially, the authors provide, for the first time, an in-depth and contextualised account of the development and dismantlement of South Africa's nuclear weapons programme, both of which activities were conducted under a cloud of secrecy. While it is important from a historical point of view to reflect on apartheid South Africa's rationale for its weapons programme and to explore the motivations for its nuclear posture, including whether the programme was morally, militarily and economically justifiable, the story's larger significance derives from the country's unprecedented unilateral dismantling of a fully mature nuclear arsenal – the first country ever to take such a decisive step. The manner in which South Africa dismantled its weapons, joined the Treaty on the Non-Proliferation of Nuclear Weapons (NPT), accepted comprehensive safeguards on all its nuclear material and cooperated fully with the International Atomic Energy Agency (IAEA) in its investigation of the abandoned nuclear weapons programme may serve as a useful future model and may also clarify the role of the IAEA, as an international and multilateral organisation, in the verification of future nuclear disarmament activities.

Disarmament and non-proliferation constituted a core dimension of South Africa's democratic transition and since 1994 the democratic dispensation has been committed to peace, human security and disarmament. Post-apartheid South Africa actively supports the implementation of international, continental and subregional agreements that promote disarmament and non-proliferation of weapons of mass destruction and plays a leading international role in these efforts. Importantly, South Africa is of the view that the only absolute guarantee that such weapons will not be used is their complete elimination and the assurance that they will never be produced again because as long as these weapons exist, the possibility of their use, whether by accident or design, will remain. While some states continue to possess them, citing security reasons for doing so, others may aspire to acquire them – as evidenced by the emergence of states such as Israel, India, Pakistan and the Democratic People's Republic of Korea (DPRK) with nuclear weapons capabilities.

It is our hope that this book will go some way towards achieving the further steps needed to rid the world of nuclear weapons and prevent states from seeking to acquire them or the materials and technology needed for other nuclear explosive devices.

Noel Stott, Senior Research Fellow
Institute for Security Studies
Pretoria, 20 August 2015

ACRONYMS AND ABBREVIATIONS

AAC	Academic Assistance Council
AAM	Anti-Apartheid Movement (UK)
AEB	Atomic Energy Board
AEC	Atomic Energy Commission (USA)
AEC	Atomic Energy Corporation of South Africa
AFTAC	Air Force Technical Applications Center (USA)
amu	atomic mass units
ANC	African National Congress
AP	Additional Protocol (to the safeguards agreement)
Armscor	Armaments Corporation of South Africa
AWE	Atomic Weapons Establishment (UK)
AWRE	Atomic Weapons Research Establishment (UK)
BARC	Bhabha Atomic Research Centre
BJP	Bharatiya Janata Party (India)
BNFL	British Nuclear Fuels
BWC	Biological Weapons Convention
°C	degrees Celsius
CIA	Central Intelligence Agency
CCI	correctness and completeness investigation
CEA	Commissariat á l'Énergie Atomique (Atomic Energy Commission, France)
CEO	chief executive officer
CNS	Council for Nuclear Safety
Comsa	Commonwealth Observer Mission to South Africa
CSA	comprehensive safeguards agreement
CSIR	Council for Scientific and Industrial Research
CTBT	Comprehensive Nuclear-Test-Ban Treaty
CTBTO	Comprehensive Test Ban Treaty Organization
CU	controlled unit
CWC	Chemical Weapons Convention
DIA	Defense Intelligence Agency
DSP	Defense Support Program

€	euro
ECI	Emergency Committee for Israel
EDF	Électricité de France
EDP	especially designed or prepared (materials and equipment)
EMIS	electromagnetic isotope separation
ERL	Engineering Research Laboratories (Pakistan)
Eskom	Electricity Supply Commission
FAS	Federation of American Scientists
FBI	Federal Bureau of Investigation
FMCT	Fissile Material Cut-off Treaty
GCHQ	Government Communications Headquarters (UK)
GfK	Gesellschaft für Kernforschung mbH (Society for Nuclear Research Ltd)
GPS	Global Positioning System
GPU	State Political Directorate (Russia)
GRU	Main Intelligence Directorate (USSR and Russian Federation)
GWh	gigawatt hour
H	hydrogen
H2	hydrogen gas
ha	hectare
HEU	highly enriched uranium
HF	hydrogen fluoride
HINW	Humanitarian Impact of Nuclear Weapons
HTGR	high-temperature gas-cooled reactor
IAEA	International Atomic Energy Agency
IBM	International Business Machines Corporation
ICBM	intercontinental ballistic missile
IDC	Industrial Development Corporation
IFP	Inkatha Freedom Party
IMF	International Monetary Fund
INFCIRC	Information Circular (IAEA)
INIR	Integrated Nuclear Infrastructure Review
IOC	International Olympic Committee
IONDS	Integrated Operational Nuclear Detection System
IRP	Integrated Resource Plan
IS	Islamic State

ISC	International Signal and Control (USA)
ISI	Inter-Services Intelligence (Pakistan)
ISIL	Islamic State in Iraq and the Levant
ISS	Institute for Security Studies
KGB	Komitet Gosudarstvennoy Bezopasnosti (State Security Committee, Russia)
KRL	Khan Research Laboratories (Pakistan)
kWh	kilowatt hour
LEU	low-enriched uranium
LHC	Large Hadron Collider
Li	lithium
MI5/MI6	British foreign intelligence service
MAD	mutually assured destruction
MBA	material balance area
Mintek	Council for Mineral Technology (previously National Institute for Metallurgy)
MIRV	Multiple Independently Targetable Re-entry Vehicle
MIT	Massachusetts Institute of Technology
MK	Umkhonto we Sizwe
MLIS	molecular laser isotope separation
Mo	molybdenum
MOX	mixed oxide fuel
MPa	megapascal
MPLA	Movimento Popular de Libertação de Angola (Popular Movement for the Liberation of Angola)
Mt	megaton
MTCR	Missile Technology Control Regime
MUF	material unaccounted for
MW	megawatt
NAC	New Agenda Coalition
NAM	Non-Aligned Movement
NATO	North Atlantic Treaty Organization
NDP	National Development Plan
Necsa	Nuclear Energy Corporation of South Africa
NIDR	National Institute for Defence Research
NIS	National Intelligence Service
NKVD	People's Commissariat for Internal Affairs, Russia

NNEECC	National Nuclear Energy Executive Coordination Committee
NNP	New National Party
NNR	National Nuclear Regulator
NNWS	non-nuclear-weapon states
NOSIC	Naval Ocean Surveillance Information Center
Np	neptunium
NP	National Party
NPT	Treaty on the Non-Proliferation of Nuclear Weapons (Non-Proliferation Treaty)
NRL	Naval Research Laboratory (USA)
NSA	National Security Agency (NSA)
NSC	Nuclear Safety Council
NSG	Nuclear Suppliers Group
NWS	nuclear-weapon states
OAU	Organisation of African Unity
OPCW	Organisation for the Prohibition of Chemical Weapons
ORR	Oak Ridge Research Reactor
OSRD	Office of Scientific Research and Development
PAC	Pan Africanist Congress
PAEC	Pakistan Atomic Energy Commission
PAROS	Prevention of an Arms Race in Outer Space Treaty
PBMR	pebble-bed modular reactor
PLO	Palestine Liberation Organization
PNE	Peaceful Nuclear Explosion
PPNN	Program for Promoting Nuclear Non-Proliferation
PSI	Proliferation Security Initiative
PTBT	Partial Test Ban Treaty
Pu	plutonium
PWR	pressurised water reactor
R	rand (South African currency)
RBMK	Reaktor Bolshoy Moshchnosti Kanalnyy (high-power channel-type reactor)
RERTR	Reduced Enrichment for Research and Test Reactors
SAAF	South African Air Force
SAC	Strategic Air Command
SACP	South African Communist Party

SADF	South African Defence Force
SAGNE	Standing Advisory Group on Nuclear Energy
SAGSI	Standing Advisory Group on Safeguards Implementation
SAGTAC	Standing Advisory Group on Technical Assistance and Cooperation
SAIIA	South African Institute of International Affairs
SAPA	South African Press Association
SAPS	South African Police Service
SCI	Sensitive Compartmented Information
SDS	Satellite Data Systems
SIOP	Single Integrated Operational Plan
SIPRI	Stockholm International Peace Research Institute
SLV	satellite launch vehicle
SSA	State Security Agency (South Africa)
SSAC	State System of Accounting for and Control of Nuclear Material
START	Strategic Arms Reduction Treaties
Steag	Steinkohlen-Elektrizität AG
SWU	separative work units
Tc	technetium
TNT	trinitrotoluene
TRC	Truth and Reconciliation Commission
U	uranium
Ucor	Uranium Enrichment Corporation of South Africa Ltd
UF_6	uranium hexafluoride
UK	United Kingdom
UN	United Nations
UNAEC	United Nations Atomic Energy Commission
UNGA	United Nations General Assembly
UNITA	União Nacional para a Independência Total de Angola (National Union for the Total Independence of Angola)
UNODA	United Nations Office for Disarmament Affairs
UNSC	United Nations Security Council
Unscom	United Nations Special Commission
US	United States
US$	US dollar

USA	United States of America
USDOE	United States Department of Energy
USS	United States Ship
USSR	Union of Soviet Socialist Republics
VDT	Van Doornse Transmissie
VIC	Vienna International Centre
VOC	Vereenigde Oost-Indische Compagnie (Dutch East India Company)
VVER	Water-Water Energetic Reactor (Russia)
WMD	weapons of mass destruction
WNA	World Nuclear Association
WSU	weapon systems unit
WWER	(see VVER)
ZAR	Zuid-Afrikaansche Republiek

PROLOGUE

A moonless night – the four masked men worked soundlessly and deftly.

It was 01:00 on 8 November 2007 and the Highveld heat had been replaced by a cool night breeze. The men were working at the bottom of a ditch, unseen by the passing traffic. Using plastic pegs, they needed no more than a few minutes to raise the bottom strand of the Pelindaba electric fence. The leader crept forward cautiously, well aware that any mistake could send 10 000 deadly volts through his body. He was sweating from exertion.

Then he was through.

Moving as cautiously as a nocturnal animal, he inched his way to the distribution box. He cut the cable that would normally have sent an alarm signal to the security control room. All that remained to do was to switch off the power to the electric fence. Within minutes the remaining three gang members had joined him. They ignored the security camera. Their movements were rapid and professional.

Inside the emergency control room, Anton Gerber and his fiancée, Ria Meiring, were sitting around, somewhat weary and bored with their shift. The emergency control room was manned 24 hours a day and was the point from which fire engines and an ambulance were dispatched when needed. The staff occasionally gave assistance with fire fighting and traffic accidents in the vicinity. Usually, however, their days followed a monotonous and predictable pattern.

It had been a long day, rounded off by a very convivial year-end party. The staff member who should have taken the night shift was in no fit state to go on duty and Ria was standing in for him, with her fiancé for company.

A noise from somewhere inside the building startled Anton. He had joined the workforce at the site 30 years previously as a young fireman. Over the years he had developed a very keen ear. He peered through the crack in the control room door. For a few seconds he thought his eyes were deceiving him. But then he saw them clearly. Four masked men were moving rapidly down the passage. They were on their way to the control room.

Damn!

Anton could see the weapons in their hands. He realised this was trouble. He ran to the telephone on the desk and phoned the security staff. They were three minutes on foot from the control room. A drowsy-sounding officer answered the call.

Anton's voice was panic-stricken.

"Help, quickly! They're attacking us! There are four masked guys in the building."

The next minute the four intruders were on top of Anton and his fiancée. Anton still had the receiver in his hand.

"Why are you phoning?" shouted one of the men aggressively.

The fireman tried to regain his composure.

"Is this a joke?" he replied in disbelief.

One of the men grabbed Ria by the hair while the other three thugs tackled Anton. Ria felt the cold barrel of a gun against her temple as one of the men forced her to the ground on her knees. Not now, so soon, Lord, she prayed silently. I wasn't even supposed to be on duty tonight.

Another of the masked men had a steel pipe, which he held threateningly over Anton. The first blow landed and the pain thudded through his body. He felt sheer anger coursing through his arteries like fire. The adrenaline took over and he put up a determined fight. He overpowered two of the thugs; his punches sent them staggering. While he was dealing with the third he was hit by a bullet in the chest. In a dazed state Anton kept on fighting for a short while, oblivious of the pool of blood forming on the floor.

Eventually he collapsed and fell to the floor. Ria watched him take a merciless beating. She cringed.

It seemed to take an eternity – in fact 24 minutes – before the security guards appeared. By that time the attackers had fled.

What happened here? Was it just another incident in crime-ridden South Africa?

Yes, according to Rob Adam, the then head of the Nuclear Energy Corporation of South Africa (Necsa). "If these people had been sophisticated terrorists, Gerber would not be alive to tell the tale today. I really think it was random criminality."

Anton is by no means so sure. Later on in hospital he discovered that a second group of intruders had gained entry while he was wrestling with the masked gang. The second group fired a shot at a security guard. Anton and his fiancée later took legal advice and filed a suit against Necsa.

Matthew Bunn, a professor at Harvard's John F. Kennedy School of Government, does not agree with Rob Adam. He believes that there was an alarming motive behind the attacks of 8 November 2007. The intruders were after the enriched uranium stored on the site. He said that this was a credible explanation, since highly enriched uranium (HEU) is very difficult to produce because of the technology required and is worth a fortune on the black market. In the hands of terrorists highly enriched uranium could be used to make a simple nuclear bomb. Bunn said on the CBS actuality programme *60 Minutes* that making a nuclear bomb simply means slamming two pieces of highly enriched uranium together at high speed. The amount of highly enriched uranium that a terrorist group would need to make a weapon would fit into a six pack. Bunn added that handling the material is not particularly dangerous. Highly enriched uranium is only slightly radioactive and can be handled with one's bare hands.

Bunn was also of the opinion that the attackers probably had inside help at Necsa.

Abdul Minty, the then South African governor at the International Atomic Energy Agency (IAEA) in Vienna, did not agree. According to him the thieves had no specific agenda. He said they saw a facility with gates and security and believed there might be something of value there. Their criminal curiosity went unrewarded, however, because the prowlers didn't steal anything in the end.

Besides, according to him it was highly unlikely that a second team would have got through the fence at another spot on the same night in order to gratify their curiosity.

Minty vehemently rejected the USA's offer to transfer the uranium to a safer place.

"Why should we get rid of our uranium when other countries are not doing so? Why are we less safe than others?" What he didn't add was that South Africa was one of the few non-nuclear-weapon countries in the world that signed the NPT while possessing large quantities of weapons-grade uranium.

The report *Securing the Bomb 2008*, which was published in November 2008 by the Belfer Center for Science and International Affairs at Harvard, refers specifically to the break-in at Pelindaba. "[It] is a reminder that nuclear security is a global problem, not just a problem in the former Soviet Union." The same report recommends that security measures in respect of nuclear materials in China, Pakistan, India and South Africa should be tightened up.

Three Necsa security guards were discharged after the 2007 incident. To this day no suspects have been detained.

Who were the mysterious attackers? What were they looking for? Could they have been reconnaissance parties testing Necsa's security systems with a view to a later full-scale assault? Military experts are inclined to think so.

Or were they after something else? One of the many top secret South African State Security Agency (SSA) reports going back to 2009 and leaked to the media network Al Jazeera in February 2015 attributes the break-in to China, whose apparent aim was to steal technology to gain advantage in a new kind of nuclear power generation, the pebble-bed modular reactor (PBMR), which was under development in South Africa. It is claimed in the report that the knowledge so acquired enabled China to accelerate their development to the extent that "they are now one year ahead of the PBMR project, although they started several years after PBMR". China obviously denied these far-fetched allegations when they appeared in the media. After all, who breaks into a facility housing the fire brigade and an ambulance and gets away with the plans for a new type of nuclear reactor?

And where did the highly sought-after stockpile that appears to have attracted the robbers come from?

That is a long and improbable story.

PART 1

25 CENTURIES FROM ABDERA TO HIROSHIMA

"The Universe is made of stories, not of atoms."
Muriel Rukeyser, American poet and political activist

THE ATOM HAS A STORY OF ITS OWN ...

Stereotypes

Thanks to Hollywood everyone knows what a scientist looks like. Typically he would be a benign, absent-minded elderly gentleman with a wild Einstein hairdo, thick spectacles and a white coat. In the background intricate experiments involving numerous bubbling and boiling glass vessels occasionally produce a small explosion. But he is harmless, if a little odd. Naturally one also gets the Dr Strangelove type, with a precarious mental balance and an urge to destroy the world.

What do these bespectacled men in white coats really do as their daily occupation? There are two distinguishable types: the thinkers or theoreticians, and the doers or experimental workers. In the rare instance when these two qualities are combined in one person, one has a star. But what, one may ask, drives these people?

Holy curiosity

Albert Einstein once replied to a question about his phenomenal intellectual abilities in these words:

> I have no special talent, I'm just passionately curious. The important thing is not to stop questioning. Curiosity has its own reason for existing. You cannot help but be in awe when you contemplate the mysteries of eternity, of life, of the marvellous structure of reality. It is enough if one tries merely to comprehend a little of this mystery every day. Never lose a holy curiosity.

That "holy curiosity" has driven people throughout the centuries to try to

understand how things fit together, to try to explain the apparent relationships between the things we encounter in nature every day, to ask:
How?
What if?
Why?
Richard Feynman, a Nobel prize-winner and an outstanding physics lecturer, tried to explain this search for comprehension to his students in the following terms: The complex collection of moving objects we call the "world around us" is like a giant game of chess played by the gods, with us as observers. We don't know the rules of the game; we are simply permitted to observe. But if we watch for long enough we may possibly discover a few of the rules of the game. We call these rules fundamental physics. But even if we do know the rules (or at least some of them) the objects around us are so complex that we can do no more than understand the basic elements of the physical world.

A long history

The ancient Greek philosophers had never heard of white coats; they wore togas. But even in those far-off days people speculated about the composition of matter. In the city of Abdera – part of present-day Greece – Democritus was speculating 2500 years ago on what would happen if one took an element (say, iron) and kept on dividing it into smaller and smaller pieces. Would a point be reached where one was left with the smallest possible fragment of iron which could no longer be subdivided? He believed that this point would be reached and called that smallest possible fragment *atomos*, the Greek word for indivisible. He is noted for the following pronouncement: "Nothing exists except atoms and empty space; everything else is opinion." Democritus was a typical theoretician.

Democritus was not the only one who carried out experiments. Over 2600 years ago the Greek philosopher Thales discovered something that is a frequent source of irritation during the dry winter months: hair that stands straight up on end when a comb gets close to it, or the mild shock that comes from touching metal. Thales observed that if a piece of amber is rubbed against wool, the amber is then able to attract light objects such as hair. If he kept on rubbing long enough he could even generate a spark. The Greek word for amber is *elektron* and 2200 years later William Gilbert used this Greek root in his writings, which explains the origin of the English words "electricity" and "electric". It became clear that there were two kinds of electricity, which either attracted or repelled each other. Today we refer to this phenomenon as static electricity.

In the mid-1700s a very remarkable man discovered that these two repulsive or attractive manifestations of static electricity were "positive" and "negative" electrical charges. That man was Benjamin Franklin, an American printer, author, diplomat, philosopher and constitutional draftsman, as well as the inventor of a more efficient type of stove and of lightning rods.

Of apples and planets

Around the time when Jan van Riebeeck was making the first wines at the Cape, one of the greatest scientists of all time deciphered a number of the universal chess rules which Feynman referred to and recorded them. In order to do so he had to design a special type of mathematics, known today as differential calculus.

That scientist was Sir Isaac Newton, who became a professor of mathematics at the University of Cambridge at the early age of 26. In 1665 and 1666 the Great Plague broke out in Cambridge. (Did the students' digs look much the same as they do today, one wonders?) Newton fled to his birthplace in Lincolnshire. These two years were to prove extremely productive and he wrote two outstanding works (which were not published until the 1680s, however).

The story goes that Newton discovered gravity by observing the falling apples in his orchard. Being the scientist he was, he was prompted to ask why the apples always fell vertically and not upwards or sideways. He made a mental quantum leap in coming to the realisation that the same type of force that kept the moon in its orbit was responsible for the way the apples fell. His first publication, *De Motu Corporum in Gyrum*, dealt with gravity and explained the orbits of planets, comets and asteroids.

The second publication, *Philosophiae Naturalis Principia Mathematica* (later known simply as *Principia*), contained the three laws of motion which, even after over 300 years, are still taught in the science classes of our schools.

For over 300 years Newton reigned as the undisputed king of the entire scientific world. His laws accurately describe how heavenly bodies move through the universe, how the tides are created and how the gravitational forces of one planet can influence the orbit of another. A shell fired from a gun would land precisely on the spot predicted by Newton's laws. He also explained why white light, when shone into a prism, decomposes into all the colours of the spectrum.

Newton had wide-ranging interests and he actually wrote more on the subject of religion than on physics! In 1704 he wrote the following: "It seems probable to me that God in the beginning formed matter in solid, massy, hard, impenetrable, movable particles." Newton therefore recognised the existence of atoms and visualised them as small, hard billiard balls.

Another of Newton's interests was alchemy, the age-old search for a secret process to turn a base metal into a precious metal (usually gold).

It was 300 years after Newton's time that scientists succeeded in changing one metal into another. That element was not gold. It was an element that does not occur naturally on earth and it was given an ominous name. This element was named after the Roman god of the underworld, Pluto. However, before this alchemistic change could take place, 300 years of earnest inquiry and experimentation were required.

In 1693 Isaac Newton suffered a nervous breakdown and abandoned his research in favour of a well-paid post as a civil servant, namely as warden of the Royal Mint in England.

Faraday, Maxwell and the Cavendish Laboratory

Michael Faraday, a young, uneducated bookbinder's apprentice from an impoverished area of London, was appointed as a laboratory assistant by Sir Humphrey Davy after neatly transcribing Davy's public lectures, binding them and presenting them to Davy. In the course of his work for Davy, Faraday discovered that magnets and conductors that carry an electric current have a reciprocal influence on one another and he began to consider the notion that they were surrounded by a mysterious field which made this interaction possible. This theory attracted no interest at all.

At an advanced age he began to correspond with a brilliant young Scot. James Clerk Maxwell understood the essence of Faraday's discovery and formulated his famous four mathematical equations, which elegantly summed up the theory of electromagnetism – magnetism can be converted into electricity and vice versa. Strangely enough, Maxwell was later to say – on his deathbed at the age of 48 – that "something in him" had prompted these formulations. He said he didn't really know how he had arrived at these insights.

Life today would have been very different without the discoveries of these two men. We would not have had electric motor cars, power stations, refrigerators or computers …

The multifaceted Maxwell was only 25 years old when he was appointed to his first professorship and in 1871 he landed in Cambridge as professor of experimental physics. There he set about designing and equipping one of the most famous research institutions of his time, the Cavendish Laboratory. This was the beginning of great things – fundamental discoveries were made and Nobel prizes by the dozen went to his successors.

The Republic of Science

A Polish scientist and philosopher, Michael Polyani (1891–1976), gave much thought to the way science should be practised. He used an analogy to explain his findings. Suppose a number of workers are given the task of completing a very large and complex jigsaw puzzle. What would be the most effective way of proceeding? Each worker could possibly take a number of pieces and try to fit them on his own. His chances of success would be slim, however, if the jigsaw was very large and his pieces had been chosen at random. This method would only succeed if each worker was kept informed of the progress of all the others. Every time a piece fitted, everyone would be prepared for the next successful fitting. They would then have a far greater chance of completing the task.

Inside the frame of the jigsaw there will be places where pieces have already been fitted and have in fact become growth points from which the whole jigsaw will grow to completion. The Cavendish Laboratory in England was destined to become an outstanding growth point, one of the best ever. Naturally there were also other excellent growth points elsewhere, especially in Germany. The University of Berlin and the Kaiser Wilhelm Institutes were among the foremost sources of knowledge and discovery. There were around two dozen of these institutes, each focusing on a particular field, such as physics or chemistry. The competition was fierce. In Copenhagen the Institute for Theoretical Physics was a formidable source of new knowledge. The exchange of scientists between these two growth points was a regular occurrence. Even during the Second World War reciprocal visits still took place.

Polyani's analogy explains exactly how science works, with strong growth points and a network of knowledge which is exchanged, evaluated and accepted or rejected. The name given by Polyani to the open community within which every scientist has the right to be informed about the work of his fellow scientists, evaluate it on the basis of collective standards and expect the same for his own work was "The Open Republic of Science".

Joseph John Thomson

Joseph John Thomson was born in 1856. He attended Cambridge where he was a brilliant student and was appointed professor of experimental physics at the Cavendish Laboratory at the age of 28. J.J. Thomson (as he was generally known) not only went on to receive the Nobel prize for his work in physics at the laboratory but became an outstanding lecturer and research leader. His extraordinary achievement as a teacher was that over the years seven of his research assistants, including his own son, walked away with the Nobel prize for physics.

Thomson himself received the Nobel prize in Physics in 1906 for his discovery of the electron. He was also the first person to discover isotopes (forms of the same element but with different atomic masses) of stable elements. He was able to show that electrons are particles with a negative electrical charge, that they can be accelerated by positive electrical fields and that the path of an electron can be deflected by a magnetic field. He carried out these experiments with cathode tubes, the remote ancestor of the "box" used by millions to watch their favourite soaps.

The most important part of Thomson's work was that he had identified a subatomic particle, established that it carried a negative electrical charge and that it was very light in comparison with the simplest atom, the hydrogen atom. However, he was unable to visualise what an atom looks like. He speculated that it resembles a plum pudding, with a positively charged sea in which the negatively charged electrons float like plums in a pudding.

Ernest Rutherford

One of J.J. Thomson's seven research assistants who later qualified for the Nobel prize was a young New Zealander, a farm boy from an impoverished background but a man of remarkable abilities. He was a rugby player, a prominent member of a debating society and a student who demonstrated a talent for innovative research from an early age. This young man was Ernest Rutherford, the son of a Scottish immigrant to New Zealand. He was born in 1871, about 50 years after the first settlers arrived in New Zealand.

He earned three degrees: in mathematics, physics and several languages (including Latin). Rutherford left his home country in 1895 at the age of 23 on a British bursary to go and work at the Cavendish Laboratory under J.J. Thomson.

After working there for a while he left Cambridge where there were few opportunities for promotion and took up appointments at the McGill University in Canada and the University of Manchester.

In 1898, while in Canada, he discovered two types of radiation derived from radioactive material. He called them alpha and beta rays or particles. It was later established that alpha particles were the positive nuclei of helium atoms and that beta particles were merely negatively charged high-speed electrons.

Rutherford also unravelled the mysteries of radioactivity. He discovered that some unstable, heavy atoms spontaneously decay into lighter atoms while emitting alpha and beta particles. He also found that with a particular radioactive substance it takes exactly the same time for half the substance to decay – the so-called half-life. Half-lives are so characteristic of radioactive substances that the substance can be identified from them, like fingerprints. In 1904 he published his book, *Radioactivity*, and in 1908 he received the Nobel prize in Chemistry for his discoveries, which left him somewhat bemused because he really regarded himself as a physicist.

Rutherford realised that the stable lead atom is the end product of the decay of radioactive uranium. By measuring the relative proportions of uranium and lead in a geological sample, using the known half-life of uranium, it was possible to determine the geological age of the sample and of the earth itself. This showed that the earth was far older than most of the scientists of the time accepted it to be.

While Rutherford was in Manchester, he and one of his students, Hans Geiger, developed an electrical method of counting single particles emitted by radioactive atoms. Geiger was later to carry out further analysis on this particle counter in collaboration with Erwin Müller to invent the famous Geiger-Müller counter.

While Rutherford was still at McGill in Canada, he observed that a narrow bundle of alpha particles were not sharply defined after passing through a thin sheet of mica. In Manchester he instructed Geiger to find out what the reason was. Geiger in turn commandeered Ernest Marsden – an 18-year-old undergraduate – to do the experiment and in particular to find out whether positively charged alpha particles would be deflected by metal foil. Marsden used very thin gold foil and to his astonishment found that within the thickness of that foil (which was only about 0,0006 mm thick) some of the alpha particles were deflected by almost 90 degrees, an inexplicable result upon which Rutherford ruminated for a year. He was later to describe it as one of the most incredible things he had ever experienced; he compared it to firing a shell at a piece of tissue paper and then seeing the shell turned round by the paper so that it came back to strike the person who had fired it. Rutherford realised that the only possible explanation was that virtually the entire mass of an atom is concentrated in a very small positively charged nucleus – a nucleus so small that if five million of them were arranged next to each other they would be no wider than the full stop at the end of this sentence. The negative electrons orbit round this positive nucleus and the combination of nucleus and electrons forms the atom.

Rutherford decided to announce this, the discovery of the century, at a meeting of the Manchester Literary and Philosophical Society in March 1911. His address had to be postponed, however, in favour of a report from a fruit importer from Jamaica on a rare snake he had discovered among his imported bananas!

Rutherford's atom had an inherent problem. The nucleus consisted of positive particles called protons. However, it was common knowledge that positive electrical charges repel each other and that the closer the charges are to each other the greater the repulsive force. How was it possible to confine a bunch of positive charges in a very small nucleus without them flying apart? He postulated that apart from the protons in the nucleus there would have to be other particles that did not carry an electrical charge and were compensating in some manner for the repulsive forces among the protons by forming an attractive force between the particles of the nucleus. He called these neutral particles neutrons and thought of them as a positive proton and a negative electron which were bonding in an unknown manner to form a neutral particle.

In 1919 Rutherford returned to the Cavendish Laboratory as director and in 1931 the farm boy from New Zealand was raised to the aristocracy as Baron Rutherford of Nelson. This rise in status led indirectly to his death, however, because in 1937 he became seriously ill as a result of a strangulated abdominal hernia. Because of his elevated status he could only be operated on by a surgeon with a title. Nobody was immediately available and the delay caused the death of the imposing and jovial former rugby player who was known to his students as "the Crocodile".

Ernest Rutherford was the first physicist to realise that the energy that accompanies radioactive decay is millions of times greater than the energy associated with chemical bonds between atoms in which the electrons participate. This energy must be coming from the nucleus itself. During the dark days of the First World War he said that he knew of no means of effectively extracting this energy from the nucleus. He added prophetically that if any such method were discovered one day his personal hope was that this would only happen once neighbours had learned to live together in peace.

Exhilarating decades

The last few years of the nineteenth century and the first few decades after the turn of the century were exhilarating years of discovery. In 1895 the German Wilhelm Röntgen discovered X-rays and a year later the Frenchman Henri Becquerel stumbled upon radioactivity. The discovery of the electron and the atomic nucleus at Cavendish and the making of counters for radioactive particles paved the way for a group of excited scientists to explore new fields.

In Germany Walther Bothe bombarded various elements with alpha rays in 1928 in order to study the gamma rays created in that way. Gamma rays are related to X-rays and also to visible light, infrared and ultraviolet radiation: all part of the electromagnetic spectrum. When beryllium was bombarded with alpha radiation Bothe made a strange discovery. The beryllium emitted intense radiation which appeared to contain more energy than the bombarding alpha particles did. But one of the "sacred laws" of physics states that the amount of energy generated by a process cannot exceed the energy that goes into it (conservation of energy). How could Bothe's finding be explained?

At Cavendish one of Rutherford's students, James Chadwick, remembered his professor's prediction that neutrons must exist. There was just one problem about the predicted neutron. Because it is not electrically charged it is very difficult to observe experimentally. It cannot be influenced by a magnetic or electrical field and it cannot be detected by Geiger counters either. How could its existence be proved? In 1932 Chadwick started a series of innovative experiments over a period of ten days. Working virtually round the clock, he came to the conclusion that the strange radiation coming from the beryllium could not be gamma radiation. He concluded that the mysterious "beryllium radiation" consisted of particles with more or less the same mass as protons and because of their penetrative power they had to be electrically neutral. Chadwick had discovered the neutron and four years later he received the Nobel prize for this remarkable achievement.

After 2 500 years, a workable model of the atom

In 1932 the model of the atom looked like this:
- It consists of a very small, compact nucleus which represents virtually the entire mass of the atom.
- The nucleus itself consists of densely compacted protons, carrying a positive electrical charge, and neutrons which are electrically neutral.
- Round the nucleus, at a great distance, negatively charged electrons are circulating. The mass of an electron is about one-2 000th that of a proton or a neutron.
- In its normal state an atom is electrically neutral. The number of positive protons is therefore equivalent to the number of negative electrons. When an electron is removed, the neutrality is broken and the atom then has a net positive electrical charge. Because an electrically charged atom is accelerated by a negative electrical field and its trajectory can be deflected by a magnetic field, the charged atom has been named "ion", which is derived from a Greek word meaning "going".

The lightest atom is hydrogen: There is one proton in the nucleus and one electron that moves round the nucleus. However, hydrogen with one neutron or even two neutrons in the nucleus is also found. The chemical character, in other words the fact that chemically the atom reacts like hydrogen, is determined by the number of protons in the nucleus, referred to as the atomic number. Nuclei of the same element, such as hydrogen, which have different masses as a result of additional neutrons are called isotopes of the element. Hydrogen with an atomic number of 1 therefore has three isotopes: one with only a proton in the nucleus, one with a proton and a neutron (deuterium), and a third with one proton and two neutrons (tritium). Isotopes differ only in respect of the mass or number of protons plus neutrons in the nucleus, but behave in a chemically identical manner.

In a graphical representation of the number of protons plotted against the number of neutrons in the nuclei of the various elements, the isotopes are dispersed around a line on which the number of protons and neutrons is initially the same (1:1). More or less in the region of the atomic number 20, representing calcium, the number of neutrons in the nucleus begins to dominate the number of protons. In the heaviest element found in nature, namely uranium, the ratio of neutrons to protons is 146:92 or about 1,6:1. As the number of positive protons in the nucleus increases, the mutual electrical repulsive forces also increase and more neutrons are required to counteract them.

> ## Things get more complex
>
> *The model of the atom created in the early 1930s looked like a small solar system. The nucleus could be compared to the sun and the electrons orbiting round it to the planets. The complexity of the model increased after that, culminating in the development of the so-called standard model in 1970. After that further development of the model stagnated while scientists looked for a breakthrough that would enable them to refine the model.*
>
> *According to the standard model there are fundamental particles from which the known subatomic particles are built up. For example, each neutron or proton consists of three quarks.*
>
> *Matter normally consists of two kinds of quarks and normal electrons.*
>
> *At high energies additional building blocks can be identified, with a total of six quarks and six leptons (which include electrons).*
>
> *In addition to these twelve quarks and leptons, the standard model also describes exchange particles which are responsible for the forces between particles:*
>
> *<u>Photons</u> (one type): Responsible for electromagnetic interactions (e.g. attraction or repulsion between electrical charges);*
>
> *<u>Bosons</u> (three types): Responsible for weak interactive forces which operate in certain types of radioactive decay; and*
>
> *<u>Gluons</u> (eight types): Derived from the word "glue", which creates the strong interaction between quarks and particles made up of quarks. This is the force, with an extremely short range, which "glues" protons and neutrons together.*
>
> *The standard model therefore makes provision for 24 different particles and it describes three relevant forces but excludes gravitational forces. A further particle, the 25th, was predicted in the 1960s by Peter Higgs. The Higgs boson was experimentally demonstrated for the first time in July 2012 by the enormous and costly LHC (Large Hadron Collider) near Geneva.*

Neutron bombardment

Scientists were quick to perceive the value of neutrons. Because these particles are not electrically charged, neither the negative electrons around the nucleus nor the positive nucleus forms a barrier to the neutrons. Neutrons are therefore the ideal particles for penetrating the nucleus and investigating it further. A neutron bundle moving at a low speed, say around the speed of sound, could more easily cause nuclear reactions than a bundle of protons with millions of times the energy of the neutron bundle.

The physicist Isidor Rabi described the bombardment of the nucleus of an atom by neutrons in the following terms: When a neutron strikes a nucleus and penetrates it, the effect is just as catastrophic as if the moon were to strike the earth. The nucleus is violently shaken. There is a great increase in energy which has to be dissipated in one way or another. This can take place in various ways, all of them interesting.

It was because they found this phenomenon "interesting" that in 1934 a group of physicists, all of whom subsequently became famous, started bombarding the nuclei of various elements with neutrons to see what would happen. In Italy Enrico Fermi bombarded uranium nuclei with neutrons and in Germany Hahn, Meitner and Strassmann did the same. They also had competition from France, where Marie Curie's daughter, Irène, carried out similar experiments – in frantic haste to make new discoveries and publish the results.

A detour to Switzerland

Eight years after the birth of Ernest Rutherford and in the same year J.J. Thomson discovered the electron, an exceptional child was born in Ulm, Germany. Initially he showed no special talents; on the contrary he only started to speak at the age of three. His school career was very average and his first attempt to gain admission to the Federal Polytechnic University in Switzerland failed. His second attempt succeeded and after four years he qualified as a teacher of physics and mathematics in 1900. He would have liked to become a university lecturer, but because he appears to have irritated his professors immeasurably he did not receive good references.

Through the good offices of a friend he managed to get a job as a technical examiner (third class) at the patents office in Bern. His application for promotion to the second class was rejected, however, because he was considered to lack experience.

The young man had neither a connection with a university nor access to a laboratory of the calibre of the famous Cavendish Laboratory in England or the Kaiser Wilhelm Institute for Physics in Germany. All he had at his disposal was the patent office's limited library. Despite these drawbacks, in 1905 the unknown Albert Einstein published four papers in the highly rated scientific journal *Annalen der Physik*. Some of his colleagues were to acknowledge in later years that at least three of the four papers merited a Nobel prize. The prize in Physics was in fact awarded to him in 1931 for his explanation of the photoelectric effect.

One paper, entitled "The electrodynamics of moving bodies", contains Einstein's special theory of relativity. As somewhat of an afterthought he published an addendum to this paper later in the same year entitled "Does the inertia of a body depend upon its energy-content?" He advanced the proposition that if a body moving at velocity V emits a quantity of energy L in the form of radiation, the mass of the body diminishes by the quantity L/V^2.

For about eighteen years this equation remained no more than a scientific curiosity. In 1923 the brilliant Italian Enrico Fermi, who was later to build the first nuclear reactor in the USA, suggested for the first time in a preface to an Italian translation of the paper on the theory of relativity that the equation could also be read differently, namely energy and mass could be seen as interchangeable (just as money can be expressed as rands or dollars). The penetrating afterthought on Einstein's work, which subsequently changed the world, is today known, thanks to Fermi, to every schoolchild as $E = mc^2$.

Einstein's paper and addendum departed from the conventions observed in scientific papers in that it contained neither footnotes nor references. Furthermore, there was little in the way of mathematical equations or references to any work which might have preceded or influenced it. This is probably one of the reasons why 25 years were to pass before scientists began to take the equivalence of mass and energy proposed by the unknown physicist seriously.

Could this energy-mass equivalence explain Rutherford's earlier observation that the energy that accompanies radioactive decay is millions of times greater than that produced by chemical reactions between atoms, as for example when coal is burned? Does this huge amount of energy come from the nucleus because mass is converted into energy?

Once Einstein became known for his theory of relativity and the famous equation, recognition soon followed. He was appointed Professor of Physics at the University of Berlin in 1914. From 1914 to 1933 he was also the Director of the Kaiser Wilhelm Institute for Physics there. However, the changing political climate in Germany in the 1930s meant that people of Jewish descent could no longer hold university posts, and he subsequently emigrated to the USA. Here he became the first (reluctant) scientist to achieve the status of a pop star. In later life Einstein described himself as a lonely old man who was hauled out and displayed in public every so often because he never wore socks.

> ## *How much more damage?*
>
> *Johnny had been coerced to accompanying his parents to visit his grandmother in her elegant home. His parents had the same argument with him every time because he always raised the same objection, "There's nothing to do there." So Johnny was allowed to take a friend along. The two boys smuggled in their cricket gear because Johnny's grandmother had a big lawn. His friend was bowling and Johnny batting, and how could he resist smashing a good ball? Unfortunately his grandmother's upstairs window was in the way. The cricket ball broke the window and with an unearthly crash it hit his grandmother's glass display cabinet with all her treasures, collected over the years. While the adults were staring at the damage in shock and disbelief, somebody accidentally kicked the cricket ball on the floor. It rolled down the stairs and struck a Ming vase at the bottom. Let's draw a veil over the rest ...*
>
> *While the ball was flying through the air and before it struck the display cabinet it possessed kinetic energy. After breaking the cabinet, the ball came to rest but had not lost all its energy because when it rolled down the stairs it did further damage. This energy is known as potential energy – energy stored in an object as a result of its position.*
>
> *But despite the damage done by the cricket ball before it finally came to rest, Johnny and his parents – and their neighbours and in fact the whole city – could be very glad that the mass of the cricket ball (160 g on average) was not somehow fully converted into energy according to Einstein's formula $E=mc^2$. That would have represented the equivalent of over 270 Hiroshima-type bombs.*

Neutron bombardment continues

There was no let-up in the competition between Hahn in Germany, Fermi in Italy, Rutherford in Cambridge and Irène Curie in France to see what would happen if uranium nuclei were bombarded with neutrons.

This friendly but intense competition was overshadowed in the early 1930s by political events in Germany and Austria as well as countries like Italy and Hungary. After the First World War Europe passed through a turbulent period. Many scientists left for greener pastures, especially in the USA. When the National Socialists (Nazis) came to power in Germany and Austria, numerous Jewish scientists had more compelling reasons to emigrate. Most of them lost their posts at universities and research institutes by decree and the influx into the USA increased. The centre of gravity in physics research gradually shifted along with these emigrants.

Lise Meitner, an Austrian Jew who had been working with Otto Hahn for a long time, had to leave the Berlin Kaiser Wilhelm Institute in 1938. She arrived in Stockholm in August 1938.

Hahn nevertheless contacted her from Germany shortly before Christmas to ask her advice.

One of his reasons for bombarding uranium nuclei with neutrons was to see whether heavier elements than uranium might be formed. Hahn and Strassmann, his collaborator, discovered that the nuclei formed were lighter, not heavier. Barium was a prominent example. As a chemist he was unable to suggest an explanation.

Meitner and a relative called Otto Frisch, a physicist like his aunt, were spending Christmas in Stockholm. On a walk through the snow they were mulling over the problem. They called to mind the view of the atomic nucleus of their colleague and mentor, Niels Bohr, namely that it was not a rigid collection of protons and neutrons. Bohr saw the nucleus as resembling a heavy drop of water which was about to burst but was held together by the surface tension that encompassed the drop like a membrane. The nucleus could be seen as a droplet that was starting to oscillate, almost like a balloon full of water which was pinched closed in the middle and then released, pinched again and released again, etc. When a neutron was added to the oscillating nucleus, the nucleus became so unstable that it broke into two pieces. Instead of a heavier element forming, two lighter elements formed – in other words the nucleus of the atom had split.

Meitner sat down there and then on a tree stump in the snowy landscape, took a piece of paper and a pencil and calculated the energy that would be released when the two positively charged, smaller nuclei repelled one another. It was not a great deal of energy in itself but was enormous in comparison with that released in a violent chemical reaction (as when dynamite explodes), namely 40 million times as much.

Where did this large quantity of energy come from? Meitner, a fine physicist, knew most of the important physics reference figures off by heart. If the heavy uranium nucleus broke up into two lighter nuclei, the lighter nuclei would collectively have a smaller mass than the original uranium nucleus. She remembered attending a lecture by Einstein almost 30 years previously in which he explained his formula $E=mc^2$. She did a rapid calculation and found that the loss of mass from the two lighter nuclei was exactly equivalent to the energy released during the splitting. As it becomes a professional physicist, Frisch did a number of experiments to confirm their theory. The results were positive and with Meitner's permission he decided to discuss those results with Niels Bohr in Copenhagen. Bohr was one of the leading physicists of his time. He was immediately impressed and fully convinced that his two acquaintances were correct in their conclusion. Two publications were prepared for the scientific journal *Nature* and on 11 February 1939 the scientific world officially learned that the uranium nucleus could be split by neutrons and that this was accompanied by a substantial release of energy.

Multiplication

Leo Szilard was one of a handful of brilliant Hungarian Jews who were to play a prominent part in nuclear science and its application, although not in Hungary, where there were no opportunities. His career path and those of a number of other Jews converged in the USA, via European and British universities.

Szilard, who had once cooperated with Einstein in Germany to design a new kind of refrigerator, was obsessed with the idea of a chain reaction, as is not unknown in chemistry. In 1933 he emigrated to Britain and it was there that the idea struck him that if one could find an element that could be split by neutrons and in the process release two neutrons for every one that was absorbed, then a sustainable chain reaction would follow if the mass of the element was large enough. In 1934 he submitted an application in Britain for a patent on a sustainable chain reaction that would effect the release of nuclear energy for the generation of electricity and other purposes through nuclear transmutation. Szilard envisaged a sustainable chain reaction in which neutrons would be the links in the chain. He described the requirements for the minimum quantity of material that would be necessary for a sustainable reaction; this later became known as the critical mass. According to him an explosion could follow if this critical parameter were exceeded.

Szilard's biggest problem was that these ideas were six years ahead of Hahn and Strassmann's experiments, and Meitner and Frisch's explanation of their results. At that stage Szilard did not even consider uranium as a possible candidate. He and some of his collaborators embarked on a fruitless search for a suitable element for such a chain reaction and Szilard eventually asked for his patent to be withdrawn.

Even among the leading physicists such as Bohr there was no certainty as to what was required to split the uranium atom. Then the mass spectrometer he had invented enabled Arthur Dempster to discover something no one had suspected. Apart from the uranium nucleus with 238 protons and neutrons (U-238), there is an isotope of uranium with 235 such particles (U-235). This isotope is very scarce. In 1938 Alfred Nier measured the proportion in which U-235 occurs and realised that only one U-235 atom is found for every 139 atoms of U-238.

This U-235 was the missing piece in the jigsaw and Bohr published his findings in the *Physical Review* of February 1939. He showed that U-235 can be split by both slow and fast neutrons (fast neutrons are easily slowed down by substances such as water or paraffin wax). This publication had the scientific world in uproar and rekindled Szilard's interest in a possible chain reaction. Fermi had emigrated to the USA in the meanwhile. In Fermi's laboratory at the University of Columbia, Szilard and Walter Zinn, Fermi's assistant, carried out an experiment and found that approximately two neutrons are released in every fission reaction for every neutron that is absorbed. Szilard's long-cherished dream of a chain reaction was eventually becoming a reality. In later years he remembered the night of his discovery as follows: "There was very little doubt in my mind that the world was headed for grief."

He was thrilled by the results of the experiment and, in the manner of scientists, he wrote them up for publication in the *Physical Review*. But in the end he got cold feet and asked for publication to be withheld – the possible implications were simply too dreadful.

Szilard was not the only scientist whose interest was aroused. In Paris, Frédéric Joliot and two colleagues also caught the fever and in March and

April 1939 two articles appeared in *Nature*. The French researchers concluded that for every ten fissions about 35 neutrons were released, more than enough to set a chain reaction in progress. This was the end of Szilard's notion of keeping the matter quiet. The secret was out, and it soon assumed nightmarish proportions.

By April 1939 it was known that the U-235 atomic nucleus was responsible for the fissions; that large quantities of energy were emitted with every fission and that more than enough neutrons were released for a chain reaction.

On 1 September 1939 Hitler invaded Poland. Britain and France declared war on Germany. The scene had been set for an interesting scientific curiosity to be turned into the deadliest weapon imaginable.

The next problem was how to obtain enough of the scarce U-235 …

Isotope separation

For every 140 atoms of uranium that occur in nature, there are 139 nuclei of the isotope U-238 and only one nucleus of U-235. To state it differently, in one kilogram (1 000 grams) of natural uranium there are only 7 grams of U-235.

For use in a typical light-water reactor, the relative U-235 content must be increased to about 40 grams per kilogram of uranium (4% enrichment). For a nuclear bomb, however, the U-235 portion must be increased to about 900 grams per kilogram of uranium (90% enrichment) or more. The process for increasing the proportion of U-235 relative to U-238 is known as uranium enrichment and is achieved by means of a process of separation of the U-238 and U-235 isotopes.

U-238 and U-235 are chemically identical. Any separation process can only rely on the fact that the masses of the two atoms differ by three atomic mass units (amu). To get an idea of how small this difference is, we can express it in more familiar units.

The difference is:
5/1 000 000 000 000 000 000 000 000th of 1 gram.

This explains why very few countries in the world have mastered the process of uranium isotope separation. The technology involved is just too complicated. But more on that subject later on.

Bellicose atoms

> *This new phenomenon (a nuclear chain reaction) would also lead to the construction of bombs, and it is conceivable – though much less certain – that extremely powerful bombs of a new type may thus be constructed. A single bomb of this type, carried by boat and exploded in a port, might very well destroy the whole port together with some of the surrounding territory.*
>
> Albert Einstein to President F.D. Roosevelt, August 1939

When the Second World War broke out a large number of scientists, many of them of Jewish or half-Jewish descent, who had had to leave Germany, Hungary and Italy, were hard at work, mainly in the USA, but also in Britain. Some of their names will already be known to the reader:
- From Hungary: the "Men from Mars" as they were called by their colleagues because of the incomprehensible Hungarian they spoke: Leo Szilard, Theodor von Kármán, George de Hevesy, Michael Polyani, Eugene Wigner, John von Neumann and Edward Teller
- From Italy: Enrico Fermi and Emilio Segrè
- From Germany: Albert Einstein, Hans Bethe, Rudolf Peierls, Otto Frisch, Klaus Fuchs and Max Born
- From Denmark: Niels Bohr
- From Poland: Joseph Rotblat

There were nine Nobel prize-winners among this group (some of them only received the award after the Second World War). With this pool of talent it was only a question of time and money – lots of money – before the USA built a nuclear bomb. The group had plenty of motivation. Not only had they been deprived by decree of their careers in the foremost laboratories of the "Old World", but more and more of their closest relatives and friends were starting to disappear in the concentration camps.

The spadework

But the machinery first had to be set in motion. An important consideration was the fear that Hitler's Germany would be the first country to build a nuclear bomb. After all, most of the emigrants to the USA had studied and conducted research in Germany. They were thoroughly familiar with the abilities of the scientists there. Otto Hahn and Werner Heisenberg commanded respect from everyone and since early in 1940 a large part of the work at the Kaiser Wilhelm Institute in Berlin had been devoted to uranium research.

A month before Germany invaded Poland on 1 September 1939, Szilard (who was already in the USA) wrote a letter together with Einstein, to be sent under Einstein's signature. The letter was directly prompted by Szilard's discovery in Fermi's laboratory that a chain reaction with uranium was a practical possibility. The letter was directed to President F.D. Roosevelt:

> F.D. Roosevelt,
> President of the United States,
> White House,
> Washington, D.C.
>
> Sir:
>
> Some recent work by E. Fermi and L. Szilard, which has been communicated to me in manuscript, leads me to expect that the element uranium may be turned into a new and important source of energy in the immediate future. Certain aspects of the situation which has arisen seem to call for watchfulness and, if necessary, quick action on the part of the Administration. I believe therefore that it is my duty to bring to your attention the following facts and recommendations: In the course of the last four months it has been made probable – through the work of Joliot in France as well as Fermi and Szilard in America – that it may become possible to set up a nuclear chain reaction in a large mass of uranium, by which vast amounts of power and large quantities of new radium-like elements would be generated. Now it appears almost certain that this could be achieved in the immediate future.
>
> This new phenomenon would also lead to the construction of bombs, and it is conceivable – though much less certain – that extremely powerful bombs of a new type may thus be constructed. A single bomb of this type, carried by boat and exploded in a port, might very well destroy the whole port together with some of the surrounding

territory. However, such bombs might very well prove to be too heavy for transportation by air.

The United States has only very poor ores of uranium in moderate quantities. There is some good ore in Canada and the former Czechoslovakia, while the most important source of uranium is the Belgian Congo.

In view of this situation you may think it desirable to have some permanent contact maintained between the Administration and the group of physicists working on chain reactions in America. One possible way of achieving this might be for you to entrust with this task a person who has your confidence and who could perhaps serve in an unofficial capacity. His task might comprise the following:

a) To approach Government Departments, keep them informed of the further development, and put forward recommendations for Government action, giving particular attention to the problem of uranium ore for the United States.

b) To speed up the experimental work, which is at present being carried on within the limits of the budgets of university laboratories, by providing funds, if such funds be required, through his contacts with private persons who are willing to make a contribution for this cause, and perhaps also by obtaining the co-operation of industrial laboratories which have the necessary equipment.

I understand that Germany has actually stopped the sale of uranium from the Czechoslovakian mines, which she has taken over. That she should have taken such early action might perhaps be understood on the ground that the son of the German Under-Secretary of State, Von Weishlicker (sic), is attached to the Kaiser Wilhelm Institut in Berlin where some of the American work on uranium is now being repeated.

Yours very truly,
Albert Einstein
August 2, 1939

This letter was handed to President Roosevelt on 11 October 1939 through the mediation of Alexander Sachs, a presidential adviser. The President responded by forming the Advisory Committee on Uranium which met on 21 October with the princely budget of $6 000 – and an ineffectual chairman. Not much came of that committee's work.

Bat bombs

President Roosevelt's approval of the nuclear weapons project could be seen as the decision of a man with the vision and farsightedness to try to end the war as fast as possible. But the same man also approved the eccentric plan of an American dentist by the name of Lytle S. Adams to release bat bombs over Japan. It was supposed to work as follows: A large number of bats were to be placed in a carrier similar to a bomb casing – but with sufficient ventilation holes. Each bat would be fitted with a lightweight device that would release a flammable mixture when the bat roosted. The device was developed by none other than the inventor of napalm. When the bat bomb was released by an aircraft the intention was that the tube would open low above the ground and release the bats and that the animals would then roost on the wood and paper Japanese houses and set whole cities alight in this way. The American army was required to catch hundreds of thousands of bats for testing purposes.

In the process $2 million was spent (rather more than the $6 000 allocated to the Uranium Committee). It was estimated that the bat bombs would only be available towards the middle of 1945 and the project was therefore abandoned in 1944 – shortly after a test bat set fire to a general's motor car.

Behind the scenes in Britain

In February 1940, Otto Frisch, a nephew of Lise Meitner's, and Rudolf Peierls, working at the University of Birmingham, concluded that it would be possible to make a nuclear bomb and that no more than "a pound or two" of U-235 would be required to form a critical mass so that the chain reaction could take place. They drew up the historic Frisch-Peierls memorandum and submitted it to their professor, Mark Oliphant. He was an Australian from Ernest Rutherford's stable. A chain reaction of committees ensued and the most important committee charged with defence research received the report. They passed it on to a new committee called the Military Application of Uranium Detonation Committee or the Maud committee for short. That committee swiftly got to work and focused on two areas: the splitting of U-235 by means of fast neutrons and U-235 isotope separation. But war is war and Frisch, the Austrian, and Peierls, the German, who had been responsible for the theoretical work, were not even permitted to serve on the committee.

The committee delegated the task of separating the U-235 isotope to a man named Franz Simon (another refugee). By December 1940 he had already concluded that separation was possible through the use of gaseous diffusion. He supplied the technical specifications for a separation plant and even estimated the cost of a big uranium enrichment plant. Following new measurements of the properties of U-235, Peierls was able to make a better estimate of the quantity of U-235 that would be required for a nuclear bomb. His new estimate was 8 kg for a spherical metal shape, and 4 to 4,5 kg for a sphere with a suitable reflector to reflect neutrons back to the sphere.

In July 1941 the Maud committee completed two reports – one on the use of U-235 for a nuclear bomb and the second on its use to generate electricity. The committee was dissolved shortly afterwards. The reports were passed on to the USA since the British realised that they would have to undertake the development in collaboration with the Americans in view of manpower and financial considerations. The British received no response from the USA. The Americans were not (yet) embroiled in a war with Germany and were more inclined to consider the possible use of nuclear energy in nuclear reactors to power aircraft carriers and submarines.

In August Mark Oliphant made an urgent trip to the USA to find out what was going on. To his amazement he found that the Maud reports were lying unread in the safe of the chairman of the Uranium Committee. The British, who had been at war with Germany for two years, were simply unable to understand this inertia on the part of the Americans.

Oliphant arranged discussions with the Uranium Committee and visited a number of influential friends in the USA, all eminent scientists, to muster their support.

In the meantime a parallel nuclear weapons programme under the code name Tube Alloys was developed in Britain.

The necessary spark

Early in December 1941 there was a rapid succession of events. On 7 December Japan attacked the American fleet in Pearl Harbor without warning and destroyed much of it. The next day the USA declared war on Japan and Hitler replied by declaring war on the USA four days later. This was the proverbial spark to the powder keg which started the nuclear weapons programme. Before the end of December the Office of Scientific Research and Development (OSRD) was established by Vannevar Bush and the scientists soon got down to work. At the University of Chicago plutonium and the building of a basic nuclear reactor were studied under the leadership of Arthur Compton. On the Berkeley campus of the University of California, Robert Oppenheimer and his collaborators started working on theoretical calculations. Six months later a conference was held and a unanimous conclusion was reached: It was possible to build a fission bomb.

At the conference the physicist Edward Teller, a Hungarian Jew, proposed that an even more powerful bomb could be built, the "Super" bomb. One of his colleagues at the conference was Hans Bethe. Before the war he had advanced the theory – for which he later received the Nobel prize – that the carbon-nitrogen cycle could explain the enormous and continuous release of energy in the sun and certain stars. Enormous amounts of energy are released during the fusion of light elements, far more than during fission. Teller's view was that a fission bomb could be used to initiate the fusion of the hydrogen isotopes deuterium and tritium. Bethe was sceptical, but the concept of the thermonuclear bomb (frequently called the hydrogen bomb) was born.

From theory to practice

The challenge was mind-blowing: They were being asked to separate two uranium isotopes that differed by 5 millionths of a millionth of a millionth of a millionth of a gram, and also create large quantities of a new man-made element (plutonium).

After Mark Oliphant's visit and Vannevar Bush's establishment of the OSRD, Oliphant approached President Roosevelt with the request that the rapidly growing, but uncoordinated work being done in various parts of the USA should be run as a military project.

On 9 October 1941 Roosevelt approved the project and decided that it should be placed under the control of the US defence force. The army engineering corps appointed Colonel James Marshall to supervise the building of the uranium isotope separation factories and the plutonium production plants. This was an unfortunate choice. Marshall had no conception of the processes involved and was unable to get along with the prima donna scientists. Furthermore, the USA was now embroiled in two wars and the army had other, more practical priorities. Vannevar Bush and his OSRD rapidly decided that things could not continue as they were. They had someone else in mind, the man who had just built the Pentagon, the world's biggest office building of its time.

This was where the larger-than-life Colonel Leslie Groves came onto the scene, much against his will. He was a soldier in every fibre of his being and wanted to be deployed in the field. He protested bitterly against a project for which he saw little chance of success, but in the military an order is an order. After the war Groves was described in the following terms by one of his aides: "He was the biggest sonovabitch I've ever met in my life, but also one of the most capable individuals. He had an ego second to none ..." Groves took command of the project on 17 September 1942, was rapidly promoted to the rank of brigadier-general and got down to work with characteristic zeal.

The project was designated "The Manhattan Engineer District", after the headquarters in New York. There were at least ten sites in New York where either uranium was being stored in warehouses or uranium atoms were being split in laboratories. The head office was located in a skyscraper opposite the city hall. In all about 5 000 people were working on the project. They each knew only what was necessary to enable them to perform their duties.

On his first day in the office Groves sent an assistant to go and purchase 1 200 tons of uranium ore that had come from the Belgian Congo and was being stored on Staten Island. He paid the Belgian owner $2,5 million. Over time this Belgian supplier was to be the source of two-thirds of all the uranium required for the project.

A week after his appointment Groves purchased an enormous piece of ground in Tennessee (over 200 km^2), originally called Site X but later renamed Oak Ridge.

About a month after his appointment he announced, to general astonishment, that J. Robert Oppenheimer would be the scientific head of the project. Oppenheimer, an American of Jewish descent, was a brilliant theoretical physicist. He trained at the Cavendish Laboratory and did his doctorate in 1926 under Max Born at the University of Göttingen in Germany. In those days not much research was done in the USA in the field of physics. The surprising aspect of the appointment was that Oppenheimer's political views were pretty far to the left. He had close ties with the communists and their fellow travellers. That was to lead to his dismissal in the late 1940s. Another problem was his lack of administrative experience. Furthermore, he had never received a Nobel prize and was being expected to head a team that included almost a double handful of Nobel prize-winners! Nevertheless Groves trusted him as the scientific leader, although throughout the project he was continuously monitored by the Federal Bureau of Investigation (FBI) and the Manhattan Project's own security people.

In addition to the land in Tennessee, enormous tracts of land were purchased in the state of Washington (Hanford, which covered almost 600 km^2) and in New Mexico (Los Alamos) for the building of new facilities. People who had occupied the land for generations were summarily removed.

While Groves was engaged in buying uranium and land and appointing staff, the team at the University of Chicago was hard at work on the first graphite-moderated natural uranium pile. The aim was to show that a self-sustaining chain reaction was possible. This first elementary nuclear reactor (known as the Chicago Pile-1) was prepared for testing by Enrico Fermi and his team. The assembly took place at an old squash court under the stands of the university's sports field. In later years Russian intelligence records revealed that they had taken the Americans' squash court for a pumpkin field!

The pile consisted of 400 tons of graphite blocks, 6 tons of uranium metal and 50 tons of uranium oxide. On 2 December 1942 the reactor went critical – the chain reaction was self-sustaining and lasted for 28 minutes. Then the team stopped the process. Fermi and his team celebrated the occasion very modestly with a bottle of Chianti and absolutely no speeches. As the group filed out at the door one of the security guards asked: "What's going on, Doctor, something happen in there?"

The "something" only produced about half a watt, but this was the first time that man had released energy from the atomic nucleus and controlled it. Today the two Koeberg reactors are capable of producing 1 800 million watts. We have come a long way since that achievement in 1942.

The momentum builds up

Money was no longer an obstacle. The only restrictions were the need for suitable staff for the rapidly expanding programme and the short time available. By the end of the war about $2.2 billion (in 1940 dollar values) had already been spent on the project. By the middle of 1944 monthly expenditure amounted to about $100 million. And the Americans were also fighting two wars simultaneously, one in North Africa and Europe and the second against the Japanese in the East. In those days America's strength still lay in real money, not in the esoteric and artificial financial instruments favoured by modern bankers.

Groves soon realised that in making the transition from laboratory-type work to industrial production he would require more than the services of prima donna scientists – however intellectually gifted. Powerful American engineering firms with impressive capacities, such as Du Pont, Monsanto, Union Carbide, Westinghouse, Kellogg, Allis-Chalmers and Stone & Webster, were therefore recruited. Within a short time the staff complement had grown to 125 000, spread over 37 large facilities. The most important of these sites were:

Oak Ridge in Tennessee: No fewer than three uranium enrichment plants were built at Oak Ridge, one for each of the three methods of isotope separation. The first of these, employed at the S-50 plant, was based on the thermal diffusion effect. Liquid uranium hexafluoride was put under pressure in the space between two long, concentric pipes. The outer pipe was cooled by means of water and the inner pipe heated by means of steam. The result was that the light isotope (U-235) tended to concentrate against the hot wall and the heavier isotope (U-238) against the cold wall. After a while the lighter isotope moved to the top of the column as a result of convection. The longer the column and the more uranium hexafluoride it contained, the better for the process. This system proved very expensive to operate, and not particularly successful. It was only capable of enriching uranium from 0.7 to 0.89%. The plant was therefore shut down immediately after the war.

The second, the K-25 plant, was a monster, larger than the Pentagon, which accounted for one-sixth of total electricity consumption in the USA. It cost $500 million in the currency of the time and provided employment for 12 000 people. The isotope separation process used was gaseous diffusion. It made use of porous barriers (similar to sturdy sieves with very small holes).

When two gas molecules (for example UF_6 molecules) are at the same temperature, the lighter one (U-235) has a higher speed and therefore a greater chance of moving through the barrier. One side of the barrier therefore acquires more UF_6 molecules with U-235 nuclei. There is only a minute difference, however, and the process has to be repeated literally thousands of times to cause any notable separation between the two isotopes. Major problems were initially experienced in building suitable barriers and in running the plant. The idea of producing highly enriched uranium at that plant was abandoned early on and the 50% enriched material that could be produced was used as feed material for the Y-12 plant.

The Y-12 was the third enrichment plant. The method it used was the electromagnetic separation of U-235 and U-238. A uranium compound such as UCl_4 (uranium tetrachloride) is ionised (electrically charged) and then accelerated through an electromagnetic field. The accelerated particles moved between the poles of a very powerful magnet, which deflected their course into a circular path, the radius of which depended on the mass of the particle. U-235 and U-238 particles therefore followed different paths and were collected at different points.

The electromagnets of the Y-12 plant needed an enormous number of electrical conductors to carry the powerful electrical current required. Copper was in very short supply, since it was required for cartridge and shell casings. Undaunted, Groves borrowed 15 000 tons of silver bullion from Fort Knox. (To get some perspective on this, think of a solid block of silver with a base the size of a tennis court and a height equivalent to two storeys.) After the war, being the conscientious civil servant that he was, he returned the whole lot to the American treasury.

The separators were named Calutrons, after the University of California, Berkeley, where these concepts originated. The machines were fed with material which had been partially enriched by the S-50 and K-25 plants. Y-12 was finally responsible for the enriched uranium used in the Hiroshima bomb.

The difficulties in getting the plants to achieve their targets can be ascribed mainly to lack of time. It was necessary to scale up from laboratory structures to industrial plants without the required interim stage of operating pilot plants. This caused endless delays and necessitated fault detection, thereby testing everyone's patience and motivation to the limit. A fourth plant made up the total number at Oak Ridge. This was the X-10 graphite reactor which was used to produce small quantities of plutonium for research purposes. This was based on the concept of the first Fermi reactor, although it was much larger. In November 1943 this plant started producing plutonium for the first time, in quantities measured in grams, for vital research purposes – a huge advance on the total quantity of only 2,5 milligrams of man-made plutonium which was available at that stage.

Hanford in Washington State: Three plutonium production reactors were built there. They each generated 250 times as much thermal energy as the X-10 at Oak Ridge and for cooling purposes they were built next to the cold Columbia River. Enough water to sustain a city of 300 000 people was required for cooling purposes. Each reactor consisted of 200 tons of uranium and 1 200 tons of graphite. These three reactors supplied the plutonium for the Nagasaki bomb and all the plutonium weapons built during the Cold War. Because of safety considerations the three reactors were built about ten km apart along the Columbia River.

When uranium is irradiated with neutrons in this kind of reactor, only one in every 4 000 uranium nuclei is converted to plutonium. This plutonium, as well as the highly radioactive fission products which are formed, has to be separated from the uranium. Fortunately, a fairly simple chemical separation method can be used. At Hanford there were two reprocessing facilities where plutonium recovery was carried out. Irradiated uranium slugs from the reactors were first cooled under water. The bars were then chopped up and the contents dissolved in a chemical solution. The solutions were then subjected to chemical separation processes to separate the newly-produced plutonium from the unused uranium and the radiotoxic fission products. A very high level of expertise and the best possible equipment were required for plutonium recovery because the levels of radioactivity inside the buildings were so high that people could not work there and repairs had to be done by remote control.

For reasons of safety the two chemical separation plants were built about 15 km away from the reactors. The plant where the uranium slugs were manufactured was located over 30 km away from the chemical separation plants in order to protect the personnel. Although it is relatively easier to produce and separate plutonium than U-235, the highly radioactive waste that is created and has to be safely and securely stored for very long periods is the price that has to be paid.

Plutonium

The element plutonium does not occur in nature like uranium. It is formed in nuclear reactors through the bombardment of certain elements with suitable particles. The American Glenn Seaborg bombarded uranium with deuterium ions in December 1940, thereby creating a new man-made element. He named it plutonium (Pu). This was big news in the scientific world and Seaborg and his collaborators prepared a publication in March 1941 for the journal Physical Review. However, the realisation that the plutonium-239 which they produced could also undergo fission (in fact more easily than in U-235) with a chain reaction made it necessary to withdraw the article before publication. Their important discovery could only be revealed after the Second World War. In the beginning it took over two years to produce sufficient material to be visible to the naked eye as small metal granules.

A range of isotopes are available today. Two of them are specially produced, namely Pu-239 and Pu-238.

Pu-239 is formed in special plutonium production reactors by bombarding U-238 with neutrons. The following reaction takes place: U-238 + neutron > U-239 > Np-239 > Pu-239.

The U-239 and Np (neptunium)-239 are radioactive and soon decay to the end product Pu-239. This isotope is not only important for use in nuclear bombs – the critical mass is only a third of that of U-235 – but it is also essential in nuclear reactors. It is normally formed in a nuclear reactor from U-238 and neutrons that were not used up in the chain reaction. The fissioning of the Pu-239 formed in a nuclear reactor in this way is an important addition to that of U-235 in releasing energy for the generation of electricity.

About two-thirds of the Pu-239 formed contributes to energy generation but the remaining third of the Pu-239 absorbs a neutron without fissioning and forms Pu-240. The longer the fuel remains in the reactor the more Pu-240 is formed. Pu-240 present in nuclear-weapons plutonium can cause major problems. It undergoes spontaneous fission and releases neutrons in the process, thereby contributing to a high flux of neutrons which cause predetonation of nuclear bombs – the bombs become damp squibs instead of crackers. The nuclear fuel in a nuclear power reactor like Koeberg is irradiated in the reactor by neutrons for months or even years. The Pu-240 proportion gradually increases to almost 30% of all plutonium isotopes in the spent fuel. This is the reason why plutonium reclaimed from spent fuel (so-called civil plutonium) is not suitable for weapons, which may not contain more than 7% Pu-240.

Pu-238 is an interesting isotope because it emits relatively few dangerous radioactive particles, but generates a lot of heat. One kilogram of Pu-238 can produce a remarkable 22 million kilowatt-hours of heat energy and is ideal for use in satellites and instruments in remote areas to generate electricity by means of thermoelectric generators. This isotope is obtained by bombarding U-238 with deuterium ions.

Los Alamos in New Mexico: This was where the nuclear bomb laboratory was established. By April 1943 the buildings were just about ready. It was here that the concentration of hand-picked Nobel prize-winners and American scientists, headed by Robert Oppenheimer, argued heatedly but also slaved away on basic research and weapons concepts. Their ranks were reinforced in November 1943 by a contingent of scientists from England: William Penney, Niels Bohr, Robert Frisch, Rudolf Peierls, James Chadwick, James Tuck, Egon Bretscher en Klaus Fuchs (of whom we'll hear more later on).

They were all kept informed of the latest discoveries and the goals of the project by means of the *Los Alamos Primer*, based on lectures by Bob Serber. The primer left them in no doubt: "The object of the project is to produce a practical military weapon in the form of a bomb in which the energy is released by a fast neutron chain reaction in one or more of the materials known to show nuclear fission."

Basic nuclear weapons design

The aim in designing a nuclear weapon is to get the nuclear material to reach a critical mass very quickly and keep it there for a while before everything explodes. This can be done in various ways.

A simple way is to shoot a projectile of nuclear material at very high speed from the barrel of a gun into another piece of nuclear material so that the combination exceeds the critical mass. The projectile could be a cylindrical piece of nuclear material which fits into a cylindrical aperture in a sphere of additional nuclear material. The critical mass could be considerably reduced by using a suitable neutron reflector to

> *reflect back any escaping neutrons. The speed of the missile must be high so that predetonation does not take place as the pieces of material approach each other. This design is not very efficient, however. A lot of the costly nuclear material is not used in the chain reaction and is wasted. This type of design is referred to as a gun-type or gun-assembled bomb.*
>
> *A second possibility is to implode a hollow sphere of nuclear material into a solid critical mass. This is done by enclosing the hollow sphere in a spherical layer of chemical explosive which implodes inwards at all points simultaneously. In practice this is very difficult to achieve.*
>
> *The implosion method can also be used to compress a subcritical solid sphere of nuclear material to a greater density so that it becomes critical.*
>
> *Most nuclear bombs use a trigger to set off and enhance the chain reaction, namely a neutron generator. When the critical mass is reached in a gun-type or implosion bomb, there is a mechanism that releases a volley of neutrons to start the chain reaction. This could be the alpha emitter polonium, which rapidly combines with beryllium and then releases neutrons.*
>
> *The explosion can be further intensified by including a quantity of tritium and deuterium in the nucleus of the bomb, which then undergoes fusion during the nuclear explosion, thereby magnifying the effect of the bomb – a so-called boosted bomb.*

On 4 April 1944 Emilio Segrè received the first plutonium produced by the Hanford reactors. It took him less than a week to realise there was a problem with the plutonium – in addition to the required Pu-239, Pu-240 was also present. Because the high neutron background due to Pu-240 could cause predetonation of the bomb, the gun-type assembly could not be used. This discovery meant that the whole approach to a plutonium bomb had to be rethought.

Work was already under way to find a more effective method of achieving critical mass. The gun method used only about 15% of the nuclear material for the explosion – a big waste of material that had been produced at enormous cost. It soon became clear that a plutonium bomb would only work if the implosion method was used. But getting this method to work was an uphill battle. The two British physicists, Geoffrey Taylor and James Tuck, were able to suggest a solution. Tuck in particular had a knowledge of the so-called implosion lenses consisting of specially shaped chemical explosives. In July 1944 work on gun-type plutonium bombs (the "Thin Man") was abandoned and from then on the scientists concentrated all their efforts on developing the implosion mechanism. They only had twelve months to develop a new, complex technology.

The gun-type design for a uranium bomb was retained, however, because it was so simple. The designers were in fact so sure that it would work that they did not even carry out a uranium bomb test as they did with the plutonium bomb. (Note: They did dummy runs without HEU.) For one thing, they only had enough enriched uranium for one bomb, because there were a number of production problems at the three enormous enrichment plants. By September 1944 the K-25 plant was only half complete. Further, no acceptable porous barriers had as yet been found. The Y-12 plant was operating at only 0,05% of its capacity. The UF_6 in S-50 had undergone further leakage and the total amount of enriched uranium amounted to no more than a few grams.

Groves was an eternal optimist, however, and in October 1944 he approved plans for the first nuclear weapons test at the Alamagordo weapons test site. His optimism was not unfounded. The Y-12 plant started producing 90 grams of highly enriched uranium per day, and in December the first successful test of the implosion lenses for a plutonium bomb took place. In the same month large-scale production of plutonium commenced at Hanford.

In January 1945 there was enough enriched uranium available for Robert Frisch to start his so-called "Dragon" experiment. The aim of the experiment was to find out how much enriched uranium was required to form a critical mass – an experiment not without hazards! An assembly of uranium hydride rods was created with a hole in the middle through which another uranium hydride rod could free-fall. For the fraction of a second during which the rod was falling through the opening, critical mass was achieved. A chain reaction by prompt neutrons took place but was over too quickly to cause an explosion. The name given to the experiment was therefore most appropriate. It was rather like tickling a dragon's tail! By April Frisch's experiments had been completed, but sufficient U-235 for a weapon was not expected to be available before August. In the meanwhile Frisch also received sufficient plutonium for criticality testing, and in June he finalised the design of the plutonium core for a weapon.

Criticality and critical mass

When a neutron splits a U-235 nucleus into two lighter nuclei, typically two or three neutrons are released along with the fission products. Not all the fission neutrons are necessarily available for further U-235 fission. Some are absorbed by U-238 nuclei, for example, to form plutonium Pu-239 (without undergoing further fission) and others simply escape and leave the system. To make the reaction sustainable, sufficient neutrons have to be available. The multiplication factor k is important here and is defined as:

k = rate of production of new neutrons / rate of loss of the previous generation of neutrons

The rate of loss consists of two parts, namely
a) the rate at which fission neutrons are absorbed to form new fissions as well as non-fission reactions; and
b) the rate at which neutrons escape from the system into the environment.

There are three possibilities:

$k < 1$: The loss rate is greater than the production rate. This means that there are not enough neutrons available to sustain the chain reaction. The system is described as subcritical.

$k = 1$: The loss rate is equivalent to the production rate. For each fission there is one neutron available on average (after losses) to sustain the chain reaction. The system is described as critical. Nuclear reactors such as Koeberg operate at $k = 1$.

$k > 1$: The production rate of neutrons is higher than the loss rate. For each fission there is more than one neutron available and this can cause a runaway chain reaction, as in the case of a nuclear bomb. The system is then described as supercritical.

The critical mass also depends on the geometric shape of the material. Of all the geometric shapes the sphere has the minimum area for a given mass and there is the least chance of neutrons escaping. A sphere therefore also has the smallest critical mass. A flat disc or a long, cylindrical piece of material allows far more neutrons to escape, thereby increasing the loss rate. When the U-235 is enclosed in a suitable neutron reflector (tamper), the critical mass becomes smaller than with an unreflected mass. Neutrons that escape into the environment are reflected

> back to the U-235, which considerably reduces the effective loss rate. In the case of U-235 the critical mass of a metal sphere is about 50 kg, but when it is enclosed in a suitable reflector (e.g. tungsten), it becomes as little as about 18 kg.

In July 1945 the hard work of the previous few years reached a peak. The uranium neutron reflector for the device (nicknamed "Gadget" for the sake of secrecy) was completed, the implosion lenses were cast and the assembly of Gadget could begin. The core and the rest of the device were transported separately to Alamogordo in New Mexico. On 13 July the components were assembled on the ground. The whole device was then hoisted to the top of a 30-metre high steel tower.

In appearance the Gadget was dark and threatening – it was a large, round device, taller than a man. It contained a 6.1-kg plutonium core at the centre, a little larger than a tennis ball. This core, which the Americans referred to as "the pit", was concentrically enclosed first by a massive uranium neutron reflector and then by 2 268 kg of conventional explosives – a mixture of various kinds. Detonators were fitted at specific points on the outside, encircling the explosives. The specially designed detonators all had to detonate at exactly the same instant to start the implosion which would focus the shock wave on the plutonium pit and reduce it to the critical mass.

The Trinity test was successfully carried out on 16 July 1945. The implosion-type plutonium weapon exploded with a blinding detonation and the steel tower on which it had been mounted evaporated in the process. A shallow crater about a kilometre in diameter was formed and the strength of the nuclear explosion was estimated to be equivalent to about 19 million kg (or 19 000 metric tons, also expressed as 19 kilotons) of trinitrotoluene (TNT). The effect of the plutonium pit was to multiply the blast yield of the surrounding 2 268 kg of conventional explosive by a factor of over 8 000. One of these plutonium bombs would have been the equivalent in blast yield of the total bomb load of about 2 000 of the biggest bombers of that time, namely the Boeing Superfortress or B-29.

Why did Oppenheimer come up with the name "Trinity test"? He had a strong interest in Eastern religions and learned Sanskrit specially to be able to read the original text of the Bhagavad Gita, one of the Hindu scriptures, with greater understanding. He always kept a copy of this book to hand on his bookshelf. Later, when asked about the choice of the code name Trinity for the first nuclear test he was suddenly unable to remember the reason and referred vaguely to a poem by John Donne. However, the name probably referred to the Trimurti, the Hindu trinity of divinity: Brahma (god of creation), Shiva (god of destruction) and Vishnu (god of protection of the world). The Los Alamos team had to create things that had never previously existed, from a material that did not even occur on earth. The result of their creation was total destruction but, just as Alfred Nobel believed that the invention of dynamite would stop all wars, Oppenheimer believed that the bomb could save humankind from further destructive wars.

Dilemma

The big incentive for the success of the Manhattan Project was originally the desire of the exiled scientists for revenge against the Nazi regime in Germany. In addition, it was feared that the Germans were engaged in building their own nuclear bombs. One must remember that the basic discoveries were made in Germany and a number of highly gifted scientists in that country were carrying out research on uranium at the Kaiser Wilhelm Institute.

In December 1944 Germany was in a precarious position with the Allied forces advancing from the west and the Soviet forces from the east. Hitler decided on a last desperate act, and on 16 December launched a major surprise attack with everything he had through the densely forested Ardennes mountainous region on the Western Front. Although the Germans were initially successful, the Battle of the Bulge, as it became known, ended within a month as a decisive Allied victory when the German armoured columns ran out of fuel. Tanks and vehicles were abandoned and soldiers had to return to Germany on foot.

At a presidential press conference a dozen years after the December 1944 Battle of the Bulge, President Dwight D. Eisenhower confessed, "I didn't get frightened until three weeks after it had begun, when I began to read the American papers and found ... how near we were to being whipped."

All further German resistance ceased on 7 May 1945. This was the end of the Second World War in Europe and there was no further motivation for building nuclear weapons to use against Germany. In any case, the first nuclear weapon was only ready for testing two months after the German surrender, far too late to use on Hitler, who had died by his own hand on 30 April 1945. However, one can only speculate that had the Ardennes Offensive been more successful and extended the war for a few more months, the original intention, namely to destroy Hitler and Nazi Germany by means of a nuclear bomb, might have been carried out. Germany was saved from this ordeal through a lack of fuel …

After December 1942, when President Roosevelt approved the Manhattan Project with a budget of over $2 billion, two cities with 50 000 inhabitants each were built at Oak Ridge and Hanford. In all 125 000 workers, equivalent to the entire workforce of the American motor industry, were appointed. Apart from the sheer numbers, what was unique about this project? The fact that only Roosevelt and the Manhattan Project employees knew about it. Roosevelt's deputy, Harry Truman, and Congress, which had oversight of how the taxpayer's money was being spent, had absolutely no knowledge of the project. Oak Ridge and Hanford only started appearing on maps after the Second World War.

When President Roosevelt died of a massive stroke on 12 April 1945, the secret could not be buried with him. On 13 April his successor, President Truman, was informed about the project by his war minister, Henry L. Stimson, and on 25 April Truman was given an in-depth briefing by Stimson and Groves. It is difficult to imagine being in Groves' army boots at that point. How was he to explain a project that had been running for over three years, had swallowed up billions of dollars, and about which even the deputy president had been in the dark? What was more, there was no final product to show for all this, merely promises of a devastating bomb that would be ready "very soon". This must have been a huge incentive for Groves to push ahead with the Trinity test and demonstrate his bona fides to the new president.

But what was he to do with the other two nuclear bombs which had reached the final stages of completion?

A physics experiment becomes a political cudgel

The war against Japan in the East was raging unabated. In March 1945 the Americans bombarded Japan's largest cities, namely Tokyo, Nagoya, Osaka and Kobe, with incendiary bombs. These tactics caused firestorms in cities where most of the houses were built of wood and paper. In Tokyo alone 100 000 people were killed and a million injured. After the attack a large area of the city was reduced to ashes. General Curtis LeMay, the Chief of Staff of the US Air Force, estimated that by 1 October 1945 60 major Japanese cities would be wiped out.

Despite the destruction the Japanese obstinately refused to surrender.

Up to that stage America had only been able to take a few smaller Japanese islands – after fierce resistance and with great loss of life. The next step would be the invasion of Japan. It was estimated that this would cost a million American lives.

Groves was convinced that the two nuclear bombs he had available would finally crush all resistance on the part of the Japanese. The Target Committee had already been formed in April 1945 to select suitable targets in Japan for the two nuclear bombs. The list of possible targets grew shorter and shorter as LeMay systematically burned Japan to ashes.

However, some scientists expressed doubts about Groves' plan. The Nobel prize-winner of German-Jewish descent, James Franck, and members of his committee, the Committee on the Social and Political Implications of the Atomic Bomb, which included Seaborg and Szilard, drew up a report recommending that the nuclear bomb should first be demonstrated to Japan. They had reservations about the consequences of dropping these bombs without warning. They also felt that it would give rise to an unprecedented arms race. They were right, of course.

The Franck report was simply swept aside. The decision was taken to use the two nuclear bombs as soon as possible, and without advance warning. The recommendation was that President Truman should announce at the upcoming Potsdam Conference of the Allies in July 1945 that America was planning to use a new type of weapon against Japan. Truman and his party arrived in Potsdam, Berlin, on 15 July, a day before the Trinity test. The objectives of the conference included dividing the defeated Germany into four zones, under the military administration of the USA, Russia, Britain and France. The war against Japan was also an important topic. The USA wanted to keep Russia out of Japan at all costs, but the Russians were poised to invade Manchuria (which was under Japanese control).

The news of the successful Trinity test on 16 July 1945 was a godsend to Truman. Churchill was also delighted with the news but wanted to keep it secret from Stalin. Nevertheless Stalin was informed in the end, on 24 July. He received the news of the "new weapon" without any visible emotion – his moles in the heart of Los Alamos and elsewhere had been reporting regularly on the progress of the project since 1942.

News of the Trinity test made it possible to issue an ultimatum to Japan: unconditional surrender or total annihilation. The ultimatum was issued on behalf of the President of the USA, the President of China and the British Prime Minister. The Russians were not included, because technically they were not at war with Japan. After five days Japan rejected the ultimatum. The countdown to the first use of a nuclear weapon in wartime had begun. The parts for the first two nuclear bombs had already been dispatched by air and by battleship to Tinian Island near Japan.

Groves had already chosen possible targets: Hiroshima, Kokura, Niigata and Nagasaki.

The assembly of the first nuclear weapon, a gun-type 4.4 ton uranium bomb, nicknamed Little Boy, was completed by 31 July. Six days later, on 6 August, Col. Paul Tibbets in a B-29 bomber, the Enola Gay, dropped Little Boy on the city of Hiroshima from an altitude of about 10 km. It was 08:15 and the people on the ground took no notice of the single aircraft flying so high above their city. Moments later all hell broke loose around them. The death toll was 70 000 and just as many people were injured. By the end of that year the death toll from radiation had risen to 140 000. Within a few hours it was officially announced over the radio in the USA that a new type of weapon had been dropped on Hiroshima – a nuclear weapon with a blast yield of 15 000 tons of TNT. Truman warned Japan that if it did not respond to the ultimatum further nuclear attacks would follow. Because of domestic problems Japan failed to respond. By 8 August the second nuclear weapon, called Fat Man, was ready. This was a 4.5-ton plutonium implosion weapon. On the following day, 9 August, Fat Man was on its way to Kokura in Japan in another B-29 bomber, Bock's Car, under the command of Charles Sweeney. But Sweeney was having problems with a reserve fuel tank on the aircraft and Kokura was under cloud cover. Sweeney decided to aim for the secondary target, Nagasaki. Fat Man was dropped at 11:01, from an altitude of about 9 km. The bomb exploded right above the Mitsubishi factory where the torpedoes for the Pearl Harbor attack had been made. Fat Man's blast yield was equivalent to about 21 000 tons of TNT. About 40 000 people were killed instantly and 60 000 were injured. Eventually the death toll from radiation sickness rose to about 140 000, as it had in Hiroshima.

Even then the Japanese leaders did not agree unanimously on an unconditional surrender and the Emperor broke with tradition by intervening, but stipulated that his own position should be protected. The Americans found this unacceptable. In response they planned to send another plutonium bomb to Tinian Island, but in the meanwhile they carried out the biggest bombardment ever in Japan, using 1 000 B-29s and 6 000 tons of conventional bombs. The Americans also dropped thousands of leaflets over Tokyo from the air setting out the conditions for surrender. Eventually, on 14 August 1945, the Emperor issued an imperial rescript affirming the Japanese surrender.

The war was over, both in Europe and in the East. The Soviets had been beaten to the draw by the Allies and had no claim to Japan. The most comprehensive and costly physics experiment of its time had become the most powerful cudgel ever to be placed in the hands of political leaders.

Three days after Japan's surrender Robert Oppenheimer uttered a prophetic warning to the American war minister Henry L. Stimson that nuclear weapons would multiply and improve in the future, that there is no effective defence against them and that the production of such weapons would spread to other countries. Two months later Oppenheimer resigned his post to take up an academic appointment. On the day after his resignation, 17 October, Norris Bradbury was appointed as his successor, a post he was to occupy for the next 25 years.

Did the nuclear bombs force Japan to surrender?

In the 1960s there was a school of historians that contended that Japan was already on its knees, ready to surrender, when Little Boy and Fat Man were dropped. Truman's decision to use the bombs was therefore not required to force Japan to surrender and was merely intended to impress the Soviet Union.

Since then an eminent historian from the University of California, Santa Barbara, has advanced a new theory. Tsuyoshi Hasegawa, who speaks English, Japanese and Russian, has come to a different conclusion after studying archival material. He disputes the generally accepted view that the Japanese leaders were fanatics. They were aware of their precarious position, but held out for strategic reasons: they were anxious to hold on to their territory, and they wanted to escape prosecution for war crimes and protect the Emperor's position. They planned to try to persuade the Soviet Union, which was not embroiled in the war in the Far East at that time, to negotiate with the USA on their behalf for a better outcome.

On 7 August 1945, a day after the Hiroshima bomb, the Japanese Minister of Foreign Affairs, Shigenori Togo, sent urgent instructions to his ambassador in Moscow to put pressure on the USSR to respond to Japan's request for mediation.

But Stalin had already taken a decision. The following day the USSR declared war against Japan and launched a surprise attack on Japanese forces in Manchuria. The strategy the Japanese had intended to follow had to be abandoned and the decision was taken to surrender – but to whom, the Soviet Union or the USA?

On 9 August, while the Japanese council of war was attempting to reach a decision, the second bomb fell on Nagasaki. Six days later Japan announced its unconditional surrender to the USA.

According to Hasegawa the two nuclear bombs were part of a bigger picture, not the deciding factor. Four months previously Tokyo had been set ablaze by American incendiary bombs and the loss of life had been just as great or even greater than that caused by the two nuclear bombs. Furthermore, about 60% of Japanese cities had already been destroyed.

Alex Wellerstein wrote the following on 6 August 2012 in *Hiroshima at 67: The line we crossed*:

> Within the context of the time, however, the atomic bombs were merely a refinement of an existing 'art': the mass firebombing of cities. This 'terror bombing,' as it was sometimes called, reached its highest form under the leadership of Curtis LeMay in the Pacific theatre, where B-29s in massive numbers flew repeated, low-altitude nighttime raids against 67 Japanese cities. They dropped explosives, napalm and thermite onto streets of wooden houses, creating massive, inextinguishable conflagrations that sucked the air out of shelters and burned people alive. The incendiary bombs were specially designed to break through the ceilings, stop on the first floor, and spray a cone of flaming, jellied gasoline into the interior. The thermite and magnesium were added so that the existing fires would burn too hot to be put out. Over two long nights in March 1945, over 300 B-29s were sent to burn the megalopolis of Tokyo. Estimates vary as to the exact numbers, but in the neighbourhood of 100 000 people were killed, with another million people injured, and another million made homeless. Success was measured in raw percentages of the total destroyed. In such a context it is hard to see Hiroshima and Nagasaki as the attacks that crossed the line. The line was already crossed – we were already burning men, women and children by the thousands.

The death throes of the Manhattan Project

The American media, politicians and public were naturally enthusiastic about this new weapon that was almost capable of winning a war on its own. Operation Crossroads was planned in 1946 to demonstrate to the taxpayers – at least indirectly – what miracles had been performed with the aid of their hard-earned money. It was to take the form of two plutonium bomb detonations which would take place before an audience of almost 42 000 journalists, politicians, naval personnel and other officials. The site chosen was the Bikini Atoll in the Pacific.

Almost 100 old warships, including an American aircraft carrier and German and Japanese ships, were used as targets. The first bomb, Able, was dropped on the area from a B-29 and the second, Baker, was used in an underwater test which blew thousands of tons of water into the air and caused the sinking of most of the ships in the demonstration fleet. Both bombs had a blast yield equivalent to about 21 000 tons of TNT. The tests were spectacular and the politicians were impressed.

These were to be the last two explosions linked to the Manhattan Project. American politicians were fully engaged with hearings and legislation to wind up the project, and transfer responsibility for the manufacture and control of nuclear weapons to a civil body – despite serious objections from General Groves. He was overruled. The Atomic Energy Act was adopted in August 1946. It made provision for a civil oversight body, the Atomic Energy Commission (AEC), which merely included a military liaison committee. On 1 January 1947 the AEC took over. The Manhattan Project was shut down, but it was decided to continue to run Los Alamos as a national weapons laboratory. From then on the task of the Los Alamos team would be to improve nuclear weapons and build up an arsenal. The weapons were to be assembled at the Sandia base, which was situated some distance away at Albuquerque in New Mexico.

Groves stayed on as Chief of the Armed Forces Special Weapons Project. In his opinion, however, he should have consolidated the organisation he had headed and safeguarded the USA's advantage in the field of nuclear weapons. Furthermore, he was still involved with the Alsos Project.

A time to reap

Throughout human history victory over the enemy has always implied an opportunity for pillaging. In this respect the Second World War was no exception.

Early on – when it became clear that Germany would lose the struggle – Groves put together a team to enter Germany on the heels of the eastwardly advancing Americans and to "harvest". The team was commanded by Colonel Boris Pash (responsible for military affairs) and Samuel Goudsmit (charged with scientific matters). Their instructions were simple: seize all the uranium and round up all the nuclear scientists in Germany before the Russians get a chance to do so. Covert operations were always given a code name. In this case it was Operation Alsos, which was indicative of the American's ego because the Greek word *alsos* means an orchard or grove in English.

Pash and his team moved in swiftly and even harvested in occupation zones which had been allocated to other Allied nations by the Yalta and Potsdam Conferences. At Stassfurt, near Magdeburg in North Germany, which lay in the Russian occupation zone, they discovered about 1 100 tons of uranium concentrates and oxides. This was seized and rapidly dispatched to the USA.

Farther to the south, in the Black Forest town of Haigerloch – this time in the French occupation zone – the Alsos team came upon the nuclear reactor Heisenberg and his team were building. The site was hidden in a cave beneath Hohenzollern castle.

At Hechingen, in the immediate vicinity, Pash came across the scientists who had worked on the German nuclear weapons programme. They included prominent figures like Heisenberg, Hahn, Von Weizsäcker, Diebner and others. In May and June 1945 they were transferred to Britain, where the German scientists were questioned at length about their programme. What they did not know was that the entire Farm Hall (near Cambridge) had secret microphones installed to listen to their private conversations. By January 1946 the Alsos team had the information they sought. The Germans were far from ready to build a nuclear bomb. Groves had received transcriptions of all the interviews and the eavesdropping. It was clear from these that the Germans had been astonished when they heard the news in August 1945 that atomic bombs had been dropped on Hiroshima and Nagasaki.

This information uncovered by Operation Alsos was reassuring. However, of special interest to the Americans was another group of scientists engaged in building rockets at Peenemünde in North Germany. This group included prominent figures like Walter Dornberger, Eugen Sänger and Wernher von Braun. From 1945 onwards some of the German rocket specialists were systematically brought over to the USA under the auspices of Operation Paperclip until ultimately there were 1 600 of them working in the rocket and aircraft industries. Without their expertise America's subsequent space and missile programmes would not easily have got off the ground.

Gimbel states in *Science, Technology and Reparations: Exploitation and Plunder in Post-war Germany* that the value of intellectual reparations – a euphemism for the plundering of patents, trademarks and industrial processes – amounted to about $10 billion in monetary value at that time. This was equivalent to about a quarter of the USA's gross national product for 1948.

It was not only the Americans and the British who garnered the spoils of war. The Russians came from the east and the goods they sent back to the USSR ranged from watches, mirrors and bicycles to entire factories. Like the Americans, they were interested in uranium, scientists and any technology they could lay their hands on. Their sights were set on the Kaiser Wilhelm Institute in Berlin in particular. Unfortunately for the Russians the cream of the equipment and scientists had already been moved to Haigerloch and Hechingen in the Black Forest in 1944 – and had fallen into the hands of the Americans in 1945.

The Russians consequently had to turn their attention to the search for uranium and for any remaining scientists who might prove useful to them. Manfred von Ardenne (the inventor of the electron microscope) was transported to the USSR along with his entire private laboratory, as was Gustav Hertz (winner of the Nobel prize in Physics), Peter Adolf Thiessen and Max Volmer. In time Nikolaus Riehl, Max Steenbeck and Gernot Zippe were added to this group, as were about 300 other Germans. What they believed would be a one-year contract was extended to ten years in most cases before they were allowed to return home.

At Riehl's headquarters of the Auergesellschaft to the north of Berlin the Russians discovered 100 tons of uranium oxide; they found a further 100 tons at Neustadt-Glewe. This uranium was later used in plutonium production reactors for the first Russian plutonium bomb. The Russians acknowledged that the uranium they harvested through these discoveries put their nuclear programme ahead by at least a year.

What did the Germans achieve?

Einstein wrote as follows to President Roosevelt in August 1939:

> I understand that Germany has actually stopped the sale of uranium from the Czechoslovakian mines, which she has taken over. That she should have taken such early action might perhaps be understood on the ground that the son of the German Under-Secretary of State, Von Weishlicker (sic), is attached to the Kaiser Wilhelm Institut in Berlin where some of the American work on uranium is now being repeated.

At that stage the USA had not yet entered the Second World War – that happened two years afterwards. Nevertheless one of the main driving forces for the Manhattan Project was the perception that Germany was engaged in building a nuclear bomb. But how far did the Germans actually get?

Judging from the results of the Alsos Project and the German documents seized, which were only released by the Russians years afterwards, they did not get very far. It would appear that the main thrust of the German research, unlike that of the Americans and the Russians, was not uranium isotope separation and plutonium production, but rather the commissioning of their *Uranmaschine* (a nuclear reactor). In 2009 the Institut für Transuranelemente in Germany analysed uranium from the Haigerloch reactor and found no traces of plutonium. The reactor, which consisted of 664 natural uranium cubes and used heavy water as a moderator, therefore never achieved a sustainable chain reaction. What is the explanation for the German failure to put more muscle behind this project?

There were several reasons. If one looks at the achievements of the German scientists who were "voluntarily" transported to Russia by the Russians, along with their families and laboratories, it is clear from the dozens of Stalin prizes awarded to them that they were among the very best. In Russia they had everything they required to set up a nuclear weapons programme without, by their own choice, working on the bomb itself. Their most notable breakthroughs included gaseous diffusion barriers and cascade theory (Thiessen, Schütze, Reichmann, Hertz and Barwich), uranium metal processing (Riehl) and the manufacture of a new uranium isotope separation process, the gas centrifuge (Von Ardenne, Steenbeck and Zippe). Some 60 years after its invention the latter process is still the world's most effective and cheapest method of enriching uranium.

THE BOMB

The politics of that time also played a part. In the 1930s a movement arose in Germany in which "German physics" was promoted at the expense of "Jewish physics". The latter included new discoveries such as quantum physics and the theory of relativity. As a result of the political climate one of the most notable scientists in Germany, Werner Heisenberg – a Nobel prize-winner famous for the development of his "uncertainty principle" – also came under suspicion and was excluded from a sought-after university post. For ideological reasons, therefore, there was little political support for a nuclear weapons programme.

Heisenberg was nevertheless one of the leading figures in the German *Uranverein* engaged in nuclear research. In 1942 he told an audience which included Albert Speer, the German Minister of Armaments and War Production, that Germany would not be able to build a nuclear bomb before 1945, that it would be very expensive and that the project would require considerable manpower. (It is estimated today that the USA spent 4 000 times as much on the Manhattan Project as the Germans spent on their programme.)

This statement by Heisenberg was a fatal blow to the nuclear weapons project. The German army used to pin their faith on the *Blitzkrieg* – after all they had taken Czechoslovakia and Poland in 1939 without a shot being fired and had overrun Norway, Denmark, the Netherlands, Belgium and France between April and June 1940. The army was not prepared to wait three years for a very expensive weapon when there was no certainty as to what results it would produce.

Nevertheless, work on the *Uranmaschine* continued – and one of the scientists involved was Kurt Diebner, a sworn enemy of Heisenberg's. The year 2005 saw the publication of a book, *Hitler's Bomb*, by Rainer Karlsch in which the far-fetched claim was made that Diebner tested a nuclear weapon in March 1945. No evidence was advanced, however, other than the accounts handed down by a few unsatisfactory eyewitnesses.

Soviet moles

When President Truman informed Stalin on 24 July 1945 about the successful Trinity test, he was astonished by the nonchalance with which Stalin received the news. What he did not know was that Stalin had numerous moles and collaborators working deep inside the Manhattan Project.

Harold Agnew, who worked on the world's first hydrogen bomb and later became Director of Los Alamos, was convinced that the USSR had a fair number of spies inside the American nuclear weapons programme. He said the Americans had always found the rapid progress made by the Soviet Union astonishing.

Klaus Fuchs was born in Germany in 1911, the son of a professor of theology. He was a brilliant physicist, but came from a very unstable family. His grandmother, mother and one of his sisters committed suicide; another sister suffered from schizophrenia. A committed communist, he fled to England to escape the Nazis after an incident. There he received a PhD and a DSc in physics. When the Second World War broke out he was initially interned on the grounds of his German citizenship, but then released after the intervention of Professor Max Born. In 1942 Fuchs was even granted British citizenship and invited by Rudolf Peierls, an exiled German Jew, to participate in the British nuclear weapons programme, code-named Tube Alloys. In 1941 he quietly resumed contact with the Russian military secret service, the GRU.

In 1943 Fuchs and Peierls were transferred to the Manhattan Project where Fuchs was assigned to Hans Bethe's theoretical physics group, as close to the core of the programme as he could possibly be. He was one of the small group of people permitted to witness the Trinity test and was able to admire his contribution to this achievement.

Through Harry Gold and David Greenglass (both Los Alamos employees) Fuchs supplied comprehensive information on the nuclear weapon (including working drawings) to Julius and Ethel Rosenberg. The Rosenbergs passed this information on to the Russians.

Unhappily for Gold, Greenglass and the Rosenbergs their espionage was discovered. Gold and Greenglass (Ethel Rosenberg's brother) were found guilty of espionage and were each sentenced to fifteen years' imprisonment. The Rosenbergs, who had also supplied other military information to the Soviet Union, were sentenced to death and in 1953 they paid the penalty for their actions in the electric chair.

Fuchs returned to Britain in 1946 as the first head of the Theoretical Physics Division at the Atomic Energy Research Establishment at Harwell. The British secret service (MI5) were waiting for him. MI5 had recently begun to decipher the Soviet Union's secret codes and discovered Fuchs' role. He was interrogated at length and in 1950 he acknowledged that he had been spying for the USSR. One of the consequences of his confession was the arrest of Gold, Greenglass and the Rosenbergs on a charge of espionage. Fuchs was found guilty after only 90 minutes and sentenced to fourteen years' imprisonment.

He was released in 1959, after serving a little over nine years. Having been stripped of his British citizenship, he immediately moved to Dresden in East Germany. He soon went back to his old ways and trained a number of Chinese physicists, thereby enabling them to have their own nuclear weapon ready for testing a mere five years later.

Fuchs can therefore lay claim to the dubious honour of having contributed to four nuclear weapons programmes, namely those of Britain, the USA, the USSR and China. His motivation was that it would not have been good for international political balance if only one country had possessed this terrifying weapon. He may have been right at that …

Fuchs was only one of a large number of spies who worked for the USSR. Their dark deeds were coordinated by the KGB master spy, Alexander Feklisov, who operated in the USA and later in Britain. Years later Feklisov referred to the Rosenberg network as one of the biggest and best networks in the history of Russian espionage.

Spies are usually secretive people who seldom receive public recognition for the work they do. To the astonishment of the Americans, President Putin of Russia announced in November 2007 that George Koval (1913–2006), an American by birth but of Russian descent, was to receive the highest Russian award posthumously. Koval grew up in America and spoke like an American without a trace of a foreign accent. He was accepted as an ordinary American citizen wherever he went. During the Great Depression he returned to the USSR with his parents for a while. Here Koval was given thorough professional training by the dreaded GRU before he returned to the USA and was appointed to a military post. Unlike Fuchs and some of his fellow moles, who were somewhat disdainfully referred to as "walk-in spies", Koval was a thoroughly trained professional spy. As a result of his responsibility for radiation safety on the Manhattan Project, Koval had access not only to the bomb factory in Los Alamos but also to all facilities and buildings attached to the project in places like Oak Ridge, Hanford and others. He even had his own Jeep in which he could go wherever he pleased and gather information on all aspects of the project. Not without reason is he considered by experts to be one of the most important spies of the twentieth century – although this only became known more than 60 years afterwards.

The Soviet Union catches up with the USA

Ioseb Besarionis Dze Jugashvili was born in Georgia in 1878 during the tsarist era. He came from an impoverished family of peasant farmers. He was an intelligent child and at the age of 16 he won a scholarship to study at a Georgian Orthodox seminary. He left the seminary before taking the final examination and exchanged the Orthodox Bible for the Red Bible of Lenin and Marx. At the age of 25 he joined the Bolsheviks and helped swell their coffers by means of bank robbery and extortion. In one big and particularly violent bank robbery 40 people died.

As was customary at that time, Ioseb Dze Jugashvili used various revolutionary pseudonyms, but the one that stuck was Joseph Stalin.

After the October Revolution in Russia in 1917 and the succeeding civil war, which lasted until 1919, he played an active part in the struggle, but owing to a physical defect he was unable to serve as a soldier. He advanced rapidly and after Lenin's death in 1924 soon took over the leadership of the USSR. He was to retain this post until 1953 through merciless oppression, organised murders and the starvation and large-scale deportation of millions of people. It is estimated that 60 million people lost their lives during one of the most violent regimes in the history of the world – exact mortality figures are unknown.

To keep such a violent regime in power, and for such a long period, Stalin required a repressive state machinery. From the early years he began expanding the state's security police and intelligence agencies. Espionage networks were established and operated in all the major powers such as Britain, France, Japan, Germany and the USA.

Stalin did not distinguish between communist propaganda, espionage and state violence; for the sake of convenience he united these functions under the People's Commissariat for Internal Affairs (NKVD). This organisation originated from predecessors such as the original security police (Cheka) and mutated like a malignant virus into a succession of organisations with strange Russian names such as the GPU, the OGPU and later the MVD to become the Committee for State Security, better known as the KGB.

Lavrenti Beria was the perfect choice as manager of the dreaded NKVD. A fellow Georgian, he was about 20 years younger than Stalin. Beria met Stalin in 1926 and from then on he devoted himself to helping establish the Soviet regime, with dedicated patience and murderous zeal. He was ultimately rewarded in 1938 with an appointment as head of the NKVD.

Stalin's daughter, Svetlana Alliluyeva, writes in her book, *Twenty Letters to a Friend*, that the family (excluding her father) despised Beria. She describes him as follows: "Beria was more treacherous, more practised in perfidy and cunning, more insolent and single-minded than my father."

On the strength of his position as head of the NKVD and the successful Soviet penetration of the Manhattan Project, Beria was appointed at the end of 1944 as the administrative head of the USSR's nuclear weapons project. He was assisted by Igor Kurchatov, the scientific head. They were the USSR's equivalent of Groves and Oppenheimer.

Beria had not only captured German uranium and scientists but also had thousands of prisoners from the Gulags (labour camps) at his disposal to mine uranium and build the dozens of facilities required for the Soviet programme.

While work on the enrichment of uranium proceeded simultaneously by means of gas diffusion, electromagnetic (calutron) and gas centrifuge processes, the first plutonium production reactor (A) was loaded with 150 tons of German uranium. It became critical on 10 June 1948.

The Americans had demonstrated in practice that their designs for both uranium and plutonium bombs were successful. This was enough evidence for Beria. Because the goal was to build a Soviet bomb as fast as possible, Beria's instructions to his scientists were to reproduce the American designs as closely as possible. He even turned down the scientists' suggested improvements.

Just over a year after Reactor A became critical, sufficient plutonium had been produced and on 29 August 1949 the USSR successfully detonated its version of the Trinity bomb, RDS-1, code-named First Lightning, at the Semipalatinsk test site in Kazakhstan. Joseph Stalin had his "big cudgel" – which the Americans referred to as Joe-1.

On 1 March 1953, after an all-night dinner and discussions with Beria, Malenkov, Bulganin and Khrushchev, Stalin collapsed following a massive stroke. He was partially paralysed and in a coma. The dreaded leader died on 5 March. His daughter described her father's death as follows in her book: "My father died a difficult and terrible death. God grants an easy death only to the just."

In typical Soviet style Beria and six of his associates were arrested out of the blue in June 1953. He had simply become too powerful. *Pravda* reported on 10 July that the arrests were the result of the group's cooperation with foreign intelligence agencies and that they had been conspiring for years to seize power in the USSR and bring back capitalism. Beria and his colleagues were hauled before a special session of the Supreme Court with no right to a defence team or right of appeal. Conviction was virtually automatic. Stalin's executioner and his co-accused were put to death by a firing squad on 23 December 1953.

In later years a joint American-Russian team investigated Stalin's death and concluded that his stroke was the result of the administration of warfarin (a blood thinner which is also used as a rat poison). It had been deliberately added to Stalin's food. The indications pointed to Beria.

Scaling up

The building of an even more powerful weapon, namely a thermonuclear or fusion bomb, was mooted as early as the middle of 1942, at a conference convened by Oppenheimer. The main proponent of this type of weapon was Edward Teller.

Teller was a Hungarian Jew who had migrated to the USA in 1933, before the outbreak of the Second World War. He did his doctorate in nuclear physics under Werner Heisenberg in Germany and was famous – or perhaps infamous – for his foul temper.

While he was working on the Manhattan Project at Los Alamos, he and Oppenheimer locked horns about numerous matters. One bone of contention was the appointment of Hans Bethe as head of the theoretical physics division, a post which Teller felt should have been his. He therefore refused to do the calculations for the implosion bomb and new members of staff, including Klaus Fuchs, had to be appointed to fill in for him.

Oppenheimer thought that Teller's obsession with the "Super" was premature. All the physicists realised that a fission bomb was required to create the extreme conditions for a fusion bomb. At that stage they didn't have a workable fission bomb.

Furthermore, Oppenheimer thought it would be best to build up a large supply of fission weapons first. In any case they did not yet have a workable design for a thermonuclear bomb.

After a fairly unsuccessful attempt by Teller to "sell" the concept to his colleagues at a conference on the subject, he left Los Alamos and joined Fermi at the University of Chicago.

When the Soviets tested Joe-1 in 1949 this changed the whole picture. President Truman gave instructions in 1950 that urgent attention should be given to building a thermonuclear bomb (also generally known as the hydrogen bomb or H-bomb). Teller therefore returned to Los Alamos to work on the project. As usual, he clashed with his colleagues and he was also frustrated by the slow pace of the project. The original idea was that the heat generated by a fission bomb would fuse the deuterium and tritium and cause a massive explosion. After a series of very difficult and intricate calculations had been carried out – on a slide rule and the mechanical calculators available at that time – it was concluded that Teller's design would not work.

In January 1951 there was a breakthrough. The Polish mathematician Stanislaf Ulam proposed that the energy of the fission bomb should be used not to heat the deuterium and tritium but to compress it. Teller accepted this idea and realised that the X-rays produced by the fission bomb (the primary bomb) could be reflected inwards by the heavy casing and thereby cause a radiation implosion which would compress the fusion material. For an extra "kick" he proposed a "spark plug", consisting of uranium and plutonium, which would be brought to a state of fission by the X-ray implosion and would then cause the compressed fusion materials to combust in the final explosion. The primary fission bomb would therefore ignite a second fission bomb in the secondary part and that would cause the final deuterium/tritium or lithium-6-deuteride fusion. After more than 50 years this concept is still used and is known as the Teller-Ulam configuration.

Two years later, on 1 November 1952, the first fusion device, bearing the code name Mike, was successfully tested on an island in the Pacific. Mike was called a device rather than a bomb because it looked rather like a factory – a structure with a mass of around 70 tons. The results were astounding. The explosion was equivalent to 10,4 million tons of TNT, almost 500 times more than the blast yield of the Nagasaki bomb. The island on which the device was built disappeared permanently from the face of the earth.

Teller did not attend the test, but followed it on a seismograph at Berkeley in California. After the announcement by President Truman of the success of the test in January 1953, Teller became known in the press as the "father of the H-bomb". He had left Los Alamos the previous year and joined the new Lawrence Livermore Laboratory, which developed in time into a second nuclear weapons laboratory in competition with Los Alamos.

Although Teller is remembered today chiefly as the brain behind the H-bomb, one of his other contributions, which dates from 1945 and which did not attract much publicity at the time, has proved to be important. This was the addition of a few grams of fusion fuel to an ordinary fission bomb to increase the blast yield – the so-called boosted bomb. Today all American fission bombs are boosted in this way and although only about 1% of the explosion is derived from the fusion, this kind of bomb has the additional advantage of releasing a flood of neutrons which instantaneously cause fission in a large part of the core and therefore utilise the material more effectively.

Less than a year after the Americans detonated the first H-bomb, on 12 August 1953, the USSR astounded the Americans by exploding its own H-bomb, code-named Joe-4. This time they didn't detonate a "factory" but a proper weapon which could be delivered by an aircraft. It was discovered later that this bomb was a boosted fission bomb rather than a fusion bomb. The initial consternation was therefore unnecessary.

The Russian attempt was nevertheless a sufficient incentive to the Americans and on 28 February 1954 the USA detonated the first deliverable H-bomb, in a test code-named Castle Bravo, on the Bikini Atoll of the Marshall Islands. It was a successful test with a blast yield of 15 million tons of TNT, but at the same time it was a major catastrophe. About 20 000 km^2 was contaminated with radioactivity and the local inhabitants were subjected to radiation. The area had to be evacuated and the whole region is uninhabitable to this day.

The Cold War had begun and the Soviet Union did not want to be left behind. Andrei Sakharov designed a fusion bomb which worked on the same principle as the Teller-Ulam device. They tested the first real Soviet fusion bomb, known as RDS-37, on 22 November 1955 at the Semipalatinsk test site in Kazakhstan. It had a blast yield of several million tons of TNT, and was therefore a true H-bomb.

This was not the end of the desire to build bigger and better bombs. To prove its technical capabilities once and for all, the Soviet Union detonated its biggest nuclear bomb ever in October 1961 – the Tsar Bomba with a blast yield of 50 million tons of TNT. To put this in perspective: This blast yield is put at ten times the joint blast yield of all the explosives used during the Second World War!

Another goal was to stockpile more and more bombs. The USA alone developed 112 different types of nuclear weapons over the years and the bombs naturally had to undergo testing to ensure that they worked and determine how much mortality and destruction they would cause.

Between July 1945 and September 1992 the USA carried out 1 054 tests. It is still possible to measure the resultant contamination of the atmosphere, although since 1962 all tests have been performed underground.

An important aim of the tests was naturally to qualify the nuclear bombs according to military standards and ensure that the devices were "G.I.-proof". In a combat situation there would not always be a bunch of Nobel prize-winners on hand to undertake the last fine-tuning. The designs had to be modified in such a way – and of course tested – that it would be impossible for an uninformed soldier to start a global nuclear war by accident.

According to official figures, the Soviet Union carried out 715 nuclear tests.

Immense arsenals of nuclear weapons were built up by both the USA and the USSR. At the beginning of the arms race between the two powers in the 1960s the USA had twelve times as many weapons. The USSR caught up rapidly, however, and outstripped the USA so that by the mid-1980s the Soviet Union had over 45 000 nuclear weapons and the USA only 23 000. The point at which the MAD nuclear war strategic capability had been achieved – where MAD stands for Mutually Assured Destruction – had long been passed.

It is estimated that today there are about 27 000 nuclear weapons left in the world, of which about 8 500 in the USA and Russia are functional. The rest are obsolete and will probably have to be rebuilt, because the non-nuclear components especially are out of date, non-functional or unreliable. The Americans usually dismantle such weapons at their Pantex plant in Texas and retain the usable cores. The Russians apparently simply store the old weapons and hope for the best.

"With the bloody Union Jack on top of it ..."

Despite the American successes in building the first nuclear bombs – and the USSR's swift imitation of these achievements – it should be remembered that the foundations of nuclear physics were laid in Britain in places like the Cavendish Laboratory and by people like Ernest Rutherford and James Chadwick, who discovered the neutron. In fact Chadwick was the first Briton to advocate the development of the nuclear bomb and make a substantial contribution to the Manhattan Project. In a parallel development to the American programme, foreigners like the exiled German-Jewish scientists Otto Frisch, Rudolf Peierls, Franz Simon and others who belonged to the so-called Paris Group provided the technical and intellectual fuel. Although the fire was burning brightly the supply of firewood was drying up since Britain had been fighting the Second World War for a few years. The secret British

Tube Alloys programme therefore did not really get off the ground.

The renowned Maud report, referred to previously in this text, was mainly the work of Frisch and Peierls. The conclusion advanced in this report was that a nuclear bomb was not only possible but unavoidable. After initial bureaucratic delays in the USA, this report set the wheels in America in rapid motion.

This by no means suggests that cooperation with the Americans was plain sailing – on the contrary there were notable fits and starts. In the beginning there were reciprocal visits between the two programmes, but when Groves and the American army took over the project the flow of information abruptly dried up.

The work done at the Cavendish Laboratory with heavy water and slow neutrons appeared to be the route to the production of plutonium. The British were eager to transfer the Cambridge group to the University of Chicago, where similar work was being done. The Americans were suspicious and baulked at doing this – only one of the group of six was British. The result was that the closest the group could get to the USA was Montreal in Canada. There the group stagnated when the flow of information dried up and the Canadians were on the point of cancelling the project. After months of negotiation an agreement – the so-called Quebec Agreement – was eventually signed by Churchill and Roosevelt in August 1943. This resulted in an exchange of materials and information and the British effort was incorporated in the Manhattan Project. This included the transfer of the following eminent scientists: Niels Bohr, William Penney, Robert Frisch, Rudolf Peierls, James Chadwick, James Tuck, Egon Bretscher and the Trojan horse, Klaus Fuchs.

Another consequence of the Quebec Agreement

The easing of relations between the USA and Britain had important consequences for South Africa as well.

We know today that uranium is about 40 times as common as silver and over 500 times as common as gold in the earth's crust. But the problem is to find it in sufficient concentrations to make it economic to mine.

In the early 1940s uranium supplies were limited and furthermore the worldwide distribution of the source material was largely unknown. The result was a scramble to find sources of this miracle substance. General Jan Smuts, the South African Prime Minister who was elevated

> to the rank of Field Marshal by the British in 1941, served in Winston Churchill's war cabinet. The Manhattan Project was discussed at a meeting in London early in 1944. Smuts was scarcely back in South Africa when he received a top secret telegram from Sir John Anderson, the Chancellor of the Exchequer. Smuts was requested to begin an urgent search for possible uranium deposits in South Africa and South-West Africa (the present-day Namibia). As a geologist, Professor G.W. Bain, one of General Leslie Groves' advisers, had a personal interest in South Africa.
>
> An exchange of knowledge took place, radioactive measuring instruments were supplied and ore samples went all the way to the USA. The results of the search were relatively clear-cut: Although uranium occurred in low concentrations along with gold in the Witwatersrand supergroup, such large volumes of ore were routinely processed that the production of uranium could be seen as a useful and desirable by-product of the gold-mining industry. A few pilot plants were set up in 1949 and 1950 to test the technology and the required processes. The first uranium production plant which came into operation, West Rand Consolidated, began producing in September 1952. South Africa had suddenly become one of the important international players in the field of uranium production.
>
> Although the war had been over for a few years, the political implications of the possession of uranium necessitated meticulous and effective control over it. This gave rise to the promulgation of the Atomic Energy Act of 1948, which established the Atomic Energy Board (AEB) – an indirect offshoot of the American search for uranium for weapons, but also a big boost for South Africa's mining industry and international prestige.

Just how forced the cooperation between the Americans and the British was, is apparent from the fact that Groves refused point blank to allow the British to go along on the Hiroshima flight. After loud protests William Penney was allowed on an observation plane that followed Bock's Car when it dropped its bomb on Nagasaki on 9 August 1945. Penney later wrote: "All of us were in a state of emotional shock. We realised that a new age had begun and that possibly we had all made some contribution to raising a monster that would consume us all."

After the war the British were convinced that the Americans would share the technology behind the bombs with them since they had contributed the lion's share to what they saw as a joint project. However, a new law adopted in the USA in 1946 (the famous/infamous Atomic Energy Act under which South Africa also suffered in later years) abruptly put an end to any such expectations.

The British were incensed and the Foreign Secretary in the Attlee cabinet (Churchill's successors) exclaimed angrily: "We've got to have this thing over here, whatever it costs. We've got to have the bloody Union Jack on top of it."

Indignation was rapidly translated into action and in 1950 the Atomic Weapons Research Establishment (AWRE) was founded in Aldermaston. Two years later, on 3 October 1952, the British exploded their own, improved version of Fat Man on an island off the west coast of Australia. This was followed by further atmospheric and underground tests (45 in all) and ultimately by their own H-bomb in 1958 – each with its own "bloody Union Jack" on top of it.

France, the fourth country with the force de frappe

After the accidental discovery in 1896 by Henri Becquerel that uranium salts emitted radiation of an unknown kind, there was considerable interest in France in this new field. Maria Sklodowska left her native country, Poland, graduated at the Sorbonne in 1893 and married Pierre Curie in 1894. Two years after Becquerel's discovery Marie Curie named this phenomenon "radioactivity". She and her husband were acclaimed for their work on isolating radium and polonium.

Before the Second World War there was a lot of activity in this field in France. Marie Curie's clever but sullen daughter, Irène, and her husband, Frédéric Joliot (who changed his surname to Joliot-Curie in honour of his formidable mother-in-law), did pioneering work but because they misinterpreted experimental results they missed two important discoveries: the discovery of the neutron (that honour fell to Chadwick) and the splitting of the uranium atom, which was recognised and explained by Hahn and Meitner. After receiving the news of the discovery of the splitting of the atom, Joliot-Curie repeated the experiment and was able to identify the fission products. Like a moody teenager he shut himself up for a few days and did not communicate with anyone – except for Abram Fedorovich Ioffe, the doyen of the Russian physicists in Leningrad. Joliot-Curie was a committed communist.

After the publication of Hahn and Meitner's sensational findings in January 1939, Francis Perrin defined the concept "critical mass" in May of the same year and published a formula for calculating the critical mass of uranium. Clearly, there was an abundance of talent in France, but Hitler's invasion in May 1940 and his conquest of France in the space of a little more than a month changed the picture completely. Most of the French scientists fled to England. Whereas France had initially been one of the leading countries in the area of nuclear research, the USA, Russia and Britain overtook France by far during the Second World War and after the war France had to start building up from scratch. They began by establishing the first civil nuclear energy authority in the world, the "Commissariat à l'Énergie Atomique" (CEA), in October 1945, with Charles de Gaulle playing an important role. The first high commissioner of the CEA was none other than Frédéric Joliot-Curie ...

But far more was required to restore France's international prestige. Apart from the humiliating defeat by Hitler, internal political chaos reigned. Between 1947 and 1958, 25 cabinets were appointed and then kicked out. In addition, in 1955 France lost the Indochina War, which had lasted for nine years, and the same year saw the start of the Algerian uprising against French rule. The Algerian situation almost led to a military coup d'état by discontented generals in France. The situation was eventually saved by Charles de Gaulle, who obtained emergency powers to rule the country for six months and draw up a new constitution. He became president in 1958 and occupied that position until 1969.

De Gaulle proposed to restore France's international prestige through a foreign policy of independence, a risky balancing act between the dominant powers, America and the USSR. He recommended the closure of all American bomber bases in France and withdrew French forces from the North Atlantic Treaty Organization (NATO). His trump card was to be the establishment of an independent French nuclear force.

Although the CEA started a few modest projects to produce plutonium – producing between 10 mg and 200 g in various small-scale natural uranium reactors with heavy water as the moderator – and carried out laboratory-scale experiments to reclaim the plutonium that was produced, there was a certain tardiness about making real progress. The reason? Joliot-Curie had surrounded himself with a select group of communists in the CEA – people like Tessier, Auger, Langevin (Joliot-Curie's former professor) and Francis Perrin. The CIA in America reported on this as early as August 1946 in a secret document.

From the beginning the Communist Party in the USSR put great pressure on its party members and sympathisers in the West to put up a fierce resistance against the promotion of nuclear energy, and especially nuclear weapons. In time it became so much part of the political DNA of leftist groups that even today the greatest resistance to nuclear energy is still encountered among these groups in the West.

De Gaulle eventually became aware of the problem and acted swiftly to get rid of the high-profile communists. Joliot-Curie was dismissed and a new triumvirate drew up a plan which included the construction of a large-scale plutonium production reactor at Marcoule. This plan had been approved by 1951, but formal approval for the development of nuclear weapons was only received late in 1954. The military defeat in Indochina played an important part in these events.

Bertrand Goldschmidt was a key member of the French team at Marcoule. He was the last assistant appointed by Marie Curie before she died of leukemia – the result of receiving excessively high doses of radiation over a long period.

He was the only Frenchman ever permitted to work on the Manhattan Project, but only on the periphery. Goldschmidt collaborated with Glen Seaborg in the USA on plutonium reclamation from irradiated uranium and developed a process which is still in use today.

A year before the Hiroshima bomb exploded, Goldschmidt met General de Gaulle in the men's bathroom of a hotel while on a visit to Ottawa and informed him in the space of three minutes about what was happening in the USA. De Gaulle immediately realised the importance of this information. Goldschmidt was later to play a significant part in the development of France's nuclear weapons and is considered by some to be the father of the French nuclear programme.

Goldschmidt and the South African diplomat Donald Sole – the first freely elected chairman of the Board of Governors of the International Atomic Energy Agency (IAEA) from 1959 to 1960 – became friends during the establishment years of the IAEA; this proved to be a life-long friendship. Goldschmidt was France's governor on the board of the IAEA for 23 years and became the chairman in 1980.

After the CIA's identification of communists on the French programme, France could expect no help from the Americans. While the last battle in Indochina was being fought at Diên Biên Phú, the French actually sent a shopping list to Britain to help them build an atomic bomb. This list included a small quantity of plutonium which the French would use to carry out studies before starting large-scale plutonium production on their own account.

The British agreed (without informing their American "friends") and even offered to check the working drawings and construction of the plants at Marcoule. According to certain sources the meticulous attention these received from the British may well have prevented a catastrophic explosion which could have contaminated the whole environment of the Rhône valley.

It was not only the British who collaborated. Dozens of Israelis were involved in the construction of the G1 plutonium production reactor and the UP1 reprocessing plant at Marcoule. This cooperation reached a peak in the 1950s. By the end of that decade the Israelis were not merely observers but also participants in the French nuclear weapons design programme.

When the French eventually detonated their first plutonium bomb on 13 February 1960 in the Sahara Desert in Algeria, two countries were said to have become nuclear powers thanks to the explosion, namely France and Israel. The test, which was code-named Gerboise Bleue (blue jerboa), had an unprecedented yield of 60 to 70 kilotons of TNT, the biggest first test ever to have been carried out by a nuclear power. This was followed by an additional three tests in the same area, code-named White Jerboa, Red Jerboa and Green Jerboa. These successful tests were the spearhead of De Gaulle's new *force de frappe*.

The French carried out further atmospheric and later underground tests and between February 1960 and January 1996 they detonated no less than 210 nuclear bombs. Among the weapons tested was the first thermonuclear (hydrogen) bomb, which was exploded in August 1968 in French Polynesia. The blast yield was equivalent to 2.6 million tons of TNT.

China, the fifth nuclear power

The Americans built the bomb as a bulwark against Hitler (unnecessary in the event). The USSR's bomb was clearly an attempt to deny the Americans the sole right to the most powerful weapon ever made. The British built their bomb out of wounded national pride after the Americans gave them the cold shoulder. The French attempt was motivated by the desire to raise France from a position of national inferiority and chaos and restore its image of power. And what about the Chinese?

China has the third largest land area in the world, the biggest population and the biggest economy but one. For almost 3 500 years China was one of the most technologically advanced states in the world. To name one example, gunpowder was invented there 400 years before it was invented in Europe and was rapidly used in a variety of weapons such as flame throwers, rockets, bombs and mines – even before it was used in firearms.

Whereas the West is noted for its short-term focus on the next financial "bottom line", the Chinese have a long-term vision – and long memories. They haven't forgotten the instances of foreign intervention and the defeats by the Mongols, French, Germans and Japanese – and especially by Britain. In the early and mid-1800s for almost half a century the British East India Company – with the full approval of the British government – exported opium to China illegally to recover the silver they had expended on importing tea, silk and porcelain. In 1820, for example, the illegal annual opium exports to China amounted to about 900 tons. Naturally the Chinese government was not prepared to accept this and the result was the two disastrous Opium Wars, which ended in exposing China to gross exploitation by the West.

From a historical perspective it was therefore unavoidable that as soon as possible the Chinese would start working on developing their own nuclear bomb, with the assistance of the infamous Klaus Fuchs, and strong support from an old friend, the USSR. China and Russia concluded their first treaty back in 1689! In the late 1950s Mao Zedong, supported by the Soviet Union, officially ordered the development of a nuclear bomb. This assistance took the form of the provision of technical advisers, materials and equipment. The latter included an experimental nuclear reactor and equipment for uranium processing, as well as a gas diffusion plant. The Soviet Union even went as far as to offer a prototype of a nuclear weapon so that the Chinese could study it.

As a result of ideological differences, relations with the USSR began to go sour and by 1959 there was an open breach between the two countries. The data and instructions on how to build a nuclear bomb were withheld and the Soviet advisers were withdrawn. But this merely fuelled Mao's desire to build his own nuclear bomb as a deterrent against American and Soviet threats.

Five years later, in October 1964, success was eventually achieved. The Chinese carried out their first nuclear test, with a bomb with a blast yield of about 22 kilotons of TNT, at the test site at Lop Nor. It was the first time any country had carried out its first nuclear test with an implosion weapon made of highly enriched uranium, and not of plutonium. The code name for the first explosion was Project 596 – to commemorate the severance of Soviet-Chinese relations in June 1959.

In the 32 months after the first test the Chinese made remarkably rapid progress. Their first nuclear missile was tested in October 1966 and the first thermonuclear bomb in 1967. The West was astounded at the speed of the progress made and in 1999 the Director of the CIA stated that the Chinese could only have done this because they had received information on a variety of American weapons concepts through espionage.

A statement issued by the Chinese government on 16 October 1964 read as follows:

> The atomic bomb is a paper tiger. This famous statement by Chairman Mao Zedong is known to all. This was our view in the past and this is still our view at present. China is developing nuclear weapons not because it believes in their omnipotence nor because it plans to use them. On the contrary, in developing nuclear weapons, China's aim is to break the nuclear monopoly of the nuclear powers and to eliminate nuclear weapons.

Their intention to "break the nuclear monopoly" is more ominous than it may sound at first. According to *Racing for the Bomb*, by Robert S. Norris (2011), China took a policy decision in 1982 to help the developing countries to acquire nuclear expertise. Their clients included countries like Algeria, Pakistan, Libya, North Korea and Iran. The philosophy behind this was evidently that if everyone possessed nuclear bombs, this would eliminate nuclear war between states. One of China's nuclear bomb designs was specifically intended for export purposes. A design of this kind landed up in South Africa in the late 1990s, via Libya, as was discovered during the Tradefin-Krisch Engineering investigation.

Whatever China's motives were for distributing nuclear expertise so lavishly, the Chinese did not foresee the later problem of non-state Islamic terrorism, something the world, and especially the USA, is in fear of now.

Be this as it may, China is the last country on the list of the five internationally recognised "nuclear-weapon states". The next question to ask is how this classification came about.

PART 2

On 2 August 1939 Albert Einstein and Leo Szilard wrote a letter to President Franklin D. Roosevelt expressing concern about Germany's nuclear programme and suggesting that the Americans expand their nuclear research.
Source: http://www.lowdensitylifestyle.com/FREE,%20flexibility,%20fluidity/albert-einstein/

General Leslie Groves (left), the military head of the Manhattan Project, with Professor Robert Oppenheimer, who acted as scientific head of the project.
Source: http://en.wikipedia.org/wiki/File:Groves_Oppenheimer.jpg

The first plutonium bomb, named Gadget, on the test tower just before the Trinity test was carried out. Norris Bradbury, seen on the photograph, was to become Robert Oppenheimer's successor and to occupy that post for several decades.
Source: http://nuclearweaponarchive.org/Usa/Tests/GadgetC351c10.jpg

On 6 August 1945 the world's first uranium nuclear bomb was used. The bomb, codenamed Little Boy, was dropped on the Japanese city of Hiroshima. The explosive yield was equivalent to 13 000 tons of TNT.
Source: http://historiana.eu/sources/show/little-boy-the-atomic-bomb-that-destroyedhiroshima

2　P

Fat Man, which was dropped on Nagasaki on 9 August 1945, was a plutonium bomb similar to the model used a month previously in the Trinity test. The explosive yield was equivalent to 20 000 tons of TNT.
Source: http://wvcivildefensefreak.webs.com/fatmanbomb.htm

Edward Teller in 1958. He was of Hungarian-Jewish descent and was one of the leading figures of the Manhattan Project. Teller is recognised as the father of the thermonuclear bomb (also called the hydrogen bomb).
Source: http://de.wikipedia.org/wiki/Edward Teller

Dr Wally Grant (1922–2008) developed the unique South African uranium enrichment process. As head of Ucor he was the driving force behind the building of the two enrichment plants at the Valindaba site, namely the Y-plant (pilot plant) and the Z-plant (semi-commercial enrichment plant). After retiring he spent the rest of his life working on the refinement of the vortex isotope separation process.
Source: Photograph from private collection

Dr J.W. (Wynand) L. de Villiers (1929–1995) is regarded as the "father of the South African nuclear bomb". From 1958 he was part of the then Atomic Energy Board and in 1982 he became Chief Executive Officer of the Atomic Energy Corporation. From 1990 until his death he was the Chairman of the Board of the AEC.
Source: Photograph from private collection

The pilot enrichment plant or Y-plant at the Valindaba site with its characteristic ventilation towers. Highly enriched uranium for nuclear weapons and low-enriched uranium for Koeberg fuel were produced here from the mid-1970s to the end of the 1980s.
Source: Ucor publication: 10 Years 1970–1980

Equipment consisting of compressors, pressure damping vessels and filter vessels as well as pipes and control valves inside an enrichment stage of the Y-plant.
Source: Ucor publication: 10 Years 1970–1980

The shed over the test shaft at the Vastrap site in the Kalahari where South Africa planned to carry out a "cold" nuclear test in August 1977. The test never took place, since satellite observations of the preparations confirmed the prior information provided by spies working for the USSR and the USA.
Source: http://isis-online.org/uploads/isis-reports/documents/Vastrap_30November2011.pdf

The Soviet spy and former commanding officer of the Simonstown Naval Base, Commodore Dieter Gerhardt, with his wife Ruth and their son Gregory.
Source: http://www.beeld.com/By/Nuus/Spioen-spioen-n-Ware-verhaal-20111111-2

The German-born physicist Klaus Fuchs worked on secret nuclear weapons projects in Britain and the USA. A Soviet spy, he was partly responsible for the rapid progress made with the USSR's nuclear weapons programme. He subsequently shared this knowledge with China.
Source: http://atomicarchive.com

Dr Jannie Wannenburg of Ucor inspects his handiwork, an axial flow compressor similar to those used in jet engines, which he designed and had built for the compression of process gas in the Z-plant.
Source: Ucor publication: 10 Years 1970–1980

Dr A.J.A. Roux (1914–1985): He became President of the Atomic Energy Board in 1959, planned and set up South Africa's nuclear research programme and headed it for the next 20 years.
Source: Ucor publication: 10 Years 1970–1980

Otto Hahn (1879–1968): Hahn is regarded as the father of nuclear chemistry. He and his colleague Strassmann discovered the nuclear fission of uranium in 1938, but were unable to interpret their results and had to rely on Lise Meitner to explain them.
Source: http://www.biographyonline.net/scientists/otto-hahn.html

Ernest Rutherford (1871–1937): Rutherford is regarded as the father of nuclear physics, responsible for the discovery of the atomic nucleus and the decay of radioactive elements.
Source: http://www.independent.co.uk/news/education/education-news/manchester-britains-greatest-university-2101828.html?action=gallery&ino=3

Robert Oppenheimer and Leslie Groves (centre) inspecting the remains of the tower on which the first nuclear test (the Trinity test) took place on 16 July 1945.
Source: Wikipedia, public domain

Staff members of the AEB who underwent training in the USA. From left to right, Dr S.J. du Toit (physics), Dr J.W.L. de Villiers (reactor engineering), W.H. Tabor (Oak Ridge, USA), Dr L. le Roux (chemistry) and Dr W.L. Grant (engineering). This historic photograph was taken on 7 April 1961 at Oak Ridge.
Photograph: Supplied by Marlet le Roux

ATOMS IN THE SERVICE OF PEACE (OR HOW TO TAME A MONSTER)

"... the hopeless finality of a belief that two atomic colossi are doomed malevolently to eye each other indefinitely across a trembling world ..."

President Dwight D. Eisenhower at the United Nations General Assembly (UNGA), 8 December 1953

A very old story

Hecataeus, a contemporary of Democritus who lived in the same city, was a historian with a special interest in Egyptian history. In one of his writings he turns the story of the Jewish exodus from Egypt – as recounted in the book of Exodus – on its head. According to his version the Jews did not escape from Egypt but were thrown out as undesirables, or rather foreigners practising strange rites. Under Moses' leadership, wrote Hecataeus, these people were following a "misanthropic and inhospitable way of life". This was the beginning of numerous "expulsions" which the Jews were to suffer with regularity throughout the millennia.

A few months after Adolf Hitler came to power in Germany in March 1933, legislation was passed which prohibited people of Jewish descent from holding various positions at universities and in the civil service, legal profession and medical sector. The Nuremberg laws of 1935 classified people as Jews on the basis of their grandparents' religion. Highly acclaimed scientists, some of them Nobel prize-winners, suddenly found themselves without a job.

In Hungary, where the highly conservative Admiral Horthy had been in power since 1920, agreements were concluded with Hitler's Germany and Mussolini's fascist Italian state. Hungary entered the Second World War as Germany's ally. As in Germany, anti-Semitic laws were adopted and 250 000 Hungarian residents lost their jobs in this way in 1939.

In Britain William Beveridge and Lionel Robbins formed the Academic

THE BOMB

Assistance Council and succeeded in bringing 2 000 scientists of Jewish descent into Britain. For many of these people, however, Britain was merely a way station. Between 1933 and 1941 over 300 of them ended up in the USA – with a significant proportion joining the Manhattan Project.

The scientific leader of the Manhattan Project was Robert Oppenheimer, himself an American Jew. The Nobel prize-winner Richard Feynman, who played an important part in the project, was also of Jewish descent.

What those fugitives, along with their American colleagues, achieved between 1943 and 1945 calls to mind a very old story.

During the sixteenth century the Jewish inhabitants of the ghetto in Prague were in mortal danger as a result of an anti-Semitic edict issued by the emperor. Rabbi Judah Loew then took clay from the banks of the Moldau River (the present-day Vltava) and used it to fashion what was known as a golem according to the prescribed rituals. Using the required secret Hebrew incantations, he was able to breathe life into the clay manikin. To keep him alive, Rabbi Loew had to write the Hebrew word *emet* (truth) on his forehead. To deactivate the golem, one had to erase the first letter, leaving *met*, which meant death.

The purpose of the golem was to protect the Jewish community by wiping out their enemies. Although a golem is not an intelligent being, he carries out orders to the letter. He therefore began to exterminate the non-Jews, thereby arousing great fear among the people. According to the legend he even attacked his maker.

The story is told that the deactivated golem still lies beside the remains of Rabbi Loew in the attic of the synagogue in Prague, in readiness in case his assistance is ever needed again.

Did the many scientists of Jewish descent who worked so zealously on the Manhattan Project out of curiosity – and out of fear and hatred of Hitler – have any idea what the golem monster they were helping to create would lead to? Was there a possibility that the golem would turn on them, and how would they ever be able to change the writing on his forehead to "death"? After 70 years this is still a matter for speculation.

On the other hand, would it be possible to harness the golem to serve instead of destroy humankind?

ATOMS IN THE SERVICE OF PEACE (OR HOW TO TAME A MONSTER)

Peaceful applications – a possibility?

After the first successful Trinity test and the dropping of the two nuclear bombs on Japan in 1945, events rapidly moved in a dangerous direction. In 1949 the Soviet Union tested its first nuclear weapon, followed by England in 1952. Only a month after the English test the Americans tested the first fusion bomb (or hydrogen bomb as it is also known), which was almost a thousand times as powerful as the earliest bombs. The Soviet Union was swift to follow suit and, as previously mentioned, tested a prototype of a hydrogen bomb in August 1953. In the meanwhile the USA's stockpile of nuclear weapons increased from 400 in 1950 to about 20 000 in 1960. Over the same period the USSR's arsenal grew from five to 1 600, but the Russians rapidly caught up with the Americans so that by the mid-1980s the Russians were ahead with around 45 000 as against 23 000 nuclear weapons. Humanity – or the Americans and the Russians at any rate – appeared to be rushing headlong towards their own destruction with little hope of halting the process. Something had to be done. The only chance of survival lay in a change of course.

Naturally there were also scientists and engineers who were working not on armaments but on controlling the uranium chain reaction and using it in nuclear reactors to generate electricity or to power ships. Furthermore, the USA and the USSR already had a stockpile of nuclear weapons sufficient to wipe out life on the planet – several times over. What were they to do with the vast – and hugely expensive – facilities especially built for the weapons programmes?

By that time the cat was out of the bag. Six days after the first nuclear bomb devastated Hiroshima, the *Smyth Report*, containing extensive information on the USA's secret nuclear weapons programme, was published in the USA. The American taxpayers suddenly discovered where their tax dollars had been spent – and would continue to be spent. There was considerable political pressure to justify these costly facilities. Nuclear reactors to power ships and submarines were at the top of the list. In 1954 the first American nuclear submarine, the Nautilus, was launched. This was followed by the commissioning of the first nuclear power plants: in 1956 at Obninsk in the USSR and at Calder Hall in Britain. In the USA the Shippingport nuclear power plant came into operation in 1957.

> ### "Good" and "bad" electricity
>
> Some years ago a much-publicised device was advertised in Austria – a country which is vehemently opposed to nuclear power. It was intended for connection to the household electricity supply. It would then identify any electricity generated by a nuclear reactor and summarily return such electricity to source – or so it was claimed.
>
> How does electricity generated by a nuclear reactor differ from that produced by a coal-fired power station? There is basically no difference. In both cases high-pressure steam is required to turn the turbines used to generate electricity. In a nuclear reactor the heat used to produce steam comes from the reactor core and in a coal-fired power station it comes from the combustion of coal.
>
> This remarkable patent was nothing but a swindle.

Besides the building of nuclear reactors, extensive programmes were run in the USA and the USSR to find ways of using nuclear explosions for peaceful purposes.

From the early 1960s to 1988, the USA and the Soviet Union conducted well in excess of 100 so-called peaceful nuclear explosions (PNEs). In the USSR alone, in their programme "Nuclear Explosions for the National Economy", slightly over 20% of the more than 700 nuclear tests conducted (some of which involved multiple, simultaneous detonations) were PNE-relevant. Over half of them were used for the implementation of two industrial applications: the creation of underground cavities in salt for the storage of gas condensate and deep seismic sounding of the earth's crust and upper mantle.

Other applications included oil and gas stimulation (fracking), extinguishing burning oil and gas wells, disposal of toxic chemical waste, block cave mining of underground minerals, as well as the excavation of water reservoirs and canals. Naturally – in typical Soviet style – many of the purportedly peaceful tests were probably disguised nuclear weapons tests.

The Soviet PNE programme was more extensive than the American Project Plowshare which was carried out in the 1960s and early 1970s. Only about 2% of the over 1 000 American nuclear tests were PNE-related. The USA did not make use of explosions for industrial purposes and fired only three industrial field experiments. One of them, Operation Gasbuggy, was a nuclear-sized fracking experiment. The result was apparently positive; however, the gas released turned out to be radioactive. Other proposals included using five thermonuclear bombs – at the insistence of Edward Teller – to dig out a harbour on Alaska's North Slope (Operation Chariot); digging an alternative to the Panama Canal across Nicaragua; and using underground blasting to release the oil from tar sands in Canada. None of these proposals was put into practice.

In Vienna, during the first half of the 1970s, the IAEA actively studied the status and technology relating to PNEs. Guidelines and procedures were issued and a series of technical meetings were held to review "the-state-of-the-art".

There were also potential uses for radioactive isotopes in the medical field, in industry and in agriculture – true peaceful applications. The application of nuclear technology in these specialised areas was in its infancy and much research and development was still required. Scientists had to be trained, facilities built and research done on the effective and safe use of isotopes. The potential applications were promising but there was still a long road ahead.

Heir presumptive of a remarkable family; wars and peacekeeping bodies

For 600 years the remarkable royal house of Habsburg reigned over most of Western Europe, the Balkan states, Hungary and Poland and even produced an English king who reigned for a short while. Their motto was: AEIOU – Austriae Est Imperare Orbi Universo, *that is, Austria will rule the world.*

Archduke Franz Ferdinand of Austria, a member of this sizeable family, was born in 1863. He appears to have been born with the proverbial silver spoon in his mouth. When he was twelve years old he was left a legacy by an uncle which made him one of the richest people in Austria, on condition that he added the name "Este" to his own. His cousin Rudolf, the heir apparent to the imperial and royal crown (K und K – kaiserlich und königlich), committed suicide after an extramarital affair with a young girl. Franz Ferdinand then became the official heir to the throne. He fell in love with Countess Sophie Chotek, a Czechoslovakian, but his uncle, Emperor Franz Josef, felt that her blood was not blue enough and therefore opposed the marriage. Thanks to the intervention of the Pope, the Czar of Russia and Emperor Wilhelm II of Germany, Franz Josef finally consented to the marriage albeit reluctantly.

THE BOMB

Franz Ferdinand and Emperor Franz Josef had other differences, which frequently led to heated arguments. One of the differences concerned the rebellious Serbs in Bosnia, one of the Balkan states under Austrian control. As recent history has again demonstrated, the inhabitants of those regions are perpetually restless and inclined towards violence.

While visiting Sarajevo on 28 June 1914 – in an attempt to reduce tensions – Franz Ferdinand and Sophie rode through the town in an open car, despite warnings. A bomb was thrown at the car. It was fortunately deflected by Franz Ferdinand's arm but it landed on the ground and injured a number of people. After the party had visited the injured in hospital, Franz Ferdinand's driver got lost and turned down a side street. When he realised his mistake and tried to turn round, a Serbian fired shots at Franz Ferdinand and Sophie at short range, killing them both.

Austria could not overlook the murder of its crown prince and declared war against Serbia two months later. The dominoes then began to fall, one after the other. The Serbians were of Slavonic descent and had blood ties with the Russians. This aspect drew the Russians into the conflict and because an alliance existed between Russia and France (the traditional enemy of the Habsburgs), France was also involved. The Germans in turn declared war on Russia and before long the pistol shots fired by Gavrilo Princip in Sarajevo had started the First World War, in which 32 nations ultimately became involved. The death toll reached 16 million and the injured numbered 21 million. This war also brought the Habsburg domination of Europe to an end after six centuries.

After the end of the Great War, as it was known, the victors met in France in 1918 and the Treaty of Versailles was signed in 1919. This treaty was important for several reasons: It established a new international organisation, the League of Nations, in an attempt to prevent further large-scale wars; the former South African Boer general, Jan Christiaan Smuts, was responsible for framing and implementing the treaty; and lastly the humiliating nature of the treaty produced a fertile dragon's egg out of which Hitler was to hatch. In less than 20 years he had seized power in Germany and started an even more extensive war, the Second World War. This time about 60 million people died, almost four times as many as in the Great War.

ATOMS IN THE SERVICE OF PEACE (OR HOW TO TAME A MONSTER)

> *The League of Nations was indisputably a failure and was later dissolved to make way for a new international organisation, the United Nations (UN), which was established on 24 October 1945.*
>
> *Jan Smuts again played a prominent part. He wrote the introduction to the UN Charter and was the only person to sign the charters of both international organisations.*
>
> *The world pinned its hopes on this new international organisation. International control and coordination were seen as the new panacea for managing conflicting nationalism with the aim of attaining and preserving lasting world peace.*

A delicate balancing act

What else could be done to prevent the further proliferation of nuclear weapons, while promoting the peaceful application of nuclear energy?

The priority for the nuclear-weapon states was to ensure that nobody else developed and built nuclear weapons – competition in this area would rob them of their dreadful advantage. Three months after the end of the Second World War, the USA, Britain and Canada entered into an agreement in November 1945 to buy up all the available uranium and to maintain a policy of strict secrecy regarding all matters concerning nuclear energy until an effective international system was introduced to control this new source of devastation – but also of unexplored potential peaceful applications.

By 1946 Dean Acheson, the US Secretary of State, had formed a select group, which was led by David Lilienthal and included Robert Oppenheimer of Los Alamos, to study ways of promoting the peaceful application of nuclear energy and eliminating nuclear weapons. Their conclusion was that no system of banning nuclear weapons would work. They were convinced that international inspections in individual states would not be practicable either. They therefore recommended that all nuclear energy programmes that could potentially be used to develop nuclear weapons should be taken out of the hands of individual states and transferred to a suitable international authority. This authority would have charge of the nuclear industry and would undertake development work and run nuclear projects on behalf of states and in accordance with their needs. This international authority would also own all uranium ore and nuclear fuels and would manufacture fuel and operate nuclear reactors. Any attempts by states to carry out any such activities would be illegal and would be detected by international inspectors.

While this group was giving careful consideration to the problem of controlling nuclear energy, ideas on the matter were being exchanged inside the UN as well. The proposal put forward by the USA and Britain that an atomic energy commission should be established at the UN was eventually accepted by the Soviet Union. The United Nations Atomic Energy Commission (UNAEC) came into being in 1946.

It was to this commission that Bernard Baruch of the USA submitted the Acheson-Lilienthal plan, in a somewhat modified form. Baruch proposed that the transition from national to international control should take place in phases. The last phase would be completed when all nuclear weapons had been handed over to the international authority.

From the start, the Soviet Union, supported by Poland, was vehemently opposed to the American proposal, and particularly to the idea of international ownership and control. The result was a marathon session and some of the matters debated were simply absurd. Should the underground ore that occurred in the respective states belong to the international authority? Should the international authority be the sole manufacturer of nuclear explosives? After two years and 200 meetings the UNAEC finally admitted defeat in 1948 and in 1952 the commission was dissolved without consensus having been reached – a victim of the ferocious Cold War which was in its early stages.

After 1949 the idea of an international nuclear authority began to lose support while the number of nuclear weapons increased rapidly and new nuclear-weapon powers entered the game. Britain carried out its first nuclear test in 1952 and France started building plutonium production facilities as well.

The signs were ominous and it was evident that action was urgently needed.

The general triumphs in the talking shop

The man who had the courage to tackle the problem was General Dwight David Eisenhower (popularly known as Ike). He was the former Supreme Allied Commander of the Expeditionary Force that inflicted a shattering defeat on Hitler's forces in May 1945 on the Western Front, with the aid of the Soviets on the Eastern Front. Thanks to the prestige that Eisenhower acquired as a result, he was elected President of the United States in 1953 with an overwhelming majority. He was 63 years old, an age at which most people are thinking of retiring.

ATOMS IN THE SERVICE OF PEACE (OR HOW TO TAME A MONSTER)

Eisenhower proved his worth as a leader and diplomat beyond all doubt during the Normandy invasion on D-Day. In addition to commanding almost a million troops, he had to deal with the opposition of self-willed generals like Bernard Law (Monty) Montgomery, who wanted to do things their way.

Although Eisenhower was a militarist in every fibre of his being, he was never greatly in favour of nuclear weapons. When news of the successful Trinity test was received by telegram in July 1945 during the Potsdam Conference (after the victory over Germany), Henry L. Stimson, the US Secretary of State, informed Eisenhower that they planned to drop the bomb on Japan shortly. When Eisenhower did not respond, Stimson asked his opinion. His reply angered Stimson. Eisenhower was opposed to dropping the bomb for two reasons. The first was that in his opinion the Japanese were on the point of surrender and the second was that he felt that America should not be the first country to use such a devastating weapon.

During the Korean War in the early 1950s Eisenhower's military chief of staff and his Secretary of State urged him strongly to consider the use of nuclear weapons to end the stalemate. Eisenhower's reaction was: "You boys must be crazy. We can't use those awful things against the Asians for a second time in less than ten years. My God!"

Eisenhower's famous "Atoms for Peace" speech in the UNGA, delivered only eleven months after his inauguration address on 20 January 1953 as the 34th President of the United States, should be seen against this background.

In his historic speech he emphasised two facts which are still equally relevant today, over 60 years later:
- The knowledge of nuclear weapons possessed by the USA and a few other countries at that stage would inevitably spread to other countries in time.
- Even a vast superiority in the existing number of nuclear weapons and the capacity for devastating retaliation would not be a sufficient preventive against a surprise attack, with accompanying large-scale loss of life and terrible material damage.

Eisenhower's proposal contained elements of the American Baruch plan which had been mooted seven years previously but was far more pragmatic. The main objectives of his plan were to begin reducing the nuclear weapons arsenals, to promote the peaceful use of nuclear energy and to establish an international UN agency as facilitator.

His vision was that fissile material from the stocks held by the nuclear-weapon powers should be transferred to a UN agency, the International Atomic Energy Agency (IAEA). This organisation would then ensure that the material was used for peaceful purposes in the agricultural sector, in medical science and especially for the generation of electricity in countries where there was a shortage of electrical power.

Eisenhower's speech was greeted with a standing ovation by the 3 500 delegates – one of the most enthusiastic responses to any address in the history of the UN. Even the Soviet delegates joined in. The elderly general was openly moved and the press immediately labelled his speech "Atoms for Peace".

Before Eisenhower's vision could take on a concrete form a great deal had to be done:

- An extensive investigation had to be undertaken into how and where fissile material could be used most effectively.
- It was necessary to ascertain whether the nuclear-weapon powers would be prepared to surrender their stocks of fissile material.
- The proposed UN agency would have to be set up, with a clearly defined mandate and the necessary means to carry out its task. Achieving consensus on this matter among the numerous members of the UN with their widely divergent viewpoints and needs was later to prove something of a nightmare.

The period from 1946 to 1953 can be regarded as a period of denial – in which the nuclear powers refrained from transferring knowledge, fissile materials and technology to any state outside the group. Eisenhower's Atoms for Peace changed all that. Bertrand Goldschmidt described this phase as "…the passage from the depressing era of denials to the euphoric era of transfers, from the nuclear Middle Ages to the nuclear Renaissance…" The "euphoric era" could be said to have dawned.

In 1954 the USA amended its Atomic Energy Act to enable peaceful cooperation with other countries on nuclear matters. Other states, notably Canada, Britain and France, soon followed suit. By the end of 1959 the USA had concluded agreements with 42 countries. Turkey was first in line, and South Africa was included in this group. Bilateral agreements were concluded for the transfer of knowledge, training and support – including financial support – for the acquisition of equipment and materials, especially research reactors. One of the important stipulations of the bilateral agreements was an undertaking by the recipient countries not to use the facilities or materials for nuclear weapons or military purposes. The exporting countries had the right to apply a system of inspections to ensure this undertaking was complied with. The intention was that once the IAEA was up and running it would take over these functions in time.

The Safari-1 research reactor at Pelindaba was supplied by the USA in terms of a bilateral nuclear cooperation agreement between the USA and South Africa.

Research reactors made available under the Atoms for Peace programme were not of much value for military purposes. There were two reactors, however, namely the Cirus reactor which Canada supplied to India (with American heavy water as the moderator) and the Dimona reactor which France supplied to Israel, that were a lot bigger and could be misused to produce plutonium. That is precisely what happened. Despite having solemnly pledged that the reactor would only be used for peaceful purposes, India made clandestine use of it to produce plutonium for the country's first nuclear explosion in 1974. India denied culpability, claiming it was a "peaceful explosion". The Atoms for Peace programme was suspended for a while after this. It was a sobering end to the "euphoric era".

Today there are those who charge Eisenhower with naivety regarding human nature and international politics. His opponents contend that his proposals were responsible for the fact that India, Israel and Pakistan possess nuclear weapons today.

During his training in the USA Dr Wynand de Villiers of Pelindaba legally acquired a computer program whose object was to ensure reactor safety by preventing unintended and uncontrolled chain reactions. Back in South Africa the program was later studied and adapted for use for peaceful nuclear explosions. Later still the program was expanded and used in the manufacture of South Africa's nuclear devices.

The criticisms levelled at Eisenhower may not be entirely misplaced.

How altruistic were Eisenhower's plans?

In addition to being the father of the Atoms for Peace programme, Eisenhower was also the only American president to publicly condemn the dropping of atomic bombs on Hiroshima and Nagasaki. But appearances can be deceptive ...

General Eisenhower became president in January 1953 when the war in Korea had been in progress for almost three years. At that stage there were 350 000 Chinese soldiers and 140 000 North Koreans on the point of moving southwards. Eisenhower asked his military and political advisers for their opinion on the use of nuclear weapons to wipe out these troop concentrations. As mentioned previously, for both personal and military reasons he did not favour the use of such weapons. But as the president he was forced to be realistic: "We cannot go on the way we are indefinitely." Nevertheless, he allowed himself to be guided by the advice of the Secretary of State, Dean Acheson, namely to use nuclear weapons as a political threat. This approach ultimately succeeded and the Chinese withdrew.

Eisenhower also used these tactics in the battle for Diên Biên Phú (French Indochina), in the Suez crisis and twice in conflicts over the islands of Quemoy and Matsu near Taiwan. In all these cases nuclear weapons were available and the possibility of using them was seriously considered, but opposition by the USA's European allies and public opinion in the USA successfully prevented this folly.

Under cover of the Atoms for Peace programme the number of nuclear weapons in the USA increased from around 1 000 to 22 000 during Eisenhower's term as president. When he stepped down in 1961 America's nuclear strike force was the equivalent of almost 1,4 million Hiroshima bombs.

The 2011 April edition of the Bulletin of Atomic Scientists quotes from the minutes of the USA's National Security Council meeting held in March 1953:

"... the President and Secretary [John Foster] Dulles were in complete agreement that somehow or other the tabu [sic] which surrounds the use of atomic weapons would have to be destroyed. While Secretary Dulles admitted that in the present state of world opinion we could not use an A-bomb, we should make every effort now to dissipate this feeling."

One of the aims of the Atoms for Peace programme was therefore indirectly to make the use of nuclear weapons more acceptable.

In 1960 Eisenhower approved the Single Integrated Operational Plan, which envisaged a full nuclear assault on the Soviet-Chinese bloc in the first 24 hours of a nuclear war. The possible consequences of such a strike were estimated at 325 million deaths in the Soviet Union and China; 100 million in Eastern Europe; 100 million in Europe (as a result of radioactive fallout); and 100 million in countries bordering the USSR

> – in all a death toll of over 600 million.
>
> There are some who contend today that Eisenhower was not a willing partner in the nuclear escalation. By January 1961 he was bone-weary, the first American president ever to reach 70. He had survived a heart attack, an abdominal operation and a stroke. In his farewell address in that month, his famous warning against the "military-industrial complex" may well have been a reference to the last battle the old warrior lost against the MAD*-obsessed military and an industry rolling in dollars.
>
> * Mutually Assured Destruction

Birth pangs

Although the Soviet Union joined in the applause that followed Eisenhower's "Atoms for Peace" speech, this was merely a polite gesture, because the Russians were inwardly seething. They were vehemently opposed to the ideals of the programme right from the beginning. Stalin had died a mere nine months before the Eisenhower speech and Russia had not yet emerged from the dark shadows cast by the Stalinist regime. Under no circumstances would Stalin have supported the Atoms for Peace programme.

The USA did not want to lose momentum and therefore announced in the UNGA in November 1954 that it would proceed without the Soviet Union and would establish the IAEA in cooperation with the interested countries. An interesting change of emphasis took place at this point. The USA conceded that the projected IAEA should possibly not be the owner and guardian of fissile material but should instead serve as a clearing agent for requests for nuclear material by those setting up programmes relating to peaceful applications.

The USA, together with seven other countries, then proceeded to draw up a draft statute for the IAEA. The Group of Eight consisted of the USA, the UK, France and the uranium suppliers Canada, Australia, South Africa, Belgium and later Portugal as well. Early in 1955 this group met in Washington. They already had a draft statute which had been drawn up by the USA and the UK as a working document. The group aimed to gain consensus on the statute, establish the IAEA and later invite other states to join them.

The Soviet Union was in a difficult position because the process was already under way and was gathering momentum. In July 1955 they grudgingly consented to start cooperating, but in characteristic fashion they stipulated their own conditions. Two Soviet satellite states, namely Czechoslovakia and Poland, were to be included. The group was further enlarged by the addition of India (to represent Asia) and Brazil (as the representative of Latin America). This enlarged group was known as the Group of Twelve.

A month later the International Conference on the Peaceful Uses of Atomic Energy, at which the peaceful use of nuclear energy and materials was discussed, was held in Geneva. This conference, which was organised by the UN, was very successful. It was attended by 1 500 scientists, engineers and diplomats from across the world and thousands of papers were read. In many instances the technology discussed was still secret. For example, France revealed the method of extracting plutonium from irradiated nuclear fuel through reprocessing. The only topics that were not touched on were the enrichment of uranium and plans to build nuclear weapons.

> ## Pronouncements at the First Geneva Conference
>
> **Admiral Lewis Strauss, Chairman of the Atomic Energy Commission of the USA:** "It is not too much to expect that our children will enjoy electrical energy too cheap to meter ... will travel effortlessly over the seas and under them and through the air with a minimum of danger and at great speeds."
>
> **Winston Churchill, Prime Minister of Britain:** "Atomic energy will be a perennial fountain of world prosperity."
>
> **Homi Bhabha (India), Chairman of the Conference:** "... during the next two decades scientists would have found a way of liberating (thermonuclear) fusion energy in a controlled manner. When that happens the energy problems of the world will truly have been solved for ever."

The new Group of Twelve got straight down to work and over a period of eight weeks between February and April 1956 designed the framework within which the IAEA was to function. They agreed that:
- the IAEA would promote research on, the development of, and practical applications for the peaceful use of nuclear energy;
- materials, services, equipment and facilities for such research would be made available (especially to developing countries);
- the exchange of scientific and technical information would be fostered;

- a system of safeguards would be designed and implemented to ensure that any nuclear assistance and materials supplied would not be used for military purposes and, if requested, to apply such safeguards in any bilateral or multilateral arrangement; and
- standards would be drawn up for the safe use of nuclear energy.

The statute still incorporated the old idea that the IAEA should be the "pool", "bank" and distributor, where required, of fissile materials.

The IAEA would be expected to wear two hats, one as the promoter and the other as the regulator of nuclear energy, always a difficult combination. Furthermore, the peaceful application of nuclear energy was to be regulated by "safeguards", but at that stage nobody knew what that would mean in practice.

The statute was nevertheless approved on 23 October 1956 by a special conference, arranged by the UN in New York, and on 29 July 1957 it came into force. This was the official birth date of the IAEA.

Regarding the day-to-day running of the IAEA, the statute provides for a Board of Governors which functions as an executive board, as well as a General Conference, which functions much like a shareholders' meeting. The IAEA also has the necessary technical and administrative staff complement (the secretariat) and is managed by a director-general. The Austrian city Vienna was chosen as the seat of the headquarters.

Most of the key members of staff were appointed at the beginning of 1958 and the new organisation moved into the prestigious Grand Hotel in the Ringstrasse, one of the principal boulevards of Vienna. While the international technical bureaucrats – a new occupational category – were making themselves at home in these luxurious surroundings, a heated debate was being conducted in Austrian government circles regarding the proposal to create a permanent home for this organisation with funds provided by the Austrian taxpayers. Eventually political considerations outweighed the objections raised.

Vienna traditionally came under attack from the east and north via the Reichsbrücke across the Danube River (the last time by the Soviet Union in 1945). At the height of the Cold War the Iron Curtain was in place only a few dozen kilometres to the east of Vienna, on the borders with Czechoslovakia and Hungary. For this reason the government decided to build the new headquarters on the site of an old municipal rubbish dump right next to the Danube and the Reichsbrücke in the hope that the presence of an international UN agency might prevent Vienna from being invaded there, as in the past.

Building operations were completed in 1979. The bureaucrats moved in on a 99-year lease at a nominal rental of one Austrian schilling (less than one South African rand) a year. Today the building is still an imposing complex consisting of seven blocks, with 28 storeys that afford a wonderful view over Vienna. This building, which is generally known as the Vienna International Centre (VIC), also houses fifteen other UN agencies with 4 000 employees from 110 countries (including a number of South Africans). The building with its high towers is often mockingly referred to as the Tower of Babel because of the many languages spoken by its occupants but in practice only one language is spoken there – poor English. To improve communication, the staff have developed an extensive technical vocabulary where terms have specific meanings. Anyone wishing to make himself understood within the IAEA has to master this jargon and be able to use it.

The years spent at the Grand Hotel were not wasted. Many proverbial mountains had to be crossed and the valleys in between were liberally sprinkled with political landmines. One of the "mountains" was the creation of an international system of safeguards.

What are safeguards?

The statute of the IAEA requires the organisation to develop and apply a system of safeguards without defining exactly what these entail.

In principle it is a simple matter. Supplier state A exports fissile material, equipment and facilities to recipient state X. The IAEA, as the objective international nuclear watchdog, has to ensure (by applying safeguards) that the recipient state, in terms of its undertaking, will not misuse the goods for military purposes or for the manufacture of nuclear weapons. In practice this is easier said than done.

The application of safeguards was a brand-new concept so there were no previous examples to serve as a guide. The recipient country was required to give a political undertaking that would have to be verified by an international organisation by means of technical inspections – carried out on the sovereign territory of the recipient state. This created landmines by the dozen!

In those years the world was sharply divided by the Iron Curtain, with the West on one side and the Soviet Union and its satellites on the other, and a high level of tension and hostility between them. Espionage was widely practised to enable each side to discover what the opposing group was doing. Many countries felt that the IAEA with its multinational staff provided the ideal opportunity for inspectors whose work involved travelling to all parts of the world to bring juicy snippets of information back to their home countries. Yet more political landmines ...

After much discussion and wrangling in numerous meetings a kind of consensus was reached and the following decisions were taken:

- There should be a binding agreement between the supplier state, the recipient state and the IAEA. To avoid the need to draw up agreements in an ad hoc (and time-consuming) manner, a model safeguards agreement that would be applicable to all states was required. This would go a long way towards preventing discrimination in the application of safeguards.
- The model agreement should set out the rights and obligations of the states and the IAEA.
- Inspection procedures and advance notification of inspections should be prescribed.
- A state should have the right to refuse an inspector (in his personal capacity or because he comes from a particular country) access to its country and facilities.

The first attempt at such a model agreement was published by the IAEA in 1961 as INFCIRC/26 and is applicable to small research reactors. It was a very complex document, which someone described as "one of the most convoluted pieces of verbal expression in history which few people could comprehend except in a long discussion with the handful that did". Not a very encouraging start!

A new group was formed to overcome this obstacle and within a year they had drafted a new model agreement, which was published in 1965 as INFCIRC/66. It covered reactors of all sizes, not only research reactors. As a result of a new spirit of cooperation displayed by the Soviet Union, the agreement was extended in 1966 to include reprocessing plants (for the reclamation of fissile materials from spent nuclear fuel) and in 1968 it was expanded still further to include the manufacture of fuel. A characteristic of agreements of the INFCIRC/66 type is that they only cover specific items (facilities, materials, etc). Today they are still applied to certain facilities in India, Pakistan and Israel. In the past, before South Africa signed the Treaty on the Non-Proliferation of Nuclear Weapons (Nuclear Non-Proliferation Treaty or

NPT), two such agreements applied in this country, namely to Safari-1 (IN-FCIRC/98) and the Koeberg power station (INFCIRC/244).

Were the safeguards adequate?

Once the IAEA's safeguards system was ready the supplier states could, in good conscience, hand over responsibility for verifying compliance with the requirements of their bilateral agreements with the recipient states to an international (technical) organisation that would ensure uniform implementation worldwide.

However, there was continuing unease about the further proliferation of nuclear technology and nuclear weapons. Type INFCIRC/66 safeguards were simply too limited. They were only applicable to specific facilities where safeguards were stipulated by a supplier country or where the IAEA was involved in an aid programme. There was no guarantee that there were no home-grown facilities in the recipient country to which the IAEA did not have access. Precisely this situation prevailed for decades in South Africa, India, Pakistan and Israel.

It was therefore necessary to make the safeguards more universally applicable. The only way to achieve this ideal was to replace the bilateral undertakings with an international treaty. The most suitable organisation to generate such a treaty was the UN, which delegated the task to a disarmament committee consisting of eighteen member countries. Complex discussions began in earnest in 1964 and eventually – four years later – the exhausted committee members submitted the seventh revised draft of the treaty to the UNGA. The treaty was adopted and on 5 March 1970 the Nuclear Non-Proliferation Treaty or NPT entered into force.

On the one hand the NPT is a very idealistic instrument. The treaty makes provision for the following progression: The discontinuation of the manufacture of nuclear weapons; the reduction of the stocks of nuclear weapons and fissile material; the complete elimination of all nuclear weapons and means of delivering them; and lastly complete disarmament (note that this was intended to apply to all weapons, not only nuclear weapons). Realistically, the NPT acknowledges that the last step would have to be covered by a further (final) treaty.

When the NPT came into operation the immediate effect was to divide the world into two classes:

- The nuclear haves: They are the states that already possessed nuclear tech-

nology and nuclear weapons. They are formally classified by the NPT as nuclear-weapon states (NWS).
- The nuclear have-nots: This group is made up of the rest of the world, especially countries that do not yet possess nuclear technology, but would like to acquire it. These states are not ever permitted to acquire or produce nuclear weapons. The NPT refers to these states formally as non-nuclear-weapon states (NNWS).

There are no complex technical criteria for distinguishing between the two classes. The distinction is simple – those states that exploded a nuclear weapon before 1 January 1967 automatically qualified as NWS. Although France and China only signed the NPT in 1992, which is 22 years after it entered into force, they are also regarded as NWS.

This built-in discrimination ensures that the two groups have entirely different responsibilities under the NPT.

All NNWS are required, for example, to sign a comprehensive or full-scope safeguards agreement with the IAEA. This agreement covers all fissile material possessed by a state and not merely certain facilities, as required under the old type of INFCIRC/66 agreement. Furthermore, this requirement does not apply to the NWS, which are not subject to inspections by the IAEA.

This discrimination has been a thorn in the flesh of the NNWS for more than four decades, chiefly because the only important obligation imposed on the NWS has not been honoured. This was that the arms race should be ended ("at an early date" according to Article VI) and that nuclear disarmament should take place. Since 1946, however, the number of weapons has increased systematically at an accelerated pace, with the global arms race reaching a peak in 1989 when over 62 000 weapons were in existence (nineteen years after the NPT came into force). After that point, the number of weapons did start to drop. However, as of mid-2015, the estimate is that there are still approximately 15 850 nuclear weapons. Of these, 4 300 are deployed with 1 800 on high alert. The remaining weapons are either in military stockpiles or are retired awaiting dismantling.

A few other Articles of the NPT should be noted here as well:
- Article III requires firstly that safeguards must be applied with respect to all source or special fissionable materials in all peaceful nuclear activities within the NNWS. The Article further requires that when any party to the NPT exports such material, or equipment or material "especially

- designed or prepared for the processing, use or production" of special fissionable material, comprehensive safeguards must be applied in the recipient country. (The term "especially designed or prepared [EDP] materials and equipment" is a widely used acronym.) This requirement is only applicable to exports to NNWS. NWS are permitted to import and use such material freely and without any form of supervision.
- Article IV provides that any party to the NPT has the inalienable right to carry out research and development for the production and use of nuclear energy for peaceful purposes "without discrimination". This Article also provides that all parties have the right to participate fully in the exchange of equipment, materials and scientific information for the aforementioned purpose. For many years this very Article has been the cause of great dissatisfaction among the NNWS, especially those on the receiving end of export restrictions. An NNWS such as Iran has every right in terms of this Article to build and operate its own enrichment plants. If it were not for certain undeclared, apparently nuclear-weapon related activities that Iran refuses to explain or admit, the Iranians would have been allowed to operate those plants freely although under safeguards supervision. Japan and Brazil are operating such safeguarded enrichment plants with no apparent opposition from the NWS.
- Article V shows how strong the movement in favour of the peaceful use of nuclear explosions was in 1970. This Article permits NWS to make the potential benefits of such explosions available to NNWS. In practice this Article was never really applied. The USA and the Soviet Union had polluted the atmosphere and the oceans to such an extent with the radioactive substances released during weapons tests that everyone became wary of the consequences of nuclear explosions, even those for potentially peaceful uses.
- Article VII permits parties to conclude regional agreements with the same purpose as the NPT. The Treaty of Tlatelolco in Latin America and the Treaty of Pelindaba on the African continent are agreements of this kind.
- Article X.1 provides that a party has the right to withdraw from the NPT if "extraordinary events are jeopardising the supreme interests" of that party. In later years this happened in the case of North Korea, and many fear that if the negotiations between Iran and the P5+1 (the nuclear powers together with Germany) which have been going on since 2013 do not lead to a substantive, mutually acceptable agreement, Iran may in time follow North Korea's example.

The NPT envisaged a shelf life of 25 years, unless the parties decided to extend it. In 1995 South Africa played an important part in extending the NPT indefinitely.

Once the NPT entered into force the next step was to apply its provisions in practice, especially the requirement of comprehensive safeguards.

Back to the drawing board: the design of comprehensive safeguards agreements

The required application of the comprehensive safeguards agreements immediately presented two problems:
- The existing model agreement, INFCIRC/66, did not make provision for the application of safeguards to all nuclear activities, but only to specific facilities or items. A new model agreement would therefore have to be drawn up.
- Furthermore, the NPT does not define the terms "source material" and "special fissionable material". Neither does it define "equipment or material especially designed or prepared for the processing, use or production of special fissionable material", that is the so-called EDP items. How was the NPT to be applied in practice in the absence of a specific indication of which items and materials were intended?

Four weeks after the NPT entered into force a special committee was formed by the IAEA to undertake the drafting of the required new model agreement. The first meeting of this committee took place in June 1970 under the chairmanship of Kurt Waldheim. The committee certainly didn't waste time and in March 1971 the model agreement was submitted to the Board of Governors. This was approved and published by the IAEA in June 1972 as INFCIRC/153.

The contents of the model agreement are extensive and also highly technical – the agreement is not exactly a riveting read. The crux of it lies in the requirement that the state should implement and operate a system to account for and control nuclear material that is subject to safeguards to the nearest gram. The quantity, degree of enrichment, chemical and physical form and especially the location of such material must be described. Records must also be kept for every facility as prescribed in the Subsidiary Arrangements and Facility Attachments. Any movement of material between facilities and/or changes in inventories must be periodically reported to the IAEA in the prescribed format. The IAEA is then responsible for verifying these reports (the agreement refers to the "findings") by means of prescribed technical inspections. This makes the NPT the first international treaty under which the political undertakings of NNWS are inspected for compliance in terms of an international technical verification regime.

> ## *IAEA inspections*
>
> *The various Facility Attachments make provision for strategic points or places where nuclear material can most easily be accessed for inspection. Inspections are concentrated mainly at these points. Nuclear material can be verified at such a point by means of measurement or sampling, instruments can be checked and records and reports audited.*
>
> *The concept of strategic points was a concession to the reservations that existed – and still exist – about allowing strangers to access a state's sensitive facilities, view them and make deductions about material flows and inventories. Some states got so carried away that they had lines painted on the floors of the facilities and required the inspectors to walk along the lines to reach the strategic points. On the way an inspector had to refrain from looking left or right, like a racehorse in blinkers!*
>
> *A host of inspection models were also prescribed in very specific terms. For example, a distinction was drawn between visits and inspections. Inspections included ad hoc, routine, unannounced, simultaneous, continuous, special or short-notice inspections, to name but a few. Each type had its own suitable technical rituals, requiring advance notice (for a longer or shorter period) and the state retained the right to have its own inspector(s) accompany the IAEA inspector.*

A system of comprehensive safeguards is operated on the basis of a trust relationship: The state undertakes not to manufacture nuclear weapons or clandestinely divert material that is subject to safeguards to undeclared nuclear activities, and to keep all nuclear material in the state (including that in the possession of private bodies) under control and declare it to the IAEA. The IAEA then conducts an "audit" so that it can rubber-stamp the state's solemn undertaking and nuclear material accountability findings in good faith. At least, that was the theory at the time.

Meaning of the woolly terminology in the NPT: Over 40 years after the NPT entered into force the terminology is still not specifically defined by the treaty. Initially this caused problems for those countries that were in a position to export nuclear technology and materials but did not know exactly what they would have to control.

Consequently 15 countries met in 1971 to discuss the matter. They formed the Nuclear Exporters Committee, under the leadership of Professor Claude Zangger of Switzerland. Today this is widely referred to as the Zangger Committee.

In one respect the committee could draw information from the IAEA, because its statute already contained the following definitions of source material and special fissionable material:
- *Source material* is uranium containing the mixture of isotopes occurring in nature; depleted uranium (left over after enrichment); and thorium.
- *Special fissionable material* is plutonium-239, uranium-233 or uranium enriched in the isotopes U-235 or U-233 (U-233 is not found in nature and is specially produced in reactors).

The Zangger Committee accepted the IAEA definitions without argument. They took a little longer to define EDP items but by September the guidelines for exports, as well as a list of EDP items, had been defined and approved. Items on this checklist require the application of safeguards in the recipient country. This is often called the "trigger list" because it "triggers" safeguards in the recipient country or in other words activates them immediately. At the request of the committee the guidelines and trigger list were published by the IAEA as INFCIRC/209.

The Zangger Committee had no formal association with the NPT. They were simply a group of states (not all of them parties to the NPT) that wanted to define in clearer terms what the NPT was trying to say in woolly language. At one of its five-yearly review conferences held in 1975 the NPT referred for the first time to the work being done by the Zangger Committee but did not mention that committee by name. Twenty years later parties were advised to use the trigger list as the basis for their exports. By this circuitous route the NPT eventually acquired working definitions for the undefined terms.

THE BOMB

Smiling Buddha, and the cat is set among the pigeons

The world was looking forward to an era of peace and tranquillity. Two devastating world wars lay in the past, the UN had been founded to serve the cause of international peace, the NPT was in place and the euphoric Atoms for Peace period was well under way. In terms of the NPT the nuclear-weapon states undertook to reduce and eventually destroy their nuclear arsenals, and the non-nuclear-weapon states undertook never to acquire or manufacture nuclear weapons. But, as history has demonstrated innumerable times, nothing in this world is ever simple.

India's hostile neighbours

When the British withdrew from British India in 1948 two new states were formed, namely India and Pakistan. The partition of Pakistan into West Pakistan and East Pakistan was awkward from the beginning, since the two states were widely separated, resembling two elephant ears attached to the Indian state. Skirmishes over territory, fuelled by religious differences, soon broke out; the most serious of these took place in 1971. As a result of this war Pakistan lost half its territory. East Pakistan became independent under the name of Bangladesh and even today the relationship between India and Pakistan is extremely fragile.

Ten years previously India had been compelled to send troops to its border with China to counter incursions there. In 1962 China invaded the Indian state Assam, which led to a full-scale war. The Indians came off worst and in December 1962 the Chinese declared a ceasefire. In the process China seized 22 000 km^2 of territory – which is still in its possession today. Two years later, on 16 October 1964, China tested its first nuclear weapon. As a result of these deep-seated differences and this new development in China, Pakistan and the USA on the one hand and India and the Soviet Union on the other drew closer to each other.

As early as 1948 India established its own atomic energy commission for the purposes of uranium exploration. Shortly after Eisenhower announced the Atoms for Peace programme India stated that it would reject any oversight of its activities by an international organisation. India nevertheless showed a keen interest in acquiring nuclear technology and in 1956 negotiations were successfully concluded and India acquired a Canadian reactor which used natural uranium as fuel and heavy water as the moderator. This type of reactor is ideally suited to the production of plutonium. The agreement with Canada specified that the plutonium produced in the Cirus reactor would be used exclusively for peaceful purposes but did not include a mechanism for verifying compliance. The Americans were accommodating enough to supply the heavy water and in 1959 they also trained Indian scientists in techniques for reclaiming plutonium from spent fuel and handling it. The scene had been set for the inevitable result.

Indira Gandhi, the then Prime Minister of India, was taken on a conducted tour of the Indian equivalent of Pelindaba on 7 September 1972 – the Bhabha Atomic Research Centre (BARC) in Mumbai. She was impressed by what she saw. In view of the regional political problems India was facing, she gave the scientists and engineers headed by Raja Ramanna verbal instructions to go ahead and prepare a nuclear device for testing. Two years later the device was ready. Test shafts had already been prepared at Pokhran in the mountainous part of the Thar Desert, to the north of Mumbai in the province of Rajasthan. Significantly, the site chosen was not far from the border with Pakistan. The test was given the code name Smiling Buddha, for reasons no one can remember too clearly. The only people informed about the planned test were the staff at BARC who were working on the project, the prime minister and two advisers. Apparently not even the Minister of Defence knew anything about it.

But then the bomb was detonated at 08:05 on 18 May 1974. The world soon learned that India, the first non-nuclear-weapon state, had tested a nuclear explosive device with a blast yield equivalent to about 8 kilotons of TNT and coals of fire were heaped on the prime minister's head. Canada and the USA, which had supplied all the equipment, technical support and materials, were particularly incensed because India had not honoured its undertaking to refrain from using the reactor for weapons production. India tried to turn aside the international wrath by claiming it was a "peaceful explosion" that was not against the spirit of its undertaking. Many years later, in 1997, Raja Ramanna conceded the following: "The Pokhran test was a bomb, I can tell you now ... An explosion is an explosion, a gun is a gun, whether you shoot at someone or shoot at the ground ... I just want to make clear that the test was not all that peaceful."

> ### Chain reaction of another kind
>
> Zulfikar Ali Bhutto, who was President and then Prime Minister of Pakistan from 1971 to 1977, reacted to Operation Smiling Buddha by giving his nuclear scientists instructions to make a nuclear bomb, even if they had "to eat grass or leaves, even go hungry, but we will get one of our own". In the end their task was greatly simplified by the theft of nuclear technology in the Netherlands by the Pakistani A.Q. Khan. That story warrants a whole book to itself; it will be discussed at greater length later in this text.

The Pokhran test brought the "euphoric era" of the Atoms for Peace programme to a sudden end. Everything came to a halt because one country had shown how the assistance and equipment supplied in good faith could be misused and that solemn undertakings by states are often not worth the paper on which they are written and signed with great pomp and ceremony. It should be mentioned, however, that at that time India was not – and still is not – a signatory to the NPT. India has never been under any legal obligation to have its nuclear material and facilities placed under comprehensive IAEA safeguards.

The Zangger Committee's list of equipment and materials, and its guidelines for exports to NNWS appeared four months later, in September 1974. This was far too late to have had any influence on the Indian nuclear test.

The realisation that recipient countries could misuse nuclear materials and technology, despite solemn promises to the contrary, caused a group of seven countries to meet in great secrecy early in 1975. None other than Henry Kissinger played a slightly reluctant but nonetheless highly influential role in establishing this group which was motivated equally by concern about nuclear proliferation and a desire to keep American officials from "charging around the world, like Don Quixote". The "London Club", as it was originally known, agreed that, taking the IAEA safeguards and export policy as a basis, they would draw up common standards for the export of nuclear items to countries outside the framework of the IAEA and the NPT. They decided to do something about the gaps in the NPT as regards control over the transfer of technology (and not only physical items), the re-export of supplied items and physical security. However, the secret group was exposed by *The New York Times* in June 1975. A number of countries were dissatisfied about having been excluded from the discussions. The group was therefore enlarged and in time they decided on a joint approach. Their conclusions were published in 1978 as INFCIRC/254, which sets out the guidelines and trigger list of what eventually came to be known as the Nuclear Suppliers Group (NSG). Because of internal differences regarding comprehensive safeguards as a condition of supply, the NSG became dormant in 1978 and was only jolted back to life after the Gulf War in 1990.

From the beginning potential recipient countries have seen the NSG as an invention of the devil – a means of denying them the benefits of nuclear technology without giving them any say in the matter, and therefore contrary to Article IV of the NPT. But over the years this organisation has gone out of its way to improve its image, largely by holding seminars to make its origin, aims and methods more transparent.

How do the Zangger Committee and the Nuclear Suppliers Group operate?

These two groups do not have central organisations to control nuclear exports. The members of the groups merely agree on joint guidelines and trigger lists for nuclear exports which all members undertake to apply in a uniform manner and to implement through national legislation. Export control is therefore applied individually by members in accordance with their own legislation.

The members are not bound to the Zangger Committee or the NSG by a formal agreement or an international treaty. Members unilaterally undertake to apply the guidelines and trigger lists.

The trigger lists for nuclear items used by the two groups are the same; it is merely the guidelines that differ. The NSG, however, did expand its export control lists in 1992 to include nuclear-related dual-use items such as equipment that could just as well be used in an ordinary industrial context as in the nuclear industry.

Since the early 1990s South Africa has been a member of both groups.

International control over the proliferation of nuclear weapons

To sum up, the international nonproliferation regime embraces the following elements:
- The NPT, with the emphasis on: (1) The distinction between nuclear-weapon states and non-nuclear-weapon states in respect of the application of the treaty. (2) An embargo on the acquisition or manufacture of nuclear explosive devices by non-nuclear-weapon states. Nuclear-weapon states are not permitted to supply nuclear explosive devices to non-nuclear-weapon states or help them to develop such devices. (3) The requirement that comprehensive IAEA safeguards must be implemented in non-nuclear-weapon states. (4) Export control over certain loosely defined items. (5) The right of parties to develop and use nuclear energy for peaceful purposes. (6) Vague speculation on the cessation of the manufacture of nuclear weapons, followed by nuclear disarmament at some unknown time in the future.
- The Zangger Committee was set up to provide technical definitions for the undefined terms in the NPT and lay down guidelines for exports.
- The NSG made additions to the Zangger Committee's guidelines as regards the transfer of technology, control over re-exporting and the physical protection of nuclear materials. Special attention was paid to the transfer of so-called sensitive technology, namely enrichment and reprocessing. In addition to the nuclear items on the trigger list of the Zangger Committee, the NSG export control list includes nuclear-related dual-purpose items.

States accede to the NPT voluntarily and in good faith, but Libya, North Korea and currently Iran, all of which are (or were) parties, have not honoured their respective undertakings. As a matter of interest, their undeclared nuclear activities were also never detected by the IAEA during the normal inspections it carried out over many years.

PART 3

THE BOMB IN THE BUSHVELD

EARLY BEGINNINGS

The home-grown product

Because of the advances in nuclear research in the 1940s Britain and the USA were on the lookout for a stable supply of uranium for their envisaged nuclear weapons programmes. It was in this context that the British Chancellor of the Exchequer, Sir John Anderson, sent a secret telegram in 1944 to the then South African Prime Minister, Jan Smuts, to request South Africa's assistance.

Smuts set up a uranium research committee which reported to him directly. Up to 1948 control over uranium production had been in the hands of the Prime Minister, a small group of high-ranking government officials and a few officials from the gold-mining industry. In 1948, however, the Atomic Energy Board (AEB) was established to control and coordinate future uranium exports.

Between 1959 and 1964 the British and American nuclear weapons projects were almost completely dependent on South Africa as a source of uranium. The income earned by the South African mining industry in this way was naturally very welcome to the local economy.

The year 1959 was a watershed year for the South African nuclear programme. Senator Jan de Klerk, Minister of Works and Mines – the father of F.W. de Klerk who later became State President – announced in Carletonville on 5 September of that year that the cabinet had approved the AEB's proposed development programme. After this announcement South Africa's nuclear research programme officially took shape.

It was by no means an easy process, however. Dr Ampie Roux submitted his proposals to the members of the AEB and the Minister of Works and Mines on 12 June 1958. He formulated his ideas after discussions with government officials, the Council for Scientific and Industrial Research (CSIR), the Electricity Supply Commission (Eskom) and the mining industry. He also held discussions with an astounding 235 experts and authorities in no fewer than ten countries to make his plan for nuclear research in South Africa as viable and relevant as possible!

Roux's proposed programme on the peaceful applications of nuclear energy followed four principal lines of enquiry:-
- **Materials:** This included research on improved methods of mining and uranium extraction, a study of the steps in uranium processing, the use of uranium as nuclear fuel, prospecting for thorium, as well as a study of the possibilities of heavy water production.
- **Nuclear power:** Research on and the development of a concept for a South African nuclear power reactor.
- **Radioactive isotopes and radiation:** The promotion of established uses of radioactive isotopes and radiation in agriculture, industry and medicine, and the investigation of possible new uses.
- **Basic research:** This research was to serve as the foundation for advances in the field of nuclear energy.

Ampie Roux considered it important that South African industry should contribute to the financing of the nuclear programme. His proposals had already been recommended to the government when a dispute arose within the AEB. The point at issue was responsibility for the implementation of the programme. Some members did not attach much importance to nuclear energy and therefore did not want to see the programme develop independently. They insisted that the programme should be integrated into existing organisations such as the CSIR. Neither side was prepared to make any concessions and the resulting deadlock lasted for over a year. By the end of August 1959 the full cabinet eventually accepted the arguments of the majority of AEB members.

Ampie Roux

Abraham Johannes Andries (A.J.A.) Roux was born shortly after the First World War broke out. He grew up on a farm close to the Free State town of Bethlehem. He passed his primary school years at the local farm school and then attended Bethlehem High School, where he matriculated. As a youngster Ampie had his heart set on farming, but his father persuaded him to study engineering at the University of the Witwatersrand instead. He obtained the BSc, MSc and DSc degrees in mechanical engineering. While doing practical work in the mining industry for two years, he attended night classes and earned a BSc (Hons) degree in applied mathematics. He was subsequently appointed to a lecturing post at the University of Stellenbosch

(US). After this he accepted a post at the Building Research Institute at the CSIR in Pretoria. Although he was interested in nuclear energy at that stage, his field was really aerodynamics.

In January 1952 Roux was appointed head of the CSIR's Mechanical Engineering Research Unit and a few months later he became the Director of the National Physical Laboratory, of which the research unit formed part. Three years later he was appointed head of the new National Research Institute for Mechanical Engineering of the CSIR. In addition, he was nominated to serve on the Physics Committee of the AEB on behalf of the CSIR, and was appointed shortly afterwards as part-time director of Atomic Energy Research. Three months later he was also promoted to Vice-President of the CSIR. He had reached the stage where there were simply too many calls on his time and he left the CSIR to do full-time research for the AEB.

When the Atomic Energy Act was amended in 1967 he became Chairman of the AEB and three years later President of that institution. He ultimately became Chairman of the Uranium Enrichment Corporation (Ucor). Roux died in 1985.

Wally Grant

One of the youngest scientists appointed by Ampie Roux, Dr W.L. (Wally) Grant, was to play a key role in South Africa's nuclear programme. Grant can scarcely be said to have had a conventional schooling. His father made a living by drilling for water in dry areas and the family moved frequently. Born in 1922, he was eight years old before he had the opportunity to attend school. After that the young boy went to over thirteen schools in the space of eight years! After passing standard eight (now grade 10) at the Johannesburg Technical High School, he joined the South African Air Force as an apprentice in 1940. Although he had a full-time job he did his matric by correspondence and in 1942 he passed with distinctions in five of his six subjects. What is more, he gained the highest marks in the then Union of South Africa in the subjects mechanics and heat engines.

During the Second World War he spent a year in Britain as part of a South African Air Force team working on gas turbines. He worked under Sir Frank Whittle on the development of aircraft jet engines. In October 1945 he returned to his homeland and registered as an engineering student at the University of the Witwatersrand. In 1948 he took up a post at the CSIR and it was there that his path crossed that of Ampie Roux. During his time at the CSIR

Grant carried out research which led to an MSc in applied mathematics. He also obtained a DSc in engineering while in the service of the CSIR. During the ten years he spent in the service of that body, he concentrated on heat transfer and thermodynamics, a valuable foundation for his groundbreaking research in later years. He advanced to the post of Director of the National Research Institute for Mechanical Engineering.

When the national nuclear programme got off the ground, the eternally curious Wally Grant saw this as an opportunity to explore new territory and accepted a post as chief engineer at the AEB. It was around this time that President Eisenhower's Atoms for Peace programme was launched in earnest. Together with other eminent South African nuclear scientists like Dr Wynand de Villiers (reactor physics), Dr S.J. du Toit (physics) and Dr J.P. Hugo (physical metallurgy), he was trained in the USA for seventeen months. During this time his fertile brain conceptualised the Pelinduna project. What he envisaged was the development and building of an indigenous nuclear reactor using natural uranium as fuel, heavy water as the moderator and liquid sodium as the coolant.

In 1967 Grant became Director-General of the AEB when Ampie Roux was appointed Chairman. Grant later rose to the position of Deputy President and then Managing Director of the Uranium Enrichment Corporation (Ucor). He retired in 1987 and joined the company IST.

In 1992 he retired for the second time at the age of 70 to farm at Aantree, his farm in the Lydenburg district. However, his lively mind led him to return to research in 2001 and he began work on the refinement of the vortex tube which he had previously developed for uranium enrichment in collaboration with the firm SDI, currently known as Klydon. When he reached his eighties his spirit of adventure was still alive and well and he even attempted a tandem parachute jump, breaking his ankle in the process!

In March 2008 Grant was travelling to Pretoria from his farm to carry out further research when he was taken ill. He died at the age of 85. A remarkable man whose equal South Africa will not see again ...

The father of South Africa's nuclear weapons

Dr J.W.L. de Villiers also had a marked influence on the history of the South African nuclear programme. Wynand de Villiers passed his childhood years in the Free State town of Smithfield. He studied physics at the University of Stellenbosch and was awarded an MSc *cum laude*. His topic was the application of isotopes in agriculture. He later obtained a DSc for his work at the CSIR while in the service of the Mass Spectrometry Division. His work on the uranium deposits on the Witwatersrand was presented in 1955 at the Second Conference on the Peaceful Uses of Atomic Energy at the UN.

After being awarded an AEB bursary, De Villiers worked at the Nuclear Physics Division of the CSIR for some time before leaving for the USA with other South Africans to receive training in the nuclear sciences, including specialised training in reactor physics at the Argonne National Laboratory.

De Villiers was appointed Director of the Reactor Development Division of the AEB in 1967, where he played a leading part in the development of the Pelinduna reactor. Early in 1970 he decided to move to the private sector, but found that he missed nuclear science too much and after two years he returned as head of Ucor's Safety Division. After a year he was promoted to the post of Vice-President of the AEB; three years later he became Deputy President and when Ampie Roux retired in 1979 De Villiers succeeded him as President of the AEB. In 1982 the Atomic Energy Corporation (AEC) was established, with the subsidiaries Ucor and Nucor (an amalgamation of the operations at Pelindaba and Valindaba) under the chairmanship of De Villiers.

He died in October 1995.

> ## *Wynand de Villiers brings a souvenir home*
>
> *In the course of his studies at the Argonne National Laboratory in the USA in the 1960s Wynand de Villiers encountered a computer program called AX-1. This program covered reactor safety, an area which the Americans were working on at the time and which would undoubtedly prove useful in operating Safari-1. When he returned from the USA in 1962 De Villiers brought the program back to Pelindaba.*
>
> *His colleagues relate that when he got back to his South African office he appeared to be lost in thought for a few days, with a faraway look in his eyes. His thoughts were turning to the possibility of doing something else with that computer program. He had it analysed and realised that it could also be used for calculations in relation to peaceful nuclear explosions. The program would have to undergo further development and his staff were quick to rise to the challenge. This was the origin of the versatile PELX-1 computer program which was refined over the years until it was able to serve as the backbone, first of South Africa's peaceful nuclear*

> explosives programme, and later of the nuclear weapons programme.
> In 1993, thirty years after the creation of PELX-1, the magnetic tapes carrying the program were destroyed under the supervision of the IAEA.

"Let's get down to work"

Initially the AEB had offices in the Merino Building in the heart of the Pretoria central business district. However, it soon became a priority to find a suitable site for South Africa's nuclear programme.

In his book *Chain Reaction*, A.R. Newby-Fraser describes some of the criteria for the site:

- Proximity to the uranium mines and manufacturing plants, the CSIR and the three northern universities, namely the Universities of Pretoria, the Witwatersrand and Potchefstroom, was essential.
- It was important that the area should be situated close to a perennial river with a constant minimum flow of 5 000 m^3 per day.
- It was also preferable that the plant should be situated at least ten miles – or 16 km – from the nearest big settlement.

Pelindaba, the area immediately to the south of the Hartbeespoort Dam and to the west of Pretoria, was chosen from a short list of six possible sites. The then Department of Lands bought the farm Welgegund on the eastern bank of the Crocodile River on behalf of the AEB. The fact that the land was really purchased for use by the AEB was initially kept secret in order to prevent land speculation.

A name had then to be found for the site, which was about 1 000 ha in extent. The name "Pelindaba", representing a small hamlet, appeared on a map; this settlement was the derelict remains of a 1920s project to build a village of that name. It was decided to call the site Pelindaba, which is a compound of two words in an indigenous black language meaning "finished" and "discussions". "That's right," said Ampie Roux contentedly when he heard what the name meant. "We've talked enough; now let's get down to work."

> ### Tragedy on the farm Pelindaba
>
> After the Anglo-Boer War three Pretorius brothers, descendants of the Voortrekkers Andries and M.W. Pretorius, after whom Pretoria was named, were farming 1 500 morgen in the vicinity of the present-day

Hartbeespoort Dam. After the dam was completed in 1923 as a government job creation project, the brothers wanted to sell the farm, but the daughter of one of them urged her husband to buy part of the farm in order to keep the land in the family. Her husband was Gustav Preller, a newspaper editor and later an official state historian. The Prellers chose 600 morgen and built a house and rondavels on the farm, which they christened Pelindaba and used as a weekend home in the early 1930s.

One of Preller's deputies was the famous naturalist, poet, writer and advocate, Eugène Marais. Like Preller, he is remembered today for his active promotion of Afrikaans. By the age of 20 he had already published his first newspaper, Land en Volk. His books on the behaviour of termites and baboons are still on sale today and everyone is familiar with his poems "Diep Rivier" and "Winternag". Marais studied medicine in Britain but later discontinued his studies in that field and qualified as an advocate. He was trapped in England by the Anglo-Boer War and only returned to Pretoria after the war.

In the 1890s he delivered a fiery public tribute to the "pleasures of opium". In the year in which he came of age, 1892, adults could still obtain opium freely and without a prescription. The distillate of opium, morphine, was then regarded as a non-addictive wonder drug. Today we are no longer under this misapprehension. Marais became addicted to morphine and obtaining a supply of the drug became a constant concern to him.

When the Prellers moved permanently from Arcadia to Pelindaba in 1935 (making the journey by ox wagon in those days), Marais, who lived with them, did not want to go along. The farm was too far from his morphine supplies. However, years of drug abuse had ruined his health and he was dependent on the Prellers. One depressing rainy and misty day on the farm, Marais, who was suffering from severe withdrawal symptoms, went to borrow a shotgun from a neighbour, Lood Pretorius. He asked to borrow the gun to shoot a snake at the rondavel. In the long, wet grass under a karree tree – in the proverbial shadow of the Safari reactor today – Marais took his own life on 29 March 1936. He was 65 years old.

The Preller house and the rondavels where Marais lived are still standing today – and so is the karree tree under which a brilliant, sensitive but lonely man ended his life on that cheerless day.

The heart of Pelindaba

After the Americans had dropped the first nuclear bombs on Japan in August 1945, events moved swiftly. As referred to previously, the Soviet Union exploded its first nuclear bomb in August 1949. Britain tested its own bomb in October 1952. A month later the Americans tested the first hydrogen bomb. Less than a year afterwards, in August 1953, the Soviet Union replied by testing a hydrogen bomb of its own. President Eisenhower of the USA decided that something drastic would have to be done to curb this rising trend and on 8 December 1953 he delivered his famous "Atoms for Peace" address to the UNGA. This is discussed in greater detail elsewhere in the text. Eisenhower was later to remark that atoms are not political in nature – they are neither moral nor immoral. It was up to people to choose how atoms should be used. His choice would be to expand the peaceful uses of atomic energy. He proposed to do this by supplying nuclear facilities to countries and training their scientists and engineers.

South Africa could fruitfully participate in this programme, especially since at that stage the country was one of the most important international suppliers of uranium. A local programme would have to begin with a research reactor. This would be required for the training of nuclear scientists, research and the production of isotopes for use in industry, agriculture and medicine. The reactor was to be used purely for peaceful purposes and this was to continue unchanged for the remainder of its operational life.

While site investigations were still in progress, the AEB was looking at possible reactors and negotiating with the USA. The eventual decision was to buy an Oak Ridge-type reactor that would be operated at 6.66 megawatts but would also have the capacity to be operated at 20 megawatts eventually (with minor modifications). Fuel for the reactor consisted of plates made from an alloy of highly enriched uranium (90% enriched) and aluminium. This had the advantage (for the Americans) of making South Africa totally dependent on the USA for fuel, a situation which was open to political exploitation in later years.

A year after the decision was taken, a small ceremony took place at the Pelindaba site. T.E.W. Schumann, the Deputy Chairman of the AEB, Ampie Roux and J.D. Roberts, the Managing Director of Roberts Construction Co, were the leading figures present. Schumann enthusiastically dug up a few spadefuls of earth and officially launched the project.

The indigenous trees and grass on the site were soon replaced by an enormous reactor hall. The outer walls were decorated with hieroglyphics. It was initially surmised that these symbols had a mystical meaning, but the designer eventually had to admit that he had put them there simply to bring the scale of the building more into line with human stature and that the hieroglyphics had no symbolic meaning! In addition to the hieroglyphics, round apertures, each several millimetres in depth, appeared in the concrete at regular intervals. When asked to explain the purpose of these apertures, scientists used to take the mickey by telling their alarmed visitors that the apertures were there to let the radiation escape.

While the reactor building was taking shape, the administration building, the chemistry block and the Van de Graaff accelerator were under construction as well. The latter has a tower that looks like the tail of a Boeing. Occupation took place from the end of 1963. The buildings erected to the south of the Pelindaba hill were the technical services building, the water treatment plant (which was capable of purifying and filtering more than a 1 000 megalitres of water from the Crocodile River annually to cool the reactor) and the radioactive waste treatment plant.

Additional structures were built over the next few years to house the library and the physical metallurgy, process metallurgy and isotope production sections.

The American-made Safari-1 reactor went critical on 18 March 1965 at 18:30. It was a historic moment. This was the first self-sustaining chain reaction to have taken place in Africa. The original plan was to finish the reactor by the end of 1963, but there was a delay of more than a year due to an industrial accident in the USA. The reactor vessel, a heavy aluminium cylinder about 4.5 m high and 1.5 m in diameter, had to undergo a series of tests before it could be shipped to South Africa. Things went wrong in this process.

In his book Newby-Fraser explains how the accident happened. It was necessary to check whether the reactor vessel's stainless steel cover, which was 100 mm thick, fitted properly. The cover was manufactured separately. The vessel had to be taken to another workshop for the cover to be fitted. The steel cable strap used to raise the vessel broke unexpectedly and the heavy cargo fell sideways onto the floor. In the process the beam tube protuberances were damaged and the core box distorted. The weight of the vessel after the cover had been fitted was too much for the strap, which was designed to bear only the weight of the vessel.

It took the Americans a year to repair the vessel. By Christmas 1963 the enormous cargo had finally been pushed into the Pelindaba reactor hall, millimetre by millimetre. After only fifteen months the reactor was finished and the American operating team allowed it to become critical on 18 March 1965.

The commissioning of Safari-1 was celebrated with a ceremony conducted by Dr H.F. Verwoerd, the Prime Minister of South Africa from 1958 to 1966. The celebrations were attended by numerous dignitaries such as Sir William Penney, the Chairman of the Atomic Energy Authority in Britain, Professor André Gauvenet of the French Commissariat à l'Énergie Atomique, Professor Carlo Salvetti, Vice-President of the Italian Comitato Nazionale della Energia Nucleare, Dr Alvin Weinberg, Director of the National Laboratory in Oak Ridge, as well as a certain B. Dargan of the Australian Atomic Energy Commission, Professor A. Boettcher, Director of the Jülich Research Centre in West Germany, and representatives of the IAEA.

> ### The Safari-1 reactor
>
> The Safari reactor is one of about 250 research reactors in the world that are used for research, training and the production of radioactive isotopes for use in industry, agriculture and nuclear medicine. About two-thirds of these reactors are over 30 years old and therefore date from the euphoric Atoms for Peace days.
>
> Research reactors differ considerably from power reactors like Koeberg, because their main purpose is to serve as an intense source of neutrons and not to generate electricity. They are also considerably smaller and were originally designed to use highly enriched uranium as fuel. Their capacity is typically 20 to 100 megawatts in contrast with the approximately 1 000 megawatts of a power reactor.
>
> There are various types of research reactors, the most popular of which is the pool type. The cluster of fuel elements are contained in a pool of water, where water serves as the moderator for the neutrons and also as the coolant. In the case of Safari-1 the pool lies inside a raised above-ground concrete structure – almost like an above-ground swimming pool. The reason is that there are apertures in the side of the pool through which neutron bundles can be accessed for research purposes.
>
> Safari-1 was obtained from the USA as an Oak Ridge Research Reactor type, designed and built by Allis-Chalmers. (Some of the older readers may remember that in former years there were many Allis-Chalmers tractors on South African farms.) Safari-1 was commis-

sioned in March 1965 and operated at just under 7 megawatts. After the secondary cooling circuit was upgraded in 1968, it was possible to raise the power output to 20 megawatts.

For the first ten years of the reactor's operating life all was well. But then political sanctions were imposed by the USA in 1975 and the export of fuel elements was discontinued. The power output was downscaled to 5 megawatts and the operating hours were drastically reduced. However, the sanctions were to have a hidden benefit. Because Safari-1 was operated at such a low output and only run for short periods, its operating life was considerably extended in comparison with its contemporaries. Where many of them have already been switched off, Safari-1 is still briskly producing radio-isotopes today and earning cartloads of foreign exchange in the process.

As a result of the American boycott the AEC leapt into the breach and began to manufacture local fuel elements with 45% enriched uranium, obtained from the Y-plant. These elements consisted of an alloy of enriched uranium and aluminium. When this achievement was made public in 1981 it made the whole world sit up. A country capable of producing 45% enriched material would also be capable of the 90% enrichment required to produce nuclear weapons.

With the reactor operating on the AEC fuel, output was kept at 5 megawatts, but the operating hours were expanded. In 1993 the output was raised to 10 megawatts and later on to 20 megawatts. Today Safari-1 is only one of five reactors worldwide that produces molybdenum-99 (Mo-99) for use in over 40 million nuclear medical procedures annually to diagnose cancer and cardiovascular disease. Mo-99 is produced when enriched uranium plate targets in the reactor are exposed to neutrons. After irradiation the Mo-99 is extracted in a separate facility, the Hot Cell Complex.

Mo-99 is radioactive and decays to technetium (Tc), the isotope which is eventually used in medical diagnoses. Mo-99 is exported globally, but the logistics involved are somewhat of a nightmare, since a technetium generator loses about 22% of its usefulness every 24 hours. Fortunately it has the advantage that the market it supplies will never become saturated.

In the early 1970s the Americans started to panic about the use of highly enriched uranium in the fuel of research reactors, especially because many of the reactors were situated at universities where security was not of primary importance. A programme called Reduced Enrichment for Research and Test Reactors (RERTR) was therefore initiated in 1978. The idea was to persuade all users to switch to lower enrichment and return the American highly enriched uranium. However, this carried a high price tag.

Research reactors are designed to use highly enriched uranium (90% +). If the U-235 content is reduced (lower enrichment), it also reduces the flood of neutrons produced in the reactor and accordingly limits the reactor's usefulness. As a compromise the Americans were prepared to accept the highest level of enrichment that still fell into the category of "low-enriched" uranium, namely 20%. This arbitrary borderline between "highly enriched" and "low-enriched" uranium has been in existence for almost half a century and nobody can remember the reasons for it, except that it was introduced at the insistence of the USA. There is no possibility of anyone making a nuclear device from, say, 21% enriched uranium, but the definition is cast in stone and untouchable.

To compensate for the reduced U-235 isotopic ratio, the density of the U-235 has to be raised (that is to say, more U-235 per cm^3), but this has an influence on the stability of the fuel elements in the severe conditions of the reactor core. The usual uranium-aluminium alloy is no longer suitable and a new type of fuel assembly is therefore necessary. Up to now an assembly of uranium and silicon (plus other metals) has been used – so-called uranium-silicide fuel.

Apart from the very expensive conversion process, there are two other major drawbacks. The 20% enriched uranium required is not commercially available – ordinary power reactors use 3 to 5% enriched uranium. The 20% enriched uranium therefore has to be specially produced, which pushes up the costs. Furthermore, 20% enriched uranium can only be supplied by certain nuclear-weapon states (read: the USA). What is more, the reactor operators are dependent on the USA, which manufactures the special uranium-silicide fuel. This is rather like giving away your title to a property and then being dependent on the whims of the new owner, who can raise your rent and cut off your water and electricity just as he pleases. And hasn't South Africa (and other countries) had much experience of bully tactics like this? Especially now that reactors of this kind are not used so much for research but rather to generate income this process is fraught with political and economic hazards.

What appears to be hysterical angst about terrorism in reality conceals a coldly calculated determination to exercise control at all costs. What terrorist group could possibly have the technical capability to steal the irradiated fuel with its radioactive fission products and extract the uranium from the uranium-aluminium alloy? This is a process similar to trying to separate the copper and zinc in bronze, except that in addition to the technical difficulties one would also have to be able to handle the radioactivity present in this hell's brew! Then these terrorists would need the technical ability to build a nuclear device from the reclaimed uranium. A tall order for your everyday, common or garden terrorist.

People with this level of sophistication would rather steal radioactive waste from somewhere, such as old radiation sources used in hospitals (these quite often turn up at scrapyards) and then add sufficient simple ingredients (sodium nitrate fertiliser and diesel oil) to cause a powerful conventional explosion that would scatter radiation. This is known as a radiological or dirty bomb.

Nevertheless the AEC bowed to pressure and agreed to switch, but insisted on technical and economic feasibility studies in advance; these were carried out in collaboration with the Argonne National Laboratory. The government approved the switch to lower enrichment fuel in 2005 and in 2006 the first fuel elements were tested. On 25 June 2009 Safari-1, after having undergone maintenance, was commissioned with its first full load of low-enriched uranium to begin the next phase of its operational life.

Safari-1 has built up an outstanding safety record over the years. In 1988 a water leak was discovered in the pool, however. Bert Winkler, a senior health physicist and member of the Licensing Branch, had been a strong swimmer and diver in his day. Without thinking twice he put on his wet suit and dived into the pool (obviously with the reactor switched off) and found the source of the leak. It was successfully repaired. The Licensing Branch was succeeded by the Nuclear Safety Council (NSC), of which Winkler became the Chief Executive Officer, and then by the National Nuclear Regulator (NNR).

The Safari-1 reactor was originally operated under a bilateral safeguards agreement with the USA, since by March 1965 the IAEA did not yet have a model agreement and the NPT would only enter into force five years later. On 3 December 1965 the IAEA did, however, approve a model agreement of this kind and the Americans were able to transfer their oversight of the reactor to the IAEA eleven days later. This agreement was numbered INFCIRC/70.

The Safari-1 reactor has therefore been subject to inspections from the time it was first commissioned to the present day to ensure that the reactor is used exclusively for peaceful purposes.

A difficult choice

Safari-1 was operating productively, the greater part of the overseas training had been completed and it was possible to focus on running a nuclear programme suited to South Africa's needs on native soil.

The AEB initially decided to develop two parallel projects. On the one hand there was the uranium enrichment programme and on the other the development of the power reactor at Pelinduna.

Wally Grant was initially responsible for the development of the Pelinduna project. The plan was that his reactor should use natural uranium as fuel, heavy water as the moderator and liquid sodium as the coolant. The use of sodium made heat transfer more efficient and resulted in cost savings since it eliminated the need for costly items like a reactor pressure vessel. It was initially thought that the cost of the core of a power station could almost be reduced by a factor of three if the Pelinduna concept could be incorporated into the design of a power station. There were also other advantages: The experience with liquid metals would be applicable to fast breeder reactors and the development of the design could serve as an incentive to South African industry to solve the problems associated with nuclear grade materials and their manufacturing techniques. It was thought that since large pressure vessels would not be required, the local industry would be able to manufacture all the nuclear components in South Africa that are required for a power reactor.

The Pelinduna assembly was designed and built and went critical on 30 November 1967, in other words, a self-sustaining chain reaction was achieved – a milestone in the history of South African reactor physics.

Because South Africa was an important supplier of uranium, it made sense to explore the possibilities of enriching uranium as well instead of merely relying on exporting uranium concentrates. The added value would make an enormous difference to the potential income from uranium.

However, Pelinduna and the enrichment programme simultaneously reached the stage where the construction of a big demonstration plant became necessary for both projects. Important decisions had to be taken. An analysis of the international uranium market indicated that a shortage of cheap uranium was imminent. This would inevitably have led to greater competition in the market. It would therefore be in South Africa's interests to rather focus research efforts on a fuel development programme. Two years later it was decided to terminate research at Pelinduna, since the government could no longer carry the enormous cost of both projects. The literal meaning of the word then became a reality: *Pelile Induna* – the chief is dead.

With the benefit of hindsight it appears that the discontinuation of the Pelinduna project may well have been a blessing in disguise. The reactor was intended to operate with unclad uranium rods, heavy water as the moderator and sodium as the coolant. Under today's safety standards Pelinduna would probably never have been able to obtain an operating licence. It was simply too dangerous to use sodium and water together, because of the risk that this may cause a violent chemical reaction.

By 1961, when the AEB scientists returned from their training overseas, gas diffusion was the only commercially established uranium enrichment process on the international scene. It was an enormously expensive process and furthermore the associated technology was top secret. South Africa simply did not have the manpower and financial resources to follow this route.

A possible alternative was to start a gas centrifuge project for uranium enrichment. In the late 1960s and early 1970s this method was considered in Western European countries. It was based on the pioneering work of Manfred von Ardenne, Max Steenbeck and Gernot Zippe, who developed the gas centrifuge after the Second World War when they were German prisoners of war in Russian penal camps. In terms of the Treaty of Almelo, West Germany, the Netherlands and Britain decided in 1971 to cooperate in this area and the Urenco company was founded. Three demonstration plants were built in 1980 in the three countries. Today Urenco is one of the biggest uranium enrichment companies in the world.

As well as enriching uranium, Urenco also (inadvertently) enriched the knowledge of a certain Abdul Qadeer Khan. In 1972, Khan, a devout Muslim from Pakistan, received his doctorate in metallurgical engineering from the Catholic University of Leuven in Belgium and found a job at Urenco's Almelo plant in the Netherlands. There he began the leisurely and unhindered theft of blueprints for the design and construction of centrifuges before returning to his fatherland in 1975. He soon set about building an indigenous enrichment plant for a nuclear weapons programme in Pakistan. Pakistan's arch-enemy, India, had tested a nuclear bomb in 1974 and Pakistan could not allow itself to fall behind. Today nobody can understand why Almelo should have given the "father of the Islam bomb" access to their sensitive centrifuge technology. Possibly Hendrina (Hennie to her friends), his South African-born wife of Dutch descent, helped open a few doors for him in the Netherlands.

Khan was later to cast a long shadow in the clandestine world of nuclear technology smuggling – in South Africa as well.

Northern Tyres and Accessories – what the façade concealed

Ampie Roux believed that the South Africans should develop their own enrichment technology, which would result in a smaller plant than the enormous gas diffusion installations of the Americans and one that would not impose the same stringent technological requirements as the European gas centrifuge process. Furthermore, gas centrifuge technology was still under development at that stage and was not accessible to outsiders – apart from A.Q. Khan, that is to say.

It was here that Wally Grant's previous experience at the CSIR proved very useful. Grant had formerly done research for a Chamber of Mines project which had studied the high temperatures in deep level gold mines and the physiological effect on the people working there.

Between the two world wars a Frenchman called Ranque developed a tube with a special vortex chamber in the middle and an attached T-piece. If compressed air is let in at the T-piece, a mini whirlwind or tornado develops inside the specially designed tube, resulting in hot air being emitted from the tube at one end and cold air at the other. This device fell into the hands of a scientist called Hilsch during the German occupation of France. He was engaged in research on cooling facilities under wartime conditions. He made a few improvements to Ranque's vortex tube, but did not find it more effective than conventional cooling methods. However, the Ranque-Hilsch tube, as it is known today, set a chain of thought in motion in Wally Grant's fertile brain.

He carried out further development on the vortex tube so that it was able to supply cool air for the dewpoint meters which are used in mines. During the experiments he carried out, Grant noted that water vapour is separated from air in the tube. Later on at the AEB he recalled the vortex tube and considered it as a possible method of separating isotopes during the manufacture of heavy water. Furthermore, if the tube was able to separate water vapour and air with different molecular masses, it could possibly also be used to separate the uranium-235 and uranium-238 isotopes. The advantage of this separation element was that, unlike the gas centrifuge, it contained no rapidly spinning parts.

It was decided to repeat the previous work at the CSIR to clearly establish the conditions for separating air and water vapour. At first Wally Grant and his team were baffled by their inability to repeat their previous success and achieve separation. Then the reason slowly dawned on them when the season changed – the relative humidity of the air had simply been too low. Such were the humble beginnings of the history of uranium enrichment in this country.

Since uranium isotope separation was a politically sensitive issue (because of its link with the manufacture of nuclear weapons) this project was code-named the "Gas cooling project" and classified as secret. The spadework was done behind the modest façade of a smallish warehouse in Du Toit Street in the centre of Pretoria. The building was formerly a motor spares shop known as Northern Tyres and Accessories, and it still bore that name. The equipment was housed in the back section of the building, which had seen better days. The workshop was situated in the front section. There were no security guards and officially the staff were making "scientific equipment". Later the modest warehouse was exchanged for the Shamrock Building in Skinner Street (today Nana Sita Street), also in the Pretoria central business district. The research component of the work was carried out there. Security was better than at the previous premises.

In 1964 the research project reached a critical stage when the scientific team began working with uranium hexafluoride (UF_6). UF_6 is a toxic and extremely corrosive substance to work with and is the essential supply material for enrichment plants. The team thought that the process of separating uranium-235 and uranium-238 would work better if a mixture of UF_6 and a carrier gas with a low molecular mass, such as hydrogen, was used as the process gas. The first attempts to use this mixture were a dismal failure, however. After experiments had been conducted for just one day the compressor had to be switched off and cleaned. UF_6 reacts very fast with oily residues of any kind, but under certain conditions it even reacts with hydrogen. When this happens, the UF_6 vapour instantly disappears from the process gas. These experiences were the forerunners of bigger problems which emerged when the pilot plant was built and even put the plant out of action for a few months. The laboratory facilities simply had to be improved to keep this mixture of UF_6 and hydrogen under control.

> ## UF_6 and hydrogen
>
> Uranium hexafluoride is a highly corrosive gas which undergoes a chemical reaction with most metals, with the exception of nickel and aluminium.
>
> It also reacts with oily substances of any kind such as are typically found in any workshop. Process equipment therefore has to be very thoroughly cleaned and the metal surface has to be specially treated (pacified) before it comes into contact with UF_6.
>
> Hydrogen gas also reacts with UF_6, but this reaction is slow at room temperature. At a high temperature and in the presence of certain contaminants it is a different matter, however. All the UF_6 can be rapidly converted in an autocatalytic reaction into a powdery fluoride compound which forms deposits on all the internal filters and can even block the vortex tubes. Another product of the reaction is hydrofluoric acid (HF), which is not only extremely corrosive – it eats through glass – but can also cause serious burns.
>
> Hydrogen gas itself is dangerous in that when it comes into contact with oxygen in the air it can form an explosive mixture. The pressure within the equipment should therefore be kept higher than atmospheric pressure to avoid inleakage of air which could cause internal explosions. For this reason the respective enrichment stages in the pilot plant that was subsequently built were also physically screened off from each other with sufficient upward ventilation to allow any possible release of hydrogen to escape safely through the ventilation towers.

Ampie Roux and T.E.W. Schumann, the Deputy Chairman of the AEB, requested an interview with the Prime Minister, H.F. Verwoerd. Within a matter of days Verwoerd approved the R1 million that the team needed to carry on with their uranium enrichment experiments. The improved facilities allowed the research team to make more rapid progress.

By October 1965 they were able to separate argon isotopes but unfortunately they were not yet able to separate the uranium isotope.

Verwoerd was expected to visit the laboratories in November 1965 and the tension began to build up among the scientists. They worked around the clock in pursuit of a breakthrough. A week before the Prime Minister's visit uranium isotope separation was finally achieved. There were still problems, however. Unfortunately the low-mass isotope emerged from the outlet where the high-mass isotope was expected! The scientists worked like madmen to find a way to correct this. On D-day the problem was finally solved. It then became possible to separate uranium-235 from uranium-238 in a helium-UF_6 mixture. The scientists were able to start looking at developing UF_6 cold traps (to extract the UF_6 from the process gas), valves, instrumentation, and the investigation of corrosion-resistant construction materials.

Compressor development was one of the most important aspects of the programme. The concern here was how to find solutions to problems caused by the corrosive nature of the UF_6 process gas. Compressors would have to function without the conventional lubrication. The solution found was to make the rings of the compressor from Teflon, which is resistant to UF_6.

Wally Grant monitored every step of the process and helped to seek solutions. One problem was that the separation capacity of the vortex tube is strongly dependent on the molecular mass of the process gas, but there was no instrument available to measure this. This problem occupied his thoughts for some time.

Grant was sitting in church with his family one Sunday morning when in a eureka moment the solution suddenly struck him. His thoughts were turning on the question of how the small church organ could be capable of producing such pure notes. He recalled from his knowledge of physics that the frequencies (tones) of the notes are a function of the density of the air in the organ pipes. Everyone knows what happens to the human voice if one breathes in helium with a molecular mass considerably lower than that of air for a while. This gave him a few ideas.

If the frequency of the natural vibrations of the gas mixture in a pipe, roughly based on an organ pipe, could be determined, he would be able to measure the molecular mass accurately. The next morning he described his new insight to his laboratory staff and this led to the development of an extremely efficient measuring instrument – the "fluitjiesmeter" (whistle meter).

By the end of 1967 it had been demonstrated that the vortex tube method was entirely feasible on a laboratory scale.

Separative work

The capacity of an enrichment plant is measured in so-called separative work units (SWU). This is rather a complex concept (expressed in kilograms). The value depends on the concentration of U-235 in the enriched output and in the depleted tailings. For example: A typical reactor like Koeberg requires 3.5% enriched material as fuel. If the uranium is depleted in the course of the enrichment process to 0.31% (natural uranium contains 0.71% U-235), then about 8 kg of natural uranium is required for 1 kg of the product and about 4.2 kg of SWU. However, if the uranium is depleted to 0.2%, the figures change to about 6.5 kg of feedstock and 5.4 kg of SWU. As the required quantity of feedstock per kilogram of enriched product is reduced, the separative work required increases. The cost of the feedstock therefore has to be balanced against the cost of the separative work, and these are factors which pull in opposite directions.

An important factor here is the energy efficiency of the separative process. The amount of energy used to perform 1 kg of separative work depends on the type of separative process. The gas diffusion process requires about 2 500 kWh per kg of SWU, the aerodynamic (Ucor) process about 3 000 kWh and the gas centrifuge only about 50 kWh per kg of SWU. In principle it is therefore cheaper for centrifuge plants to do more separative work and use less feedstock in comparison with the other processes.

To gain a better grasp of the concept of separative work units, take the following two nominal cases as examples:

A big nuclear reactor – such as one of the Koeberg reactors – requires about 100 000 kg of SWU per year. In practice this means that with fuel enriched to 4% and depleted tailings of 0.2%, about 15 tons of 4% enriched material would be necessary, for which almost 114 tons of feedstock (natural uranium) would be required and almost 99 tons of depleted tailings at 0.2% would be produced.

An enrichment plant of this capacity is not, however, necessary to produce highly enriched uranium for a nuclear bomb. A plant with a capacity of only 20 000 kg of SWU/year can produce about 120 kg of 90% enriched uranium (sufficient for at least ten simple gun-type bombs). For this output 34 120 kg of natural uranium would be required as feed and 34 000 kg of depleted tailings would be produced.

The sheer size of some of the commercial enrichment plants and the

> *separative work done are astounding. For example, the Tricastin gas diffusion plant in France has a capacity of almost 11 000 000 kg of SWU, sufficient to produce fuel for about 90 Koeberg-type reactors in one year. The electricity consumption of this plant is 3 000 megawatts. It is supplied by four dedicated nuclear reactors.*

FLEXING THEIR MUSCLES

In 1968 two senior AEB officials went to Tokyo to present a lecture on the Pelinduna reactor. On the way home the South Africans visited nuclear installations in Britain. At that stage South Africa could still buy nuclear reactors from overseas manufacturers, but obtaining nuclear fuel or information on enrichment technology was another matter. Although the decision had already been taken by 1967 not to proceed with work on Pelinduna, basic knowledge of reactor technology was still important to the South Africans.

In the previous year it had been demonstrated that it was possible to carry out uranium isotope separation by the vortex tube method on a laboratory scale. This discovery set the South African scientists free to dream – after all if sufficient enriched uranium could be produced, what else might be possible ...

Sitting in the back of their official black limousine, having just returned from Britain, the two eminent gentlemen decided to start a small project that would keep the dejected South African nuclear scientists, who had recently seen the Pelinduna project close down, busy and motivated in future. This was the origin of the Peaceful Nuclear Explosion (PNE) project. A civil engineer from the AEB was already in the USA to undergo training on the peaceful application of nuclear explosions.

Either plutonium or highly enriched uranium is required for a peaceful nuclear explosion. At that stage the production of plutonium was out of the question and the scientists knew they would have to look to uranium. They soon realised that the enrichment results already obtained by the AEB's scientific team in the laboratory would have to be tested on a larger scale by building a pilot plant. But they could not expect the government to take such an important (and expensive) decision purely on the recommendation of the group of scientists working on the project. Early in 1968, on the recommendation of Ampie Roux, the government therefore appointed a specialist committee whose members had not been involved in the development work.

Dr Hendrik van Eck, the Chairman of the Industrial Development Corporation (IDC), was appointed chairman of the committee.

Van Eck was a man who wore two hats. In 1965 the Minister of Mines and of Planning, Jan Haak, asked the AEB to undertake a study on the desirability of commercial nuclear energy for South Africa. Van Eck was appointed chairman of a commission of inquiry which carried out a study between 1965 and 1968 and submitted a report containing recommendations. This report was accepted in April 1968. It included the following statements:

- From a purely economic standpoint it is clearly DESIRABLE to use enriched uranium as fuel, but it is ESSENTIAL that the supply of fuel should be assured for the operating lifetime of any commercial power station, i.e. for 25 to 30 years.
- Any enriched uranium power reactor built in South Africa in the near future would be dependent on enrichment facilities in one of three countries (the USA, the UK and France). Although long-term supply contracts for enriched fuel can be arranged with overseas organisations, such arrangements could be subject to veto by the governments concerned.
- An alternative, of course, would be to build an enrichment plant in South Africa. A plant of the desired capacity would require a capital investment in excess of R500 million. It is unlikely that this country will be in a position to consider either such vast capital expenditure, or the enormous technical effort required, in the foreseeable future.

The enrichment technology referred to in this report was the very expensive gas diffusion technology. It was here that Van Eck's "second hat" came into play. After the success of Wally Grant's vortex tube at laboratory level, it became possible to develop a cheaper alternative to gas diffusion. Van Eck's committee of independent specialists made a study of all the available information on the work done on the vortex tube and then held intensive discussions over three days with the people directly involved in the development work. Unlike Van Eck's former report on commercial nuclear power for South Africa, which took three years to complete, this report was essentially finished one Friday in February 1968 after three days of searching discussions. The following Monday the document was on the minister's table. It was clear that the draftsmen had been in a hurry. The report was marked TOP SECRET in view of its technical and political sensitivity.

The committee made an enthusiastic and positive recommendation to the minister on the possibility of enriching uranium in South Africa, based on Wally Grant's vortex tube technology. The recommendation was that a pilot plant should be built to test the new process on a far larger scale.

Not all members of the government were equally excited about this recommendation. Internationally the possession of enrichment technology by a country outside the circle of nuclear-weapon states was a political hot potato. Naturally there was also the matter of funding. It is therefore understandable that the government did not react to the recommendations immediately. Only after the Minister of Finance, Nic Diederichs, had been won over by persuasive arguments was there a breakthrough. A year after the Van Eck Committee's secret report, on 11 February 1969, the cabinet under the leadership of John Vorster, the then Prime Minister, voted in favour of the Van Eck recommendations.

Then things started happening rapidly. A number of new staff members had to be recruited. A full-time top management team under Wally Grant was appointed. The distinguished firm Roberts Construction was appointed as the construction contractor. This company had built the Safari-1 reactor facility ten years previously and was later to put up numerous other structures on the nuclear site.

As increasing numbers of outside organisations and individuals became involved in the process, it became more and more difficult to keep the operations secret. John Vorster therefore decided on a public announcement. His statement in parliament on 20 July 1970 had international repercussions, as might be expected. The world had now been informed, but did not necessarily believe, that South African scientists had developed their own process for enriching uranium. This was the beginning of decades of espionage and speculation to find out what the exact nature of the process was, from whom it had been stolen or bought, or who had collaborated on its development. To the USA in particular this announcement was like the proverbial red rag to a bull. Right up to the present – as Iraq discovered a while ago and Iran is now experiencing – the USA becomes extremely uncomfortable when another country starts enriching uranium – even when this is done under the supervision of the IAEA.

At that time South Africa's relations with the USA were deteriorating in general. Just a few days before John Vorster's announcement the Americans had stated through their Secretary of State that the USA would no longer supply weapons or military hardware to South Africa. Vorster may well have taken great pleasure in waving the red rag with an extra flourish.

> ## *John Vorster's announcement of 20 July 1970*
>
> *Vorster sketched the background to the development of the enrichment process, stating that South Africa was an important producer of uranium and explaining that it did not make sense merely to export uranium ore concentrates from the mines for further processing by other countries. South Africa could add a lot of value and negotiate considerably better prices by marketing the uranium in an enriched form. Furthermore, South Africa was on the point of launching a comprehensive nuclear power programme of its own. To ensure that fuel would be available for this programme, it had to be locally produced.*
>
> *He emphasised that very few countries had mastered the expensive and technically difficult process of enriching uranium and that the South African process not only compared well with those of other countries but had the potential for considerable improvement. The local press immediately fastened on this statement and trumpeted it as "the cheapest process in the world".*
>
> *Vorster announced that the proposed small pilot plant, based on the new enrichment process, would be used for peaceful applications. He said he needed to reiterate this because, as everyone knew, his announcement would be incorrectly interpreted.*
>
> *An important part of the announcement concerned South Africa's willingness to share the benefits of the new enrichment process with the global community – under certain conditions.*
>
> *South Africa was also prepared to accept an international safeguards system and inspections, but since the IAEA was still in the process of designing the safeguards system at that stage (it was not ready for another year), accession to the NPT could only be considered when particulars of the system were known. The NPT had only been in force for four months at that stage.*

Suddenly all eyes were turned on South Africa. The international community was not slow to respond. Only three days after the announcement the UN Security Council (UNSC) adopted Resolution 282 in which an appeal was made to member states to rescind all licences and military patents that had been sold to the South African government or South African companies to manufacture weapons, ammunition or any form of military equipment. Investment or technical aid for the manufacture of such items was also prohibited under this resolution. The UNSC resolution was adopted by 12 votes to nil. France, Britain and the USA abstained, however. This resolution was the successor to the 1962 resolution, Resolution 161, which even then forbade the international community to sell weapons to South Africa.

Only a few months later, on 24 October 1970, the UNGA passed Resolution 2627, in which apartheid was described as "a crime against the conscience and dignity of mankind".

The South African government did not allow itself to be deflected from its course, however.

The Uranium Enrichment Act was passed by the South African parliament in July 1970. In November of the same year Ucor was officially established, with a share capital of R50 million. The organisation was to be situated right next to Pelindaba, on the site called Valindaba. Staff members of the AEB who were working on uranium enrichment were transferred to Ucor. In time the so-called "red buses" began to ferry thousands of staff members every day from suburbs in Pretoria and even Johannesburg to Pelindaba and Valindaba.

In September 1970 Ampie Roux and Wally Grant turned the first sods at the new site. Less than a year later Valindaba was commissioned. The name of the new site meant "we don't talk about this". It was a compound name made up of indigenous words.

From 1971 onwards a stream of young Afrikaans- and English-speaking graduates in engineering, physics, mathematics and applied mathematics joined the country's uranium enrichment programme. Only South African citizens qualified and strict security clearance checks were applied to prospective candidates under the gimlet eye of General Els. It is very difficult to say exactly how many Ucor employees were ultimately involved in the South African nuclear programme. Everyone who had top secret clearance at Ucor was aware that the company manufactured highly enriched uranium. Most of them probably guessed what it was intended for. According to Wynand de Villiers, at any given time about 400 people with top secret clearance were working actively on the programme and this number probably grew to a total of 1 000 over the years. Information was compartmentalised and only a few people were fully informed of what was going on.

Meanwhile there were developments on various fronts. An internal committee of the AEB that had investigated the possible development of devices for peaceful explosions had identified the following different types of devices by 1970:

- Gun-type and implosion-type fission devices, also called type A devices. There was a boosted version of this type of device with a mixture of lithium, deuterium and tritium in the core, which was known as A* (A-asterisk).
- A thermonuclear device (hydrogen bomb with a fission detonator), known as type B.

There was another important development in March 1971. Carl de Wet, the Minister of Mines, approved the secret programme for the development of peaceful nuclear devices. The idea was to use them in areas like mining and harbour construction. The peaceful nature of the intended devices was demonstrated by the fact that responsibility for them fell under the portfolio of the Department of Mines. The Minister of Defence was obviously informed about the explosives programme. In August 1973 the Minister of Mines reaffirmed his 1971 decision and also gave permission for theoretical studies on type B devices to proceed.

The basic concept of the gun-type A devices involved shooting an enriched uranium projectile from a gun barrel at high speed (about 300 m/s) with precision into a specially shaped enriched uranium target. A chemical propellant (explosive) is used to do this. For security reasons this part of the development work could not be carried out at Pelindaba, because of the attention the gunshots would attract. In 1972 three postgraduate bursary holders of the AEB were consequently sent to the National Institute for Defence Research at the CSIR's facility in Somerset West (Somchem) to do research and development on the mechanical and pyrotechnical subsystems of the nuclear device. The Minister of Defence made a few obsolete naval gun barrels available for research purposes. The barrels had to be sawn off and drilled out. Some of them were used in the construction of the first South African nuclear devices. In addition to the development work, information on the construction of explosive devices from open sources, such as declassified information from the Manhattan Project, was also used after undergoing refinement by South African scientists. The internet did not yet exist.

The second half of 1977 was chosen as the cut-off time by which the first South African nuclear device for peaceful purposes should be ready for testing. It was considered that sufficient enriched uranium should be ready by this date.

P.W. Botha, the forceful Minister of Defence at that time, had gained a reputation as an obstinate and proud man. As a response to the UN resolutions on arms exports to South Africa he had already informed the South African parliament on 7 May 1971 that the country would be able to meet its own military needs at that stage and had no need of weapons from foreign suppliers. This was typical of the "laager" mentality of the South African government. The harsher the criticism they received from the international community the more determined the white government became to stand alone. This again demonstrated that sanctions often have the effect of making a country more self-sufficient.

ISOLATION AND RESOURCEFULNESS

Criticism

The international community's criticism of South Africa's political dispensation became increasingly ferocious. On 5 October 1973 the UNGA rejected the credentials of the South African delegation. On 28 November of the same year the Arab states introduced oil sanctions against South Africa. On 30 November the UNGA passed Resolution 3068 (XXVIII), thereby ratifying the International Convention on the Suppression and Punishment of the Crime of Apartheid. This was followed by a further resolution of the UNGA on 14 December 1973 to the effect that the South African government "had no right to represent the people of South Africa" and that the freedom movements were "the authentic representatives of the South African communities".

In October 1974 an attempt was made in the UNSC to terminate South Africa's membership of the UN. South Africa was accused of violating the principles of the UN Charter, and of contempt for the Universal Declaration of Human Rights. South Africa was also accused of sending troops to the former Southern Rhodesia to prop up Ian Smith's government, thereby not only flouting the UNSC's sanctions against Rhodesia but at the same time posing a threat to the security of Southern Africa. Pik Botha was South Africa's representative at the UN at the time and on 24 October 1974 he sounded a heartfelt plea for South Africa's continued participation in the organisation. This was to be the most important speech of his career. He denied that the South African government's apartheid policy was based on concepts of inferiority and superiority and explained that the different communities in the country preferred to retain their own culture and beliefs.

Botha went on to point out to the UNSC that they might be able to remove South Africa from the UN, but not from the planet. According to him South Africa had not violated the principles of the UN or waged war on black Africa: "We were in fact the first African nationalists. Black Africans need not conduct a freedom struggle against my government. Being an African country, we understand African aspirations. We have stolen land from nobody. We have conquered no people.

"We threaten no one. We have absolutely no designs of aggrandizement."

He compared South Africa to a zebra: "If the zebra were shot, it would not matter whether the bullet penetrated a white stripe or a black stripe: the whole animal would die."

The debate lasted a whole day and afterwards ten representatives voted in favour of suspending South Africa's membership. Only three dissenting votes, those of the USA, Britain and France, saved South Africa from political excommunication because these three countries all possessed the veto. This was the first time in its history that a proposal was vetoed in the UNSC by three countries simultaneously. The three did, however, express their opposition to South Africa's policies and said that they expected the South African government to use its continued membership to introduce changes into the country.

Wooing the Germans

As a result of the secrecy surrounding South Africa's nuclear programme, local scientists often had to do wonders with basic equipment. Ampie Roux stated years later that about 90% of the components of the uranium enrichment plant were manufactured locally and that the imported parts required were certainly useful but not essential. The scientists did make use of every possible opportunity for knowledge exchange and collaboration with international colleagues.

The Bavarian political legend Franz-Josef Strauss was a minister in the West German coalition cabinet at the time. He was regarded as a good friend of South Africa's. He brokered the arrangement by which a few South African scientists were allowed to work at the Karlsruhe headquarters of the West German Federal Nuclear Research Centre (GfK) between 1969 and 1974. These scientists included Dr Waldo Stumpf, who later headed the plant for the manufacture of Koeberg fuel (Beva) at Pelindaba and eventually became the Chief Executive Officer of the Atomic Energy Corporation (AEC), the successor to the combined AEB and Ucor.

A German energy company named Steinkohlen Elektrizität AG (Steag) was involved in a pilot study in 1973 with a view to cooperation on the erection of a big enrichment plant, based on the South African vortex tube enrichment process. The Germans were to provide most of the capital and the South Africans the technology. Steag is a wealthy enterprise, the fifth biggest power generator in Germany with eight fossil fuel power stations.

This cooperation was later misinterpreted as evidence that the South Africans had merely taken over the German uranium enrichment technology. Professor E.W. Becker had developed an aerodynamic isotope separation process in Germany which made use of the so-called Becker nozzle. This process was never applied in Germany, although a pilot plant was built in Brazil. Although they are based on the same physical principle, namely the separation of lighter and heavier isotopes by creating a rapid spinning action in the gas, separating the isotopes through centrifugal action, the Becker and Ucor processes differ considerably.

Steag was contracted by the West German Federal Nuclear Research Centre to license the German Becker process.

The legendary Professor Becker was invited to South Africa in 1974. The instructions from the South African embassy in Bonn were that no publicity should be given to the professor's visit. He was not permitted a close inspection of the Ucor facilities or the Ucor vortex tube, but he was taken on a tour of the site. The unique silhouette of the pilot plant with its three buildings and nine high ventilation towers led the German scientist to conclude that the Ucor process was related to the inefficient thermodynamic diffusion separation process which was tested during the Manhattan Project, but rapidly abandoned. When he saw the towers he shook his head ruefully and remarked incredulously: "It is not going to work!" The South Africans did not enlighten him.

A formal cooperation agreement between Steag and Ucor was signed in August 1973. The West German government had to give its final approval to the agreement, however, and since they were unable to reach consensus Steag withdrew their formal application for federal government consent. Who knows what part Becker's erroneous assumption may have played in this process!

In March 1976 the agreement between Steag and Ucor was officially cancelled, partly because the two institutions were unable to agree on conditions for investment and the supply of natural uranium to a commercial enrichment plant.

The Y-plant

By the end of 1974 the first stage of the lower cascade portion of the pilot enrichment plant, the Y-plant, had been completed. Work on the plant began in 1971. The plant was commissioned in stages, from the stripper and feed section, eventually leading to the high enrichment section. The whole cascade only became fully operational in March 1977, however. After the cascade has been filled with the process gas – a mixture of UF_6 and hydrogen – it takes some time before the so-called gradient can be established, namely with the starting point at the concentration of depleted uranium and the top of the cascade at the eventual high degree of enrichment. The first small quantity of highly enriched uranium was only extracted on 30 January 1978.

Technical aspects

The heart of an enrichment plant is the enrichment stage. In the Y-plant this stage consisted of a suction compressor and several pressure vessels. The process gas had to be compressed to such an extent that it could be shot at supersonic speed through the separation elements (also called vortex tubes), where the separation of isotopes took place. When the gas was compressed its temperature increased and heat exchangers were consequently used to cool the process gas. An internal cold trap was also linked to each stage, so that the UF_6 could be internally frozen out if the stage had to be opened for maintenance.

In order to protect the fine holes in the vortex tubes, each stage was fitted with two sets of filters to catch dust from the piston rings or any reaction products.

Enrichment stages were linked in series (tandem) to form enrichment blocks. The blocks were then linked in series to form a cascade.

Ideally the entire plant should have been housed in a single building, but owing to the geological structures at the old Valindaba site the plant was spread over three buildings, namely Buildings C, D and E. Building C contained the stripper, the feed and the first enrichment block, and the cascade in building E ended where the highly enriched uranium was extracted.

Each building had three tall ventilation towers. Because the process gas was a mixture of UF_6 and hydrogen, and the latter can react explosively with the oxygen in the air under certain conditions, the enrichment process was operated at a pressure above atmospheric pressure to prevent inleakage of air into the equipment. Each enrichment stage was compartmentalised and ventilated from below in order to remove any possible hydrogen leakages from the building as rapidly as possible via the ventilation towers.

The process gas fed into a stage was divided into two parts by the separation element: an enriched stream which flowed into the cascade further downstream under pressure – becoming progressively more enriched – and a depleted component which was conducted back upstream to the beginning of the cascade, becoming increasingly depleted in the process. The hydrogen also had to be removed from the process gas. This was achieved with the aid of the same type of vortex tubes that were used in the uranium isotope separation process.

Building C – the beginning of the cascade – contained the following: the stripper section (Block S) where the depleted uranium was extracted; the starting point where the process gas was fed in; and the first enrichment block (Block 1). UF_6 – which is a solid at room temperature and pressure – was placed in autoclaves (ovens) in 2-ton cylinders and heated, which caused the UF_6 to sublimate, after which it mixed with hydrogen to form the process gas. In a cascade most of the separation work is done at the beginning: the units are therefore physically larger and each stage consists of two units. Blocks 2 and 3 in Building D and Blocks 4 and 5 in Building E contained single stages which became physically smaller because the flow of the enriched stream also gradually became smaller.

The cascade was operated by means of the Pelsakon cycle. This means that the constant flow of the process gas from the beginning to the end of the cascade was periodically interrupted and the process gas was allowed to recirculate in each stage (also referred to as reflux). This was achieved by the central activation of special valves, which interrupted the flow and isolated each stage for a while. This process was operated by a central computer system which originally came from the USA and, after a carefully designed detour, ended up in the control building – Building H - where it was installed. From a Central Intelligence Agency (CIA) report dated 11 August 1978 it is clear that the CIA knew about the computer at the time and also knew for what purpose it was being used.

The separation capacity of a cascade is measured in so-called separative work units (kg SWU). The initial design capacity of the Y-plant was

> raised considerably, to about 20 000 kg SWU per year, by the installation of a new generation of vortex separation packs. The plant was therefore able to produce, for example, about 7 tons of low-enriched uranium for Koeberg and 53 tons of depleted uranium from 60 tons of natural uranium feed. Alternatively, with the 20 000 kg SWU about 120 kg of highly enriched uranium (90%) per year could be produced from 34 120 kg of natural uranium, meanwhile producing about 34 000 kg of depleted material. (These figures naturally depend on the final percentage of depleted tails.)
>
> As the name "pilot plant" indicates, this plant was originally intended to provide a practical demonstration of the Ucor separation process. In practice, however, the plant was used to produce nuclear weapons material (90% enriched), enriched material for Safari fuel (45% enriched material) and enriched material for Koeberg fuel (3.25%).

As might be expected with groundbreaking technology, the new plant had to overcome a number of serious mechanical and chemical problems in the early days. For instance, from August 1979 to April 1980 production had to be suspended completely. As a result of the chemical reaction between UF_6 and the hydrogen in the process gas (and possibly other contaminants) the uranium was deposited as a fluoride compound in powder form inside the equipment, blocking both the internal filters and the separation elements. The plant had to be switched off, dismantled and cleaned. It had to be filled with process gas again afterwards and the gradient then had to be re-established. Not until July 1981 could highly enriched uranium eventually be produced again.

> ## Courage in action
>
> *At the time of the catastrophe Richard Robinson was the manager of the Y-plant. He was a real character, one of a kind. He was a large, naturally bald man and wore a full beard which made him look like a Voortrekker of old. This was misleading since he was an English-speaking South African from Natal who knew very little Afrikaans. Unlike most of the senior members of staff, he didn't wear a suit. As a nod in the direction of the formal dress code he did wear a tie – which he always combined with a pair of Nike trainers. People who favoured formal shoes occasionally remarked on his choice of footwear (this was the 1970s) but this was always met with the following reaction: "They cost a darn side more*

than your shoes!"

As explained previously, the uranium in the process gas was deposited in powder form on the internal filters and blocked the separation elements. HF (hydrogen fluoride) is another product of the chemical reaction. It should be remembered that the critical mass – the amount of enriched uranium that is sufficient for a spontaneous, uncontrolled chain reaction – is closely dependent on the ratio of uranium to hydrogen atoms. Hydrogen (H) acts as a moderator for the neutrons and drastically influences the critical mass. (The reader will remember that the chances of a fission reaction are considerably higher for slow neutrons.) For example: For spherical U-235 metal in the absence of hydrogen atoms (H:U-235 ratio 0) the minimum critical mass is around 18 kg. With a solution of uranium in water, on the other hand, the minimum critical mass is dramatically reduced to around 800 grams (H:U-235 ratio 500) in spherical form because of the moderating effect of the hydrogen.

The problem was that nobody knew what the H:U-235 ratio was, that is the ratio of the enriched uranium which had been deposited on the filters to the hydrogen (available from the HF). Uncontrolled criticality on the blocked filters at the highly enriched end of the cascade could not be ruled out. There had been a number of criticality accidents across the world in which people had been killed or suffered serious radiation injuries. It was then that Richard Robinson showed his metal. As manager of the plant he refused to allow any of his people to tackle the job of removing the blocked filters. A procedure was set up to reduce the chances of criticality as far as possible. Richard put on an air suit himself, unscrewed the filter vessels and successfully removed the filters. (An air suit is a plastic suit which covers the body and supplies fresh air under pressure through a pipe. The wearer looks like a blown-up "Michelin man". The suit protects the wearer from exposure to radioactive uranium dust or HF, which can cause severe chemical burns.)

Not long afterwards Robinson suddenly became very agitated at an internal meeting one day: "Why are we making this stuff (highly enriched uranium)? What are we going to do with it?" This was a somewhat naïve question, coming from the plant manager who knew exactly what and how much the plant was producing. As an engineer, he was only too well aware of the possible uses. Nevertheless he tendered his resignation shortly afterwards. He probably realised that he would be in management's black books from then on.

A love-hate relationship

South Africa is greatly indebted to the USA for the impetus to set up its own nuclear programme. Eisenhower's Atoms for Peace programme and the USA's Atomic Energy Act of 1954 gave rise to a nuclear cooperation agreement between South Africa and the USA in 1957. The fruits of this agreement were the provision of the Safari-1 reactor, the supply of fuel for the reactor and the training given to South African scientists. Roy E Horten (Pretoria's Nuclear Weapons Experience, USAF Institute for National Security Studies, Occasional Paper #27, August 1999) claims that over the years about 90 South African scientists and technicians underwent training in the USA and elsewhere. In 1964 Dr T.E.W. Schumann said in an interview with *Südafrika*, a Swiss periodical, that 83 local scientists had been trained in Europe and the USA. In 1976 Ampie Roux remarked: "We can ascribe the level of progress we have reached today largely to the training and assistance so willingly provided by the USA during the early years of our programme."

On 22 May 1974 the USA and South Africa signed amendments to their initial 1957 cooperation agreement, extending the 1957 agreement, which would otherwise have lapsed in 1977, to 2007. This enabled South Africa to increase the amounts of imported enriched fuel for Safari-1. South Africa was also able to import small quantities of U-235 (not in fuel elements) for fuel research and reactor tests, as well as plutonium for fuel. The American Department of State felt that it was important to avoid alienating South Africa, since the South African government had opposed communism. An internal departmental memorandum contained the significant remark that "South Africa owns over 27% of the free world's uranium".

However, in line with international pressure and the political climate in the USA, these cordial relations slowly began to unravel as a result of the political system prevailing in South Africa.

In October 1974 the Director of the CIA issued a special national intelligence document in which the capabilities and motivation of a number of countries that wanted to acquire nuclear weapons were examined. South Africa was one of them and according to this report the motivation for the possible manufacture of nuclear weapons was the country's "growing sense of isolation and impotence, perceptions of a big military threat and the desire for regional prestige".

This document was hastily compiled after an event which extinguished the euphoric flame of the Atoms for Peace programme. This blast came from the Indian subcontinent.

Indian breach of faith affects South Africa

As indicated earlier, on 18 May 1974 India detonated a nuclear explosive device equivalent to about 8 kilotons of TNT. This happened despite the assurance given by the Indian government that all facilities, materials and technology acquired under the Atoms for Peace programme of the USA and Canada would be used solely for peaceful purposes.

The nuclear explosion at Pokhran in the Rajastan Desert therefore took both friend and foe by surprise and caused great consternation. India pleaded innocence and claimed that it was merely a "peaceful explosion".

After this the eyes of the world – and especially those of the USA – were sharply focused on all countries that might possibly follow India's example. The honeymoon was over for Atoms for Peace. In future South Africa was to be closely watched.

Apart from this, the international climate gradually became more negative for South Africa and the South Africans' isolation made them increasingly self-centred in their actions. It also had a significant influence on the country's nuclear programme.

In 1975 both Mozambique and Angola became independent and white South Africans gazed with morbid fascination at press photographs of stunned Portuguese nationals who were forced to flee across the borders of the former Portuguese colonies by night with no more than the few belongings they could scrape together.

The openly expansionist policies of the Soviet Union made South Africa uneasy. In South-West Africa the actions of the black nationalist movement were a further source of anxiety to the South African government.

In 1975 South Africa, with the covert support of the Americans, attacked the MPLA liberation movement within the context of the Angolan civil war. However, when this clandestine alliance was uncovered, the Americans (partly as a result of the so-called Clark Amendment which prohibited military aid to any party in Angola) suddenly distanced themselves from the operation. The result was that Cuban troops began to stream into Angola. By 1987 Angola consequently had one of the biggest armies Africa had ever seen: seven brigades of local soldiers, equipped with the latest Soviet tanks, missiles and aircraft – and a reserve force of 50 000 Cubans.

To cap it all, in 1975 Britain cancelled the Simonstown Agreement on bilateral naval protection in the South Atlantic Ocean. P.W. Botha, the then Minister of Defence, regarded this action as treachery. International restrictions on the exporting of conventional weapons to South Africa aggravated the paranoia in government circles.

On 27 March 1975 P.W. Botha announced in parliament that the country's defence budget would be increased by 36%. South Africa's expenditure on defence would now make up one-fifth of the total national budget. In June 1976 tension inside South Africa increased notably with the outbreak of the Soweto riots and the declaration of a state of emergency. The South African government was feeling increasingly beleaguered.

After the Atoms for Peace programme was formally wound up the American Congress adopted the Nuclear Non-Proliferation Act, which prohibited the transfer of nuclear technology to states that had not signed the NPT. This Act was applied retroactively to all previous agreements and contracts. Not only did it make it difficult to obtain fuel for Koeberg in future, but in 1976 it also led the Ford administration to cancel fuel exports for Safari-1 which had been paid for in advance. The American action was rightly seen in South African circles as very negative and unreasonable, since both Safari-1 and Koeberg had always been subject to IAEA safeguards inspections. The couple of million rand paid for fuel for Safari-1 was only paid back five years later, in 1981 – following a decision by President Ronald Reagan.

In 1973 the IAEA decided to increase the number of governors on its board from 25 to 34, which gave the developing states a small majority. Three years later this resulted in the so-called Group of 77 flexing its new muscles. In 1977 the members proposed that South Africa should be deprived of its governorship. As the most advanced nuclear country in Africa, South Africa had held the governorship since the commencement of the IAEA's operations and also produced the first freely elected chairman of the board. The Group of 77 won the election by 19 votes to 13. It was an important consequence of the Soweto uprising of June 1976. Egypt, which had no nuclear programme to speak of and was not a uranium producer, was appointed governor in South Africa's place. At the same meeting the Palestine Liberation Organization (PLO) obtained observer status; this was clearly a departure from the IAEA's traditional purely nuclear-technical agenda to a more politically oriented one.

Two years later, in 1979, in India of all places, five years after the Indian breach of faith caused by the country's "peaceful explosion", the credentials of the South African delegation were rejected and South Africa was denied the right to participate in the Annual General Conference of the IAEA. South Africa was expected to join the NPT and then submit all their nuclear operations – and not only Safari-1 and Koeberg – to international safeguards. Interestingly enough, the host country, India, was not reprimanded at the meeting for its breach of faith and was not pressurised to sign the NPT either.

These events finally persuaded the South Africans that the sanctions against the country were of a political nature and that they had nothing to gain from joining the NPT.

A more aggressive approach

The first half of the 1970s, with the constant stream of UN resolutions, arms embargoes and other sanctions, trouble in the neighbouring countries of Angola and Mozambique, as well as the setbacks at the IAEA, had a cumulative effect on the South African government. The year 1977 was therefore characterised by a deliberate change in South Africa's attitude regarding its nuclear capability. Peaceful objectives had to make way for a more aggressive, challenging approach that included the proven Cold War deterrent – nuclear explosive devices. This decision was taken against the background of the threatening actions of the Warsaw Treaty countries in Southern Africa, the build-up of Cuban troops in Angola and the installation of sophisticated missile systems to the north of the South African borders.

On 26 August 1977 the South African government started discussions on a document containing proposed national strategic guidelines in which the new policy was outlined. This marked the birth of the nuclear weapons programme. This document was the work of Brigadier Bossie Huyser, the Chief Director of Planning of the South African Defence Force. In April 1978 these guidelines were finally approved. This strategy made provision for various phases:

- Phase 1: Strategic uncertainty: the country's nuclear capability would be neither admitted nor denied.
- Phase 2: Covert acknowledgement to certain international powers (such as the USA) if South African territory were threatened.
- Phase 3: If partial acknowledgement in terms of phase 2 did not lead to the removal of the threat, the country's nuclear capability would be used as an overt deterrent. That could take the following forms:
  - Public acknowledgement of South Africa's nuclear capability.
  - Demonstration of that capacity (underground tests).

No offensive tactical application of the country's nuclear capacity was envisaged, however. In practice the strategy never advanced beyond the first phase of the strategic guidelines.

This more aggressive attitude was exemplified by the government's decision in 1977 to discontinue talks with the IAEA on proposed safeguards for the semicommercial Z enrichment plant at Valindaba. This plant was designed to produce low-enriched uranium for Koeberg. However, in the event of a major threat to the country the low-enriched material produced by this plant could be used as feedstock for the Y-plant – instead of natural uranium – thereby trebling the Y-plant's output of highly enriched uranium.

In view of the increasing international pressure the nuclear programme in its new form began to look more and more like a survival strategy.

SPIED ON AND SHUNNED

Progress

As part of the original programme for peaceful nuclear explosions, once initial approval had been obtained in 1971, work went ahead apace at the AEB on the construction of facilities and the performance of development work and testing. The projects undertaken included the following:

- The development of the following computer programs (codes): internal ballistics, neutronics, thermodynamics and hydrodynamics (developed from basic principles). The construction of Building Complex 5000 at Pelindaba, in a suitably secluded valley. The complex included the following buildings: Building 5000 (A hall), Building 5100 (B hall), Building 5200 (D hall) and Building 5300 (C hall).
- By 1972 engineers from the AEB had carried out experimental research and development work at the Somchem facilities of the National Institute for Defence Research at Somerset West on the mechanical and pyrotechnical subsystems of the explosive devices. An internal ballistics testing facility was constructed for the purpose. In 1973, 50-kg tungsten projectiles were fired and the ballistic parameters were determined for the development of a theoretical model for the gun-type devices.
- This preparatory work enabled the team to design a scale model of a gun-type explosive device which was tested for the first time in May 1974 using a tungsten projectile.

- The first full-scale model was only tested two years later, in 1976, using a natural uranium projectile.

By the middle of 1977 the first test device, but without the highly enriched uranium warhead, was ready for a fully instrumented underground test. The device was 2,79 m in length and had a diameter of 480 mm. The protective steel casing surrounding it was 4,44 m in length, with a diameter of 610 mm. The total mass was 3 450 kg – a pretty robust first attempt!

Nuclear devices and nuclear weapons

The terms "nuclear device" and "nuclear weapon" are both used. What is the difference?

In general a nuclear device is an experimental assembly; it is often the first pre-production model which is tested to determine whether the theoretical calculations and execution of the design have produced the desired result.

A nuclear weapon is a militarily qualified item that is ready to be delivered by aircraft, missile or glide bomb. Whereas a nuclear device would be surrounded by highly qualified engineers and scientists in white coats clucking over their handiwork and making final adjustments, a nuclear weapon must be able to withstand the hard knocks of military life without intervention from nuclear scientists. The weapon must be ready at short notice for offensive application by soldiers and airmen who are not nuclear experts.

The first American hydrogen bomb (the Ivy Mike test in 1952) is a good example of the difference between the two concepts. It was not a bomb in the military sense, but rather a 70-ton "factory" built on solid ground. It was a nuclear device built to demonstrate the principles.

The hydrogen bomb was developed into a usable military weapon afterwards. In 1966 an American B-52 bomber and a tanker aircraft collided in the air and exploded near the Spanish coast. Four hydrogen bombs aboard the B-52 fell about nine km. Not one of those bombs exploded because they were nuclear weapons designed with multiple safety mechanisms to enable them to survive such incidents safely and above all to be "G.I.-proof".

This was not the only incident involving nuclear weapons. At least 40 weapons went missing in aircraft and submarine accidents during

> the Cold War and have never been recovered. Thanks to strict military specifications not one of these nuclear weapons has exploded.

The next question was where South Africa would carry out the first test.

Dirty work in the desert

Vastrap is a hot and dusty Air Force base in the Kalahari Desert. The nearest big town is Upington, to the south-west. The area is remote and sparsely populated, with virtually no agricultural potential. Another advantage is that the stable geological formations make it ideal for carrying out nuclear tests.

By 1973 officials of the AEB had already started scouting around for a suitable test site for nuclear experiments. They immediately recognised the Kalahari's potential, but did not want to attract attention by buying that specific site. The job of acquiring the Vastrap land was therefore delegated to the Defence Force. The Air Force set up a military testing ground there. Vastrap was the name of one of the six farms that were purchased by the Defence Force and consolidated into a unit.

An old diamond drill, previously used on the mines, was rebuilt and transported to Vastrap. In November 1976 the first test shaft, with a diameter of almost a metre and a depth of 391 m, was completed with the aid of this drill. A second test shaft with a depth of 216 m was added in 1977.

The enormous rig, capable of drilling holes a metre wide, attracted the cynical attention of the Kalahari farmers in the district – everybody knew there was no water in those parts. It is possible that a driller, after a hard day's work in the heat and a few cold beers, let something slip because right from the start the local farmers referred to the boreholes as "the atom shafts" …

By the middle of 1977 all the planned site buildings, the roads, the water reticulation system – and a runway – had already been completed. A group of Defence Force employees and about 20 employees of the AEB, who relieved each other every two weeks, worked tirelessly to prepare for the country's first "cold" nuclear test (in other words a test of the complex system required for a nuclear test, but without an enriched uranium warhead). The placement tower and hoisting gear were set up above the first test shaft. All that was still missing were the instrumentation modules, which were waiting at the Pelindaba site to be transported to Vastrap in Venter trailers. The test was intended to verify the placement of the device in the test shaft, the detonation process and certain instrumentation, communication and safety aspects.

To camouflage the increase in the number of personnel on site and the upsurge in activity, the Defence Force arranged to carry out manoeuvres simultaneously at the Vastrap site from 15 to 18 August 1977. They were to concentrate on the version of the "Stalin organ" produced by the National Institute for Defence Research (NIDR) of the CSIR. The Stalin organ was a multiple rocket launcher mounted on a lorry.

On the afternoon of Sunday 14 August two scientists saw something unusual from the office building at the base. An unidentified light aircraft was flying very low (about 50 m above the site) over the sleeping quarters in the direction of the runway. Other scientists also observed the aircraft flying over the first placement shaft, along the instrumentation route and up to the office complex. In that arid, remote area this was certainly a strange phenomenon. Efforts to identify this unknown aircraft were unsuccessful. The Department of Counterintelligence and 8 SA Infantry Battalion were unable to throw any light on the matter. Subsequent investigations showed that no flight plan had been submitted for such a trip.

Someone had clearly come to see what was going on at the base. The work continued the next day (Monday), however, and the excitement was tangible. The first device was completely ready, but did not carry a uranium warhead. Because of production delays at the Y-plant there was not sufficient highly enriched uranium available for a warhead.

On Wednesday 17 August, while the staff at the site were still busy with preparations, Dr Richardt van der Walt, the AEB's Director of Reactor Development, was told to expect a call from headquarters on the site's cipher telephone. It was scheduled for 21:30 that evening. Van der Walt was uneasy. He had a feeling something was wrong. The message he received that evening from the Vice-President of the AEB, Wynand de Villiers, confirmed his worst fears. De Villiers' message was short and to the point over the creaky line: Somebody had found out what they were doing at Vastrap. A local inspection had been requested by certain foreign countries. The staff would have to leave the site immediately. An inspection would undoubtedly serve to confirm that preparations had been made for a nuclear test (even if it was only a cold test) but it would be difficult to convince the inspectors that the aim was peaceful. The Department of Counterintelligence's red herrings with the military testing of the Stalin organ at the site would not stand up to thorough scrutiny.

The result was panic. The sleeping AEB personnel were hastily woken up. In expectation of a possible inspection (although it was not clear by whom and by what authority) sensitive apparatus was hastily identified. The smaller pieces of equipment were packed in ammunition boxes and loaded onto every available army vehicle, along with the larger items, to be taken to Somerset West as a temporary measure. The very big items were hastily buried in the loose Kalahari sand. Early in the morning of 18 August the AEB staff and all their vehicles travelled back to Pretoria. After the staff had left, a few items on the site had to be repacked or reburied because they still looked conspicuous or because the wind might blow the shallow sand away and expose them. NIDR staff who were at the site were quick to lend a hand and everything got done. The only AEB employee who remained behind at the site was Richardt van der Walt and he made certain that all the equipment had been removed or properly buried. A few days later Vastrap looked like a military site again. It was only the two unusual shafts that might have raised an eyebrow among people who knew what to look for.

Several explanations have been suggested as to why the South Africans' preparations for the "cold" nuclear test were discovered. Some people claim that the Soviet Union approached the USA in 1976 on the subject of South Africa's nuclear weapons programme. At that meeting the Russians are said to have submitted information on the South African programme and asked the Americans to help put a stop to it. They even went so far as to suggest a preemptive attack on the Y-plant. That met with no support from the USA. This idea of possible cooperation between the USSR and the USA at the height of the Cold War is odd, to say the least of it.

Another variation is that South Africa informed the USA at some stage that nuclear tests would take place at a future date. The Americans were disconcerted, but kept the information secret. When the Soviet Union noticed the preparations at Vastrap in 1977 by means of a satellite observation, it informed the USA. The Americans naturally had no choice but to react. It is probable that the USA, which had an embassy in South Africa (unlike the USSR, which was persona non grata in this country at the time), hired the offending aircraft to find out precisely what was going on at Vastrap.

Dr Frank Barnaby of the respected Stockholm International Peace Research Institute (SIPRI) was of the opinion that an American satellite probably observed the activities at Vastrap just as the Russian satellite did. He wrote as follows in the edition of *New Scientist* of 19 October 1978:

> On 3 July, 1977, the Soviet spy satellite Cosmos 922 passed over the Kalahari Desert in South Africa. The sky was cloud-free and the

conditions ideal for space photography. The weather was equally fine the next day when Cosmos 922, designed for aerial surveillance, again scanned the Kalahari.

On 20 July, a week after Cosmos 922's mission ended, Cosmos 932, a manoeuvrable satellite carrying close-look equipment, was launched. Two days later, according to ground tracks published in the 1978 *Sipri Yearbook*, the satellite was manoeuvred to take it over the Kalahari. Again, the sky was virtually cloud-free. Cosmos 932 was recovered on 2 August. Four days later Soviet diplomats informed American officials that a South African nuclear test was imminent.

This news may have come as no shock to the Americans. One of their spy satellites had also been active over the region. Big Bird 1977-56A made four passes over the Kalahari during July 1977. And it passed over it again on 13 August, possibly checking activities in the area.

When the Kalahari was in sight of the Soviet and American satellites the sun happened to be low in the sky so that any object would have cast long shadows in the desert. A tower built to hold a nuclear explosive, for example, would have stood out in the photographs like a sore thumb.

Regarding the observation satellites, one needs to remember the following: At that time it was not possible to send digital images back to earth as it is today. Photographs were taken on kilometres of film and then sent back in a re-entry vehicle capable of withstanding the return journey through the atmosphere without burning out like a meteorite. The film was then parachuted down to earth and developed. When all the film in the satellite was used up, the expensive satellite had fulfilled its function and a new one had to be launched.

The official designation of the American Big Bird observation satellites was the KH-9 Hexagon series. Twenty observation satellites of this kind were launched between 1971 and 1986. They contained two cameras and four film capsules. When a capsule's film had all been shot, the capsule returned to earth through the atmosphere where, hanging in the air on a parachute, it was recovered by an aircraft. (The parachute of one of the capsules in the first series failed to open and it fell into the Pacific and sank to a depth of 5 km.) The American Big Bird (KH-9-13 or 1977-056A) was launched on 27 June 1977 and its usefulness expired in December 1977 once all the film had been shot.

Former Minister Pik Botha relates in a thesis by G.R. Heald, "South Africa's voluntary relinquishment of its nuclear arsenal and accession to the treaty on the non-proliferation of nuclear weapons in terms of international law", that he was informed by the American ambassador to South Africa that the USA was aware of South Africa's nuclear weapons programme. At this meeting with the South African Minister of Foreign Affairs the American ambassador was quite blunt. He simply took a dozen photographs of the Vastrap site out of his briefcase and showed them to Botha, who had not been informed of South Africa's prospective cold nuclear test since the "need to know" principle applied. However, he realised at once what the photographs showed and had to think on his feet:

> I said to the Ambassador, "They (the Boere) might be drilling for water." This at least elicited a smile from him. He said, "I respectfully disagree with your assessment. Our experts and technicians have pored over these photographs and studied them meticulously. They have confirmed that there is no place on God's earth that you would need a drill of that size to get water. The official US government view is that it is a nuclear weapons test site intended for exploring and exploding a nuclear device."

According to Botha the ambassador informed him at the same meeting that the Soviet Union had supplied the satellite photographs to the USA, with a request that the Americans take the matter up with the South African government.

At all events, the Vastrap discovery of August 1977 resulted in heavy diplomatic pressure from the USA, the USSR – and even from France. The then French Minister of Foreign Affairs, Louis de Guiringaud, issued a warning on 22 August to the effect that there would be "serious consequences" for South African-French relations, which was taken to imply that the Koeberg contract might possibly be cancelled.

A message which the American ambassador, William Bowdler, conveyed to Pik Botha on 18 August 1977 contained the warning that South Africa could no longer rely on any help from the West if the country decided to go ahead with the planned nuclear test:

> In the light of the grave implications President Carter instructed me to make clear that the detonation of a nuclear device whether a nuclear weapon or a so-called peaceful nuclear explosive or any other further steps to acquire or develop a nuclear explosive capability would have the most serious consequences for all aspects of our relations and would be considered by us as a serious threat to peace.

On 19 August 1977 Cyrus Vance, the American Secretary of State, also wrote to Pik Botha to express his anxiety. Vance referred to all the facilities at Vastrap in minute detail, thereby demonstrating that the Americans knew exactly what the site looked like. He made an official offer to provide the South Africans with photographs of the facilities. Vance also proposed that "a small technical American team" should be allowed to inspect the Kalahari site.

This pressure had the desired effect. On 23 August 1977 President Jimmy Carter announced at a press conference that, following enquiries from the USA and other countries, the South African government had informed the USA that it had no plans to develop nuclear devices and that the Kalahari test site had not been developed for the testing of nuclear devices. South Africa had also given them the assurance that no tests would take place in future …

On 28 August 1977 *The Washington Post* published an article on the incident. An American official was quoted as having made the following remark: "I would say that we are 99% certain that the buildings were in preparation for a nuclear test." According to this article South Africa had become the world's "seventh nuclear power".

Pik Botha assured the Carter government that the rumours about South Africa's nuclear test were unfounded. According to him the USSR had fabricated the rumours to put South Africa in a negative light in advance of the UN conference on apartheid which was to be held in Lagos in August 1977. In an American TV interview on 30 August Botha stated that nuclear power would only be used for peaceful purposes in South Africa. He had the following to say about the Vastrap area: "I don't know the area. But any installations that may be found in the Kalahari Desert would not be used for nuclear tests." When the journalist asked Botha what advice he might have for President Carter, Botha's reply was as dramatic as usual: "Get your hands off my country! And the sooner the better!"

What the spooks in the USA thought

On the day the AEB officials departed in haste from Vastrap (18 August 1977), a secret American CIA report *Interagency assessment: South Africa: policy considerations regarding a nuclear test* appeared. This report was declassified in 2004.

There are references in this report to the "pressure of time" and a whole ten pages are devoted to the Americans' view of Prime Minister Vorster and the Afrikaners. A few passages from the report are quoted below:

"... It is consistent with Vorster's personality to favour proceeding with nuclear weapons development and to undertake testing. Vorster throughout his career has shown a strong inclination toward actions which project power and tough-mindedness and has made no secret of his personal contempt for world opinion ...

"... For many South Africans, the rationale for going ahead in the development of nuclear weapons stems from a fear that ultimately South Africa faces the threat of being invaded by Communist-backed black regimes and even by Soviet and Cuban forces. Historically, the Afrikaner response to a perceived threat has been to assume the worst and to prepare for it ...

"... We are virtually certain that Vorster is aware that a nuclear test would sooner or later be detected and made known throughout the world. A decision to test must therefore be seen as a conscious decision to defy the world and to increase greatly the risk of bringing on various combinations of censure and sanctions, as well as jeopardizing any sensitive negotiations South Africa might be engaged in at the time. We find this attitude entirely consistent with the defiant, tribally-orientated cast of the Afrikaner world view ...

"... We perceive no credible threat which would be sufficient to deter South Africa from carrying out a test; indeed our reading of the Afrikaner personality suggests that threats would have the opposite effect to that intended ...

"... We do not foresee any circumstances which would induce South Africa to terminate, or even to postpone for a prolonged or indefinite period, its nuclear weapons program ...

... If South Africa were within two or three weeks of a scheduled test, the costs of a prolonged delay and the long lead-time needed before reaching the test phase would probably be prohibitive ..."

How did the Soviet Union know where to look?

In 1977 the USA and the Soviet Union were deeply engaged in the Cold War. So why would the USSR devote its precious satellite observation time to searching for gemsbok or the odd straying lion in the empty Kalahari? Somebody must have given them a hint. It must have been someone fully informed about the imminent test at Vastrap.

The information came from Dieter Felix Gerhardt. He and his Swiss-born wife Ruth served as secret agents for the Soviet Union for many years.

Later on in his career Gerhardt was to become the commodore in charge of the Simonstown naval base. This was a key position during the Cold War, since Simonstown was the biggest naval base in the South Indian and Atlantic Oceans. Gerhardt had an extensive knowledge of South Africa's defence strategy, the country's ties with Britain, the USA and NATO – and of the local nuclear programme. In the early 1970s, when it was decided to acquire gun barrels from the navy for use in the nuclear devices being built, Gerhardt, who was the Armscor naval liaison officer at the time, was informed about the matter and drew his own conclusions. It must have been an interesting snippet of news for his paymasters in Moscow.

For over 20 years, since 1962, Gerhardt sold secrets to the Soviet Union and made a pretty penny out of this. His house was filled with fine furniture and beautiful silverware. He explained this away to visitors by saying that it was affordable thanks to a legacy from his mother and to successful share trading.

In 2009 Vitaly Shlykov told the Swiss newspaper *Der Bund* that the Gerhardts had been associates of his for many years. From the early 1970s he was Gerhardt's handler on behalf of the GRU (the USSR's military espionage service in which he held the rank of colonel). Shlykov's contact with Gerhardt and his wife Ruth lasted for fifteen years; their meetings took place in many parts of the world: Madagascar, Copenhagen, Paris, Madrid, Geneva, Bern and Zürich. According to the Swiss Department of Justice, during this period the Gerhardts received about 800 000 Swiss francs or around R6 million (in monetary value at that time) from the GRU. The Gerhardts also travelled to Switzerland frequently, ostensibly to visit Ruth's family and then travelled to Moscow on false passports. Ruth often acted as Gerhardt's courier.

Shlykov was caught by the Swiss in 1983 and arrested for espionage. He was sentenced to three years' imprisonment. After his release he returned to Russia. After the fall of the communist regime he was appointed deputy minister of defence by Boris Yeltsin. He was given the office of Chairman of the Commission for Security Policy and Analysis of Military Legislation. Shlykov was also a founder member of the Russian Council for Foreign and Defense Policy. He died in 2011.

In his capacity as commander of Simonstown Gerhardt once visited the Vastrap military site and informed his Soviet masters accordingly. By passing on this information he dramatically changed the course of the nuclear weapons programme in South Africa.

There are certain drawbacks attached to a career in espionage, as Gerhardt was to discover. During one of his numerous overseas trips he went to the USA in 1982 to "study mathematics" at the Syracuse University in New York. This time the Federal Bureau of Investigation (FBI) were waiting for him.

How did the Americans know?

In 1980 a colonel in the Soviet Union's KGB approached France and offered his services to transfer secret information. He did this purely for ideological reasons and neither asked for nor received any payment. Between 1981 and 1982 Vladimir Vetrov supplied almost 4 000 documents to France – the so-called Farewell Dossier. The French were cooperating with the USA and they made the information available. As a result almost 400 Soviet agents were eventually unmasked, including the Gerhardts.

After Gerhardt's arrest in New York he was interrogated for weeks. After interrogation he was deported to South Africa. In January 1983 the Prime Minister, P.W. Botha, announced that the Gerhardts had been arrested for espionage. The hearing was held in camera. Proceedings began on 5 September and ended on 29 December 1983. Gerhardt was sentenced to life imprisonment for high treason. His wife received a sentence of ten years' imprisonment for her role as courier. After an agreement between the then government and the ANC Ruth was released in 1990, however. Her release followed a visit to Switzerland by the then President F.W. de Klerk. After a further plea by Boris Yeltsin, Dieter Gerhardt was released in 1992.

Even now it is still not clear why Gerhardt decided to spy for the communists. There are various stories about his possible motivation. In an interview with the *Mail & Guardian* he referred to his contempt for the "illegal Nazi-fascist system" in South Africa, which he apparently found less acceptable than the oppressive communist system of his secret employer. He had apparently also built up a hatred for the USA over the years.

It is also claimed that the internment of Gerhardt's German father in Koffiefontein during the Second World War caused him to decide to spy for the communists. Ironically enough, this indicates that his father was probably a supporter of the "illegal Nazi-fascist system". Gerhardt stated in later years that he was opposed to apartheid and wanted to help bring about black liberation.

According to Janet Coggin, Gerhardt's British first wife, he was motivated by ideology. "I think it was a mixture of a lot of things. He liked the way of life, the power and money and the feeling that he was fooling people," she said in an interview with *The Independent* on 28 March 1999.

General Herman Stadler headed the South African investigating team that interrogated Gerhardt after the Americans sent him back to South Africa. He saw Gerhardt's motives for working for the Russians in a different light. According to Stadler, as a child Gerhardt was unpopular at school. He did not fit in because of his German origins. While his father was interned his mother had to support the family on her own and years later he was still resentful about the hardships they endured. He became a rebel in his early teens, even occasionally stealing cars. He was later caught by the police and received corporal punishment.

According to Stadler, who spent hours talking to Gerhardt after his capture, Gerhardt decided to become a spy because he wanted the best of everything for Janet, who came from a wealthy family. Ironically enough, he offered his services to the Americans first, but they were not interested. After that he literally walked into the Soviet embassy in London and declared himself available. In the end he was to work for the Russians for 20 years (from about 1963 to 1983).

Gerhardt was granted amnesty by the Truth and Reconciliation Commission in 1999. He is reported to be living a peaceful life on the South African West Coast as a well-heeled pensioner, commuting to Switzerland every now and then.

If Gerhardt was so well-informed and had even visited the Vastrap site, he should have known that the planned test was a "cold test", that is one in which a nuclear warhead is not used. The first highly enriched uranium was only produced two years later. Why did the USSR make such a fuss about the proposed test?

There was a good reason.

The Vastrap incident took place on the eve of a planned meeting in London between the British, American and South African ministers of foreign affairs to discuss internationally recognised independence for Rhodesia and

South-West Africa – countries where the Soviet Union was eager to get a foot in at the door. In fact the Soviets were the chief supporters of the resistance movements in those countries. It is significant that the Soviet Union informed the USA about Vastrap as early as 6 August, about two weeks before operations started in earnest at Vastrap. Therefore it was not activities on the ground that attracted the attention of the satellite but prior knowledge that was passed to the Americans with a specific purpose.

By painting South Africa black they ensured that nothing much was likely to come of the discussions. In fact Minister Pik Botha returned with a feeling that the more the South Africans tried to assist in finding a solution to the two problems, the more opposition they encountered from the Western governments.

Another Trojan horse?

At the end of October 1991 the *Los Angeles Times* reported that ten Americans and several South African companies, including Armscor, had been indicted for illegally exporting American weapons and technology (chiefly missile-related) to the value of over $10 million to South Africa.

The accused included the American Robert Clyde Ivy of the firm International Signal & Control (ISC) of Philadelphia in the USA, a man with an interesting past. Ivy was an electrical engineer who had taken part in the Korean War. After the war he worked for several engineering companies in the USA, including General Electric, before coming to South Africa in the 1970s as head of the NIDR at the CSIR. Kentron, a division of Armscor that was later responsible for building South Africa's nuclear bombs, split off from the NIDR under Ivy. In 1980 Ivy left Kentron. He returned to the USA, where he accepted a senior managerial post at ISC.

If the complaint against Ivy had been proved, he would have faced a maximum term of imprisonment of 515 years and a fine of $44 million. Of the 20 individuals and companies indicted, Ivy had the most counts against him.

After about six years Ivy was sentenced in 1997 to a mere six months' imprisonment and a further six months under house arrest. Following mediation by Vice-President Thabo Mbeki and Al Gore the three South African companies, Armscor, Kentron and Fuchs Electronics, were fined $12.5 million, however.

Ivy was considered by Hannes Steyn, his successor at Kentron, to be a man with strong intelligence ties. This is confirmed by Purkitt and Burgess in their book, *South Africa's Weapons of Mass Destruction*. Ivy's light sentence at the end of his career was clearly a symbolic rap across the knuckles.

Why should Ivy have been suspected of being a Trojan horse? As head of the NIDR and Kentron in the late 1970s he must have had full knowledge of the proposed "cold test" at Vastrap in 1977. After all, the NIDR was present at the Vastrap base where the testing of their Stalin organ was to serve as cover.

It is therefore highly probable that long before the much-publicised, so-called discovery by a Soviet observation satellite the Americans knew all about the South African nuclear weapons programme and the test planned at Vastrap. But to protect their mole they had to pretend that the Soviet discovery was news.

Further interference by the Americans

In 1975 and 1976 the USA repeatedly vetoed the institution of compulsory sanctions against South Africa in the UNGA, because it did not see South Africa's race policy as a threat to international peace. However, in 1977 the new Carter administration adopted a different view, largely to thank black Americans for their support, to which Carter owed his unexpected election to the White House. 25 October 1977 was an important date in the history of relations between South Africa and the USA. This was the day on which the former peanut farmer, Jimmy Carter, announced that South Africa was a threat to world peace.

Two days later Carter announced that the USA would support compulsory arms sanctions in the UN. This culminated in the passing of a resolution in the UNSC in November of that year. All countries, even those that were not members of the UN, were unanimously instructed in terms of Resolution 418 not to supply arms, military vehicles, equipment or spares to South Africa. Countries were also specifically forbidden to assist South Africa with the development of nuclear weapons. This was the first time in the 32-year history of the UN that compulsory sanctions were ever instituted against a member state.

This news was not well received by Prime Minister P.W. Botha. A few days after the resolution he announced that South Africa had all the weapons the country needed. These ranged from handguns to heavy artillery, as well as missile power. The Republic was in the process of developing other strategic weapons, which was something he didn't wish to expand on. He ended with a few telling words: "As long as we have money, there will always be suppliers." In April 1979 there was a bit of a sensation when P.W. Botha announced that three members of the American mission in Pretoria had been given a week to leave the country. This followed an incident in which an aircraft belonging to the American embassy was observed flying over the Valindaba site outside Pretoria. Members of the South African security police were waiting for the aircraft when it landed and found that it was equipped with spy cameras. They had been used to take unauthorised photographs of the AEB buildings and probably of other sensitive facilities in South Africa. Botha was furious about these underhanded actions on the part of the Americans.

In his thesis G.R. Heald comments as follows on the incident:

> In a toughly worded statement read on prime-time television in South Africa, Prime Minister P.W. Botha announced the expulsion of several members of the American mission in Pretoria for aerial espionage. A grim-faced Botha told South Africans that a twin-engine Beechcraft turboprop used by US Ambassador William B. Edmondson had been converted for use as a spy plane by the installation of an aerial-survey camera under the seat of the co-pilot. The Prime Minister charged that the embassy aircraft was engaged in a systematic program of photography of vast areas of South Africa, including some of our most sensitive installations. Botha's disclosures seemed designed both to embarrass the Carter Administration at a time when the US is pressing South Africa to accept a United Nations plan for the independence of Namibia, and to deflect attention from his scandal-ridden government at home.
>
> The State Department flatly refused to deny the charges, and Secretary of State Cyrus Vance said that 'no apology' would be issued, as the South African Prime Minister had demanded.
>
> The following day, Willem Retief, South Africa's chargé d'affaires, was summoned to the State Department and told that two of his mission's military attachés were being ordered to leave the US within a week, in direct retaliation for the expulsion of three American defence attachés. The brusque US response to Botha's charges, as well as the refusal to deny that espionage was involved, reflected the Administration's worries about South Africa's nuclear capacity.

The information obtained by the spy flight was to be used thirteen years later by the USA, again in an underhand manner, in an attempt to defeat a positive outcome in an IAEA investigation.

In case of need

Preparations for the proposed instrumented "cold test" at Vastrap had had to be abandoned unexpectedly, and therefore little useful technical information was obtained. The 3.5-ton device never even left the Pelindaba premises. However, it was necessary for the AEB to carry out a real test in case the country's situation required it.

The decision was consequently taken to carry out a cold test in 1978 at Somchem in Somerset West. A device with the same design as the one that would have been used at Vastrap was primed with natural uranium, but without the outer steel casing in which the instrumentation would have been housed. The device was successfully detonated and then transported to Pretoria by Hercules C-130. The device was under severe elastic strain on account of the projectile which had been shot into the natural uranium target at high speed and captured. The plan was to cut the device open in Pelindaba's Building 5001 and study it intensively. However, a few hours after the device had been delivered at the site, during the early hours of the morning, there was a loud bang and it disintegrated mechanically with great force as a result of the built-in tension; an enormous lathe was destroyed in the process! When the staff arrived the next morning they could only count their blessings since they had not been around at the time of the accident.

For the purposes of rapid deployment, a smaller device (with a length of 2 m, a diameter of 360 mm and a mass of about 750 kg) was built by the AEB in 1978. The main purpose was to be able to carry out a rapid instrumented test at Vastrap if necessary. By November 1979 the Y-plant had produced sufficient highly enriched material to be built in as an actual nuclear warhead. This was the first – and last – complete nuclear device to be built by the AEB. The code name for the device was Video. For security reasons the name of this device would be changed several times.

But first an interlude ...

MYSTERIOUS INCIDENT NO. 747 OF 22 SEPTEMBER 1979

Over the years the five recognised nuclear weapons states, namely the USA, Russia, Britain, France and China, carried out over 2 000 nuclear weapons tests. A large number of these tests were carried out in the atmosphere, some under the ocean while another group took place underground in shafts or tunnels beneath mountains. When a test was carried out in the atmosphere, there was a significant chance that the radioactive fallout from the explosion would be dispersed through the atmosphere by wind. Here it was mainly the big explosions on a megaton scale that caused problems. The characteristic mushroom cloud disperses right into the stratosphere, about three times the height at which aircraft normally fly on intercontinental flights.

The nuclear weapons states gradually realised that the radioactive pollution of the environment could not continue and began negotiating on the drafting of a treaty to ban tests in the atmosphere and in the oceans. As usual, there was tension between the West and the USSR regarding the contents and execution of the treaty. The West wanted to introduce a system that would make provision for local inspections, but the proposal was vehemently opposed by the USSR. The Russians were of the opinion that remote sensing and seismic methods would be a better option. After much dispute the Partial Test Ban Treaty (PTBT) came into operation in October 1963 – and it did not include a right to carry out local inspections. This victory by the USSR led to the launching of a variety of specialised satellites which observed the earth from distances of up to 100 000 km in order to detect any "illegal" tests.

> *Plutonium for the crocodiles*
>
> After Saddam Hussein's secret attempts to build nuclear weapons the IAEA found it necessary to establish whether environmental monitoring could be used to detect undeclared nuclear plants. The AEB collaborated on this programme in 1995. Water, plant and soil samples were taken from the Pelindaba area to provide an indication of the type of activities being carried out at the site.
>
> One of the results of the study proved somewhat embarrassing. Plutonium was detected in the Crocodile River (which flows past Pelindaba). And this despite the fact that the AEB had never done any work to speak of with this highly unusual metal! What possible explanation could there

> be? Would the IAEA conclude that the AEB was hiding something? The South African scientists held their breath. Luckily the IAEA was unperturbed about this finding. It corresponded to the level of plutonium being found all over the world as a result of the atmospheric nuclear weapons tests carried out before 1963.

In 1979 an American satellite spotted something that could have been indicative of an "illegal" nuclear weapons test. This was during the polecat years and South Africa immediately got the blame. Had the satellite really detected signs of a nuclear test? Had South Africa carried out a nuclear weapons test somewhere in the Indian Ocean? Alone, or possibly along with another country? Or had someone else tested a weapon? These teasing questions are still being asked and contradictory explanations and opinions are still being offered.

Vela 6911 registers a double flash

In the late evening of 21 September 1979 the USA's Air Force Technical Applications Center (AFTAC) in Florida began a routine downloading session with data from Vela satellite number 6911. The Vela satellite's memory showed that the two bhangmeters on board – optical sensors that are capable of registering light levels at a speed of a sub-millisecond – had registered an event at 00:52, thus a little before 01:00 on the morning of 22 September. This incident had presumably taken place somewhere over the Indian Ocean or the South Atlantic Ocean. The spot was later more exactly determined by means of other methods as the Indian Ocean in the vicinity of South Africa's Prince Edward Island. The observed double flash was likely to have been a nuclear detonation with a yield of about 3 kilotons. AFTAC assigned the reference number 747 to this event and sent the information to other interested agencies in the USA.

With the aid of the Vela satellite programme the USA began tracing possible nuclear explosions in the atmosphere and in space after the Partial Test Ban came into force in 1963. There were two groups of Vela satellites. The first ones were not technologically very advanced and in 1967, 1969 and 1970 they were replaced by a second group of satellites equipped with bhangmeters. It was estimated that these satellites would be able to function for about eighteen months, although this was subsequently changed to seven years and the devices in question were all eventually in use for over ten years. The last

Vela satellite was decommissioned in 1984 after having been in use for fourteen years. Signals from these satellites were relayed to the AFTAC air force base in Florida.

At the time of the alleged explosion Vela 6911 had been in use for ten years and the device was orbiting about 100 000 km above the earth.

> ## *Double flashes and bhangmeters*
>
> *When a nuclear bomb explodes, the temperature of bomb material rapidly reaches about 10 million degrees Celsius. Part of the energy released is in the form of electromagnetic radiation (an umbrella term that includes light rays, X-rays, ultraviolet rays and radio waves). This energy is absorbed by the surrounding air, which reaches a temperature similar to that of the bomb matter. When air is heated the pressure increases, in this case to a few thousand times normal atmospheric pressure. The heated combination of bomb matter and air forms the original fireball. An intense shock wave forms on the surface of the fireball; this is a thin shell of highly compressed air which breaks away from the fireball at high speed and moves outwards like the rubber skin of a balloon which has been blown up very rapidly. The area behind the shock wave is saturated with energy and therefore opaque to normal light. In this way the core of the explosion is concealed. As the shock wave moves outwards the area behind the shock wave cools down and becomes transparent again in time.*
>
> *The result is that a short period elapses after the original light flash of the exploding bomb before the explosive core becomes visible again. This causes the so-called double flash which is characteristic of low-altitude nuclear explosions. A graphical representation of the light intensity would resemble the two humps of a camel. The time that elapses between the two peaks in light intensity is an indication of the size of the explosion. The greater the number of kilotons, the longer the interval between the two light peaks. These events happen in considerably less time than it takes to read this description – that is to say, they happen in the space of thousandths of a second.*
>
> *This unique characteristic of nuclear explosions makes it possible to use a relatively simple method to register them. A photodiode – a sensor which is sensitive to light – is linked to an electronic circuit and is capable of detecting the two light pulses that occur in rapid succession*

THE BOMB IN THE BUSHVELD

and estimating the magnitude of the explosion from the time interval between the two light peaks. The Americans who designed this device gave it the name "bhangmeter". This odd name is explained in a document published by the Department of Energy of the USA in October 1985:

> Early in 1950 an intense afternoon was spent by the entire Group J-7, with its group leader Fred Reines, picking a name for this world-shaking device that was going to produce simple, cheap and easy yield measurements. At the end of the afternoon, Reines picked a name which we all knew would be misinterpreted for the rest of history. Bhangmeter is not synonymous with bang meter. "Bhang" is a variation of Indian hemp, the leaves and seed capsules of which are chewed or smoked, and which produces the same euphoria as other variations of hashish. The now obvious connotation is that we were off our rockers to think that this thing would ever be particularly useful and anyone who ever believed it must also have a little something wrong with them.

Since the decommissioning of the Vela satellite system in the mid-1980s, the ability to detect nuclear explosions on board the new series of GPS military satellites has been improved by fitting an Integrated Nuclear Detonation Detection System (IONDS). The first satellites of this series, NAVSTAR 5 and 6, were launched in 1980 and contained bhangmeters but also GPS location capabilities to pinpoint the actual location of the detonation.

In September 1983 the USSR shot down Korean Airlines flight 007 with 269 people on board because it had strayed into Soviet airspace. As a result, when GPS navigation devices became available President Reagan offered them to civilian aircraft free of charge. In 1996 President Bill Clinton declared the GPS a dual-use system for military and civilian use. Today we have GPS navigation devices in our cars and on our cellphones. The original need to observe secret nuclear explosions has evolved into something peaceful and very useful.

There were certain problems about the Vela observation, however. The shelf life of the two bhangmeters on board had long since expired, their observations of the light intensity of the double flash did not correspond, and a backup sensor for the observation of an electromagnetic (X-ray) pulse was not functioning.

Was it really a nuclear explosion and exactly where did it take place?

The bhangmeter sensors were not able to look down with telescopic eyes from a height of 100 000 km to determine the exact location of the explosion. The sensors merely observed the light flash, which in this case occurred in a very large area, namely the South Indian Ocean.

Event 747 immediately caused consternation among the various agencies involved in the USA's nuclear weapons programme. The agencies were manned by professional bomb snoops, each jealously guarding their own specialised technological territory and skills.

One of the agencies had a method which could be used to narrow down the point of origin of a supposed explosion. Shortly after the incident was registered, hydrophones under the sea registered hydro-acoustic signals which are similar to those caused by nuclear explosions. The American Naval Research Laboratory (NRL) analysed these signals and came to the conclusion that the signals came directly from a source close to Prince Edward Island.

The most compelling evidence of a nuclear explosion is provided by measuring radioactive fallout in the atmosphere. However, this did not provide clear-cut evidence either. For some strange and unknown reason AFTAC did not immediately send aircraft over the area to take atmospheric samples. After an unnecessary delay the American air force did undertake 25 reconnaissance flights which took over 230 hours of flying time (the most ever for such a purpose), but they did not detect any radioactive atmospheric samples.

An American researcher, Van Middlesworth, did find low levels of iodine-131 (a transient radioactive fission product) in the thyroid glands of sheep in the Australian states of Victoria and Tasmania shortly after event 747 took place. The wind patterns indicate that radioactive fallout from an explosion in the South Indian Ocean could land up in that part of the world.

When the origin of the explosion was traced to the vicinity of South Africa's Prince Edward Island, fingers were immediately pointed at South Africa, despite the numerous uncertainties and contradictions. The South African government, as well as the recognised nuclear powers, all denied that they had tested a nuclear weapon. It was soon rumoured that Israel might also have been involved, either alone or in cooperation with the South Africans. Even Taiwan was suspected.

The incident was kept secret until 25 October 1979, when the American television station ABC broadcast the story after obtaining confirmation from Pentagon contacts.

Search for the truth

For Jimmy Carter's Administration, this announcement opened a can of worms. The USA was preparing for an election campaign and Carter was a vociferous advocate of non-proliferation and a strong opponent of South Africa. Further, he could not afford to be embarrassed by Israel. If Israel proved to be guilty and Carter were obliged to institute sanctions, he would run the risk of alienating millions of Jewish Americans, with unavoidable consequences at the ballot box.

Carter decided to appoint a panel of hand-picked scientists to determine whether the flash had come from a nuclear explosion. The panel consisted of eminent scientists. The leader was Jack P. Ruina of the Massachusetts Institute of Technology (MIT). The eight other members included people like Luiz Alvarez, Wolfgang Panofsky and Richard Garwin. Alvarez had participated in the Manhattan Project. He was the scientific observer on the observation flight when Little Boy was dropped on Hiroshima, and was also responsible for the design of certain instrumentation. He won the Nobel prize in Physics in 1969. Panofsky was an eminent physicist from Stanford University, and Richard Garwin of the American International Business Machines Corporation (IBM) is still one of the most eminent living authorities on nuclear weapons today.

After holding three meetings in 1980 the panel members released their report and came to the conclusion that the flashes were probably not due to a nuclear explosion, although "the possibility could not be ruled out". The panel considered possible explanations for the flashes and suggested that the optical data could possibly have been the result of a small meteorite striking the satellite.

In later years Alvarez referred in his autobiography to the panel's investigation. He and other members were certain that no nuclear explosion had taken place. His pragmatic account of the panel's findings makes interesting reading. The following is an extract:

> I doubt that any responsible person now believes that a nuclear explosion occurred because no one has broken security, among South Africans or elsewhere. U.S. experience teaches that secrets of such import can't be kept long. After the United States tested its first megaton-scale thermonuclear weapon, which completely evaporated the small Pacific island of Elugelab, stories about a disappearing island reached U.S. newspapers as soon as the task force steamed into Pearl Harbor and sailors had time to call home.

> Many people think that solving a scientific puzzle is an exercise in logic that could be carried out equally well by a computer. To the contrary, a scientific detective's main stock-in-trade is his ability to decide which evidence to ignore. In our Defense Intelligence Agency (DIA) briefings were shown, and quickly discarded, confirming evidence from a wild assemblage of sensors: radioactive Australian sheep thyroids, radiotelescopic ionospheric wind analyses, recordings from the Navy's sonic submarine-detection arrays that supposedly precisely located the blast from patterns of sound reflected from bays and promontories on the coast of Antarctica.
>
> (Luiz Alvarez: *Adventures of a Physicist*, Basic Books, New York, 1987, chapter 14).

Not everyone agreed with the findings of the Ruina panel, however. The professional bomb snoops in the CIA, the NRL, Los Alamos, Sandia National Laboratories and the DIA all believed to a greater or lesser degree that a nuclear explosion did take place. In certain circles Carter was accused of trying to cover up the incident. This seems highly unlikely in view of Carter's hostility to South Africa – unless the American President wanted to keep the possible involvement of Israel secret.

G.H. Mauth of the Sandia National Laboratories (not far from Los Alamos) made several interesting comments in a comprehensive 70-page study (May 1980). Apart from Vela 6911 there were other satellites equipped with bhangmeters, namely those of the Defense Support Program (DSP) and those of Satellite Data Systems. Not one of these satellites registered the Vela incident. Mauth also mentions that during the 40 satellite-years for which Velas were in use, "many hundreds of thousands of bhangmeter events have been recorded from non-nuclear sources". Nevertheless, his conclusion was that event 747 was a nuclear explosion.

The CIA only released its own secret report on the 1979 incident to the public in June 2004, as usual in heavily redacted format. The document was directed to Ralph Earle II, the Director of the Arms Control and Disarmament Agency of the USA, "at the request of the National Security Council". The report was based on the assumption that the incident, which was observed over a portion of the Southern Hemisphere, was a nuclear explosion and stated explicitly that "technical information and analysis" indicate that:
- an explosion was produced by a nuclear device which was detonated in the atmosphere, close to the earth's surface;

- the device had a yield of less than 3 kilotons; and
- the incident took place in a large area, chiefly ocean, which was experiencing cloudy weather that day.

If it was a weapons test, who did the testing?

If South Africa or Israel were involved, this would mean that they had infringed the Partial Test Ban Treaty, to which both countries were signatories. Israel's involvement could also have had a serious impact on the situation in the Middle East and could have led to a reduction in military assistance to Israel by the USA.

Part of the above-mentioned CIA report was devoted to South Africa as the possible culprit. The report refers to a statement by P.W. Botha three days after the incident, on 25 September 1979, at a provincial National Party (NP) congress. He said that "South Africa's enemies may possibly find out that we have military weapons that they don't know about".

One could speculate as to precisely what Botha meant by this statement. He was probably simply boasting and taking the opportunity to cash in on the speculative rumours doing the rounds about South Africa's nuclear capacity. He and some of his ministers had referred on other occasions to an unknown South African "secret weapon".

The CIA report, which began with the assumption that there had been a nuclear explosion, ultimately concluded that the Vela observations had not been accidental, but did not provide sufficient evidence to indicate who could have been responsible for the explosion.

After South Africa signed the NPT in 1991 and concluded the safeguards agreement with the IAEA, a full investigation was launched into the former weapons programme, with full cooperation from South Africa. It was proved unequivocally to the IAEA that at the time of the Vela observation South Africa did not yet possess the necessary highly enriched uranium to build a nuclear bomb. South Africa was therefore not the guilty party. There were many sceptics at the time, however. On 26 October 1979 the Secretary-General of the UN was instructed by the General Assembly to report on the Vela incident, and on 5 December of the same year South Africa was expelled at the annual meeting of the General Conference of the IAEA in India. Technically, Vela could possibly not make the grade, but it became an important political instrument.

If a nuclear explosion did take place and South Africa was not implicated, was it possible that South Africa was supporting another country? There was a lot of speculation that Israel might be the country involved. But was this the case?

The South-African-Israeli theory was given much credence in certain circles. Some pundits pointed out that Israel would need South Africa's help to carry out a nuclear test, since it could not risk doing so on its limited territory in the Middle East.

Around the time of the Vela incident the USA was already well aware of the increasingly close military cooperation between the two "polecat countries", namely South Africa and Israel. For one thing, the South Africans and Israelis were engaged in developing a series of ballistic missiles. The South Africans might have agreed to make their territory available for an Israeli nuclear test in exchange for Israel's assistance with other aspects of South Africa's military programme. There was an international UN embargo on military assistance to South Africa and the South Africans were therefore very dependent on Israel's goodwill.

In 1991 Seymour Hersh, a well-known reporter, made a sensational disclosure. After carrying out an investigation into Israel's nuclear weapons programme, he claimed to have been informed by two different sources that Israel and South Africa had carried out a joint test in 1979.

This theory enjoyed the support of South Africa's best-known Red spy, Commodore Dieter Gerhardt, who was referred to previously in this text. He was in command of the Simonstown naval base when the alleged nuclear test took place – part of Operation Phoenix, according to him. He says that a few Israeli ships had touched at Simonstown shortly before the incident. He is convinced that a nuclear test did take place on 22 September. He believes it was a joint operation by the Israelis and the South Africans. In 1994 Gerhardt even told the newspaper *City Press* that the two parties did not expect anyone to notice the explosion, but that the weather conditions on the night in question thwarted their plans. He did admit, however, that he had no first-hand knowledge of the alleged test, despite being in charge of the Simonstown naval base. He also told the newspaper that no South African ships had been involved.

If a nuclear test had really taken place, ships belonging to the fleet of the country concerned would have had to be in the vicinity to ensure that there were no hitches. Apart from Gerhardt's rather meaningless statement, there was no concrete evidence to this effect, however.

In any case, why should the Israelis have wanted to carry out a nuclear test in 1979? Israel and France cooperated very closely on nuclear energy matters in the 1950s and 1960s, while the relationship between Israel and the USA was not exactly cordial. There is sufficient evidence of Israeli involvement in the French weapons programme and of French activity in Israel during that period. The French were intensely involved in the building of the Dimona reactor which made plutonium for Israel's nuclear weapons programme from 1962 onwards. The technology for plutonium weapons differs considerably from that used for uranium weapons, and is also far more complex. A country producing plutonium weapons for the first time therefore needs opportunities to test them. Weissman and Krosney claim in their book *The Islamic Bomb* (1981) that when the first French nuclear test was carried out in Algeria in 1960 not one but two new nuclear powers were born.

At the time of the Six-Day War in 1967 Israel already possessed nuclear weapons. When the Yom Kippur War broke out in 1973 sophisticated nuclear weapons were ready for use. This implies that those weapons must already have been tested. Why would Israeli ships have come all the way to Prince Edward Island six years later, in 1979, to test a single nuclear device?

Military cooperation is known to have taken place between South Africa and Israel during those years in respect of conventional weapons; it is also now generally known that South Africa sold uranium ore concentrates to Israel at that time. However, the technology used for Israel's plutonium weapons differed so widely from that required for South Africa's uranium weapons that the two countries could not have learned much from each other. Furthermore, in 1979 Israel had possessed nuclear weapons for more than a decade, while South Africa was still busy producing highly enriched uranium for the country's first nuclear device.

On 26 October 1979, Wynand de Villiers, the father of the South African nuclear weapons programme, strongly denied on behalf of the Atomic Energy Corporation of South Africa (AEC) that South Africa had been involved in the Vela incident. He emphasised that at that stage the country did not have the capacity to carry out a test of that kind. To support his statement he released a report containing the negative results of ad hoc atmospheric fallout tests carried out by AEC scientists.

The rumoured linking of Israel and South Africa with the Vela incident was therefore nothing other than an opportunistic political low blow.

In 1997 the slumbering controversy flared up again when the *Ha'aretz* newspaper in Israel reported that South Africa's Deputy Minister of Foreign Affairs Aziz Pahad had referred to the incident as "an undoubted nuclear test". However, Pahad's press secretary denied the claim on 11 July 1997 in an interview with the *Albuquerque Journal* and said that Pahad had been quoted out of context. He apparently only said that the possibility of South Africa's involvement in the incident should be investigated since so many rumours were circulating. On the same day the Los Alamos National Laboratory released a press statement to the effect that Pahad's statement confirmed what they had long thought!

In the course of the IAEA's investigation into South Africa's former nuclear weapons programme from 1991 to 1993 the Vela incident of 1979 naturally came up. While the IAEA was still engaged in checking production records and other historical data, which were later to convince them that at that time there was insufficient material to build a weapon, Wynand de Villiers was asked to give his opinion in confidence. He was the one person who had to know, since he had started the weapons programme and later run it in his capacity as Chief Executive Officer and Chairman of the AEC's board of directors. His reply was short and sweet: "No, the AEC had nothing to do with it." With a twinkle in his eye he added: "As far as I am concerned – if there was a test and the Israelis were involved – it was probably cooperation between Israel and the Americans. They would never admit cooperation and South Africa was a convenient scapegoat. Why did the Americans find it so difficult to get their planes into the air to take samples, which came to nothing in the end in any case?"

Waldo Stumpf, the former Chief Executive Officer of the AEC, referred to the Vela incident in his chapter in C.M. Meyer's book *Is Chernobyl Dead*? He reported specifically on a closed meeting he attended with President F.W. de Klerk and Magnus Malan, the Minister of Defence. At this meeting De Klerk asked Malan to look him in the eyes and tell him whether South Africa had been involved in the incident. Malan emphatically denied any South African involvement.

Stumpf also refers to the fact that the Americans exerted enormous diplomatic pressure on South Africa after the incident. The pressure ceased abruptly two weeks later, as if the Americans had discovered what had really happened and realised that South Africa was not involved after all. The truth is sometimes more mundane than one is inclined to believe …

Vela postscript – a ghost from the past

On 20 January 2013 Barack Obama was sworn in as President of the USA for a second term. As usual he appointed new ministers to key posts. One of them, Chuck Hagel, was appointed as Secretary of Defense. Hagel immediately ran into a lot of opposition.

In an article in Salon.com, dated 7 January 2013, the situation was described as follows:

> Here's a rule of thumb: On the rare occasion when everything including the kitchen sink gets thrown at a cabinet nominee to block an appointment, there's a solid chance that the opposition is not merely about the collage of negative headlines. That is particularly the case when a nominee is seen as a threat to the lucrative business of permanent war …

Chuck Hagel's unforgivable sin? He had been critical of Israel in the past and he also intended to cut the defence budget. On a website supported by the Emergency Committee for Israel (ECI), Hagel was accused of wanting to alienate the USA and Israel; of blaming Israel for Palestinian terrorism; and also of exerting pressure on Israel to return the occupied territory. A number of other "anonymous groups" even donated large sums of money to oppose Hagel actively.

The Hagel support group, who were enraged by the activities of the Israeli pressure groups, possessed plenty of ammunition of their own. A ghost that had long since been laid to rest was raised again, and they even tried to show that the ghost had had South African DNA. The big name in this regard was Jonathan Jay Pollard. Pollard had been detained in an American jail since 1987 after having been convicted of spying for Israel.

In 2006 the CIA issued a report on the Pollard case. The document had been heavily redacted, as usual, and contained little useful information. On 14 December 2012 the report was coincidentally (?) reissued. Considerably more information was revealed this time. The pro-Hagel group suddenly put two and two together and got five in order to make the pro-Israeli pressure groups look silly.

Jonathan Jay Pollard

Pollard was an American of Jewish descent, a noted spinner of yarns with a cannabis habit who was rejected by the CIA when he applied to them for a job after university. He had more success with naval intelligence. Unlike the CIA, they did not require polygraph tests. By the middle of September 1979 the young Pollard had been appointed to the Navy Ocean Surveillance Information Center (NOSIC) and by the end of November of the same year he had received a temporary Sensitive Compartmented Information Clearance SCI). His job description was to analyse the movements of merchant shipping.

To impress his boss, he resorted to lies: He claimed that his father was the head of the CIA in South Africa (his father was actually a microbiologist in the USA); he said that he, Jonathan, had grown up in South Africa and was able to speak Afrikaans fluently. Pollard also claimed to have had contact with South African intelligence agents.

In February 1980 Pollard was temporarily allocated to HUMINT, a division of the navy responsible for HUMan INTelligence. Four months later, however, his SCI clearance was withdrawn "due to bizarre behaviour". This meant that his case would have to be investigated. Before he could be made to undergo a compulsory polygraph test he made a clean breast of the whole thing and confessed to all his lies. He revealed that in September 1979, long before his appointment to the intelligence division, he had made contact with the South African military attaché in the USA.

Pollard was referred for psychological evaluation several times and his high security clearance was withdrawn. He was carefully monitored for several years, and only in 1985 was his security clearance fully restored, which was very convenient for his next adventure.

Around mid-1984 Pollard made contact with Colonel Avi Sella, an Israeli Air Force officer who was in the USA for further training. They reached an understanding – information in exchange for money, even for a valuable engagement ring and a honeymoon trip to Paris later on.

The man's audacity was astounding. One day he carried five briefcases containing secret documents out of his place of work, while the security officer courteously held the door open for him. He took the documents to a secret destination where the Israelis were waiting for him, ready to make copies before he nonchalantly returned the originals.

Pollard's activities did not go completely unobserved. When things got too hot for him, he and his wife applied to the Israeli embassy for asylum in November 1985. This was refused, however, and they were arrested outside the embassy. The espionage case created a big sensation in the USA. After a protracted hearing Pollard was sentenced to lifelong imprisonment in March 1987 and his wife to five years.

Although Pollard applied for Israeli citizenship in 1995 and this was *granted in the same year, up to 1998 Israel continued to deny that he had been spying for the Jewish state.*

How does this story relate to Chuck Hagel's appointment as Secretary of Defense?

In January 2013 reports suddenly appeared in the American press under sensational headlines such as the following:

"Israel spy was central cog in nuclear weapons proliferation" and "CIA Report – Israel guilty of nuclear proliferation"

On the basis of the CIA report that was reissued in December 2012, sensational conclusions were drawn to the effect that Pollard had been in cahoots with South Africa, that he had known about the "South-African-Israeli nuclear test" of 22 September 1979 and that he had deliberately withheld damning information which had been in the possession of the navy and provided confirmation that the test had taken place.

However, the only reference to South Africa in the CIA report was to Pollard's unauthorised meeting with the South African military attaché in September 1979 about two weeks after his appointment to the navy. It was only at the end of November of that year that Pollard received temporary security clearance. How could he possibly have had access to information on a secret nuclear test so soon? He was not yet working for the Israelis at that time (this started five years later). If Wynand de Villiers (the Chairman of the AEC) did not even know about a test of that kind, how could a junior South African military attaché have had that knowledge? Furthermore, it was proved, and the IAEA bore that out, that at that stage South Africa did not have sufficient highly enriched uranium for a nuclear test. But could South Africa have held Israel's hand while the Israelis carried out a test? It is a possibility but at that stage Pollard would have had no access to such information. Besides, it was made clear in court that he had never supplied information on America to Israel, although he had passed on information obtained by the Americans on Arab countries, the PLO, Soviet arms supplies to Syria and other Arab states and also details of Pakistan's nuclear programme.

The old dead polecat – namely South Africa – had to be resurrected again to lend a bit of flavour to a dirty American political fight – but all in vain. Hagel has since been unceremoniously dropped as Secretary of Defense. After decades of lobbying by Israel, it was finally announced on 28 July 2015 that Pollard had been granted parole and that he would be

> *released from jail on 20 November of the same year. Secretary of state, John Kerry, formally denied rumours that Pollard's release was an attempt to pacify the Israeli government over the July 2015 agreement reached with Iran to curb its nuclear programme.*

ARMSCOR STEPS UP

The compulsory UN arms embargo imposed by Resolution 418 on 4 November 1977 had far-reaching consequences for the South African conventional arms industry as well as for the country's nuclear industry. While the previous Resolution 282 did have the same objective, it was only applied on a voluntary basis. Under the new resolution all member states of the UN were formally constrained from making weapons and technology available to South Africa.

There were severe consequences for South Africa. France immediately cancelled the sale of frigates and submarines and there was no further possibility of buying aircraft to defeat the Cuban MiG-23 jets during the Border War in Angola.

This offensive resolution brought home even more clearly to the South African government the fact that they were on their own. Strategic independence had become the first priority. The arms boycott was the trigger and an important turning point in the establishment of an extensive and sophisticated arms industry in South Africa. This was the origin of Armscor, which developed rapidly to meet local demand. The organisation was later to become an important exporter of armaments. Where there is the political will and the necessary technical infrastructure, especially manpower, sanctions have always led to the development and strengthening of unique national capacity – the opposite effect to the one intended.

In the 1980s the South African arms industry saw unprecedented growth. The aviation industry was manufacturing more than one type of aircraft locally and was able to maintain five other types efficiently without outside assistance. The testing of five types of missile was being researched. With locally built and maintained anti-landmine vehicles and tanks, the armoured vehicle industry was well in the forefront. Remarkable progress was made in the areas of radar, communication and electronic warfare. Numerous assault rifles, anti-aircraft guns and artillery programmes underwent further development in South Africa.

That a small, isolated country was able to run so many programmes simultaneously was an outstanding achievement. Furthermore, all these projects were aimed at making the country's arms industry self-sufficient. About 15 000 people were in service at Armscor in the 1980s and another 15 000 posts in the private sector were connected with Armscor programmes.

In the late 1980s the South African Defence Force was facing a dilemma. There were budget deficits, along with a shortage of highly skilled scientists and engineers. On the one hand the Defence Force had to continue to operate successfully in the field against overwhelming conventionally equipped Soviet surrogate forces in Angola. On the other hand all the development projects had to be funded and managed in order to make the country self-sufficient in respect of armaments. Innovative thinking was required in order to get the most out of the dwindling research budget. The question arose whether a nuclear weapon would not provide a partial solution.

The reasoning was that if South Africa were to be faced with a serious military threat, the country could proceed to phase 2 of the national strategic guidelines, namely partial disclosure of the country's nuclear capability. If phase 2 did not produce a successful result and the international community was not prepared to come to South Africa's aid, phase 3 could kick in and the country could then openly acknowledge or even demonstrate its nuclear capability. An underground test would confirm this capability and the international community would have no means of knowing whether an experimental device or a full-scale weapon had been tested.

Hardly a month after P.W. Botha had become prime minister in 1978, he gave instructions for the appointment of a committee to draw up a plan of action for embarking on the manufacture of nuclear weapons based on the devices the AEB had developed for peaceful purposes. These proposals were approved on 4 April 1979 and Armscor as the appropriate body was tasked with designing and building militarily qualified gun-type nuclear weapons, while Ucor would provide the highly enriched uranium and the AEB would share its existing knowledge of theoretical and neutron physics with Armscor. Approval was also granted for the construction of suitable facilities. From then onwards all the documents concerned bore a big red stamp: UITERS GEHEIM / TOP SECRET.

On 31 January 1979 the Chief of the South African Defence Force (SADF) wrote a formal letter to the AEB. The Defence Force registered Project Festival (also known as Accabo) for the development of a militarily qualified nuclear weapon on behalf of the SADF that would be compatible with the existing delivery systems (aircraft, missiles and glide bombs). This job was assigned to Kentron. At a meeting held on 25 June of that year Armscor reported that a suitable site had been identified at the circular Armscor vehicle testing track (known as Gerotek today). It was to be known as the Kentron Circle facility.

The Kentron Circle facility

In July 1979 the action committee appointed by P.W. Botha finalised its plans for the production of nuclear weapons. The members' recommendation was that seven weapons in all should be developed.

The Kentron Circle facility, where the nuclear weapons were to be manufactured, was situated about 15 km to the east of Pelindaba. Armscor was to bear the full cost of the Kentron Circle, but the AEB would supply certain equipment which Armscor could not purchase for security reasons. Specialists were also transferred to the Circle facility from the staff of the AEB. Enriched material remained the property of the AEB and certain theoretical core aspects were still handled by the AEB. The conversion of enriched UF_6 (received from Ucor) to uranium metal was also still carried out at Pelindaba.

In May 1981 the premises were taken into use. The Gerotek site was normally used to test vehicles at high speed on different road surfaces. The signpost at the turnoff to Circle simply said "Workshop".

The Circle facility consisted of three components: the main facility, the environmental testing facility and a magazine for the HMX explosives. From the outside the windowless main building was deliberately unimpressive. Inside it consisted of two storeys with a floor area of about 8 800 m^2. The ground floor was used for the manufacture of the nuclear warheads and related systems. It housed storage vaults for storing the warheads. There were also eight specially designed cells on the floor where propellant explosives and up to 2,5 kg of high explosive could be tested. Above these cells was a plenum designed in such a way that overpressure (as a result of a conventional explosion on the ground floor) would be dissipated through ventilation grilles to prevent a possible collapse of the roof and walls. Offices and conference rooms occupied the top floor. Thanks to a large embankment the building was not visible from the nearby road. To avoid attracting unnecessary attention, the management of the Circle facility decided against using antennas for communication on the roof of the building.

The environmental testing facility was intended to test the weapons system components under conditions that would correspond to operational use.

A great deal of implosion research was also conducted – an undertaking which had been started on a limited scale at the AEC. Much of the work concerned measuring techniques to determine the equation of state of the materials under high pressure.

Nuclear weapons that work on the implosion principle use only one-third to one-quarter of the amount of highly enriched uranium used by gun-type devices and therefore represent a far more effective use of the extremely scarce weapons-grade material. It would therefore be possible to build more devices with the existing material and, because of the smaller dimensions, the technology would also be more suitable for use in missiles.

Experiments were carried out with plane-wave lenses at the Circle facility and spherical implosion technology was planned for the future.

At one stage an enormous amount of explosive (three tons) was bought for experimental purposes. Experts on conventional explosives were specially recruited to carry out certain tests with the explosives purchased.

The area in the Circle building where work was performed with enriched uranium was known as "the red area" on account of the higher levels of radiation. Workers had to wear protective clothing there. When necessary, radioactive waste was sent back to the AEC's special dumping site for radioactive waste (Radiation Hill) by night.

In the early 1980s there were about 100 people employed at the Circle facility, of whom about 40 were directly involved with the building of nuclear weapons. The staff complement increased to about 300 over the years.

Extraordinary security measures meant that numerous components had to be developed on the site, since the work could not be put out on contract. The development and fine-tuning of the hardware therefore took years. The Circle facility was officially based at the Kentron offices in Centurion, where three people sustained the illusion that the project was being run from there. It was necessary that as few people as possible should know what was happening at the Gerotek site.

The strict security measures even regulated the social life of the employees at the Circle facility. AEC officials and Armscor employees were not permitted to socialise after hours or to give any sign in public that they knew each other. They were not permitted to tell their family and friends where they really worked – they could merely say that they were working on a government research project and that the work was "classified". Workers were transported by day in discrete white minibuses with the windows obscured by paint. Former employees relate that at one stage the head of security at the Circle facility even had an Uzzi machine gun mounted under his desk for quick access!

Product containers, each with about 3 kg of highly enriched UF_6, were transported under guard from Valindaba to the Pelindaba site and passed through a special small hatch in the metallurgy building to a person whose hands were all that was visible. Here the UF_6 was converted to metal. Regarding the transfer of the metal to the Circle facility, only two people at Circle knew when the next consignment of highly enriched uranium would be available. Transfers never took place on the same day of the week and deliveries were made late at night. A designated official was instructed to rent an ordinary truck from Value Truck Rentals. Another employee drove the truck between the AEC and Circle. When their colleagues arrived for work at the Circle facility the next day and saw the truck they knew immediately that a delivery had taken place the previous night!

The Kentron Circle facility was formally opened on 18 May 1981 by Prime Minister P.W. Botha.

In his speech Botha referred to the history of the project with obvious pride. He saw the project as the equivalent of the Los Alamos and Lawrence Livermore Laboratories in the USA, or Britain's Atomic Weapons Research Establishment (AWRE). Today we would be inclined to say, "Get real!" because Botha's comparison did not take into account the USA's numerous academic feeder sources, its nuclear infrastructure – and above all the American financial resources.

He went on to say that as Minister of Defence he had initiated discussions back in 1975 on the possibility of manufacturing nuclear weapons for South Africa and had given instructions in July 1977 to draw up national strategic guidelines for nuclear weapons. These were approved on 4 April 1978. In October of the same year he requested the appointment of an action committee to determine how nuclear weapons could be manufactured for South Africa. The aim was to build on the work already done by the AEB on the development of peaceful applications of nuclear explosives. On 4 July 1979 the action committee submitted draft proposals on the weapon and the facilities that would be required and these were approved by Botha as Project Festival, or Accabo. (Code names were changed from time to time for security reasons.)

In his speech Botha also referred to the events at Vastrap when the testing of the first cold device was abandoned. The reason he gave for the cancellation of the test was that it was necessary for the development programme to be kept secret for another few years in order to continue with the refinement, reduction in size and improvement in the handling of the device.

In typical, forceful Botha style he said that it was time to beat the South African ploughshare (with reference to the USA's peaceful Operation Plowshare) into a sword with the aim of forcing the USA and Russia to come to the negotiating table. This would enable South Africa to deal with the conflict from a power base of nuclear strategy instead of a "power base of black politics". It would also provide a key to the peaceful solution of the conflicts in Southern Africa and should be utilised as such.

Botha also said emphatically that above all nuclear weapons were "an inducement and a means of persuasion and coercion" because they were primarily a political weapons system and not a military system. He saw the NPT as a way of depriving South Africa of its right to develop its own deterrent.

What the Prime Minister failed to say, however, was that the big obstacle in the way of developing nuclear weapons was and had always been the acquisition or production of weapons-grade material. The main problem did not lie in actually making the weapons. Strangely enough, he made no mention of South Africa's outstanding achievement in developing its own, unique uranium enrichment process, a process that does not exist anywhere else in the world. Possibly he did not want to give too much credit to his predecessor, John Vorster, who had announced the process eleven years previously.

On the day when P.W. Botha opened the Kentron Circle facility, his Minister of Foreign Affairs, Pik Botha, left for Washington along with Brand Fourie and Carl von Hirschberg to hold talks with the new American administration. Theresa Papenfus relates in *Pik Botha and His Times* that South-West Africa was at the top of the South African agenda during the discussions with the newly elected President Ronald Reagan and Alexander Haig, the Secretary of State.

> There was an atmosphere of mutual trust, acceptance and respect between the President and Pik, as Fourie observed. The minister informed President Reagan about the situation in South Africa and they discussed South-West as well. The South African Prime Minister, Pik assured Reagan, was committed to making South-West independent. South Africa was not opposed to a majority government in the territory, only to a communist one-party government. Then Pik raised the Koeberg issue.

> "Haig almost lost his temper and intervened that I had not cleared my agenda with him first. Reagan overruled him, and asked me directly: 'Are you producing a bomb?'"
>
> "I replied: Mr President, we have the capacity to do so. But I commit my government in assuring you that we will never test such a device without first consulting the US government."
>
> "Reagan's response was: 'That sounds fair.'
>
> "Haig again objected. 'We cannot be associated with this at all.' I appealed to Reagan: 'Mr President, I believe the Soviet Union also believes we are in the process and have the capacity. And this suspicion may act as a deterrent not to go too far in fomenting unrest in Southern Africa. And we believe that is a deterrent.'
>
> "Ronald Reagan bought what I was saying and silenced Haig. 'I think this is a fair explanation, Mr Secretary, and we should speak to our French colleagues about Koeberg.'"

This conversation contributed to South Africa's obtaining approval for Koeberg's fuel supply.

The programme makes headway

The first – and last – complete nuclear explosive device, known as Video, which was built by the AEB in 1978 and fitted with a highly enriched warhead in November 1979, spent the first years of its life in rather gloomy surroundings. The Circle facility was not yet available and it was decided to store Video temporarily in an old army ammunition depot. The depot was situated in an abandoned coal mine near Witbank.

One of the people involved in building Video, and the temporary storage of the device in the mine, describes the night when Video was stored there:

> It was 03:00 in the morning. We had driven through the night and were tired. But when we got there (the Witbank mine) the vault's doors were not yet finished. The army had simply not done their job. Richardt (van der Walt) decided that we couldn't just leave the device there with a couple of guards. We had to make it more difficult to steal. That was when I decided to take the wheels off the trolley carrying the device. It was dark; all I wanted was to get

> home. I started unscrewing the nuts on one wheel in the dark. I kept on unscrewing without any apparent results. The mine was pitch dark and there was no light to speak of; the guys had feeble headlamps and that was all. Eventually I said to the sergeant major: "Give us a little bit of light here because something must be wrong." Then I saw that I was busy trying to unscrew a split rim. If it had blown out it would have taken my head off! (translation)

By April 1982 the Circle facility had been opened and Video was moved from its humble hiding place to the brand-new facilities at Gerotek, where the highly enriched uranium warhead was replated to prevent corrosion of the uranium. The device was then renamed Melba and would in future be preserved as a demonstration model.

Video therefore had to be transported twice through the centre of Pretoria in the space of three years, while the unsuspecting population slept, past Heroes Acre where former President Paul Kruger is buried. Church Street West was the only route to the Circle facility. The old President of the ZAR would probably have turned in his grave if he had known what was passing on the military convoy. With that weapon at his disposal 80 years previously he would have been able to chase "perfidious Albion" head over heels into the sea and might never have needed to sound the retreat in the *Gelderland* – the ship so graciously provided by Queen Wilhelmina of the Netherlands ... It took time for Armscor to develop a militarily qualified, deliverable nuclear weapon. During the qualification process several pre-production models were built to test the reliability of the components, to integrate the device with the delivery system and also to test the systems. Six such complete or semi-complete devices (but without the uranium warheads) were built in the so-called 300 series. These devices were never formally tested. Waldo Stumpf explains the reasons in C.M. Meyer's publication *Is Chernobyl Dead?* which appeared in 2011:

> The nuclear devices were based on technology little different from the first uranium gun-type design developed by the Americans in 1944. And because we based our design on simple, conservative and reliable technology nearly 50 years old, we were confident that it would work without a formal test. In any case, the basic design had been tested on Hiroshima, on 6 August 1945.

THE BOMB

PRE-PRODUCTION MODELS IN THE 300 SERIES*	
Series number	Purpose
301	Semi-complete, used for flame tests
302	Complete, used for integration tests and for several firing tests of the gun section
303	Used for flight tests
305	Complete, intended as a spare device for flight tests, although it was never used for this purpose. The quality of 305 was so high that it was fitted with a warhead in 1986. It was consequently the second active device produced by Armscor. The warhead was later removed and transferred to production model 502. Device 305 was retained as a training model, up to the termination of the programme.
306	This was the final pre-production model before the industrialisation process. The model was also of such a high quality that it could be upgraded to an active device in 1988/89.
304, 307, 308, 309, etc	These series numbers referred to subsystems in various degrees of development and not to additional models.

The models in the 300 series were not equipped with warheads, except as indicated by later conversions.

The first complete nuclear weapon built by the Armscor team was completed in December 1982, a Christmas gift for P.W. Botha. The device was "G.I.-proof" (the euphemistic term was "militarily qualified"). It was also capable of being dropped (or "delivered" to use another euphemistic term) on military targets from an aircraft or by glide bomb. The code name for the first deliverable device was Hobo, which was later changed by Armscor to Cabot.

After Hobo one nuclear weapon a year was completed until the decision was taken seven years later to terminate the programme.

Every nuclear weapon consisted of two parts: a front part containing the uranium warhead and a rear part containing the gun assembly with its uranium missile. The highly enriched uranium was therefore divided between the two parts, which were locked away in two separate vaults. There was consequently no possibility that an unforeseen explosion could take place. As a further precaution, the front and rear parts of the weapon were never worked on simultaneously. Precautions were taken to make it impossible for a single person to open the vaults in which the parts were stored. Furthermore, the front warhead could not be removed from the vault without specific orders from the State President, via two separate chains of command, namely a military and a civilian chain. The chains of command were as follows:

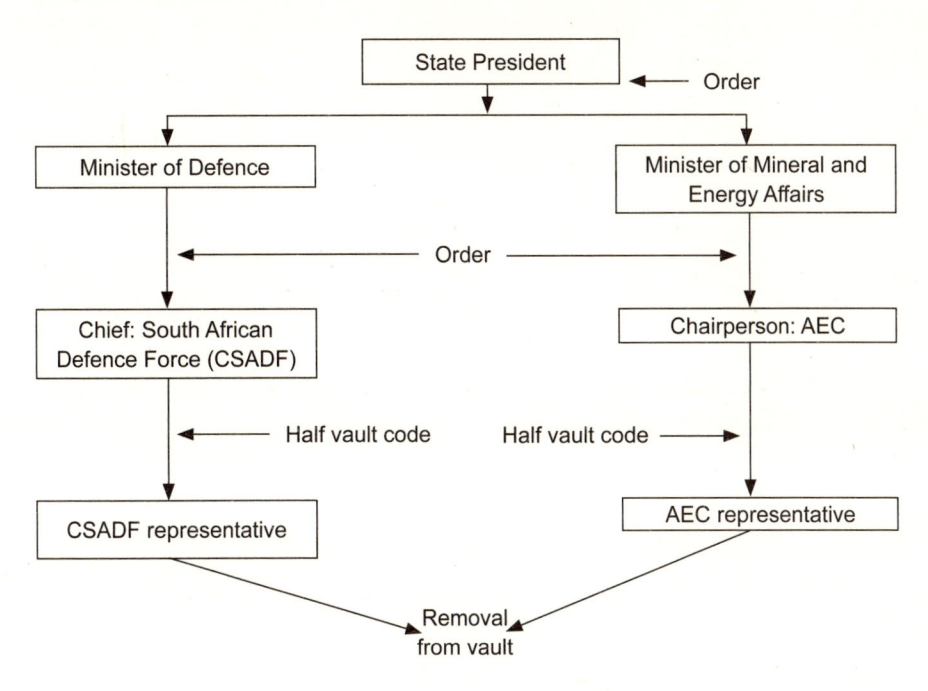

```
                        ┌─────────────────┐
                        │ State President │ ◄──── Order
                        └────────┬────────┘
              ┌──────────────────┴──────────────────┐
              ▼                                     ▼
    ┌───────────────────┐                ┌──────────────────────┐
    │ Minister of Defence│               │ Minister of Mineral and│
    │                   │                │    Energy Affairs     │
    └─────────┬─────────┘                └──────────┬───────────┘
              │ ◄──────────── Order ──────────────► │
              ▼                                     ▼
    ┌───────────────────┐                ┌──────────────────────┐
    │ Chief: South African│              │  Chairperson: AEC     │
    │ Defence Force (CSADF)│             │                       │
    └─────────┬─────────┘                └──────────┬───────────┘
              │ ◄── Half vault code    Half vault code ──►        │
              ▼                                     ▼
    ┌───────────────────┐                ┌──────────────────────┐
    │ CSADF representative│              │  AEC representative   │
    └─────────┬─────────┘                └──────────┬───────────┘
              └────────────► Removal ◄─────────────┘
                            from vault
```

The highly enriched uranium was also strictly supervised. At the beginning of every working day the uranium to be used that day was weighed to the nearest one-tenth of a gram before being removed from the vault. At the end of the day the material was removed from the manufacturing area and weighed in the same manner before being returned to the vault.

By the time the programme was finally dismantled, six devices had been built that qualified as nuclear weapons: Melba (demonstration model), 306 and the production models 501, 502, 503 and 504. There was sufficient highly enriched uranium available for a seventh weapon but it was never built.

THE BOMB

Nuclear weapons

WEAPON IDENTIFICATION	FRONT OR REAR WARHEAD	PRODUCTION DATE	REMARKS
Video/Melba		November 1979 (built by the AEB)	Replated in 1982
Hobo/Cabot		December 1982 (first weapon built by Armscor)	Warhead later built into another device (502)
306	Front Rear	September 1986 November 1986	Upgraded pre-production model
501	Front Rear	August 1987 June 1988	First production model
502	Front Rear	November 1988 October 1988	Production model
503	Front Rear	November 1988 March 1989	Production model
504	Front Rear	March 1989 March 1989	Production model

The Gouriqua project: materials for sophisticated devices

Although Armscor took over responsibility for the development and production of nuclear weapons from the AEB, the latter continued to supply materials and support in respect of neutron physics.

In addition to the production of highly enriched uranium for gun-type devices (A-type), as far back as 1975 the Minister of Mines gave approval for funds and facilities to be used to acquire and produce plutonium, as well as fusion materials, namely lithium-6, deuterium and tritium. A pilot plant for the production of lithium-6 in gram units was constructed on the Pelindaba site in 1977 but was later demolished. The plan was that a bigger plant would be constructed at the Gouriqua site, which would be able to produce about 5 kg a year by 1994. These materials were intended for use in a thermonuclear device (B-type or a so-called "hydrogen bomb") or for building a boosted gun-type device (A*). The explosive yield of the latter would have been five times that of the A-type.

In 1980 approval was granted for the Gouriqua project which was to be built at Gouritsmond, close to Mossel Bay. This project was designed for the large-scale production of these fusion bomb materials. A pressurised water reactor of the same type as Koeberg but far smaller (150 megawatts) was to be built for this purpose. The reactor was intended to serve various purposes, such as producing plutonium and tritium, but would also be used to develop commercial pressurised water reactor technology.

Plutonium would have been required if it had been necessary to switch to physically smaller nuclear weapons for use in missiles or artillery weapons. Armscor would have had to develop the necessary implosion technology and a neutron initiator or trigger would also have been needed. In the 1980s Armscor contracted the AEB to build such a trigger. A laboratory model was manufactured but the project was abandoned during the initial stage.

In order to boost the blast yield of the gun-type uranium weapons, two possibilities were investigated. The one was to encapsulate a highly compressed gas of fusion material in a capsule in the projectile section of the weapon. However, there was no compressor available that could compress the gas to about 100 megapascals (MPa) and so that option was abandoned. The second option was to make a pellet consisting of Li-6, tritium and deuterium. Tritium is radioactive, however, with half of it decaying to helium within about twelve years. This would mean that the pellets would have to be replaced frequently. This would have caused difficulties because it is not practicable to dismantle militarily qualified weapons every so often; a new design was therefore required. The extra costs involved, and the fact that the weapons were not intended for offensive use, meant that the project for producing booster materials was ultimately discontinued.

The target dates for the building of the Gouriqua reactor and the production of advanced materials was set for some time in the 1990s. Although land had been purchased and basic infrastructure in the form of roads, houses and a few workshops constructed, because of economic pressure and the termination of the nuclear weapons programme in 1989, little came of this ambitious project.

Ad hoc cabinet committee: September 1985

In the 1960s South Africa had the second highest economic growth rate in the world, surpassed only by Japan. The Border War, which began in 1966, and the compulsory arms embargo imposed in 1977 began to eat into the budget inexorably, however. In 1977 the defence and police service budget votes rose by 21% and 15% respectively. Although Armscor was able in time to supply all the country's arms requirements with outstanding products which proved themselves on the battlefield, the fact that many of the products had to be designed from scratch, developed, built, tested and then manufactured meant that the costs were very high in comparison with the cost of buying similar, ready-made products from overseas.

The ongoing domestic unrest was a further deterrent to foreign investors and the result was a net outflow of foreign capital.

The country was also under constant pressure from the UN and the international community. Over the years the UNGA adopted a multitude of resolutions against South Africa. The resolutions that had a major impact were those passed by the UNSC. Typically three or four resolutions were passed each year between 1976 and 1983, although 1981 was unnaturally quiet with no resolutions adopted. In 1984 the pace picked up and five resolutions were passed; in 1985 the number grew to ten.

There was a good reason for the unnatural silence in 1981. On Sunday 7 June 1981 Israeli planes carried out an air strike against the Tammuz reactor in Iraq. This was the first time a nuclear reactor had been bombed. This incident caused uproar in the international community. For a long time Israel had attempted to dissuade France, which supplied the 40-megawatt (MW) reactor, which the French called the Osirak reactor, from exporting the reactor to Iraq. When their objections were ignored, the reactor core was blown up by the Israeli intelligence service (Mossad) in Toulon (but without the fissile material) and the engineer in charge of the Iraqi nuclear programme was murdered. After the equipment had been repaired and the exports were going ahead, Israel decided to destroy the reactor in situ. As expected, the UN and the Board of Governors of the IAEA strongly condemned Israel. All technical assistance from the IAEA was suspended and Israel was threatened with expulsion. For a short while the spotlight was off South Africa.

In November 1984 Pik Botha was a member of a South African delegation that held talks in the Cape Verde Islands with Chester Crocker, the then American Assistant Secretary of State for African Affairs. The subject of the talks was a settlement in Angola, where there was still a Cuban and South African presence and the MPLA (Movimento Popular de Libertação de Angola) was gaining the upper hand over UNITA (União Nacional para a Independência Total de Angola). The Americans had submitted a proposal and the South Africans, who mistrusted the Americans' true motives, had to make a counterproposal. In her biography *Pik Botha and His Times* Theresa Papenfus, drawing on passages from Chester Crocker's book *High Noon in Southern Africa – Making Peace in a Rough Neighborhood*, describes the prevailing atmosphere during those talks:

> "Like paint remover, the non-stop alcohol intake stripped away any veneer of Afrikaner solidarity." They disagreed about everything – Savimbi's prospects in Angola, the relative importance of the Angolan war for South Africa, the role being played by the United States, the hopes for Namibia's internal parties, how to handle growing black unrest at home, and the right course in Mozambique. He didn't find the talks on South-West much more constructive. Dr Willie van Niekerk, the Administrator of the area, "a hardline gynecologist-politician whose dream it was to abort Namibia", suggested to P.W. Botha that Resolution 435 should be amended so that a constitutional conference could be set up before the elections.

At the conclusion of the talks Crocker had little hope for the future of Southern Africa ...

South Africa was also being subjected to pressure by the IAEA. At the annual General Conference in September 1984 it was demanded by a majority of 57 votes to 10 (with 23 countries abstaining) that the South Africans should open all their nuclear facilities for IAEA inspection.

In 1984 and 1985 two expensive Eskom projects – Koeberg 1 and Koeberg 2 – started producing power for the first time.

Overview of the most important UNSC resolutions

UNSC RESOLUTIONS	CONTENTS	VOTING	REMARKS
181 (August 1963)	Concern over arms build-up in SA. Member states asked to impose voluntary embargo on exports of military equipment.	For: 9 Against: 0 Abstentions: 2	This was a follow-up of Resolution 134 (1960) but had little effect.
191 (June 1964)	Previous voluntary embargo repeated. An expert committee appointed to investigate the effectiveness of measures which could be undertaken.	For: 8 Against: 0 Abstentions: 3	
282 (July 1970)	Concern over the violation of the arms embargo. Member states requested to stop providing any military training to South Africans.	For: 12 Against: 0 Abstentions: 3	
418 (November 1977)	Compulsory arms embargo instituted.	Unanimous	Cancellation of corvettes and submarines. No more fighter aircraft made available. Growth of SA arms industry (Armscor). No USA fuel for Safari-1.

UNSC RESOLUTIONS	CONTENTS	VOTING	REMARKS
569 (July 1985)	The state of emergency that was declared in 36 districts in South Africa was condemned. In addition to the compulsory arms embargo States Members of the United Nations were urged to suspend or restrict investment as well as maritime, aviation, sport and cultural relations.	For: 13 Against: 0 Abstentions: 2	
591 (November 1986)	Strengthened sanctions under Resolution 418. Explicitly forbade cooperation in the nuclear field. Prohibited the importing of military equipment produced in SA. Requested States Non-Members of the UN to comply with sanctions.	Unanimous	Recalled in 1994 by Resolution 919.

In July 1985 the American House of Representatives passed the Anti-Apartheid Act. Under this Act no further bank loans could be granted to South Africa, Kruger rands could no longer be imported and no computers or nuclear technology could be sold to South Africa. The Bill was supported by the Senate a few days later.

On 20 July 1985 the South African State President announced a state of emergency in a large number of districts, which was to remain in force for the next five years. Six days later the international community reacted by passing Resolution 569 in the UNSC and thereby introducing economic sanctions against South Africa. Unlike the arms embargo, however, the contents of this resolution were not compulsory. Two months later South Africa announced the imposition of exchange control in an attempt to curb the efflux of foreign capital. Repayments on short-term foreign loans were provisionally suspended.

It was against this background of economic and weapons sanctions, together with a serious efflux of foreign capital, that a secret ad hoc cabinet committee met in the State President's office on 3 September 1985. The committee had to reconsider the existing nuclear weapons programme and the additional materials and facilities that would have to be provided in future. They were going to have to pinch the pennies until they squeaked.

That Tuesday afternoon, on a beautiful spring day, several VIP official vehicles arrived at the State President's office. The VIPs who emerged were grim-faced. The President and his right-hand man, the Minister of Defence, had already finished one work session when the other members of the ad hoc cabinet committee, namely the Ministers of Finance, Foreign Affairs and Mineral and Energy Affairs, joined them. The three other participants at that meeting were the Director-General of Mineral and Energy Affairs and the Chairmen of Armscor and the AEC.

Among the men seated around the table, State President P.W. Botha was the one with the most political experience. He was appointed Minister of Defence in 1966, a post which he held for fourteen years. After this he served as Prime Minister for six years, from 1978 onwards. In 1984 he was appointed Executive State President. The Minister of Foreign Affairs, Pik Botha, had been the South African Ambassador to the UN and the USA in the mid-1970s, where he was personally exposed to the growing opposition to South Africa's political system on the part of both the UN and the USA. In 1977 he was appointed Minister of Foreign Affairs, a post he was to occupy for seventeen years. General Magnus Malan, the Minister of Defence, became the Chief of the South African Defence Force in 1976 and was appointed minister four years later. The other two ministers had little experience in their specific portfolios. Barend du Plessis had only held the post of Minister of Finance for a year and it was a mere two years since Pietie du Plessis had succeeded his predecessor, Fanie Botha, as Minister of Mineral and Energy Affairs.

The other three people present at the meeting were the technical officers responsible for carrying out the politicians' wishes. The scope of their responsibilities was determined by the amount of money the politicians were prepared to disburse from the treasury – and on their judgement. Dr Louw Alberts was the Director-General of Mineral and Energy Affairs at the time. He had made his mark as a professor of physics at Bloemfontein and at the then Rand Afrikaans University (RAU), currently the University of Johannesburg (UJ), after which he served as Vice-President of the AEB for a while, and as Director-General of the National Institute for Metallurgy (Mintek).

While he was at the AEB, he announced openly in 1974 that South Africa had the capacity to build nuclear bombs, but emphasised that the nuclear programme was about peaceful applications.

As its chairman, Commandant Piet Marais represented Armscor. His title dated from the days when he was the commandant of the rifle commando at De Aar, but from these humble beginnings he and his successors built Armscor up into a powerful organisation. The last person at the meeting was the "father of the bomb", Wynand de Villiers, the Chairman of the AEC. After his training as part of Eisenhower's Atoms for Peace programme at the Argonne National Laboratory in the USA, he became the Director of Reactor Development at the AEB in 1967, after which he became Vice-President and then Deputy President. In 1979 he succeeded Ampie Roux as President of the AEB. Back in 1970, while working on reactor development, he had already developed a concept for a nuclear warhead.

It was a formidable group that met around the conference table on 3 September 1985. One of the items on the agenda was a report from the Witvlei Council, but the underlying theme was money. After Armscor formally took over responsibility for the building of nuclear weapons in 1979, the Witvlei Council supervised this sensitive activity and submitted periodic reports. Against the background of the economic situation the committee had to reconsider the nuclear weapons programme at this meeting.

How many?

Where to?

What for?

Years later Waldo Stumpf recalled that, according to the account Wynand de Villiers gave him, it was a stormy meeting and President P.W. Botha was anything but impressed with the Witvlei Council's "exotic" plans. He also said that strangely enough the senior military personnel did not appear to be very enthusiastic about the nuclear weapons programme (*Is Chernobyl Dead?* by C.M. Meyer, 2011).

The ad hoc committee had a difficult task ahead of them. They were juggling a number of issues simultaneously and had to strike a balance between funding restrictions, international and American sanctions, the war in Angola, the internal state of emergency, and the scope and purpose of the nuclear weapons programme.

After a heated discussion the ad hoc committee decided to limit the number of nuclear weapons (A- or gun-type with an explosive yield equivalent to 5 to 20 kilotons of TNT) to seven. Admittedly this was one more than the number envisaged seven years previously, in 1978. The AEC's Y-plant would have to adapt its operating strategy to supply the nuclear material for seven weapons, as well as for a "sensible stockpile" – for whatever might come. At the same time it was a "writing-on-the-wall" situation for the Y-plant. Final decommissioning was just a matter of time and took place as soon as the production target had been reached.

It was also decided that production planning for plutonium warheads would be discontinued. That tore the heart out of the Gouriqua project.

The production of lithium-6 – required for boosted weapons – would be permitted to continue, but only until around 40 kg had been produced for possible future use.

One of the most significant instructions given was that the integration of nuclear weapons with a long-distance carrier (ballistic missile) should go ahead. Missiles require considerably smaller and lighter nuclear warheads than the gun types that were in production at that stage. For this reason it was important that engineering development work on smaller implosion weapons should go ahead.

These drastic cutbacks naturally affected the morale and professional future of the top-ranking scientists and engineers, whom Armscor and the AEC did not want to lose. The bitter pill was therefore sugared with the concessions that "expertise must be retained", "limited research could be carried out", and "theoretical work could be done" on aspects such as the development of boosted weapons. But these were merely theoretical studies.

In its report to the ad hoc committee, the Witvlei Council revisited the nuclear strategy of 1978, dusted it off and put a somewhat revised proposal to the ad hoc committee. This largely amounted to the same strategy as before, namely that if South Africa should ever find itself with its back to the wall –
- the existence of its nuclear capacity should be made known in a covert manner to Western powers (especially the USA);
- an underground test should be carried out to demonstrate South Africa's nuclear capability (overt declaration) if the first step did not lead to an improvement in the situation; and
- an above-ground test should be carried out if the threat continued.

The existing strategy was therefore reaffirmed, but with two important provisos: Any decision in this regard (the escalation from one phase to the next) was the sole responsibility of the State President. Furthermore, the strategy specifically excluded the operational use of nuclear weapons.

The decision to discontinue the production of highly enriched uranium in the near future and cancel all plans to produce plutonium, but to go ahead with the development of missiles and smaller nuclear warheads, led some observers to question whether a fourth, undivulged phase was not envisaged. Why would a very costly ballistic missile programme employing uranium implosion nuclear warheads (for which a great deal of development work would still have to be done) be used to demonstrate phase 3? After all, Vastrap was always available. Was the approval of the missile programme intended to leave the back door open for operational use?

Apart from the weapons programme, the ad hoc committee discussed certain other matters, including the application of IAEA safeguards to the Z-plant, which was still under construction and about which discussions with the IAEA were already under way. The decision was that those discussions should be discontinued or suspended, depending on sanctions and boycotts, and on what happened at the IAEA's General Conference later that month. The resolution passed at the previous year's conference was probably still fresh in everyone's memory.

As one might expect from a Minister of Finance, Barend du Plessis was a trifle disconcerted at the scale of the AEC's budget, and found the manner in which it was being funded especially disturbing. For some reason a decision had been taken in the past that the government would not fund the AEC directly, but that loans would have to be taken out. (In later years these debts were to become a millstone around the AEC's neck when the organisation was trying to become commercially viable.) One can well imagine the minister's next thought: Can these guys really be building atom bombs on credit?

The AEC was therefore instructed to reduce its expenses by re-evaluating its priorities. As a guideline it was suggested that over the next three years the AEC should try to achieve a real reduction of 10% a year.

Wynand de Villiers pointed out to the relatively inexperienced Minister of Finance that the AEC was already engaged in a rationalisation process which would only show results in two or three years' time. Further cutbacks would result in additional retrenchment of staff and this after the staff had strained every sinew in 1978 to overcome the problem regarding fuel for Koeberg which arose in the USA under the Carter administration. The state president's political memory stretched back further, and he agreed with De Villiers.

The decision either to discontinue the main components of the nuclear weapons programme or to phase them out before long, but nevertheless to continue with the long-range ballistic missiles programme, makes it necessary to shed a little more light on the missiles programme at this point.

The RSA missile series

In May 2010 Sasha Polakow-Suransky published a sensational book entitled *The Unspoken Alliance: Israel's Secret Relationship with Apartheid Africa*. This book was the fruit of six years' research for a doctorate in modern history at Oxford and is based partly on previously inaccessible documents and partly on interviews with various people who were involved with cooperation between Israel and South Africa. More information on this cooperation, and the politics behind it, is provided in Part 5 of this book.

The aim of Polakow-Suransky's book was to prove that South Africa and Israel had cooperated in the field of nuclear weapons and ballistic missiles. As regards nuclear weapons, the book is a lamentable failure as it contains wild, unsubstantiated assumptions. When it comes to ballistic missiles, however, the book fills in some of the details of a picture with which we were already familiar.

Missiles and South Africa's interest in them

Missiles occur in a variety of sizes because they are especially designed for particular applications, but there are two basic types: ballistic missiles and cruise missiles. The latter have a jet engine which propels the missile for the full period while it is in the air. Ballistic missiles, on the other hand, are launched by means of rocket power which operates for a short period, after which they fall back to earth under the influence of gravity – just as a cricket ball that has been hit for a six also has to come back to earth somewhere. (The word "ballistic" is derived from the Greek for "throw".)

Ballistic missiles can have one or more rocket stages, depending on the purpose of their application and the distance they have to cover. A missile used to launch a satellite usually has three stages, for example. The third stage is fired when the missile reaches the highest point of its trajectory. The extra horizontal boost given to the missile prevents it from falling back to earth (it misses the earth) and the missile is then placed in an orbit around the earth that enables it to launch a satellite.

There are three classes of ballistic missiles: satellite launch vehicles (SLVs); intercontinental ballistic missiles (range greater than 5 500 km) and intermediate-range ballistic missiles (range 500 to 5 500 km).

There are two broad categories of rocket fuel, namely liquid and solid fuel. A popular liquid fuel consists of kerosene (power paraffin) and liquid oxygen, which are ignited simultaneously. For large rockets, such as those used in the American shuttle programme, liquid oxygen and liquid hydrogen are ignited simultaneously. From a military perspective this type of fuel has some serious drawbacks. For one thing a lengthy and very specialised process is required to fuel a missile with liquid hydrogen and oxygen, which have to be stored at −253 °C and −183 °C respectively. When the need arises to retaliate rapidly, this type of fuel is highly unsuitable and the answer is solid fuel. An example of a solid fuel is a mixture of ammonium perchlorate and aluminium in powder form held together in a rubber base. The mixture is cast into a mould and is relatively easy and cheap to manufacture. A rocket propelled by this type of fuel can be launched immediately, but has the drawback that once the fuel is alight it is difficult to extinguish or to reignite.

After the SAAF's initial successes in the early 1980s during the Border War in Angola, it gradually became more and more difficult to retain control of the air. There were a few major reasons: the small complement of obsolete aircraft which could not be supplemented because of international sanctions, the build-up of air defence systems, and the provision of highly sophisticated aircraft to Angola. A 1991 report by the UN indicated that Angola had acquired 140 modern Soviet fighter aircraft (MiG-21, MiG-23 and Su-22) as against the SAAF's approximately 80 Buccaneers, Mirage III and Mirage F1 aircraft. The Angolan fighter aircraft were integrated with an air defence system consisting of dozens of radar installations, five battalions of ground-to-air missiles, over 140 launching platforms and over 300 anti-aircraft guns.

This situation explains the feverish haste with which Armscor got down to the job of acquiring suitable technology and ballistic missiles. Without effective control of the skies, aerial reconnaissance was impossible. Observation satellites would be able to overcome this problem and furthermore long-range missiles with suitable payloads would be a deterrent and would, when necessary, be able to wipe out big military concentrations effectively.

The proven Israeli Jericho series of ballistic missiles and the Shavit satellite launch vehicles were eminently suitable – and the technology was available.

In the early 1970s Israel began developing both medium-range ballistic missiles and an SLV. The latter is relatively easy to adapt for use as an intercontinental ballistic missile. The details of the missile programme were veiled in impenetrable secrecy. Nobody knew, for example, whether "Jericho" was the real name of the missile or whether it was simply the name used by the American intelligence agencies.

Jericho I was a short-range ballistic missile obtained from France in the 1960s. With this missile as the base, Israel developed the Jericho II ballistic missile in the 1980s. This was a robust two-stage missile with a range of between 1 500 and 3 500 km. It is still in service today.

A further development was the Shavit SLT, a three-stage missile capable of placing a payload of about 250 kg in orbit round the earth. The Shavit (which means comet) contains a third stage in addition to the two stages of the Jericho II. A handful of Ofeq spy satellites have already been successfully launched by means of Shavit missiles.

In view of the close cooperation between Israel and South Africa in the 1970s and 1980s, it is hardly surprising that the indigenous RSA-1, RSA-2 and RSA-3, which were built by Armscor, were technological blood brothers of Jericho I, Jericho II and Shavit.

RSA-1 was a single-stage and RSA-2 a two-stage missile. They both had sufficient range to hit nearby countries (like Angola). RSA-3 was a three-stage ballistic missile that could be used as a satellite launch vehicle to launch observation satellites, for example. One of the RSA-3 models was not destroyed and can still be seen today at the SAAF museum at Zwartkop, Pretoria. All these models used solid fuel. Plans had been drawn up for RSA-4, which was to have been a more powerful version of RSA-3. RSA-4 was to have had four stages consisting of a first stage with 66 tons of solid fuel, a second stage with 10 tons, a third stage with 3 tons and a fourth stage (hydrazine fuel) with 300 kg. The total mass of RSA-4 was to have been 80 tons, with a length of 23.5 m and a diameter of 2.4 m. It would have been able to put a payload of over 500 kg in orbit and there was some speculation that RSA-4, when used as a ballistic missile, would even be able to reach Moscow or New York with a nuclear warhead. However, RSA-4 never got farther than the drawing board.

Facilities of various kinds were required to support the missile programme. The impressive Houwteq developments and manufacturing facilities were constructed near Grabouw in the Western Cape. The aim was to accomplish the development work and the integration of the respective components of the missile with the planned observation satellite or the nuclear warhead. The Overberg test range near Bredasdorp was used for test flights and Somchem was again used to build the solid fuel rocket engines; there was an engine test facility at Rooiels. The nuclear warheads would be manufactured at the Circle/Advena facility. In addition to the numerous other components and systems that were built and tested at Kentron subsidiaries, it was necessary to develop a suitable extra heavy duty vehicle for use as a mobile launching platform. This was an extensive high technology programme and the costs were high.

Unlike the nuclear weapons programme, which was deliberately kept very quiet, Armscor was quite open about the need for ballistic missiles. For instance, in 1988 Fires van Vuuren, the Chief Executive Officer of Armscor, told a reporter that South Africa required medium-range missiles and long-range artillery. Five years previously Armscor's CEO had announced that South Africa could produce about three-quarters of its weapons requirements locally and acquire a quarter covertly from elsewhere. Armscor were past masters of the art of acquiring technology and systems, and then adapting them for their own use.

On 5 July 1989 the cat was let out of the bag for the benefit of the inquisitive satellites that were keeping an eye on South Africa. A missile was observed that was fired from the Overberg site and travelled a distance of about 1 600 km in the direction of the Prince Edward Island group. American intelligence sources noted that the rocket trace was similar to that of an Israeli Jericho II and also claimed that a high-level Israeli delegation was present at the test in South Africa.

The institutional panic created in the USA whenever another country acquires the ability to enrich uranium or to build long-range missiles was later to lead to the unprecedented and total destruction of all missile-related Armscor facilities.

But that is a story that will have to wait until later.

Further reflections on Project Festival

Although the technical staff of the AEC and Armscor were dumbstruck by the decisions taken on 3 September 1985, nothing happened immediately. It was only about four months later, early in 1986, that these issues were discussed at the highest level of the Festival project. The project's strategic working group were instructed to re-examine the national strategy – but from a different perspective to that of the politicians.

They worked hard throughout that year and in November 1986 an amended strategy was submitted to the Minister of Defence and approved by him. The President read this approved document and expressed verbal agreement. Significantly, however, he did not sign it.

The proposed strategy amounted to more or less the same thing as the initial strategy of 1978 and 1985, but was spelt out in greater detail this time. Furthermore, the proposed number of nuclear weapons required to execute the strategy differed drastically from the numbers previously decided on in 1978 and September 1985.

The proposed strategy now took the following form:

- While the military threat was at a low level a strategy of opacity would be followed – nothing would be either admitted or denied and signature of the NPT was therefore out of the question. (This strategy has been successfully followed by Israel for almost 40 years and is known as *amimut*.)
- If the military threat were to increase and the balance of power appeared to have turned against South Africa, Western countries would be secretly informed about South Africa's nuclear capability.
- When the military threat became serious and South Africa was being subjected to an overwhelming threat, the strategy of deterrence would be applied in practice through an announcement of the country's nuclear capabilities, a show of force, a demonstration, and a threat to use this capability.
- If South Africa were to find itself losing the war, the nuclear capability could be put to tactical use as a deterrent. Strategic application was not envisaged, however. (In this context "strategic" means an attack on the enemy's territory and infrastructure and "tactical" refers to support for a specific military or naval operation.)

The following weapons would be required to carry out this strategy in practice:
- Six nuclear warheads for missiles (three A-type plus three boosted A*-type warheads)
- Seven nuclear weapons for use by aircraft (A-type)
- One warhead for demonstration purposes

The number of nuclear warheads planned, fourteen, was therefore double the number approved in 1985.

In order to accommodate nuclear warheads in missiles where space and weight were important factors, implosion technology had to undergo further development so that smaller devices could be built.

The limited facilities at Kentron Circle were not suitable for this job –

especially the work on missile development – and an important part of the proposed strategy therefore consisted in establishing the necessary infrastructure in a new plant a few kilometres to the east of the Circle facility. This plant was to be known as Advena. Funds were approved for the project and ample facilities were systematically built in 1988 and 1989. By the time the nuclear weapons programme was discontinued in 1989 on the instructions of the new State President, F.W. de Klerk, the building was not yet fully operational. After R36 million (in monetary value at the time) had been spent, excellent purpose-built facilities had been constructed – for which there was no longer any purpose.

The ease with which the 1985 decisions of the ad hoc cabinet committee regarding the number of weapons and the establishment of a new, expensive infrastructure were contravened involuntarily reminds one of the winged words of General Eisenhower in his farewell speech as American president: "In the councils of government, we must guard against the acquisition of unwarranted influence, whether sought or unsought, by the military-industrial complex. The potential for the disastrous rise of misplaced power exists and will persist."

The requirements of the South African Defence Force

After the September 1985 decision the military-industrial complex quietly continued with their deliberations on the place and use of nuclear weapons. The SAAF was appointed in April 1986 as the user of the nuclear and missile programmes.

The planning division of the SADF undertook an internal review of the situation and presented a report to the political and military heads of the Defence Force in July 1987. This set out the requirements foreseen by the planning division and made provision for an increased number of warheads (above the number approved in 1985) and their required delivery systems (missiles and aircraft). The report was approved by the Minister of Defence, General Magnus Malan, on 27 August 1987 with the proviso that the new proposed number of weapons would be regarded as final and that no further changes would be permitted.

Exactly two years after the decision by the ad hoc cabinet committee, the Minister of Defence and the SADF submitted the proposals to the Witvlei Council in September 1987 for further action. A detailed description of the existing status of the weapons programme and the prospective developments

THE BOMB

was attached to the agenda for the meeting. In terms of security requirements the existing code words used in the weapons programme were also changed, as will be shown later.

Status in September 1987

The Defence Force's written submission of September 1987 to the Witvlei Council gave the existing status and new code names of weapons as follows:

CODE NAME	DESCRIPTION OF THE TYPE OF WEAPONS AND DELIVERY SYSTEMS (EXISTING AND ENVISAGED)
Gardenia/Melba	The eight-year-old Melba device (previously known as Video), made by the AEC in previous years, with its placement and control systems, was collectively known as Gardenia. The design was for a device with a blast yield equivalent to 6 kilotons of TNT. Gardenia was designed for an explosion without backfilling of the test shaft. Since radioactive material could possibly be released in a test of this kind, it was regarded as a "dirty" test.
Cabot	This was a ballistic or gravity bomb design with an explosive yield equivalent to 6 kilotons of TNT. There was only one such design; it was almost six years old and was formerly known by the code name Hobo (the first weapon that was designed and built by Circle). As the weapon was technologically obsolete, it was to be withdrawn and replaced by Hamerkop weapons in time. (Because Cabot was a gravity bomb – it was to be released by an aircraft and then fall under the influence of gravity – it was called a "dumb bomb").
Hamerkop	Hamerkop weapons (formerly known as Bakker) were guided glide bombs with an explosive yield equivalent to 20 kilotons of TNT. Five such weapons were envisaged and the first one would have been ready in October 1987. They would have been launched from a Buccaneer aircraft and later from Mirage F1 and Cheetah aircraft. (Glide bombs could be guided and were therefore called "smart bombs".)
Husky	Husky was a medium-range ballistic missile that was still under development. Although certain tests had already been completed, the production of the weapons system was not intended to begin before 1996. Development work on the warhead for Husky – Project Ostra – had started but was only expected to be completed in 1996.

On the basis of this survey numerous changes were also submitted for consideration by the Witvlei Council:

ITEM	RECOMMENDATIONS
Vastrap	The test shafts had to be inspected without attracting international attention. If necessary an alternative test site had to be found and developed.
Modulus	Modulus was intended as a test device to replace Melba in 1991. The test shaft was to have been backfilled in order to ensure a clean demonstration explosion.
Warheads	Fourteen warheads were required. See below for more particulars.
Technology	The technology used for gun-type weapons had to be retained, but implosion technology had to undergo further development. Theoretical studies on other types of weapons also had to be carried out.
Y-plant	The plant would have to be kept in operation for longer. The need for stockpiling therefore fell away.

For the period 1981 to 2006 the Department of Defence budgeted an estimated amount (just for the warheads) of R406 million, of which about R26 million had already been spent (calculated in 1987 rand value). The cost of the nuclear materials required and the theoretical studies for the same period was estimated at R402 million, of which about R240 million had already been spent.

Of the fourteen proposed warheads, one was intended for Modulus, ten were intended for gun-type devices which could be used interchangeably between aircraft and ballistic missiles, and three boosted A*-type warheads would be used in medium-range missiles.

The proposals were finally discussed on 18 April 1988. The original approval given by the ad hoc cabinet committee on 3 September 1985 and the new requirements were compared and discussed. It was noted that the proposals had already been approved in writing by the Minister of Defence on 27 August 1987. However, there was one dissenting voice. Wynand de Villiers of the AEC dug in his heels and insisted that the order to increase the production of highly enriched uranium should come from his own minister (Economic Affairs and Technology at that time) and not from the Department of Defence. What was more, the Y-plant was engaged in producing low-enriched uranium as fuel for Koeberg until the new Z-plant was able to meet this need. That would only be in 1988.

The sealed test shafts at Vastrap were revisited by Armscor personnel in April 1987 and their possible future use was included in the Defence Force's report. There was thought to be an obstruction in one test shaft. Three senior Circle officials had previously obtained the coordinates of the shafts from insiders at the AEC. Their assignment was to visit the site in a van as inconspicuously as possible and inspect the shafts. The trio had to be careful because it was assumed that the Americans were still watching the area closely. One of the three officials was a meteorologist. He examined the area thoroughly, ascertained where the surveyor's beacons were and with the aid of a compass the three eventually reached the exact location of the test shafts and began to shovel the heaps of Kalahari sand out of the way to uncover the concrete protective plates. A corrugated iron shed with hoisting equipment was erected on the concrete block covering one of the shafts to shield the activities from prying eyes. The Defence Force carried out a glide bomb test at the same time, providing good cover for the discrete exploratory operation.

On inspection it was found that the shafts were partially filled with water. When that had been pumped out, the shafts were found to be intact for the rest and the shaft covered by a building was therefore ready for testing procedures in 1988.

In an interview that Or Rabinowitz had with Pik Botha in 2010, which was published by the Woodrow Wilson Center, Botha referred to the promise he made to President Reagan in 1981 that South Africa would not carry out a nuclear test without informing the USA beforehand and then added:

> There was a major meeting around about 1988, Armscor people and others wanted to make a test. We had a meeting that lasted 2–3 hours; [President] P.W. Botha was present. I strenuously objected and referred to the meeting with Reagan, [I said] "we cannot do this without informing the Americans, I am sure our office recorded the meeting, and if this [the test] happens I will immediately resign". [President] Botha fully supported me. The decision was that under no circumstance will a device be tested. Armscor people were upset about not getting the permission.

However, Rabinowitz also adds: It should be noted that Botha's account regarding this alleged test proposal by "Armscor and others" has not been corroborated by Armscor sources.

Little came of the Department of Defence's ambitious plans. While the new strategic plans were advancing at a snail's pace, events on the international and local political front were moving fast in the opposite direction. In the end the planners simply lost control of the situation just as rapidly as a skateboard can slip out from under its rider.

An indication that South Africa's policy was changing came almost simultaneously with Magnus Malan's acceptance of the revised nuclear proposals. On 21 September 1987 the 31st General Conference of the IAEA kicked off in Vienna. On the same day the South African ambassador in Vienna issued a press release on behalf of President P.W. Botha which contained the following surprising proposal, given that back home plans had been approved to extend the nuclear weapons programme:

> The Republic of South Africa is prepared to commence negotiations with each of the nuclear-weapon states on the possibility of signing the Nuclear Non-Proliferation Treaty (NPT). At the same time the Republic of South Africa will consider including in these negotiations safeguards on its installations subject to the NPT conditions. The nature of these negotiations will depend on the outcome of the 31st General Conference of the IAEA which is being held as from 21 September (1987).
>
> South Africa hopes that it will soon be able to sign the NPT and has decided to open discussions with others to this end. Any safeguards agreement which might subsequently be negotiated with the IAEA would naturally be along the same lines as, and in conformity with, agreements with other NPT signatories.

At the General Conference of the IAEA a resolution to suspend South Africa's membership of the agency was postponed. Sixty member countries supported the resolution, 20 were opposed to it and four countries abstained. The statement by P.W. Botha was obviously instrumental in preventing South Africa's expulsion from the IAEA. But what had been going through his mind, since he made this statement in the knowledge that plans had been approved to extend the weapons programme? Was it simply to buy time or did Pik Botha and his Department of Foreign Affairs spot a gap and go for it?

ELSEWHERE ON THE FARM

Koeberg, the Z-plant and Beva

Despite South Africa's abundant coal reserves, by the nineteen fifties it had become clear that the availability of cheap uranium and the advances in nuclear energy usage elsewhere in the world would mean that nuclear energy would eventually become important in meeting South Africa's energy needs. A sandy farm called Duynefontein, about 27 km outside Cape Town, was identified as a suitable site for a nuclear power station back in 1971 and purchased by Eskom. However, it was only when the Arab oil boycott was imposed on South Africa in 1973 that Eskom was able to justify the building of a nuclear power station.

The contract for the building of the power station was initially awarded to a Swiss-Dutch consortium, but this arrangement fell through as a result of a political difference of opinion in the Netherlands, which raised questions regarding insurance cover for the financial risk surrounding exports. It was decided to award the contract to a French consortium instead. On 5 August 1976 Eskom and the Framatome-Framateg consortium signed a contract for the building of the Koeberg nuclear power station. On 15 October of the same year the South African and French governments formalised the agreement by signing a bilateral treaty. This was followed by a tripartite safeguards agreement between South Africa, France and the IAEA in terms of which nuclear safeguards would be applied to the new power station.

The French were notably eager to start work. Two days after the signature of the agreement the excavation equipment was already on site! France provided favourable credit conditions and training facilities. The French were also fairly sympathetic towards South Africa's defence requirements, as illustrated by the fact that they supplied submarines, missiles and Mirage aircraft, despite the UN sanctions in force at the time. It should be remembered that the French only signed the NPT in 1992 and France was therefore not bound by the export restrictions prescribed by the treaty in respect of nuclear facilities.

After the Indian nuclear explosion in 1974 the Americans abandoned Eisenhower's Atoms for Peace project and four years later the American congress adopted the Nuclear Non-Proliferation Act, which banned the transfer of nuclear technology to states that had not signed the NPT. This Act was made retroactively applicable to all previous agreements and contracts and led directly to the cancellation of export permits that would have enabled South Africa to export enriched uranium (belonging to Eskom but having been enriched in the USA) to France for the manufacture of fuel elements for Koeberg. Eskom and the American Department of Energy (USDOE) concluded a contract in 1974 for the enrichment of the supplied uranium. By imposing this embargo the Americans were wrongfully withholding exports of enriched uranium that belonged to Eskom. A surrealistic situation arose when on top of everything else the USDOE held Eskom fully responsible for paying the account for the enrichment work done on American soil.

At the end of 1981 South Africa succeeded in acquiring 130 tons of low-enriched uranium from Kaiseraugst in Switzerland, along with a certain quantity of low-enriched uranium from Synatom in Belgium, for the manufacture of fuel for Koeberg.

It was only in 1982 that the absurd situation with the Americans was (partially) resolved after the election of Ronald Reagan and the intervention of Pik Botha as described earlier. The US government decided that France could be allowed to manufacture and deliver fuel for Koeberg. However, it was stipulated that the enriched uranium which Eskom was to supply to France should not have been sourced in the USA. Fortunately the enriched material that Eskom had already obtained in Europe did meet this requirement. The deadlock regarding Eskom nuclear material sourced in the USA was finally resolved in 1984 when the Americans allowed Eskom to sell their unenriched UF_6 material, together with their enriched uranium, to an NPT country, naturally depending on American approval. Eskom suffered a big financial loss as a result of this transaction.

The following month the US government allowed Westinghouse Corporation (the original designers of the reactor) to provide Koeberg with technical equipment and assistance with maintenance. Between 1983 and 1984 the South African government quietly recruited 25 American reactor operators and technicians to work at Koeberg. (Unsuccessful attempts were subsequently made in the USA to bring criminal charges against these people on the grounds that they had consented to do contract work in South Africa.)

On 9 September 1985 President Ronald Reagan of the USA announced a decision which placed new restrictions on nuclear trade with South Africa, although it did permit certain exports. The restrictions still made it possible to enlist IAEA assistance in respect of safeguards or technological aid programmes that promoted non-proliferation, or exports the American government considered necessary "for humanitarian reasons to ensure public safety". However, John Herrington, the Minister of Energy, decided that any such assistance excluded American citizens from taking up employment at Koeberg.

THE BOMB

> ## Koeberg nuclear power plant
>
> *The Koeberg nuclear power plant is situated at Melkbosstrand on the West Coast, just north of Milnerton. It is currently the only power station of its kind in Africa, with the biggest turbine generators in the Southern Hemisphere. The station was built by the French firm Framatome, but is basically an American Westinghouse design. It consists of two units, each with a capacity of about 900 megawatts. A single unit's initial fuel requirement is about 100 tons of uranium dioxide between 3,5 and 4% enriched. When the plant is refuelled annually (these days every eighteen months), about 25 tons of fresh fuel is required.*
>
> *The reactor core consists of fuel elements in water which serves as both the moderator for the nuclear chain reaction and the coolant. The water is under high pressure, which permits the temperature to rise to 450 °C. This type of reactor is also known as a pressurised water reactor or PWR. The fuel elements in the reactor core release heat as a result of the chain reaction in the enriched uranium.*
>
> *Each fuel element consists of an assembly of 17 x 17 zirconium alloy tubes, each about 4 m long and 10 mm thick, filled with ceramic uranium oxide pellets. Each pellet is the size of a fingertip and is cylindrical in shape. A single pellet contains the energy equivalent of over 800 kg of coal. Depending on the design, about 150 fuel elements are loaded into the reactor.*
>
> *Used fuel elements are physically hot and are kept in deep pools of water for cooling purposes. The elements are not described as "used" because all the uranium has been used up. In reality only a fraction of the enriched uranium has been used up. The problem is rather to be found in the build-up of fission products which are formed by the chain reaction and which later begin to retard the reaction. In some countries – such as France, England and Japan – after being stored for some years to allow it to cool, the used fuel is processed in reprocessing plants to extract the unused uranium and newly formed plutonium for use in new fuel, which is known as mixed oxide (MOX) fuel.*

The two Koeberg reactors were eventually supplied with fuel from France and commissioned in 1984 and 1985. But before the official opening could take place the project had to survive a very destructive attack. At the beginning of the 1980s Koeberg's operational staff, headed by Paul Semark, had just returned from intensive training in France. These courses were presented by the nuclear energy department of Électricité de France (EDF). This was a busy, stressful period for the team members. They had had no previous experience of power stations, but they now had to develop infrastructure as well as operating procedures, maintenance guidelines and emergency procedures.

In December 1982 their job was made a lot more difficult when members of the ANC's military wing, Umkhonto we Sizwe, sabotaged the Koeberg power station by planting limpet mines in strategic positions. Four explosions took place in the space of two days. The damage amounted to about R500 million and delayed the completion of the plant by about eighteen months. Fortunately the explosions occurred before any nuclear material had been loaded and no one was killed or injured in the incidents.

The ANC issued a statement from Dar es Salaam describing the sabotage as "a salute to all our fallen heroes and imprisoned comrades, and to those buried in Maseru". ("Maseru" was a reference to ANC members who were killed during a previous cross-border raid by the SADF.)

Two of the saboteurs, the Wilkinson couple, applied for and received amnesty from the Truth and Reconciliation Commission (TRC) in 1999.

Rodney Lawrence Wilkinson and his wife Heather were members of the ANC's military wing. Douglas Birch of the Center for Public Integrity revealed the following in an article, "South African who attacked a nuclear plant is hero to his government and fellow citizens", which appeared on 17 March 2015: Wilkinson stole blueprints for Koeberg and presented them in Harare to Mac Maharaj, who was until recently presidential adviser to President Zuma. According to Maharaj, he had the blueprints authenticated and subsequently gave instructions to Wilkinson to carry out the act of sabotage. Years later the Wilkinsons openly admitted to the TRC that they had been members of a special operational unit of Umkhonto we Sizwe which had been ordered by the party to sabotage the power station. This was part of the ANC's overall strategy to attack "apartheid installations". The couple planned the attack together. It fell to Rodney Wilkinson to put their plans into action in December 1982 and plant four limpet mines at specific points.

According to Ian McRae, the executive officer of Eskom between 1985 and 1994, the first explosion at Koeberg took place in the reactor head mechanism of the first reactor. The second explosion occurred inside the head mechanism of the second reactor. The third and fourth explosions occurred in the cellars, inside the cable trays within which the cables were laid.

A few days after the explosions McRae received an interesting call from the operational head of the EDF in France. They knew each other well. According to the Frenchman he was convinced that the sabotage was not the work of locals or anti-government groups. In his opinion an anti-nuclear power group had been imported from Europe to carry out this act of sabotage and had infiltrated the construction team at the Koeberg site.

A virtually identical attack had taken place on French soil in 1975 when the Baader-Meinhof gang sabotaged the Fessenheim nuclear power plant close to the German border. Four bombs were placed at four different points within the power plant and set to go off within hours of each other – exactly like at Koeberg. One was placed inside the reactor head of the first reactor. The others were placed in the cable trays and in the information centre. The saboteurs did not place a bomb in the second reactor head, however, and it was therefore possible to use this head in the first reactor. In the case of Koeberg the saboteurs did place a bomb in the second reactor head, thereby causing enormous damage and huge delays in the construction work.

In view of McRae's strong conviction that the Baader-Meinhof gang had been involved, the question arises who authenticated the Koeberg blueprints for Mac Maharaj, as the ANC did not have any expertise of that kind within Umkhonto we Sizwe.

EDF sent some of their senior staff to South Africa to assist Eskom and the police with their investigations and remained convinced that the saboteurs had been "imported" from Europe.

In August 1983 the French firm Framatome repaired a set of eighteen control rod drive mechanisms and returned them to Koeberg. In the meanwhile the power plant was examined for leaks following the news that the French cladding material had begun to show cracks.

After all this drama Unit 1 of the Koeberg power plant was eventually formally commissioned on 7 April 1984. The second phase of the power plant began to deliver power for the first time on 25 July 1985.

More "sabotage" – of a kind that casts a long, dark shadow

On Christmas Day 2005 Koeberg-1 was ready to start generating power again after maintenance and refuelling. But when the turbines started turning there was chaos. There was a loose bolt in a turbine which did catastrophic damage to the rapidly rotating blades. Minister Alec Erwin, who was responsible for the Department of Public Enterprises at that time, immediately described the incident as a possible act of sabotage by a mysterious, right-wing "Boeremag" that allegedly deliberately planted the bolt in the turbine. Not long afterwards he – in the manner of a wily politician – denied that he had ever made any such allegation. The damage was done, however, and by a stroke of bad luck Koeberg-2 was also scheduled for maintenance and refuelling. That left the Cape without power and electricity had to be urgently imported from the north. The President had to appeal shamefacedly to the French for help. The French president, Nicolas Sarkozy, was kind enough to arrange for a new rotor to be supplied and by May 2006 Koeberg-1 was again able to start producing power. The "sabotage" turned out to be nothing more than poor and negligent workmanship, testimony to Eskom's managerial shortcomings – a portent of things to come…

This problem proved to be the proverbial first neutron in the chain reaction. The power situation slowly deteriorated and by the end of 2007 and beginning of 2008 it had assumed catastrophic proportions. In January 2008 the country's electricity supply was on the brink of total collapse and the mines had to stop operating. Industry and business lost millions of rand; for example, big chain stores had to discard all their frozen products. Suddenly a new term was on everybody's lips. The sporadic blackouts were given the euphemistic name of "load-shedding" – a new concept in this country.

The politicians were falling over themselves in an effort to explain. The most popular explanation was that the South African economy had grown more rapidly than had been planned, but the figures refuted that explanation. Actual growth had been only half the planned growth. The truth was somewhat different. Eskom had decided in 2000 that its coal supply was too large and had started selling some of it. In that year the supply was sufficient for 61 days' production, but seven years later that had dropped to eighteen days. This action, together with the poor quality

> of the coal supplied by the new black economic empowerment companies, triggered a catastrophe. When heavy rains fell in December and January 2008 on top of everything else, Eskom's goose was cooked. An Eskom spokesman acknowledged that the coal that had been supplied was mainly coal dust and that in conjunction with the very heavy rains it had turned into mud – and they couldn't get the mud to burn. Things began to improve after May 2008 and the public was able to pack away their old-fashioned candles as well as their trendy – and very costly – new generators, at least for a while.
>
> The lessons of 2008 were soon forgotten, however, and six years later Eskom was again trying to explain why further load-shedding had to be introduced in March 2014 and continues to this day with generating units failing randomly due to neglect to maintain them properly, organisational disarray and political skulduggery.

The Z- and U-plants and Beva

The protracted problems and uncertainty surrounding the acquisition of nuclear fuel for Koeberg in the midst of the sanctions campaign were a real headache. At Pelindaba three large and specialised plants were being constructed with all possible speed. These were the uranium conversion plant (U-plant), the semi-commercial or Z uranium enrichment plant and Beva, the fuel manufacturing plant, which had to be built specially for Koeberg to secure the fuel supply. If Koeberg had run out of fuel and had to stand idle the cost in the rand value of the day would have been R1 million per day for the repayment of loans and loss of income. It was therefore cheaper to build a large enrichment plant in South Africa than to rely on capricious foreign suppliers.

The Z-plant, like the pilot plant, consisted essentially of the following elements: compressors to send the process gas at supersonic speed through the Ucor separative elements, heat exchangers to cool the hot compressed gas, connecting pipes and valves to connect the various modules into a cascade, autoclaves (ovens) to evaporate the UF_6 in the process and cooling stations to extract the enriched and depleted UF_6. However, there were a few notable and highly innovative differences.

THE BOMB IN THE BUSHVELD

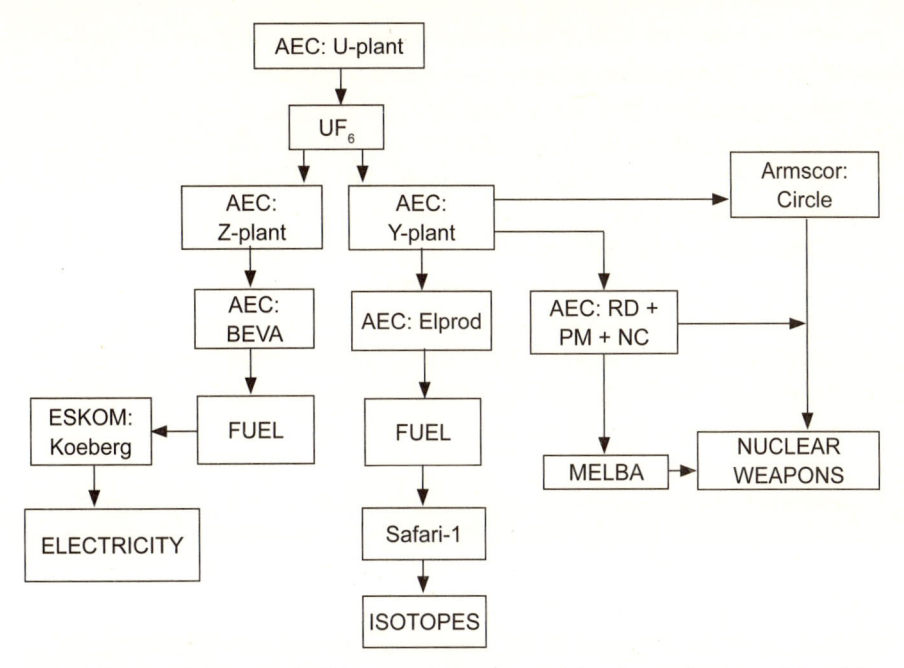

AEC, Eskom and Armscor facilities were interconnected for the production of electricity, isotopes and nuclear weapons.
(Remark: Safari fuel elements were manufactured at Elprod ; RD=reactor development; PM=Physical metallurgy; NC=nuclear chemistry)

Firstly, the separative capacity had to be considerably greater, namely 300 000 kg SWU (instead of the 20 000 SWU of the Y-plant), to supply the basic refuelling needs of the two Koeberg reactors. Drastic upgrading was required to produce these volumes. The equipment and buildings were physically far bigger than those of the Y-plant.

The Ucor separation element was characterised by a small cut. This means the enriched stream that leaves a separation element is only one-twentieth of the inlet stream. This is the price that has to be paid for a higher separation factor. However, the implications of this situation were that nineteen separate streams at slightly different levels of enrichment had to be moved along without their mixing. If separate compressors and pipelines had had to be used for each of these streams the cost would have been prohibitive.

This was where ingenuity – the typical "Boer maak 'n plan" approach – resulted in a breakthrough in which Dr Pierre Haarhoff and Dr Jannie Wannenburg played a prominent part. Haarhoff and Wannenburg discovered that gas streams with different compositions can be compressed simultaneously by an axial flow compressor (think of a Boeing or Airbus engine) and emerge on the other side without any notable mixing. Intuitively it was difficult to accept that such a large "egg beater" could handle gases with such a light touch. The engineers therefore borrowed an old Boeing engine from the SAA to demonstrate the principle in practice.

With the aid of this technique – which they christened the Helikon technique – all nineteen streams could be moved along at a particular point in the cascade in a single, compact module. It should be remembered that "compact" is a relative concept. Each module was 4 m in diameter, 22 m in length and had a mass of about 120 tons. A module contained 400 separation element assemblies and two water-cooled heat exchangers. At both ends of the module there were two axial flow compressors, called Mamba and Cheetah, which were turned by electric motors. These were not your everyday electric motors but monsters that gobbled up electricity by the megawatt. In fact the electricity consumption of this plant was equal to that of Port Elizabeth, including the consumption of all the local industries.

Large connecting pipes with internal divisions linked the modules to form a cascade. Four-way valves had the ability to separate individual modules from the cascade and permit internal circulation without interrupting the flow in the cascade. There was a story attached to these valves. At one stage during the design process problems arose which were solved with the aid of a certain Gerhard Wisser of Krisch Engineering in Johannesburg and his contacts in Germany. Many years later Wisser was to clash with the South African justice system over other, more sinister enterprises.

The size of the building housing the 56 modules was truly impressive. From a control corridor above the level of the modules one had a bird's eye view of the whole process. This corridor was so long that the operating staff had to use bicycles to monitor the various control panels. It was truly a monument to engineering excellence and ingenuity – the first and last of its kind in the world.

Civil construction work on the Z-plant began in July 1979. It was one of a large number of building projects being constructed at the site almost simultaneously.

The uranium conversion plant (U-plant), where uranium concentrates obtained from the mines were converted into UF_6, was one of those projects. This was essentially a big chemical plant where extremely corrosive and dangerous chemicals such as fluorine gas and hydrofluoric acid were used to produce the feed material (UF_6) for the Z-plant.

The U-plant started operating in 1986. The highly capable chemical engineer, designer and manager of the plant was Dr Rod Colborn. Once the plant was running smoothly he decided to leave and go and study medicine! He qualified as a doctor at the Cape Town University and shortly afterwards he was appointed as deputy dean of the local medical faculty.

In view of the size of the Z-plant and the complex machinery required, it took eight years before the plant became fully operational in 1987 with Piet Bredell in charge. The big, cumbersome enrichment modules weighing 120 tons each were assembled in a separate part of the building and then slowly moved on air cushions and placed in their operating positions. The floor of the building had to be given a smooth and even finish so that the surface made this type of transport possible – one of the many innovations that were necessary.

Just over the hill a whole complex of new buildings was springing up at the same time. This was Beva, the fuel element manufacturing plant. The enriched UF_6 received from the Z-plant was converted at Beva into a uranium oxide powder which was then sintered (baked) at a high temperature to a ceramic form. This was the material from which the thousands of small cylindrical pellets were manufactured with precision. These were packed into zirconium alloy tubes (fuel rods) and welded closed to form the basic constituents of a Koeberg fuel element. The plant was completed in 1986 and commissioned. Noel Pienaar was in charge of Beva, which was established with the aid of much French expertise. Waldo Stumpf was later to succeed him before being appointed CEO of the AEC.

The substantial progress made was reflected in the proud announcement by John Marais, Chairman of the AEC, on 26 May 1987 to the effect that South Africa's nuclear fuel cycle programme would be able to operate independently by 1988, without international help. He also stated that Koeberg would use locally enriched uranium and that Safari-1 had been running on locally made fuel since 1981.

Beva's output was initially modest. At first only a few individual fuel rods were manufactured and then irradiated at Koeberg before being examined in the hot cell complex at the Pelindaba site for integrity and possible damage. The fuel rods passed this test with flying colours. The first four full fuel elements made in South Africa were completed in 1988 and sent to Koeberg.

It is no easy task to manufacture full fuel elements that pass all the safety and operating tests. It is a very time-consuming and difficult process. An agreement was therefore concluded with the French firm Framatome (currently Areva) to certify the Beva fuel elements as "equivalent to French elements". Certification was naturally dependent on continuous French inspection and testing during the manufacturing process, and a fee had to be paid.

The enriched uranium was initially not obtained from the Z-plant, but from the usual old willing horse, the Y-plant, which had to be specially reconfigured to produce low-enriched uranium throughout 1986, since the Z-plant was not yet production-ready.

Once South Africa had signed the NPT in 1991, the threat of sanctions soon diminished. By December 1991 the USA had approved a partial reduction of sanctions and in September 1993 Nelson Mandela requested the UNSC to lift sanctions completely. This was approved by the UNSC a month later.

Relations between the mighty Eskom – at one time the biggest sole provider of electricity in the world and currently among the seven top producers – and the much smaller but cooperative AEC were always somewhat strained over the years. Matters were further complicated by differences in their corporate cultures. The group of reactor scientists at Eskom were mainly British, and the AEC was staffed by Afrikaners and a few English-speaking South Africans.

At one stage Eskom seriously considered enriching its own uranium. When the sanctions problem began to disappear, Eskom summarily turned its back on the AEC because it was able to get nuclear fuel more cheaply elsewhere. In this respect the AEC was not able to compete with the big nuclear-weapon states on an economically viable scale. All the hard work, innovative technical breakthroughs and millions of rands spent to help get Eskom out of trouble suddenly counted for nothing. On 31 March 1995 the Z-plant therefore had to be closed and the associated U-plant and Beva similarly became redundant – a sad day when years of pioneering work undertaken to establish a unique, indigenous nuclear fuel cycle capacity in South Africa came tumbling down like a house of cards because of Eskom's reckless pursuit of its own interests. This may help explain why, thirteen years later, Eskom sold its own coal reserves and plunged South Africa into primeval darkness.

Although in time Eskom abandoned its plans to enrich its own uranium, it still cherished a grandiose vision, namely to design and build its own reactor. The driving force behind this ideal was Dave Nicholls, a Brit with an engineering background who had worked on British nuclear submarines earlier in his career. In 1993 work began on the development of a new type of reactor, the pebble-bed modular reactor (PBMR). A number of specialised AEC staff members, who had lost their jobs as a result of the compulsory closure of the AEC facilities, were again able to earn an income from this development. But seventeen years and R9 billion later the government finally decided in September 2010 that it would have to pull the plug. Possibly someone eventually realised how difficult it would be to sell a new type of reactor, for which there had never been a demonstrable commercial application anywhere in the world, on the international market. Furthermore, the reactor would always carry the ambivalent label "Made in Africa".

Eskom's PBMR

A pebble-bed nuclear reactor, generally known as a PBMR, differs considerably from the pressurised water reactors used in Koeberg. The coolant is not water but helium gas and the moderator (to reduce the speed of fast neutrons) is graphite. Another name for the reactor is a high temperature gas-cooled reactor (HTGR).

Unlike the assembly of long fuel rods which are bundled together in fuel elements and used in Koeberg, small, enriched uranium dioxide granules are encased in several layers of carbon, pyrolitic graphite and silicon carbide, mixed with graphite, compressed and sintered (baked) to form spherical fuel balls which are the size of a tennis ball. Each ball contains about 15 000 such encased uranium dioxide granules. Fuel balls are let into the reactor from above and move slowly to the bottom under gravity and are then removed and returned to the top. After the remaining uranium content has been measured, the balls can be recirculated or discharged into waste containers. A full load could consist of about 452 000 fuel balls.

As a result of the chain reaction produced in the fuel the helium gas is heated to about 900 °C. This heated gas is used directly to drive a turbine which generates electricity. The fuel balls are designed to withstand temperatures of up to 1 130 °C.

The technology was originally developed in Germany where a prototype of a 15-megawatt PBMR was designed and built and operated intermittently from 1967 to 1988. The technology was developed with a view to sales to Russia, but when that hope was frustrated the project was abandoned in 1991.

A number of important modifications were made to the original design for the South African PBMR, which was intended to produce between 125 and 165 megawatts.

A significant difference between the German and the South African varieties was that with the German design the hot helium gas underwent considerable cooling before it reached the turbines. The South African design, which did not use interim cooling, would probably have encountered numerous materials-related problems at the high operating temperature (900 °C).

Several foreign companies showed interest and bought shares in the project. The American company, Exelon, was initially a shareholder but withdrew after a time. British Nuclear Fuels (BNFL) was another shareholder, but their shares were later taken over by Westinghouse, the big American reactor builder. Towards the end of the project the main shareholders were Westinghouse, together with the South African government, Eskom and the Industrial Development Corporation (IDC).

The original plan was to start building a demonstration plant in 2006 on the Koeberg site, to commission it in 2010 and then to hand the plant over to Eskom in 2011. In February 2009 a significant change in strategy was announced, however. The building of a 165-megawatt demonstration reactor at Koeberg had been called off and the PBMR company had announced that the focus would shift from electricity generation to the generation of heat which could be used in the Sasol process or to desalinate water. The writing was on the wall as far as government funding was concerned and besides, some serious technical problems that had the potential to increase the eventual costs substantially still had to be solved.

Ultimately the coffers ran dry and a potentially promising and innovative product followed the same route as the famous Rooivalk helicopter – an excellent local product that nobody wanted to buy. Today Westinghouse – which as the biggest player in that field would never have lightly risked money on something they didn't believe in – has the technology and the Chinese are systematically and judiciously building their own version. Possibly South Africa's mistake was not to have followed the Chinese approach. The South Africans wanted to progress too rapidly to the finished product without proceeding step by step. That book has still to be written, however, and will probably provide material for many an MBA case study in future.

PART 4

THE END OF AN ERA

Butterflies and chaos

In 1960 the meteorologist Edward Lorenz was engaged in investigating complex mathematical models for the purpose of predicting the weather when the pressing desire for a cup of coffee interrupted his work. With sufficient caffeine in his system he decided to repeat his work, but to save time he resumed his task in the middle of his calculations instead of at the beginning. To his astonishment his results were completely different from those of the earlier calculations. After a bit of head scratching he realised that he had rounded off one figure from six decimal places to three. He was astounded to find that such a small difference could have had such an enormous effect. He had discovered what is now known as the butterfly effect. The small difference in the initial figures used in the calculation can be compared with the flapping of a butterfly's wings, causing a very slight change in local atmospheric conditions that could, in time, lead to a tornado on the other side of the globe. As a result of this sensitivity to initial conditions, and especially when relatively little information is available (for example on temperature, atmospheric pressure, humidity etc), a meteorological system would no longer be predictable after a while. This is why it is not really possible in practice to predict the weather for more than a week ahead.

This was the origin of so-called chaos theory, or the study of the behaviour of dynamic systems which are very sensitive to small changes in initial conditions. Today this theory is applied in various disciplines, including mathematics, biology, economics, politics and psychology.

The butterfly in the USSR

> "It's only a matter of time before the Soviet Union falls apart.
> They've got no food, because you can't farm with civil servants."
> (translation)
>
> Dr S.J. du Toit, member of senior management at Ucor, 1975

Was the dramatic dissolution of the Union of Socialist Soviet Republics (USSR) on Christmas Day 1991, three-quarters of a century after the outbreak of the revolution in 1917, the result of the flapping of a butterfly's wings? Did the flapping possibly take the specific form of the death of Stalin in March 1953? Joseph Stalin held the USSR together – with its over 100 nationalities distributed over a territory one-and-a-half times the size of the USA – by a combination of brutal, murderous actions and an exaggerated personality cult.

Or was it possibly the rough but pragmatic Nikita Khrushchev who was in the habit of pounding on the table with his shoe to drive home some point of argument? During a closed session of the Twentieth Congress of the Communist Party in 1956 he denounced Stalin, settling the score for his murderous past and thereby destroying a sacred party symbol. So drastic was the effect of this turnabout that a dozen or so delegates collapsed during the proceedings. The General Secretary of the Polish Communist Party died of a heart attack and a famous Stalinist writer shot himself the following day. The butterfly had flapped its wings with deafening effect!

But it was also possible that the butterfly effect in the USSR was triggered by the election of Mikhail Gorbachev on 10 March 1985. He had good intentions when he took up the post of Soviet president. The terms *glasnost* (openness) and *perestroika* (restructuring) became part of the international political vocabulary. However, he had an albatross around his neck, namely the war in Afghanistan, which had been in progress for six years by that time. In addition, a year after he took office as president of the USSR the biggest nuclear accident up to that time occurred at the Chernobyl nuclear plant. But Gorbachev's biggest headache was caused by his struggle with the closed and hidebound political order. His progressive methods did not suit some of the arch-conservatives and during a short but unsuccessful coup d'état Gorbachev and his family were placed under house arrest for a few months. Although he was able to resume his duties as President of the Soviet Union with the support of Boris Yeltsin and other sympathisers, Gorbachev had sustained a mortal political wound. In order to regain control, he therefore left the Communist Party and dissolved the party's central committee. He also began attempting to loosen the party's grip on the KGB and the army. This proved to be more than the intractable system could cope with. The central, brutal force that had held the whole system together for three-quarters of a century shattered. As if propelled by centrifugal force, the parts split into a loose confederation of independent states bespeckled with a collection of nouveau riche oligarchs. In 1991, on Christmas Day, Gorbachev resigned. At the end of the same year the lights went out for all the institutions of the old communist regime.

It had been clear to the West for a long time that the USSR was in extremis, and the end was therefore not entirely unexpected. The Iron Curtain was torn open on 19 August 1989 when a rickety farm gate at Sopron on the border between Hungary and Austria was opened for East German refugees. Within three weeks 10 000 of them had crossed over to freedom without the usual hail of AK-47 bullets. A month or two later the East German government fell and on 9 November 1989 the detested Berlin Wall was demolished.

The death throes of the USSR brought relief to South Africa as well. In May 1988 an American mediation team led by Chester Crocker took the opportunity to initiate dialogue between South Africa, Angola and Cuba, with the USSR as observer. The aim was eventually to implement the UNSC's Resolution 455 on peace in Southern Africa. The first of twelve talks took place in London on 2 May 1988. Neil van Heerden, the Director-General of the Department of Foreign Affairs, led the South African delegation. In *Pik Botha and His Times* Van Heerden's impressions are described as follows: "For the first time we saw the Cubans across the negotiating table: very aggressive men with heavy beards and thick cigars."

These talks got an important boost during a Moscow summit between the American President, Ronald Reagan, and his Russian counterpart, Mikhail Gorbachev, in May-June 1988. It was agreed that the Cuban troops would withdraw from Angola and that Soviet military aid would be discontinued as soon as South African troops withdrew from Namibia. This tripartite agreement between South Africa, Angola and Cuba, the so-called Brazzaville Protocol, was signed on 22 December 1988, after seven months of diplomatic jousting. Control over Namibia was then transferred from South Africa to the UN. The practical implementation of the agreement commenced on 1 April 1989.

In an interview with Padraig O'Malley in November 2001, Pik Botha gave a clear account of the differences that became evident in the South African camp between the diplomats and the soldiers during the negotiating phase. In *Pik Botha and His Times* Theresa Papenfus describes Botha's impressions of his military co-negotiators:

> Military people are cast in a different mould. To put it simply: they have been trained to identify a target or the enemy, and see whether they have the necessary men, weapons, ammunition and capability to attack and destroy it. That particular kind of military thinking, planning and action leaves little room for flexibility.

"What always struck me was that before we left for a round of talks they would want a document that spelled out the purpose of the negotiations, with all the advantages and disadvantages. Well, I always rejected that. I said: This business is like playing soccer or rugby; you can have the best coach and plan on the sidelines, but the match is won on the field, where you have to take quick decisions and you cannot rehearse your reactions in advance. That, I think, with respect, describes the difference between typical military thinking and Foreign Affairs thinking. It also applied in South Africa, where the military community saw a serious threat in the 50 000 Cuban troops in our region, supported as they were by the Soviet Union.

While the peace negotiations were still in progress, another initiative pointed to a marked change in South Africa's policy. On 16 September 1988 (shortly before the conclusion of the IAEA's annual general conference), Hans Blix of the IAEA received a letter from South Africa expressing the country's willingness to sign the NPT if certain conditions were met, primarily that South Africa be allowed to market its uranium, subject to IAEA safeguards.

This letter followed talks held on 11 and 12 August between a South African delegation (which included the Ministers of Foreign Affairs and Economic Affairs and Technology) and the three NPT depositary states, namely the USSR, Britain and the USA in Vienna. Since the delegates were unable to reach agreement on all the items on the agenda, from 5 September the South Africans went ahead and discussed this issue with the representatives of another thirty or so countries. At a press conference held on 13 August, Pik Botha said he was not convinced that Hans Blix wanted to see South Africa as a fully fledged member of the IAEA ...

The very next day Blix issued a press release in which he rather sarcastically pointed out that the talks the South African representatives had held in August concerned only the NPT's so-called depositary states and that neither he nor anyone else from the IAEA was involved. He also declared that he would personally welcome South Africa's entry to the NPT – but he said nothing about IAEA membership ...

At that stage, South Africa, after the signing of the Brazzaville Protocol, was rid of an expensive and unpopular war. The rearing of the new baby, Namibia, would be the responsibility of the UN in future. The time had come to focus on other matters. As fate would have it, there was a change of leadership as well. President P.W. Botha resigned as the leader of the NP on 2 February

1989 following a stroke on 18 January of that year. He stayed on as President, however, and F.W. de Klerk was elected party leader. This was the beginning of a period of conflict between the two politicians. On 6 April P.W. Botha announced that parliament would be dissolved at the end of May and a general election held in September. He announced at the same time that he would not stand for the presidency. The conflict between Botha and De Klerk increased to such an extent that by 14 August Botha had resigned as President. F.W. de Klerk was sworn in as Acting President; he was officially confirmed in the post of President on 20 September 1989 after the election of 6 September. The table had been laid for a new era, with a new leader and a new vision.

The new broom

F.W. de Klerk took the helm and set a new course as a statesman when he started discussions with Nelson Mandela - still in jail at the time – on 13 December 1989. On 2 February 1990 De Klerk announced the unbanning of the African National Congress (ANC), the Pan Africanist Congress (PAC) and other anti-apartheid organisations in parliament. Nelson Mandela was released on 11 February. At that stage De Klerk could not have guessed what violent storms he would have to weather and where the course he had set would eventually take him. On 18 April 1990 in a speech to parliament he was still excluding the possibility of a black majority government, but after violence from left and right-wing political groups, coups d'état in the homelands and serious black-on-black violence in Natal, there were times when a shipwreck appeared inevitable. The ensuing political events could fill volumes, but they fall outside the scope of this book.

President De Klerk also decided not only to set South Africa's political house in order but also to try to improve its international image. An important step in this direction would be to sign the NPT.

Over the years there was sustained international pressure on South Africa to sign the NPT. Back in October 1977 African states tried to persuade the UNSC to forbid any form of nuclear cooperation with South Africa, but the USA opposed this step because limited cooperation was seen as a means of exerting pressure on the pariah state with a view to getting it to sign the NPT. In 1979 matters took a more serious turn when South Africa was expelled from the General Conference of the IAEA in India by means of a resolution which demanded that South Africa sign the NPT and open up all its facilities for IAEA inspections. The Vela incident, which took place in the same month in which the meeting was held, naturally also had a significant influence on events. There were even speculations in the press that the allegations by the USA about a South African-Israeli nuclear test were actually intended to put pressure on South Africa to sign the NPT.

In South Africa there was an ongoing debate on the advantages and disadvantages of signing the NPT. The big obstacle was Valindaba's Y-plant or pilot plant where the highly enriched material for the nuclear weapons programme was produced, and then naturally the programme as well. As long as South Africa saw a purpose in the production and possession of nuclear weapons, it was impossible to sign the NPT. The IAEA did carry out inspections at the Safari reactor and at Koeberg but had no right to go any further than these facilities.

In January 1984 the IAEA published a statement by Wynand de Villiers in terms of which South Africa undertook to conduct the country's nuclear activities in accordance with the spirit, objectives and principles of the NPT, but without officially signing the treaty. De Villiers also indicated that South Africa was prepared to resume negotiations with respect to the application of IAEA safeguards to the Z-plant, but not the Y-plant.

This statement was followed a year later by a "fishing expedition" by the USA; a popular US strategy is to offer information and technical assistance in an area which is new or unfamiliar to a particular country. During interaction with the grateful recipient country the Americans naturally learn a great deal about – and also see a great deal of – that country's processes and facilities. Accordingly a substantial delegation, consisting of officials from the USA's Department of State and Department of Energy, as well as nuclear-related industries like Martin Marietta, visited the AEC in 1985.

When any nuclear plant is placed under IAEA safeguards, comprehensive technical information has to be supplied in advance so that the IAEA has a thorough understanding of the process before deciding how and where safeguards should be applied. In the 1960s the US Department of Energy, USDOE, started to develop gas centrifuge technology to replace the very expensive gaseous diffusion plants. Construction of a centrifuge enrichment plant began in the early 1980s. The intention was to place this plant under IAEA safeguards and discussions with the Agency in this regard were well advanced. The carrot on a stick held out to South Africa was the experience gained in their interaction with the IAEA – it was also a first for the US since none of their enrichment plants had ever been placed under safeguards. This carrot was not real, however, because firstly the USA as a nuclear-weapon state was not obliged to subject any plant to IAEA safeguards and secondly the project was abandoned in the same year, 1985. Nevertheless, the delegation took the following line: "We (that is, the USA and South Africa) are the good guys; the IAEA are awkward customers; let us show you how to handle them."

The American delegation was led by the ageing, affable and highly experienced Carl Thorne, noted for his preference for wearing old-fashioned red braces. He was accompanied by a bunch of colourful characters. They included Carlton Stoiber, a man of few words, who habitually drew pencil sketches of the participants at meetings. Jörg Menzel from the American State Department was a bit of an oddball because during relaxed intervals before and after meetings he used to tell stories about his early years in Germany when he belonged to the Hitler Youth movement, and because, despite that background, he was working for the Americans. He even spoke with a slight German accent. The perception in the USA at that time was that South Africa was governed by a bunch of Nazi sympathisers. The fact that Menzel came out of the closet as an old Hitler Youth member was probably a tactic intended to gain the confidence of any AEC staff members who might be harbouring right-wing sentiments. This plan fell flat, however.

The South Africans were also struck by the fact that many members of the US delegation turned up often in later years at international conferences and meetings but in different capacities, shuttling between a number of state, semi-state and nuclear-related bodies. It seemed probable that some of them were "spooks" in the service of the CIA or one of the many other American intelligence agencies.

Any information the AEC supplied on the Z-plant was lapped up by the American delegation. There was an "innocent" reference to the Y-plant (about which the Americans were obviously curious), but the South Africans simply ignored that. As a gesture of goodwill – and probably also in an attempt to show off – the Americans were taken on a tour of the Z-plant. As explained previously, the plant had a very long control corridor where the operational staff had to use bicycles. From this corridor one could look down through windows onto the impressive 56 separation modules, each larger than a railway carriage. The Americans were duly impressed and were keen to see more. They were told that they were restricted to the control corridor. The process floor was out of bounds because of the risk that the hydrogen used in the process could cause an explosion. One of the visitors remarked drily: "And all these guys with the shotguns, then?" There was a security officer armed with a shotgun lurking around every corner – the risk of an explosion notwithstanding ...

They were probably even more amused when they drove back to Pretoria after the visit. Their minibus was escorted to the main road by the Broederstroom horse commando, with riders armed to the teeth on both sides of the bus. Why Wally Grant ignored the objections of top management at the AEC and decided on this somewhat archaic show of force is something of a mystery. Possibly he was trying to pander to the supposed American affinity for cowboys? Years later one of the American delegates made the laconic comment: "We thought the show was really bizarre. Here we come, suspecting that you were building a nuclear bomb in secret and we see those magnificent enrichment modules – something we've never seen anywhere in the world – and then the charge of the cavalry?"

The somewhat irascible Hans Blix was invited to visit South Africa in 1989. In June of that year he was taken on a guided tour of the AEC's facilities. An AEC tie that was presented to him at a dinner later became a permanent item of his daily office attire, to be repeatedly recognised by AEC visitors to the IAEA in the next decade. He may well have developed a soft spot for South Africa.

However, the Y-plant and the weapons programme remained an obstacle to any further discussions.

President De Klerk was to change all this.

The "Mantel" Project

Waldo Stumpf relates that shortly after F.W. de Klerk became President in September 1989 he attended a meeting at which the new head of state candidly described his vision. Nelson Mandela was to be released and South Africa should sign the NPT and in so doing become part of the international community again. At an ad hoc cabinet committee meeting in November 1989 (at which Magnus Malan and Dawie de Villiers, the new Minister of Mineral and Energy Affairs, were present) F.W. de Klerk put his plans into action. The AEC, Armscor and the Defence Force were instructed to terminate the nuclear weapons programme immediately.

The Y-plant was to cease production and the weapons were to be dismantled in preparation for South Africa's entry to the NPT. The parties concerned were asked to supply an urgent schedule for this and outline the procedures to be followed.

Consequently the last highly enriched uranium was drawn off at the Y-plant in November 1989 and the plant was subsequently operated in such a way that the isotopic concentration of the UF_6 was lowered to that of natural uranium by mixing the contents of the cascade. The plant was finally switched off on 1 February 1990.

After this the dismantling process began in all earnest and top secret documents were circulated back and forth among the people concerned without any notable bureaucratic delays. The almost certain detection of highly enriched uranium by international inspectors and the instinctive reaction of trying to hide the weapons programme from the world were thorny problems for many people.

In a memorandum marked "TOP SECRET", which was sent by Richard Carter on 17 November 1989 to Herbert Beukes, the then Deputy Director-General of Foreign Affairs, different scenarios for the dismantlement of South Africa's nuclear programme were sketched. Armscor's attitude was summed up as follows: "Armscor is no longer committed to a nuclear weapons program. Feel that a satellite and/or conventional delivery system program is worth focusing on. Considerable financial saving."

From the document it was also clear that much thought had been given to different possible ways of hiding the abandoned weapons programme from future international inspections. One of these would be to thoroughly decontaminate all relevant facilities.

According to Carter (who was in the service of the Department of Foreign Affairs at the time) even a three-year decontamination project would not remove all traces of highly enriched uranium metal. IAEA inspectors would find evidence of it with the aid of sensitive equipment. The suggested solution was that the highly enriched metal in the weapons should be converted back to highly enriched UF_6 and that the UF_6 should be declared to the IAEA. South Africa would deny the existence of a weapons programme. This would make it possible to explain any "chance discovery" of highly enriched uranium by the IAEA inspectors without first carrying out a dubious decontamination process. The highly enriched UF_6 could then be downgraded in time. Certain records would have to be destroyed, however.

A further proposal was that South Africa's strategy for accession to the NPT should take the following form while the dismantlement programme was proceeding:

> That SA "come clean" and admit that it has enriched uranium to weapons grade, but that it has not made weapons. Doing this does

away with the lengthy, expensive, dubious contamination program. The process could be completed in 12-18 months, after which accession could take place followed by ± 18 months safeguards negotiations. If we came clean on the 95% enriched product, we would have to do very little arguing over safeguards. The "secret" would be out. Manufacture of weapons however need never be admitted. Only 2/4 [2 out of 4] of the Y-facility's units would have to be shut down and dismantled or "transformed." This could probably be achieved within the 18 months period before accession.

Carter then remarked that the AEC had neither the manpower nor the will to carry out the time-consuming decontamination programme. In his view such a programme would be both counterproductive and bad for the morale of the AEC employees in any case.

Lastly, the memorandum made a cryptic reference to Wynand de Villiers, the Chairman of the AEC. He was described as "yesterday's man" in relation to Waldo Stumpf, who was apparently regarded as an easier – and more pragmatic – person to do business with.

In the meantime a lot had been done to flesh out F.W. de Klerk's instructions. In a letter to the Minister of Mineral and Energy Affairs dated 15 February 1990, Wynand de Villiers referred to the meeting of the ad hoc cabinet committee with W.E. Stumpf from the AEC and J.L. Steyn from Armscor, which took place on 22 January of that year. A modus operandi for phasing out the nuclear weapons, known as the "Mantel" Project, was submitted for consideration by the minister and final approval by the President. The target was to complete the process before the end of September 1991.

Nuclear weaponry command and control procedures

Procedures had been introduced over the years for the building and safe maintenance of the nuclear weapons, but these procedures did not make provision for this unexpected turn of events. The weapon sections could not simply be removed from the safes. Dismantlement would inevitably be a complicated process.

The nuclear weapons consisted of two main parts. The most important part was the nuclear warhead containing the highly enriched uranium – in local military jargon this was known as the front warhead or controlled unit (CU). The second part was a gun assembly with a short barrel out of which an enriched uranium missile was shot into the nuclear warhead at high speed by means of high explosives. That section was locally known as the rear warhead or weapon systems unit (WSU). For security reasons the two parts were physically separated, placed in special containers and locked in separate safes.

There were strict command and control procedures to ensure that the nuclear weapons did not fall into unauthorised hands. Double safe security was applied to eliminate unauthorised handling of the nuclear warheads by a single party. The front part could only be removed from the safe on the orders of the State President via two parallel chains of command – one military and one civil – namely via the Minister of Defence and the Head of the Defence Force on the one hand and the Minister of Mineral and Energy Affairs together with the Chairman of the AEC on the other. Both parties, each of which only possessed half of the safe code, appointed representatives to unlock the safe so that the devices could be removed.

This procedure was somewhat more conservative than the American equivalent, which Dick Cheney (then Vice-President of the USA) described in December 2008 on Fox News:

> The President of the United States now for 50 years is followed at all times, 24 hours a day, by a military aide carrying a football that contains the nuclear codes that he would use, and be authorised to use, in the event of a nuclear attack on the United States. He could launch the kind of devastating attack the world has never seen. He doesn't have to check with anybody, he doesn't have to call the Congress, he doesn't have to check with the courts.

That is to say, provided the President has not mislaid his "biscuit". This "biscuit" is a plastic card (similar to a credit card) containing codes that allow the President to activate the "football". It is claimed in two books written by senior military personnel that former President Bill Clinton was very careless with this card and that on one occasion – during his relationship with Monica Lewinsky – it was missing for months. Clinton did not have the slightest idea what had become of the card. Jimmy Carter once sent a suit to the drycleaners card and all.

President De Klerk accepted the proposals for dismantlement. On 26 February 1990 the nuclear weapons programme was officially condemned to oblivion. De Klerk gave written consent and instructions to the effect that

- all existing nuclear weapons – both the front warheads and the rear assemblies – could be taken from the safes where they were kept – when required – along with any nuclear material for incomplete weapons; and
- the weapons and incomplete weapons should be dismantled and the highly enriched uranium handed over to the AEC for safekeeping under specific instructions.

He also gave instructions that the entire process should be supervised by an expert steering group, consisting of representatives of the Defence Force, Armscor and the AEC. This steering group was to approve the dismantlement plan, approve the process step by step and report on it regularly to the President. After a while Waldo Stumpf was appointed to lead the steering group.

To ensure independent supervision over the whole process, Professor W.L. (Wynand) Mouton, a former professor of physics, Vice-Chancellor of the then University of the Orange Free State and Chairperson of the Committee of University Principals, was appointed as external auditor. He had direct access to the President.

Early in 1990 President De Klerk met a group of AEC and Armscor personnel who had been working on the weapons programme or were to start working on the "Mantel" Project.

The meeting took place after working hours and took the form of a small social gathering in Armscor's offices in Pretoria.

It was an opportunity for the President to chat informally about his decision and thank the staff, some of whom had put in many years of dedicated work on the project, and also to appeal for their understanding and cooperation in the changed circumstances.

De Klerk was clearly under a great deal of pressure. He had come straight from his office to attend the function in the Armscor building. He was chain-smoking just before and after his brief address and appeared strained. The President was also visibly uncomfortable in the presence of his audience, most of whom had guessed what was in the offing. There was palpable tension among many of those present, who were facing not only the unexpected end of a challenging piece of technical history but also uncertainty about their own future job prospects.

THE END OF AN ERA

An era marked by outstanding scientific and technical achievements was dismissively brought to an end in a brief and awkward speech, in which no real appreciation of the historical meaning of that occasion was apparent. This was the first time in the history of the world that a country that had built up its own nuclear capability – at great cost and with remarkable ingenuity – had voluntarily decided to abandon the capability and destroy its weapons.

De Klerk was in a hurry to get away.

He turned to a member of staff and asked: "Can I have one for the road?"

He swallowed the drink. About 30 minutes after his arrival De Klerk disappeared.

A colleague who had driven behind the official presidential car in the Pretoria traffic a few days previously told the shocked audience that he had seen the President in the back of the car doing some serious neck exercises.

"The poor man is very tense, let me tell you."

The project that had irreversibly shaped the careers of those present had come to an abrupt end. The reality of this, the unexpected end to their hard work done in great secrecy and spanning more than two decades, had yet to sink in. One of the employees, wearing an expression of defeat and holding a glass of whisky, compared the situation to that of Louis XVI of France. One moment he was a reigning monarch and a fraction of a second later he had lost his head on the guillotine, a victim of drastically changed circumstances.

Stephen Shapin's essay on Edward Teller and the spirit that prevailed among the scientists working on the Manhattan Project strikingly reflects the feelings of those present in the Armscor building that night:

> Nevertheless, there's something else about the experience of working on the Manhattan Project that is as disturbing as it is understandable and even attractive. For many of the scientists, it was the most enormous fun. They said so themselves and they said it repeatedly. Bethe wrote that, for all of its scientific inhabitants, Los Alamos "was really the great time of their lives". The English physicist James Tuck called it "a golden time". All the great men were there; all happy to be in each other's company; all united in an urgent common cause that broke down the artificial disciplinary boundaries that existed in the academy. The problems were interesting; the funding was inexhaustible. They were, Teller announced, "one big, happy family". After Hiroshima, when Oppenheimer left Los Alamos to return to Berkeley, the scientific staff

formally thanked him for the wonderful time they'd had: "We drew much more satisfaction from our work than our consciences ought to have allowed us." They were having so much fun that some regarded the fence around the place not as something that kept its inhabitants in, but as a barrier to stop others from joining them. It was that fun – that total absorption in the elaborately funded "technically sweet" – which kept potential moral reflectiveness in check.

For the AEC and Armscor staff, their "golden time" had also come to an end.

Historic moments are sometimes bitterly mundane.

One for the road – and on with the motley!

The dismantlement process

Carefully considered and thoroughly tested plans and procedures for the building and maintenance of South Africa's nuclear weapons were developed and refined over a number of years. In the nature of things no protocol existed for the total dismantlement which had to take place out of the blue. The dismantlement included the handling of high explosive chemical substances and highly enriched uranium which carried the risk of radioactive contamination and criticality hazards. In view of the sensitive and dangerous nature of the process, carefully considered procedures had to be drawn up and approved. By the middle of 1990 the procedures to ensure the safety of the personnel and the security of the nuclear material had been finalised and it was possible to start the delicate task of taking the bombs apart safely.

President De Klerk wanted the nuclear weapons fully dismantled one by one. An alternative suggestion, supported by Professor Wynand Mouton, was to begin by dismantling half of each weapon before dealing with the second half. Admittedly this was a slower process, but it would give the staff more time to try out the procedures and get used to the process. In the end this was the procedure followed.

By July 1991 the dismantlement process had been completed – South Africa's nuclear weapons programme was a thing of the past.

Working with uranium metal for any length of time makes radioactive contamination of equipment and work surfaces inevitable. It was decided that at the Circle facility, where the devices had been built, all traces of radioactive contamination had to be cleared and accordingly contaminated equipment used for the weapons programme was removed. Floors and temporary walls that had become contaminated were demolished and sent to the AEC along with any equipment, such as smelting furnaces, that could not be fully decontaminated. Because of the nature of the AEC's business procedures and facilities, the material could be safely stored there. The idea of hiding the fact that nuclear weapons had been manufactured in the past was still prevalent at that stage.

The enriched uranium which was recovered from the front and rear warheads – which had been very accurately machined into special geometric shapes for the weapons – was then melted down into a number of smaller, innocuous cylindrical castings.

The castings were transferred from the Circle facility to the AEC in four batches during the nights of 12-13 and 14-15 March, and 3-4 and 5-6 September 1991. As a safety precaution to ensure that accidental criticality would not be reached, the castings had specific masses and dimensions and the material was transported in special compartmentalised containers – known in the trade as birdcages – to ensure that the castings were kept a safe distance apart. Upon arrival at the AEC each casting was weighed and the degree of enrichment of the material confirmed. Each of the castings was then locked into a safe which was placed inside a larger safe. The whole collection of safes was housed in an enormous drive-in safe which allowed vehicles to drive in and unload the precious cargo, unseen and behind securely locked and strengthened doors.

Chuck Norris to the rescue

For security reasons the transfer of materials had to take place in the middle of the night. Because this was a sensitive operation the Broederstroom Commando (whose commandant was an employee of the AEC) was on standby. Even General Rooi-Gert Opperman with his Northern Transvaal Command was somewhere out there in the dark, out of sight but primed for action. The idea was to have sufficient protection available without any conspicuous armed convoys that might attract undesirable attention.

The AEC recipients had to wait at their premises for the various cargos, which were being transported from the Circle facility in the "baker's van". To keep them awake late at night the men from the Commando

> *and the AEC security service provided a series of videos featuring the action hero Chuck Norris. For many of the scientists present this was their first encounter with the iconic film star's oeuvre. Some of them couldn't help speculating aloud on why they needed nukes with real men like Chuck Norris around!*

A critical question arose during the dismantlement process. This concerned the need to preserve documentation that could later be used to prove South Africa's bona fides to the IAEA. Few of the regular inspectors who had been allocated to South Africa came from nuclear weapons states and therefore they had no specific knowledge of nuclear weapons. As a future signatory of the NPT, South Africa had an obligation not to pass on detailed plans and procedures for the building of nuclear weapons to anyone – including IAEA inspectors. It was therefore necessary to be very circumspect in deciding which documentation to keep and which to destroy. For example, the destruction of certain classes of documents relating to the design and construction of the weapons was not intended to conceal the history; it was necessary for the sake of non-proliferation. Eventually it was decided to keep only the following records:

- All health records in respect of people classified as radiation workers
- All operating and production records for the enrichment plants (Y and Z), including nuclear material accounting records
- Build histories for the weapons
- Dismantlement records in respect of the nuclear warheads
- Documentation on the transfer of the nuclear material from Armscor back to the AEC.

The destruction of documentation

It is often alleged that the documentation on the nuclear weapons programme was destroyed because the apartheid government wanted to cover its tracks. There was a legitimate reason, however.

After the NPT entered into force in March 1970, no new state was permitted to join the treaty as a so-called nuclear-weapon state. There was a simple reason for this. Only states that had exploded a nuclear weapon before 1 January 1967 were legally classified as nuclear-weapon states. This is the reason why the USA, Britain, France, Russia and China are defined as such. Although India, Pakistan, North Korea and prob-

ably Israel as well developed and tested weapons after that date, they are excluded as nuclear-weapon states by the NPT. Apart from North Korea, which was a signatory of the treaty but later withdrew, none of the other countries ever signed the NPT. India for one took a decision in principle from the beginning never to sign the treaty.

South Africa's decision to sign the NPT therefore meant that the country was only able to join as a non-nuclear-weapon state. Any accession to the treaty while South Africa still possessed nuclear weapons was out of the question and the weapons therefore had to be destroyed first.

That was not all, however. One of the intentions of Article I of the NPT is that no signatory with knowledge relating to nuclear weapons should transfer this information to non-nuclear-weapon states. This would refer to technical information on nuclear weapons in the form of scientific calculations, engineering construction plans etc. This hypothetical transfer of information even included the IAEA, which is obliged by its statute to promote only the peaceful application of nuclear energy. There was therefore no choice but to destroy all the proliferation-related documentation.

Hans Blix, the former Swedish Minister of Foreign Affairs, who was the Director-General of the IAEA when South Africa joined the NPT, viewed the South Africans' actions in this light and supported them. Strangely, his successor, Mohamed ElBaradei, made the astonishing statement at a meeting of the IAEA's Board of Governors in 2002 that the IAEA had dismantled and destroyed South Africa's nuclear weapons. Except in the case of Iraq, where the IAEA had a mandate from the UNSC to destroy relevant equipment (there were no nuclear weapons), the IAEA had never had a mandate of that kind, certainly not in the case of South Africa. In fact there is no provision in the statute of the IAEA for the direct dismantlement and destruction of nuclear weapons. The South African delegation pointed out his error to ElBaradei. The Egyptian was clearly irritated. Apparently in a mere ten years the institutional memory of the actual process had been lost – and that at the highest level of the organisation.

A few important non-nuclear components were also retained. Some of the sensitive components were partly destroyed but those parts containing serial numbers that referred to the construction history were kept for reference.

Professor Wynand Mouton was satisfied with the process and submitted his report to the President. This was the signal that South Africa was ready to lift the veil on its nuclear programme and satisfy the world's curiosity via the sharp eyes of the IAEA.

On 17 September 1990 Pik Botha issued a statement reiterating South Africa's willingness to sign the NPT. Botha referred to the numerous discussions which had taken place during the preceding two years between the South African government and the three so-called depositary states of the NPT (Britain, the USA and the then USSR). According to Botha, South Africa would be willing to accede to the NPT if the other states in Southern Africa did the same.

At that juncture, the IAEA had suffered a serious setback with implications for its very existence, however, and there were other matters urgently claiming that organisation's attention.

Saddam Hussein causes trouble

It had been widely suspected that Saddam Hussein had a screw loose, and on 2 August 1990 these suspicions were decisively confirmed when the Iraqi leader threw down the gauntlet to the world by invading Kuwait – thereby starting the Mother of All Wars, as he called it. The invasion caused international consternation, and South Africa was one of the countries that had to pay the price for Saddam's folly.

After the invasion a series of resolutions was adopted in the UNSC in November 1990. The most important of these was Resolution 678. This gave Saddam until 15 January 1991 to withdraw his forces from Kuwait. As might have been expected, he refused and on 16 January the UN coalition replied with a large-scale aerial bombardment under the leadership of the USA. Four days after the deployment on 28 February 1991 of the land forces of the UN coalition force, the fighting was over.

After the defeat the Iraqis were forced to subject themselves to a UN-led inspection and monitoring system aimed at destroying all programmes involving nuclear, chemical and biological weapons and ensuring that these projects would not be resumed. The United Nations Special Commission (Unscom) was formed for this purpose and remained operational for the next eight years.

Unscom and the IAEA's action team

After the Iraqi forces had been expelled from Kuwait, the UNSC adopted three resolutions which placed Iraq under certain obligations and also established Unscom, which was tasked with ferreting out and exposing Saddam Hussein's secret biological, chemical and missile programmes.

The IAEA was asked to take responsibility for the nuclear section of Unscom. Hans Blix immediately appointed his action team headed by Maurizzio Zifferero (a former Deputy Director-General of the IAEA). The action team was not part of the IAEA's safeguards department, but reported directly to Blix. The mission of the team was not to monitor the usual application of safeguards, but to carry out the instructions of the UNSC. They were given an enormous task: to expose the secret elements of Iraq's nuclear programme; to destroy any equipment used for the programme and remove from Iraq any nuclear weapons material that might be discovered; and then to monitor all nuclear activities continuously. The latter meant, for example, that Iraqi staff members involved in the secret programmes would also have to be continuously monitored in their new postings.

As usual, there was a lot of dissension behind the scenes. There were suspicions that Unscom was in fact a US team in UN guise. For example, the USA vehemently opposed the role envisaged for the IAEA. In the USA Unscom started energetically recruiting members for the IAEA inspection team and Blix had to resist for all he was worth. There were always serious tensions between Unscom and the IAEA action team. Unscom thought the IAEA team looked too much like civil servants. The action team viewed the Unscom members as Rambo types. Their inspection cultures were markedly different: The Unscom team favoured a radical, confrontational manner and the IAEA team tended towards a clinical, scientific approach.

Later on a scandal erupted when it emerged that certain intelligence services, principally those of the USA and Britain, had infiltrated Unscom as team members and illegitimately obtained information, which was transmitted directly to their capitals and kept from Unscom. This provided the final evidence that Unscom was an instrument of the USA rather than the UNSC.

These inspections turned out to be a source of great embarrassment to the IAEA, which was responsible for the nuclear section. It was soon discovered that Saddam had been producing material for nuclear weapons in secret for some time, using various uranium enrichment processes.

Iraq had signed the NPT back in 1969 and concluded the Safeguards Agreement with the IAEA in 1973. By acceding to the NPT the country had given an undertaking that no nuclear weapons would ever be built or acquired. After 1973 the IAEA regularly carried out inspections in Iraq to verify compliance with this solemn undertaking – and never discovered that Saddam was engaged in a clandestine programme. The safeguards inspections methods applied in the past were obviously completely ineffective.

The discovery of Saddam Hussein's nuclear weapons aspirations is a story on its own, and one which is told in Hans Blix's book *Disarming Iraq*. The most interesting part is the way in which the meddling hand of the USA is apparent in all matters.

There was an American in the employ of the IAEA at the time of the Iraq saga, a certain David Kay. He held a fairly low-ranking administrative position. Kay had nothing to do with safeguards inspections. In fact, he had no experience of such inspections. Despite this he was appointed out of the blue as an inspector on the IAEA's action team and was then suddenly made team leader. Kay, who was later to acquire the nickname "Ramrod", adopted an aggressive approach – very unlike the IAEA – and made startling discoveries about Saddam's illicit nuclear activities. Another illuminating aspect is that Kay, an employee of the IAEA, first announced these findings in America before revealing the information to the IAEA's Board of Governors.

All the equipment used in the illicit nuclear weapons programme was physically destroyed and buildings were blown up. The IAEA then did some serious soul-searching to find out why they had suspected nothing in the course of almost twenty years of inspections. The IAEA's credibility – and in the opinion of some people the reason for its very existence – had been seriously compromised.

In defence of the IAEA's safeguards system it should be emphasised that safeguards are determined by a system negotiated by the member states themselves and applicable to all. For the protection of the sovereignty and sensitive nuclear facilities of member states, a system was negotiated which effectively meant that each member state undertook to exercise control over its own nuclear material and keep records– just as any firm controls its own finances – subject to an external audit. The IAEA inspectors then conduct a technical audit on the member state's nuclear material reports. The accepted approach was that the inspectors were not nuclear spies or detectives. It is no wonder that for years the inspectors did not detect anything amiss in Iraq. The clandestine activities were never declared and were carried out separately from the declared process. The IAEA was only permitted to inspect the officially declared programme.

It was in the midst of these turbulent conditions that South Africa decided to sign the NPT and permit IAEA inspections. After all the years of international suspicion that the South Africans possessed nuclear weapons, the IAEA could not afford another failure. This spelled trouble for South Africa.

The Additional Protocol

The IAEA's intensive self-examination after the Iraq debacle began immediately. One aspect stuck out like a sore thumb. The comprehensive Safeguards Agreements model (INFCIRC/153) which had been applied since 1972 did not give the IAEA legal powers to obtain additional information on and enter premises where no nuclear material was present, but where nuclear weapons related work might possibly have been carried out.

After negotiations lasting a few years, the Additional Protocol (AP) model was agreed upon. As the name indicates, this is additional to the Safeguards Agreement, but signature of the AP is voluntary. It was published for the first time in September 1997 as INFCIRC/540. The AP requires the signatory to provide considerably more information and to update that information regularly. The information includes the following: all activities around research and development in the nuclear fuel cycle; uranium mines and production plants; the manufacture of enrichment and reprocessing equipment and related equipment and materials; the importing and exporting of a comprehensive list of prescribed nuclear equipment; the description of the purpose and contents of all buildings on a nuclear site – and even all related buildings outside the site as well; etc.

The AP gives the IAEA additional rights of access to all activities on which information is supplied, but also makes provision for clearing up any questions or obscurities that crop up in the application of the safeguards.

The purpose of the AP is to ensure that no undeclared nuclear material or nuclear activities are present or in progress in an inspected state.

Signing the NPT and the IAEA's Safeguards Agreement

In the biography entitled *Pik Botha and His Times* there is a reference to an interview which Dr Sue Onslow conducted with the former Minister of Foreign Affairs in 2008. In this interview Pik Botha spoke of the pressure exerted on South Africa by Herman ("Hank") Cohen on behalf of the American administration to sign the NPT. Botha was convinced that in the run-up to 1990 the American intelligence was expecting that Nelson Mandela would be released. After a meeting in 1988 or 1989 a South African diplomat reported as follows on a remark by an American official: "You'd better hurry up in signing the NPT because if the ANC comes to power in South Africa, they will not do so."

When Pik Botha discussed the matter with Cohen, he strongly denied this. In his interview with Sue Onslow Botha went on to say: "It is possible that the USA wanted the whole issue of nuclear capability to be resolved before there was an ANC government. Perhaps Britain and France, as well as the Russians, were of the same view."

As explained previously, the NPT forbids any non-nuclear weapons state signatory to possess, acquire or manufacture nuclear weapons. It was therefore not legally possible for South Africa to become a signatory to the treaty while there were still nuclear weapons in the safes at the Circle facility. However, the possession of highly enriched uranium was not illegal provided it was declared and made accessible to IAEA inspections.

There was intense political pressure to sign the NPT as soon as possible and this was a period of symbolic gestures. In March 1991 Advocate Harry Schwarz was appointed ambassador to the USA by President De Klerk. He was the first member of the Opposition – and the first Jewish person – ever to have been appointed to a senior South African ambassadorial post. Four months after his appointment, Schwarz received instructions to sign the NPT in the USA. There were people who read sinister implications into the fact that the signature on 10 July 1991 had to take place in the presence of the British ambassador. There was in fact a simple reason for this. Britain is one of the three states designated by the NPT as so-called depositary states, able to receive a signed treaty and then register it according to UN rules.

From Monday 16 September to Friday 20 September 1991, a South African delegation was able to attend a General Conference of the IAEA in Vienna for the first time since 1979. The South African delegation, which had arrived before the weekend, was in a state of great uncertainty regarding the signature of the Safeguards Agreement with the IAEA. Messages flew back and forth between the South African embassy in Vienna and the headquarters of Foreign Affairs in Pretoria. Some decision makers felt that to sign the Safeguards Agreement barely two months after accession to the NPT signalled a "too hasty" attitude of "capitulation" since the NPT allows up to 18 months for signature after accession. However, the delegation in Vienna judged the mood among the delegates to be conducive to the South African government's demonstrating its true intentions by not unnecessarily delaying the signature of the Safeguards Agreement. Eventually they were able to get in touch with Minister Pik Botha on Sunday evening. He immediately agreed that the Vienna delegation should sign the Agreement before the conference started. He therefore instructed Ambassador Cecile Schmidt to sign the Agreement the following morning. Half an hour before the conference was to begin that Monday morning, the South African ambassador and Hans Blix accordingly signed the Agreement. Blix's announcement minutes later that the South African government had just signed the Agreement was greeted with thunderous applause by the conference attendees. At that stage many delegates were still very sceptical about the true intentions of the South African government (since at the time North Korea had already delayed its signature of the Safeguards Agreement by up to six years and many critics were suggesting that South Africa would likewise use accession to the NPT to simply "buy time").

After more than a decade of exclusion from the IAEA's General Conference the South Africans were not entirely sure what to expect. For the leader of the South African delegation, Dr Wynand de Villiers, this was a poignant moment as he had also been the leader of the delegation in New Delhi in 1979 that had to suffer the humiliation of being escorted out of the conference when the South African government's credentials were rejected. This time around, however, the South Africans found some members of the American delegation surprisingly helpful. One of the American representatives in particular went out of his way to support them. "Sit at the back of the chamber," was his initial advice to the South Africans. As the days went by his advice every morning was to sit a little closer to the front. Their confidence and visibility increased accordingly. On the last day, when the South African credentials came up for discussion, there was a suppressed muttering among the African countries. The Egyptian representative was speaking at that stage and she clearly had her (razor-sharp) knife in for South Africa.

While she was still busy with her tirade, the friendly American stepped forward and whispered in her ear within earshot of the South African delegation: "But we did not agree on this." She fell silent ... and then announced that South Africa's credentials would be accepted!

An important requirement for a new entrant to the NPT is that negotiations with the IAEA on the comprehensive Safeguards Agreement should be started immediately. All the "negotiations" really amount to is the making of a choice between a few alternative administrative clauses. The remainder of the agreement is captured in a standard model which is applicable to all new entrants. The NPT also provides that the Safeguards Agreement should enter into force no longer than eighteen months after the commencement of the negotiations. The reason for allowing eighteen months is that in the case of a country like South Africa, with a long-running and complicated nuclear programme, sufficient time has to be allowed to make the necessary technical and administrative preparations before the Safeguards Agreement, with all its attendant obligations, comes into force. However, this matter was finalised with lightning speed on 16 September, about two months after the signature of the NPT. The sudden decision to sign the Safeguards Agreement had put the cat among the pigeons at home.

The IAEA requires that a formal system of control of and accounting for nuclear materials should be implemented. This is referred to as the States' Systems of Accounting for and Control of Nuclear Materials (SSAC). The SSAC is defined by the IAEA as the organisational arrangements at the national level which may have both a national objective, to account for and control nuclear material in the State, as well as an international objective, to provide the basis for the application of IAEA safeguards. The SSAC also has to provide national inspectors who ensure that nuclear facilities comply with their obligations and who accompany IAEA inspectors on official inspections. The modus operandi of the IAEA is not to confront plant operators about problems. Instead, the SSAC functions as an intermediary in seeking solutions. In order to meet the SSAC obligations, a special department was created at the AEC, namely Nuclear Nonproliferation, to which the functions of the SSAC were delegated. This department had direct access to the chief executive officer of the AEC. The department was divided into an inspection section and a data processing section.

One of the department's immediate obligations was to draw up a complete inventory of the country's nuclear material – to the nearest gram. This nuclear inventory had to be submitted to the IAEA as the Initial Report and was to form the basis for the IAEA's inspections, which would then start in earnest.

The physical and chemical forms (e.g. metals, alloys, powders, liquids, fuel elements, scrap, waste, UF_6, oxides and nitrates), the U-238 and U-235 isotopic content, the masses and the specific locations of each gram of uraniferous material had to be compiled in a prescribed format – an enormous undertaking. Staff of the AEC had to fly back and forth between Pretoria and the IAEA's headquarters in Vienna to gather information and negotiate on the inclusion or exclusion of materials.

Because they were being subjected to extreme pressure, the Nuclear Nonproliferation Department only had until the end of October 1991 to compile the Initial Report. Time for controlled panic ... The handful of staff that made up the Nuclear Nonproliferation Department therefore had to get to work immediately and begin compiling the report. They spent their weeks, weekends and nights working and sleep deprivation sometimes caused them to do strange things. For example, in the early hours of one morning one of the exhausted members of staff fed an old-fashioned floppy disc into a computer to download data and found that nothing was happening. She had to get a computer technician to take the computer apart – the disc had been pushed through a thin opening in the PC box and not into the slot provided for discs.

The survey of nuclear material and facilities included the following:
- Three so-called item facilities: Koeberg, Safari-1 and the Hot Cell Complex at Pelindaba;
- Seven so-called bulk facilities: The U-plant (uranium conversion); the Z-plant; Beva (the fuel manufacturing plant); the decontamination facility; alloy manufacturing; Safari fuel manufacturing; as well as a plant for processing depleted uranium;
- Three storage facilities: For the reclaimed highly enriched uranium; uraniferous waste (Radiation Hill); and the decommissioned Y-plant, which still contained uranium internally on filters etc; and
- Thirty-two other places such as laboratories where uranium was located.

The total inventory amounted to over 2 700 tons (2 700 000 000 grams) of uranium, all specified to the nearest gram. Even the plutonium that is normally formed in the Koeberg reactors during operation had to be accounted for, although in this case the values were calculated and not measured.

On 22 October 1991 the report was submitted to the South African Department of Foreign Affairs in time for transmission to the IAEA. The rapid signature of the Safeguards Agreement and the compiling of the Initial Report after signature of the NPT may not have made it into the *Guinness Book of Records* but nevertheless they were a record for the IAEA. The report was compiled in a little over three months. The usual allowance for a report of this kind is eighteen months. The IAEA was later to state that, despite the haste with which it was compiled, the Initial Report was the most comprehensive and professional report of its kind they had ever received.

Before the report reached the IAEA through the official channels, one of the compilers, Nic von Wielligh, had to depart for Vienna in haste. There he met a few IAEA officials who were to be involved in processing the information in the report and in the ensuing practical inspections. The section head for safeguards inspections in South Africa was a Fin, a man over two metres tall with a neatly trimmed full beard and the habit of waxing philosophical about everything. At that stage South Africans were more or less an unknown factor at the IAEA and Juha Rautjaervi invited his South African guest for dinner at a famous restaurant just outside Vienna. The restaurant was situated on the Wagramer Straße close to the battlefield where Napoleon and the Austrians joined battle 182 years previously and 74 000 soldiers lost their lives within two days. The restaurant used to be a favourite of Mimi Coertse's when she was still a "Kammersängerin" with the Vienna State Opera – an engraved copper plaque commemorates her regular visits.

The restaurant's stuffed pheasant breast and "Grüne Veltliner" were undeniably superb, but the man from the AEC scarcely tasted them. His mind was fully occupied with the question whether he should inform Rautjaervi about what the IAEA was going to find when they examined the Initial Report. The long years of speculation about South Africa's nuclear capability made this a delicate matter. In any case the IAEA was going to find out from the report – and naturally also during the inspections that followed – that South Africa did possess large quantities of weapons-grade uranium. However, President De Klerk's express orders were that the time was not yet ripe to discuss the former weapons programme. One is reminded of the dilemma of a policeman who, upon finding a corpse with a dagger in its back, is not allowed to ask whether a crime has been committed!

After much hesitation the visitor decided that he had better share the existence of the nuclear material with Rautjaervi. The IAEA was going to find out about it within the next few days and advance knowledge might better prepare them to handle the data with the necessary circumspection – especially in view of the fact that the IAEA was known to be as leaky as a sieve.

The conversation became a little stiff.

"Juha, we have only met a couple of times and we don't really know each other. But I think I need to warn you in advance about something. In a few days' time the IAEA's information technology division is going to receive South Africa's Initial Report. They will process it before the information reaches you people in the inspection division. To prepare you for any possible misinformation you may hear over the bush telegraph, I want to tell you that the report will show that we do possess weapons-grade uranium – and in large quantities at that. Unfortunately that is all I can say at this stage."

The voluble Fin lost his voice, raised his eyebrows, and then did the diplomatic thing and made no response at all. After dinner the two men drove back to the IAEA's headquarters in silence. But this favour to the inspection division was the beginning of a period of cordial and professional cooperation.

The Information Technology Division of the IAEA plays a central role in the organisation. Not only does this division receive the data on a country's initial stock of nuclear material and its whereabouts, but any change that takes place afterwards in the numerous so-called material balance areas (MBA) has to be reported within 30 days. This division therefore has an almost real-time knowledge of the nuclear material stocks and materials flow between MBAs in any non-nuclear weapons state anywhere in the world. This can be compared to a kind of super-regulator that has a real-time knowledge of how much money each bank on the planet has and how much money is being transferred between banks.

It was significant that at that time the two superpowers were prominently represented in the person of the director of the division, a taciturn and stoical Russian, with as his second-in-command a jovial American who went a bit overboard at times with his garish Hawaiian shirts. The South Africans used to refer to them as "Brolloks en Bittergal" (two old scoundrels who used to scare children in the author C.J. Langenhoven's story). Nobody was in any doubt that these appointments had not been made for nothing. The two Cold War opponents had to know at all times whether any country could possibly become a third threat and thereby disturb the balance of power.

235

> ## The IAEA: organisation and legal rights
>
> *The Department of Safeguards is managed by a Deputy Director-General and, in addition to the necessary administrative component, it has six divisions, each of which has its own director and staff. Three of the divisions (A, B and C) are responsible for safeguards inspections in various geographical regions of the world. The other three divisions are the Division of Technical Support, the Division of Information Management and the Division of Concepts and Planning.*
>
> *The IAEA's comprehensive Safeguards Agreement covers all the nuclear material in a particular state. All plants, laboratories, storage areas and other places where nuclear material can be found therefore have to be declared. The safeguards "follow the nuclear material". Therefore if nuclear material has to be transferred to a location that did not previously contain any, the new location also has to be declared. IAEA inspectors have access to all declared areas to verify material, take samples and measurements, check records, fit containment and surveillance devices such as seals and cameras, etc.*
>
> *However, IAEA inspectors do not legally have right of access to plants, workshops and laboratories that contain no nuclear material. It is the prerogative of the state in question to admit inspectors to or exclude them from such areas.*
>
> *If a country has signed the Additional Protocol – which is voluntary – the IAEA has far more access to information, buildings and facilities, even if there is no nuclear material present, but access is still subject to certain guidelines. The AP only became available after 1997 and by early 2015 it was in force in over 120 countries. South Africa signed the AP in June 2002.*

Unavoidably, the Initial Report, which was compiled with indecent haste, contained errors and inaccuracies. The report was refined and corrected over time, thanks to continuous efforts by the Nuclear Nonproliferation Department and verifications by the IAEA. An important component of these errors was caused by the fact that some plant operators were only able to correct estimates by replacing them with measured values after the submission of the report.

The IAEA also caused a problem that put the AEC in an unfavourable light for years afterwards. Before the report was compiled the IAEA was asked whether low-concentration waste should be included in the Initial Report. This comprised mainly items like gloves, cloth overshoes, plastic, teflon filters and vacuum pump oil which had come into contact with uraniferous material during maintenance operations and therefore become slightly contaminated. This waste was sealed in 100-litre drums made of metal or plastic, not because it was dangerous but simply as a good housekeeping practice.

The question was answered in the affirmative and the South Africans were told to include low-concentration waste, but the problem was that after years of sanctions the AEC could not obtain the necessary instrumentation (drum scanners which cost millions in any case) to measure the uranium content of each drum individually. There were literally tens of thousands of drums which had accumulated over a period of about twenty years. The contents of the drums were therefore estimated on the basis of random sampling. This was not regarded as good enough. The IAEA wanted measurements and they exerted pressure on the AEC for years, including in the form of unfavourable reports in the annual global overview of problems with the implementation of safeguards. Eventually, after some years, the instrumentation was acquired through an IAEA aid programme and the gigantic task could begin.

A game with new rules

The signature of the NPT, and subsequently the Safeguards Agreement of the IAEA, was seen by many countries as the culmination of long years of political pressure on South Africa. Although South Africa was welcomed back by the General Conference of the IAEA (after having been expelled in 1979), a new condition was set which had never previously been applied to any country.

The failure of the IAEA in Iraq and the long-standing suspicions about South Africa's nuclear capability suddenly gave rise to new rules: The IAEA was not only expected to start verifying the initial inventory immediately, as they did for all countries, but in addition had to verify the correctness and completeness of South Africa's declaration of its nuclear material and nuclear facilities – as contained in the Initial Report. This instruction was endorsed by the UNSC.

Evidently there were still suspicions that the South Africans had not declared all their nuclear material and facilities. The IAEA wanted to avoid a repetition of its embarrassment over Iraq. This was a game with new rules for everyone, including the IAEA, which had had no previous experience with an investigation of this kind.

Hans Blix appointed a special team consisting of senior officials from the organisation's safeguards department to carry out the correctness and completeness investigation (CCI). The team lost no time and its first visit to South Africa took place towards the end of November 1991. The leader of the team was the formidable and highly experienced Dr Dimitri Perricos, who had also been appointed in April (a few months previously) as the operational head of the action team which had to uncover Saddam Hussein's clandestine nuclear activities following the Gulf War. His experiences in Iraq had shown him how inadequate the IAEA's inspection methods had been in exposing Hussein's contraventions over almost twenty years.

Dimitri Perricos was born in Greece in 1935. At the time of his visit to South Africa he was in his mid-fifties and his short, curly hair was virtually grey. He had been educated in Athens, where he obtained a doctorate in chemistry. In 1972 he joined the IAEA as an inspector in the safeguards department and in time he advanced to the level of director. He had been in the service of the IAEA for 28 years and had done pioneering work on refining the safeguards system and making it more efficient. Perricos had an arrogant manner and was not easy to get along with. Hans Blix, his boss, described him as follows: "He was no easy-going fellow, not infrequently scaring people with his sharp arguments. I used to say he made up for any impatience I lacked."

Perricos's bark was just as bad as his bite.

Furthermore, his first visit to South Africa took place barely six months after he had headed the first inspection team in Iraq. Relying on prior information supplied to the action team by intelligence agencies (read, the USA), Perricos and his team came across a plant in Iraq that had been destroyed. Photographs taken by the team members were analysed and the equipment was identified as dinosaur technology, namely calutrons (the old electromagnetic separation process used in the Manhattan Project). It was clear that Saddam was enriching uranium and since Iraq had no nuclear power stations, he could only have had one reason – the development of his own nuclear weapon. In June the action team discovered a number of trucks carrying undamaged calutrons. When they tried to take photographs, they were fired upon by the Iraqi guards. In September the team discovered numerous documents containing details of the Iraqi nuclear weapons programme. The team's success was celebrated in Vienna later on at an event where they received several awards.

THE END OF AN ERA

One can well imagine that this was still the prevailing mindset two months later, when Perricos visited South Africa: Invade, conquer and celebrate the success, even if you do have to dodge a few bullets in the process!

The big difference, however, was that the Iraqi action team had been working under a directive from the UNSC, which gave them unrestricted powers and access. The situation in South Africa's case was entirely different. The IAEA had no special powers in South Africa. Apart from the usual verification of the Initial Report the only additional requirement was that the correctness and completeness of South Africa's nuclear inventory list had to be proved – but nobody was quite sure how this was to be done. However, Perricos had a competent team to assist him. The team members changed from time to time, but the anchors were Dr Adolf von Baeckmann, Garry Dillon, Richard Hooper, Svein Thorstensen and André Lagattu.

Von Baeckmann was a German and, like the team leader, a chemist by profession. He had years of uranium enrichment experience behind him. He was a benign elderly man (in his late sixties), short and a little plump, silver-haired and always painfully tidily dressed. He had a slight lisp and spoke English with a distinct German accent. His benign image might almost have tempted people to call him "Onkel Adolf" but in this case appearances were deceptive. He was an extremely professional man with a razor-sharp brain.

Garry Dillon was an agreeable Brit, tall and affable, but highly professional. He had unexpectedly replaced Juha Rautjaervi as the IAEA section head for South Africa – a sign that the nuclear-weapon states wanted to be more involved in the investigation.

The Americans were represented by Richard Hooper, a statistician by training who had cut his technological teeth at Boeing, before being attached to the IAEA for decades. He made valuable contributions as a member of the Iraq action team, but is remembered especially for the crucial contributions he made to the expansion and improvement of the safeguards system after the failure in Iraq. He was the main architect of the Additional Protocol to the Safeguards Agreement which was later to give the IAEA far more legal access to information and localities for the purposes of inspection. In 1994 he was appointed director of the IAEA's think tank, namely the Division of Concepts and Planning.

André Lagattu, the hyperactive Frenchman of the team, had gained his nuclear experience in the French navy. He was built like a rugby forward and had in fact been a keen rugby player in his day. Lagattu never let an opportunity pass to attend a big match at the Loftus Versfeld stadium, Pretoria and with his UN passport and French charm he got past all the security checkpoints and often managed to park right in front of the Loftus pavilion. He spoke English with astonishing rapidity – and a strong French accent – which required extreme concentration on the part of his listeners and often left them exhausted. The staff at the AEC used to watch with bated breath when Lagattu had to handle delicate equipment. When someone remarked one day on his heavy-handed assault on a computer keypad he simply replied: "The book says: Hit the button!"

The team's secret weapon – as the South Africans were later to discover – was a Norwegian by the name of Svein Thorstensen, a bald man with all the bulk and strength of a Viking of old and restless eyes behind large-framed spectacles. He was a man of few words, but nothing escaped him. As director of one of the inspection divisions, he was a senior member of the team, but his real value lay in the years he had spent working in the Netherlands and becoming fluent in Dutch. The South African team were unaware of this at first. It made him the man with the radar ears who picked up snippets of information when the AEC team spoke Afrikaans to each other. He was well able to read and understand AEC reports, which were written mainly in Afrikaans and submitted to substantiate certain aspects. His initial modus operandi was to range himself with the AEC team in an ostensibly protective manner when the going got rough. This won him both goodwill and information – until his ploy was discovered.

At the insistence of the African states Blix also appointed an African to the team, although only a little later. Kaluba Chitumbo came from Zambia and was the only black section head in the IAEA's inspection division. He was the proverbial brick and a tickey in height, but had the disposition of a Napoleon to go with it. He was made a director of a safeguards division in later years and his staff – which included a few South Africans – found him a difficult boss to deal with.

The corpse with the dagger in its back

The first meeting between Perricos's team and their AEC counterparts, the latter reinforced by experts from the Department of Foreign Affairs, was rather stiff. The two teams glared at each other across the broad table in the AEC council chamber like the proverbial battle ranks of the Israelites and the Philistines. Everyone was waiting for the opening attack by Goliath – or rather Perricos. After a conciliatory remark by Perricos in an attempt to break the ice, AEC team leader, Dr Jannie Wannenburg – a brilliant engineer, a wag of note and a lover of classical Greek – responded with this sally: "Beware of Greeks bearing gifts!" Perricos almost had a seizure and sat bolt upright on the front few millimetres of his chair. Behind the steel-rimmed spectacles the level of his blood pressure was clearly apparent, but the Greek chemist controlled himself. After a while the atmosphere became a little less strained.

The Initial Report remained lying on the table like the corpse with a dagger in its back but all eyes were averted and nobody asked the obvious question. It was stated on the first page that South Africa had declared a few hundred kilograms of weapons-grade uranium, but the IAEA team asked no questions and the AEC team volunteered no information. Years later Von Baeckmann summed up the position in an article which appeared in the IAEA journal: "South Africa had no obligation to declare what had been the purpose of this material. Equally, the primary task of the IAEA was to ascertain that all nuclear material had been declared and placed under safeguards; priority was given to this task in 1992."

The moderate line taken by some members – faithful to the established diplomatic IAEA culture – contrasted sharply with the new Iraq-fired adrenaline coursing through the veins of other team members, and the result was serious problems within the team later on.

The following morning (12 December) a member of the AEC team, who happened to have seen Perricos's passport, noticed that it was his birthday and whispered this information to Jannie Wannenburg. With a stony face Wannenburg said that he had a serious announcement to make on the basis of information he had received from South African intelligence sources. The IAEA team braced themselves. Wannenburg was to the point: "I just want to announce that today is Dr Perricos's birthday! Many happy returns!"

Openly relieved, Perricos replied: "For once their information is correct!"

This broke the ice and the work was able to proceed in a professional manner. But the corpse with the dagger in its back was still on the table and almost two years were to pass before the "crime" was acknowledged and an autopsy could be performed. Waldo Stumpf said years later that he did have permission from F.W. de Klerk to disclose what the highly enriched uranium had been used for in the past in response to a direct question. But nobody on the IAEA team asked this specific question and so Stumpf kept the information to himself.

> ## In search of the MUF
>
> ### What is MUF?
>
> The IAEA divides nuclear facilities into so-called material balance areas (MBAs). A material balance is compiled annually for each MBA. One could compare this with people managing their finances by doing the following calculation for a given period – a month or a year:
> Opening balance + deposits – withdrawals = closing balance
> We all know from experience that unless one's bookkeeping is very meticulous this calculation does not always work out. The closing balance calculated is seldom the same as the figure that appears on one's bank statement. Somewhere along the way money has either disappeared or been added. The root cause is inaccurate bookkeeping, of course. Or otherwise there is a forgotten envelope with a pile of banknotes inside still waiting to be discovered.
> With MBAs the commodity is uranium and not money, but the principle is exactly the same. With an MBA there is an initial inventory of uranium. The transfers in (additions) and transfers out (withdrawals) of uranium are measured over a given period and at the end of the period the closing inventory is determined by means of a physical stocktaking. The difference between the initial and closing inventories is then expressed as follows:
> (Book inventory) – (physically measured closing inventory) = MUF
> or:
> (Beginning inventory + transfers in – transfers out) – (ending inventory) = MUF. MUF stands for "material unaccounted for", in other words uranium for which no account can be given.
> The IAEA does not get unnecessarily wound up about MUF that falls within certain prescribed limits. For example, it is possible for uraniferous material to stick to filters inside equipment from which it can later be reclaimed. On the other hand this could simply be a wily strategy on the part of the plant operator to divert material deliberately under the guise of MUF. Consequently methods have been developed to determine whether this might be the case.

In the meanwhile the verification of the declared inventory was proceeding smoothly and the IAEA team decided on a method of determining the correctness and completeness of the reported figures. In the Initial Report every gram of uranium reported had to be divided into the U-235 and U-238 components. By adding all the U-235 and U-238 masses separately, it was possible to calculate the following ratio:

(Sum of U-235 mass) / (sum of U-235 mass + sum of U-238 mass)

or:

Total mass of U-235 / total mass of uranium

Since all enriched and depleted uranium was produced from natural uranium, this ratio should be that of natural uranium, namely 0,71%. In theory this was an elegant solution, but in practice it gave rise to considerable problems.

The reason was of a purely practical nature. For every kilogram of weapons-grade uranium produced (93% enrichment in U-235), about 300 kg of natural uranium feed material was required. At the end of the enrichment process one was therefore left with 1 kg of highly enriched uranium and 300 − 1 = 299 kg of depleted uranium. The highly enriched uranium is drawn off in kilogram quantities, the U-235 concentration is very accurately measured and the mass is determined to the nearest gram. In contrast, the depleted uranium, which is produced in the proportion of 299:1, is regarded as "waste" and consequently no special efforts are made to ensure that the U-235 concentration is always accurately measured. The usual practice is to assume an average value.

While it is true that depleted "waste" contains a smaller percentage of U-235 than natural uranium, given the large quantities of such waste its total U-235 content is still significant.

In the equation above the U-235 content was therefore not accurately known in the biggest component of the equation, namely the depleted waste produced over the years (a few hundred 2-ton cylinders).

The IAEA team calculated from the South Africans' Initial Report that the U-235 that had been declared did not make up 0.71% of the total amount of uranium. This suggested that some of the U-235 was "missing" or had not been declared. Could the AEC or Armscor possibly be hiding a stock of highly enriched uranium or even a bomb buried under a tree in the bushveld? The IAEA team requested a meticulous audit of the U-235 content of the depleted waste on the basis of sixteen years' operating records or whatever was left of them. The new figure was submitted to the IAEA team. Within a week or so the exact figure – to the last kilogram – appeared in an American scientific journal, despite the presumption of confidentiality laid down in the Safeguards Agreement.

This hotline to the USA naturally upset the AEC team, but by the conclusion of the correctness and completeness investigation, matters had become clearer to them. The IAEA has been restricted for years by a so-called "zero-growth budget". The annual budget is merely adjusted every year to make provision for inflation. The unexpectedly high travel and subsistence allowances of the CCI team for the South African investigation could not be financed from the limited funds available. However, the USA was eager to bear the cost (the USA provides about a quarter of the IAEA's normal budget in any case). In exchange the team was expected to report periodically to the USA and receive tips from the American intelligence agencies which they were to use in their ongoing investigations. At the time the AEC was completely unaware of this skulduggery. They learned about it by chance long afterwards.

There were a lot of people in the USA who for a full twenty years made a living partly from speculating regularly in the media on South Africa's nuclear capability. Among the best known were Frank Pabian, David Albright, Mark Hibbs, Leonard Spector and Thomas Cochran. These writers have subsequently turned their attention to countries like Syria, North Korea, Myanmar and Iran, but it has always been evident that they had close ties with the numerous intelligence agencies in the USA. Some experts even suspect that the organisations some represent are mere front organisations for the CIA and others. Even today it is striking that publications by these individuals always contain the very latest news, some of it highly confidential. These journalists quite frequently "fly kites" at the instigation of the intelligence agencies to see what reaction they get.

By revising and updating the original data, the AEC was able to reduce the MUF substantially in time, but without reaching the point where the "missing U-235" could be reduced to nil. There was simply too much uncertainty about the actual U-235 content in the tons of depleted uranium produced over the years. To arrive at a better estimate, each of the few hundred 2-ton cylinders would have had to be heated to liquefy the UF_6 and the contents would then have had to be homogenised by shaking the cylinders before taking a representative sample for analysis. This would have been completely impractical, impossibly expensive and even dangerous. Any cylinder that had been filled above a certain limit would split open like a banana during heating – liquid UF_6 expands enormously when it is heated to the point where it passes from a solid to a liquid state. Besides, the Y-plant had been decommissioned and the heating facilities were no longer available.

It was therefore up to the IAEA team to decide whether they could live with the "missing U-235".

Pale faces and furious blushes

During the first visit by the IAEA team, one morning shortly after the discussions had begun, Dimitri Perricos suddenly froze and turned very pale. The South African delegation wondered whether he was feeling ill. The Greek murmured something to a fellow team member, excused himself and left in a hurry. The discussions continued without him. It emerged later that he had left his wallet and passports (Greek and UN) in his hotel room. The IAEA team first stayed in Pretoria in the Holiday Inn Crowne Plaza Hotel on the corner of Church and Beatrix Streets. Perricos's dash to go and recover the missing articles was in vain. His wallet and passports were gone. Fortunately an official of the South African Department of Foreign Affairs was able to help him get a new Greek passport immediately.

In the same hotel an expensive short wave radio belonging to Kaluba Chitumbo later disappeared. In another incident Richard Hooper, who had brought his wife along on that trip, found a prowler in his hotel room one night. The intruder appeared to have a key. Fortunately this individual left in a hurry without taking anything of any importance. After a while the team moved their base to a hotel in Centurion. It was a more hospitable environment and there were more restaurants and shops in the area. An additional incentive was that for some obscure reason the daily allowance for Centurion was higher than for central Pretoria …

Richard Hooper, who seemed to be dogged by bad luck, had his second unpleasant experience, this time at the new hotel. When the team got back to the hotel one evening, exhausted after the day's discussions at Pelindaba, Hooper found an attractive young woman, rather scantily clad, in his hotel room. She was shaving her legs with his razor. The American went pale with shock, thinking at first that he was the victim of a "honey trap" – a traditional method used by intelligence agencies to lure people into their nets. The young lady evidently had no intention of leaving. After appropriate objections to the management, it finally emerged that the young woman was the hotel manager's mistress and

> that she usually stayed over in that particular room. She had been away for a while and the room was given to Hooper in her absence. Unfortunately for Hooper she had returned unexpectedly. And she did have her own key.

Ballpoint pens to the rescue

There was another matter troubling the IAEA team – the long stoppage at the Y-plant from August 1979 to July 1981 when the production of enriched material resumed. Was this not possibly an attempt by the AEC to conceal almost two years' production of weapons-grade material? It looked almost like a ruse worthy of Saddam Hussein.

The process gas in the Y-plant consisted of a mixture of hydrogen and UF_6. It is a known fact that a chemical reaction between the two components can take place under certain conditions, especially at high temperatures, and the UF_6 disappears from the process gas and is deposited in powder form (UF_5) inside the equipment. This was a major problem because the Ucor separative elements had fine holes which became blocked and were then no longer able to separate isotopes. To solve this problem, and also to catch ring dust from the compressors, the enrichment stages were each equipped with two sets of teflon filter candles.

The problem of the formation of deposits was encountered early on in test assemblies like Maverick (the name says it all) in building J. The UF_6 would simply disappear from the gas phase overnight and the next morning only hydrogen gas would be left in the process gas. Numerous studies were carried out to try to overcome this nuisance. One of the procedures tried was the special treatment of the inner surfaces of the enrichment stages before filling them with process gas. The big problem was that the UF_6/H_2 chemical reaction was autocatalytic. Once it started it became a runaway reaction.

The Y-plant suffered a catastrophe of this kind in August 1979. Operations came to a halt because the equipment was clogged with powder. All the elements had to be physically opened and cleaned. The cascade then had to be refilled with process gas and the time-consuming process of building up the enrichment gradients resumed. This meant that the bottom of the cascade again had to stabilise at waste concentration and the top at weapons-grade concentration.

But how, after twelve years, were the scientists to prove that the Y-plant had been out of commission for some time? One possibility was to look at the electricity consumption of the plant for the period August 1979 to July 1981. The graph did in fact reflect the stoppage, but then anybody can concoct a graph afterwards. The question was how to prove that the graph was authentic.

Here the humble ballpoint pen came to the rescue. Over the years the plant operators had been faithfully making daily recordings of the status of the cascade in the familiar old black Croxley counter books. These books were still available and provided confirmation that the stoppage had occurred. The IAEA team asked for one of the old books.

The South Africans were later to discover that there are only a few manufacturers of ink for ballpoint pens in the world. The manufacturers put certain markers in the ink and change them from time to time. If a dispute ever arises, say over the authenticity of a signature on a contract or a will, the ink can be analysed to provide confirmation of the date of the signature. In the business world this is a common practice in court cases, especially in the USA where the analysis was carried out.

It was possible to establish the authenticity of the entries in this way. The Y-plant had indeed stood idle for some time.

Deep in the desert

Early in 1992, during a follow-up visit by the IAEA team, an unusually timid Perricos produced an old UN report on groundwater studies in the Kalahari. On one of the maps in the report a cross had been drawn in a large, open space.

"We would like to visit this place. They have given me this GPS but I don't know how the confounded thing works. Could you help us?" It was clear that the cross marked the old Vastrap testing site to the north of Upington, but the South Africans feigned innocence and simply said they would look into the matter. They were caught off guard by the request. The South Africans wanted to give the Defence Force time to make preparations and think up a story to explain away the relatively new shed on the site. In 1988 Armscor had erected the shed and put a concrete slab over one of the test shafts in order to inspect the condition of the shaft. The inquisitive Russian and American spy satellites had naturally observed these activities at some stage.

The Defence Force was contacted and a visit arranged. Members of the IAEA team, accompanied by a few AEC team members, flew to Upington and then proceeded by car, travelling up and down across the red dunes which lay across the road like petrified waves of the sea, deeper and deeper into the Kalahari.

As explained, Vastrap was a military testing range used by the Air Force for bombing exercises. Enough old damaged vehicles, and even plywood targets, were on display all over the site to make its purpose clear. Deliberately, there were no senior military personnel on the site. There was only a staff sergeant who lived there, with one or two helpers.

The staff sergeant explained the purpose of the site to the IAEA team – with some difficulty because English is not the lingua franca of the Kalahari! The IAEA team listened politely and then made two requests: They wanted to visit the shed on the site and also to take plant samples. These requests were granted at once – they were what the AEC personnel had been expecting.

The shed contained a few military vehicles, some with their bonnets up and some on blocks. At first glance it looked like a workshop, except that there was a rather unusual structure in the middle of the floor: an oblong solid concrete block a few metres in length and about a metre tall, with a short, very steep slope running upwards at one end. Perricos was clearly amused by this structure.

"What is this?" he asked.

In his best Kalahari English the staff sergeant offered an explanation:

"It is a ramp, sir."

Perricos looked at the short, steep slope and shook his head:

"What do you use it for?"

"For fixing our trucks, sir."

"But a truck can't drive up there!"

"Oh no sir, our army trucks is very strong; they go everywhere!"

But there were no rubber tyre marks on the ramp to indicate that it had ever been mounted by a "strong truck". Furthermore, there was no pit in the solid block to give a technician access to work on a vehicle from below. The actual pit was beneath the concrete block, and it was very deep indeed …

Thorstensen pulled out a few tufts of grass to take along for analysis and the party started on the return journey. Perricos was deep in thought the whole way, with an occasional wry smile the only clue to his thoughts.

Thorstensen's grass tufts were analysed in Vienna (or possibly in the USA for all anyone knew) for the presence of uranium and fission products. Nothing suspicious was found, however.

THE END OF AN ERA

Nuclear forensics

Technology was developed in the 1990s to trace uranium and plutonium on a minuscule scale and carry out a highly detailed analysis. The IAEA calls this process environmental monitoring, but it is a far more specialised field than the name indicates.

These days incredibly small quantities of uranium and plutonium can be traced and analysed for the isotope composition. The limit is about 1/1 000 000 000 000 000 000th of a gram. Particles as large as a micrometre (also referred to as a micron) can be isolated under a microscope and analysed. The period at the end of this sentence is about 300 to 400 micrometres in diameter. We are dealing with extremely delicate and sensitive techniques. But why is this necessary?

When plutonium or uranium is used in any way, minuscule particles are always released, for example through the machining of metals, or through the release of small quantities of UF_6 that react with the moisture in the atmosphere and form a fine powder, which is then distributed in the surroundings. These emissions can be traced, even when they are far below the levels that pose a danger to human health or that are visible to the naked eye.

These minute particles can be deposited on exposed surfaces in buildings such as window ledges or air ducts, or else spread by the wind – sometimes over considerable distances – where they filter down onto plants, the soil or watercourses.

The first step in the analysis is simply to wipe the surface with a special kind of tissue, pluck leaves from plants or take small soil or water samples. The samples are then sent to an IAEA laboratory for analysis. Many of the more specialised analyses are carried out by AFTAC in the USA.

Two types of analysis are carried out: bulk analysis, where the whole sample is used, or particle analysis, where a few particles are selected from the sample under a microscope and analysed.

Uranium occurs freely in nature: in soil, concentrated in ores or simply in drinking water – but naturally at very low levels. The U-235 and U-238 isotopes occur in a very specific proportion (1:140), which is constant in all parts of the world. If any particle found shows a change in this natural proportion, this is a clear indication that a nuclear activity such as uranium enrichment has taken place. Uranium particles of this kind are known as anthropogenic uranium, in other words uranium that has been influenced by human activities. This could be an indication that a plant is in operation, or could even be a sign of activities that were discontinued some time previously. If the selected particles came from metal processing and not from UF_6 emissions, this could indicate that uranium metal has been machined for nuclear warheads.

Two other isotopes of uranium are also important: U-234 and U-236. U-234 occurs in natural uranium in extremely low concentrations, but these concentrations are not constant (unlike the U-235 and U-238 concentration). U-234 usually occurs in the proportion of 52 to 54 parts per million, but some uranium ores contain more. The U-234 content can therefore be an indication of the area where the ore was mined. It serves another important purpose: It provides an indication of the type of uranium enrichment process used. In electromagnetic calutron and laser processes the U-234 is not found in the enriched material. In the Ucor vortex tube technology on the other hand, the U-234 is even more rapidly enriched than the U-235 – because it is even lighter – and at the highly enriched end of the Y-plant it reached about 1%, considerably more than the value of around 0.005% in natural uranium.

U-236 does not occur in nature at all. It is formed in a reactor when fuel is irradiated and a U-235 nucleus absorbs a neutron to form U-236. When spent fuel is removed from a reactor, it still contains a lot of valuable uranium that can be recovered along with the plutonium which has been formed. The reclaimed uranium contains not only the unused U-235, but also the U-236 formed in the reactor. The detection of U-236 in enriched uranium is therefore an indication that it came from reprocessed nuclear fuel and that plutonium was probably also produced.

One minuscule uranium particle can therefore reveal a great deal about the origin of the original ore, and also indicate whether enrichment has taken place and even pinpoint the type of enrichment process that was used. If U-236 is also present, there is a strong possibility that a process involving plutonium is also taking place.

Because the IAEA's inspectors are restricted by the terms of the Safeguards Agreement as regards access, there is always the possibility that a country may have undeclared facilities of which they have no knowledge – as happened in Iraq previously. Environmental monitoring makes it possible to detect undeclared nuclear activities and materials.

Nuclear forensics has acquired another important potential applica-

> tion which is undergoing further development in the USA in particular. If terrorists were to get their hands on a nuclear device and explode it, an analysis of the uranium or plutonium residues could reveal a great deal about the origin and processing of the nuclear material and thereby help to pinpoint those responsible. For example, 65 years after the first Trinity detonation, scientists have recently been able to identify plutonium, uranium (which was used in the bomb as a reflector) and fission products such as cobalt-60, cesium-137 and europium-152 in grains of sand that were melted in the explosion and vitrified.

The pressure builds up

In the meanwhile the IAEA's verification of South Africa's declared facilities and nuclear material was proceeding very well. Even certain AEC facilities that contained no nuclear material were voluntarily opened for the inspection team.

There were a few surprises, however.

One of the facilities was housed in Building X, where the AEC had previously run a small programme for the building and testing of gas centrifuges. The Ucor isotope separation process gobbled energy and was costly to run. The AEC had therefore begun to investigate other promising enrichment processes, namely gas centrifuge and the use of the MLIS (molecular laser isotope separation). At a certain point economic considerations made it necessary to choose between the two projects. Unfortunately the gas centrifuge project was axed, not because it was unsuccessful but simply because of the daunting technical backlog in comparison with advanced technology such as the Urenco process in Europe, which had already reached the fourteenth improved modification of the original design. Gerhard Wisser of the firm Krisch Engineering did try to peddle gas centrifuge plans to the AEC at one stage, which would have helped them to catch up with Urenco. But the AEC management considered this too expensive and risky and decided against it. In contrast, the MLIS process was equally unfamiliar in all the countries involved in developing it.

The unexpected announcement in 1991 that the centrifuge project had been discontinued caused a lot of rancour among the technical people who were working on it. Not only were they proud of what they had achieved but the announcement caught them completely unawares. The laboratory was closed at very short notice.

When the laboratory was reopened two years later at the request of the IAEA, there was a surprise awaiting the inspection party. They were reminded of the brigantine *Mary Celeste*, which was discovered in December 1872 near Gibraltar under full sail without a living soul on board, but with the tables still set, with six months' food and water and all the crew's possessions still on board.

Equipment was lying around in the laboratory, there were lunchboxes on the tables and white coats and even a jacket or two hanging on hooks against the wall. It was an eerie scene and the IAEA team found it difficult to believe that the project had been abandoned two years previously. However, interviews with the project leader and technicians were enough to convince them that the staff had not stepped out for a quick meal. They were simply furious and had hurriedly picked up their belongings and walked out.

Another surprise was in store for the IAEA team when they visited the storage yard for depleted uranium cylinders, each with a capacity of two tons of UF_6. There were cylinders with inscriptions in a foreign language, some of them still visible. Samples of the contents of the cylinders were taken and analysis revealed that the cylinders had contained between 2.7 and 3% enriched material. The big surprise was that the samples also contained traces of U-236. As explained previously, U-236 does not occur in nature but is formed in reactors while the fuel is being irradiated. The UF_6 must therefore have come from reprocessed nuclear fuel. Since South Africa did not have a plant where this process could have been carried out the material must have been imported – at a time when South Africa had been subject to stringent nuclear sanctions. After analysing the samples and examining the foreign script the IAEA team were in no doubt as to the origin of the material – it had come from the Peoples' Republic of China. Von Baeckmann didn't comment on the origin specifically, he merely smiled as he looked at the weathered characters and said: "You can see for yourself where the stuff came from." From 1983 to 1984 the AEC was concerned that the Z-plant would not be ready in time to supply fuel to Koeberg. Because the sanctions in place at the time made it difficult to obtain the low-enriched material on the international market, it had to come in through the "back door"; in total 44 cylinders containing two tons of low-enriched UF_6 each were imported in this way.

The enriched material was probably not produced in China as there were no known reprocessing plants there at the time. The irony of this transaction was that Red China had somehow come to the aid of the South Africans, who were blamed at the time for seeing "a communist behind every bush". Then, as now, the Chinese were not much concerned about who was in power in Africa. Financial gain was the sole priority.

It should be added that Red China only acceded to the NPT in March 1992 and was consequently not bound by any international restrictions on the exporting of enriched uranium. Political sensitivity was of course another matter.

By September 1992 the IAEA investigation had progressed so well that the team was able to submit a report to the IAEA's Board of Governors, namely GOV/2609 dated 3 September 1992, in which the following findings were documented:

- The top-end of the Y-plant cascade, where the highly enriched uranium is drawn off, has been dismantled and the stages removed. The open space has been prepared for the installation of MLIS equipment, to be brought into operation from 1993 to 1994.
- Historical material balance reports, some dating back fifteen years, have been checked. They show an "apparent deviation in the U-235 balances" at the Y- and Z-plants (a euphemistic way of saying that a quantity of U-235 was "missing"). However, this was put into perspective by pointing out that the nuclear material accounting systems used at that time did not make accurate provision for a later investigation by the IAEA in accordance with the strict safeguards standards applied by that organisation.
- The team visited the gas centrifuge project, which included a proposed cascade of 48 units. Visits to all the premises associated with the project clearly showed that it had been discontinued.
- The AEC supplied information on "an unspecified amount" of low-enriched uranium which had been imported as fuel for Koeberg. This material was not placed under safeguards by the exporting country. Information was also made available on natural uranium, in the form of UF_6, which was imported before 1979 as feedstock for the Y-plant. (Remark: In both cases the origin, China and France respectively, was not revealed by the AEC. However, these were the only two countries that were not members of the NPT at that stage and were therefore not obliged to make the export of uranium subject to safeguards.)

As far as the AEC and the IAEA were concerned, the investigation had gone off satisfactorily and the end was in sight. There were just a few details left to be attended to. The two parties had been negotiating informally about the wording of a final statement for the IAEA's Board of Governors and the UN.

However, the IAEA team's financial sponsor in Washington D.C. was visibly dissatisfied with the situation. The "apparent deviation in the U-235" was a very sore point with the Americans and they were determined to rake up past issues. They wanted value for their money. The USA then threw the proverbial spanner in the works.

Shortly after the neutral report GOV/2609 had been tabled and discussed in Vienna, two IAEA inspectors, including André Lagattu who happened to be visiting, received a fax late one afternoon at the IAEA office at the Pelindaba site. The fax included a map of an isolated and fenced-off area to the south of the AEC's ordinary site. There was a group of buildings on the site, most of which had been locked up for years. The only building in use served as sleeping quarters for the Broederstroom Commando. The instruction on the fax was explicit. The inspectors were to insist on immediate access to the "secret" area.

Arrangements were hastily made with AEC Security to unlock the buildings in question – the complex of buildings numbered 5000, 5100, 5200 and 5300. Security ran around looking for the keys. The AEC team didn't know what they would find, since the buildings had been disused for so long.

The IAEA inspectors had received instructions from headquarters to concentrate on one building, namely building 5000, a fair-sized structure a couple of storeys high. It was clear from the appearance of an office cubicle in the foyer that the place had not been in use for years. A red telephone stood on a small table, next to a hand-written telephone guide – on which the dust was lying so thick that the numbers were barely legible.

Inside the tall building it was clear that it had been used for storage for years. There was a stack of 100-litre drums and a few odd pieces of equipment whose purpose had long been forgotten. Other than that there was nothing of much interest in the building.

While the South African team were standing around in conversation and the IAEA inspectors were busy with their investigation and taking photographs, Lou Denner, a long-standing member of AEC Security, related that years ago they had found a hidey-hole, concealed by dense bush. It was situated on a rise that looked out over the building complex and it was clear from the cigarette butts and other litter lying around that someone had used a telescope over a long period to keep the buildings under observation from that vantage point. The buildings had also been the subject of the illicit aerial photographs taken in April 1979 from an aircraft belonging to the American

THE END OF AN ERA

embassy – the same photographs that had resulted in the expulsion from the country of the American military attaché and another two members of the diplomatic staff. Could this fruitless exercise have been the Americans' way of retaliating for the humiliation inflicted on their diplomatic staff at that time?

On 8 October 1992, just a few days after the visit by the IAEA team, Mark Hibbs published an article in *Neucleonics Week* in the USA:

> IAEA inspectors discover evidence of critical assemblies, testing gear and equipment for metallurgical research and processing at Building 5000, an abandoned site southwest of the enrichment complex at Pelindaba. Unnamed sources say that South African technicians used the equipment to work on the shape of spherical cores for a nuclear explosive device.

This was of course totally untrue, as no such equipment was actually found. It merely reflected the US's long-standing belief with regard to the purpose of the building. However, Hibbs had a point. If F.W. de Klerk had been willing to acknowledge the existence of the old weapons programme right from the start, there would have been no need for Hibbs and others to keep chipping away at the deliberate maintenance of strategic uncertainty until the truth was revealed. (The term used by the Americans was "calculated ambiguity".) Transparency would also have made life a good deal easier for the AEC team, which had to interact with the IAEA inspectors on a daily basis.

But there are always two sides to an issue. F.W. de Klerk first had to complete the last white referendum of 1992 and news of the dismantlement of the weapons programme might have had a profoundly negative effect on the voting in this important ballot. Furthermore, the heads of the AEC and Armscor were not sure whether the UN cowboys, who had unceremoniously blown up Saddam Hussein's facilities and physically destroyed all the enrichment equipment, might not arrive in South Africa with similar intentions.

The 5000 building complex

The four buildings, which were constructed on an isolated portion of the Pelindaba site and separately fenced, served a particular purpose in the nuclear weapons programme.

Building 5000, also known as Hall A, was designed to accommodate

255

a pulse reactor, but was never used for that purpose. Pulse reactors generate short, intense pulses of neutrons and were intended to be used to calibrate theoretical computer programs. In 1979 the building eventually housed a critical assembly for fast neutrons. Unlike in power reactors where slow neutrons are used for fission, fast neutrons perform this function in nuclear weapons. Years after the project had been wound up one of the key people concerned with testing at that time described how close they had come to a nuclear accident ...

At the time the staff were ready to start experiments with that critical assembly. On the day of the test everything went off well. The next day Wynand de Villiers, Wally Grant and Richardt van der Walt were invited to come and watch a repetition of the experiment. As planned, everything went well – up to a point. It was possible to make the assembly more reactive by inserting a control rod into an aperture. The rod was inserted slowly and, as expected, the locally manufactured counter tubes showed higher counts. To the surprise of the spectators, the counts suddenly started levelling off. One of the researchers slowly pushed the rod in deeper, millimetre by millimetre, but with no result. On impulse Johan Slabber decided to stop the experiment immediately. This was providential because closer examination revealed that the counter tubes were saturated and had simply stopped counting!

They had been a hair's breadth away from a criticality accident (uncontrolled chain reaction) in Building 5000 that day. Several accidents of this kind, in which a number of people were killed by radiation, occurred in the USA in the 1950s.

Building 5100 (Hall B) contained the control room for Building 5000, as well as offices, laboratories and facilities for machining uranium metal. The building also housed a small-scale gas gun, a prototype for the full-scale model which was subsequently installed in Building 5200.

The purpose of this was to determine the equation of state of the metals in a high pressure and temperature context.

Building 5200 had previously contained a critical assembly for determining the multiplication factors of the two parts of the nuclear weapons (the spherical section and the missile) separately. The multiplication factor measures the rate at which neutron production grows as criticality is reached.

Building 5300 was specially designed to serve as a laboratory for high explosives.

> *Collectively the four buildings housed the core of the experiments carried out in the early days to determine and to calibrate all the parameters for the first nuclear devices. The buildings largely fell into disuse afterwards, with the exception of Building 5100, which was used as an office and dormitory by the local commando.*

As part of the pressure being exerted on South Africa, the ANC was being fed information from overseas, especially from the USA. In a SAPA report dated 22 December 1992 the ANC voiced its concerns " … regarding reports emanating from Europe and the United States disclosing South Africa's nuclear activities and ambitions". The report referred to a few hundred kilograms of highly enriched uranium which had been produced and the IAEA's "discovery" of an old facility where "it found equipment to develop nuclear explosive devices". At the same time the CIA released information to the effect that the chairman of the AEC, Wynand de Villiers, had been involved in the development of nuclear weapons up to 1979. The ANC said in the report that F.W. de Klerk should disclose full information on the previous and current nuclear programme to South Africans and the international community. In January 1993 the campaign was carried further. The ANC released a CIA document, obtained in the USA in terms of the Freedom of Information Act, in which it was claimed that South Africa had carried out a nuclear test in the South Atlantic Ocean in 1979 with the assistance of Israel. The AEC issued a denial – as it had done repeatedly over the previous fourteen years.

In March 1993 the Foreign Minister, Pik Botha, went to the USA. There was some speculation in the media at the time that the USA wanted to buy the reclaimed weapons material from South Africa. On 18 March the minister had a discussion with the Americans, but the possible sale of such material was not mentioned. A week later Pik Botha referred to the discussions and said that the US's concerns were that:

- South Africa might later sell weapons or weapons material to a country hostile to the USA;
- South Africa had not declared all the weapons material to the IAEA; and
- the country had not been open with the IAEA and had concealed a nuclear weapon (or weapons) somewhere.

Botha assured the Americans that their fears would be laid to rest within two weeks.
- While the political pressure was building up, the AEC and Armscor per-

sonnel were finalising the collection of a large quantity of classified documents which had accumulated over a period of twenty years or so. This job was completed early in March 1993 and the documents were classified into categories. On 17 March President De Klerk issued instructions that all technical documentation that represented a nuclear proliferation risk should be destroyed under the supervision of the independent auditor, with the exception of

- documents relating to the initiation and termination of the project;
- medical and health records of the personnel who had worked on the project;
- nuclear material accounting and operating records; and
- the certification of the dismantlement process by the independent auditor.

This was completed on 22 March, just in time; fortuitously a day before a special joint parliamentary session convened by President De Klerk.

A rough neighbourhood – and a surprise announcement

Chester Crocker, who had helped bring about a negotiated peace in Angola, published a book about his experiences in 1992 entitled *High Noon in Southern Africa: Making Peace in a Rough Neighborhood*.

The description was very apt. The going undoubtedly got rough around this time, not only in Angola but also in South Africa, especially in 1992 and 1993.

In June 1992 unknown attackers shot and killed over 40 people at Boipatong, near Vereeniging. It was immediately rumoured that the attackers had perpetrated these murders under the protection of the police. Nelson Mandela suspended all talks with the government and requested the UN Secretary-General to convene a meeting of the UNSC. The Goldstone Commission instituted an inquiry and foreigners like P.N. Bhagwati, the former Chief Justice of India, Dr P.A.J. Waddington from Reading University in Britain and Cyrus Vance, the UN Special Envoy, were invited or assigned to assist with the inquiries.

Drastic measures by the government followed. In July 1992, 31 and 32 Battalions and the special police unit Koevoet were disbanded. In Augustus 1992 the Minister of Law and Order, Hernus Kriel, also announced the discharge or early retirement of 18 out of 55 police generals.

As if this were not enough, in September 1992 Ciskei troops fired on uninvited ANC demonstrators who were on their way to Bisho. The death toll was 29 and the number of wounded 200.

In December 1992 President De Klerk announced that 23 high-ranking officers of the SADF, including two generals and four brigadiers, had been either suspended or forced to take retirement.

Undoubtedly a rough neighbourhood. In February 1993 the Commonwealth Observer Mission to South Africa (Comsa) confirmed this in its statement that South Africa was one of the most violent countries in the world.

In the midst of all the murder, killing and other unrest, talks between the government and the ANC resumed through mediation, largely with the aid of Cyrus Vance. A multiparty planning session was held on 5 March 1993. It was decided that negotiations should be resumed no later than 5 April.

It was generally expected that the subject of the special parliamentary session arranged for Tuesday 23 March 1993 by President De Klerk would be the prevailing violence and the approaching multiparty negotiations. This was indeed the case, but the President surprised everybody by opening with a bit of a bombshell. He was clearly unwilling to resume the suspended talks with the proverbial albatross round his neck.

To general astonishment – and great relief on the part of the AEC negotiators – he announced at the joint parliamentary sitting that South Africa had been running a nuclear weapons programme from 1974 to 1990. This announcement was the culmination of a carefully crafted plan. De Klerk explained that historical, international and political considerations, such as the expansion of the Soviet Union's influence in Angola through the agency of its Cuban lackeys, made a limited nuclear capability necessary from 1975 onwards. The government's strategy was that in the event of a serious threat to national survival it would reveal this capability in confidence to one or more of the nuclear powers with the aim of securing their intervention. However, the drastic change in the international political scene in 1989 had influenced South Africa's strategy accordingly and it was possible to dispense with the nuclear capability. He emphasised that there had been no cooperation with foreign countries in creating the local nuclear capability.

De Klerk went on to announce that six nuclear weapons had been made and work on the seventh had been in progress. All the nuclear weapons had, however, already been dismantled. The weapons material had been melted down and transferred from Armscor to the AEC for safekeeping before the signature of the NPT around 18 months previously. All nuclear material that was subject to safeguards – including the weapons material – had been declared to the IAEA. During this period inspectors from the organisation had had access to enable them to verify the declared stock and the facilities. Furthermore, all proliferation-sensitive documents, in other words detailed technical information on how to make nuclear weapons, had been destroyed in accordance with the spirit of the NPT.

At the ensuing jam-packed press conference where the President was supported by Foreign Minister Pik Botha and the heads of Armscor and the AEC, Tielman de Waal and Waldo Stumpf respectively, De Klerk was peppered with questions.

To the inevitable question regarding the cost of the programme, President De Klerk replied that it was difficult to arrive at a specific figure. Much of the work done also overlapped with other programmes, such as the project for the production of low-enriched uranium and the manufacture of fuel for Koeberg. Research and development in respect of the enrichment process, as well as the building and operation of facilities for producing uranium hexafluoride, were further examples of overlapping. It should also be remembered that the AEC and Armscor had their own budgets. He nevertheless estimated that about R700 to R800 million had been spent on the programme. (Remark: In 1944 this was roughly the monthly cost of running the Manhattan Project!) The intention was to keep the highly enriched uranium as fuel for the Safari reactor for use in the production of medical isotopes. Speculative rumours about the possible sale of the weapons material to a nuclear power were therefore untrue.

The President emphasised that the provisions of the NPT only apply from the day on which it enters into force for a specific country. South Africa acceded to the NPT as a non-nuclear-weapon state and therefore had no legal reason to provide more information and access than the treaty required. In spite of this the IAEA would be given full access to former facilities and relevant records so that their staff could be convinced that South Africa had nothing to hide. The IAEA was later to codify this policy as "access anywhere at any time, but within reasonable limits".

A sceptical journalist asked "why the government misled the citizens of the country for so many years by deliberately denying the existence of the weapons programme". De Klerk was visibly annoyed by this question and pointed out that the nuclear weapons were intended as political – and not as offensive – weapons. Within that context the overriding factor is deter-

THE END OF AN ERA

rence and by neither admitting nor denying that the country possessed such weapons the government had increased their value as a deterrent. The government's silence regarding the existence of the weapons was a deliberate strategy – not a deliberate lie.

De Klerk's announcement did not come out of the blue. The historic moment was preceded by a lot of careful planning and preparation. The previous evening Dr Jannie Roux, the ambassador in Vienna, had informed Hans Blix of the IAEA on the nature of the announcement. The preparations included ensuring that senior inspectors of the IAEA would be available at the AEC premises to take immediate action if required. On the morning of the announcement De Klerk had shared the news with the heads of all the political parties beforehand. Wynand de Villiers had the unenviable task of visiting former President P.W. Botha at his home in the Wilderness. As might have been expected, Botha did not take the news well. De Villiers was therefore unable to get back to Cape Town in time for the announcement. The foreign ambassadors were also asked to assemble before the parliamentary session and were addressed by Waldo Stumpf and Jeremy Shearer. De Klerk wanted to ensure that South Africa would not put a diplomatic foot wrong this time ...

Putting things in perspective

The sensational and unexpected nature of President De Klerk's announcement pushed a few important aspects of the weapons programme into the background.

The ultimate building of a nuclear weapon is the final stage of the process, but by no means the most technically challenging one. The enrichment of the weapons material – highly enriched uranium or weapons-grade plutonium – is the most complex and expensive part of the operation and can be described as the highest technological hurdle to overcome.

Very few countries in the world have succeeded in developing their own, unique uranium enrichment process. Several methods were developed at the time of the Manhattan Project, but only one of them has survived, namely the gas diffusion process which was developed jointly by the USA and Britain. After the Second World War German scientists in captivity designed the gas centrifuge process in the USSR; worldwide this is still the process of choice today. Although the nuclear-weapon states have jealously protected this technology in order to keep the power of nuclear weapons in their own hands, the knowledge has been disseminated over time through espionage, covert cooperation for political ends or simply as a result of technological theft.

The South African uranium enrichment process stood alone in that it was not related to any of these processes. It was a unique indigenous process that had never previously been developed or used anywhere else.

Advanced nuclear expertise was naturally required in order to develop the processes and produce weapons material. While South African scientists and engineers had initially been trained in the peaceful uses of nuclear energy (under the American Atoms for Peace programme), this training did not cover the technology required for uranium enrichment or the making of nuclear weapons. Despite the repeated claims in the past that they had received foreign assistance, the fact is that these scientists and engineers had to increase their basic knowledge of nuclear science by independent study, develop their own enrichment process, produce the weapons material and build the devices without any outside help. They didn't even have half a dozen expatriate Nobel prize-winners to call on! Front companies were sometimes used to acquire certain industrial items in a clandestine manner, but the South African scientists had only their own ingenuity to fall back on when making specialised components or inventing new processes.

A second matter that was not specifically mentioned in the announcement was that South Africa was the first – and so far the only – country in the world to develop its own nuclear capability and then to dismantle it voluntarily, while opening up all its facilities to international inspection. Furthermore, the ensuing inspections were of a nature that no country in history has ever before permitted.

The cat was out of the bag and members of the IAEA team were now free to ask all the tantalising questions they had been intentionally holding back on for 16 months. They were able to ask whatever they wanted to know and visit everything they wanted to see, at the open invitation of the State President. The second phase of the correctness and completeness investigation could begin.

A whole new game was about to start.

Prelude to 23 March 1993

On 26 February 1990 President De Klerk signed the death sentence for the South African nuclear weapons programme; the weapons had all been laid to rest by mid-1991, but the obituary notice was only read in parliament on 23 March 1993. Why the delay? one might ask.

De Klerk's predecessor, P.W. Botha, had been the Minister of Defence for 12 years, and then served as Prime Minister for six years, up to 1984, after which he held office as the Executive State President of South Africa for the next five years. While holding the last two offices he still retained a tight grip on the reins of the Defence Force. Under his leadership the State Security Council was given an increasingly important role in the daily running of the country through the National Security Management System. Botha was a militarist in every fibre of his being and was also the driving force behind the local armaments industry which was created to fill the gap left by international arms sanctions and succeeded impressively in doing so. Armscor was soon able to boast of a large variety of locally developed combat vehicles, missiles, light and heavy artillery, torpedoes, glide bombs, remote-controlled reconnaissance aircraft and electronic combat systems.

De Klerk had had no exposure to the development of the armaments industry. To him this was *terra incognita* and he felt very ill at ease. He almost gave one the impression that he might have had the following quote from the old soldier Eisenhower's farewell speech as President of the USA, delivered in January 1961, framed and hanging somewhere on his wall:

> Until the latest of our world conflicts, the United States had no armaments industry. But now we can no longer risk emergency improvisation of national defense; we have been compelled to create a permanent armaments industry of vast proportions.
>
> In the councils of government, we must guard against the acquisition of unwarranted influence, whether sought or unsought, by the military-industrial complex. The potential for the disastrous rise of misplaced power exists and will persist.
>
> We must never let the weight of this combination endanger our liberties or democratic processes. We should take nothing for granted. Only an alert and knowledgeable citizenry can compel the proper meshing of the huge industrial and military machinery of defense with our peaceful methods and goals, so that security and liberty may prosper together.

THE BOMB

At the cabinet meeting held in November 1989 at which F.W. de Klerk confirmed the decision to terminate the nuclear weapons programme, the President was asked to put the decision in writing. Consequently letters were sent to the AEC and Armscor via their respective ministers, Dawie de Villiers and Magnus Malan. The AEC's letter was delivered a few days after the cabinet meeting, but the letter to Armscor was "missing" for six weeks. On top of this, it was during this period that an attempt was made by the Air Force (which was appointed on 21 April 1986 as the "user" of the nuclear and missile programme) to transfer the nuclear weapons (quite unnecessarily) from the Circle facility to the army's big ammunition depot near Roedtan on the Springbok Flats. This was a strange initiative. Why had it suddenly become necessary to move the weapons after the decision to dismantle them had already been taken at the highest level? Furthermore, the reasons given by the spokesperson for the Air Force lacked credibility: The Air Force was officially in control of the weapons and wanted to be able to say that they had used the storage facility, which had been specially built for the safekeeping of nuclear weapons in the ammunition depot, for that purpose for a short while. Armscor did not support the Air Force in this and after a threat to report the matter to the State President the Air Force representative undertook to discuss the matter with his bosses. Only then could the process of dismantlement begin. Someone who played an important part during this critical period is still convinced today that the country came very close to a coup d'état led by members of the Defence Force.

Shortly afterwards, in 1992, a number of high-ranking military and police officers were suddenly discharged by De Klerk. The "Roedtan initiative" was probably partly responsible. In addition, the Defence Force budget was halved overnight. The military coterie had been well and truly bloodnosed.

The attitude of the right-wing political parties in parliament, including the Conservative Party and the Afrikaner Volksfront, was far closer to the views of certain elements in the security machinery. Notably, the eminent and respected former head of the Defence Force, General Constand Viljoen, who was later to enter politics, threw his weight behind the more conservative political faction. It was clear that De Klerk had been very careful not to antagonise this group too soon by an announcement that the weapons programme was to be terminated and the weapons dismantled. The vehement response of the right-wing parties in parliament following De Klerk's announcement was a telling manifestation of the way they felt – but so was De Klerk's biting reaction to their outcry. The views of political thinkers on the

THE END OF AN ERA

right were put in a nutshell in an interview which Jan Lamprecht conducted with P.W. Botha five months before Botha's death:

> President P.W. Botha personally told me that he was extremely unhappy with De Klerk's dismantling of the nuclear bombs. Like the scientists, President Botha believed that De Klerk dismantled much more than just the nukes – by destroying Pretoria's nuclear deterrent, he destroyed the Afrikaner state.
>
> PW's own words to me about the nukes was that he never intended to use them. He told me that he wanted to use them as a "negotiations tool". He felt that De Klerk had foolishly destroyed one of the most potent negotiation tools that our side had possessed. Foolishly, he destroyed everything instead of using it as a bargaining chip.

De Klerk therefore had to perform a delicate balancing act: On the one hand there was the fear of a right-wing backlash but on the other there was increasing international pressure to come clean. He therefore had to wait for the most suitable time – in his opinion – to make the announcement.

Shortly after De Klerk's announcement, Waldo Stumpf mentioned another reason for the delay to David Albright, namely that the government had been afraid that an earlier announcement might have led to the type of inspections that took place in Iraq, where there were serious and unpleasant confrontations and buildings and equipment were physically destroyed.

Whatever the real reason, during the 16 months of tightrope-walking by the President the AEC staff, who had to confront the IAEA team almost every day, were gnashing their teeth. The IAEA team in turn were under enormous pressure, especially from their financial sponsor, the USA, to act in a more confrontational manner, something which was foreign to the IAEA's customary diplomatic and scientific stance.

Finally Perricos's team could openly turn their attention to the "corpse with the dagger in its back" and begin their forensic investigation – which was a huge relief to all concerned.

In Vienna the IAEA welcomed the new developments in a press release, especially the State President's offer of "access anywhere, at any time, but within reasonable limits".

The Department of State of the USA stated in a secret report, dated December 1993, that South Africa even agreed to allow American experts to get directly involved in analysing documentation relating to the Y-plant. Fortunately by that time the IAEA had already learned an important lesson from their cooperation with Unscom in Iraq and they did not want to see the tail wagging the dog again. Accordingly the IAEA courteously declined the USA's offer, "for the sake of the IAEA's institutional impartiality and integrity".

Not all the problems that arose were foreign-based. After De Klerk's announcement reports appeared in local right-wing newspapers on "Projek Kerktoring" (Project Church Tower), along with threats that "everything would be revealed". Sixteen former Armscor employees (mainly technicians) who had lost their jobs tried to blackmail the state in March 1994 by demanding retrenchment benefits of 1 million dollars each. Unless the state met their demands they planned to sell their secret information to the highest bidder. However, the Chief Justice of the Transvaal prohibited the group from revealing any information on the provision, exporting, importing or manufacture of nuclear weapons or on nuclear weapons research. A secret settlement was negotiated with the 16 individuals, but they did not receive anything like the large sum they were hoping for. The threats died a silent death but for many of the retrenched staff the bitterness lingered.

There were also other influential individuals who were unhappy about the way the dismantlement procedures and South Africa's re-entry into the international community were handled. Jannie Roux, who was the South African ambassador in Vienna between 1992 and 1996, regarded it as a humiliation that the IAEA had been permitted to place their seals on the special storage facility containing highly enriched uranium at Pelindaba. He was of the opinion that South Africa had "given too much away and received nothing in return". However, the attachment of the seals immediately confirmed South Africa's bona fides and was in line with F.W. de Klerk's instructions to raise South Africa's international standing as far as possible. These seals are rather flimsy and can easily be opened; they serve mainly to indicate afterwards that they have been tampered with.

Wynand de Villiers, the chairman of the board of the AEC, was personally concerned about the consequences if the highly enriched uranium were to land in the ANC's hands. In July 1993 he visited the USA along with Waldo Stumpf and Jeremy Shearer (from the Department of Foreign Affairs). Before the meeting with their American counterparts De Villiers told Stumpf and Shearer that he wanted to offer the South African highly enriched uranium to the Americans. Stumpf held a very different opinion. He wanted to keep the uranium for Safari for use in the manufacture of medical isotopes. Stumpf had to think fast. At the meeting at the South African embassy in Washington he deliberately chose a seat between his two South African colleagues. Since Stumpf was in the middle of the group the Americans assumed that he was the leader of the delegation and he was able to dominate the discussion.

According to a report that appeared in *NuclearFuel* on 16 August 1993, Stumpf said that South Africa had approached the USA and Britain in 1992 about the possible sale of weapons material. The British showed no interest and the Americans said that they would only be able to take a decision after the presidential election in November 1992. Furthermore, the first newsletter of 1993 issued by the Programme for Promoting Nuclear Non-Proliferation (PPNN) indicated that the Americans would be prepared to buy the weapons material, on condition that the USA was permitted to launch its own investigation (parallel to that of the IAEA) to establish the "completeness and correctness" of the information and to ensure that no further enrichment was taking place.

Stumpf deliberately refrained from opening up this can of worms at the Washington meeting and made it clear to the Americans (and his own boss) that the highly enriched uranium would be retained as fuel for Safari for use in the manufacture of medical isotopes. The Americans therefore left empty-handed. What is more, they were denied the opportunity for further meddling in South Africa's affairs. This privilege was reserved for the IAEA.

Resuscitating the CCI

A day after De Klerk's sensational announcement in parliament, Von Baeckmann and André Lagattu, both of whom were available since they were still finalising the CCI, visited the Armscor facilities (the Circle and Advena) where the weapons were built. It was no more than a symbolic visit but the IAEA had a specific problem.

The IAEA's two main objectives are to promote the peaceful use of nuclear energy and to ensure that any nuclear material and equipment supplied is not being used for military purposes and that nuclear material is not diverted for nuclear explosive purposes. By definition, therefore, the staff of this body are not supposed to be nuclear weapons experts, and exposure of the staff to technical data on nuclear weapons is regarded as nuclear proliferation. So how was the second stage of the CCI to be approached?

As in Iraq, this problem was solved by co-opting nuclear weapons experts from outside as part of the IAEA team. The CCI team was therefore rapidly augmented with weapons experts from four of the five nuclear-weapon states, namely the USA, France, Britain and Russia. Why China was bypassed, is a matter for speculation. These experts came and went. One got the impression that some of them were simply there out of curiosity and did not make much of a contribution to the work of the IAEA team. The team was also reinforced by the addition of a few people from the IAEA's Iraq action team. The augmented IAEA team was permitted to hold interviews with any South African who had worked on the previous programme. Bob Kelley, an American team member who had gained a lot of experience in Iraq and who had (since 1992) apparently been leaking information on Iraq, gleaned in his capacity as an IAEA employee, to institutions in the USA, abused this privilege. He wormed himself into the confidence of the local Armscor personnel on a personal and social level. In the process he obtained more information than he strictly needed, for example on the South African missile programme – which was not the IAEA's responsibility.

A new series of discussions followed in which the augmented team was given in-depth information on the technical history of the weapons programme by people who had participated in it directly. Questions could be freely asked and all the facilities were made available to the IAEA team. The team obviously attached great value to being able to liaise directly with the staff who had worked on the previous programme. They were also visibly impressed by the quality of the people they met in this way, so much so that Dr Johan Slabber – the leading AEC scientist who supplied information to the team – soon received a job offer from the IAEA and joined that institution before the year was out.

The information provided by the South Africans concerned the design and building of the nuclear weapons, along with the dismantlement history of every weapon. There were naturally also questions about the controversial "test in the Indian Ocean in September 1979" which is discussed elsewhere in this book.

Dimitri Perricos, who was still the team leader, was dumbstruck when the team started inspecting the Circle and Advena facilities. He had been expecting far more sophisticated machinery and equipment. His precise words were: "From now on we will have to look at equipment again, differently. How did they manage to make the bombs with this?"

He obviously did not know what South Africans are capable of improvising with equipment that others might regard as primitive. Sanctions and lack of funding necessitated innovative thinking during the "polecat" years. For example, they simply bought the best lathes from overseas that were not on the sanctions lists and then adapted them locally for high-precision work.

The spanking new Advena facilities, which had not really been occupied yet, impressed the team. One building was especially conspicuous. It had clearly been designed for the integration of missiles and nuclear weapons.

A Russian bomb-maker takes the wheel

Eventually there were only two Russian nuclear weapons scientists on the augmented team, both fairly young. One individual was very tall and the other on the short side. The AEC people referred to them jocularly as "Langeraat" and "Fielafooi" (terms used in Afrikaans to designate the middle and ring fingers).

Fielafooi, while he was apparently capable of building nuclear bombs, had one gap in his education. His sophisticated technical knowledge did not include the ability to drive a motor car and he had a burning desire to learn to drive. There was plenty of space at the Advena site and its roads had recently been tarred. One day he came up with a diffident request that somebody should show him the basics on the Avis car the team members had hired.

After some terse instructions he got behind the wheel and pulled off jerkily like a typical learner driver – a clutch is an awkward thing to master, even for a seasoned bomb-maker.

He soon improved, however, and the joy on the Russian's face was a pleasure to see – he evidently found driving as much fun as successfully designing and building a new-generation hydrogen bomb.

The remainder of that chaotic year: 1993

The augmented IAEA team was systematically compiling a full picture of the building up and termination of the South African nuclear weapons programme from interviews with the staff, the building and dismantlement history of the weapons, records of nuclear material and other documentation. The information had to be compared with what they had already learned over the previous 16 months by means of thorough verification of the declared stocks of nuclear material. The two most important questions were:
- Did the declared material correspond to what had been produced over the years?

- Was the declared weapons-grade uranium reconcilable with the details of the weapons programme they were investigating?

On the basis of the President's open invitation the IAEA team was kept busy visiting numerous facilities. Apart from the obvious AEC, Circle and Advena facilities, the team members inspected other sites in all parts of the country. This was no scenic tour; the areas they visited were mainly remote. Some of their destinations were:
- a testing centre for explosives at a military site in Potchefstroom;
- the army ammunition depot near Roedtan where a special storage area for nuclear weapons was built but never used;
- the old coal mine near Witbank where the Melba device was stored for a few months;
- the Vastrap test shafts;
- Armscor facilities such as the Kentron factory in Centurion, Naschem at Potchefstroom and Somchem in the Western Cape;
- the Gouriqua site near Mossel Bay; and
- the Alkantpan ammunition testing grounds where armour-piercing missiles made from depleted uranium were tested. This programme was not connected to the nuclear weapons project, however.

Despite this gruelling programme, within five months of De Klerk's announcement the team had an answer ready for the IAEA's Board of Governors and the General Conference which was to take place in September 1993. This was followed by the report by Hans Blix, the Director-General of the IAEA, which he delivered to the UNSC in person on 1 November. In this report he came to the following conclusions:

> When a State joining the safeguards system has many nuclear installations and much nuclear material, it is always difficult to verify that everything has been declared.

> However, the Agency's activities in South Africa show that such difficulties can be successfully tackled through sustained efforts by the IAEA and a high degree of co-operation and transparency by the inspected party. Since September 1991, when South Africa concluded its comprehensive Safeguards Agreement with the IAEA, 22 IAEA safeguards missions have visited South Africa. Many apparent discrepancies and inconsistencies which were ear-

THE END OF AN ERA

lier identified have been resolved. No reason has been found to doubt the veracity of South Africa's initial declaration.

A new dimension was added when President De Klerk declared that South Africa had developed a nuclear weapons capability but had destroyed it totally before acceding to the NPT. The Agency was invited to examine that the programme had, in fact, been terminated and that all the nuclear material had been placed under safeguards. A team of Agency staff and nuclear weapons experts visited South Africa for these purposes in April, June and August this year. It found no indication casting doubt on South Africa's statement that all the highly enriched uranium from weapons had been reported in its initial declaration.

A specialist international team finally concluded that there were no bombs buried under a tree in the bushveld – or anywhere else for that matter.

Not everyone agreed with this finding, however.

In the first half of 1993 the following information appeared in the PPNN newsletter: "As an apparent point of concern, (South African) newspapers note that the scientist originally in charge of the weapons programme, Dr. Wally Grant, is now the leader of the movement for a separate Afrikaner homeland."

After leaving the service of the AEC in 1987, Wally Grant had joined several right-wing organisations, such as the Afrikaner Volkswag, the Volkseenheidskomitee, the Afrikaner Vryheidstigting and the Volkstaatraad. As a member of the last body he participated in the discussions in April 1994 which led to an agreement between the Freedom Front, the ANC and the South African NP government. The agreement was known as the "Accord on Afrikaner self-determination". In one of the many exploratory talks with the ANC he made a joke about "one (nuclear weapon) which I keep in my garage". Everyone laughed, but some of those present were not sure that he was joking …

The worst accusations were still to come. Two years after the IAEA had published a clean report, the armchair experts Peter Hounam and Steve McQuillan (famed for literary productions like *Who Killed Diana?* and *The Secret Cult*) published their book *The Mini-Nuke Conspiracy: How Mandela Inherited a Nuclear Nightmare*. This contained the statement that the six nuclear weapons produced "in the early 1980's" were simply a cover for a more advanced programme which included nuclear bombs capable of being fired by G5 guns, as well as neutron bombs. A further melodramatic allegation was that "hundreds of nuclear weapons" had not been dismantled or declared and were hidden away in a secret place. They alleged that over 1 000 tactical weapons had ended up in the hands of the far-right parties. The authors gave a detailed account of South Africa's attempts to obtain the magical (but unfortunately mythical) substance "red mercury" for the nuclear programme.

A magical substance

What was the magical substance – red mercury – referred to by the scandalmongers Hounam and McQuillan? Thereby hangs a long tale of deceit, intrigue and even the death of innocent – if greedy – people.

During the decade-long presidency (1990 to 2000) of the habitually vodka-befuddled Boris Yeltsin, the first democratically elected Russian president, the affairs of Russia and its former satellite states were going to hell in a handcart. When the iron lid of central communist control was gradually lifted, a veritable Pandora's box was opened from which fabulously wealthy oligarchs came pouring out. Mafia-like criminality and fraud in various guises spread like an evil virus.

Scams involving nuclear materials were especially popular. Many of these scams involved offering small quantities of natural uranium, low-enriched uranium and depleted uranium to ignorant buyers as weapons material. Even hazardous radioactive sources such as cesium-137 and cobalt-60 were offered for sale as weapons material. Ill-informed and greedy buyers paid astronomical prices for them. This created an ideal breeding ground for criminal entrepreneurs.

In 1993 the leading Russian newspaper Pravda (ironically enough the name means "truth" in Russian) published extracts from a so-called secret government memorandum containing a reference to "red mercury". This magical substance was described as "a superconductive material used for producing high-precision conventional and nuclear bomb explosives" and for making aircraft invisible to radar. Primary end-users were given as the aerospace and nuclear-industry companies in the USA and France, as well as a number of countries aspiring to build nuclear weapons, including South Africa, Israel, Iran, Iraq and Libya. It began to be rumoured (possibly at the deliberate instigation of the KGB) that a "pure" thermonuclear bomb, the size of a cricket ball, could be made *with the aid of red mercury.*

The magical red mercury was smuggled by Russian businessmen in Europe and the Middle East and sold for fabulous sums. "Red mercury can do almost anything the aspiring Third World demagogue wants it to do" (New Scientist, 1992). What dictator wouldn't want to own a few thermonuclear bombs (fusion bombs) the size of a cricket ball – an enormous improvement on the first thermonuclear bomb (code-named Mike) which weighed 70 tons and was the size of an average house?

The feverish search for red mercury continued everywhere: In Angola uninformed people tried to reclaim red mercury from old landmines and unexploded bombs – with accompanying loss of life. In the Arab world the price of Grandma's old-fashioned Singer sewing machine increased a thousandfold because these machines were thought to contain red mercury.

In an article in Nucleonics Week which appeared in 1993, red mercury became a Soviet code word for a compound between a particular isotope of lithium and deuterium (heavy hydrogen) which is used in thermonuclear bombs (formerly called hydrogen bombs). A thermonuclear bomb uses an ordinary nuclear bomb as a "spark plug" which creates the necessary conditions to cause the secondary fusion of deuterium and tritium in order to produce a far higher explosive yield.

Deuterium is a stable isotope and is present in ordinary water from which it is fairly easy to extract. Tritium, on the other hand, is radioactive and has to be specially produced in nuclear reactors. Because of radioactive decay, tritium has to be replaced from time to time. The ideal is therefore to make a so-called "dry" thermonuclear bomb in which tritium is produced in situ. When lithium and deuterium form a solid compound (lithium deuteride) the result is the ideal material for thermonuclear reactions. Freely available neutrons from the fission reaction of the "spark plug" react with the deuterium to form tritium. When particular high pressure and temperature conditions are created, the deuterium and tritium fuse and cause powerful thermonuclear explosions.

But where does mercury come into the picture? There are two isotopes of lithium, namely lithium-6 and lithium-7. The isotope required for a thermonuclear bomb is lithium-6. The two isotopes are separated in a process in which lithium is used in an amalgam with large quantities of mercury. Both Britain and the USA used processes of this kind to obtain lithium-6. The American Colex process used 11 million kg of mercury, for example, and was ultimately unable to account for about a million kilograms – a highly toxic legacy of the insane race to build ever-bigger nuclear bombs.

So, does red mercury exist? The IAEA, the world's nuclear watchdog, dismissed it in the following words: "The whole thing is a bunch of malarkey." The USA's Department of Energy (USDOE) has stated that no such substance exists.

The international groups which are trying to prevent nuclear proliferation by controlling exports of nuclear-related and dual-use materials and components are the Zangger Committee and the NSG. They have drawn up comprehensive export control lists of items that could be used for nuclear proliferation. Nowhere on these lists does red mercury appear. If simple objects like stainless steel pipes and valves appear on these lists, why has the extremely potent red mercury been omitted?

What was the position in South Africa? The brutal murder in November 1991 of Alan Kidger, the sales manager of Thor Chemicals, was the first of a series of unexplained murders in South Africa. (Thor Chemicals was responsible for the contamination of the Cato Ridge area in KwaZulu-Natal with mercury.) Most of the murder victims were involved in the arms trade and in transactions with Middle Eastern states. It has been suggested that trade in "red mercury" could have played a part in their deaths. However, no conclusive evidence linking these murders has been found as yet. There is a theory that the Israeli intelligence agency Mossad was responsible for the murders. The red mercury peddlers tried their luck even in the most elevated circles. Waldo Stumpf remembers that during Thabo Mbeki's presidency he received a letter in which the President asked his advice after an agent had offered to sell him the magical substance.

Professor André Buys, formerly attached to the AEC and Armscor and currently a lecturer at the University of Pretoria (UP), had the following to say about this dubious material:

> The red mercury story is a hoax that has got out of hand ... I have no doubt that there could well be a connection between murders in South Africa and red mercury, because we know these people are arms smugglers. We know that this commodity, which is a phantom substance, has achieved a value

> of ridiculous proportions – it is more than 10 times the price of gold (André Buys in *Is Chernobyl Dead?* by C.M. Meyer).

Despite the doubts cast on the IAEA's conclusions by certain organisations, the American Department of State took a more realistic view. In a secret report dated December 1993 they came to the following conclusion:

> The amount of enriched uranium produced at the Valindaba plant (the nation's key highly enriched uranium [HEU] producer) ... corresponds to the mid range of previous estimates of actual plant production but is well below plant capacity. South African officials have described, in impressive detail, plant operating problems that are technically plausible but were hitherto unknown to the United States; nonetheless, there are consistencies between other data provided by South Africa and US information.

A spectacular affair

The backfilling of the test shafts at Vastrap, which took place under the supervision of the IAEA, did not prove to be a simple process. Initially front-end loaders were used to drop great scoops of fine Kalahari sand down into the shafts – with unexpected results. As the sand fell down the shaft it formed a "plug" which compressed the air at the bottom of the shaft. Suddenly a red fountain of Kalahari sand – which one of the spectators compared to a dragon's breath – shot up from the shaft high into the air. It looked as if the shafts were objecting vigorously to the backfilling.

After many experiments, which included lowering drums filled with concrete and scrap steel, the shafts were eventually filled in July 1993 and sealed with concrete.

An interesting visit

After the revelation by President De Klerk regarding South Africa's abandoned nuclear weapons programme, Waldo Stumpf became a popular speaker on the subject of the history and dismantlement of the programme. He appeared in numerous television interviews and participated in news conferences and symposia, including some in the USA and Italy.

How did the government of the day feel about the possibility that their former arch-enemy might inherit South Africa's sophisticated nuclear weapons programme? Waldo Stumpf is quoted on this matter in G.R. Heald's thesis entitled "South Africa's voluntary relinquishment of its nuclear arsenal and accession to the treaty on the non-proliferation of nuclear weapons in terms of international law":

> Professor Stumpf claimed that the potential nuclear proliferation risks by the ANC were not raised by Mr de Klerk as a specific concern in his meetings with him. It is noted, though, that Professor Stumpf did explore the matter of nuclear proliferation fears associated with a national liberation movement. In this regard, Professor Stumpf's assessment was similar to that of Mr Pik Botha, inasmuch as:
>
> - he acknowledged the OAU's desire to possess a nuclear capability;
> - he acknowledged that there were elements within the leadership of the ANC who shared this view.

During an interview which the authors of this book held with Waldo Stumpf on 7 March 2013, the former CEO of the AEC emphasised that it had not been fear of the ANC that motivated F.W. de Klerk to order the dismantling of the nuclear weapons programme:

> In all my meetings with De Klerk I never even picked this up from his body language. This was not the factor. The factor was the handing over by a white minority to a black majority. That was already a complex business. Why make the process more difficult? It would have been a hot potato. What would they have done with the things? The international community would have climbed in immediately, because this was not something that could be done in secret. It would simply have put too much pressure on them. I never got the impression that De Klerk was afraid that the ANC would act irresponsibly with the nuclear bombs. But there were just too many complications. How would you hand the bombs over? Emotions would have run high in South Africa. In any case, would Mandela have been accepted on the world stage with "nukes in his backyard"? (translation)

THE END OF AN ERA

Johan Slabber, who was recruited by the IAEA during their inspection in South Africa and who accepted a post at their head office in Vienna, says that a different story was doing the rounds in Vienna at the time. He had been told "on good authority" that the Americans had made it a specific condition that the nuclear weapons programme should first be dismantled before the black majority government came to power. There are even people who go as far as suggesting that at the time F.W. de Klerk accepted millions from "the Americans" to dismantle the programme and "hand the country over to the ANC". According to the late P.W. Botha, the Americans made the same offer to him at that time but he rejected it. However, there is no evidence to back this up apart from verbal communications made by Botha to a few individuals shortly before his death.

By the middle of 1993 it was clear in which direction the political winds were starting to blow. Waldo Stumpf therefore decided to invite the ANC for a formal discussion. The invitation was accepted and a delegation visited the AEC on 30 July 1993. It was a fairly large delegation and included the future Minister of Defence, Joe Modise, and the future Deputy Minister of Foreign Affairs, Aziz Pahad. Their technical adviser was Professor Ahmed Bawa, a young physics lecturer from Durban.

The atmosphere was jovial and relaxed. Waldo Stumpf gave his usual presentation on the nuclear programme. The delegation listened attentively and were visibly astonished when Stumpf invited the ANC to carry out their own completeness investigation.

After the presentation, lunch was served and there was an opportunity for more informal discussion. The future Minister of Defence remarked: "Doctor Stumpf, Africa is actually cross with you that you dismantled the nuclear weapons. Africa would have liked very much to have its own weapon."

Dr Niel Barnard, who was Director-General of the National Intelligence Service (NI) at the time, confirmed that Joe Modise had in fact been angry about South Africa's decision to sign the NPT. Barnard is quoted as follows in G.R. Heald's thesis:

> If our nuclear weapons capacity had been handed over to the ANC, it would have had very serious and negative implications for South Africa's international relations, its constitutional status, and indeed its legitimacy as a state. This was an important reason for dismantling the nuclear arsenal.

THE BOMB

Barnard was also worried about what might happen to the nuclear weapons if the ANC took control of them:

> I was worried about these weapons ending up in the hands of the ANC, particularly as Mandela and Gaddafi were quite close at that time.

Heald's own opinion is stated as follows in his thesis:

> The endemic corruption that has been evident in South Africa since the inception of democracy has been of such an intense and all-pervasive level that the researcher's personal view is that a criminal nuclear proliferation scenario would almost certainly have arisen had South Africa retained these weapons. The temptation to sell these nuclear weapons to the highest bidder, whomsoever it might have been, at the greatest profit would simply have been too great.

An African bomb?

In the biography Pik Botha and His Times which appeared in 2010, Theresa Papenfus relates that during a meeting with his old friend Pik Botha, Julius Nyerere expressed himself in favour of a "bomb for Africa", just as Joe Modise had. The demolition of the South African nuclear weapons was clearly a disappointment to him. In an interview with Sue Onslow, Pik Botha recalled: "He (Nyerere) said it had been a tremendous achievement for Africa."

G.R. Heald expands on this incident in his thesis, with reference to a discussion he had with Pik Botha:

> Mr Pik Botha also referred to two important instances where the putative matter of the nuclear weapons being proliferated by the incoming regime of the ANC was brought into stark relief. The first was when Mr Pik Botha had a joint staff luncheon with the United States Assistant Secretary of State for Africa Affairs, Mr Hank Cohen, and the matter of the ANC potentially proliferating nuclear weapons was informally raised by one of Mr Cohen's staff members as a US concern.
>
> The second occasion pertained to a meeting with Mr Julius Nyerere, who was President of Tanzania and an important

indicative "voice" of the Organisation of African Unity (OAU), who also chastised him for South Africa's relinquishment of its nuclear arsenal and accession to the NPT. Mr Botha was bemused by Mr Julius Nyerere's views on this matter.

"Julius Nyerere, the President of Tanzania, came to visit me (Pik Botha) personally in either late 1994 or 1995. He requested a friendly meeting with me and a discussion. In the first part of the meeting, Mr Nyerere provided an excellent overview of the seminal changes that had taken place in Southern Africa. He was highly influential in the Organisation of African Unity (OAU), which had been an important institution in Africa's decolonisation struggle in the Post-World War II period – from the 1950s up into most of the 1960s.

"At one point Nyerere said to me: 'You have displayed great courage and wisdom in what you have done. You have assisted in setting South Africa on a democratic path and restoring human dignity. But I cannot understand why you decided to demolish South Africa's atom bomb. The whole of Africa would have been so proud to own and display to the world that it had such power, mastery and high technology.'

"I explained to Mr Nyerere that there was no way that we could have proceeded with the constitutional negotiations if we had retained the nuclear bomb. The nuclear bomb was anathema to the creation of trust that we were seeking from the constitutional negotiations. I said to Nyerere: 'The nuclear bomb is perceived and seen as the product of apartheid. It is the apartheid bomb. The perceptions are indissolubly linked.'

"I found it interesting that Nyerere harboured these thoughts and deep-seated views. For me it was a *raaisel* (English translation: a riddle, a poser, an enigma) which could not stand up to logical scrutiny. Nyerere never explained to me in what way Africa could have gained prestige from retaining our nuclear bombs. His logic also flew in the face of the emerging nuclear reality, which had as its central purpose the objective of getting Africa to be declared a nuclear-free zone. Nyerere's deep-seated view seemed to be a negation of the massively positive steps of nuclear relinquishment, accession to the NPT, accession to the Treaty of Pelindaba, and the abrogation of South Africa's apartheid Constitution with the negotiation of one of the most advanced constitutions in the world. Nyerere persisted with this bondage thought pattern."

> Speculation on who would have been physically responsible for nuclear weapons in the African context, what they would have been used for and how agreement would have been reached on their use, could well form the subject of another book. However, since 2009 the Treaty of Pelindaba Treaty (African Nuclear-Weapon-Free Zone Treaty) has forbidden the existence and use of nuclear weapons in Africa. Furthermore, South Africa is a founder member of this treaty.
>
> Interestingly enough, the Treaty of Pelindaba came by its name as a result of a bit of wheeling and dealing. Egypt took the lead during the preparations for the signature of the treaty. (Egypt replaced South Africa on the IAEA Board of Governors in 1977, after the South Africans were expelled for political reasons.) The Nigerian, Benson Agu, who had come to Pretoria for discussions with Waldo Stumpf, said that he would prefer that South Africa, the only African country with a nuclear capability on the continent, should be given the credit for the agreement, rather than Egypt. He therefore requested Stumpf to hold the closing function for the treaty negotiations at Pelindaba and also suggested that the South Africans should make full use of the opportunity to display their knowledge and experience. This was done, to the consternation of the Egyptian ambassador who was present that morning and who believed – probably with some justification – that South Africa had wanted to steal a march on Egypt. Although the treaty was officially signed in Cairo later on, it was called the Treaty of Pelindaba.

Nothing came of the parallel investigation proposed by Waldo Stumpf. The ANC was preparing to take over the reins of government a year later and a lot more was at stake.

Apparently the ANC was also fully satisfied with the IAEA's report, because two months later, on 24 September 1993, Nelson Mandela put the request to a session of the UNSC that all sanctions against South Africa be lifted. This request was granted and the resolution was ratified by the UNGA on 8 October 1993.

And this concluded a chapter in South Africa's nuclear history.

The inevitable question is: was it all worthwhile?

In 1988 the Cuban delegation to the talks on ending the Border War in Namibia and Angola was headed by Jorge Risquet. Many years later, in December 2010, he visited South Africa and had a meeting with his former opponent, Pik Botha, to mull over the old days. On that occasion Risquet was generous enough to admit that fear of the South African nuclear weapons had restrained Cuba from invading the then South-West Africa. The Cubans were convinced that the weapons could be fired from South Africa's formidable G5 and G6 guns. Pik Botha arranged for Risquet to have a discussion with Waldo Stumpf in Pretoria. Risquet and his delegation told Stumpf that since 1985 the Cubans had been so sure that South Africa had deliverable nuclear weapons that they always split their divisions in two so that their troops would not all be wiped out at the same time by a nuclear bomb! Stumpf assured the Cubans that although South Africa did have nuclear weapons at that time, they were not sophisticated or small enough to be fired from G5 and G6 guns. Cuba had overestimated South Africa's capability, which was naturally to the advantage of the South Africans. On 1 January 2011 *Rapport* published the following piece:

> For Botha and Stumpf this interaction showed that the South African nuclear programme had achieved its aim and made a real contribution to the Cuban military "caution" in the south of Angola. In their opinion, if Cuba or Angola had in fact intended to invade South-West Africa, this was prevented and therefore apparently never became the official policy. (translation)

Jorge Risquet Valdés

From 1965 Jorge Risquet Valdés was closely involved in intervention in the Congo area (Brazzaville and Leopoldville) together with the Cuban brothers, Fidel and Raúl Castro, and Che Guevara. Their aim was

> to plant their communist revolutionary ideology there. Later on they turned their attention to Angola.
>
> Risquet was born in 1930 and by the age of 15 he was already an active member of the executive committee of the communist party in Cuba. In time he rose to become a respected member of the central committee of the party and was Cuba's chief negotiator, opposing Pik Botha, at the four-party talks held in London in May 1988. These talks were to lead to the ending of the Border War and ultimately to Namibia's independence.
>
> The London talks were tough at times. At one stage when the negotiations between the various parties were deadlocked Risquet threatened to throw an additional 30 000 Cuban troops into the struggle. Pik Botha's answer was that in that case South Africa would have to send an additional 3 000 soldiers to Angola. Risquet was enraged at this "contempt" for Cuba's military prowess. He stormed out of the meeting. Little did he know that the 3 000 soldiers were really all South Africa would have been able to muster at that stage! The following morning Pik Botha and his team had to use all their diplomatic skills to get the talks back on track. The South African Foreign Minister offered to allow the Cubans to withdraw with honour.

Within the political context of its time the nuclear programme can therefore be said to have played a useful part.

The dismantling of South Africa's nuclear capability was reflected in tangible form when Pik Botha visited Vienna in April 1994. At a function he presented a small sculpture of a miniature plough to Hans Blix of the IAEA. The base of the sculpture bears a quotation from Isaiah 2:4 in both Afrikaans and English: "And they shall beat their swords into ploughshares, and their spears into pruning hooks. Nation shall not lift up sword against nation, neither shall they learn war any more."

This sculpture is on display in front of the entrance to the IAEA's council chamber. An inscription has since been added which reads: "This sculpture, made out of non-nuclear material from a dismantled nuclear device, symbolizes the commitment of the Republic of South Africa to the nonproliferation of nuclear weapons." This country, which was reviled for decades, is still the only state in the world to have voluntarily destroyed its own nuclear weapons.

PART 5

COOPERATION BETWEEN ISRAEL AND SOUTH AFRICA

The Israeli nuclear programme

Israel's involvement in nuclear technology dates back to the establishment of the Jewish state in 1948. In the 1930s and 1940s many Jewish scientists emigrated to Palestine from various parts of the world. Ernst David Bergmann was one of this number. He was later to become the director of the Israeli Nuclear Energy Commission, and to initiate Israel's nuclear weapons programme. He was a close friend of David Ben-Gurion's who became prime minister in 1955 and his advice to the premier was that nuclear energy was the answer to Israel's inadequate natural resources and limited military manpower. As early as 1948 scientists were prospecting for uranium deposits in the Negev Desert on the instructions of the ministry of defence. In 1950 they found low-grade deposits close to Beersheba and Sidon and began work on a method of producing heavy water that did not require much energy.

The government sent promising Israeli students overseas to study nuclear science. In 1952 Israel secretly established its own nuclear energy commission and placed it under the direct control of the ministry of defence. Shimon Peres, deputy director-general of the department, was put in charge of nuclear weapons production. He was insistent that Israel should find a partner in order to speed up the programme. He identified France as a supplier of the required equipment and technology. France felt indebted to Israel for the assistance rendered during the 1956 Suez Crisis and in 1957 Peres and the French government under Guy Mollet signed three secret agreements which would form the backbone of the Israeli nuclear weapons programme.

The young state of Israel was financially constrained at the time and decided not to use internal funds but to rely on secret foreign donations. In this way Peres managed to obtain an astounding 40 million US dollars – but that was only about half of what was needed. For many years the question remained: Where did the rest of the finances come from? A possible source was exposed by the German media (*Die Welt* and *Der Spiegel*) in 2015. Since 1961 the German government under Konrad Adenauer had been financing projects for the "development of the Negev Desert" which included a "textile factory" and a "seawater desalination plant using nuclear energy". These plants were never built but the money kept flowing until about 1973. Estimated in present currency values, it represented about five billion Euros of which four billion was regarded as a "grant". So did Germany finance the Israeli nuclear weapons programme? As might be expected, Peres and the German government denied this.

The heart of Israel's nuclear weapons programme is the Negev Nuclear Research Centre, which is located near the desert city of Dimona. The centre is usually referred to simply as "Dimona". In the 1950s and 1960s the French built a nuclear reactor and plutonium production facility at Dimona. All Israel's weapons material is produced there, although the design and production of nuclear weapons may take place elsewhere. There is a substantial amount of evidence that over the years Britain has also been only too willing to supply equipment, materials and expertise to the Israelis. Official government papers released by the British National Archives in 2005 revealed that 20 tons of excess heavy water, originating in Norway, was exported to Israel without the knowledge of the USA and no condition of "peaceful use" was attached to the export.

One might well ask why France became involved. The answer is simply that General Charles de Gaulle regarded Israel as part of France's strategic vision. If Israel possessed a nuclear capability it could serve as a buffer against Egypt. It should be remembered that Egypt had supported the rebel forces in their fight against French domination in Algeria. Furthermore, France was aiming to develop its own nuclear capability. The USA had banned the supply of certain kinds of computer technology to France. The Israelis were able to obtain this technology and in turn pass it on to France. Another factor was that the USA was supplying heavy water to Israel under the Atoms for Peace programme – in addition to that supplied by the UK – for use in the small research reactor at Soreq. France had its eye on this heavy water for its own purposes.

Since the French still needed a few years before they could carry out a successful nuclear test, they regarded the knowledge the Israelis were acquiring as an insurance policy in case they encountered technical problems on the road to achieving their nuclear aspirations.

It has been claimed that the first French nuclear test which took place in Algeria in 1969 marked the creation of two nuclear powers. Israeli observers were present along with the French scientists and they had unrestricted access to information on the nuclear test. The Israelis even provided the French team with technology and hardware for the test.

Officially the Israelis referred to the facilities at Dimona as a manganese plant, and sometimes even as a textile plant! The USA became aware of the existence of Dimona for the first time in 1958 from photographs taken from their U-2 spy planes. On 2 December 1960 the US Department of State issued a statement disclosing that Israel had a secret nuclear facility. This was reported in *The New York Times* a few days later. The Israeli prime minister, David Ben-Gurion, was obliged to make an announcement and on 21 December he stated that Israel was building a 24-megawatt reactor "for peaceful purposes".

In May 1961 the then Israeli prime minister, David Ben-Gurion, and the new president of the USA, John F. Kennedy, met in New York to discuss the future of the Dimona project. Ben-Gurion had repeatedly tried to convince Kennedy, both in public and in private, that the project was intended for peaceful purposes. Kennedy remained sceptical.

The minutes of their official meeting were kept secret for 30 years and only made public in the mid-1990s. They indicate that the two leaders spent only 15 minutes discussing the topic. Ben-Gurion pointed to Israel's energy needs and repeated that the aims of the project were peaceful. However, he concluded the discussion on the following note:

> We are asked whether it is for peace. For the time being the only purposes are for peace. Not now, but after three or four years we shall have a pilot plant for separation, which is needed anyway for a power reactor. There is no such intention now, not for four or five years. But we will see what happens in the Middle East. It does not depend on us. Maybe Russia won't give bombs to China or Egypt, but maybe Egypt will develop them herself.

Over the years Dimona was discussed at several meetings between American presidents and Israeli prime ministers. Israel repeatedly made use of delaying tactics and obfuscation to keep the Americans at arm's length. Later on they began to use their nuclear capability as a secret trump card in negotiations to acquire conventional weapons from the USA.

Israel did permit the American physicists Eugene Wigner and Isidor Rabi to visit Dimona, but Ben-Gurion refused to allow regular international inspections at the plant. Eventually the USA and Israel agreed that Israel should only operate Dimona for peaceful purposes and that the Americans would be permitted to carry out an inspection twice a year. However, the

THE BOMB

American inspectors were only allowed access to the aboveground sections of the buildings and these visits dwindled to once a year. There were simulated control rooms in the aboveground sections and the access points to the underground areas were carefully concealed while the inspectors were on site. The Israelis even went so far as to build a brick wall to hide the lifts leading to the subterranean plutonium reclamation plant!

These inspection visits began in 1962 and continued into 1969. They were discontinued following an agreement between President Richard Nixon and the Israeli head of state Golda Meir. Nixon made the pragmatic decision to accept Israel's nuclear status provided that it remained a secret.

The fact that the collusion between Israel, France, the UK and Norway left the USA in the dark for many years has recently been described by Avner Cohen and William Burr as "a major blunder of American intelligence. In comparative terms, it was probably as severe as the failures to anticipate the Indian nuclear tests in 1974 and 1998." In this respect the winged words of Donald Rumsfeld – an erstwhile secretary of defense under George W. Bush – seem to apply:

> There are known knowns. These are things we know that we know. There are known unknowns. That is to say, there are things that we know we don't know. But there are also unknown unknowns. There are things we don't know we don't know.

Israel has been surrounded by hostile neighbours since Biblical times. It consequently makes sense for Israel to maintain the so-called Samson option, a strategy of deterrence and massive retaliation with nuclear weapons as a last resort if the country's existence were to be threatened. The name of this strategy refers to the blinded Biblical figure Samson who caused a Philistine temple to collapse, thereby killing himself and thousands of Philistines. An important part of the strategy is to maintain *amimut,* i.e. not to confirm or deny the existence of the nuclear capability.

In 1958 Charles de Gaulle came to power, made peace with the Arabs and relinquished French claims to Algeria. The close relationship with Israel came to an end and aid was cut off. Mirage fighter jets and missile boats on order and paid for in full were not delivered. Although France, like the Americans, received a solemn undertaking from the Israelis that they would not develop nuclear weapons the Israelis proceeded to run their nuclear programme in the Negev Desert on their own. By the time the Yom Kippur War broke out in October 1973, Israel already possessed sophisticated nuclear bombs. Premier Golda Meir's cabinet resolved on 8 October 1973 that thirteen 20-kiloton nuclear bombs should be prepared for delivery. The words "Never again!" (a reference to the extermination of the Jews by the Nazis during the Second World War) are said to have been welded on the first bomb.

The Egyptian and Syrian forces against whom they were fighting suspected that Israel possessed such weapons. Who knows to what extent this influenced their tactics?

Upon the outbreak of the Yom Kippur War in the Middle East in October 1973 the Americans hastily supplied Israel with conventional weapons for fear that if the Israelis were driven into a corner they might exercise their nuclear option.

Christian convert/successful spy

A sensational espionage scandal that caused the Israelis great embarrassment erupted in 1986. The central figure was a nuclear technician, Mordechai Vanunu. He focused international attention on Israel's top secret nuclear programme.

For nine years Vanunu had been employed at the Machon 2 facility at Dimona, where plutonium was produced and bomb components were manufactured. However, his increasing involvement in pro-Palestine politics led to his discharge in 1986. Because the security measures were inadequate, before he left he was able to take about 60 photographs, covering almost every section of the Machon 2 facility. He then spent a few months travelling round the world and ended up in Australia, where he was converted to Christianity and joined the Australian Anglican Church which was vehemently opposed to nuclear weapons. Under their influence he decided to make his information on the Israeli nuclear arsenal public.

Vanunu made contact with the London paper, *The Sunday Times*. The newspaper flew him to London and prepared for an exclusive interview. But the Israeli government got wind of Vanunu's plans and instructed its secret service, Mossad, to arrest Vanunu and take him back to Israel. They did this without difficulty. An Israeli agent named Cheryl Bentov approached the lonely Vanunu and introduced herself as an American tourist, "Cindy". Cindy invited Vanunu to join her for a holiday in Rome – a classic "honey trap" frequently used by Mossad. Vanunu was overpowered by Cindy's accomplices, drugged and spirited away to a waiting Israeli ship a few days before the publication of the tell-all article in *The Sunday Times* on 5 October 1986.

A few months later Vanunu was tried in Israel. Despite the fact that he was unable to communicate with anyone outside, he nevertheless succeeded in dramatically revealing the details of his arrest by writing them on the palm of his hand and holding his hand up to newspaper photographers while being led from the court by policemen.

According to the information that Vanunu supplied to *The Sunday Times*, at the time of his discharge there were 10 facilities (or machons, in Hebrew) at Dimona. The staff numbered about 2 700. He explained the layout and function of each of the ten facilities. Vanunu also claimed that Israel possessed 100-200 nuclear weapons (for which about 400-800 kg of plutonium had been required) and that the country was capable of producing about 40 kg of plutonium per year. Experts thought that this production figure was too high, however, and regarded the information with scepticism.

Vanunu also claimed that Israel possessed boosted nuclear weapons and had even developed hydrogen bomb technology. He supplied information that confirmed lithium-6 and tritium were being made at Dimona. Tritium was being produced in sufficient quantities for a boosted weapons programme. He also referred to evidence of uranium enrichment at Dimona by means of gas centrifuges and laser isotope separation.

Vanunu was convicted of treason and espionage and sentenced to 18 years' imprisonment. He was released in 2004 and is not permitted to leave Israel. He currently lives in quarters in St George's Cathedral in East Jerusalem, having progressed from whistleblower to bell-ringer.

Vanunu was only one of Israel's numerous problems.

It had long been a known fact that Israel would do everything in its power to prevent its neighbours from developing a nuclear capability. Iraq had been a serious annoyance to Israel for many years. In 1981 Israel decided to bomb the Osirak reactor in Iraq. The attack was carried out by eight F-16 and six F-15 aircraft. Fifteen 1 000 kg bombs were dropped into the depths of the reactor structure. The reactor was blown to pieces. Ten Iraqi soldiers and one French scientist were killed in the attack. As described earlier in this text, while the Osirak reactor core was still in France it was mysteriously sabotaged. It is strongly suspected today that the Mossad were responsible.

Three days after the Israeli attack on Osirak, Raful Eitan, the head of the Israeli Defence Force, triumphantly wrote to a friend in faraway South Africa, Magnus Malan, the Minister of Defence:

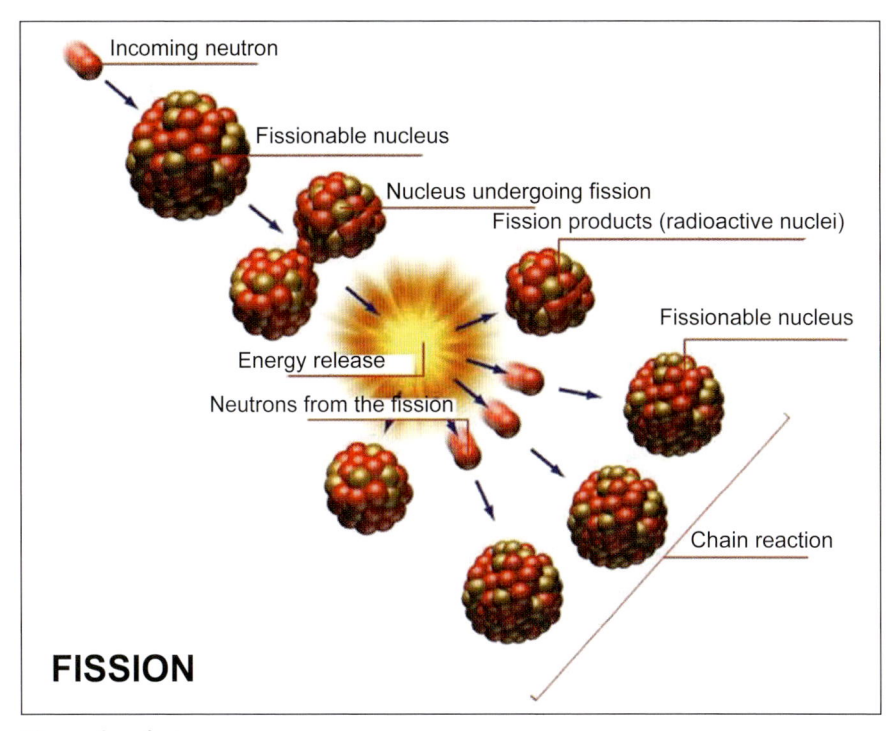

The nuclear fission process
Source: http://visual.merriam-webster.com/images/science/chemistry/matter/nuclear-fission.jpg

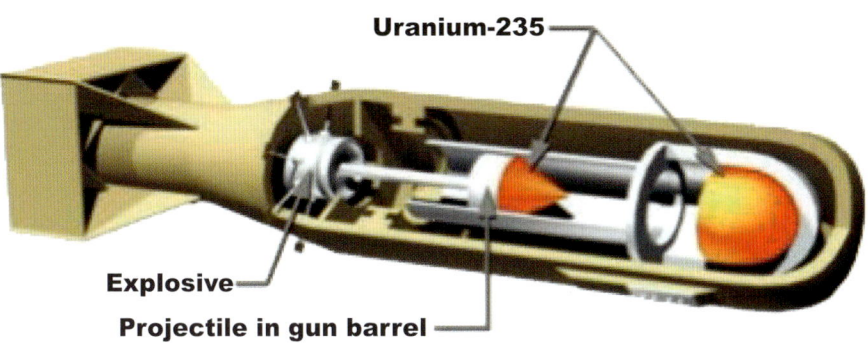

Schematic representation of a gun-type nuclear weapon
Source: http://atomicarchive.com

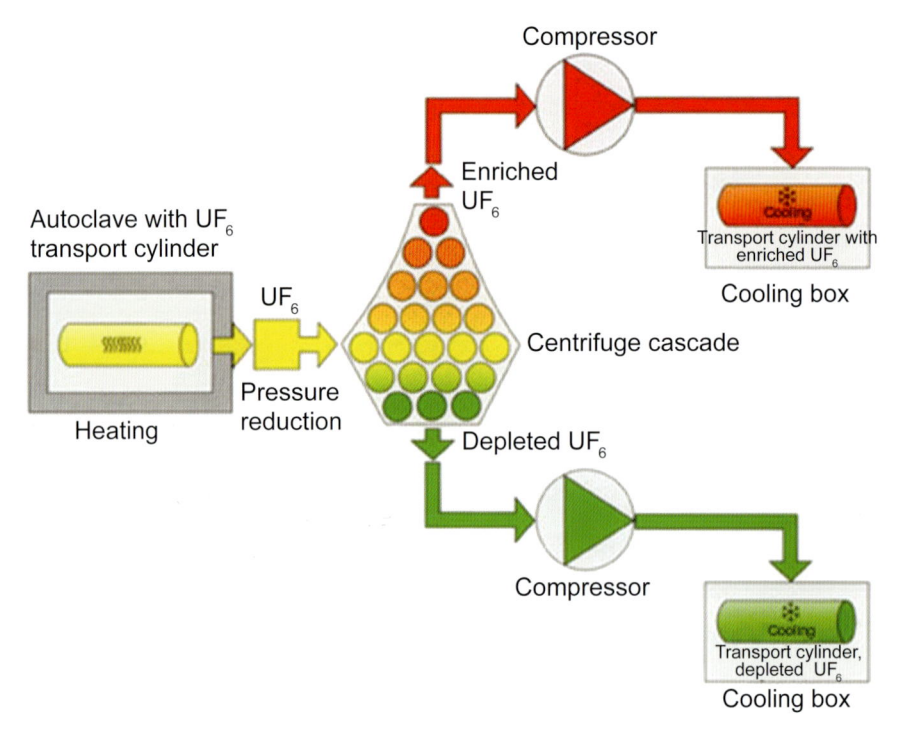

Schematic representation of the uranium enrichment process as it progresses from natural uranium (yellow) to enriched uranium (red) and depleted uranium (green). The diagram represents a gas centrifuge plant.
Source: World Nuclear Association

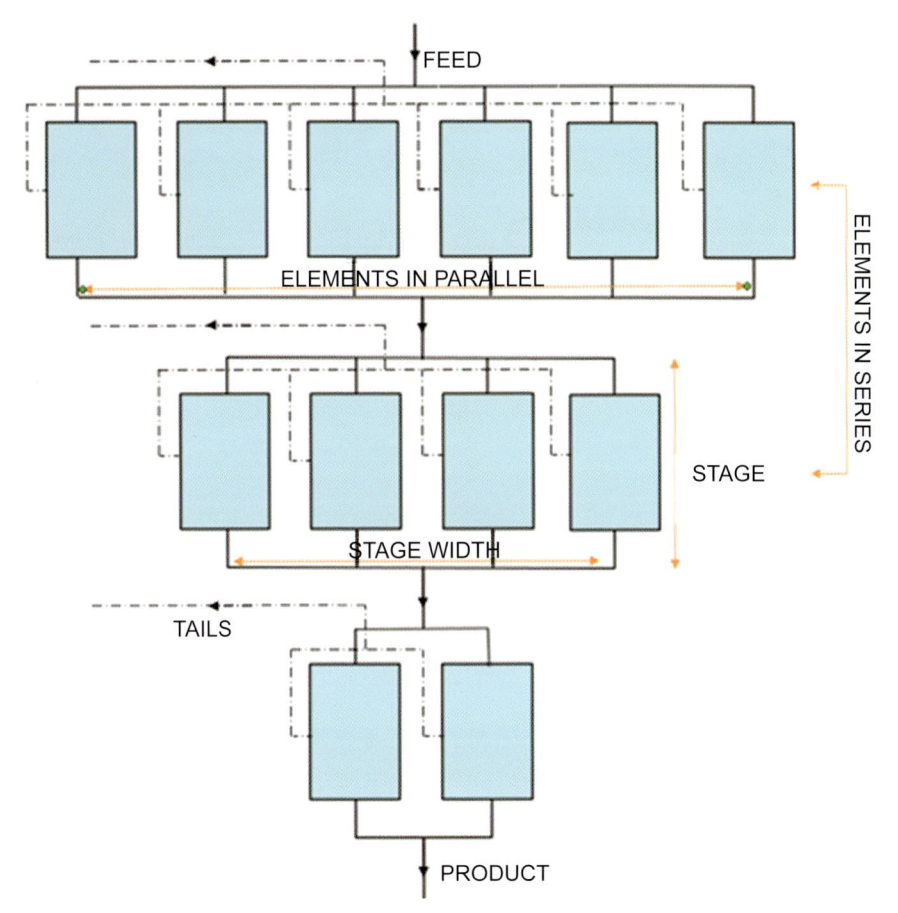

A simple cascade. Little enrichment is achieved by a single separation element. The slightly enriched uranium therefore flows to the following separation element where it is again slightly enriched. The process is repeated many times in a so-called cascade in order to achieve the desired degree of enrichment.
Source: http://www.fas.org/programs/ssp/nukes/fuelcycle/centrifuges/cascades.html

The first Soviet nuclear bomb was called RDS-1 (Joe-1). It was a plutonium implosion bomb, a copy of the American Fat Man. It was tested on 29 August 1949.
Source: http://phobos.ramapo.edu/~theed/Cold_War/b_Stalin_era/e_Berlin_Blockade/cc_Soviet_ABomb.html

Modern American B-38 thermonuclear bombs ready for loading onto a bomber
Source: http://evolutionofme.net/blog/index.php?blog=10

4   CP

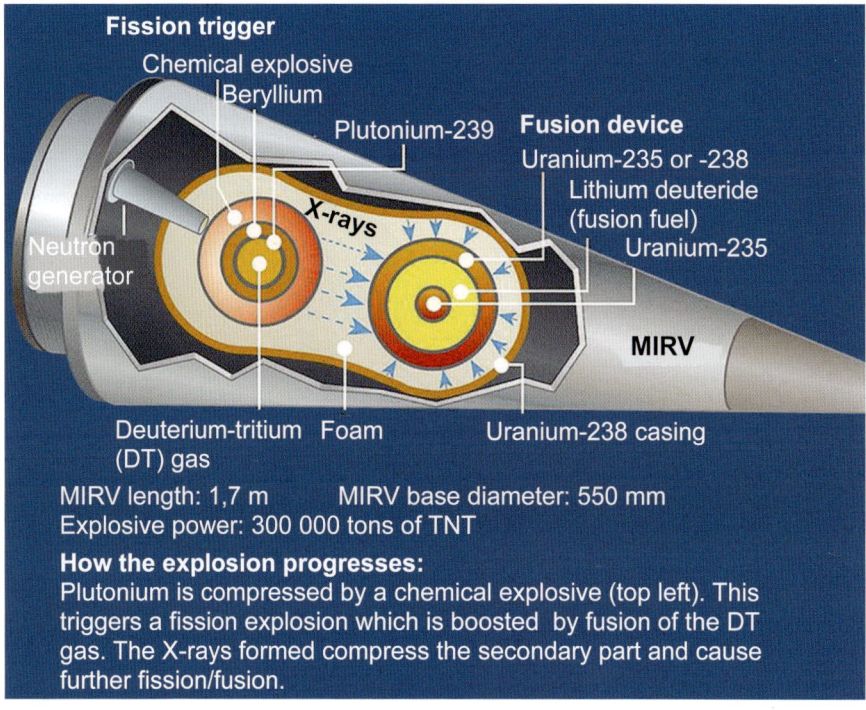

Fission trigger
Chemical explosive
Beryllium
Plutonium-239

Fusion device
Uranium-235 or -238
Lithium deuteride (fusion fuel)
Uranium-235

X-rays

Neutron generator

MIRV

Deuterium-tritium (DT) gas   Foam   Uranium-238 casing

MIRV length: 1,7 m   MIRV base diameter: 550 mm
Explosive power: 300 000 tons of TNT

How the explosion progresses:
Plutonium is compressed by a chemical explosive (top left). This triggers a fission explosion which is boosted by fusion of the DT gas. The X-rays formed compress the secondary part and cause further fission/fusion.

MIRV (Multiple Independently Targetable Re-entry Vehicle): A ballistic missile is used to launch several nuclear warheads which can strike various targets independently of each other. Example of an American B-87 nuclear warhead.
Source: http://nuclearweaponarchive.org/Usa/Weapons/W87.html

Building 5000, located on an isolated part of the Pelindaba site, housed a critical assembly for fast neutrons in the early days of the nuclear weapons programme.
Source: http://isis-online.org/5000

CP 5

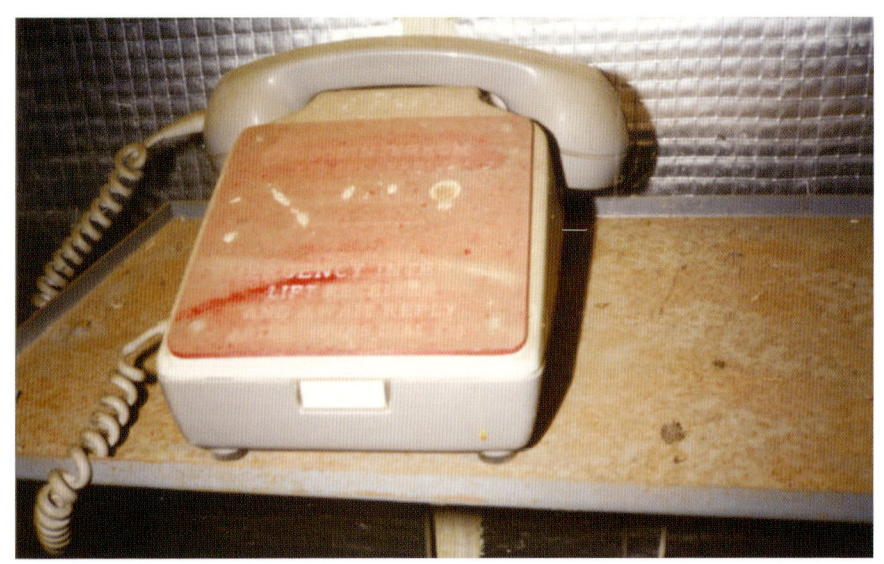

In 1992 IAEA inspectors found this dusty emergency telephone in Building 5000 after the Americans had insisted on an urgent inspection of the building.
Source: http://isis-online.org/phone

The abandoned Kentron Circle facility (May 2013) where nuclear weapons were made and stored in the 1980s.
Source: Author's own photograph

Notice on the gate at the Circle facility restricting access to the top secret nuclear weapons facility in terms of a 1957 Act.
Source: Author's own photograph

Circle facility: Remains of a panel in the building's control room (May 2013).
Source: Author's own photograph

Circle facility: The building was designed in such a way that overpressure (resulting from an unexpected conventional explosion on the ground floor) could be dissipated through the ventilation grilles – seen on the photograph – to prevent the roof and walls from collapsing.
Source: Author's own photograph

Storage lockers in 1993. This photograph was taken after the building had been declared and made accessible to the IAEA. The front and rear parts of the nuclear weapons were stored separately in these storage lockers at the Circle facility.
Source: http://nuclearweaponarchive.org/Safrica/SABuildingBombs.html

The author, Nic von Wielligh, standing next to one of the old storage lockers ten years later, in May 2013.
Source: Author's own photograph

Massive electrically operated steel sliding doors were used to contain the effect of conventional explosions in ballistic cells.
Source: Author's own photograph

This photograph shows an RSA-3 missile which is still on display at the Zwartkop Air Force Museum. The RSA missiles made by Armscor were similar to the Jericho missiles produced by Israel. In response to pressure from the USA the South African government stopped the local missile programme in 1993.
Source: http://www.militaryphotos.net/forums/showthread.php?64954-South-African-National-Defence-Force/page124

Behind this partly demolished false wall J.A.M. Meyer of the firm Tradefin Engineering concealed 11 shipping containers full of components made in his Vanderbijlpark factory for the Libyan enrichment plant.
Source: Author's own photograph

A photograph of assembled process equipment (destined for Libya) in the Tradefin Engineering factory prior to dismantling and packing in shipping containers.
Source: Court case against J.A.M. Meyer and Gerhard Wisser

Gerhard Wisser who, as managing director of the South African firm Krisch Engineering, had a hand in A.Q. Khan's "atomic bazaar". Wisser was arrested in 2004 for his involvement in the manufacture of components for the Libyan nuclear programme.
Source: http://www.atoomspionage.com/nuclearbazaar/nuclearbazaar.htm

Abdul Qadeer (A.Q.) Khan, known as the father of Pakistan's nuclear programme, which was founded on information stolen from Urenco.
Source: http://www.pakistantoday.com.pk/2012/12/08/news/national/kalabagh-dam-vital-for-economic-stability-dr-aq-khan/

In 2003 the Americans detained a German cargo vessel, the *BBC China*, bound for Libya with six containers full of gas centrifuge components from Kuala Lumpur in Malaysia.
Source: http://www.doe.gov

Packing list
Crate 3

Box 1	Pressure regulators	10 off
	Pressure gauges (0-16 bar)	10 off
	shut-off valves	10 off
Box 2	Pressure Gauges (0-16 barg)	10 off
Box 3	Pressure gauges (0-1 bar (prseudo-a))	10 off
Box 4	Temperature transmitters	25 off
	Cables - Weigh transmitters	10 sets
	Cables - PLC to electrical	5 sets
Box 5	Pressure transmitters (0-25m bar)	10 off
Box 6	Pressure transmitters (0-4000mbar)	28 off
Box 7	Pressure gauges (0-4 barg)	
Box 8	Pressure transmitters (0-1 bar(a))	10 off
	Pressure transmitters (0-1.6 bar(a)	
	Interface cable	1 set
Box 9	Pressure transmitter (0-100mbar(a))	33 off
Box 10	Touch screen for control systems	5 off
	Touch screen cabinets	5 off

A typical packing list of components and equipment found in the Tradefin Engineering shipping containers.
Source: Court case against J.A.M. Meyer and Gerhard Wisser

Dimitri Perricos joined the IAEA in 1972. In April 1991 he became a member of the Iraq Action Team before heading the IAEA team that carried out the IAEA correctness and completeness investigation from November 1991, after South Africa's signature of the Nuclear Non-Proliferation Treaty and disclosure of the former nuclear weapons programme.
Source: http://www.un.org/depts/unmovic/new/pages/chairman_perricos.asp

Hans Blix, Swedish Minister of Foreign Affairs from 1978 to 1979. From 1981 to 1997 he was the Director-General of the International Atomic Energy Agency (IAEA) in Vienna.
Source: http://sydney.edu.au/images/content/cws/news/newsevents/articles/2007/may/Hans%20Blix%20main.JPG

Prof. Johan Slabber, a key figure in the South African nuclear programme between 1964 and 1989 and safeguards inspector at the IAEA in Vienna during the 1990s. Currently extraordinary professor in mechanical and aeronautical engineering at the University of Pretoria.
Source: http://web.up.ac.za/default.asp?ipkCategoryID=8776&articleID=6840

Prof. Waldo Stumpf, who joined the Atomic Energy Board in 1968 and later became Chief Executive Officer of the AEC and leader of the AEC/Armscor team responsible for shutting down the nuclear weapons programme. Currently professor in metallurgical engineering at the University of Pretoria.
Source: http://ivarfjeld.com/tag/south-africa/

Lydia von Wielligh-Steyn standing next to bomb casings in the Ammunition Defects Museum in Pretoria in May 2013. These casings, which were used for flammability and flight tests, are often erroneously reflected in the literature as actual nuclear weapons casings.
Source: Author's own photograph

July 1993: A concrete mixture being poured into test shaft 1 at the Vastrap test site to make the shaft unusable.
Source: IAEA, against the spread of nuclear weapons: IAEA safeguards in the 1990s.
http://www.iaea.org/Publications/Booklets/Safeguards/pia38e14.html

Former minister Pik Botha visited Vienna in 1994. At a function he presented a small sculpture of a miniature plough to Dr Hans Blix of the IAEA. The sculpture is made from non-nuclear metal recovered from the nuclear weapons. The base of the sculpture bears a quotation from Isaiah 2:4 in Afrikaans and English: "And they shall beat their swords into ploughshares, and their spears into pruning hooks. Nation shall not lift up sword against nation, neither shall they learn war any more."
Source: http://www.unis.unvienna.org/unis/en/visitors_service/art_tour.html

> Well, we did the deed with iron determination not to allow those crazy Arabs to possess nuclear weapons ... we are not perturbed by all the "righteous souls" that all the crocodiles in South African rivers could not provide with enough tears to wipe out their hypocrisy.
>
> ... I am certain that you understand us very well.

Malan wrote a congratulatory letter to Eitan and advised him not to be deflected by criticism from the UN since this body was an "international platform and propaganda machine of South Africa's enemies". He added: "It is comforting to know that South Africa does not stand alone in facing criticism from the international community. Our respective countries will have to withstand this in all its many manifestations."

Many similar letters passed between Israeli and South African generals over the years. They exchanged information on recent hostilities, and on the number of terrorists killed during the various incidents. They also supported each other in the councils of international bodies. For example, Ariel Sharon, the Israeli minister of defence, visited South Africa in 1981. He appealed to the West to support South Africa in its struggle against the Cuban and Angolan communist forces. Magnus Malan wrote to his Israeli counterpart to thank him and lauded Sharon for his "serious concern about Soviet expansion in Southern Africa and his willingness to speak out on the subject".

Strange bedfellows – the Jewish parallel

How did this unlikely friendship come about? When one examines the history of the Afrikaners in South Africa, one is struck by the continual parallels which this community drew between their own fortunes and those of the Jewish nation in Old Testament times. Like the Jews, the Afrikaners migrated restlessly to a promised land where they could be the masters of their destiny. As believing Calvinists in a hostile environment they recognised their own fate in that of the elect Jews. In addition, the systematic international isolation of the Jewish state of Israel and South Africa, the apartheid state, created close ties between the two countries during the second half of the twentieth century.

In 1952 Israel acquired diplomatic representation in South Africa. In 1974 the local office was upgraded to the status of a fully fledged embassy. In 1972 South Africa in turn opened a consulate in Tel Aviv and in December

1975 this became a fully fledged embassy.

In the 1960s it became clear, however, that the Israeli leaders were ideologically opposed to South Africa's policies. In 1961 David Ben-Gurion, the father of the Jewish state, replied to critics in the Knesset who took issue with the fact that Israel had voted against South Africa at the UN. One of the points he made was that "a Jew cannot support discrimination".

In 1963 Golda Meir, who was Israel's minister of foreign affairs at the time, addressed the UNGA. She said that Israel was "naturally opposed to policies of apartheid, colonialism and racial or religious discrimination". Meir did everything in her power to forge close ties with the newly independent African states. Israel offered aid, which included assistance with agriculture and military training, in order to win the support of these countries. Numerous heads of African states visited Israel, and some of them even hired Israeli security guards. African states supported Israel at the UN during an era when the Jewish state had few allies.

In 1967 the Six-Day War broke out. Israel thrashed its Arab neighbours soundly and trebled its territory within the space of a week. Israel's occupation of Egyptian, Jordanian and Syrian territory earned the country the label of colonialism. And, more significantly: Israel's image as a nation of gallant victims/survivors of the German concentration camps was beginning to wear a little thin.

Following the Yom Kippur War of October 1973, the African states, with the exception of Malawi, Lesotho and Swaziland, cut off diplomatic relations with Israel.

In view of this open hostility the Israelis no longer felt obliged to keep their budding relationship with South Africa secret at all costs. Furthermore, the older generation of leaders of the Labour Party in Israel, most of whom came from Eastern Europe, had begun to make way for younger leaders like Shimon Peres, Moshe Dayan and Yitzhak Rabin. Dayan and Rabin were sabras and war veterans.

In November 1974 Shimon Peres, then minister of defence in the Yitzhak Rabin government, and the South African head of state, John Vorster, met secretly in Geneva. At the conclusion of the meeting they signed a strategic cooperation agreement. The gist of this was that the two countries would come to each other's aid in wartime by making spare parts and ammunition available to each other. They also undertook to store armaments for each other in their respective territories.

In 1975 the two countries were driven even closer together by the adoption of a resolution in the UNGA which equated Zionism and apartheid.

In May 2010 Sasha Polakow-Suransky published a sensational book, *The Unspoken Alliance: Israel's Secret Alliance with Apartheid South Africa*, which included secret minutes of a meeting which took place on 31 March 1975 between senior officials of both countries. Lieutenant-General R.F. Armstrong drew up a memorandum on behalf of the South African delegation on the same day he described the advantages for South Africa of obtaining Jericho missiles from Israel. The missiles had been offered to South Africa at this meeting. Armstrong emphasised in his memorandum, however, that the missiles would have to be armed with nuclear warheads.

On 3 April 1975 Peres and P.W. Botha (at the time South Africa's Minister of Defence) signed a security agreement in Zurich which covered all aspects of cooperation between the two countries. The agreement was known as Secment (Security and Secrecy Agreement). One of the provisions of the agreement was that its mere existence was to be kept covert and could not be revealed by either of the parties. Another provision was that it could not be unilaterally suspended by either party.

The Jericho Project was now officially known as Operation Chalet. At a second meeting between Peres and Botha in June "Chalet" was discussed again. Extracts from the secret minutes of the meeting read as follows: "Minister Botha expressed interest in a limited number of units of Chalet subject to the correct payload being available," and continue: "Minister Peres said the correct payload was available in three sizes. Minister Botha expressed his appreciation and said that he would ask for advice."

Polakow-Suransky simply jumped to the conclusion that the "three sizes" above referred to conventional, chemical and nuclear warheads, but the reference could merely have been to the size or type of conventional warheads, for instance whether they were intended for blowing up reinforced bunkers, armoured vehicles or troop concentrations. The last three applications have to do with the so-called force-multiplying factor, or how to get more from a single weapon.

Botha ultimately decided not to go ahead with Project Chalet in view of the high cost. The transaction would have had to be approved by the Israeli prime minister, Peres's political rival Yitzak Rabin, and there was no guarantee that permission would be obtained.

Interestingly enough, Shimon Peres, who was president of Israel from 2007 to 2014, responded to the ruckus over Polakow-Suransky's book and the subsequent revelations in *The Guardian* on 24 June 2010 by denying in the strongest terms that he ever offered to sell nuclear weapons to South Africa during his term of office as minister of defence in the 1970s. His office issued a press release saying that "there was no basis in reality" for the allegations based on the declassified South African documents. "Israel never discussed the exchange of nuclear weapons with South Africa. No Israeli document or Israeli signature on a document exists to show that such negotiations took place."

In 1977 the reactionary Menachem Begin and his Likud Party shocked friend and foe alike by winning the national election. When he accepted the office of prime minister Begin brought 30 years of domination by the Labour Party to an end. With Begin in charge of affairs, the relationship between South Africa and Israel blossomed into one of more regular cooperation. Begin attached great value to military strength and supported a new realism in the context of foreign affairs. As a supporter of ethnic nationalism, he believed in an enlarged Israel and he enthusiastically supported the Israeli settlements on the West Bank and in the Gaza Strip.

Although it was Begin's Labour Party predecessors who had forged ties with South Africa in the early 1970s for strategic reasons, under Begin the two countries began to cooperate increasingly closely in military, scientific and industrial areas. Harry Hurwitz, a prominent member of the South African Jewish community and a strong proponent of closer ties between Israel and South Africa, migrated to Israel and became an adviser to his old friend Begin.

In the late 1970s and 1980s Israeli generals visited South Africa regularly and established friendships with their counterparts. They even exchanged military strategies, blueprints for conventional weapons and advice on terrorism.

It has been established beyond doubt today that military cooperation did take place between South Africa and Israel. However, in the recent past a number of untruthful statements have appeared regarding cooperation between the two countries in the nuclear field.

Operation Tea Leaves

In 1976 Fanie Botha, the Minister of Mines, visited the offices of the Israeli Atomic Energy Commission as well as the Soreq Nuclear Research Centre. Afterwards his hosts accompanied him to a meeting with Shimon Peres, who was then minister of defence. Subsequently he even had an hour-long meeting with Prime Minister Rabin. The topic under discussion was the stock of 500 tons of uranium concentrates which Israel had acquired since 1965 in terms of a bilateral agreement with South Africa on condition that the uranium should be used for peaceful purposes only. Since the IAEA was not involved, South African staff from the AEC visited Israel annually to keep an eye on the uses to which the material was being put.

Israel does produce uranium as a by-product of the phosphate mining near the Dead Sea, but production amounts to no more than about 10 tons per year. The Israelis are therefore obliged to buy uranium for their Dimona reactor in the Negev Desert on the world market as discreetly as possible.

The team working at the Dimona reactor needed uranium for the production of plutonium for the weapons programme. The 500 tons of stockpiled South African uranium could help to keep Dimona going for an estimated five to 10 years and produce sufficient reprocessed plutonium to make dozens of nuclear bombs.

Only the previous year the Israelis had approached General Hendrik van den Bergh with a request to buy an additional 100 tons of uranium concentrates. Although Prime Minister John Vorster had approved the transaction, Fanie Botha's predecessor, Piet Koornhof, was hesitant about entering into an agreement with Israel on such a sensitive issue. Fanie Botha had no such reservations, however. The Israelis therefore sounded him out again in 1976 on the 100 tons of uranium concentrates and also requested him to lift the condition of strictly peaceful uses that had been applicable to the stockpiled uranium since the bilateral safeguards agreement of 1965. Because the AEC fell under the control of the Department of Mines, Fanie Botha had the final say.

In *The Unholy Alliance – Israel's Secret Relationship with Apartheid South Africa*, Polakow-Suransky explains that the cancellation of the restriction would mean that South Africa would forgo the right to inspect the sealed drums of uranium concentrates. Furthermore, the South Africans would not be able to verify that the Israelis were using the uranium for peaceful purposes. Immediately after his visit to Israel in 1976 Fanie Botha did remove the restriction. The Israelis were then free to use the 500 tons of uranium in their possession as they dearly wished to do.

Ampie Roux, who was the Chief Executive Officer of the AEC at the time, was very troubled about Fanie Botha's decision to drop the South African inspections of Israel's uranium concentrates and wrote several letters to the minister in which he expressed strong opposition. However, he had to give in when Botha began threatening him with dismissal. According to Waldo Stumpf these letters are among the historical documents that were not destroyed during the dismantlement process.

In exchange for the cancellation of the restriction 30 grams of tritium was handed over to Fanie Botha.

On 3 June 2010 the British paper, *The Guardian*, published an article in which the journalist and former editor of the *Rand Daily Mail*, Allister Sparks, eventually disclosed the details of an event that took place several decades previously. Eschel Rhoodie, the former Secretary of Information, apparently told Sparks in 1979 that he had transported nuclear-related material, which he referred to as a "trigger" and which in all probability was the 30 grams of tritium, from Tel Aviv to South Africa. Sparks describes the incident as follows:

> Rhoodie said talks had taken place between the two sides which had ultimately led to he and (South African intelligence head) Hendrik van den Bergh being assigned the task of bringing "the trigger" to SA – which he said they did by packing it in a tea chest and transporting it as part of their hand-luggage on a South African Airways commercial flight (*South African Business Day*).

Inevitably, this exchange came to be referred to as "Project Tea Leaves".

According to Sparks, Rhoodie visited Israel regularly in the 1970s, sometimes together with General Hendrik van den Bergh.

Mervyn Rees, a former reporter of the *Rand Daily Mail*, to whom Rhoodie later described the same event, relates the following: "(Rhoodie) said I can't give you any of the details but suffice it to say it was a vital component, it was a trigger that would be used for South Africa's nuclear capability."

According to Rees, Eschel Rhoodie made a number of disclosures to him in Ecuador, and later in the south of France, after being compelled to resign from the government on account of the Information Scandal. This event occurred in 1978 and led to the political demise of Prime Minister John Vorster. The scandal erupted at the time when it was discovered that millions had been channelled from the Defence budget to Rhoodie's Department of Information for "propaganda purposes". The irony is that it was Rees's initial disclosures in the *Rand Daily Mail* that led to Rhoodie's resignation. According to Rees, Rhoodie, who was still bitter about having been made the scapegoat by the South African government, was only too willing to talk to him.

Rhoodie's important role as the link between South Africa and Israel is emphasised in a letter which Peres wrote to him in 1974 in his capacity as minister of defence to thank him for the leading part he played in promoting cooperation between Israel and South Africa.

Polakow-Suransky reports fairly extensively in his book on the part played by Brigadier Jan Blaauw in this context. Blaauw was a former South African air force officer and fighter pilot, a veteran of the Korean War. He is said to have received $1 million from Israel as a reward for assisting Fanie Botha during the tritium–uranium exchange operation. (Blaauw and Botha's relationship went sour later on and they ended up in court in 1987, when Blaauw was acquitted on charges of attempting to extort money from the former minister. Botha was alleged to have promised Blaauw diamond mining concessions, which never materialised.)

Shortly after Rhoodie's visit to Israel to which Sparks referred, Wynand de Villiers received a call from Minister Fanie Botha: "I've got some tritium from Israel; send someone to fetch it," he said. De Villiers was still protesting that the AEB did not need tritium when the minister cut him short. Four cylinders of tritium, each containing about five grams, simply had to be fetched. A small sample was drawn for verification purposes. The cylinders were then stored at the Valindaba site for 10 years. The tritium was later declared to the IAEA team and what was left of it (the half-life of tritium is around 12 years) was eventually used to make cinema seat numbers that glow in the dark!

A number of years later Magnus Malan, the Minister of Defence, wanted nuclear warheads to be produced for use in ballistic missiles. These would necessarily have to be implosion bombs (uranium gun-type bombs that were small enough to fit into the missile could not be made). It is possible that Armscor discussed the matter with Israel, but implosion bombs were never produced although some preliminary work on implosion technology was started at the Circle facility. Implosion technology is essential for the Israeli bombs in which plutonium is used, whereas the South African gun-type uranium bombs did not require that technology.

Although the Israelis did not have a direct influence on South Africa's nuclear programme, they did play a major part in the development of the local missile programme. In April 1976 Prime Minister John Vorster visited Israel. As a direct consequence of his visit, South Africa would in future have access to Israel's advanced missile technology and other military equipment.

By 1979 South Africa was Israel's single biggest weapons client. When the Socialist Party came to power in France in 1980, French weapons sales to South Africa dried up. This made the South Africans even more dependent on the Israelis.

In 1979 when the Shah of Iran was deposed in a revolution Israel lost its most important partner in missile development. After this the Israelis began to look at their South African ally with new eyes. In March 1979 the Israelis carried out a test in strict secrecy and launched a modernised version of the Jericho missile over the Mediterranean Sea. I.R. Gleeson, the head of special operations of the SADF, was invited to attend the test in Israel. General Magnus Malan wrote a personal letter to his Israeli counterpart to apologise for being unable to be present. Malan did travel to Israel later in the same year for a second test of the same nature.

The cooperation which ultimately took place between the two countries centred on the creation of an updated version of the Jericho II missile. Jericho II was a ballistic missile with a range of over 1 500 km, which meant that tests over the Mediterranean were no longer possible. South Africa's land area, financial strength and well-developed infrastructure made it possible for the Israelis to carry out these tests with ease, which they could hardly do in their own small country. The tests that took place at the Overberg testing site near Cape Agulhas received no publicity and it took the Americans a while to become aware of the cooperation between the two countries.

In July 1988 South Africa sent a team to Israel to learn more about airspace control techniques. By this time Israeli engineers had already modernised half the Cheetah aircraft that had been sent to Israel for upgrading. Another group of South Africans were to visit Israel to purchase laser-guided weapons. The two governments even initiated discussions on cooperation on the building of a new South African fighter aircraft.

Three missiles were launched during the life of the South African missile programme. Another missile was destroyed at a public ceremony in 1994. This was a requirement for South Africa's accession to the MTCR (Missile Technology Control Regime). Another missile was preserved and is still on display at the South African Air Force Museum at the Zwartkop Air Force Base. The South African programme was remarkably sophisticated for a relatively small country. By 1992 about 1 000 engineers, technicians and scientists were employed on the country's missile project. Another 5 000 officials were indirectly involved in the project.

Yitzhak Shamir became Prime Minister of Israel in 1983. In his days as a young freedom fighter he allegedly had a hand in an assassination attempt on the British High Commissioner, the murder of the British Resident Minister in the Middle East and also that of the Swedish count Folke Bernadotte, the UN mediator in the Arab-Israeli war back in the 1940s. Furthermore, Shamir's harsh attitude towards the Palestinian question not only strained his relations with the USA, but also resulted in an open rebellion by the Palestinians towards the end of 1987.

As if this were not enough, early in 1989 the American ambassador, Thomas Pickering, voiced his country's disquiet regarding Israeli involvement in the South African missile programme to Shamir. According to him President Bush was highly dissatisfied. This followed satellite evidence of missile tests near Arniston.

Israel's response was cryptic and significant. The following statement was issued: "The defense establishment strictly abides by the inner cabinet decision of March 18, 1987, whereby no new contracts will be signed between Israel and South Africa in the defense realm."

However, collaboration on missiles at Arniston had begun before 1987 and was excluded from the above sanction measures.

According to the CIA, South Africa had no real need for a long-range missile unless the missile was intended to carry a nuclear warhead …

The end of the friendship

The missile programme eventually had to be abandoned in response to pressure from the USA. The winding up of the programme is discussed in greater detail in part 6 of this text.

The Americans played an important part in the eventual change in Israel's stance in relation to South Africa.

The adoption in 1986 of the Comprehensive Anti-Apartheid Act in the USA was enough to persuade Israel that it would have to modify its attitude towards its ally. In terms of one provision in the Act the USA reserved the right to cut off aid to states that continued to supply weapons to the Apartheid state.

Shamir decided to capitulate and to follow the advice of the leftist contingent in the Israeli Department of Foreign Affairs. The time had come for changes in the relationship with South Africa. Israel imposed sanctions against South Africa on 16 September 1987. No new investments were to be made in South Africa, no new agreements in the scientific field were to be concluded, Israeli civil servants would pay no further visits to South Africa, tourism to South Africa would no longer be marketed and South Africa would receive no further assistance in circumventing sanctions. There was even a clause that provided that only brown, Indian and black students would be permitted to attend leadership courses in Israel.

This evoked an angry and emotional response from President P.W. Botha. He wrote a personal letter to Prime Minister Yitzhak Shamir in which he accused him of back-stabbing. "How could you do this to us, after so many years of friendship and alliance?" Botha asked his Jewish counterpart.

South Africa had invested a lot in this friendship and Botha viewed this turnabout in the attitude of the Israeli government as a betrayal.

P.W. Botha was a proud man, however, and continued to show loyalty to friends who had left him in the lurch. He had no wish to disclose this letter to the media. It was only years later that the Israeli Ministry of Defence discovered the existence of the letter.

On 2 November 2006 *The Jerusalem Post* conducted an interview with Alon Liel. He was the Israeli ambassador to South Africa from 1992 to 1995. Liel was also in charge of the South Africa desk at the Israeli Ministry of Foreign Affairs from October 1986 to 1990. Liel described the impact of Israeli sanctions against South Africa as follows: "They were totally confounded, taken by surprise, and really, really hurt. They never believed we would go that far and join the Europeans in their form of sanctions. They thought we would just make some public declaration and quietly let things go on as they were."

Liel went on to describe the context of the changes in the bilateral relations, with some interesting insights.

In 1986 the ministry of foreign affairs appointed a committee to investigate Israel's policy towards South Africa. Alon Liel served on that committee. He described the events as follows:

> We sat for about six months and deliberated about what we should do. In September of 1987 our recommendations were approved in the cabinet by a 6-4 vote. In the end we sent them a letter saying that we were imposing 'measures' – we didn't call them sanctions. These measures went pretty far, and they included sanctions on everything from trade, tourism, culture and sports.

Liel confirmed that P.W. Botha had reacted very strongly. "He felt betrayed, like he was stabbed in the back," he told *The Jerusalem Post*. "He threatened Israel to the effect that if we went ahead and implemented this, then he would not allow South African Jews to take money out of the country."

According to Liel, Anton Loubser, the South African ambassador to Israel in 1987, told *The Jerusalem Post* that the decision of the Israeli government on sanctions clashed head-on with the wishes of the Israeli people. "We (the foreign ministry) gave him such hell for that, that he was recalled to Pretoria and went to serve in Scandinavia," Liel revealed to the newspaper with relish.

According to Polakow-Suransky, the sanctions that Israel instituted against its former ally were of a cosmetic nature and did not have a big impact on trade between the two countries. The important military contracts signed before 1987 remained in place. In a South African government memorandum issued in August 1987 it was even stated that top Israeli officials had assured their South African counterparts that the sanctions were really just for show since the cutting of trade ties between the two countries would harm Israel the most. Later on in his book Polakow-Suransky mentions that Yitzhak Rabin even gave the assurance that the changes in Israel's policy towards South Africa would be mainly of a symbolic nature and that they had been made public in order to mitigate "the negative effect of contact with South Africa" on Israel's public image.

The impact on business was not substantial either. Reg Donner, the chairman of the research section at Anglo American, wrote to the South African Department of Foreign Affairs as follows: "It is of the utmost importance for us to carry on fostering these friendly relationships on a low profile basis to the mutual benefit of both countries ... I will most certainly continue to promote (them) ... even against the fiercest pressures by the USA or others."

During the 1980s most of South Africa's polished diamonds left the country via Israel. Businesspeople were using diamonds as a means of getting money out of the country. Israeli companies made use of the favourable conditions offered by the financial rand system in place at the time to buy diamonds at a huge discount and then sell the final product overseas.

After its 1994 election victory the ANC chose to turn its back on Israel and forge ties with the Palestine Liberation Organization instead. They also preferred to turn to European arms manufacturers for new armaments instead of to the old South African ally, Israel. By the mid-1990s there was nothing left of the shared economic interests and ideological points of concurrence that had been a feature of two decades of close cooperation between Israel and South Africa.

In one of history's ironies, the international community has today thrown the political mantle of apartheid squarely over the burly shoulders of Benjamin Netanyahu, prime minister of Israel since 2009.

THE BOMB

PART 6

FROM POLECAT TO MODEL CITIZEN

A modern Aeolus

On a hot day in February 1960 Harold Macmillan, who had been British prime minister since 1957, conveyed his government's greetings and congratulations to the South African parliament near the foot of Table Mountain. The occasion was the 50th anniversary of the Union. He did not, however, pass up the opportunity to take South Africa to task about its domestic policy and did not follow the customary practice of making his speech available to the South Africans in advance to allow them to reply.

The following is an excerpt from his speech:

> Ever since the break-up of the Roman Empire one of the constant facts of political life in Europe has been the emergence of independent nations. They have come into existence over the centuries in different forms, different kinds of government, but all have been inspired by a deep, keen feeling of nationalism, which has grown as the nations have grown.
>
> In the twentieth century, and especially since the end of the war, the processes which gave birth to the nation states of Europe have been repeated all over the world. We have seen the awakening of national consciousness in peoples who have for centuries lived in dependence upon some other power. Fifteen years ago this movement spread through Asia. Many countries there, of different races and civilisations, pressed their claim to an independent national life.
>
> Today the same thing is happening in Africa, and the most striking of all the impressions I have formed since I left London a month ago is of the strength of this African national consciousness. In different places it takes different forms, but it is happening everywhere.

His speech is best remembered today for the frequently quoted statement: "The wind of change is blowing through this continent, and whether we like it or not, this growth of national consciousness is a political fact. We must all accept it as a fact, and our national policies must take account of it."

Britain's power was waning all over the world. The violence in Malaysia was one example. The "emergency situation" in that country lasted from 1948 to 1960. The conflict was referred to in this way – and not as a war – at the request of the British industrialists in the country who were afraid that Lloyds would refuse to pay their insurance claims. This conflict hit Britain hard financially, as did the Mau-Mau rebellion in Kenya between 1952 and 1960. Two British shipyards that had been operating for over 300 years had to close, with the loss of 2 500 jobs. The chairman of British Railways said that it would be necessary to close 2 000 railway stations and scrap 8 000 railway carriages – with an accompanying loss of 68 000 jobs.

The fact that Britain granted independence to about a dozen overseas colonies during Macmillan's term of office was due not so much to severe pangs of conscience, but rather to war weariness and impoverishment. Colonies that the British Empire had acquired over the centuries with unbecoming cupidity were now being declared independent with equally unbecoming haste and left to their own devices. This was Macmillan's wish for South Africa as well.

In view of his classical education in Latin and Greek at Oxford, Macmillan's "wind of change" was probably a reference to Greek mythology. Aeolus held the four winds captive in a mountain cave and released them at Jupiter's command to perform certain tasks.

Be this as it may, the wind that Macmillan released over Africa reached South Africa some three decades later – as a hurricane-force Black South-Easter. This wind of change blew down many a political and social structure, but at the same time created the opportunity for new building.

The fact that South Africa was the first and only state to build up a nuclear capability, voluntarily dismantle it and then open up all the country's nuclear programmes for international inspection gave rise to new opportunities. The outcasts suddenly became model citizens and South Africans received numerous invitations to tell their story and join gatherings and groups concerned with nuclear non-proliferation.

Harold Macmillan and the biggest ever Western nuclear disaster

Through their Tube Alloys project the British developed important technology necessary for nuclear weapons. Because Britain was within range of the German bombers, the project was transferred to the USA, staff and all, and integrated with the Manhattan Project. As a result, the British acquired valuable information.

Early in 1947 this cooperation was summarily and unilaterally terminated by America through the so-called MacMahon Act. This Act was inspired by the discovery by the Americans that certain Britons, in particular Klaus Fuchs and Allan Nunn May, had been spying for the Soviet Union. The newborn mistrust was to bedevil relations between the USA and Britain for years to come.

The British prime ministers Winston Churchill, Clement Attlee and Anthony Eden tried in succession, but without success, to restore relations with the USA. Harold Macmillan became prime minister in 1957. He believed that if the British could demonstrate that they could build and test their own thermonuclear bomb (hydrogen bomb) without help from the Americans, the USA would agree to exchange nuclear secrets with Britain again. He therefore ordered the fast-tracking of the building of a thermonuclear bomb.

The British built two reactors, Windscale Pile 1 and Pile 2, especially for the production of plutonium. They were air-cooled graphite/natural uranium reactors. Each reactor consisted of massive graphite blocks with horizontal channels for the fuel and vertical channels for control rods. The fuel consisted of natural uranium metal cylinders encased in finned aluminium housings. The fins were added for cooling purposes.

The fuel elements were loaded into the channels at one end of the graphite core and discharged after a certain time at the other end, where they fell into a water-filled duct to cool down. The plutonium produced was then separated from the irradiated fuel in a reprocessing plant.

A great deal of heat was generated during the chain reaction in the fuel, and air was therefore blown through the channels for cooling purposes. The hot air was then released through 120 m tall chimneys. Sir John Cockcroft, a famous physicist and Nobel prize-winner, insisted that filter chambers should be mounted on top of the chimneys to trap any radioactivity that might be released. The plant operators used to joke about these filters, which they called "Cockcroft's folly" – little knowing what was in store for them!

The British had had very little experience of this type of reactor. The main problem was the so-called Wigner effect. When graphite is bombarded by neutrons, it suffers dislocations in its crystal structure and in the process absorbs energy which under certain conditions may be released as a single burst of heat energy.

Tritium is also required for building thermonuclear weapons, in addition to other isotopes like polonium-210, which is used in the trigger. In response to heavy pressure from Macmillan and his political team, the British decided to produce these isotopes in the Windscale reactors as well, but soon found that the aluminium used for the finned casings absorbed too many neutrons. This prompted the decision to reduce the size of the fins of the 35 000 fuel elements, which naturally made the process of cooling the uranium fuel less effective. This decision boosted the tritium production, but at the expense of the safety of the core.

As a result of the combination of these two factors, in October 1957 the uranium fuel in Windscale Pile 1 overheated and caught fire. The fire was not detected initially and the operators merely recorded an inexplicable rise in the temperature in the reactor core. The obvious response was to push more cooling air through the reactor. This merely made things worse – now the burning uranium was getting additional oxygen. Then elevated radioactivity readings by the monitors in the chimney made the operators realise that something else was wrong. When an inspection hatch was opened it was clear that the fuel channels were glowing white hot. The graphite was smouldering and had been for the past four days.

The operators had no idea how to deal with this situation. Several attempts failed, including the use of carbon dioxide; they then tried to extinguish the burning fuel with water.

By then it was estimated that more than ten tons of uranium was on fire. Tom Tuohy, the reactor manager, sent everyone home, donned protective gear and, accompanied by the fire chief, sealed all the openings through which air could leak into the core. After 24 hours the smouldering fire was out.

While Tuohy was risking his life in an attempt to get the catastrophe under control, Macmillan was cold-bloodedly arranging a summit with Washington. He was anxious to sign the so-called US-UK Mutual

Defence Agreement, which would gain Britain recognition as a nuclear peer.

Because he was aware that the nuclear catastrophe might lead to the cancellation of the agreement, Macmillan suppressed news of the disaster and issued a brief statement in which he blamed the operators – an error of judgement on their part, he said. For the following 50 years the blame was placed on the very people who had brought the disaster under control. Right up to his death in 2008, Tuohy never received any recognition for his heroic efforts.

And thanks to "Cockcroft's folly" the radioactive contamination of the environment was limited to a fraction of the radiation released by Chernobyl, for example (the Chernobyl reactor was also a graphite reactor, but it was water-cooled). Nevertheless, Windscale was the biggest Western nuclear disaster ever. Today the core of Windscale Pile 1 still contains about 15 tons of hot uranium as well as highly radioactive fission products. It will probably be finally dismantled in 2060 – over a hundred years after the accident. Work started in 2014 on dismantling the filter gallery on top of the tall chimney; this was followed by the dismantling of the chimney itself.

Macmillan nevertheless got his desired American agreement in 1958, after the British had demonstrated in 1957 that they were capable of designing and detonating their own thermonuclear bomb. This agreement led to the renewed exchange of nuclear secrets, plutonium and delivery systems between the two states. Their cooperation has continued up to the present, and is so firmly in place that the British Atomic Weapons Establishment (AWE), which manufactures and maintains British nuclear warheads, has been controlled by American firms since 2008.

The last decade of the 20th century

In the political arena the Aeolian winds blew strongly throughout this decade. In April 1990 the last president under the old dispensation, F.W. de Klerk, announced in parliament that he did not foresee a black majority parliament. By the end of the same decade the second black president (Thabo Mbeki) had already taken over the reins.

This political reversal was preceded by a number of significant events. Two coups d'état took place in former homelands (the Ciskei and Venda); right-wing elements set off bombs in several locations and shots were fired at the British embassy in Pretoria; black-on-black violence between the Inkatha Freedom Party and the ANC increased alarmingly and thousands of people were killed on both sides. Chris Hani of the South African Communist Party (SACP) was murdered. The celebrated Afrikaans theologian Professor Johan Heyns suffered the same fate.

Despite all this violence, almost 69% of the voters in the last white referendum, held in 1992, voted "yes" in favour of a change in the political dispensation. Two years later the first democratic general election took place. The ANC won about 63% of the votes and the once powerful white National Party only 20%. Nelson Mandela was sworn in as President in May 1994. His deputies were F.W. de Klerk and Thabo Mbeki. The government of national unity included several white ministers.

Despite the fact that Mandela and De Klerk were the joint winners of the Nobel prize for Peace in 1993, there was never really peace between the two leaders. In 1991 there was a public slanging match between them at the Codesa talks. In June 1996, after two years in the government of national unity, De Klerk had had enough and he and the NP withdrew from the government. In the British *Daily Telegraph* of 11 April 2012 De Klerk referred to Mandela as a principled man of "stature and strength" but also a "savage and unfair opponent" – no saint but a man with faults.

In 1997 the NP changed its name to the New National Party (NNP) in an attempt to shake off its past. De Klerk retired from politics. After this the decline of the NNP was unmistakable and in 2005, after 90 years, the once proud and powerful party vanished like candyfloss into the gaping maw of the ANC. Old friends like Taiwan and Israel now became adversaries and alliances with them were exchanged for new partnerships with China and Palestine. The hand of friendship was extended to former enemies like Russia, Iran, Cuba and Libya. The red carpet was rolled out for Ayatollah Akbar Hashemi Rafsanjani of Iran, Muammar Gaddafi of Libya and Fidel Castro of Cuba.

Taiwan must have read the signs and tried to buy the favour of the new South African leadership by filling the empty Advena buildings to overflowing (with the consent of the government) with brand new electrical test benches, lathes and other equipment, specially for the training of returning MK cadres who had no useful civilian skills. The announcement by President Mandela that ties with Taiwan would be exchanged for connections with China resulted in the Taiwanese ambassador being recalled, aid programmes being discontinued and 36 treaties and agreements with South Africa being declared void. What became of the brand new equipment? It remained locked up in the Advena complex for a long time, unused. Its present whereabouts are not known.

The second democratic election took place in 1999. The ANC won again. Mandela retired and Thabo Mbeki took over as President.

The end of the decade was suitably marked by the demise of the AEC, which was replaced in 1999 by the Nuclear Energy Corporation of South Africa (Necsa). Of the once magnificent nuclear fuel cycle plants and facilities, the only operational unit that remained was also the oldest, namely the Safari reactor.

South Africa in the non-proliferation arena

Internationally South Africa had achieved stellar status as the first country ever to have achieved an indigenous nuclear weapons capability and voluntarily destroyed it – and then invited the IAEA to verify this.

South African expertise and experience were suddenly highly sought after in the unique world of non-proliferation of weapons of mass destruction. Waldo Stumpf, the Chief Executive Officer of the AEC from 1990 to 2001, who had been appointed by President De Klerk to terminate the nuclear weapons programme, became a popular speaker at numerous international conferences. In 1994 Nic von Wielligh and Neville Whiting of the AEC were invited by the IAEA to participate in the IAEA Symposium on International Safeguards and provide an overview of the South African experience of the IAEA verification process.

It was not only the practical experience of the total dismantling of a nuclear weapons capability that received international recognition. The expertise of the staff was in demand as well. Johan Slabber, who had been closely involved with the nuclear project while he was with the AEC, was invited to join the IAEA (as mentioned previously) while the organisation was still carrying out its verification project in South Africa. After his departure almost the entire national safeguards inspectorate of the former AEC left at short intervals to join the head office in Vienna. The South Africans were sought after for their expertise, and especially for their work ethic. Brian Rens was the first to leave, followed by Neville Whiting, Helgard du Preez, Schalk Potgieter, Alta Broodryk and Chris de Wit. Most of them eventually became section heads for safeguards inspections at the IAEA. Neville Whiting ended his career in Vienna as the director of safeguards inspections. At the end of 2013 he was succeeded by another former AEC stalwart, Dr W. van Zyl de Villiers.

The IAEA makes use of external experts in several standing advisory groups which serve as technical think tanks and advise the director-general of the IAEA directly. The Agency was quick off the mark in using such expertise where it was available in the AEC. Waldo Stumpf was appointed to the first Standing Advisory Group on Technical Assistance and Co-operation (SAG-TAC) and served as chairperson of that group for three years from 2001. This group advises the Director-General of the IAEA on peaceful nuclear energy development projects in developing countries. Similarly, Nic von Wielligh was appointed to the Standing Advisory Group for Safeguards Implementation (SAGSI) from 1992 to 2002. From 2000 to 2002 he also served as a member of the Standing Advisory Group on Nuclear Energy (SAGNE).

The international community was not slow to realise that South Africa, which possessed a large quantity of highly enriched uranium from its former weapons programme and had developed a unique enrichment process, could well become a proliferant – especially because the nuclear policy of the future government and the way it would be implemented were unknown factors. Would the new ANC government revive the nuclear weapons programme to produce an "African bomb"? Added to this, there were concerns regarding South Africa's new friends like Iran, Cuba and Libya.

These were not the only problems. Around the time when the dismantling of nuclear weapons was taking place, the defence budget was drastically cut. According to André Buys (in "Tracking nuclear capable individuals", a paper delivered in Washington in April 2011), 40% of the staff attached to the programme were retrenched because they could not be redeployed to other positions at Armscor. Almost half this group were dissatisfied with their retrenchment packages because they felt that they had built up specialised skills and should be compensated accordingly. As a result, in March 1994 sixteen of the retrenchees threatened to disclose secret information to the highest bidder, unless they received $1 million each in unemployment benefits. These factors combined to make the international community restive. The obvious step was therefore to tie South Africa into existing export control regimes together with the other countries that possessed nuclear technology. The Nuclear Exporters Committee, also known as the Zangger Committee, and the NSG were the two groups that were active in this area, inter alia by drawing up lists of items which are subject to export controls and laying down guidelines applicable to exports of materials and equipment, but also relating to technology (see Part 2 for a more detailed description). Membership of the two groups would furthermore hold significant benefits for South Africa.

In October 1993 South Africa was accepted as a member of the Zangger Committee without any opposition. Membership of the NSG was somewhat more problematic, however.

As early as January 1984, Wynand de Villiers, the Chairman of the AEC, issued a statement which was published by the IAEA in February as INFCIRC/314. The following is an extract from De Villiers's statement:

> During discussions on nuclear policy and safeguards with the United States of America, South Africa has become aware of United States concerns about its intentions, and the South African Government has given the assurance ... that it will conduct and administer its nuclear affairs in a manner which is in line with the spirit, principles and goals of the Nuclear Non-Proliferation Treaty (NPT) and the Nuclear Suppliers Group Guidelines (NSG).

After the "peaceful Indian explosion" of 1974 the NSG – consisting of countries that possessed nuclear technology – was founded in 1975 as a secret "club" the aim of which was to reach agreement on mutually acceptable export control lists and guidelines for exports to prevent the further proliferation of nuclear weapons. In 1977 the group became dormant, although its membership was slowly increasing. The organisation only became active again in 1992, after the Gulf War, when it began to meet regularly and revise its guidelines. One of the important changes effected was the extension of control to nuclear-related dual-purpose items or rather items that were in use in non-nuclear industries but could also be used in the manufacture of nuclear weapons.

As a result of the NSG's change of course, Albright and Hibbs reported in April 1993 in *The Bulletin of Atomic Scientists* that a "Western" diplomat was of the opinion that South Africa's undertaking of 1984 was no longer applicable and that this was the reason why South Africa could not qualify for membership of the NSG. It was also claimed that the exporting of uranium to Israel after 1984 was not in accordance with South Africa's undertakings. The Americans did not want South Africa in the NSG at that stage, but at the same time they were concerned that the future government could possibly supply nuclear technology and materials to countries and organisations like Iran, Libya and the PLO "to repay old debts".

With the USA obdurately blocking South Africa's possible membership of the NSG, matters were made worse by a trivial incident at the Pelindaba site. A number of drums used for storing low-level radioactive waste were stolen.

Theft and an application for membership of the NSG

While South Africa's admission to membership of the NSG was still under consideration, an incident occurred that almost derailed the process.

There is an area on the AEC site known as Radiation Hill (now Thabana) where radioactive waste is stored. At that time much of the site contained waste in the form of uranium-contaminated gloves, paper, plastic, oil from compressors and Teflon filter candles from the Y-plant. The level of contamination was very low, but nevertheless the material could not simply be disposed of before the uranium content had been measured. Because of international boycotts, it was not possible to acquire equipment to measure the uranium content. As a result, thousands of sealed drums (metal and plastic) containing contaminated material were stored on Radiation Hill.

One day in 1994 external contractors, who were increasingly being allowed access to the AEC site, are thought to have opened some of the blue plastic drums, thrown the contents onto the ground and removed the drums from the site – under the very noses of the security guards. The target was undoubtedly the plastic drums and not the contents. These days one often sees drums of that kind on the back of overloaded vans bound for rural areas to the north of the country ...

This theft from a well-guarded nuclear site immediately hit the headlines and as usual the tale grew in the telling. The discarded contents of the drums included Teflon filters in which minute quantities of highly enriched uranium might have been trapped. The sensational story spread by the media was that "highly enriched uranium had been stolen from the AEC site". This even had repercussions overseas, to such an extent that the USA put its foot down firmly about South Africa's proposed membership of the NSG.

In order to put matters in perspective, the staff of the American embassy in Pretoria were invited to visit the AEC for an information session. The second-in-command at the American embassy, accompanied by a large group of advisers, attended the meeting. In order to illustrate how slight the contamination on the filter candles was, Nic von Wielligh had placed a small piece of a filter candle, about the size of a two rand coin and about 2 mm in thickness, in a small, sealed transparent plastic container. The contamination was visible as a very thin discoloration on

> *the outer surface of the Teflon slice. When the container was produced as a demonstration it was met with mild hysteria. The spectators reacted as if a black mamba had been released in their midst! The group apparently had no technical knowledge and were in deadly fear of a few milligrams of "highly enriched" uranium. In time, after further explanations, they calmed down but could not bring themselves to touch the sealed bottle. They did realise, however, that the kilograms of uranium metal of which they had formed a certain mental picture did not exist and that all that had actually been stolen were a few handy plastic drums.*
>
> *Fortunately this demonstration helped secure South Africa's admission to the NSG without any further resistance and being able to attend the annual meeting in Madrid in 1995 for the first time.*

The NSG and Zangger export control regimes do not control exports as such. They merely compile lists of item to be controlled, as well as guidelines that should apply to exports. Member states are then expected to control exports through their national legislation, compiled in accordance with the guidelines of the Zangger Committee or the NSG. Before South Africa could lay claim to membership, legislation therefore had to be introduced.

The South African Nuclear Energy Act was promulgated in 1993 to make provision for the control of nuclear materials and nuclear equipment, and also for the implementation of the comprehensive safeguards agreement with the IAEA.

However, this Act did not include the nuclear-related dual-use items that were included by the NSG in its export control lists in 1992. As previously explained, these dual-use items can be used in the manufacture of nuclear weapons but also for general industrial purposes. Furthermore, aside from nuclear weapons, there are also other weapons of mass destruction, namely chemical and biological weapons. A special law was therefore drafted to cater for weapons in this category and for nuclear-related dual-use items. The Non-Proliferation of Weapons of Mass Destruction Act was promulgated in 1993, with a control board to supervise such activities and a secretariat seated within the Department of Trade and Industry for day-to-day management.

The legislation had been prepared, membership of the two export control regimes obtained and the IAEA's investigation into the nuclear weapons programme completed. The logical next step was that in 1994 South Africa regained its place on the Board of Governors of the IAEA – which it had held up to 1977 when it lost its seat to Egypt.

Waldo Stumpf recounts an interesting story: a Greek businessman who was based in South Africa contacted him while Perricos's IAEA mission was still active in the verification activities in South Africa. Stumpf agreed to see him. During their discussion the businessman coolly announced that he was interested in buying nuclear weapons and asked whether Stumpf could help him. The Greek claimed that he was buying the weapons on behalf of "a NATO country". Stumpf obviously refused and pointed out that transactions of that nature were illegal. He added that he would report the conversation to the IAEA. Afterwards Stumpf wrote a personal letter (not through Foreign Affairs channels, as was customary) to Hans Blix of the IAEA to complain, since he suspected that the approach had been a trap, possibly arranged for South Africa by Dimitri Perricos …

The Greeks were not the only people shopping for bombs. Waldo Stumpf ("South Africa 'very circumspect' about N-Deals", *Iran Brief*, 9 October 1995) relates that an Iranian delegation consisting of a minister and senior officials from the crude oil industry visited South Africa in December 1995. Stumpf was instructed by his minister (Pik Botha, who was Minister of Mineral and Energy Affairs at the time) to have a meeting with the delegation in Cape Town. The Iranians wanted to talk about nuclear collaboration. Stumpf says it was clear that they did not know much about nuclear matters. Nevertheless the leader engaged Stumpf in a private conversation and then astonishingly produced a nuclear shopping list! Stumpf's reply was that it was out of the question for South Africa to assist them. In September 1997 the well-known publication, *Jane's International Defence Review*, carried a report on this incident.

South Africa's missile programme and the MTCR

There was another international export control regime of which South Africa wanted to become a member – the Missile Technology Control Regime (MTCR). But a high price had to be paid for membership.

It was no secret that South Africa had long been interested in several kinds of missiles. The first missiles were tested at the St. Lucia testing range (in KwaZulu-Natal). In 1983 the government openly announced that the St. Lucia testing range would be closed and a new test site would be built in the Overberg nature reserve close to the town of Houwhoek to make provision for longer range tests. Two years later the chairman of Armscor openly announced that South Africa was interested in ballistic missiles with a range of between 200 and 300 km to compensate for the increasing shortage of strike aircraft. In 1986 in an interview with a reporter he extended the range to "neighbouring countries". In February 1989 a spokesman for Armscor stated in an interview with foreign military attachés that Armscor's future lay in missile development. From then on South Africa's, or rather Armscor's, interest in missiles was common knowledge.

According to a 1991 UN analysis (*SA's Nuclear-Tipped Ballistic Missile Capability /UN A/45/571*) it typically takes 10 to 15 years for a country to get through the design and testing phases before it can proceed to the production of a respectable longer range missile – unless the country receives technological aid from elsewhere. The analysis also stated that ballistic missiles are not sufficiently accurate for the use of conventional warheads and that they cannot carry much explosive material in any case. These devices are therefore specially built for nuclear warheads or satellite launching. According to the UN report, the purpose of South Africa's ballistic missile programme was therefore clear: the delivery of nuclear warheads to neighbouring states.

Did South Africa receive technological aid from elsewhere for this programme? There was a great deal of speculation on this matter, but in March 1994 a spokesman for the 16 retrenched Armscor employees let the cat out of the bag. He told the *Sunday Times* that between 1989 and 1992 South Africa had been secretly collaborating with Israel on missile development. He added that 200 South Africans who were involved in the missile programme had secretly visited Israel during that period. "Projek Kerktoring" was given as the name of the secret project. This cooperative project with Israel, aimed at building South African missiles, is now a matter of public record. Part 5 contains information on it.

Distress on the other side of the Atlantic

After a Soviet satellite (Kosmos 2019) observed preparations for a launch at the Overberg site in May 1989, more and more speculative reports began to appear in leading newspapers like *Jane's Defence Weekly*, *The Guardian* and *The Washington Post*. All these reports hinted at cooperation between South Africa and Israel and suggested that the missile about to be tested was an adapted Jericho II missile.

On 5 July 1989 a missile was observed which was fired from the Overberg site and travelled a distance of about 1 600 km in the direction of the Prince Edward Islands.

This successful test put the proverbial cat among the pigeons. Israel was openly accused of having helped South Africa to develop a missile with a nuclear warhead, but the Israeli Prime Minister, Yitzhak Shamir, vehemently denied this. The statement by the Israeli Department of Defence did, however, leave the back door open: "No new contracts were concluded after 18 March 1987 ..."

The Americans found another rod for South Africa's back when they discovered that sensitive equipment had been acquired illegally. Between 1984 and 1988 an American firm, International Signal and Control (ISC), had covertly supplied missile-related equipment worth more than $30 million to Armscor. In 1991 the chairman of ISC was charged, convicted and imprisoned. The USA made every effort to catch up with Robert Clyde Ivy, an American engineer with intelligence contacts, who had worked for Armscor up to and during 1980 and had later been employed at ISC.

Israel was also implicated. In November 1989 another three South Africans and two Americans were charged with having attempted to export missile components to Armscor in South Africa via Israel between 1987 and 1988. Israel was threatened by the USA with an embargo on the planned exporting of a supercomputer and in 1991 a formal notice appeared in the Federal Register to the effect that additional sanctions would be imposed against South Africa because missile technology had been imported from Israel.

Ambassador Harry Schwarz protested vigorously, but the Americans were unperturbed – until President F.W. de Klerk phoned President Bush to protest. Bush was embarrassed because he had not known about the notice. He was very angry, largely because he had wanted to reduce existing sanctions against South Africa for the sake of promoting the transition to a majority government. His officials suddenly changed their tune and told Ambassador Schwarz that the proposed new sanctions would be moderated if South Africa would undertake to build only "peaceful" satellite launch vehicles (SLVs) and would permit inspections and follow the MTCR guidelines.

Bush's officials later had second thoughts about this outcome. An SLV can be converted into an intercontinental ballistic missile in the space of a few hours – long before any periodic inspection could detect this. A different approach was proposed, one which would hit the South Africans' pockets harder.

In his article entitled "Ending South Africa's rocket program: a nonproliferation success" (Nonproliferation Policy Education Centre: 31 August 1993), Henry Sokolski described a study undertaken by the Rand Corporation the previous year in which convincing evidence was presented to show that no country with a nascent SLV programme stood any chance of commercial success. The market was simply too small at that stage and the competition too strong. The South Africans had to be convinced of this fact.

The Americans' greatest fear was that if South Africa proceeded with the programme and found that it was a commercial failure the temptation would be too strong to sell the technology to bidders like Iran, Iraq and Libya in order to subsidise the local programme.

A meeting was arranged with South Africa. Henry Sokolski (formerly attached to the US Department of Defence) referred to it as the first high-level meeting between the USA and South Africa on South African soil in 30 years. Even Minister Pik Botha was involved. The USA's message was clear: The sanctions would remain in force until missile technology imports stopped. South Africa's application to join the MTCR would only be supported if the SLV programme was terminated. Halfway through the meal Pik Botha turned to the Americans and said: "Let's talk business. If we end the programme, what do we get out of it? We've got a lot of people working on the project. If we close it down, they are out of a job. What would you give us in exchange?"

The Americans had had enough time to prepare an answer.

"You will get a billion dollars and 1 000 highly trained engineers," they replied.

Pik Botha smiled. "Now we are talking. How will we get this?"

"It's easy," was the answer. "Stop the project and all the money and manpower you are putting into it will become available for use elsewhere. If you carry on you are going to lose your money anyway, no matter what you do." This message was underlined by the results of the Rand study – apparently a local missile programme would not be commercially viable.

The Americans were sure that this message had been clearly received and understood. The South African delegation were not completely convinced and the following year Armscor investigated the satellite market in Europe, but with little success.

In January 1992, Israel – under heavy pressure from the USA – announced that the MTCR guidelines would be strictly adhered to and that any cooperation with South Africa in the area of ballistic missiles would stop immediately.

The International Monetary Fund (IMF) also announced that future loans to South Africa might be blocked if the SLV project went ahead. That was the last straw. On 30 June 1993 Minister Pik Botha, who was acting State President at that stage, announced that the SLV project had been summarily terminated.

America had succeeded in wiping out another space programme – using the same tactics it used in 1990 and 1991 in Taiwan and South Korea. However, not every budding space programme received the same treatment. These days India, which is not a member of the MTCR, launches satellites on behalf of France and Japan without encountering any resistance. The USA was also behind the pressure to bring India in as a member of the NSG despite India's reluctance to sign the NPT. The reason for this irrational behaviour is probably that the USA regards India, nuclear weapons and all, as the first line of defence against an emerging China.

Sokolski cites an important reason for American pressure on South Africa to abandon the SLV programme. "Had this program continued, South Africa would have acquired an intercontinental ballistic missile (ICBM) capability that the African National Committee (sic) (ANC) government could use to lord over its African neighbors and sell for cash to ANC supporters, such as Libya."

The CIA's *Africa Report* of 8 December 1989 expresses another American viewpoint:

> South Africa appears committed to series production of ballistic missiles. Such production will alarm neighbouring African nations, who will probably seek ballistic missiles of their own to counter any perceived South African advantage … (which) may ignite a missile race on the African continent.

Bankrolling demolition

The price South Africa had to pay for membership of the MTCR was extremely high – and almost as ironic as the macabre joke about the child who killed his parents so that he could attend the orphanage picnic. Everything that had been built up had to be destroyed before South Africa could become a member of the MTCR, which regulated missile exports, although there would be nothing much left to regulate.

Kentron, Houwteq and Somchem were obliged to physically destroy important facilities and technology and even recall and destroy engineering drawings and other documentation held by subcontractors. Houwteq had to dismantle all the big missiles in its possession; Somchem had to destroy all the solid rocket fuel; at Somerset West the casting pits used to cast rocket engines were backfilled and sealed; X-ray equipment had to be destroyed; and the testing facility for static rocket tests at Hangklip near Rooiels was destroyed under the supervision of American inspectors.

The Americans were so anxious to see the whole programme destroyed that they even contributed $500 000 towards the demolition costs.

In May 1994 a notice was published in the *Government Gazette* regulating items on the MTCR list and five months later South Africa and the USA signed a bilateral agreement in which South Africa undertook to build no more ballistic missiles and to comply with the export guidelines of the MTCR. A year later, in September 1995, South Africa was admitted as a member of the MTCR and the South Africans could eventually look forward to the orphanage picnic.

The big prize – membership of the MTCR

The MTCR was established in 1987 as a result of a decision by seven industrial countries to control exports of missiles and the relevant technology in the interests of non-proliferation. Since then membership has grown to almost three dozen countries, including South Africa (1995). Not all the countries with advanced ballistic missile programmes, like Israel, India, Pakistan, Iran, China and North Korea, are members of the MTCR today, however. Israel has undertaken to act in the spirit of the MTCR and China did apply for membership in 2004, but was not accepted because of reservations about China's clandestine technology exports.

Like other control regimes, such as the NSG, the MTCR imposes two forms of control by consensus: firstly a list of items and technology that must be controlled; and secondly guidelines for exports of technological items. The MTCR is not a controlling body (it does not even have its own secretariat). The members undertake to apply export control in accordance with their national legislation, which would have been drafted in compliance with MTCR guidelines. Another important aspect is the mutual exchange of information on missile proliferation.

The main purpose of the MTCR is to control the proliferation of unmanned delivery systems for nuclear, chemical or biological weapons of mass destruction. The delivery systems specifically include rockets and

> drones capable of carrying a load of over 500 kg over distances of over 300 km.
> Like the NSG, the MTCR has two control lists:
> **Category 1** – items include complete rocket systems and unmanned aircraft (along with related technology) capable of carrying a payload of over 500 kg for a distance of over 300 km. These include ballistic missiles, SLVs, cruise missiles and all drones. The MTCR expressly forbids the exporting of items in this category.
> **Category 2** – less sensitive items which are similar to the dual-use items of the NSG. These items can therefore be used for purposes other than in rockets and drones. Exports of items in this category are also subject to strict guidelines and are forbidden in practice in some instances.

Could South Africa resume building SLVs while still complying with the MTCR guidelines? Yes – the MTCR does not forbid this, provided the launch vehicles are built for own use or to launch a satellite for a client. But, in the euphemistic language of the MTCR, there is "a presumption of denial" when it comes to exports to another country. In practice, however, this means that if South Africa were to start its own programme again almost all the components of an SLV would have to be developed and built locally since the importing of critical components is strictly regulated by the MTCR.

In terms of the USA's interpretation of the bilateral agreement of 1994, South Africa may not build such vehicles at all. Although it may be accepted from a legal point of view that membership of the MTCR along with all its regulations has replaced the bilateral agreement, there is little doubt that the USA would do everything possible to bedevil any projected new programme.

A spectacular debut in New York

The apparent haste to gain membership of the Zangger Committee, the NSG and the MTCR was not prompted simply by the need to be seen in respectable company, but was also part of a specific strategy.

Only three months after the new government of national unity had taken over the reins in May 1994, the cabinet decided that the Department of Foreign Affairs should promote South Africa as an "active participant in the various non-proliferation regimes and supplier groupings". The aim was to lend active support to nuclear non-proliferation, to encourage African states and members of the Non-Aligned Movement to support non-proliferation, and also to ensure that advanced peaceful technology would not be denied to developing countries.

The small group of competent diplomats charged with non-proliferation and disarmament got to work and by 1995 South Africa had already been accepted as a member of the three important supplier groupings. The big challenge still lay ahead, namely the NPT Review and Extension Conference of 1995.

After the NPT came into operation in 1970, review conferences were held every five years to discuss and evaluate the implementation of the treaty. The fifth review conference, which was to be held in 1995, was an important one in terms of Article X.2 of the treaty:

> Twenty-five years after the entry into force of the Treaty, a conference shall be convened to decide whether the Treaty shall continue in force indefinitely, or shall be extended for an additional fixed period or periods. This decision shall be taken by a majority of the Parties to the Treaty.

Before the meeting there were divergent views on whether the treaty should continue indefinitely and the situation was tense. There were fears regarding the future of the NPT. The USA, the EU and some members of the Western Group did some intense advance lobbying for an indefinite extension of the treaty, whereas other members from the Non-Aligned Movement (NAM) were in favour of extension for successive, limited periods – to be negotiated each time. The NAM was seeking in this way to apply political pressure to force the nuclear-weapon states to make concessions on disarmament and technical aid.

The NAM – "a broad church"

The NAM was founded in the early 1960s by a group of developing countries under the leadership of India, Indonesia, Ghana, Yugoslavia and Egypt who saw themselves as an independent bloc between the Western and Soviet blocs during the Cold War. This group expanded over time and now has about 120 members. Provision is also made for countries or organisations with observer status.

The aims of the NAM were set out as follows by Fidel Castro in the Havana Declaration of 1979:

> ... to ensure the national independence, sovereignty, territorial integrity and security of non-aligned countries in their struggle against imperialism, colonialism, neo-colonialism, racism, and all forms of foreign aggression, occupation, domination, interference or hegemony as well as against great power and bloc politics.
>
> *This describes the NAM very well, since it tends to be "against" things in general (for example, against Israel) rather than "for" a specific purpose.*
> *Although the members of the group make up almost two-thirds of the membership of the UN and are therefore quantitatively important, they are a loose association often characterised by contradictory internal tendencies. The group includes neighbouring countries like India and Pakistan and Iraq and Iran which are living in a state of disharmony or have even been involved in outright war. Some members are driving strong non-proliferation agendas whereas others, like India and Pakistan, have not signed the NPT and are armed with nuclear weapons and missiles. Iraq, North Korea and possibly Iran, have signed the NPT but have contravened its provisions by attempting to develop nuclear weapons. Furthermore, Iran and its Arab neighbours are far from being blood brothers. Without a doubt a "broad church"...*
> *With the end of the Cold War the original raison d'être of the NAM largely fell away and some commentators today question the relevance of the organisation. In 2003 Thabo Mbeki served as chairperson. He warned the NAM that its future would depend on how its members tackled global problems and on its ability to adopt and maintain strong positions.*

As a new member of the NAM, South Africa was in a unique position after 1994 in that it was the only member of the group from Africa that was actively involved with the supplier groups (Zangger, the NSG and the MTCR). Furthermore, South Africa was the only country ever to have built up a nuclear capability and voluntarily destroyed it. The potential role of diplomatic bridge-builder between the nuclear-weapon states, with the privileged position conferred on it by the NPT, and the non-nuclear-weapon states (chiefly members of the NAM), which had second-class status under the NPT, gave South Africa a rare opportunity to make a special contribution to the 1995 conference.

South Africa's strategy and approach to this conference were discussed two weeks beforehand at a meeting held in the state guesthouse in Pretoria under the chairmanship of Deputy President Thabo Mbeki. The consensus reached was that the NPT was the most important existing instrument for nuclear disarmament and non-proliferation and that it should not be jeopardised by a limited extension, as favoured by some NAM members. Mbeki apparently argued that it was a basic human right not to be threatened by weapons of mass destruction and that South Africa therefore had no other option but to give active support to the unrestricted extension of the NPT. But the nuclear-weapon states were expected to make concessions in exchange. It was left to a small group of South African diplomats to work out an appropriate strategy, while Mbeki undertook to write a letter to Deputy President Al Gore of the USA setting out South Africa's position (information from: *A Decade of Disarmament, Transformation and Progress* by Thomas Markram, Safer Africa, 2004).

The team of diplomats was headed by the new Minister of Foreign Affairs, Alfred Nzo, and included Tom Wheeler, Peter Goosen, Thomas Markram and Jean du Preez (attached to the South African mission in New York). Abdul Minty and Nic von Wielligh accompanied them as advisers. Nzo, who was elderly and had the unfortunate habit of nodding off during discussions, merely attended the commencement of the conference to read a speech from manuscript. Tom Wheeler then became the de facto leader of the delegation.

To the uninitiated an NPT conference is a revelation. It lasts a whole month and on occasion proceedings go on right through the night. If consensus cannot be reached on the last day "the clock is stopped" and the meeting simply continues. To survive this one needs a well-padded behind (*Sitzfleisch*, as the Germans call it).

The traditional procedure followed in a review conference is that the plenary assembly proceeds while the members put forward their national positions. Three main committees – set up on the basis of the NPT's three "pillars", namely the peaceful use of nuclear energy, non-proliferation and nuclear disarmament – make simultaneous attempts to draft consensus documents on the three topics. A special committee then collates these three documents to form a final draft document for approval by the plenary assembly, which is the ultimate purpose of the review conference. All the proceedings are based on consensus. A single country which raises an objection, or even simply wants to see a special aspect included in the final document, can bring the whole process to a halt or even derail the conference.

Minister Nzo's speech caused a stir in the typical lacklustre UN meetings which some observers regarded as a big and wearisome talking shop. In the absence of a formal NAM position South Africa took the initiative in strongly supporting the extension of the NPT, and also proposed a new approach in the so-called Principles and Objectives for Nuclear Non-Proliferation and Disarmament, which covered all aspects of the treaty. These included an undertaking by the nuclear-weapon states to fulfil their undertakings with regard to disarmament "with determination" and make peaceful nuclear technology more freely available to non-nuclear-weapon states. A stricter oversight process to monitor the implementation of the treaty was proposed. The document also called for the completion of the Comprehensive Nuclear-Test-Ban Treaty (CTBT) by 1996 and the immediate commencement of negotiations on a treaty banning the production of fissile material for nuclear weapons and other explosive devices.

In the words of John Simpson in *CSSS JMCNS NPT Briefing Book 2012*, the South African proposal diverted the debate on nuclear disarmament from political rhetoric to clear-cut undertakings by the nuclear-weapon states to proceed towards incremental disarmament. This proposal was like manna from heaven to the chairman of the potentially disastrous conference, Jayantha Dhanapala of Sri Lanka. He described it as a "brilliant package" and in order to retain the momentum he immediately asked a group of about 20 delegates to collaborate with South Africa in developing the proposal. However, the final document adopted by the conference differed little from the original proposals.

Although most of the non-nuclear-weapon states accepted the outcome as "permanence – but with responsibility", at the last minute the Arab countries almost derailed the whole process. They were not in favour of an indefinite extension of the treaty. They threatened to terminate the treaty unless Israel's nuclear capability was dealt with. Eventually three nuclear-weapon states, the USA, Britain and Russia, offered to support a resolution calling for all states in the Middle East (meaning Israel in particular) to sign the NPT and introduce comprehensive IAEA safeguards with the aim of making the area free of weapons of mass destruction. The conference was saved and the South Africans – rightly – enjoyed their hour of glory. The polecat had eventually been transformed into a model citizen – at its first appearance at an NPT conference at that.

Thomas Graham, the American ambassador at the conference, summed the proceedings up as follows:

The result was better than almost anyone expected prior to the conference, and a large degree of credit goes to the South African Government. As a result of the role played during the NPT Conference, South Africa now has emerged as a major player in arms control and disarmament, and perhaps other areas of international diplomacy as well (*Defense News*, 12-18 June 1995).

Twenty years later only one member of the brilliant 1995 team of South African diplomats is still with the department. Peter Goosen has recently returned from The Hague where he was ambassador to the Organisation for the Prohibition of Chemical Weapons (OPCW). Tom Wheeler has retired as a senior researcher and political adviser at the South African Institute of International Affairs (SAIIDA) but is still very active. Thomas Markram is head of the Weapons of Mass Destruction (WMD) branch at the UN Office for Disarmament Affairs (UNODA) and has been serving as Secretary to NPT conferences for the past decade. Jean du Preez presently holds a senior post at the Preparatory Commission for the Comprehensive Nuclear-Test-Ban Treaty Organization (CTBTO) in Vienna.

Before the following review conference in 2000 the prospects for non-proliferation began to deteriorate. On 11 and 13 May 1998 India detonated five nuclear devices underground in the course of Operation Pokhran-II. Its arch-enemy, Pakistan, responded two weeks later with Operation Chagai. Five underground tests were carried out: Chagai-I on 28 May and a further test, Chagai-II, two days later. These were the first nuclear devices detonated by Pakistan (India had carried out its first test in 1974). Admittedly, neither country had signed the NPT, but another state with a proven nuclear capability was bad news.

Five months later, in October 1998, President Bill Clinton signed the Iraq Liberation Act to support the Iraqi opposition group in deposing Saddam Hussein. In the aftermath of the Gulf War against Iraq in 1990-1991 the UN uncovered numerous attempts by Saddam Hussein to build weapons of mass destruction. Equipment and facilities were destroyed under UN supervision. Clinton's successor, George W. Bush, found it hard to believe that everything had been destroyed. This eventually paved the way for the American and British invasion of Iraq in March 2003. But Iraq was still a member of the NPT family and behaved in a thoroughly stubborn and obstructive manner at the NPT conference in 2000.

The formation of the New Agenda Coalition (NAC) in 1998 was better news. This group, consisting of South Africa, Sweden, Brazil, Egypt, Ireland, Mexico and New Zealand, was created in an attempt to solve the problems associated with the traditional three-group approach (NAM, the Western bloc and the Eastern bloc), which dated back to the Cold War, and to make real progress with nuclear disarmament, as envisaged by the NPT.

However, the nuclear-weapon states were no longer convinced that the "concessions" they had made to support the principles and objectives of 1995 in exchange for an indefinite extension of the treaty equated to an unconditional undertaking on their part to disarm. The argument was that their undertaking in 1995 was of a political nature and that the only legally binding consideration was Article VI of the treaty, which envisages "nuclear disarmament, and a treaty on general and complete disarmament under strict and effective international control". For the nuclear-weapon states all this lay far over the horizon, because a treaty of this kind would have to be negotiated at some future date.

The NAC began to negotiate on this matter with the nuclear-weapon states outside the conference but when a television team found out about these discussions by chance, the NAC began to function as a group within the conference.

The obduracy of the nuclear-weapon states was eventually overcome and the conference was saved from failure by the acceptance of the NAC's proposed 13 steps as put forward by South Africa. This broke the link between nuclear disarmament and complete disarmament which the nuclear-weapon states had been trying to establish and it was accepted that nuclear disarmament should proceed independently from general disarmament. This meant an unequivocal undertaking on the part of the nuclear-weapon states to eliminate their nuclear arsenals completely, thereby bringing nuclear disarmament closer. They did not, however, commit themselves to a date ...

The final document, in other words the summary of the outcome of the conference, almost came to grief because of a reference in the text to Iraq's non-compliance with the conditions of the treaty. Iraq obstinately dug in its heels. While the arguments between the USA, Iraq and a few other states continued behind closed doors, the other delegates sat through nights of waiting for something to happen. On the last Friday night of the conference the chairman "stopped the clock" at midnight and the negotiations proceeded. By Saturday afternoon, when some of the delegates had already gone home, the final document was eventually approved.

Another group that stood out at this conference were the Iranians. They treated the proceedings like a game of chess and played like grandmasters, skilfully securing the outcomes they wanted to see in the text. Two years later the world sat up straight when it became known that Iran had been engaged in covert nuclear activities for about 15 years, never having declared them to the IAEA. More than a decade later this game of chess is still continuing.

Unlike the review conferences of 1995 and 2000, which produced a number of positive results, the 2005 conference was bedlam from the start. The customary debate could not begin before the unfinished business had been dealt with. The Iranians, who had already been unmasked for their undeclared activities, and Egypt as well, frequently put obstacles in the way of consensus. The proceedings just could not get under way. In addition, the NAM was divided on certain matters, which contributed to the delays. Eventually there was insufficient time to follow the usual working pattern.

Throughout the conference Iran and Egypt brazenly impeded every effort to reach consensus and eventually the chairman resorted to a stratagem which had not been used for 30 years and submitted his own document, which was accepted simply as a technical report on proceedings. No final consensus document was possible.

The following NPT review conference in 2010 began under far more favourable circumstances. A year previously the new American president Barack Obama had stated in Prague: "So today, I state clearly and with conviction America's commitment to seek the peace and security of a world without nuclear weapons. I'm not naive. This goal will not be reached quickly – perhaps not in my lifetime. It will take patience and persistence."

Early on in the review conference the five nuclear-weapon states issued a joint declaration in which they undertook to take serious steps towards nuclear disarmament and reduce the number of their nuclear warheads.

Britain and France were more transparent about their nuclear arsenal and there was also progress with talks regarding the 1995 resolution on the Middle East being free of all weapons of mass destruction.

The only potential obstacles in the way of a consensus document were the IAEA's findings on undeclared nuclear activities in North Korea, Iran and Syria. In 2007 Israel carried out an aerial bombardment and pulverised a complex at Dair Alzour in Syria. This facility was apparently a nuclear reactor built with the aid of North Korea but never declared to the IAEA. After the bombardment Syria removed all the equipment, razed the site and refused the IAEA access to the site.

Despite this the review conference went fairly well. The last Friday of the conference ended on a rather strange note, however. While Obama had already agreed to accept the final document, the delegation from Iran was still awaiting instructions from Teheran, although the document contained no negative references to Iran. The Arab states were satisfied with references in the document to a nuclear weapons-free Middle East and did not support the Iranians in their attempts to thwart consensus. Iran eventually gave in, but in a new twist (for the NPT) the Iranians did not support consensus, but did not oppose it either.

For the first time in 35 years the final document was open to the interpretation that it did not require full compulsory consensus. This made it possible for member countries to agree to differ on certain controversial sections, but achieve full consensus on other sections of the document. This was probably the most important result of the NPT review conference of 2010 and in future it may hopefully cut out the endless semantic wrangling and ensure that selfish blocking actions cannot bring the proceedings to a halt.

Before the May 2015 NPT Review Conference (Revcon), most observers were pessimistic about a positive outcome, but pinned their hopes on the "Action Plan" on disarmament adopted in 2010. As part of the plan, the five nuclear-weapon states pledged "to accelerate concrete progress on the steps leading to nuclear disarmament", including reductions in "all types of nuclear weapons" and entry into force of the 1996 Comprehensive Test Ban Treaty (CTBT). However, 19 years after agreement was reached on the text of the CTBT, it has still not entered into force.

Over the years it has become standard practice for the weapon states to agree to nice sounding wording for the sake of a final consensus document – but then to either ignore it or dispute the interpretation of the wording afterwards.

Since the previous Revcon the USA has announced that it intends spending $1 trillion over the next 30 years to overhaul its nuclear arsenal and to update the associated infrastructure, Russia is doing some serious nuclear sabre-rattling with regard to the situation in Crimea and the Ukraine, China is developing a new generation missile with multiple nuclear warheads and the number of warheads deployed by the USA and Russia has increased. None of this boded well for the May 2015 conference.

Not only did the old Cold War warriors fling political barbs at each other, but in an ironical twist Iran – whom they suspect of having secret intentions of building its own nuclear weapons – blamed them for the lack of progress on disarmament since the previous Revcon in 2010 and for their plans for further investment in modernising and extending the lifespan of their nuclear weapons and related facilities.

The response of the P5 (the P equals Power), as they wish to call themselves, was at times hostile and even demeaning towards the non-weapon states. Before the conference the P5 had a secret meeting in London and a statement was released afterwards to the effect that: "The P5 all reaffirmed the importance of full compliance with existing, legally-binding arms control, nonproliferation, and disarmament agreements and obligations as an essential element of international peace and security." This is a general call meant for "everyone out there" but obviously not applicable to themselves. Further: "We continue to believe that an incremental, step-by-step approach is the only practical option for making progress towards nuclear disarmament, while upholding global strategic security and stability."

This caused ambassador Abdul Samad Minty of South Africa to cry out in frustration: "If for security reasons the P5 feel that they must be armed with nuclear weapons, what about other countries in similar situations? Do we think that the global situation is such that no other country would ever aspire to nuclear weapons to provide security for themselves, when the five tell us that it is absolutely correct to possess nuclear weapons for their security?"

There are three treaties or conventions covering weapons of mass destruction, that is nuclear, chemical or biological weapons. Two of the three forbid the possession and use of such weapons. For example, the Chemical Weapons Convention (CWC), which came into force in 1997, forbids the use and possession of chemical weapons and prescribes a time frame within which all stocks of such weapons should be destroyed. By August 2015, about 90% of the world's stock of chemical weapons had already been destroyed.

More than 40 years after the NPT entered into force, concerned individuals started to ask the obvious question: Is it more inhumane to kill people with chemical or biological weapons than with nuclear weapons? If not, why are nuclear weapons not legally forbidden? Why is there no agreed time frame within which the weapon states should destroy their nuclear weapons?

This led to three conferences, the first of which was held in Oslo in 2013, the second in Mexico in February 2014 and the third in Vienna at the end of 2014. The theme was the Humanitarian Impact of Nuclear Weapons (HINW). The Vienna gathering was attended by 800 delegates from almost 160 nations. The Austrian government closed the conference with two unexpected and extraordinary pledges: the first to cooperate with all stakeholders "to identify and pursue effective measures to fill the legal gap for the prohibition and elimination of nuclear weapons," and the second "to cooperate with all relevant stakeholders, organisations and civil society, in efforts to stigmatise, prohibit and eliminate nuclear weapons in light of their unacceptable humanitarian consequences and associated risks." The Austrian Pledge, as it has become known, has received the blessing of the Pope and the UN Secretary-General.

This humanitarian initiative became a hot topic at the 2015 Revcon, described by *The Washington Post* as "an uprising" of 107 states (out of the 191 NPT members) and civil society groups. These states are "seeking to reframe the disarmament debate as an urgent matter of safety, morality and humanitarian law", and have pledged to fill the gap for the prohibition and elimination of nuclear weapons. As can be expected, the P5 hit back feebly by stating that the HINW produced no new evidence that their nuclear forces were more dangerous than previously believed and belittled the initiative as a public relations exercise and a distraction from the NPT.

The humanitarian pledge can be regarded as the most significant departure from the stale debates which characterise typical NPT review conferences and can, hopefully, in future create enough pressure so that the existing legal gap in the NPT with regard to the prohibition and elimination of nuclear weapons will eventually be filled – a gap described by the Austrian ambassador as "a reality gap, a credibility gap, a confidence gap and a moral gap". Hopefully this gap will be filled before the very chummy P5 – clubbing together in London and issuing combined statements – possibly choose mutual nuclear destruction, taking the rest of the world into the abyss with them.

Another notable feature of the Revcon was that, for the first time, Israel was present at such a conference, albeit as an observer, not being a state party to the NPT. This obviously contributed to Egypt's being more intransigent than ever. For 20 years, Arab countries, led by Egypt, have called for the creation of a Middle East zone free of weapons of mass destruction, which would eventually require Israeli to accept nuclear disarmament. In 2010, NPT states agreed to hold a dedicated conference to discuss the Middle East zone proposal. This conference did not materialise, however, with Israel blaming its Arab neighbours for the failure of progress and claiming that after five rounds of consultations with some of its Arab neighbours in Switzerland between October 2013 and June 2014 the Arab states had decided to discontinue the meetings.

Israel's attitude towards such a conference has always been that there is such a broad range of security challenges in the region that it could consider joining the NPT only if it were at peace with its Arab neigbours and Iran – something that has, alas, proved elusive since Biblical times.

Israel consequently rejected the vague final draft proposal that set March 2016 as a deadline for the conference because there was no agreement on the agenda, terms of reference and follow-up steps for the conference. Egypt stubbornly refused to relent.

Since Israel, as a non-state party, had no direct say in the conference, the US came to the rescue at the recent Revcon, stating:

> "We regret that we were not able to support the draft consensus document tabled by the President of the conference. The blame for the inability of this conference to produce a forward-looking consensus document, however, lies squarely with those states [read Egypt] that were unable to show any flexibility in pursuit of the convening of a Middle East conference that enshrined the principles of consensus and equality."

With the support of the UK and Canada this dealt the final death blow to the main purpose of the 2015 Revcon, namely to agree on a final consensus document, looking back on its implementation and sketching a path for future improvements and disarmament.

The fact that the conference had failed because of Israel was a convenient way – some cynical observers even say it was engineered that way – of deflecting attention from the main problem, namely the utter failure of the P5 to meet their obligation (and disregard for such obligations) under Article VI and undertakings in previous Revcons to advance towards nuclear disarmament.

This is not the first time in the 45-year history of the treaty that the conference has ended without a consensus document, but it has simply increased the scepticism of many observers, who doubt whether the NPT and its Review Conferences are still relevant.

In the past the Conference on Disarmament did sterling work in preparing the texts of the Nuclear Nonproliferation Treaty, the Biological Weapons Convention, the Chemical Weapons Convention and the Comprehensive Test Ban Treaty, but it has been fossilised into inaction for almost two decades. For example, no start has been made with negotiations on the FMCT as foreseen 20 years ago. No wonder then that desperate states are beginning to work outside the formal forums and start initiatives like the HINW in the hope of somehow blowing new life into nuclear disarmament, an ideal whose achievement is long overdue.

A new man on the scene

Abdul Minty is of Indian descent, despite his Scottish surname. He was born in South Africa in 1939 and grew up in Johannesburg. In 1958 he left for Britain to continue his studies, chiefly in the field of international relations. He obtained several degrees overseas.

Minty joined the British Anti-Apartheid Movement (AAM). From 1979 to 1994 he was the director of the World Campaign against Military and Nuclear Collaboration with South Africa, an organisation based in Oslo, Norway.

With the support of these two organisations he succeeded in getting the South African Olympic Committee expelled from the International Olympic Committee (IOC) in 1963. Thanks to the support of the African group, the NAM and some members of the IAEA, he was also largely responsible for the fact that in 1977 South Africa lost its position as governor on the IAEA's Board of Governors. Egypt took over South Africa's seat.

After the UNSC had imposed a voluntary arms embargo against South Africa, Minty appeared before the supervisory committee on numerous occasions and submitted information behind closed doors on contraventions of the embargo.

Over the years Abdul Minty established very close ties with the UN, the IAEA and the NAM. It therefore came as no surprise when in August 1995 he was appointed deputy director-general of the South African Department of Foreign Affairs with special responsibility for non-proliferation and disarmament. Although he was not part of the inner circle of the ruling party after 1994, his competence and experience were recognised and rewarded.

In 1995 he was appointed chairperson of the South African Council for the Non-Proliferation of Weapons of Mass Destruction and also as the South African governor serving on the IAEA's Board of Governors. Traditionally the Department of Foreign Affairs had always had a senior officer on the AEC's board, and this practice was continued with Minty's nomination to the post. He soon gave Waldo Stumpf to understand that the ANC did not agree with the way in which the history of the building and dismantlement of South Africa's nuclear weapons had been conveyed to the world. Waldo Stumpf was once invited to address a historical society at the University of the Witwatersrand on the weapons programme. When this came to Minty's ears he forbade Stumpf to deliver his paper. Stumpf told him that the arrangements had already been made, but Minty countered with the threat that the minister would force Stumpf to cancel his appearance. Minty was evidently still harbouring a grievance because the ANC had been unable to claim any credit for dismantling the nuclear weapons programme.

Minty enjoyed an international reputation thanks to his activism and was given several responsibilities as a result. In 2006 he served as the president of the General Conference of the IAEA and from 2007 to 2008 as the chairperson of the Nuclear Suppliers Group.

When Mohamed ElBaradei retired as the director-general of the IAEA in 2009 after a term of 12 years, Minty was nominated for this position by the South African Department of Foreign Affairs. He was also the favoured candidate of the developing countries.

In a tough electoral battle between April and July 2009 Minty and Yukiya Amano of Japan were neck and neck – with neither of them being able to obtain the required two-thirds majority in the IAEA's Board of Governors. The whole process was then restarted with three additional candidates. These three soon fell out, however, and on 2 July 2009 Amano was successful in the sixth round after gaining a two-thirds majority by a single vote. At the end of 2009 Amano was eventually appointed director-general of the IAEA.

Is it possible that the armed burglary at Pelindaba, which had made international headlines two years previously, played a part in the outcome? After all it was the first attack of this nature anywhere in the world on a nuclear plant containing nuclear weapons material.

On 18 November 2011 Minty made a speech in his capacity as ambassador and governor at a meeting of the IAEA's Board of Governors. He made the following statement:

> Board members may recall that since the termination of Apartheid South Africa's nuclear weapons programme, it has taken the Agency nearly 18 years to conclude, for the first time, as outlined in the Safeguards Implementation Report of 2010, that all nuclear material in South Africa remained in peaceful activities.

Minty's statement requires a brief explanation. When a country signs the IAEA's Additional Protocol, a so-called state-level evaluation is carried out. This means that the new, expanded declaration in respect of the specific country's nuclear activities and material required by the AP is compared with all the information on the state that is already in the possession of the IAEA. Furthermore, it took years to measure the low-activity waste stored in several thousand drums, as previously explained. Taking this additional information into account, the IAEA could then conclude that South Africa was not concealing anything, and they issued a statement to the effect that there were no undeclared activities and that all nuclear material was under safeguards. The completion of the evaluation referred to had nothing to do with the former verification in respect of South Africa's nuclear programme (which had in fact been completed 18 years before his statement); it concerned the implementation of the AP. Minty had cited the South African case inappropriately in this context in order to gain time for Iran, which, at the time, was refusing to supply information on past activities and grant access to certain facilities.

On this occasion Minty expressed doubts about information the IAEA had collected on possible nuclear activities in Iran. He claimed that Iran's activities were of a peaceful nature: "As for the Islamic Republic of Iran, the Agency has indeed concluded that its declared nuclear material remained in peaceful activities." In the course of this speech Minty did, however, appeal to Iran to cooperate with the IAEA to remove "ambiguities, if any" about the Iranian nuclear programme.

In the same speech Minty went on to make the following mystifying statement: "The eventual abandonment of the nuclear weapons programme by Apartheid South Africa is testimony to this principled position of the liberation movement of South Africa against nuclear weapons and of their elimination."

Since 2011 Minty has been serving as the South African ambassador in Geneva, responsible for the UN Conference on Disarmament, among others. Lastly, Minty's philosophy is briefly summed up in his résumé:

> In the present international environment there is no issue in this field (to restrict the rights of members of the NPT to use nuclear technology for peaceful purposes) that can be said to be only a technical one – they are all fraught with danger for developing countries and of supreme political importance. Thus, these negotiations involve technical and political issues and the pressure of the big powers, united in purpose, is almost overwhelming for most developing and even some developed countries. In this context, South Africa has been able to stand on principle and defend its

position on the basis of international law and specific treaties and agreements. Despite the fact that South Africa's position is often not welcomed by the big powers this is the main reason why it is respected and held in high esteem. Thus the role of South Africa is unique.

This philosophy was clearly demonstrated by Minty's several strong interventions in the 2015 NPT Revcon where he took the P5 to task. For example, on 13 May 2015 he stated on behalf of South Africa:

> Whilst we have outlawed other weapons of mass destruction, including chemical and biological, nuclear weapons are the only weapons that we have retained and modernised and which continue to present a threat to humanity as whole. How do we continue to justify the retention of these weapons?
>
> Such an approach makes nonsense of the 1995 and 2000 Review Conference decisions and the many other decisions, which constitute the NPT regime. It certainly makes nonsense of the South African proposal in 1995 to extend the Treaty indefinitely based on the historic bargain that NWS will disarm, whilst others will not proliferate. It makes nonsense of the 2000 Review Conference, together with many other agreements. Many of us also cannot forget the commitment made, not so long ago, to Global Zero and the Prague statement, which inspired so many of us. Since Hiroshima and Nagasaki, there was so much hope that we were moving in the right direction with this commitment to try to find a solution to rescue humanity from this peril. However, even this commitment was regrettably later qualified by statements to the effect that we could not expect nuclear disarmament 'in our lifetime'.

Interlude in Iraq

It had been suggested that South Africa, as the world's "model pupil", might share its experience of nuclear weapons dismantlement with other countries. President Thabo Mbeki therefore proposed in 2003 that a delegation of South African specialists in the fields of nuclear, biological and chemical weapons of mass destruction should visit Iraq. The aim of the visit would be to advise the Iraqis on the best ways to dismantle their weapons programmes in order to satisfy the IAEA's weapons inspectorate and Unscom. The political situation in the country was extremely tense and things were hovering on the proverbial knife edge. It was a mere two weeks before the outbreak of the Second Gulf War. The Iraqis were not interested in advice from anybody.

Waldo Stumpf was to have been part of the South African delegation to Iraq, but did not go in the end. President Mbeki decided that it was unnecessary. Some years after the mission Stumpf told G.R. Heald that he had been sceptical about the possibility of South Africa's being able to share knowledge of its nuclear weapons dismantlement process successfully with other states:

> Stumpf commented that while Iraq's nuclear weapons were in an advanced weaponisation phase both prior to and during the Gulf War of 1991, Iraq was simply too exhausted and financially ruined by the Gulf War to proceed with their nuclear weapons programme.
>
> They had already been defeated in 1991, and the British and American invasion of 2003 consolidated the extent of their 1991 defeat with the imposition of comprehensive and mandatory sanctions. Professor Stumpf contended that Iraq's battle fatigue would have been so pervasive and intense that the military establishment would simply not have had the wherewithal to pursue a nuclear weapons programme that required such intense focus, energy and co-ordination. He submitted this suggestion to President Thabo Mbeki at the Union Buildings in Pretoria before the group visited Baghdad in 2003.
>
> The South African mission entered Iraq with good intentions, but they were far too late to be effective. By this time, the negative pattern of obstructive behaviour exhibited by the Iraqis towards the inspectorate had already long been entrenched. The situation in Iraq had already entered a point of irreversibility. The invasion had gathered momentum and could not be stopped.

It should be remembered that South Africa's situation differed considerably from that of Iraq. Iraq had signed the NPT some years previously; South Africa had not. In addition, Iraq was the aggressor, since it had invaded Kuwait. This was why the UN imposed sanctions on Iraq. In South Africa's case the decades of international sanctions were the consequence of opposition to the country's domestic policy.

In a discussion with the authors of this text in March 2013, Waldo Stumpf emphasised that he remains sceptical about the value that South Africans as outsiders could add by sharing knowledge and experience gained from their own nuclear weapons dismantlement process with the world. "It remains a political decision," he says. "Nuclear weapons are a political matter."

Furthermore, each case is unique because it plays out in a particular period of history, against a particular political and strategic background. What most cases have in common is severe tension between parties in an unstable regional context, such as in the cases of India and Pakistan as well as Israel and its neighbours.

An unworthy end to a career

After Deputy President F.W. de Klerk and his NP colleagues left the government of national unity at the end of June 1996, the writing was clearly on the wall for the incumbent chairmen and executive heads of semi-state institutions like Eskom, Armscor and the AEC. These people were aware that they would have to make way for appointments by the new ruling party. The process that followed was vacillating, protracted and unworthy of highly trained people with decades of specialised knowledge and managerial experience behind them. What happened to Waldo Stumpf is a case in point. (Johan Alberts of Armscor and Allen Morgan of Eskom suffered similar humiliation.)

Pik Botha was the Minister of Mineral and Energy Affairs from 1994 to 1996, when the NP left the government. In 1996 he was replaced by Penuell Maduna, with Susan Shabangu as his deputy.

At the time the IAEA in Vienna happened to be looking for a deputy director-general who would be responsible for the worldwide application of safeguards. Stumpf was approached as the most suitable candidate and several member countries, including Germany and the USA (which contributes almost one-quarter of the IAEA's budget), supported him strongly. A candidate for such a senior position should preferably enjoy the support of his or her own government. Minister Maduna was consequently informed about the situation with the expectation that this would provide an ideal solution. Stumpf would be able to make a graceful exit from the AEC and devote his talents to a greater cause. The minister in turn would be able to appoint someone of his own choice. But after Maduna had discussed the matter with President Mbeki, his reply to Stumpf was: "No, as long as I am minister you will remain in that post." In 1999 Maduna was moved to a different portfolio and Phumzile Mlambo-Ngcuka became minister. Attempts by Waldo Stumpf to bring the discussion on the vacation of his post to a conclusion came to nothing. The new minister did not even answer his letters. She had other matters to occupy her, including the department's green paper.

To Stumpf's dismay, when the green paper on the future of nuclear energy (compiled without consulting the AEC) was eventually published, it stated that the chief executive officer of the AEC would lose his job. Years later Stumpf commented as follows: "I was prepared to go and had already found another means of livelihood, but now I had to read in a policy document that I had lost my job!" All he could do was to seek legal advice from a labour law practitioner. The advice Stumpf received was that he held a permanent appointment and could not simply be kicked out. The department eventually realised that there would have to be some negotiation and a satisfactory severance package was negotiated. The minister and the chairperson of the board, Roger Jardine, arranged a farewell and Waldo Stumpf was rewarded for 32 years of hard work with a cheap fountain pen. By that time the post at the IAEA had already been filled.

Waldo Stumpf was succeeded in 2001 by Lord Senti Thobejane, who holds a degree in medical physics from a university in the USA, obtained with the aid of a UN bursary for ANC students. He headed the Department of Health and Welfare in the Northern Province (now Limpopo) for several years, but a commission appointed by the premier found him guilty of a "blatant waste" of funds before he joined Necsa. He did not remain in the Pelindaba post for long, but disappeared abruptly after a disagreement with the board over his salary. He had reportedly negotiated a hefty 25% salary increase with certain board members without ministerial consent. He has since advanced as an important adviser to the Minister of Energy Affairs and at times also advises the President directly with regard to South Africa's future nuclear procurement plans.

PART 7

A SOUTH AFRICAN STALL IN KHAN'S ATOMIC BAZAAR

While every effort was being made in the international and diplomatic arena to establish South Africa's credibility as a non-proliferant of nuclear weapons, there were also people who were secretly undermining that credibility while liberally lining their own pockets.

This chapter is devoted to the story of a group of international swindlers who ran an extensive atomic bazaar from the early 1970s to the early 2000s. For the whole of this period they were doing a roaring trade, and for all we know there may be elements among them that are still active somewhere.

The UNSC

When the existence and scale of the atomic bazaar were discovered in the 1990s, the director-general of the IAEA, Mohamed ElBaradei, referred to it as "a nuclear Walmart". It was an enormous, clandestine import and export business for countries that needed equipment to produce nuclear material on the sly for their own nuclear weapons programmes. As a bonus, the plans for building the weapons were sometimes supplied with the equipment!

Someone once jocularly referred to this group as the UNSC – not the United Nations Security Council but the Unrepentant Nuclear Scoundrels and Crooks. In time about 50 individuals came to be associated with the bazaar. They included Pakistanis, Germans, Swiss, Sri Lankans, Britons, Turks, Malaysians, Indians, a few Israelis and a handful of South Africans. The group spread its tentacles to countries in the Middle East, the Far East and Europe. The heart of the network was situated in Dubai.

The partners in the bazaar were a loosely structured association of people whose only tie was the profit motive. Loyalty to one another – if such a thing is possible among scoundrels – lasted only while the dollars were flowing, but vanished like mist at the slightest setback. Then it was every man for himself as they scrambled to protect their bank balances.

The clients were what some people referred to as rogue states: Pakistan, North Korea, Iraq, Libya and Iran. Their sole purpose was to make their own nuclear weapons. But in order to do so they faced a huge technological hurdle, namely the acquisition of weapons material, and this was where the group of nuclear smugglers were anxious to assist them – naturally for a substantial fee.

But at this point we need to go back a bit in history …

Gernot Zippe's legacy

In the early days of the Manhattan Project several techniques for separating uranium isotopes were investigated. One line of inquiry was the use of the gas centrifuge process. Jesse W. Beams of the University of Virginia was the expert in this field. Although the 1941 budget for this was about four times the amount allocated for gas diffusion (the method that was ultimately successful), Beams was unable to master the use of the delicate, super-fast rotating rotors. Work on uranium enrichment by means of gas centrifuges was therefore discontinued.

After the World War II the Austrian Gernot Zippe and his collaborators in a Soviet prisoner of war camp succeeded in overcoming Beams' problems and in 1960 the Soviet Union became the first state to commission a full-scale centrifuge plant for the enrichment of uranium.

It was 11 years after the end of the war before the Soviet Union released Zippe. He returned to Germany and in 1957 attended a conference on the gas centrifuge process, where it became clear to him that the techniques developed in Leningrad were far more advanced than Western efforts. He immediately patented the gas centrifuge process and became a man with a mission: the commercialisation of his system.

In 1958 and 1959 Zippe was invited to take up a post at the University of Virginia, where he initiated the Americans into gas centrifuge separation techniques. His work was not classified as secret at first, but by 1960 the Americans realised that they had a serious proliferation problem on their hands and started classifying the information. The problem was that they had no means of controlling technology that had been developed beyond the borders of the USA.

On the other hand there was nothing to stop the Europeans from continuing to develop the gas centrifuge. They had no intention of using the technology to make weapons material, but simply wanted to produce fuel for reactors. Besides, the enrichment plants built by Urenco in Britain, the Netherlands and Germany were covered by stringent Euratom and IAEA safeguards and any illicit enrichment for the purpose of making weapons would very soon have been detected.

In the land of cheese and windmills

Abdul Qadeer Khan was born in Bhopal in British India in 1936. In later life he was to acquire the status of honorary cabinet member in a country that did not even exist at the time of his birth. In 1984 Bhopal became the scene of a massive chemical accident at the Union Carbide pesticide plant (a company which coincidentally had previously been an important contractor for the Manhattan Project). Between 15 000 and 20 000 people in a nearby squatter camp died and about half a million others sustained serious health impairments – and this was not even caused by a weapon of mass destruction.

In 1947 the British applied religious segregation and partitioned British India into three parts, namely one part for the mostly Hindu population (India) and two parts, East and West Pakistan, for the predominantly Muslim population.

The small group of Muslims that remained in India soon found their situation untenable and most of them migrated to Pakistan. For Khan as a 16-year-old boy the migration was a traumatic experience. It left him with a deep hatred of India and later steered his life in a particular direction.

Khan was a bright pupil and thanks to several European aid programmes he was selected in 1961 to further his education in West Berlin. Following this he graduated as a metallurgical engineer in Delft in the Netherlands. In 1972 he followed this with a PhD at the Catholic University of Leuven in Belgium.

The engaging Khan made friends with fellow students – people like Heinz Mebus (German), Günes Cire (Turkish) and Henk Slebos (Dutch). These friendships lasted for decades and played a big part in Khan's later life and fortunes.

Another important friend of Khan's who studied with him at Leuven and qualified in nuclear engineering was the Swiss, Friedrich Tinner. Their friendship lasted for over 30 years and included joint involvement in numerous illicit projects.

Three years after his arrival in Berlin, Khan married Hendrina Reterink. She was born in South Africa of Dutch parents. Henny, as she was known, grew up in the former Northern Rhodesia, but later returned to the Netherlands with her parents.

Henny travelled with her husband from West Berlin to Delft and Leuven and the couple eventually settled in the Dutch town of Almelo in 1972.

A colleague, Frits Veerman, with whom Khan shared an office, described him as tall and slender, with a strong nose and a broad forehead under a bush of dark hair. According to Veerman, Khan was affable and modest; he was enthusiastic right from the beginning and showed an interest in his coworkers and their doings.

In 1971 Pakistan suffered a humiliating defeat in a war against India. The Pakistani Defence Force was crushed and East Pakistan disappeared before reappearing as the state of Bangladesh. In later years Khan referred to the television images shown in Europe of Pakistani soldiers being brutally humiliated by Indians; these images were to haunt him for years to come. To crown it all, India exploded its first "peaceful" nuclear device three years later, in 1974. This was a challenge to Pakistan and the rest of the world.

A.Q. Khan, the patriot, had found his mission in life. Almelo was a means to achieving his purpose. Urenco's Dutch gas centrifuge plant for the enrichment of uranium was situated there. In May 1972 Khan took up a position at a small research laboratory called FDO. FDO was a subcontractor for the Dutch branch of Urenco. Although he did not have formal security clearance to visit the enrichment plant, he managed to do so within a week of his appointment (and frequently afterwards). His employer did not object to his unauthorised visits. Significantly, during his Urenco visits Khan walked about with a notebook, diligently making notes.

At the time Urenco was developing two designs for gas centrifuges, one named CNOR/SNOR, designed by a Dutch team, and the other the more advanced German G-type centrifuge. The G-type was more effective but also more difficult to build.

Khan was given the task of translating the design data on the advanced G-1 and G-2 types from German to Dutch and for over two weeks he had full unsupervised access. He often worked late into the night making illicit photocopies of the data and even took documents home at night so that Hendrina could help him with the finer nuances of the translation.

The Dutch intelligence service was more wide awake than Khan's employer, especially since this Pakistani citizen was asking far too many questions that had nothing to do with his own project. For another thing, cars with French and Belgian diplomatic number plates were often seen parked in front of his house at night. He was placed under surveillance and his case was even discussed with the CIA. Ruud Lubbers, who was then Minister of Economic Affairs in the Netherlands (and later Prime Minister), said on a television programme in 1995 that the Dutch had wanted to arrest Khan on two occasions, but were requested by Washington not to do so. The Americans preferred to keep him under observation so that they could keep tabs on the network he was building up.

After Pakistan's humiliating defeat by India, Zulfikar Ali Bhutto, the Prime Minister of Pakistan, gathered all his nuclear experts together in January 1972 in great secrecy and made his famous pronouncement that Pakistan had to build a nuclear bomb, even if they had to eat grass for 1 000 years. This was an enormous challenge for a country which, according to A.Q. Khan, did not even have the capacity to manufacture bicycle chains.

In terms of technological development, Pakistan was simply not equipped for such a task and therefore had to arrange to have scientists and engineers trained overseas. For example, in 1972 Pakistan and West Germany concluded a scientific and technical agreement in respect of training and soon dozens of Pakistanis were making their way to the famous nuclear research station at Karlsruhe.

The "peaceful" Indian nuclear detonation of 1974 drove Bhutto's blood pressure even further and Khan was ready to exploit the situation. Four months after the Indian explosion, while he was still in the Netherlands, Khan wrote a letter to Bhutto offering to put his knowledge and services at Bhutto's disposal.

In December 1974 Khan travelled to Pakistan and met Prime Minister Bhutto and Munir Khan, the head of the Pakistan Atomic Energy Commission (PAEC). A.Q. Khan advised Bhutto to build a uranium bomb rather than a plutonium bomb. This was just the beginning of the trouble between the two Khans. Munir Khan was A.Q. Khan's senior and he was already planning the production process for plutonium to build a nuclear weapon. A.Q. Khan undertook to continue with his work in the Netherlands and get as much information as he could.

At the beginning of 1975 Pakistan officially began its enrichment programme which was headed by Sultan Basheer-ud-Din Mahmood. Khan met him in Belgium to discuss strategy, after which he speeded up his thefts of information – and even components – from Urenco. He also asked his friend Frits Veerman to take photographs. One evening when visiting Khan at his home, Veerman noticed to his consternation that top secret blueprints of centrifuges were lying on a table in the sitting room.

By October 1975 the Dutch had run out of patience and on Lubbers' instructions Khan was moved away from any work at the FDO that related to centrifuges. He realised that his machinations had been detected. On 15

December he therefore returned to Pakistan, taking with him information on over 100 firms that made components for centrifuge enrichment. The faithful Hendrina followed him with their two daughters. Hendrina travelled with the copies her husband had secretly made in her baggage.

Eight years after fleeing from Holland, Khan was sentenced in absentia by a Dutch court to four years' imprisonment for industrial espionage. However, in 1985 the sentence was set aside on a technical point.

Nevertheless, Khan would never again be able to visit the Netherlands as an ordinary tourist. In 1988, on a cold, rainy Christmas Eve he and his Dutch friend, Henk Slebos, were detected in a car near the border between Belgium and the Netherlands, close to the home of Hendrina's parents. This came about because the authorities were monitoring Slebos' movements. To the agents' surprise, Khan was with Slebos in the car, travelling under an assumed name. He was summarily put on a plane and sent back to Pakistan.

When Khan returned to Pakistan at the end of 1975 he was received with open arms and at the beginning of 1976 he joined the PAEC. Bhutto asked Khan's opinion on the status of the Pakistani enrichment programme which had been launched under Munir Khan. After visiting the facility, Khan predictably reported that the project was in a chaotic state. Bhutto offered him a managerial post under Munir Khan. Eyewitnesses relate that when Khan accepted the post, Bhutto triumphantly banged his fist on the table and roared: "I will see the Hindu bastards now!"

A.Q. and Munir Ahmad Khan (who are not related – the surname Khan is as common as Smith) clashed from the beginning. They were later to become arch-enemies. The situation became so bad that Bhutto made A.Q. Khan fully responsible for the uranium enrichment programme, reporting directly to the prime minister. Munir Khan was put in charge of plutonium production, plutonium weapons and nuclear reactors. It is astonishing that a poor country like Pakistan could follow two parallel paths to the production of a nuclear bomb and later even run two competing missile programmes. These competing programmes were deliberately launched by the political leaders of the time and maintained by their successors.

Right from the start this hugely expensive undertaking undoubtedly had the potential to give rise to an international network to finance the enormous projects.

One can only sympathise with Munir Khan. He was expected to compete with a man whose CV contained the following astonishing claim:

> As arrow of time moves, the Will of God prevails and is focussed on the emergence of humans endowed with exceptional capabilities and creative abilities. Such are the men who, by their good deeds, fullfill the edict of God as revealed in the Holy Qurran. By their deeds and actions such persons, though not prophets, demonstrate that they are an extension of the will of the transcendental. These are the people who are destined to make history in the elevation of nations. Such is the personality of Dr Abdul Qadeer Khan… (. .) It is rare that a person in a single lifetime accomplishes so much. This is done only by men who are endowed with special abilities by God and who prepare themselves through hard work and devotion to fulfill the mission of serving mankind.

Little was to come of Bhutto's wish to "see the Hindu bastards", however. In 1977, after serious political unrest, he was replaced by the militaristic Muhammad Zia ul-Haq, and two years later the poor man was hung after being convicted of political murders by the new regime.

A.Q. Khan established Engineering Research Laboratories (ERL) in mid-1976 and three years later his P-1 centrifuges, copied from Urenco's German G-1 model, were functioning. At first small quantities of uranium were enriched at the Kahuta plant. In 1981 the new president, Zia ul-Haq, changed the name of the laboratory to Khan Research Laboratories (KRL). This was the first recognition Khan received for his achievements.

Two Germans and a South African

It's one thing to have the blueprints but quite a different matter to physically manufacture the equipment and get it to work. It was here that Khan needed help and an old acquaintance in Germany, Gotthard Lerch, was happy to assist him for a fee.

The prominent journalist, Steve Coll, who often writes about proliferation-related matters in *The New Yorker*, describes the German in the following terms: "A big man with a flattened nose and a bulky face, and, were it not for his meticulously pressed clothing, he might be taken for a brawler".

Lerch was a mechanical engineer who held a senior post at the prominent German firm Leybold-Heräus in Hanau, Germany, at the time when A.Q. Khan was stealing secret information at Almelo. One of the products for which the firm was world-famous was its vacuum pumps, without which no uranium enrichment plant can function. It was this firm that came up with a technique for making the high-speed rotating rotors of gas centrifuges (70 000 or more revolutions per minute) rotate in a vacuum. This is achieved by placing the rotating rotor inside an outer casing and evacuating the space between the two, which reduces friction so that the rotors are able to rotate at well above the speed of sound.

In the 1970s Leybold-Heräus had contracts to supply UF_6 feed-and-withdrawal systems for the Urenco enrichment plants. This enabled Lerch to acquire the top secret plans to build centrifuges. Like Khan, he collected blueprints which, even decades later, are still being passed around among countries that plan to build their own enrichment plants, rather like family heirlooms being handed down from generation to generation. At one time he even concealed the plans in South Africa for security reasons.

By 1979 the German authorities were becoming suspicious of Leybold-Heräus's activities. When Lerch was approached, he openly admitted that his firm had sold valves, vacuum pumps and a "gas purification plant" to Pakistan for an amount equivalent to about seven billion South African rand. On top of this, in March 1979 a television programme was broadcast in Germany on the subject of Khan's underhand dealings in the Netherlands. This was an embarrassment to Germany and Lerch left the firm and moved to Switzerland, taking the plans with him. Here he established his own firm, AVE, in the city of Buchs. Tons of equipment were soon being exported to Pakistan. The suspicions of the Swiss authorities were aroused, however, and they were in time to prevent three autoclaves (heating ovens to enable UF_6, which is in a solid state at room temperature, to be fed into the cascade as a gas) from leaving the country. The German authorities prosecuted Lerch, but he was tried and acquitted in 1992.

Lerch had many other contacts. One of them was a German by the name of Gerhard Wisser with whom Lerch – who was still employed at Leybold-Heräus at the time – became friendly. In 1971 Wisser established a firm called Krisch Engineering in Randburg, South Africa. He was the local agent for Leybold vacuum pumps, which he had been able to obtain for Ucor, despite sanctions. Through Wisser, Leybold also provided technical assistance when there were problems with a big four-way valve in the semi-commercial Z-enrichment plant at Pelindaba which produced fuel for Koeberg.

Through his contacts at Ucor, Wisser became friendly with a young mechanical engineer, J.A.M. Meyer. Meyer did not see his calling in a lifelong career as an engineer in a parastatal organisation. He was too much of an entrepreneur for that. He consequently left Ucor in the early 1980s and established his own company, Roxound Engineering Works, in Vanderbijlpark.

In 1986 when the Swiss seized Lerch's autoclaves that were destined for Pakistan, he had to find a way to replace them without delay. He contacted Wisser to find out whether it might be possible to manufacture the autoclaves in South Africa. Wisser and his friend Meyer put their heads together. It would be welcome business for his embattled small company and Meyer jumped at the opportunity. Between 1986 and 1989 Roxound manufactured several pieces of equipment for Pakistan – including the three autoclaves. With the aid of these large pieces of equipment it would be possible to heat so-called 48F cylinders containing over 12 tons of UF_6 each. It is quite possible that three autoclaves bearing plates with the words "Made in South Africa by Roxound" are still to be seen today at the Pakistani enrichment plant at Kahuta!

Orders from Pakistan increased after the autoclave project. The quality of Meyer's work was good. The autoclaves were followed by a pipe system for the feed and withdrawal of UF_6 from the Pakistani enrichment plant. This was built according to the plans supplied by Lerch's Swiss company AVE, but was described as a cooling system using Freon gas in order to sidestep any queries from inquisitive customs officials. In a further attempt to avoid suspicion, the manufactured items were exported to Dubai, a convenient stopover with lax customs control. From Dubai the consignment was sent on its way to its ultimate destination, Pakistan.

Consignments of South African-made valves, compressors and 30 UF_6 cylinders, each capable of holding about two tons of UF_6, followed – all destined for Dubai and originating from Vanderbijlpark.

Were the manufacture and exporting of the components from South Africa to Pakistan illegal? The answer is both yes and no. When the NPT entered into force for South Africa in June 1991, the country undertook in principle, in accordance with Art III.2, not to export any equipment which could be used to produce enriched uranium if the recipient country was not covered by comprehensive IAEA safeguards. Pakistan was not covered by comprehensive safeguards at that time – and neither is it now. The Nuclear Energy Act only came into operation two years later, however, and the regulation listing the specific items to which export control must be applied did not become applicable until 1994.

Friends, butter factories and skulduggery

Leaving aside Lerch's role, Khan had enough other European friends on whom he could rely to supply him with equipment and components. The purpose of this equipment was clear to anyone with adequate technical knowledge, but the projects all had innocuous-sounding names to protect them from unwelcome attention by curious customs officials.

Henk Slebos was a friend of this kind, an old friend of Khan's from their student days at Delft. From the mid-1970s to May 2004 – when he was indicted in the Netherlands on five counts of illegal exports to Pakistan – Slebos was a major supplier and important middleman for Khan's project. His biggest illegal transaction was the exporting of thousands of rotor tubes made from a special type of steel, maraging steel. This project was called the "Pakistan Pipeline" to conceal its true nature. Ironically, the manufacturing was done by Van Doornse Transmissie (VDT), which was largely controlled by the Dutch government at the time.

Another project for the benefit of Pakistan was described by Slebos as a "butter factory", which did not attract much attention from the authorities in the Netherlands, the home of dairy products. Through the agency of Lerch, Cora Engineering in Switzerland manufactured an entire UF_6 feed-and-withdrawal plant for Pakistan under the guise of a "gasification and solidification plant". In the late 1970s the plant was transported by Pakistani C-130s, making three trips.

Khan's other student friend, the German Heinz Mebus, supplied Pakistan with a whole plant for the production of fluorine gas and UF_6.

Espionage and letter bombs

The acquisition of entire plants along with components, especially from Europe, not to mention the building of the Kahuta enrichment plant, did not pass unobserved. The American CIA, as well as the Dutch and German intelligence services, had been onto Khan and his suppliers since the early 1970s. The authorities brought charges against the suppliers from time to time, but most of these cases were struck from the court rolls on account of technicalities.

In June 1983 a report by the US Department of State contained the following statement:

> There is unambiguous evidence that Pakistan is actively pursuing a nuclear weapons development program ... Pakistan's near-term goal evidently is to have a nuclear test capability enabling it to explode a nuclear device if (Pakistani leader Muhammad) Zia (ul-Haq) decides it's appropriate for diplomatic and domestic political gains.

As is often the case, the American CIA was well informed, and as a result the other intelligence agencies allowed the CIA to take the lead.

In 1979 the Soviet Union, the Cold War enemy of the USA, invaded Afghanistan and the Americans were forced to stay in Pakistan's good books so that they would have access to Afghanistan. Furthermore, the Soviet Union and India had traditionally maintained cordial relations (in opposition to the Pakistan-China alliance) and India had demonstrated five years previously that it was capable of making a nuclear bomb.

The intelligence agencies had done their job and drawn the right conclusions but in the end politics prevailed. For example, in 1981 the USA granted Pakistan an aid package worth $3,2 billion, the biggest donation to any country except Israel and Egypt. Their aim was to retain the support of Pakistan against the Soviet Union in Afghanistan.

Between 1983 and 1987 the USA supplied Pakistan with 40 advanced F-16 combat aircraft – adapted to carry nuclear weapons.

There is one intelligence agency that does not readily take direction, however, and that is the Israeli Mossad. It must be remembered that the possibility of a "Muslim bomb" in that part of their world was like a red rag to the Israelis, who characteristically acted with ruthless independence. In the course of 1981 letter bombs were sent to several people who had ties with the Khan network. Khan's friend Heinz Mebus received one of these bombs. The device exploded; he survived, but sadly his dog did not. In Switzerland a bomb exploded in front of the house of the head of Cora Engineering, which was supplying equipment to Pakistan. Toward the end of 1981 Albrecht Migule, a collaborator of Heinz Mebus's, who had supplied Pakistan with a plant for producing UF_6, also received a letter bomb. He survived, but the incident attracted the attention of the German authorities, who investigated the matter and convicted and fined him. These incidents all bore the typical unorthodox stamp of the Mossad.

The tide turns against Pakistan

In 1993 *The New Yorker* carried a sensational article in which A.Q. Khan made the following remarks to a journalist:

> Western countries had never imagined that a poor and backward country like Pakistan would end their (nuclear) monopoly in such a short time ... As soon as they realized that Pakistan had dashed their dreams to the ground, they pounced at Pakistan and me like hungry jackals and began attacking us with all kinds of accusations and falsehoods ... How could they tolerate a Muslim country becoming their equal in this field ... All Western countries including Israel are not only the enemies of Pakistan but in fact of Islam ... All these activities are part of the crusade which Christians and Jews have been carrying on against Muslims for about one thousand years.

Khan had advanced from Pakistani patriot to warrior for Islam. The next rung of the ladder was the position of swindler and nuclear smuggler for his own account. The withdrawal of the Soviet Union from Afghanistan which started in 1987 was the event that changed Khan's role.

In later years, after the American-led invasion of Afghanistan in 2001, a former Pakistani Minister of Foreign Affairs, Agha Shahi, said the following:

> (Pakistani) President Muhammad Zia (ul-Haq) began to see the truth in something I had long argued. We were now deep inside the US pocket. Pakistan needed to win independence so as not to suffer when the inevitable happened and the US dropped us. Pakistan needed to broker new alliances and develop a revenue stream that was dependable and outside the scope of the US-run Afghan war.

Furthermore, Khan was ruling over Kahuta with an inexhaustible fund of blank cheques and Zia ul-Haq was not prepared to match the euphoric commitment of his predecessor Bhutto (of blessed memory) to "eat grass". By 1985 Zia and a select group of ministers had already met secretly to determine whether the technology developed at Kahuta could possibly be turned into hard cash and/or advantageous ties with friendly countries.

After the final withdrawal of Soviet troops from Afghanistan in 1989 America no longer had any need to ignore Pakistan's nuclear weapons programme and extensive nuclear-related sanctions against Pakistan were introduced. This made Pakistan all the more determined to turn its nuclear technology into cash in order to finance its very costly parallel nuclear weapons and missile programmes.

Pakistan identified countries like Iran, Syria and Libya as possible clients and by 1985 these countries had already held a meeting. Khan had started using his second-generation P-2 gas centrifuges, so the obsolete P-1 centrifuges could be supplied to potential customers in exchange for hard cash and newly acquired goodwill. Iran and Libya, with their petrodollars, were the chief targets. In time much of this money found its way to Khan's pockets. He ultimately owned seven properties in Islamabad, two in London and even built a hotel, the Hotel Hendrina Khan, in Timbuktu. Furniture for the hotel was flown out at state expense on a C-130 belonging to the Pakistani Air Force.

An impending threat and missile systems

In June 1981 Israel, with its customary deadly efficiency, carried out a surprise aerial attack on the nuclear reactor that France had built in Iraq to produce plutonium for Iraq's nuclear weapons programme. The Osirak reactor was completely destroyed. This sent shock waves through Pakistan because, leaving aside the Israeli threat, India would naturally also have liked to see Kahuta and the other Pakistani nuclear facilities turned into heaps of rubble.

India and Israel

India, Pakistan and Israel became independent states at more or less the same time (1947 to 1948).

Independence went hand in hand with problems for all three states. Israel's hostile Arab neighbours started a war and the two-way migration in India and Pakistan (six million Hindus moved from Pakistan to India and eight million Muslims from India to Pakistan) caused extreme tension and instability. Despite the mass migration, India still had the biggest minority population of Muslims in the world: a group of people who had no time for Israel and whose wishes the Indian government could not afford to disregard. It can come as no surprise that relations between Israel and India were openly chilly during the first 40 years of their existence. India did acknowledge Israel's existence in 1950, but full diplomatic relations were not established until 1992.

Behind the scenes things were a little different, however. By the 1960s India and Israel had already forged secret military and intelligence ties. In 1962 and 1965 Israel secretly supplied weapons and ammunition to India for its wars against China and Pakistan and did the same thing in 1971 during the Indo-Pakistani War. India and Israel found themselves in an uncomfortable situation on account of their joint opposition to Pakistan's development of the "Muslim bomb".

To complicate matters further, India and the Soviet Union were on good terms (India had obtained most of its weapons from the Soviets), while there were also close ties between Israel and the USA. However, the fall of the Soviet Union in 1991 meant that India was compelled to reconsider its choice of friends and weapons suppliers. Israel was happy to step into the breach. As chance would have it, there was a major exodus of Russian Jews to Israel after 1991. Many of them had formerly been employed in the Soviet military industry. They were capable of repairing and upgrading old Russian weapons in India, an opportunity that India was quick to embrace.

Since that time business has been booming and today India is Israel's biggest client for armaments worth billions of American dollars. In 2008 India even launched an Israeli spy satellite.

Towards the end of the 1970s Israel and India were both aware that A.Q. Khan was building an enrichment plant at Kahuta with the aid of stolen technology. Both countries were contemplating a pre-emptive strike to take the plant out. Adrian Levy and Catherine Scott-Clark relate in their book Deception *(2007) that Indian military personnel visited their Israeli colleagues in 1983 with a complete plan of attack which they wanted to discuss. The Indians wanted to purchase electronic equipment at the same time to circumvent Pakistan's air defence systems.*

In view of the strained relations between India and Pakistan, Israel offered to carry out the attack if India put two air force bases at their disposal. Early in 1984 the then Indian Prime Minister, Indira Gandhi, approved the plan. The CIA had full knowledge of the planned attack, however, and in order to prevent a war the Americans ensured that President Zia ul-Haq of Pakistan was warned. Enormous pressure was put on Israel to abandon the plan. Indira Gandhi was compelled to withdraw her consent.

In addition, Munir Khan warned his Indian counterpart, Raja Ramanna, at an IAEA conference in Vienna that Pakistan had the power

> to strike back and would do so in a way that would cause enormous emissions of radioactive material at the Indian nuclear centre in Trombay, close to the megalopolis Mumbai.
> The Indians and Israelis consequently aborted the project and A.Q. Khan was left in peace to build up and operate Kahuta. While doing so he spent an estimated 150 million dollars on helping friendly Muslim countries to attempt to acquire their own nuclear weapons.

Pakistan decided that it would be wise to upgrade its defences and KRL was given the additional task of developing missile systems. Khan turned to Pakistan's old ally, China.

Back in 1976 Mao Zedong of China and Zulfikar Ali Bhutto of Pakistan had signed a nuclear cooperation agreement. The trigger was the detonation of a nuclear device in 1974 by India, a common enemy of both states. When Mao died later that year, Khan went to China to attend the funeral and took the opportunity to persuade certain top Chinese scientists that he would be able to boost uranium enrichment in China by supplying stolen European gas centrifuge technology. Visits were then paid back and forth. Khan was later to state that he had sent 135 consignments of equipment to China by means of Hercules C-130 aircraft. China was Khan's first client.

China showed its gratitude by supplying Pakistan with 15 tons of UF_6 which was later used for the production of Pakistan's first weapons-grade uranium.

Because Pakistan was afraid that India or Israel might carry out an Osirak-type preemptive strike, it directed a curious request to China, namely to "borrow" enough weapons-grade uranium to make a few nuclear weapons. Khan went to fetch the uranium on a C-130 and years later he still recalled with appreciation the delicious meal of roast lamb he was served by his affable Chinese hosts – and also the plans for a nuclear weapon which the Chinese supplied as a perk. In time these plans became part of the "family heirlooms" which Khan so bountifully shared with other countries.

While Khan was producing sufficient weapons-grade material, Pakistan put the "borrowed" material aside. When Khan wanted to return this material in 1985, the Chinese reaction was: "Feel free to keep it." The loan had become a gift.

Cooperation with China helped Khan with KRL's other responsibility, namely the development of missiles, specifically for the delivery of Pakistani nuclear weapons. Pakistan's Hatf missile series is a technological copy of the

Chinese M-11 ballistic missiles, and the Ghauri series is copied from the North Korean Nodong missile which Pakistan obtained through the agency of China.

The other Khan works behind the scenes

Unlike A.Q. Khan, his nemesis, Munir Khan, had a solid grounding in nuclear physics and reactor development which he obtained mainly in the USA – partly thanks to the American Atoms for Peace programme. Shortly after the establishment of the organisation he was invited to join the IAEA in 1958. Here he was to advance to the position of director of reactor technology and the nuclear fuel cycle. He was recalled to Pakistan in 1972 and headed the PAEC for almost two decades.

A.Q. Khan was flamboyant, a swindler and somewhat of a loose cannon. Munir Khan's style was quite different – he simply worked tirelessly behind the scenes, building up the Pakistani nuclear industry from scratch. An important part of this industry consisted of building reactors and a reprocessing plant for the production of plutonium to make a plutonium implosion bomb. By March 1983 the first successful cold test (i.e. without plutonium) was carried out. The second one followed in May and by 1990 Khan had already carried out 24 successful tests with various designs.

A.Q. Khan had intended to use the highly enriched uranium which he had produced at Kahuta to build a gun-type uranium bomb himself, but Munir Khan, who had ongoing responsibility for the scientific side of the design, prevailed: the design was changed to an implosion bomb. In any case this was better suited to delivery by ballistic missiles.

Indian and Pakistani nuclear tests

On both sides of the Indo-Pakistani border the required cold tests were carried out in the 1990s and the nuclear arsenals were built up by degrees without the two countries having a clear idea of when – or indeed if – the weapons would be used.

In May 1996 an ultranationalistic and strongly militarist Hindu political party was voted into power in India: the Bharatiya Janata Party (BJP) under the leadership of Atal Bihari Vajpayee. The new prime minister was determined to carry out a nuclear test by hook or by crook. Without any attempt to conceal their actions, the new Indian government made feverish preparations to detonate a nuclear weapon – the first since 1974. The device was lowered into the test shaft but before the test could be carried out the new, unstable government found itself out of office just 13 days after coming to power. The device was removed and stored for later use.

However, the spy satellites took a good look at the extensive activities being carried out openly around the test shaft and in 1996 Fabian and Gupta published an article entitled "Investigating the allegations of Indian nuclear test preparations in the Rajasthan Desert". The whole world took note of India's plans, which had come to nothing at that stage.

Two years later, in March 1998, another election took place. This time the BJP got many more votes and were able to form a coalition government along with a few smaller parties. Prime Minister Vajpayee did not let the grass grow under his feet and on the day before his swearing-in he made his intentions plain: "There is no compromise on national security. We will exercise all options including nuclear options to protect security and sovereignty."

Pakistan knew what was coming. The country had been expecting this since 1996. On the day of Vajpayee's inauguration Pakistan's minister of foreign affairs decided to use the proven carrot-and-stick approach. He expressed Pakistan's willingness to enter into an agreement with India "for an equal and mutual restraint in conventional, missile and nuclear fields". The stick was the Ghauri missile, supplied by A.Q. Khan's laboratory, which was launched early in April. India was alarmed since the missile was able to carry a payload of 700 kg and had a range of almost 1 000 km – far enough to strike any of the big Indian cities.

Vajpayee gave orders that the Indian nuclear tests should be carried out as soon as possible, and this time the defence force did everything in their power to conceal the preparations. All the work was carried out between satellite observations. Heavy equipment was always returned to the original storage places before the next satellite flyover.

On 10 May 1998 the five devices arrived at Pokhran, the test range, and were taken to the "Prayer Hall" and prepared for Operation Shakti II.

At 15:45 on 11 May 1998 three nuclear weapons exploded simultaneously in the respective test shafts. Two days later two smaller tests followed. Significantly, the first three weapons were tested on the Buddhist festival Buddha Purnima, the same festival on which the 1974 test (Shakti I) was carried out.

On 14 May Vajpayee announced : "India is now a nuclear weapons state. We have the capacity for a big bomb now." He did add, however: "Ours will never be weapons of aggression."

Although Pakistan had been expecting something of the kind, Shakti II caused consternation. A day after India's announcement the Pakistan cabinet and senior defence force officers held a meeting. The advantages and disadvantages of a test series were discussed and it became clear that Pakistan would have to pay a price. They were in an unenviable position. The only thing left to decide was who would lead the test series, the PAEC or Khan Laboratories. President Sharif and his top military advisers decided on the PAEC because the military contingent had little confidence in A.Q. Khan. This was a slap in the face for Khan. After all he was "the father of the bomb", although it was a hotly contested paternity.

KRL was given a minor role in the preparations for the tests. Because Khan was a popular public figure he was invited to attend the tests (Chagai-I) in a bunker about 10 km from the detonation site. After a cry of "Allah Akbar!" a technician pressed the button on 28 May and five nuclear explosions took place simultaneously at a great depth below the Chagai hills. To trump India's achievement, a sixth explosion (Chagai-II) took place two days later at a different site in the Kharan Desert.

There was an angry outcry from the international community. The USA, Japan, the World Bank and the IMF announced sanctions, but the people of Pakistan glorified A.Q. Khan as a national hero. The backward state of Pakistan, where more than half the population of over 130 million were illiterate, had finally shown that it was able to put the "Hindu bastards" in their place.

A party with an agenda

In the midst of all the adulation A.Q. Khan found the test series a bittersweet experience. After the top military officers turned against him he could read the writing on the wall. In addition, he had a serious problem. One of his clients, Iran, was well on its way with its illicit uranium enrichment programme by that time, but the despotic and unpredictable Colonel Gaddafi of Libya – who, according to Khan, had given about 200 million dollars to Bhutto to get Pakistan's weapons programme up and running – was waiting impatiently for his own enrichment plant.

It was clear that while India and Pakistan were the subject of international scrutiny Khan was going to find it far more difficult to continue with his nuclear smuggling in future. There was no doubt that it would be impossible to go on exporting equipment and components directly from Pakistan.

A.Q. Khan had, however, selected Dubai more than a decade previously

A SOUTH AFRICAN STALL IN KHAN'S ATOMIC BAZAAR

and had used it as a convenient stopover for equipment that was being smuggled to Pakistan from Europe. He even had a flat there. One day Khan met a young man, Buhari Sejed Abu Tahir, a native of Sri Lanka, who sold him some air conditioners. This was the beginning of a special friendship, which was so strong that Tahir came to look up to Khan as a father figure and later even called him Pappa. Tahir came to be called Junior. Junior and his pappa, who were devout Muslims, even went on a pilgrimage to Mecca together.

In Dubai Tahir was appointed the "chief executive officer" of Khan's network towards the end of the 1980s. He was responsible for ensuring that the equipment destined for Pakistan reached its destination, no matter what its point of origin, and that the money that had to flow in the opposite direction reached the correct overseas accounts. The flamboyant Junior with his proverbial "Colgate smile" was well rewarded for his trouble and was able to drive around in a swanky white Rolls-Royce.

In Dubai Tahir cooperated with Peter Griffin, a British citizen, and his company, Gulf Technical Industries. Tahir's uncle, S.M. Farouq, a businessman who had been born in India, had also settled in Dubai and was later to play an important role in the network.

A month after the Indian and Pakistani nuclear tests, Tahir married Nazimah, the daughter of a Malaysian diplomat, in Kuala Lumpur. The wedding was a grand affair which lasted for five days, and was a good opportunity for the seasoned group of nuclear smugglers to come up with new plans. Naturally Khan was there, but the wedding celebrations were also attended by Khan's old friend from the Netherlands, Henk Slebos, and Peter Griffin, together with a handful of Pakistani military officers, 300 employees of Tahir's Dubai front company SMB Computers and about 100 scientists from Khan's Pakistan KRL. With so many wedding guests present, inevitably discussions between the jovial guests leaked out …

Griffin was later to relate in an interview that A.Q. Khan remained in the background the whole time and kept a low profile. Curiously, he did not mention the nuclear tests of the previous month.

The nuclear smugglers took advantage of the opportunity to confer. They had been operating in Dubai for more than a decade and realised that by that time the intelligence agencies must have had their activities in their sights. They would have to build in an extra layer of security by diversifying to other parts of the world and using other suppliers.

They were a well-oiled team with decades of experience of underhand dealing and they sprang into action. Khan, the head of the team, handled client relations and brought in the orders; Tahir was his "minister van finance" and three "regional managers" had to ensure that products from Malaysia, Turkey and South Africa reached the export market. The project was officially called Machine Shop 1001.

Friedrich Tinner, the owner of the firm Cetec in Switzerland, was an innovative inventor and mechanical engineer who concentrated mainly on vacuum technology. His vacuum valves had even been patented in the USA. His connection with A.Q. Khan extended back over decades and over the years he had been an important supplier of dual-use vacuum-related equipment to the Pakistani uranium enrichment programme. A son of his, Marco, ran his own firm, Traco, and a second son, Urs, was a highly competent engineer who acted as a consultant. While Traco was engaged in the mass production of certain centrifuge components, Urs was sent to Malaysia. This country was ideal for their project. Malaysia had a growing industrial capacity with well-qualified artisans; it did not figure prominently on the radar of the major intelligence agencies and furthermore Tahir's wife owned shares in a local company called Scomi together with the prime minister's son. Scomi was well-known for its work in the oil and gas industry. Another factor was that Malaysia is chiefly a Muslim country.

In Turkey Khan could rely on his old friend from his time in the Netherlands, Günes Cire, and on Selim Alguadis, who was of Jewish descent and had in the past frequently supplied the Pakistani programme with electronic components and electric motors to turn the rotors.

Another valued friend of Khan's was Gotthard Lerch, who had previously used his South African connections to render excellent service to Pakistan's enrichment programme.

The table was laid but what Khan did not know was that his wide circle of friends included someone on the payroll of the CIA who was to ensure a few years later that the atomic bazaar he had built up so carefully over decades would collapse almost overnight. But that is a long story ...

Gaddafi's dream, Khan's contract

In the 1970s and 1980s Colonel Gaddafi was eager to build up his own nuclear arsenal. As ever, the biggest problem was to obtain fissionable material and for this he would have to acquire his own enrichment plant.

In the mid-1980s A.Q. Khan met the Libyan Matoug Mohamed Matoug on one of his visits to Turkey. Matoug had intended to start an enrichment project on the scale of a small laboratory, located underground. Khan told him to forget it. He would need too much space, too many workshops and too large a staff. Khan's jaw probably dropped when Matoug replied that in that case he would buy a farm and stock it with goats and camels and then erect two sheds among the livestock. Libya was wary, especially following the US attacks on Tripoli and Benghazi in 1986 to destroy supposed chemical weapons factories.

Khan's advice to Matoug was to have his people trained overseas before tackling such a technically challenging project.

But Gaddafi was in a hurry. Through his agents he obtained the services of a German, a so-called centrifuge specialist who had recently been discharged by Urenco. This expert brought his own equipment and engineering designs along with him, his intention being to build a centrifuge and getting it operational. Possibly because the poor man was working in isolation among the goats and camels, he failed to achieve anything in the space of 12 years and left Tripoli in 1992.

At the end of 1989 Khan and Libya resumed talks and a formal agreement was reached. Khan was to supply Pakistan's P-1 centrifuges to Libya. But only the previous year Libyan terrorists had detonated a bomb on the Pan American flight 103 over Lockerbie in Scotland, with the loss of 270 lives. In 1992 the UNSC imposed a full arms embargo and air travel restrictions on Libya and the whole project came to a standstill.

Gaddafi finally realised that he would not be able to build centrifuges on his own. He would have to buy a complete plant. His henchmen, Matoug and Karim, met Khan and Tahir in Turkey again in 1997. After Gaddafi surrendered two Libyan suspects and the UNSC lifted their embargo in 1999 the pressure was off and work could proceed again.

Khan supplied about 20 complete P-1 centrifuges with components for another 200, as well as UF_6 cylinders and other equipment. Gaddafi and Matoug really wanted Khan's more advanced P-2 centrifuges. In the meanwhile they were able to use the P-1s – now called L-1s – to gain experience.

Libya ordered a complete plant with P-2 centrifuges from Khan for an amount of between 100 and $200 million dollars. The enrichment plant itself was to consist of over 5 000 centrifuges, but 10 000 were ordered as a backup. This was Khan's biggest and most complicated contract ever, no less so because it involved arranging for literally millions of small and large components to be secretly manufactured in various parts of the world – and they all had to fit.

The work was distributed among various firms. The Scomi group in Malaysia had to build various components of the centrifuges, especially the outer aluminium casings that protected the rotors. The electric motors that turn the centrifuges as well as the electronics and the control systems were to be manufactured in Turkey by Günes Cire and Selim Alguadis. The job of supplying maraging steel rotors, as well as vacuum equipment and valves, was assigned to the Tinner family.

For the rest of the plant, which included the feed-and-withdrawal equipment for UF_6, all connecting tubing (literally kilometres of it), UF_6 cylinders and accessory equipment such as flow meters, Khan, Tahir and Lerch went back to their previous supplier who had served the Pakistan plant so well in the late 1980s: Gerhard Wisser and his contacts in South Africa.

The nuclear smugglers fall into a snare

One sultry day in August 2003 six big containers were loaded onto a nondescript ship in Kuala Lumpur, Malaysia. The containers came from the Scomi group where the Swiss, Urs Tinner, had been supervising the manufacture of their contents for a few months. The container ship sailed for Dubai, where the containers were unloaded and temporarily stored. Two days later the containers were loaded onto a German freighter, the *BBC China*, which headed past the Persian Gulf, through the Red Sea and up the Suez Canal, in the direction of the Mediterranean. Halfway through the canal the captain unexpectedly received a radio message from the owners in Hamburg. The ship had to call at the Italian port of Taranto before the journey could continue. The captain felt uneasy at this sudden change of course, especially as he had just observed two American frigates following the ship at a distance. The ship moored in Taranto on 4 October. The captain was given the numbers of five containers which were summarily unloaded and taken away by American military vehicles.

After 9/11 the Western states, and especially the USA, were seriously concerned about the possibility that terrorists could ship a nuclear bomb in a container to a busy harbour like New York and detonate it there. A month before the arrival of the *BBC China* in Taranto, 11 countries, including the USA, Germany, Italy and Britain, concluded an agreement ratifying the Proliferation Security Initiative (PSI). Its purpose was to intercept and investigate any suspected consignments of weapons of mass destruction and related equipment by air, land or sea. The containers on the *BBC China* were the first suspicious containers to be intercepted and examined in this way. The result was astounding – the containers were filled with thousands of components of gas centrifuges despite a waybill bearing the innocent description "Used Machinery".

The Gaddafi government was confronted with the discovery and secret negotiations followed on how to proceed. Eventually the Libyan leader realised that he had been driven into a corner and had little prospect of escape. On 19 December 2003 the Libyan Minister of Foreign Affairs therefore announced that his country had decided to abandon its chemical and nuclear weapons programmes and that Libya would disclose full information on those programmes. Colonel Gaddafi made a brief television appearance and said that this was a "wise decision and a brave step".

This disclosure and its consequences hit Khan and his henchmen like a Fukushima tsunami. Libya's promise of full disclosure must surely have caused panic. Teams of American CIA and British MI6 agents swooped down on the remnants of Gaddafi's dream. They started unravelling the intricate network to get to the source.

The interceptors did not have the numbers of all the containers and after a few months an unusually diffident Gaddafi discreetly forwarded one remaining container, which had got as far as Tripoli, for the attention of the British and Americans. And what of the *BBC China*? Exactly a year after the events at Taranto the ship was wrecked on a reef near Port St. Johns, about 200 km to the south of Durban. That was her last voyage.

The dominoes fall

In Pakistan A.Q. Khan's star had begun to wane even before the 1998 nuclear tests, chiefly in military circles. General Feroz Khan was later to remark that everyone had started to feel that the loquacious popular hero had possibly done enough and should be replaced by someone out of the public eye whose anonymity would be better suited to the secret nature of the weapons programme. Besides, the USA, Pakistan's biggest financial supporter, was putting pressure on Pakistan to neutralise Khan, especially in view of his transactions with North Korea.

A year later the opportunity finally presented itself. The "little general", Pervez Musharraf, following the Pakistani tradition, took the opportunity to carry out a coup d'état while President Nawaz Sharif was overseas. He became the new president in October 1999. By that time Musharraf was fed up with Khan's arrogance and unwillingness to submit to authority. He ordered an investigation into Khan's affairs and agents even followed Khan on one of his numerous unauthorised visits to Dubai. Musharraf took Khan to task about this. When Khan paid another unauthorised visit to Dubai in December Musharraf had had enough. But he had to reckon with Khan's status as a national hero. Consequently Khan was summoned in January and informed that he had been discharged as head of KRL and that he would never be permitted to set foot in the KRL complex again. In deference to his public image it would be announced that Khan, who had just turned 65, would retire in the normal way in March 2000 and be appointed as a special adviser to the president – a nominal position. Musharraf was following the familiar tactics for dealing with a troublemaker – get rid of the person, give him a fancy title and sing his praises in public. On 27 March Musharraf hosted a gala dinner for Khan at the Serena Hotel in Islamabad, where he praised Khan for his achievements. The Pakistan media quoted the president as follows: "You are our national hero and an inspiration to our future generations. Nobody can ever take that away from you and your place in history is assured. You will always be at the very top. We salute you and thank you from the depths of our hearts."

For Khan the bomb really only burst when Colonel Gaddafi made his public confession on 19 December 2003.

On Musharraf's instructions Khan was then summarily placed under house arrest and on 4 February 2004 he appeared before the television cameras and read a carefully prepared "admission of guilt". He apologised humbly and pleaded guilty to nuclear proliferation, stating that neither the Pakistan government nor the defence force had known anything about his activities. His statement included the following words: "It pains me to realise this, that my entire lifetime of providing foolproof national security to my nation could have been placed in serious jeopardy on account of my activities, which were based in good faith, but on errors of judgement related to unauthorized proliferation activities."

He was later to change his tune a good deal – and frequently at that.

Nevertheless, the first and most important domino had fallen and the others would inevitably follow.

The second domino

Within a month of the seizure of the five containers from the *BBC China* and a month before Colonel Gaddafi made his public announcement, the CIA and MI6 swooped down on Malaysia. Their Malaysian counterpart, Bukit Aman, was confronted with damning information and the authorities were asked to cooperate.

To their astonishment Bukit Aman's intelligence officers were informed that A.Q. Khan was proliferating Pakistani nuclear technology under their very noses and was supplying Libya with an enrichment plant. The Malaysians also learned that Tahir, who had connections with the Malaysian engineering firm Scope (a subsidiary of Scomi) was actively involved and that Scope had been responsible for manufacturing centrifuge components. This emerged from an examination of the contents of the containers seized on the *BBC China*. The name Scope was clearly stamped on the wooden boxes found in the containers.

Bukit Aman was courteously reminded that this was a serious matter which was receiving attention at the "highest levels of the American and British governments".

The Malaysian authorities sprang into action and on 20 February 2004 the police issued a sensational statement which spread like wildfire on the internet. Upon interrogation Tahir spilled the beans. The whole conspiracy became public knowledge and the German, British, Swiss and Turkish collaborators on the nuclear network were mentioned by name. Their respective contributions to the supply of nuclear technology to Iran and Libya were laid bare.

Names mentioned in the Malaysian press release

Germany: *Heinz Mebus (died in 1992) and Gotthard Lerch*
Britain: *Peter Griffin and his son Paul*
Switzerland: *Friedrich Tinner and his sons Urs and Marco*
Turkey: *Gunas Jireh (known elsewhere as Günes Cire) and Selim Alguadis*

Strangely enough, A.Q. Khan was not mentioned by name. There was simply a reference to "a Pakistani nuclear arms expert". However, the statement did contain an inadvertent reference to a relationship extending over many years between the Turks and a mysterious AQK.

It was also mentioned in the statement that the German, Gotthard Lerch, had tried to obtain the header piping for the Libyan Machine Shop 1001 project from South Africa, but had not succeeded in doing so although the work had been paid for. No further information was supplied on the South African connection and in Randburg and Vanderbijlpark certain people were probably mopping the sweat from their brows and enjoying this temporary reprieve.

Despite Tahir's revelations the Malaysian police insisted that Tahir and Scope had committed no criminal offences and therefore they were not charged. Tahir was nevertheless detained for four years in terms of Malaysian internal security legislation and was only released in June 2008. The authorities stated that he had been released because he did not pose a threat to anyone. It was suspected in some quarters, however, that American pressure was behind his detention until the completion of the investigation.

Arrests in Switzerland, Germany, Turkey and the Netherlands

Tahir's statement led to swift action in Europe.

Lerch was arrested in Switzerland in 2004 and was extradited to Germany the following year after a court battle.

Friedrich Tinner and his son Marco were taken into custody in Switzerland. Urs was arrested in Germany and subsequently extradited to Switzerland.

Peter Griffin was interrogated by the British, but he steadfastly denied any involvement in nuclear activities. He had simply imported and exported machinery into and out of Dubai – machinery that could have been used in any big machine shop. He was not prosecuted.

Günes Cire and Selim Alguadis were interrogated by the police in Turkey. Cire died of a heart attack during interrogation. Nobody was charged, however.

Within days of Khan's confession at the beginning of February 2004 the Dutch started investigating Henk Slebos's activities. Towards the end of 2005 he stood trial in Alkmaar.

How did the Americans and the British know about the cargo on board the BBC China?

In 1999 German intelligence sources learned that a number of suppliers of advanced technology who had previously had ties with Khan were involved in a major project with a new client. The identity of the client was unknown and the information was passed on to the CIA.

The biggest outpost of the CIA outside Washington is located in Vienna, Austria. A local agent with the code name Mad Dog was instructed to pick up the trail. (The Americans are fond of the first name Caleb. In the Old Testament Caleb was Joshua's army commander when the Jews invaded Canaan and the name means Mad Dog.)

According to Frantz and Collins in *The Nuclear Jihadist* the name Tinner cropped up early on in the investigation. The family had been on the CIA's radar for a long while. Mad Dog discovered that Urs, one of the sons, had fallen foul of the law in France and plotted with the French to set a trap for Urs. The French were to put pressure on Urs and the CIA would then offer to make the pressure disappear if Urs was prepared to cooperate with them.

Early in 2000 Mad Dog followed Urs Tinner to Dubai and ran into him "by chance" one night in a bar. They started making small talk. When Urs wanted to leave, Mad Dog remarked casually that he had heard about Urs's problems with the French authorities. He offered his assistance if Urs could supply information on imports to and exports from Dubai. Tinner didn't bite at first, but in time he became an unwilling collaborator. According to a report in *The New York Times* of 24 August 2008 "Nuclear net's undoing, a web of shadowy deals", in time Urs persuaded his father and brother to get involved as well. The Tinners, who had been in financial difficulties, may well have been swayed by the payment of $10 million, which they received over a period of four years – sometimes in the form of a suitcase full of notes.

Urs was permitted to complete his work at Scope in Malaysia with Swiss precision. After this he collected all the engineering drawings, wiped his computer hard drive and waved goodbye to Scope late in 2003 with his staff file under his arm.

The discovery of the centrifuge components in the containers on the *BBC China* was therefore not the first indication of the existence of the Libyan project, but simply physical confirmation of part of it. A report to Congress by the American CIA for the period July to December 2003 contains the following:

Libya

In March 2003, Libya approached the United Kingdom and United States expressing interest in coming clean about its WMD programs. In the course of discussions and visits, the Libyans made significant disclosures about their nuclear, chemical, and missile-related activities and minor disclosures about biological-related activities. A team of US and UK experts travelled to Libya in October and early December to receive detailed presentations and to visit a number of Libyan facilities.

After extensive discussion during the three weeks of meetings, our experts were shown covert facilities and equipment and were told of years of Libyan efforts to develop weapons capabilities. In late December, the Libyan Government announced its intention to eliminate its nuclear and chemical weapons programs and MTCR class missiles as part of an effort to rejoin the community of nations.

But why was the unpredictable Colonel Gaddafi prepared to come clean out of the blue – months before the discovery of the *BBC China*'s cargo? The reason was that the surprise invasion of Iraq on 20 March 2003, the much talked-of Bush-Blair war, had scared him out of his wits.

The story began when MI6, the British foreign intelligence service, received a call from a Palestinian who was acting as a middleman. He had a message from the colonel. Gaddafi's son Saif wanted to deliver the message in person. Saif later met two MI6 agents at the Mayfair Hotel in London. His message? Gaddafi wanted to talk about weapons of mass destruction.

On the day when the bombs started falling in Iraq, an aircraft with two British agents left in secret for Sirte, Gaddafi's headquarters in the Libyan Desert. They met the Libyan leader in a tent among his camels. With the information that MI6 and the CIA had already collected on the activities of the Khan network, it was not difficult to persuade the eccentric colonel to start negotiating. He appointed Moussa Koussa, his head of intelligence, as the negotiator.

Seven months later, however, with the evidence found on board the *BBC China*, negotiation gave way to capitulation. The revelation of what that cargo contained was the final nail in the coffin. The CIA and MI6 agents may well have said to Gaddafi: "Look here, we've known about your bomb project all the time, and now the whole world knows." The colonel was in a corner and had to confess his sins.

The Tinners

After the arrest of the three Tinners their fortunes followed a strange and convoluted path. Urs and Marco were indicted in Switzerland in October 2004. The Tinners' property was searched in August of the following year and the authorities seized a large quantity of electronic data, apparently including plans for building a nuclear weapon. The father, Friedrich, was also indicted.

In October 2006 the IAEA requested permission to access any information in the Tinner files that was related to proliferation. A year later the Swiss Bundesrat decided that this information should be secretly destroyed under the supervision of the IAEA. The problem was that this documentation was evidence in the case against the Tinners – the curious situation had arisen where the evidence in a sensational trial was being deliberately destroyed. The destruction of about 30 000 documents took place in secret. It was not until August 2008 that the Swiss president, Pascal Couchepin, announced that the authorities had arranged for the destruction of an enormous number of digital files and other documentation. His justification for this action was that sensitive information, which included a sophisticated design for a Pakistani nuclear bomb, could not be allowed to fall into the hands of terrorists. The president did not permit any questions during the press conference.

In a report in *The New York Times* of 25 August 2008, "In nuclear net's undoing, a web of shadowy deals", it emerged from interviews with senior government officials in the USA that the reference to terrorism was merely an excuse. The real purpose in destroying the information was to keep the working relationship between the CIA and the Tinners secret.

Despite this, Urs and Marco were only released on bail after four years in detention, respectively at the end of 2008 and the beginning of 2009, but the relentless Swiss prosecution authority did not drop the matter – against the wishes of its own government. In December 2010 the father and sons were charged again and a year later the three of them admitted guilt – probably out of sheer desperation after seven years of prosecution. The maximum penalty was five years, but the three Tinners had already been in prison for years. They were all released. On 25 September 2012 the Swiss federal criminal court accepted a plea bargain with Tinner and his sons. This officially ended the case against the family. All three accused were then free, although they had to pay their legal costs and fines.

This was the inglorious end to a case that had been unnecessarily drawn out as a result of the mulishness for which the Swiss are famous – and this in the case of a family which, ironically enough, had made a big contribution to the unmasking of A.Q. Khan's network.

Paid for but not delivered – the focus shifts

With the arrests and interrogation of the Khan collaborators in Europe and Tahir's statement that part of the Libyan plant had been manufactured in South Africa and paid for but never delivered, 2004 must have been an anxious year for a number of people in South Africa. By 14 February Agence France-Presse had already reported that: "US investigators arrive in South Africa to probe a local link in an international black market in nuclear technology". Late in March the South African Department of Foreign Affairs was informed by the USA that Gotthard Lerch had facilitated the manufacture of enrichment equipment in South Africa by two local firms, namely Krisch Engineering and Tradefin.

Late in August 2004 the National Prosecuting Authority (NPA) was contacted by its German counterpart with the news that Gerhard Wisser (the director of Krisch Engineering) had been arrested on 25 August during a visit to Germany. He made a statement in which he admitted that Tahir had asked him to manufacture components for the Libyan plant. Wisser had merely acted as an intermediary and the components had been made by Tradefin, a Vanderbijlpark firm. Wisser and Tradefin were paid generously, but the components were never exported.

Wisser was released on bail by the Germans and flew back to South Africa in style in a private jet.

A hastily formed team consisting of members of the NPA, the South African Police Service (SAPS), the National Intelligence Service (NIS) and the Departments of Trade and Industry and Foreign Affairs set off to visit premises in Randburg. Nic von Wielligh accompanied the group as an adviser. The target was the firm Krisch Engineering, the directors of which were the German, Gerhard Wisser, and the Swiss, Daniel Geiges.

Late in the afternoon of 1 September the minibuses drew up at Krisch Engineering. There were only three people on the premises: Wisser, Geiges and a secretary. Wisser was obviously taken aback by the visit and replied abruptly and arrogantly to a few questions from Captain Ben Nel of the SAPS. Nel was in charge of the investigation – a surprise "birthday gift" to Wisser (one day early).

Other members of the team strolled around looking at the equipment in the workshop and stores. The little that there was to see consisted mainly of equipment for repairing vacuum pumps. Krisch Engineering had a conspicuously extensive filing system. With typical German thoroughness it was perfectly organised. Certain files had summaries of the contents, which made it easy to investigate specific topics. A file marked AVE (Lerch's Swiss company) was drawn at random and there it was in black-and-white: an enquiry to Krisch in 1993 about purchasing 10 000 ring magnets, admittedly not for Libya but for India. Ring magnets are an essential component of gas centrifuges. At that stage it was not widely known that India was interested in uranium enrichment with gas centrifuges. In the past India's nuclear bombs had all used plutonium.

The team paid a memorable visit to the office of the Swiss, Daniel Geiges, a thin, serious man with spectacles and a goatee. His manner was notably tense. The computer on his desk was brand-new, its box and packaging still on his office floor. He was curt and did not really reply to questions.

The group left the premises of Krisch Engineering fairly late that afternoon. Clearly, they had seen no more than the tip of the iceberg and would need months to unravel the whole scheme.

A visit to Tradefin in Vanderbijlpark and further arrests

The following day, 2 September, the team left for the premises of Tradefin Engineering. The offices were situated in the depressing and dusty Vanderbijlpark industrial area. Here they met Johannes Andries Muller Meyer – better known as J.A.M. – a director of the firm. While the police were questioning him and receiving very reluctant and hostile replies, other members of the team walked through the factory. It was a typical big machine shop, oily and deafeningly noisy as a result of the drilling, cutting and welding of numerous steel castings, pressure vessels and other components. Nothing on open display resembled components intended for an enrichment plant.

Peter Goosen of Foreign Affairs decided to search for anything that looked like aluminium tubes. Such tubes had been part of the *BBC China* consignment. Behind a wall of galvanised iron sheets that did not quite reach the ceiling he saw some protruding components that looked like the offending aluminium tubes. Closer inspection revealed numerous cargo containers behind the false wall and Meyer was asked to have the sheets removed. It was apparent that the couple of tubes lying on top of one of the containers were not important. Eleven large concealed shipping containers, stacked in two layers, were found.

When the containers were opened it was clear that the components inside were not suited to the rougher activities being carried on at Tradefin. They were components intended for a centrifuge enrichment plant. Documentation with a description of the contents of each container was found along with neat packing lists. This was the "jackpot" everyone had been looking for. Photographs were taken and Meyer was summarily arrested for contraventions of the Nuclear Energy Act and Non-Proliferation of Weapons of Mass Destruction Act.

That evening Ambassador A.S. Minty (South Africa's governor on the IAEA's Board of Governors and chairman of the South African Council for the Non-proliferation of Weapons of Mass Destruction) met inspectors from the IAEA in Pretoria and informed them of the preliminary findings during the visits to Krisch and Tradefin. They were told that Meyer was in custody. The next day this was headline news, even causing a sensation overseas.

An anxious Meyer, trying to hide his tension behind a grin, appeared briefly in the Vanderbijlpark Regional Court on Friday 3 September. The ruling was that he should be detained in the Vanderbijlpark police cells until Wednesday 8 September, after which he was expected to apply for bail. This was probably sufficient time for a man who, according to *Beeld*, lived in the luxurious Woodhill estate in Pretoria and "collected imported sports cars the way some people collect Royal Doulton porcelain" to reflect on his desperate situation.

The two IAEA inspectors were kept informed throughout and on Saturday 4 September they spent the whole day with the investigation team at Tradefin examining the containers and trying to identify the wealth of components. It was decided that the freight containers could not remain at Tradefin and over the weekend 11 loads were transported under police escort to safer quarters, namely the former Z-enrichment plant at Pelindaba. There was enough space to store the containers safely and examine the contents thoroughly.

Meyer's next court appearance on Wednesday 8 September caused a sensation. All charges against him were dropped. The IAEA in Vienna described his release as "interesting", but added that there was probably a reason for it.

The reason behind the release certainly qualified as "interesting". To go back to the 1700s, one is reminded of the following observation by the English author and critic, Samuel Johnson: "Depend upon it, sir, when a man knows he is to be hanged in a fortnight, it concentrates his mind wonderfully." In our more enlightened society one could regard the loss of R38 million in a Swiss bank account as the modern-day equivalent of going to the gallows. In a bail application by Gerhard Wisser his advocate, Anand Choudree, warned the state that Meyer would do "anything" to protect his wealth, even lie to the state.

The weekend in the cold, grimy police cell had indeed concentrated Meyer's mind. He decided to turn state witness and "tell all", with section 204 of the Criminal Procedure Act hanging over his head like the sword of Damocles, and in the full knowledge that if he were caught out in a lie he might be facing fresh charges.

This was not the last of the sensational events of 8 September. Gerhard Wisser and Daniel Geiges were arrested. At first Wisser could not be found at his luxurious villa in Bryanston. The police eventually caught up with him in an apartment in the wealthy suburb of La Lucia close to Durban. The flat belonged to Gotthard Lerch. Although Wisser claimed that he had merely been looking after Lerch's various South African properties on his behalf, the reason for his visit to Durban emerged later. He had driven all the way down from Johannesburg to throw three computer hard drives into the sea. That explained Geiges's new computer.

On 9 September Wisser and Geiges appeared in court in Vanderbijlpark. They looked anxious and tense. Wisser's advocate, Anand Choudree, complained that the two men, who were both close to 70, had spent the previous night on the cold floor of a police cell – without mattresses or blankets. Choudree also claimed that they had been deliberately humiliated. They had been given soup for supper, but only forks to eat it with. They were once woken in the middle of the night by policemen and a cabinet minister who derided them. Wisser was prepared to identify the minister if he could be supplied with photographs. Choudree lodged an objection to the "barbaric" treatment. "It's as if we are back in some Third World country. Yes, we are back in the previous dispensation," he said.

Meyer received a death threat from Wisser's wife of the time, Erika, and he was placed in a witness protection programme.

Following international shock over this discovery in South Africa – the world leader in the non-proliferation stakes – Abdul Minty (with Nic von

Wielligh as adviser) had to depart in haste for Vienna to put out fires. The IAEA's Board of Governors was informed about these events and discussions were held with senior IAEA officials, as well as American and British diplomats. Minty also addressed a packed press conference. The media were told that South Africa was cooperating closely with the IAEA to uncover the smuggling ring and that all possible assistance would be given.

Meanwhile a number of crates containing equipment and blue steel cabinets with documents were discovered in a store in Silverton after Meyer had informed the police of their existence. These goods were also sent to Pelindaba for safekeeping. The time-consuming evaluation of the documents was later to yield some startling information.

In the course of a bail hearing on Wednesday 22 September, Advocate Anand Choudree revealed that Wisser and Geiges had received death threats in the Vanderbijlpark police cells. He told the court: "There is a strong possibility that the two men will not live to stand trial unless they are released on bail. They are ridiculed and intimidated. Their human rights are being severely violated." According to *Beeld* (22 September), a visibly distressed Choudree added that he had tried to reason with the police at the cells but the only answer he got was that they had received instructions from "higher up" to intimidate the accused. "I am a senior advocate and occasionally serve as an acting judge and they took no notice of my pleas."

It took almost 30 days to work through the seized documentation and compile a report on it. The task was completed towards the end of November. There was a wealth of reference documents. Some of them bore the German Leybold-Heräus stamp and dated back to the 1970s; they had clearly been inherited from Gotthard Lerch. Then there were engineering drawings; cascade calculations; centrifuge equipment results for P-1 and P-2 models; calculations from Pakistan which indicated how much feed material and time would be needed to make a certain number of nuclear weapons; plans for a building to house the cascade; as well as certain manuals, brochures and instructions for electrical and electronic process control. Important documents on a Denn flow forming machine for the manufacture of centrifuge rotors were also found.

Tradefin was also considerate enough to enclose complete lists for their Libyan client of all the equipment manufactured, with packing details and detailed instructions on how to put everything together, as if it were a big Meccano set. All told, it was a thorough package of documents that included building and cascade layout plans, calibration certificates for instrumentation, as well as operating instructions for the equipment.

This hoard of information also contained faxes and correspondence between the conspirators, quotations and orders, a report on a visit to Turkey in February 2002 to reconcile the process and control equipment supplied by Tradefin with the electrical equipment for the cascade manufactured by the Turks and, lastly, even notes bearing A.Q. Khan's signature. There was also a video advertising A.Q. Khan Research Laboratories.

All that remained to be evaluated was a computer hard drive which had been handed in by Meyer and was in the possession of the SAPS.

By the middle of January 2005 the foreigners had descended on Pelindaba (at South Africa's invitation) to join the South African team in unpacking the containers systematically one by one and identifying and evaluating the contents. There were two inspectors from the IAEA, three people from the USA (Oak Ridge and the CIA), seven Brits, most of whom were from MI6, and three Germans (including one representative of Urenco). They were assisted by members of the SAPS, the NPA, the NIS, the Department of Trade and Industry, and advisers. The work was physically exhausting and had to be done under the merciless January sun. It took ten days to complete the job.

While this was going on the NPA systematically took statements from everyone involved: Willem Mennega of Dynamic Engineering in Silverton, which was to have manufactured the autoclaves and possibly also the centrifuge rotors; Leonard Jack Harvey of Krisch Engineering, responsible for the instrumentation such as pressure and flow meters; Mrs Höller of Krisch Engineering; and André Smit of Logichem, which built the programmable electronic logic controllers.

The Americans in turn made every effort to build up a good working relationship with the NPA. Arrangements were made for a South African delegation to visit Oak Ridge, where the Gaddafi equipment was stored, and there was two-way consultation in which the CIA played an important part. The USA even arranged for the submission of statements by three experts, namely William Tobey (American Department of Energy), Jeff Bedell (Los Alamos) and Ron Miskell (Oak Ridge).

After all the hard work that went into evaluating the information and equipment, the following picture emerged:

In an ordinary centrifuge plant there is a feed point where natural uranium in the form of UF_6 is evaporated by autoclaves into the process equipment as feed material. Both the depleted and the enriched uranium – in the form of UF_6 – are extracted by means of a cooling system (i.e. by freezing).

This is a continuous process.

The plant manufactured by Tradefin was to have worked differently.

Two cascades, known as C1 and C2, each consisting of 1 968 centrifuges, were to have functioned in parallel, yielding 3,5% enriched uranium. They were to have been fed with natural uranium and the enriched product was to have been captured in product cylinders.

These cylinders containing material enriched to 3,5% would then be physically transferred to the autoclaves of a second cascade, HC01, where they would serve as feed material. HC01 was to consist of 1 312 centrifuges and the uranium would be further enriched to 20% and then captured in product cylinders again.

The process would be repeated for a third cascade, HC02, with 456 centrifuges, which would enrich the uranium to 60% and a fourth, HC03, with 128 centrifuges, which would produce the final product, enriched to 90% – in other words bomb material.

The total number of centrifuges used for the enrichment process therefore amounted to 5 832.

This cumbersome process was made possible by having five different sets of equipment, each consisting of a feed station and a product and depleted waste withdrawal station – one set for each of the five different cascades. Three of them were intended for C1, C2 and HC01 and were named ministations. The other two, intended for HC02 and HC03, were known as microstations.

The freight containers held all the necessary equipment, including the extensive header piping required to link the stations to the cascades and to interconnect the 5 832 centrifuges, several vacuum stations, electronic control systems, measuring instruments and structural steelwork to keep everything in place. Even a desk and two chairs had been included.

The purpose of the equipment was clear and the workmanship outstanding. All that remained was to get the accused into court and begin the trial.

Before the commencement of the trial Nic von Wielligh and one of his colleagues from the former South African nuclear weapons enterprise, both of whom had been requested to assist the NPA with the technical aspects of uranium enrichment and were responsible for the technical evaluation of the documents which had been seized, wanted to examine the last outstanding item. This was the hard drive in the possession of the SAPS. A visit to the NPA's offices was arranged in August 2005 and the process of making copies of the documents on the hard drive began. The first few pages consisted of obvious drawings of centrifuge rotors, complete with the dimensions and other specifications. An American delegation happened to be visiting the NPA at the time. They met behind locked doors. It may have been a coincidence but NPA officers descended on Von Wielligh and his colleague at the same time and instructed them to stop work immediately. The cooperation of the two South Africans with the NPA was suddenly considered undesirable. This was the thanks they got for a year's dedicated work. No reasons were given.

A report that appeared in *The Guardian* in June 2005 under the title "UN alert as nuclear plans go missing" could possibly explain this strange conduct:

> Electronic drawings that give comprehensive details of how to build and test equipment essential for making nuclear bombs have vanished and could be put up for sale on the international black market, according to UN investigators.
>
> A senior official said several sets of blueprints for uranium centrifuges – the so-called P-1 and more advanced P-2 systems which were peddled by the Khan network – have gone missing.
>
> "We know there were several sets of them prepared," said the official. "So who got those electronic drawings? We have only actually got the one full set from Libya. So who got the rest, the copies? We have no evidence they were destroyed. One possibility is another client. We just don't know where they are."
>
> The blueprints, running to hundreds of pages, show how to make centrifuges for enriching uranium. In addition, the investigators have been unable to trace key components for uranium centrifuge rigs and fear that drawings for a nuclear warhead have been secreted away and could be for sale.
>
> The Libyan leader, Colonel Muammar Gaddafi, confessed to his secret nuclear bomb programme and gave it up in December 2003. Three months later in Tripoli, the UN inspectors were given two CD-roms and one computer hard drive. One CD contained a set of drawings and manuals for the P-1 centrifuge system, the other for the more advanced P-2.
>
> The instructions are in English, Dutch and German, and the de-

signs are from Urenco, the Dutch-British-German consortium which is a leader in centrifuge technology and is the source of Khan's know-how from his time working there in the 1970s. The CDs and hard drive are at IAEA headquarters in Vienna, where they have been analysed. The investigators now know that the scanning of the original blueprints was done in Dubai and when.

In addition to these blueprints, Khan also supplied Libya with drawings for an old Chinese nuclear warhead design. The drawings, now in Washington under IAEA seal, were not complete, say sources, but were adequate to construct a crude nuclear device.

The contents of the hard drive may have been considered too much for the "innocent" eyes of the evaluation team. Did the CIA have their way again?

Fact or fiction?

Getting to the truth usually requires a protracted court process which moves from the customary denial by the accused to a conclusive result and a judgment. That is to say unless the accused persons decide to turn state witness to save their own skins and spill the beans. Occasionally, because of the strength of the evidence against them, the accused decide to plead guilty and enter into a plea bargain.

The account Wisser initially gave was, to put it briefly, that of an innocent and unknowing intermediary who had simply been led astray by the offer of a good commission.

The statements he made to the authorities in Germany and South Africa added further details to his account. But as time went on it became apparent that the man was lying through his teeth.

Wisser's original story was the following: He suffered from hip arthritis and often went to Dubai because the warm seawater, which at times reached temperatures of up to 44 °C, was beneficial for his condition. After a stressful divorce from his first wife he went to Dubai again, this time to recover from cardiac arrhythmia. As far as he was able to remember, this was in 2001. There he met Tahir at a dinner arranged by an acquaintance, Jabbar Gargash. He and Tahir did not know each other at the time. According to him eight people were present at the dinner. Tahir had strange ideas and Wisser got the impression that he had invited himself to the dinner. Gargash was described as a "heavy drinker with no interest in work". He came from a prominent family, but apparently he was not a serious businessman. Instead his interest lay in "women who had inherited a lot of money". By this account Gargash had nothing to do with the rest of the story.

The unknown Tahir asked Wisser whether his firm would be able to build a piping system for a refinery and provide vacuum equipment at the same time. He offered an excellent commission. Any reservations Wisser might have had about the project vanished at once. He was embroiled in a divorce and his ex-wife had instructed a private detective to trace all his foreign bank accounts. His wife was determined to have her share of his assets. Wisser knew that the police investigation would turn up all his bank accounts in time and as a precaution he offered his ex-wife R9 million, an offer which she fortunately found entirely satisfactory.

Wisser explained to Tahir that he would not be able to manufacture the equipment himself, but that he would look for a firm in South Africa that might be able to do it. When he returned to South Africa he approached two companies without success. Then he thought of his old friend J.A.M. Meyer of Tradefin.

Meyer was prepared to look into the matter and Wisser arranged with Tahir to send the drawings directly to Meyer. A while later Meyer invited Wisser to come round and showed him a stack of documents measuring about half a metre in height that he had received from Tahir. The South African's reaction was: "This is the animal. I am going to make an offer." Wisser said in his initial statement that he had no idea what the drawings were intended for or how big the project was. He also claimed that he was unable to tell Meyer to which country the finished product should be exported. He, Wisser, knew nothing whatsoever about the project and had simply acted as a facilitator who had received an unexpectedly large commission.

According to Wisser he received a call from Gotthard Lerch about two months later regarding his South African properties. Lerch enquired casually whether Wisser wanted to go on with the "pipe business". Wisser was surprised that Lerch knew about this project.

In the meanwhile Meyer continued with the project and told Wisser that he had received the first payment for the purchase of materials. The payment was made directly into his Absa account and he was astonished to see that it had come from Libya. Meyer also told Wisser about two "Egyptians" who came to inspect his premises in May 2003.

According to Wisser he was shocked by the Libyan deposit in Meyer's account and started an internal investigation. What he found led him to believe that Meyer was building equipment for an enrichment plant for Libya. He advised Meyer to melt down the metal (without even knowing whether it was stainless steel or aluminium) and destroy the engineering drawings, because he expected major problems if the equipment were to be exported. In his opinion Meyer didn't really know what he was engaged in. The "Egyptian" inspectors had misled him into thinking that the equipment was intended for a water purification plant.

So much for Wisser's original story. Geiges, on the other hand, refused to cooperate with the investigators or give any explanation.

Meyer provides the nails for the coffin

Meyer's testimony and other evidence before the court revealed a completely different picture from the one sketched by Wisser in his statement as described above.

Wisser met Lerch and the other nuclear smugglers in Zürich, Switzerland, as early as May 1999 to plan the Libyan project. The continuation of this meeting took place in July 1999 in Dubai, where technical discussions lasted for almost a week. Wisser was appointed as project director with full responsibility for the work that was to be done in South Africa. His areas of responsibility included the design, development, production and procurement of materials and components. The procurement of special machinery and design data was another of his duties. He was also responsible for controlling the project finances.

Wisser appointed Daniel Geiges, a codirector at Krisch Engineering, as chief engineer on the project. He would be responsible for the practical and technical side of the design and building of the plant, the appointment of and supervision over subcontractors, and the procurement of a thousand and one components.

Wisser and Geiges knew very well that what they were doing was illegal and they devised and used several strategies to cover up their crime.

Towards the end of 1999 Geiges contacted Meyer at Tradefin and asked for a quotation for the project on the basis of the extensive specifications and drawings he had supplied. This quotation was ready by January 2000. Meyer calculated the cost at R39 million, but subsequently reduced that to R38 million. Meyer testified that he had known from the beginning that a uranium enrichment plant was being built.

Wisser instructed one of his employees, Leonard Jack Harvey, to design a centralised control system for the feed-and-withdrawal systems for the UF_6. Harvey was well aware that Lerch was involved and used to refer to the "Mr Lerch project". Wisser once told Harvey that A.Q. Khan had acted as consultant for the project. Harvey later received additional instructions to design and build flow and pressure meters, which were unavailable on account of stringent export controls. He had sound experience in this area because he had previously built flow meters for India and had even visited India to attend to problems with the meters.

In April 2001, Wisser and Meyer paid a visit to Dubai, where Wisser attended a project planning meeting (a "kick-off meeting"). Curiously enough, Wisser did not invite Meyer to the series of meetings that took place. Meyer interpreted Wisser's odd working procedure as a way of maintaining a monopoly on the project information in order to protect his commission. The only name Meyer heard during his visit was that of Tahir. Wisser did, however, show Meyer round Gotthard Lerch's palatial Dubai home as a kind of consolation prize.

Financial arrangements to pay Meyer took the form of deposits in a Swiss bank account which Meyer had recently opened with the aid of a South African employed at a Swiss bank. Money was to flow into the account at intervals through front companies and individuals; at one stage it even came from a body called National Industrial Safety Libya. Wisser was responsible for the scheduling of the payments. Meyer received a deposit of €10 200 in May 2001, and another €950 000 later on. Meyer received over 20 payments in all. The last transaction took place in June 2003. The total amount paid to him was €6 503 109.

In turn Meyer paid several subcontractors from this Swiss bank account – by means of transfers to their overseas bank accounts – to keep the project quiet. He even established a front company in Switzerland to procure equipment which could not have been exported to South Africa in any other way. This enabled him to acquire vacuum pumps from Spain and valves and pressure meters from Germany.

One of Meyer's most important subcontractors in South Africa was Logichem. This company was managed by André Smit, who was responsible for the programmable electronic control of the process. In February 2000 Wisser arranged that Geiges and Smit should travel to Turkey to determine whether Smit's electronic control equipment was compatible with the Turkish electrical components for the centrifuges.

According to Meyer, the Swiss, Daniel Geiges, who had served as chief engineer on the project, worked for Tradefin on a semi-fulltime basis for 18 months. He received €100 000 from Meyer for this work.

In Switzerland the Tinner family was to have been responsible for the manufacture of the rotor tubes of the centrifuges out of maraging steel, but that project never got off the ground. The relationship between Wisser and Friedrich Tinner was not exactly cordial. Wisser's statement to the German authorities included the following:

> Many years ago I accepted the request to represent the Swiss company Cetec [Friedrich Tinner's company] in South Africa. The company manufactured vacuum valves ... At that time I met the senior members of the family Tinner. It was very brief ... Because he did not want to have anything to do with us I thought: you could shove the business up your arse.

Towards the end of the year 2000 Wisser told Meyer that there had been problems with the manufacture of the rotor tubes and asked whether he would be able to take over this process. Meyer did not have the necessary special equipment and Wisser therefore arranged to have a flow forming machine imported from Dubai. The Denn flow forming machine was imported from Spain by Peter Griffin's Gulf Industries in Dubai. The flow forming of the rotor tubes may be compared to the process by which a potter starts with a lump of clay shaped like a cup with thick walls and gradually pulls the clay upwards on the wheel to form a longish cylinder with thinner walls. With a flow forming machine the thin-walled rotor tube is shaped by rollers around a cylindrical mandrel.

The flow forming machine was illegally imported as a "lathe" for which no import permit is required and the value was given as about 10% of the actual value in order to reduce the excise duty. Under the Non-Proliferation of Weapons of Mass Destruction Act, an import permit is required to bring this type of machine into South Africa.

Meyer asked Willem Mennega of Dynamic Engineering in Silverton to manufacture the rotor tubes. Mennega, who also manufactured other components such as the autoclaves and UF_6 containers from Monel alloy, agreed to have the flow forming machine delivered at his business premises. When the machine, packed in a large wooden crate, arrived at Mennega's premises late in December 2000, the offices were already closed for the Christmas holidays and the machine was consequently sent to Tradefin.

Meyer had his reservations about manufacturing the rotor tubes. The flow forming machine had to be placed on a specially designed pedestal and the maraging steel was not yet available. The suggestion was that it should be supplied by Karachi Steel Mills. He nevertheless submitted a quotation for over $5 million to Wisser, but heard nothing more about it.

After the machine had been standing in a crate at Tradefin for over a year, Meyer received instructions from Wisser in December 2001 to send it back to Dubai. It was again exported illegally without a permit as a "second-hand lathe". The machine was consigned to Libya from Dubai. Today it stands at Oak Ridge in the USA along with the other equipment seized in Libya.

By June 2002 Meyer had virtually finished the project. In the meanwhile, without Meyer's knowledge Lerch and Wisser had arranged with two "Egyptians" called Ali and Abdul to inspect the plant in situ. They were later identified by the IAEA as the Libyan citizens Al-Karim Imaq'iq and Ali Al-Shamli. On 2 June these two inspectors signed into the Emerald Casino Hotel next to the Vaal River. They contacted an astonished Meyer on his mobile phone. Between that Sunday and the following Saturday they went through everything at his factory. They were well-informed and requested certain technical changes. Among the relatively unsophisticated artisans on the shop floor the plant was known ever afterwards as the "AF project", with AF standing for "Arab Fuckers".

After the visitors had left and the changes had been made, the equipment was dismantled and packed into the 11 shipping containers. On Wisser's instructions, all labels, name plates and other identifying marks had to be removed. He gave further orders that the technical documents and manuals on how to reassemble the plant should not identify the origin or the authors. All technical and other documents that Geiges still had in his office at Krisch Engineering were also transferred to Tradefin and the whole lot were packed into steel trunks and stored at Silverton in Pretoria.

The following problem was how to export the containers and especially where to send them. But Wisser had a plan to deal with this as well. In 2002 he handed a forged contract between Tradefin and an imaginary organisation in Jordan – backdated to 20 May 2001 – to Meyer for signature. Shortly afterwards Wisser returned from overseas with the contract signed by a certain "Professor Tahir" from the organisation in Jordan. The contract applied to the exporting of five "water purification plants" to Jordan. Meyer was paid over R6 million for the projected exports; this was the very last payment he received for all his trouble.

On 15 August 2002 Wisser supplied Meyer with a delivery schedule, but without disclosing the delivery address. The situation was frustrating and at the end of 2003 Wisser flew to Dubai to finalise an outstanding payment and also the delivery address. However, instead of the outstanding information, Meyer received panic-stricken SMS messages from Wisser: "The bird must be destroyed, feathers and all" and "They fed us to the dogs." Wisser was referring to the seizure of the *BBC China's* cargo in October and Colonel Gaddafi's subsequent confession.

Meyer was anything but pleased by Wisser's orders to "melt down the plant" and destroy all the documentation. He did not feel that he could destroy the plant, for which millions had been paid, without the consent of the owner. Furthermore, he was proud of his handiwork, which ironically enough was later described by his attorney as "a thing of beauty".

The case

Although Wisser and Geiges were arrested in September 2004, it was to take three years before a final judgment was handed down in the case against them. Because of the international implications of the case and the overcrowded court rolls, which usually result in court cases being postponed, Judge Joop Labuschagne was called out of retirement so that the case could receive maximum attention in the minimum of time.

There were eight charges against Geiges (first defendant), and 10 against Wisser (second defendant) and Krisch Engineering (third defendant). One charge under the Non-Proliferation of Weapons of Mass Destruction Act was in relation to the importing and exporting of the Denn flow forming machine. There were also six charges under the Nuclear Energy Act relating to the unlawful manufacture, possession and attempted exporting of nuclear-related equipment, materials and technology. A further charge of fraud arose from the fraudulent description of the flow forming machine as a lathe with a view to importing and exporting it without a permit, as well as the declaration of a false value (about one-tenth of the actual value) in order to evade customs and excise duties. The last two charges (which only concerned Wisser and Krisch) dealt with the falsification of order forms of other companies in order to procure vacuum and gas leak detection equipment.

Geiges, who denied everything from the beginning and tried to protect everyone, was suffering from cancer by then. He had lost his job at Krisch and with it his company apartment and consequently felt that he had not much more to lose. He continued to protest his innocence, however. In

March 2006 he unburdened himself to the German news magazine, *Der Spiegel*. Gotthard Lerch was openly pointed out as the mastermind behind the project, which he ran from Switzerland. In the early months of 2001 and towards the end of 2002 Lerch visited South Africa for technical discussions and inspections. Everyone was expected to follow his instructions. J.A.M. Meyer once even described Lerch as the mastermind behind the building of the Pakistan enrichment plant and – rather surprisingly – dismissed A.Q. Khan as an apprentice with a lot to learn.

On 4 September 2007, Gerhard Wisser entered into a plea bargain and pleaded guilty to the charges against him in the Pretoria High Court. He acknowledged that he had conspired with A.Q. Khan, Abu Tahir and Gotthard Lerch and illegally supplied materials and equipment to Pakistan and Libya for the purposes of uranium enrichment. Since Geiges was still pleading not guilty, his case was separated from Wisser's.

Wisser was ultimately sentenced to 18 years' imprisonment. In exchange for his admission of guilt and promise to cooperate with international investigators in order to expose the network, 15 years of the sentence were suspended and he was placed under house arrest for three years. He never saw the inside of a prison. What hurt him most was that he had to surrender the income from his criminal activities to the state: R6 million from his South African accounts and a further €2,85 million which he had in an overseas account. He instantly became poorer to the tune of over R30 million.

Geiges, however, bluntly continued to protest his innocence. Judge Joop Labuschagne was only too pleased when Wisser decided to plead guilty and thereby avoid a protracted trial. Labuschagne remarked laconically that a long trial might possibly "lead to a divorce in my old age". Another judge was appointed to take Geiges's case further.

In a cable, 07PRETORIA3091, made public by WikiLeaks, an official of the American Embassy relates what he observed outside the courtroom while Geiges and his advocate were waiting to be called:

> He was engaged in a lengthy monologue, protesting his continued innocence to his poker-faced attorney and describing at length how the charges were a grand plot orchestrated by British and American intelligence services (to what end was unclear). Geiges showed no visible signs of illness, gesturing, pacing and speaking with energy and animation and smiling frequently.

The disease took its toll, however, and on 5 February 2008 Geiges decided to give up the fight and plead guilty to five charges. Judge Van der Merwe found him guilty in the Pretoria High Court and sentenced him to 10 years' imprisonment (suspended for five years) on one set of charges and three years on the other, also suspended for five years. As in Wisser's case, the money derived from criminal activities was declared forfeit to the state: €50 000 and 74 255 Swiss francs, or over R1 million.

The American cable 08PRETORIA234 (WikiLeaks again) carried the following report:

> Contrary to his vibrant physical presence at the Wisser plea bargain Geiges appeared weak, gaunt, and mostly silent in court today. He declined all media requests for interviews – a departure from his past practice. Geiges' visible ill health underscored the plea package assessment that he has little time left before succumbing to cancer.

Later in 2008 Geiges did in fact lose his battle against cancer.

Lerch's fate

In December 2008 Gotthard Lerch – after decades of illegal operations and three previous unsuccessful attempts to bring him to book – was ultimately found guilty in a court in Stuttgart, Germany, and sentenced to 66 months' imprisonment. Since he had already spent so much time in custody he was released at the conclusion of the trial. He was fined US$ 4.7 million (over R40 million).

The case against Lerch was a very complicated one, since Tahir refused to travel to Germany to testify and also because of the extremely tense relations between the NPA and the German authorities. In a WikiLeaks report, 07BERLIN2239, the Germans complained to US embassy officials in Berlin that South Africa had refused point blank to allow them to contact Wisser. German diplomats in Vienna apparently communicated with Ambassador Minty on the matter in September 2007 but never received a reply.

Did A.Q. Khan do the unthinkable?

Colonel Gaddafi's announcement in December 2003 that he had stopped all work on weapons of mass destruction and would cooperate with the USA and Britain to expose the network must have caused shock waves in Islamabad. In a letter to his wife, Hendrina, dated 10 December, which was evidently written in haste, A.Q. Khan wrote: "Darling, if the government plays any mischief with me, take a tough stand." He only had time to write four pages and in numbered paragraphs Khan listed the countries he had supplied with equipment and technology: China, Iran, North Korea and Libya.

Although Khan had been doing things his own way for decades, Pakistan's top military command structure had cooperated actively, or at least been aware of his activities. Pakistan is a unique country, because although it has a civil government, in practice it is governed by the army and especially by the formidable Inter-Services Intelligence (ISI). Khan's fear was that Gaddafi's revelations might result in the established order sacrificing him to avoid losing vital financial aid from America. Khan did not know which way things would go, but he feared the worst and wanted the outside world to be aware of the involvement of the military rulers. A copy of his letter to Hendrina was sent to one of his daughters in London and to Simon Henderson, a journalist working for *The Times*. Henderson reported on this at length in September 2009 in *The Sunday Times*.

The image of himself that Khan projected over the years was one of a patriot who would even steal technology to protect Pakistan from a nuclear threat by India – after all he was the "father of the Pakistani bomb". But was he really the arch-patriot he claimed to be?

After the discovery of the cargo carried by the *BBC China*, the IAEA launched an in-depth investigation to expose the network and all the conspirators. They looked at the records of the equipment produced in Malaysia for the Libyan plant and compared them with what was found. There were differences. Olli Heinonen, the then head of the IAEA inspectorate, commented on the matter as follows: "The shipments were never found. Were they destroyed? Dumped? Are they being kept somewhere? We don't know."

The possibility that there was a "fourth client" (apart from Iran, Libya and North Korea) had been mooted for a long time and shipments to this client were handled in code by the nuclear smugglers. Why the secrecy and why did Khan not mention this in his letter to Hendrina? Was he afraid of an even bigger scandal?

Back in 1998 it was already being whispered in Pakistan that Khan was involved with a "fourth client". Ex-president Pervez Musharraf, the former head of the defence force who had denied any involvement with Khan's network and also discharged Khan as head of the KRL, wrote in his biography in 2006: "Ironically, the network based in Dubai had employed several Indians, some of whom have since vanished. There is a strong probability that the Indian uranium enrichment programme may also have its roots in the Dubai-based network and could be a copy of the Pakistani centrifuge design." Had the unthinkable happened? Would Musharraf wilfully have accused the "saviour of Pakistan" of possible collaboration with India without good reason?

And how does one account for Lerch's enquiry to Wisser in 1993 about procuring 10 000 ring magnets, for use in centrifuges, for India? And what is the explanation for the fact that Harvey – a Krisch employee – made flow meters for the Indian enrichment plant and even visited India to sort out problems with the meters? Years after the Tradefin network had been uncovered, Waldo Stumpf related that Gerhard Wisser had come to see him one day (while the Tradefin case was being heard) to find out how uranium exports worked. He had a client – India – that wanted to buy uranium without a permit. It was apparent that the members of the network couldn't care less who they were working with as long as they got paid.

Further, what motivated Selim Alguadiş, a Turkish Jew, to make electronic components for the Libyan enrichment plant? After all, Libya is an Arab state and a sworn enemy of Israel's.

Asher Karni resigned his post as a major in the Israeli army in 1985 and travelled to South Africa, where he held the post of assistant rabbi in Cape Town for four years. After this he founded his own company. In 2004 he visited the USA. There he was arrested for exporting illegal components for nuclear weapons to Pakistan via South Africa.

The probable reason why A.Q. Khan came to the aid of his arch-enemy India, why Alguadiş assisted Gaddafi with his "Arab bomb" and why Karni helped Pakistan with his "Muslim bomb" can be summed up in one word: greed.

PART 8

A MURKY CRYSTAL BALL

What are the prospects for the world: a nuclear war or two, on a limited or global scale? Or possibly the last war ever fought? Or can we look forward to a rosier future, with full nuclear disarmament and lasting peace, accompanied by the safe, peaceful development of nuclear energy?

Deterrent or miracle?

> *Deterrence is hope masquerading as strategy.*
>
> Zia Mian, Princeton

Towards the end of 1945 the war-weary Allies just wanted to be left to lick their wounds in peace. Germany in defeat was a country reduced to rubble and ashes. But the fly in the ointment was Joseph Stalin and his Red Army, which was in control of a large part of Eastern Europe, with tank forces that made it the dominant fighting force on the continent. Despite the sacrifice of over 20 million lives and the destruction of large cities such as Leningrad and Kharkof, the Soviet Union had attained the status of a world power.

Hiroshima and Nagasaki changed that status overnight. The Americans now possessed the mother of all weapons, one that would keep potential aggressors in their place. There were visions of reduced fighting forces and lasting peace – the peace about which Alfred Nobel had dreamed a century previously but which had never materialised: "My dynamite will sooner lead to peace than a thousand world conventions. As soon as men will find that in one instant, whole armies can be utterly destroyed, they surely will abide by golden peace."

Stalin had been informed by his numerous moles that the Americans would not be able to build enough nuclear bombs within the next few years to engage in a struggle with the Soviet Union, with its vast geographical area. He took full advantage of this opportunity to hastily develop and build his own nuclear weapons. Klaus Fuchs and other moles, who were intimately involved with the Manhattan Project, provided valuable assistance with this programme. It was to take the Soviet Union about four years, a little longer than it had taken the USA, to build its first nuclear device. On 29 August 1949, at 06:00 on a wet and windy morning in East Kazakhstan, the earth shook. The Soviet Union's first nuclear device was detonated at the Semipalatinsk Test Site with an explosive yield that was 7 kilotons greater than America's first attempt.

Stalin did not announce the test. He probably wanted to avoid provoking the USA into speeding up its own nuclear weapons programme. However, an explosion of that nature cannot readily be concealed. Three weeks later President Truman announced that the USA had information indicating that the USSR had detonated a nuclear device. The Americans were greatly alarmed because the CIA had estimated that it would take another four years at least before a test of this kind could be carried out.

The unearthly bang caused by Joe-1, as the Americans christened Stalin's bomb, was the starter's pistol that set off the biggest and most expensive arms race of all time. The USA accelerated its programme and in January 1950 Truman announced in public that he had ordered the building of a still more destructive weapon – the hydrogen (thermonuclear) bomb. This was the beginning of an insane, irrational race which was largely responsible for reducing the Soviet Union to bankruptcy four decades later and which played a major part in the ultimate decline of the USSR in 1989.

The two superpowers became engrossed in the Cold War game and feverishly built nuclear weapons behind the scenes. Between 1945 and 2000 the Americans manufactured 70 000 nuclear weapons and the USSR produced 55 000, far more than they needed to wipe each other out completely and return the earth to its initial state as described in Genesis 1:2: "The earth was formless and void, darkness was over the surface of the deep."

In a famous speech delivered in 1955 Winston Churchill described this diabolical inflexibility as "the balance of terror". After the Cuban missile crisis in 1962 people began to refer to the "MAD" strategy (mutually assured destruction). The word "deterrence" acquired a specialised meaning and a whole politico-military philosophy developed around the concept.

Amos Zeeberg describes the situation as follows in *Nautilus* (6 May 2015):

> During the Cold War, the important thinking about using nuclear weapons didn't come from old military wisdom but from game theory, a new way to understand strategic decision-making. This analytical approach suggested that the standoff between the US and USSR represented a Nash equilibrium: Neither superpower had reason to preemptively launch a nuclear attack, as it would surely provoke a devastating counterattack. At the same time, neither would disarm significantly enough to leave itself unable to

retaliate to a preemptive strike. The doctrine of mutually assured destruction (or MAD, named somewhat facetiously by mathematician John von Neumann) seemed to keep the superpowers at a peaceful balance point. But it's unsettling to live in a world whose existence is maintained only by the threatening logic of the Nash equilibrium.

At a meeting between President Lyndon Johnson and Soviet Prime Minister Alexsei Kosygin in 1967 at Glassboro nuclear weapons were one of the topics discussed. In the course of the discussion Robert McNamara, the US Secretary of Defense, stated his country's position (*The Star Wars History – From Deterrence to Defence: The American Strategic Debate* by Michael Charlton, 1986):

> Mr. Prime Minister, you must understand that we will maintain a deterrent under any circumstances. And we view a deterrent as a nuclear force so strong that it can absorb your nuclear attack on it and survive with sufficient power to inflict unacceptable damage on you. And therefore, if you put a defense in place, we're going to have to expand our nuclear offensive forces. You may think, as the Congress apparently does, that a proper response to the Soviet defense is a U.S. defense; but I tell you the proper response – and it will be our response – is to expand our offensive force.

> Kosygin normally wore a poker face. Perhaps he initially looked at McNamara as if he were from a strange, distant planet. Then, in McNamara's recollection, he absolutely erupted. He became red in the face, arguing what was then the standard Soviet line, that defense was a moral imperative and that a nuclear arms race was immoral.

The practical implications of the American approach, formulated in the innocuous-sounding Single Integrated Operational Plan (SIOP), which was approved by President Eisenhower in 1960, were astounding. When he became secretary of defence in 1961, Robert McNamara, a former president of the Ford Motor Company, went to the trouble of finding out exactly what the SIOP involved. He was enlightened about the USA's official nuclear war plan by General Thomas Power, the head of the all-powerful Strategic Air Command (SAC) in charge of the nuclear weapons arsenal. McNamara was cold-bloodedly informed that if the USSR were to invade any country in the Free

World, even without using a single nuclear weapon, the SAC would hit back with all the nuclear weapons at their disposal. At that stage they had 3 423 nuclear weapons with an explosive yield equivalent to 7 847 million tons of TNT. That was expected to kill 250 to 300 million Russians and Chinese and injure 40 million people. The consequences of the global radioactive fallout (including fallout over the USA) were not taken into account. McNamara was greatly distressed by the crudity and cold-bloodedness of the American strategy.

In a discussion on nuclear strategy between Bill W. Kaufmann, who had acted as adviser to seven successive US secretaries of defence, and General Power a year previously, the latter burst out angrily: "Why do you want us to restrain ourselves? Why are you concerned with saving their lives? The whole idea is to kill the bastards! Look. At the end of the war, if there are two Americans and one Russian, we win!"

Kaufmann answered drily: "Well, you'd better make sure they're a man and a woman."

Since the surprise Japanese attack on the American fleet in Pearl Harbor in December 1941, which led to America's entry into the Second World War, surprise attacks had always been a very sensitive subject with the Americans. This sensitivity was later to be painfully reinforced by the events of 9/11. As explained by McNamara, the doctrine of deterrence meant that if an opponent launched a surprise first strike against the USA there should be sufficient reserves to counter the attack and pay the attacker back in the same coin – or worse – that is, there should be a second strike capability. Initially this meant that the SAC had to keep long-range bombers carrying nuclear weapons in the air constantly in order to carry out such an attack. With the later development of nuclear missiles that could be launched from underground silos in the USA or from submarines, the so-called nuclear triad (long-range bombers, ballistic missiles and submarines) made it far easier to carry out a retaliatory attack of the kind envisaged and far more probable that this could be done, even if New York or Washington for example had already been destroyed. The deterrence capability was considerably strengthened by this diversification of delivery systems.

In time the doctrine of destroy and retaliate became more nuanced, thanks to the contributions of non-militarists like Brodie, Kaufmann, Wohlstetter and others. Brodie realised that the world had changed radically since 1945 and even in the same year he made the following statement: "Thus far the chief purpose of our military establishment has been to win wars. From now on its chief purpose must be to avert them."

Bill Kaufmann strongly opposed the prevailing viewpoint, as expressed by General Thomas Power, not only on moral grounds but also because of strategic considerations. His position was that the attack envisaged by Power would not be able to knock out every single Soviet nuclear weapon and that millions of innocent people in the USA and especially in Europe would lose their lives in a counterstrike. His approach was aimed at greater flexibility. If the Soviet Union were to invade Europe, for example, Soviet military targets would first be destroyed by means of precision bombing. If the Soviet forces did not withdraw, the big cities in the USSR would then be the targets of nuclear missiles fired from the USA or from submarines. This approach of a flexible response became the US doctrine in the 1960s – the screw would therefore be turned by degrees before a full-scale nuclear war with apocalyptic consequences occurred.

Was deterrence – with all the variations on the theme – the reason why, after Hiroshima and Nagasaki, there was no nuclear war for almost seven decades? There are numerous opinions on this matter. There were certainly numerous incidents and wars during this period in which the nuclear powers were involved (sometimes indirectly) and where nuclear weapons were seriously considered, but ultimately not used. The two salient examples are the Korean War of 1950 to 1953 and the Cuban missile crisis of 1962.

The Korean War, which broke out in 1950 with an unexpected attack by North Korea on its southern neighbours, is sometimes described as a nuclear war during which no nuclear weapons were used. The invasion was supported by the Soviet Union and China, which made an overwhelming ground force available. The Soviet Union had tested its first nuclear device the previous year, but did not yet possess an arsenal of militarily qualified weapons. The Chinese were still 14 years away from carrying out their first test. The Americans, who were fighting on South Korea's side, possessed a significant number of nuclear weapons by that time.

The invasion of South Korea by the North Koreans and Chinese, equipped with fairly primitive weapons, was so successful that by the evening of the first day the USA was considering the use of nuclear weapons. Four days later a journalist asked President Truman whether the USA might decide to use nuclear weapons. The reply was: "No comment." The Chinese did not believe that the USA would really resort to nuclear weapons, which Mao Zedong called a "paper tiger", a kind of bogeyman. By the end of the year the Chinese had driven the Americans and South Koreans back as far as Seoul in a surprise nocturnal attack. The next day President Truman announced that the USA was prepared to use all the weapons at its disposal. The Chinese were not daunted by this threat because they had been informed by their British double agents in the USA that Truman did not really plan to use nuclear weapons. And at that juncture a different kind of war broke out among the American militarists and politicians. Truman's head of staff, the celebrated General Douglas MacArthur, had ordered 34 nuclear bombs for use against the invading force, but also for an attack on China. This order was not well received in Washington. The Americans could have lost the support of a number of Western allies (including a handful of South African Air Force officers) and a new war against China, possibly accompanied by a full-scale war against the Soviet Union, was just too much for them to take on. When MacArthur stuck to his guns Truman relieved him of his post, thereby taking the nuclear weapons out of the hands of the military and placing them under civilian control.

In 1953 General Dwight Eisenhower became president. As an old soldier his slant on things differed from Truman's. He wanted to put a speedy end to the war and decided to threaten to use the big cudgel. His joint chiefs of staff prepared a plan of attack that would target North Korea, Manchuria and the Chinese coast. But as usual the information leaked out to the media. Eisenhower's strategy worked, aided by China's uncertainty about the line the Soviet Union would take after Stalin's death the previous year. In the end the Chinese were scared by the paper tiger; they withdrew and signed an armistice treaty in July. When Eisenhower was asked why the Chinese had backed down, he said laconically: "fear of a nuclear war".

Many of the other confrontations between the two nuclear powers concerned the status of Berlin. At that time the city was an enclave in the Soviet-occupied zone of East Germany. The situation was further complicated when West Germany joined the North Atlantic Treaty Organization (NATO) in 1955. This gave the USA the right to station nuclear weapons in West Germany.

The reaction of Nikita Khrushchev, the Soviet leader, was to send a note to the city of Bonn in which he threatened to turn West Germany into a "nuclear graveyard".

But far in the West, close to the US coast, this threat, in combination with a convergence of circumstances, almost led to the first true nuclear war. These events warrant a separate discussion.

The Cuban missile crisis of 1962 and the man who saved the world

While Cuba was still under Spanish control, there was a long period of rebellion by the inhabitants against Spanish domination. In time America was drawn into the conflict and in 1898 this led to the Spanish-American War (which concerned wider issues than just Cuba). Within ten weeks the unequal struggle was over and America had gained control of Cuba, Puerto Rico, Guam and the Philippines. Out of gratitude the first president of Cuba announced in 1903 that America would be permitted to lease the area called Guantanamo Bay (now known as Gitmo) in perpetuity; this decision was sealed by the Cuban-American treaty.

In January 1959 the young Fidel Castro and his camp followers like Che Guevara overthrew the pro-American president of Cuba, Fulgençio Batista. At that time American corporations and rich individuals owned about half of Cuba's sugar plantations and most of the cattle ranches and mines.

Castro was a radical communist who had established diplomatic relations with the Soviet Union in May 1960. Cuba was the only communist state in the West and consequently a thorn in the flesh of the Americans.

Castro's slogan of "Cuba si, Yanquis no" ("Cuba yes, Yankee no") rapidly gained popularity in Cuba. American properties were nationalised and land reforms introduced. Former supporters of the Batista government were arrested, many were executed and others were imprisoned for long periods. Those who were able to escape in time fled to the USA, where a large community of anti-Castro ex-Cubans grew up over time – especially in Florida.

Castro also wanted Guantanamo Bay back, but Eisenhower dug in his heels. The CIA arranged to train opponents of the Castro regime to overthrow his government. Numerous incidents of sabotage and factory bombings took place. When John F. Kennedy succeeded Dwight Eisenhower as president, planning for an invasion was far advanced. Fearing a Soviet reaction, Kennedy was strongly opposed to any direct American military intervention. The CIA assured him that they would only use ex-Cubans. In April 1961 the invasion took place at the Bay of Pigs. For various reasons the operation failed dismally and it was all over within four days. Kennedy was furious with the CIA and said he wanted "to splinter the CIA into a thousand pieces and scatter it to the winds".

The invasion prompted Castro to approach the Soviet Union for future protection. Khrushchev saw this as the ideal opportunity to compensate for the expansion of the USA's nuclear arsenal to Europe through NATO. This was the origin of Operation Anadyr.

From 15 September 1962 onwards a number of freighters sailed from Soviet ports.

These ships carried the following arsenal:

42 SS-4 ballistic missiles (medium-range with 60-megaton nuclear warheads)

32 SS-5 ballistic missiles (shorter range with 1- to 2-megaton nuclear warheads)

12 Frog surface-to-surface missiles (tactical application, 2 kilotons)

80 FKR cruise missiles (tactical application, 12 kilotons)

6 Ilyushin-28 bombers (in crates) with six 12-kiloton nuclear bombs.

On 4 October the Indigirka reached Cuba. On board were 45 nuclear warheads for SS-4 and SS-5 ballistic missiles; 36 nuclear warheads for FKR cruise missiles; 12 nuclear warheads for Frog (Luna) surface-to-surface missiles; and six nuclear warheads intended for Ilyushin-28 bombers.

On 23 October the Aleksandrovsk arrived with the rest: 24 strategic nuclear warheads and a further 44 FKR-1 nuclear warheads. The scene was set for the planet's first true nuclear war.

At 07:30 on 15 October 1962 Major Richard Heyser of the USAF was approaching the Cuban coast in his U-2 spy plane. For safety's sake he was flying at an altitude of 21 km, but nothing escaped the notice of his spy camera with its 910 mm lens. While flying over the island he shot over a kilometre of film. Back in the USA his high-resolution photographs showed that nuclear missiles and other military back-up equipment were spread all over the Cuban territory with no notable attempt at camouflage.

Kennedy was forced to take action. He couldn't allow the presence of this threat less than 200 km from the American coastline. The question was how to handle the situation – by mounting an attack or through negotiation? He decided to establish a naval blockade around Cuba to prevent the additional approaching ships from reaching the island. This came into force on 24 October, but only after the Indigirka and the Aleksandrovsk had already docked. Kennedy sent Khrushchev an

A MURKY CRYSTAL BALL

ultimatum demanding the withdrawal of his nuclear missiles – initially without success.

The chance of a nuclear war was balanced on a knife edge, but Khrushchev had not expected that the weapons on Cuba would be discovered so soon or that the USA's response would be so swift and decisive. Secret diplomatic negotiations took place between Kennedy and Khrushchev. The USA undertook to withdraw obsolete Jupiter nuclear missiles aimed at the USSR from Turkey and not to invade Cuba. Under these conditions Khrushchev was prepared to withdraw his nuclear missiles.

The crisis officially ended on 28 October 1962. The world was able to breathe again.

On 5 November the Aleksandrovsk returned to the Soviet Union with all the SS-4 missiles and strategic nuclear warheads on board. The hold was opened so that American helicopters and spy planes could count the missiles. Because of the naval blockade, the SS-5 ballistic missiles never arrived in Cuba.

What the Americans did not know was that there were already 158 nuclear weapons – five types – in Cuba when the naval blockade came into force. Fortunately they were not all ready for operational use. Washington was also unaware that about 100 tactical nuclear weapons had remained in Cuba after the ships returned. The USA knew nothing about the FKR-1 cruise missiles and the gravity bombs for the Ilyushin-28 bombers. These were only removed at the end of 1962. These facts were revealed 30 years later by the former Soviet general, Anatoly Gribkov. The whole operation was commanded by General Issa Pliyev. He was a senior Soviet officer and was authorised to use the weapons – no further approval required – if the Americans invaded Cuba.

The most dangerous moment during the whole drama had nothing to do with the number or explosive force of the nuclear warheads. It turned on a lack of communication.

Four Soviet submarines accompanied the freighters bound for Cuba for their protection. As a result of the big American naval blockade off Cuba, the submarines were unable to surface at the prearranged times in order to communicate with Moscow. They were completely in the dark about the game of military chess that Kennedy and Khrushchev were playing and had to rely on American radio stations for the latest (rather biased) information.

401

> One of the submarines, the B-59, was detected by the American fleet with the aid of sonar. On 27 October the USS Beale started dropping small depth charges to try to force the submarine to surface. The Soviet submarine fleet would have regarded this as the greatest possible humiliation. Captain Valentin Savitsky did not know that they were purely practice rounds and assumed that war had already broken out. He decided to fire a torpedo with a 10-kiloton nuclear warhead at the flagship, USS Randolf. The true nature of the torpedo was only known to a few senior officers on board the B-59. The torpedo was referred to as a "special weapon". According to the rules, to use the "special weapon" the captain only needed the permission of his second-in-command. Savitsky reportedly boasted at the top of his voice that they would protect the honour of their illustrious fleet. But, as luck would have it, the flotilla commander was also on board. As senior officer, Vasili Arkhipov had to authorise the firing of the torpedo and he was not willing to do so. He was afraid of the consequence if the USS Randolf disappeared in a vapour. His orders were that the B-59 should surface and surrender. When they did so they were taken wholly by surprise by the reception they got. They were greeted by a jazz band on the deck of the American warship and mechanical assistance was offered. This was refused and the B-59 was accompanied to the other side of the naval blockade on its way back to base. When they returned home the sheepish crew members were berated as follows by a Soviet admiral: "It would have been better if you had gone down with your ship!"
>
> The story of the "man who saved the world" only became known 40 years later, after Vasili Arkhipov's death. He received no recognition in his own country – only humiliation.

Castro was furious about the Soviet withdrawal. At the very least he had wanted to retain the tactical weapons to protect his country from an invasion, but in the event he was powerless to do anything. Two years later the humiliated Khrushchev lost his premiership as a result of this debacle. John F. Kennedy, the young American president (who had only been in his post for a year), was acclaimed as the winner. His defence secretary, Robert McNamara, stated before Congress: "We faced that night the possibility of launching nuclear weapons and Khrushchev knew it, and that is the reason, and the only reason, why he withdrew those weapons."

The Wilson Center's Cold War International History Project recently made documents public concerning a discussion between Khrushchev and Novotný, the head of the Czechoslovakian Communist Party. This discussion took place on 30 October 1962. After the Soviet missiles had been discovered by the USA, Castro wrote an urgent letter to Khrushchev. The USA is going to attack within 24 hours, he wrote, and proposed that the USSR and Cuba should join forces to start a nuclear war against the USA immediately. Khrushchev was shocked: "Do you know what this means?" he wrote back. The Russian president was referring to all the American nuclear missiles in silos and the submarines which the USSR did not even know about: "What would we achieve by starting a war? Millions of people will die, in the USSR as well. Could we really consider something like that?"

Therefore, according to McNamara and Khrushchev, deterrence really won the day. But McNamara learned something else as well: "The record of the missile crisis is replete with examples of misinformation, misjudgment, miscalculation … Such errors are costly in conventional warfare. When they affect decisions relating to nuclear forces, they can result in the destruction of nations."

Jonathan Schell's book *The Gift of Time* quotes General Lee Butler, who was head of StratCom in his day, on the delicate balance between deterrence and planning for war:

> … (t)he goal – the wish, really – might be to prevent nuclear war, but the operational plan had to be to wage war. After all, actual nuclear "deterrence" – which is to say a mental state of restraint brought about by terror of annihilation – was nothing that we could bring about by ourselves. In the last analysis, it was up to the enemy whether he would be deterred or not. What both sides had to do in the meantime was plan for nuclear war. Wish and plan collided at every point – psychologically, intellectually, but, above all, operationally.

In his observation on the "balance of terror" in 1955, Churchill added the following: "The deterrent does not cover the case of lunatics or dictators in the mood of Hitler when he found himself in his final dugout. This is a blank."

This "blank" is applicable not only to "lunatics and dictators" but also to unforeseen events.

At the beginning of the nuclear arms race the opposing sides had to rely on bombers which had to be kept in the air day and night with their deadly cargo. In the nature of things there were numerous flying accidents at take-off and landing and especially during refuelling from tanker aircraft. American nuclear bombs fell from aircraft in the USA, Greenland, Spain, the Pacific Ocean and Britain – but fortunately never exploded. Some of these "broken arrows" (as the Americans euphemistically refer to them) are still missing. The secretive USSR naturally did not report such occurrences, but in view of their familiar lackadaisical attitude there must have been various similar incidents on their side. It doesn't take much imagination to visualise the consequences if one of these accidentally dropped bombs had exploded while tension was at its height during the Cold War.

In time, with the distribution of nuclear weapons to underground silos and submarines and aircraft carriers in all parts of the world, matters started to become more complex. The pilots of NATO countries stationed in the Netherlands, Germany and Italy and operating as part of their own air forces could still discharge American nuclear weapons on the enemy-of-the-day. It is a wonder that in the course of almost 70 years no submarine captain, after months at sea and far from home, has ever become deranged. Or that a vodka-befuddled Soviet officer has never issued the wrong instruction, or pressed the wrong button by mistake or misinterpreted an order. Let us not forget Valentin Savitsky, the captain of submarine B-59, whose role in the Cuban missile crisis was described above …

The 20th Air Force of the USA was the component responsible for dropping nuclear bombs on Japan. Since 1991 this unit has been in control of almost 450 Minuteman III intercontinental ballistic missiles equipped with nuclear warheads. These missiles are distributed among three bases, namely the F.E. Warren base (Wyoming), the Minot base (North Dakota) and the Malmstrom base (Montana). Each Minuteman III missile is able to carry three warheads with an explosive yield of between 300 and 500 kilotons of TNT.

In October 2013 the commander, Major-General Michael Carey, was discharged for drunkenness on a visit to Russia, and for spending time with "suspicious" Russian women. While well and truly under the influence Carey also blurted out that he was the man who safeguarded the world from war on a daily basis; he added that personnel under his command "have the worst morale of any airmen in the Air Force".

This last statement was borne out by a series of lapses. First 17 officers at the Minot base were disciplined and then the Malmstrom base failed a nuclear safety inspection in August 2013. During an investigation into drug abuse at the same base in January 2014 it was discovered by chance that

34 officers had cheated in a periodic examination. In February this number virtually doubled and in March it grew to about 100. Colonel Robert Stanley had to resign and nine officers were relieved of their commands.

One shudders at the thought of unqualified and dishonest operators with their fingers on the firing buttons. We know little about the Russian operators, except that they are noted for their lackadaisical attitude and obsolete equipment.

One has to agree with Charles Iklé, who has written numerous books on this subject over the years. Back in 1973 he published an article in *Foreign Affairs* entitled "Can nuclear deterrence last out the century?" The conclusion he reached was that the reason why so many decades have passed without a mushroom cloud has not been deterrence or other factors but purely luck – a kind of miracle really. One can only wonder whether something like sustainable miracles really exists. With the current problems in the Ukraine, Russia's threats to move nuclear weapons to the Crimea, NATO's re-evaluation of the role of nuclear weapons and the ambitious plans by the USA to modernise its nuclear arsenal, the biggest test for true miracles probably lies in the not too distant future. Since Eisenhower's 1953 reference to "two atomic colossi malevolently eyeing each other across a trembling world" things have changed in that we now have the further complication that nuclear-armed minions are also eyeing the colossi and each other – putting unbearable pressure on the sustainability of miracles.

The faceless enemy

In the USA daily information sessions are prepared to update the president on the global situation, with special reference to possible threats to the USA. In his article "The deafness before the storm" (*The New York Times*, 10 September 2012) Kurt Eichenwald refers to the most important information session of all for an American president, namely the one held on 6 August 2001. On this day President George W. Bush was informed about Osama bin Laden and his al-Qaeda group. A top secret report, compiled by several American intelligence agencies, was entitled: "Bin Laden determined to strike in the US." A little more than a month afterwards – on 11 September 2001 – the incidents took place that are now simply referred to as "9/11". Many questions have been asked and accusatory fingers pointed at the Bush administration for their omission to react to the report and the numerous other warnings that they received months in advance. Recently declassified reports on that harrowing period probably provide the answer: "But which state is behind it?" Bush kept asking.

In the years before 9/11 states waged war against each other. The enemy was known and localised and you could hit him with all the weapons you had. Although Bin Laden, who was the brain behind the attack, and 15 out of his 19 Arab shock troops came from Saudi Arabia – ironically America's best friend in the Arab world – this was a new kind of stateless war declared by a loose confederation of groups scattered across the Muslim world. They had strong roots in tribal Pakistan and Afghanistan where al-Qaeda originated during the Soviet invasion – with American funding. What unites these groups is a radical, militant Islamist ideology as well as a hatred for the USA and the West. They also have little tolerance for dissenting elements in their midst. This is evident from the recent barbaric acts of the Islamic State (IS or ISIL) in Iraq and Syria.

This new, unknown enemy can no longer be threatened or wiped out with nuclear weapons. A cudgel is useless against a swarm of annoying mosquitoes.

An even greater fear exists. Suppose the terrorists were to acquire their own nuclear weapon or sufficient fissile material to build their own bomb? When the Soviet Union collapsed in chaos in 1989, thousands of nuclear weapons were scattered throughout the former Soviet republics with no structures and mechanisms in place to ensure the control and safe custody of these weapons. In the Ukraine alone there were 1 068 nuclear warheads which were stored until 1994 before they were returned to Russia in exchange for the recognition of Ukrainian sovereignty. This chaos created the ideal opportunity for people or groups with evil intentions to gain control of the weapons. Apparently it did not happen (another miracle), but there may still be nuclear weapons concealed somewhere waiting for a scaled-up repetition of 9/11. There may even be a nuclear weapon or two for sale in Pakistan or North Korea. Who knows?

In the politically unstable Pakistan the powerful intelligence service, the ISI, maintains unholy alliances with numerous terrorist groups which are characterised by religious bigotry and short-term political opportunism. Some examples of this are the Lashkar-e-Taiba (directed against India); Tehrik-e-Taliban Pakistan (operating internally); the Haqqani network (against Western forces in Afghanistan); and al-Qaeda (externally directed). According to certain experts it is only a matter of time before nuclear weapons fall into the hands of one of these groups. Since 2009 the Pakistani Taliban has carried out three aggressive suicide attacks on Pakistani military installations. In October 2009 army headquarters in Rawalpindi were attacked, in May 2010 the Mehran naval base was hit and in August 2012 the Kamra air base was attacked. The latter incident was the fourth attack since 2007. In all these cases it is suspected that nuclear weapons were stored in or near the bases.

The USA is extremely concerned about the situation. Roger Cressey, a former deputy director charged with the prevention of terrorism, made the following statement on NBC News in August 2011: "It's safe to assume that planning for the worst-case scenario regarding Pakistan nukes has already taken place inside the U.S. government. This issue remains one of the highest priorities of the U.S. intelligence community and the White House."

It is no wonder that General Ashfaq Parvez Kayani, the former head of the Pakistan ISI, is convinced that the American incursion into Abbottabad to capture Osama bin Laden – just a kilometre from an important military base – was a trial run for hitting various locations simultaneously in order to get their hands on the Pakistani nuclear arsenal.

People with evil intentions would not necessarily have to hazard their lives to get hold of Pakistani nuclear bombs. They could do this in the USA. In 2007 air force ground staff at an air base in North Dakota loaded six cruise missiles with nuclear warheads onto a B-52 bomber in error, after which the B-52 took off for a base in Louisiana. Because it was a long weekend the consignment stood there for 36 hours without any direct guard. Admittedly the air base as a whole was under guard.

However, heavily guarded facilities can be breached. This happened in July 2012 at the Y-12 plant in Tennessee, one of the best-guarded locations in the USA where nuclear weapons are handled and about 300 to 400 tons of weapons-grade uranium are stored. Sister Megan Rice, a retired nun and peace activist (aged 82), caused a sensation. She and two elderly helpers passed unobserved through several high-tech security fences and past floodlights, hordes of security cameras and other sensors until they reached the heart of the plant. The almost 500 security guards at the plant were authorised to use lethal force if intruders were found in certain areas. When one of the guards, who had possibly just returned from dreamland, eventually reached the elderly trio they had long been engaged in energetically painting slogans and attacking the storage facility with hammers.

War can get dirty

In the approximately two decades during which terrorist groups like al-Qaeda have been targeting people, buildings, trains, aircraft and ships with terrifying consequences – of which 9/11 was probably the most spectacular – there has always been the fear that the next act might be a nuclear detonation. It is a long time since nuclear weapons were heavy, clumsy affairs. Today courier companies could deliver a small nuclear explosive device unawares in one of the millions of parcels they deliver daily. The weapon could also be among the thousands of items in the cargo hold of an unremarkable freighter lying at moorage or in one of the tens of thousands of shipping containers in a harbour – just waiting for a cellphone signal. At the nuclear security summit of March 2014 in The Hague, President Obama made the revealing remark that he was not afraid of Russia but that he did fear "a nuclear bomb in Manhattan".

This would be the ultimate terrorist attack. However, there is another stratagem which the terrorist groups have not yet resorted to and which is causing great alarm at present and that is the use of conventional explosives to spread radioactive material. This is referred to as a radiological or "dirty" bomb. This type of bomb does not necessarily require uranium or plutonium; any of the numerous radioactive isotopes used in trade, industry or medicine can be used. Even the nuclear waste generated as a by-product of energy production could be used.

Al-Qaeda are adept at stuffing motor cars or lorries with mixtures of ammonium nitrate (fertiliser), nitromethane (used in dragsters) and ordinary explosives and then setting them alight. There have been numerous such cases. The first assault on the World Trade Center (New York) in 1993 is one; the American embassies in Nairobi and Dar es Salaam fell victim in 1998; Istanbul was targeted in 2003 and the Danish embassy and the Marriott Hotel in Pakistan were hit in 2008. If radioactive material had been included in the cocktail of explosives, this would have greatly complicated rescue work and mopping up. Emergency services are usually not trained and equipped to handle radioactive contamination. This allows the terrorists to cash in on the psychological fear of invisible radiation and thereby extend the disruption and sow panic.

It is far easier to get hold of radioactive material than to obtain a nuclear weapon. Throughout the world control over radioactive sources is extremely poor. From 2010 to 2011 the IAEA recorded about 172 incidents worldwide in which nuclear or radioactive material went missing, was stolen or was smuggled. Today many countries have detection equipment at border posts and harbours, but the Director-General of the IAEA stated in October 2012 that smugglers of materials of this kind are becoming more professional and are able to evade detection measures.

Human carelessness and ignorance also play a part here. Several discarded cobalt-60 sources, used in hospitals and industry, have ended up in scrapyards and been melted down along with scrap iron. In 1987 metal poachers in Goiâna (Brazil) broke into an abandoned cancer clinic and stole a cesium-137 source. The double-encapsulated source was chopped open and 93 grams of cesium-137 in powder form were distributed to friends and anyone who wanted some. People smeared it onto their faces for fun because it glowed in the dark. Two hundred people were contaminated, 28 suffered severe radiation burns, four died and one person had to have an arm amputated. Several houses had to be demolished and in the course of clearing a scrapyard 3 500 cubic metres of contaminated material had to be removed. The release of such a small amount of radioactive material (weighing about as much as a small apple) therefore had widespread consequences. This is a shocking story but the crux of it is that poor control by the authorities led to this tragedy. Inadequate control is a worldwide phenomenon. Scrapyards are an ideal place for terrorists to obtain the material for a dirty bomb.

In the case of a big truck bomb the chemical explosion would cause the most direct fatalities and damage, but the disseminated radioactivity would result in large areas and potentially thousands of people having to be evacuated until, after extended specialised cleansing processes, everything had been decontaminated. There would therefore be few fatalities, but the bomb would have a huge impact. Imagine the consequences of such an attack on Wall Street in New York, the banking district in London or the EU headquarters in Brussels.

In countries like the USA plans have been in place for some time and regular training sessions are held on dealing with the consequences of a dirty bomb. In the early months of 2010 before the Soccer World Cup tournament a South African team was specially trained by the USA to handle a situation of this kind.

The world has changed

With the advent of globalisation deterrence has undergone a mutation and also taken on a more subtle economic tinge. Today the USA is more concerned about China's economic power than about the Chinese nuclear arsenal. For over a decade China recorded large trade surpluses and foreign investments began streaming in. In order to prevent the value of its monetary unit from rising and thereby adversely affecting exports, China began to buy American dollars. Despite this trade surpluses continued to rise, with an accompanying rise in dollar reserves. These reserves chiefly take the form of US government (treasury) bonds, which are already worth over three trillion dollars. Government bonds are a method by which governments borrow money: the government (in this case the USA) undertakes to repay a specific amount plus interest on a certain date. Compare the 2015 American national debt of more than 18 trillion dollars with what China already owns – the more you owe your creditor, the stronger his hold over you.

When the Kremlin turns off the taps to prevent its vast natural oil and gas reserves from reaching Europe (as has happened in the Ukraine), much of Europe will be paralysed and will succumb to the freezing winters. Destruction could be accomplished without a single city being destroyed by a nuclear bomb. The European Union gets over one-third of its gas and about 30% of its oil from Russia. In the case of the strongest regional economy, Germany, the share is even larger: 36% of the gas and 39% of the oil come from Russia. Supplies could be shut off overnight. The energy dependence of the European Union was the reason why its members could not react too strongly when Russia invaded the Crimean Peninsula in March 2014.

Globalisation has made things immeasurably more complex. In the United Kingdom the chief suppliers of electricity are two firms, E.ON and RWE, both of which belong to the enemy of 70 years previously, namely Germany.

What better deterrent than to threaten to turn off the gas taps or switch off the power?

"Global (no?) zero"

After the collapse of the USSR the hostility that marked the Cold War began to diminish and classic deterrence slowly lost its prominence for the two powerful opponents. This has enabled a considerable mutual reduction in the number of nuclear weapons over the past decade. Thanks to the Strategic Arms Reduction Treaties (START) between the USA and Russia, the number of nuclear weapons has been reduced by literally tens of thousands. START I was signed in 1991 and lapsed in 2009. It bound the two powers to deploy a total of no more than 6 000 nuclear warheads on 1 600 ballistic missiles and bombers. In 2011 its successor, New START, came into operation. This provides that the total number of nuclear warheads may not amount to more than 3 100 over a period of seven years, deployed on 1 400 ballistic missiles and bombers. (Provision is also made for reserves.) The START treaties have therefore brought about a considerable reduction, namely from tens of thousands to thousands of weapons.

However, as of mid-2015, the estimate is that there are still approximately 15 850 nuclear weapons left. Of these, 4 300 are deployed with 1 800 on high alert. The remaining weapons are either in military stockpiles or are retired awaiting dismantling.

However, these numbers only relate to strategic weapons, that is long-range weapons with enormous explosive power – usually megatons – which are capable of wiping out cities, industrial complexes and big military bases. There is a large number of non-strategic nuclear warheads (usually known as tactical warheads and intended for short-range battlefield use) which are not affected by the START initiatives. Since 1991 the USA has destroyed more than 90% of its non-strategic nuclear warheads, but has withheld an unknown number to make provision for supplying its European allies with a deterrent. The Russians have dismantled more than 75% of the weapons in this category, but have withheld an unknown number to oppose NATO and protect their borders with China.

In December 2008 an international initiative for the complete elimination of nuclear weapons was launched in Paris by about 100 prominent people, including former presidents, prime ministers, politicians, religious and military leaders. Former president F.W. de Klerk and Archbishop Desmond Tutu were among their number. The movement was optimistically christened Global Zero. The next year, on 1 April, Presidents Obama and Medvedev met and committed their countries to a "nuclear-free world". Four days later a very inexperienced President Obama stated euphorically in Prague:

> So today, I state clearly and with conviction America's commitment to seek the peace and security of a world without nuclear weapons.
>
> I'm not naive. This goal will not be reached quickly – perhaps not in my lifetime. (…) But now we, too, must ignore the voices who tell us the world cannot change. We have to insist. Yes, we can.

How has that translated into practice? Just four years later the same President Obama submitted his 2012 budget for nuclear weapons – $7.6 billion, that is US$ 363 million up from 2011. The Congressional Budget Office estimate (2015) is that the weapons modernisation plans will cost almost US$ 350 billion over the coming decade, but the James Martin Center for Nonproliferation Studies claims that the total bill could be as much as US$ 1 trillion over the coming three decades.

President Vladimir Putin announced in July 2015 that Russia would add more than 40 new intercontinental ballistic missiles (ICBM) to its nuclear arsenal and added that Moscow will not be drawn into a new arms race although Russia is modernising its armed forces. Putin said that by 2020, 70% of the military equipment in use would be top quality and of the latest design.

The Global Zero group calculates that the nine states that currently have nuclear weapons will spend about US$ 1 trillion (1 000 000 000 000 000 000) on these weapons in the next decade. In difficult economic times this is an indication of a strong political will to retain and modernise nuclear weapons (and in some cases increase them) rather than to destroy them.

Global Zero has the appearance of an idealistic slogan thought up by well-meaning people, but as with so many other pipe dreams, it has been no match for harsh reality. It now seems probable that the time line for Global Zero will be measured in light years rather than years.

Major-General Garrett Harencak, the deputy chief of staff of the American air force charged with strategic deterrence and nuclear integration, may have summed up the dream of Global Zero very well in 2013. In a speech on final nuclear disarmament he said in Washington: "I hope that day comes. I hope that day comes soon. And when it does, I want to invite you all over to my house for a party. I'd just ask that you don't feed any of the hors d'oeuvres to my unicorn."

Nuclear weapons: states that have them and those that want them

Despite possessing nuclear weapons, states that have become involved in wars since the Second World War have effectively lost most of them or else the outcomes have been undecided: Britain in Suez; France in Algeria; the USSR in Afghanistan; and the US in Vietnam, Afghanistan and Iraq. Having nuclear weapons therefore does not necessarily translate into success in skirmishes with non-nuclear-weapon states. In the USA nuclear weapons no longer play a dominant military role. The focus is consequently on strong US conventional forces and well-stocked and staffed military bases all over the globe or in conjunction with NATO forces and others.

Russia, on the other hand, can no longer rely on the support of the surrounding pre-1991 Soviet republics, of which the Ukraine is a good example, and feels at a disadvantage in relation to the NATO allies. The Russian state believes that until it can reach parity in conventional forces, its tactical nuclear weapons are vital deterrents. The USA apparently thinks Putin means business with his nuclear sabre-rattling because, as indicated above, the Russians are putting a lot of effort into upgrading and modernising certain classes of nuclear weapons and delivery systems.

China has possessed nuclear weapons for a long time and is currently expanding its missile programmes and building nuclear submarines and aircraft carriers. In the past China's attitude towards nuclear weapons has been ambivalent, but the Chinese take a long view of life which Westerners find difficult to understand. The USA is already reinforcing its fleet in that part of the world and constructing listening stations in Australia.

The small numbers of nuclear weapons that Great Britain and France possess play a subordinate part in their military strategies, but cost a lot of money. Their small arsenals are examples of fossilised Cold-War thinking, neither substantially increasing nor decreasing quantitively or qualitatively and with no clear-cut policy as to the continuing relevance of their nuclear capabilities.

They have recently ended years of secrecy by disclosing the size of their nuclear arsenals. In June 2012 the British announced that they would reduce their 160 active nuclear weapons to 120 and that the total stock would be limited to 180. The active nuclear weapons are carried in Trident ballistic missiles on four submarines based in Scotland. In the absence of direct enemies as in the days of the Cold War, it seems likely that the British nuclear capability will die a natural death, since the four submarines are obsolete and replacement would cost billions at a time when Britain is experiencing a financial squeeze.

Former president Nicolas Sarkozy of France announced in 2008 that France had less than 300 nuclear warheads to serve as its "insurance policy". The French have four submarines carrying sixteen ballistic missiles with nuclear warheads, but they also have bombers, a flagship and three ground installations. Former ministers of defence and retired senior military officers have on occasion criticised the arsenal as "belonging to the Cold War" and as "a very expensive absurdity".

It might just be a question of time before these two countries take shelter under the American "nuclear umbrella" and give up their obsolete nuclear weapons, but this would make it unlikely that the Americans would reduce their nuclear arsenal to any great degree.

Among the newcomers to the nuclear weapons scene, India has a strong economy and its nuclear weapons fall under civilian rather than military control. The nuclear arsenal is seen as a psychological deterrent and a way of preventing potential attacks by China and especially Pakistan. India has not signed the NPT and is therefore not bound by its provisions. India has probably decided that its nuclear arsenal (estimated at about 100 nuclear weapons) is adequate and no significant expansion is expected in this area.

Pakistan is a poor country which has been under military rule for years and is furthermore in cahoots with ideologically driven religious groups. United by a hatred of India and the West, Pakistan's greatest aspiration is to outdo India in respect of its stockpile of nuclear weapons and missiles. Pakistan also has a history of coups d'état and assassinations of civil and military leaders. It is a highly unstable country and is home to several terrorist groups with their eye on the country's nuclear arsenal. Anything is possible.

Apart from its nuclear deterrent, Israel has strong conventional forces. None of Israel's neighbours possesses nuclear weapons and with the prevailing chaos in the Arab world a nuclear threat seems unlikely, unless Iran were to develop nuclear weapons despite concerted international efforts to prevent this.

North Korea is an unknown factor. The North Koreans have already notched up a few low-key nuclear explosions, which experts think were unsuccessful. The normally secretive country invited Siegfried Hecker and two colleagues from Los Alamos to visit a plant in November 2011. They were astonished to see a brand-new, medium-sized uranium enrichment plant that was clearly using advanced technology. Hecker suspects that there is more than one plant of this kind in North Korea, probably to produce weapons-grade uranium for nuclear weapons. It is unclear what the intentions of this unusual country are, but they probably boil down to a porcupine strategy aimed at its South Korean neighbours and their powerful backer, the USA. The North Korean nuclear programme could also serve as a mechanism for attempting to extort financial and other aid from the USA – as has happened in the past.

Among those states interested in the bomb, there has been sharp focus on the Iranians, who nevertheless deny that they have any interest in nuclear weapons. Much of the world believes that Iran is deliberately engaged in building such weapons. Iran does not require nuclear weapons as a defence against its Arab neighbours, which do not possess such weapons, but sees it as its mission, according to several leading Iranians, to rid the world of Israel. The situation is more complex, however. Iran is surrounded by about a quarter of a million American soldiers, stationed in the north-east in several former Soviet states, in the east in Afghanistan, next door in Iraq and at various locations around the Persian Gulf. There are also another four neighbouring states with strong American ties, namely Turkey, Saudi Arabia, Pakistan and Israel. Two of these neighbours possess nuclear weapons. It may well appear logical to Iran to use the existing enrichment facilities to build its own nuclear weapons, if necessary. Although there are indications that Iran's activities in the past probably went beyond mere uranium enrichment, the ability to enrich uranium is a deterrent in itself.

A number of alarming discoveries in the early 2000s cast considerable doubt on Iran's compliance with the NPT and the Comprehensive Safeguards Agreement signed more than 40 years ago. Traces of highly enriched uranium were discovered by IAEA inspectors on gas centrifuge equipment. Iran had never declared enriching uranium to that level. This mystery was solved when Iran admitted that the contaminated equipment had been obtained from Pakistan through the good offices of A.Q. Khan. Next, a laptop computer that had been smuggled out of Iran fell into the hands of the USA towards the middle of 2004. The following year the USA gave a presentation of material found on the laptop to an assembly of foreign diplomats. Iran had apparently been involved in weaponisation studies, including specialised high-explosive testing and the design of a nuclear warhead for use in missiles. To this day Iran has denied the existence of such activities and prohibited access to the relevant sites. To complicate matters further, Western intelligence identified an undeclared, well-hidden underground enrichment facility at Fordow. This was acknowledged by Iran in 2009, three years after the building started.

During most of this time the abrasive Mahmoud Ahmadinejad was the president of Iran and interaction with the IAEA and the EU-3 (the UK, France and Germany), who tried to put pressure on Iran to come clean on its intentions and actions, came to nothing. Instead, in 2006 Ahmadinejad announced defiantly that Iran had successfully enriched uranium to 3,5%.

The Board of Governors of the IAEA ruled in November 2003 that Iran had been in non-compliance with its safeguards agreement but deferred reporting this to the UN Security Council – as required by the IAEA's statute – until February 2006. In the following years a raft of UNSC resolutions were passed: the UNSC demanded that Iran suspend enrichment, instituted sanctions against entities and persons in Iran and in addition imposed a complete arms embargo and asset freeze.

An aggravating factor, which influenced the series of unproductive interactions, was tension between Iran and the USA after the 1979 revolution and the seizure of American diplomats, who were held captive for 444 days, and the leading role the USA played in rolling out the UNSC sanctions.

In 2006 a group of six countries joined forces in an effort to approach Iran on a diplomatic level. The group known as the P5+1 (the five UNSC permanent members, namely the USA, the UK, France, Russia and China, together with Germany) then began active engagement in talks.

The election of the more moderate Hassan Rouhani as president in June 2013 was a chance to make a new start in the years of wrangling over Iran's nuclear programme. Unlike his populist predecessor, Rouhani favoured a more diplomatic and pragmatic style. He also had wide experience. Between 2003 and 2005 he had been Iran's chief negotiator. Reuters reported on 25 November 2013 that even before Rouhani became president, the USA and Iran had started secret talks back in March 2013 – behind Ahmadinejad's back. Ali Akbar Salehi, the then minister of foreign affairs, risked his life to obtain the permission of the supreme leader, Ayatollah Ali Khamenei, to negotiate with the arch-enemy and to report directly to Khamenei.

It was as a result of the secret negotiations that Iran's formal discussions in Geneva with the P5+1 (under the leadership of Catherine Ashton, the EU's head of foreign policy) produced the first positive result at 04:30 on a cold, wet Sunday morning on 24 November 2013. It was agreed that Iran would stop or curtail certain nuclear activities if in exchange the financial sanctions to which it was subject were mitigated and the country was permitted to export higher volumes of oil.

This agreement officially came into operation on 20 January 2014. The terms were that for the following six months Iran undertook not to enrich uranium to more than 5%, to downgrade its stock of 20% enriched uranium, to uncouple almost half of its 16 000 gas centrifuges, to discontinue work on the Arak heavy-water reactor and to permit more extensive IAEA inspections, some of which would even be carried out on a daily basis at certain facilities.

The agreement was hailed as a "big breakthrough" by the Americans, but was immediately described as a "big mistake" by the Israeli prime minister. The concessions made by Iran were not irreversible; they were only valid for six months and Israel also felt that Iran could swiftly reconnect its plants and go on producing bomb material. The Israelis wanted to prevent Iran from getting to that point and were prepared to carry out their own preventive "surgical" attacks on Iranian plants. That was the euphemism used by the minister of defence, Ehud Barak. The prime minister, Benjamin Netanyahu, in an interview with the French magazine *Paris Match* in October 2010, described the reaction to any such possible attacks as follows: "Five minutes later, contrary to what sceptics think, I believe there will be a great feeling of relief throughout the region. Iran is not popular in the Arab world, far from it."

However, in a White House press release of 23 November 2013 the temporary nature of the "breakthrough" was emphasised: "As part of a comprehensive solution, Iran must also come into full compliance with its obligations under the Nuclear Non-Proliferation Treaty (NPT) and its obligations to the IAEA. With respect to the comprehensive solution, nothing is agreed until everything is agreed. Put simply, this first step expires in six months, and does not represent an acceptable end state to the United States or our P5+1 partners."

Ongoing negotiations between the P5+1 and Iran towards finding a "comprehensive solution" finally resulted in an agreement, after a series of marathon sessions in Vienna, on 14 July 2015.

The conditions of the agreement include the following:
- Iran will reduce its enrichment capacity by two-thirds and will stop using its underground facility at Fordow.
- Iran's stockpile of low-enriched uranium (LEU) will be reduced by 98% to 300 kg by diluting it or shipping it out of the country and kept at that level for 15 years.
- The core of the heavy-water reactor in Arak will be removed and redesigned so that it cannot produce significant amounts of plutonium. Iran will not build additional heavy-water reactors for 15 years.
- Iran will allow UN inspectors to enter sites, including military sites, when the inspectors have grounds to believe undeclared nuclear activity is being carried out there. Continuous surveillance of centrifuge manufacturing and storage facilities will take place.
- A separate IAEA work plan requires verification that Iran has taken steps to shrink its programme. Only then will UN, US and EU sanctions be

lifted. The plan includes clarification of past activities associated with "possible military dimensions" by the end of 2015.
- Restrictions on trade in conventional weapons will continue for another five years, and eight years in the case of ballistic missile technology.
- If there are allegations that Iran has not met its obligations, a joint commission will seek to resolve the dispute for 30 days. If that effort fails the matter will be referred to the UN security council, which would have to vote on whether to continue sanctions relief. A veto by a permanent member would mean that sanctions are reimposed (snap-back sanctions).

The UNSC passed a resolution in July 2015 incorporating the agreement and its five annexes but it would be another 90 days before it entered into force, giving the US Congress and the Iranian Majlis (parliament) the opportunity to review and approve the agreement.

As might be expected, not everybody is happy with the outcome, particularly because after 15 years Iran will be able to produce as much fuel as it wishes and in the meantime research on improving centrifuge technology can continue, so that more isotope separation can be achieved with fewer centrifuges. When the agreement expires in 2025, Iran could have an industrial-level nuclear programme in place.

So does this agreement give President Obama his desired "legacy" and simply defer the day of a Middle East nuclear conflict to the next generation?

Israel has called the agreement a "historic mistake" that will create "a terrorist nuclear superpower". Sunni Arabian neighbours are troubled as well. They do not trust Shiite Iran. Saudi Arabia regards Iran as the driver of much of the violence that is shaking the Arab world at present and when funds become available through sanctions relief, the fear is that Iran could significantly increase its military strength.

Back in 2009 King Abdullah of Saudi Arabia told Dennis Ross, an envoy of President Obama's in the Middle East: "If Iran gets a nuclear weapon, we will get a nuclear weapon." The wealthy Saudi Arabia is known to provide substantial support to Pakistan's defence industry. According to the BBC, the former Israeli head of military intelligence, Amos Yadlin, made the following statement in October 2013: "They already paid for the bomb, they will go to Pakistan and bring what they need to bring."

There are even rumours at present that Israel and Saudi Arabia, along with some of the United Arab Emirates, have begun cooperating in secret to neutralise Iran. Strange bedfellows …

Japan is a dark horse. Since Hiroshima and Nagasaki there have always been strong anti-nuclear sentiments in Japan. Around 2010, however, two successive prime ministers openly began to discuss the possibility of developing nuclear weapons to counterbalance the nuclear weapons of neighbouring countries (China and North Korea). In 2012 the Japanese Nuclear Energy Act was amended by the inclusion of the term "national security" as one of the objectives of the Act. This made the neighbouring countries sit up. Japan has already collected about 10 tons of weapons-grade plutonium locally as a result of previous reprocessing campaigns. The Rokkasho reprocessing plant will shortly become fully operational. Japan is the only non-nuclear-weapon state that reprocesses its spent nuclear fuel itself. The plant at Rokkasho has the capacity to extract 8 tons of weapons-grade plutonium per year from spent nuclear fuel. That is sufficient for about 1 000 nuclear warheads. In addition Japan has a uranium enrichment plant that has been operating for years. Although the Japanese have always been strong supporters of the NPT, it is quite possible that if they feel seriously threatened by neighbouring countries they could withdraw from the NPT one day. The treaty makes provision for this. Then there would be no bar to their building local nuclear weapons. The obstacle to overcome in undertaking a nuclear weapons programme has always been the availability of fissile material. Japan has tons of this and also possesses the means to produce it rapidly.

Unholy curiosity

Referring to man's interest in science, Einstein spoke of "a holy curiosity". Unfortunately, the reverse side of the coin is man's unholy interest in the affairs of others. The reformer, Martin Luther, complained almost 500 years ago when his letters were opened and read by the Duke of Saxony: "A thief is a thief, whether he is a money thief or a letter thief."

In the past governments had so-called "black chambers" or secret rooms in post offices where mail was opened and read. One of the most efficient of these systems was the black chamber in Austria under Metternich's reign as chancellor in the 1880s. Bags of diplomatic mail arrived at 07:00. The letters were then unsealed and read, the important parts copied, sometimes by dictation, and finally the letters would be replaced, resealed and sent to the various embassies by 09:30. Owing to pressure of time the employees sometimes made mistakes, however. When the British ambassador to Austria complained that he was actually receiving copies instead of the original documents, Metternich did not apologise but blamed the overworked staff instead: "How clumsy these people are!"

Today, it has become much easier "to read other people's mail" by intercepting electromagnetic waves moving freely through the air between cellphone towers, bounced from communication satellites, or by tapping international cable systems which interconnect continents.

The world was aghast in 2013 when Edward Snowden revealed the extent of the American National Security Agency's unbridled eavesdropping on the communications of foes and friends. It transpired that, among others, the surveillance targeted three German chancellors, three French presidents, more than 30 heads of state and even the secretary-general of the UN – and potentially every ordinary citizen with a cellphone or an email address. In this endeavour the NSA was enthusiastically and ably supported by the British Government Communications Headquarters (GCHQ).

Furthermore, using this new international connectivity, the authorities were able to carry out even blacker deeds such as waging cyber war. A computer worm named Stuxnet that was reportedly created by the USA and Israel, according to *The New York Times* of 1 June 2012, was able to take over control of electromechanical processes. Stuxnet was specifically aimed at the Iranian enrichment plants and was apparently able to destroy almost 20% of the gas centrifuges by causing them to spin much faster than the design value.

Mischief in the misuse of modern interconnectivity is of course not limited to formal government agencies. Hackers, ranging from bored teenagers to groups of dedicated troublemakers, are also using this new technological wonder to simply annoy people or purposefully break into data systems to steal vast amounts of money or sensitive information. Hackers, believed to be from China, have been obtaining access to US government databases since 2014 and have stolen sensitive personal information from the background checks of more than 20 million individuals.

In November 2014 hackers infiltrated Sony Pictures' servers to wipe computers clean and release sensitive data and embarrassing emails as well as publish the salaries of top executives. The FBI said the North Korean government wanted to prevent the studio from releasing *The Interview*, a film that satirised the leader Kim Jong-un. Sony had to spend at least US$ 15 million on repairing the damage.

A more ominous scenario was outlined in May 2015 by General James Cartwright, former commander of the US nuclear forces. "Our nuclear missiles could be hacked – launched and detonated without authorization," Cartwright said at a function. There are only two realities in the modern, interconnected world, he warned: "You've either been hacked and are not admitting it, or you're being hacked and don't know it."

Half of US and Russian strategic arsenals are continuously maintained at high alert, meaning that 1 800 warheads could be launched within three to five minutes. Silos containing ballistic missiles were designed many years ago to withstand nuclear blasts, but the designers did not envisage that the US agencies in charge of nuclear weapons would later have to withstand a reported 10 million hacking attempts on a daily basis. Is it possible that nuclear war could break out because an ICBM was maliciously launched by a hacker?

International treaties and disarmament

The considerable reduction in the number of nuclear weapons by the great powers in recent decades has been the result of bilateral treaties and, ironically, has not taken place in accordance with the NPT, which is the only existing multilateral treaty in which nuclear disarmament is one of the most important elements. In 1995 the non-nuclear-weapon states that were members of the NPT consented to the indefinite extension of the treaty in exchange for certain concessions by the nuclear-weapon states. These included the acceptance of the so-called principles and objectives for nuclear non-proliferation and disarmament. The requirements were the following:

- The finalisation by the UN's Conference on Disarmament (CD) before 1996 of the text of the Comprehensive Nuclear-Test-Ban Treaty (CTBT) – which formally bans all nuclear tests.
- The immediate commencement of negotiations in the CD, and the rapid completion of those negotiations, to compile a treaty banning the production of fissile material for use in weapons.
- Resolute efforts by the nuclear-weapon states to reduce nuclear weapons systematically, with the ultimate purpose of eliminating such weapons completely and eventually introducing complete disarmament under strict international control.

The negotiations on the establishment of the CTBT did take place in time. An organisation to monitor the implementation of the treaty was created in Vienna, Austria, with the object of determining by means of seismic, hydroacoustic (sound waves in the oceans), radioactive and infrasound measurements (low-frequency sound waves) whether a nuclear test has taken place anywhere on earth. This monitoring organisation is functioning well and has monitoring stations in all parts of the world (including South Africa). Unfortunately, by 2015 almost two decades later, the treaty has not yet entered into force. Only 36 of the 44 countries whose ratification is required for the treaty to enter into force, have done so. The eight outstanding states are China, North Korea, Egypt, India, Iran, Israel, Pakistan and, yes, the USA. Furthermore, the USA and Russia have since carried out dozens of so-called subcritical tests that do not lead to nuclear explosions but that can be used to improve weapons. These actions are against the spirit of the treaty. Egypt will not ratify the treaty if Israel does not do so as well; Israel will not do so unless Iran agrees to do the same; and Pakistan and India firmly refuse to ratify the treaty unilaterally. The future of the CTBT and the organisation responsible for monitoring – with an annual budget of more than 120 million dollars – is unknown. In all probability this treaty will never enter into force.

The story of the treaty to compel states to stop producing fissile material – the Fissile Material Cut-off Treaty (FMCT) – is even sadder than that of the CTBT. Twenty-two years after the FMCT was first mooted, negotiations at the Conference on Disarmament (CD) in Geneva have not even started. There is a bizarre reason for this. Negotiations at the CD with its 65 members take place on the basis of consensus and for two decades one country – which is not even a signatory to the NPT – has been refusing to allow negotiations to begin. That country is Pakistan, which has even blocked a decision on a working programme. In October 2012 the Pakistani ambassador, Zamir Akram, made the following remark at the UN: "If there is no consensus on negotiating FMCT, there is also no consensus on negotiating nuclear disarmament, negative security assurances or PAROS (prevention of an outer space arms race)."

This means that the world is being held hostage and any possibility of establishing an FMCT has receded over the horizon.

The systematic reduction in the number of nuclear weapons by the nuclear-weapon states with the ultimate goal of eliminating such weapons completely and placing the eventual complete disarmament under strict international controls has also remained a dream. The nuclear-weapon states that enjoy a special status under the NPT are not going to relinquish that status and have subtly come up with a new euphemism. Instead of the negative word "deterrence" they are using the expression "strategic stability". And who would want to agitate against stability?

Black swans and nuclear power

In former years the expression "rare bird" or "rara avis" (*rara avis in terris, nigroque simillima cygno*) was widely used to refer to anything considered very unusual. It means "a rare bird on earth, very like a black swan". The Europeans all knew that the graceful swans they were familiar with were white.

In 1696 the Dutch East India Company (VOC) instructed one of its sea captains, Willem de Vlamingh, to go and search for a richly laden ship which had disappeared on the way to Batavia in 1609 carrying 325 passengers. The *Ridderschap van Holland* was presumed to have been wrecked, possibly on the west coast of Nieuw Holland, the present-day Australia. De Vlamingh found no trace of the lost ship, but in the vicinity of what is now Perth he came across something "impossible" – black swans in a river which he immediately named the Zwaanenrivier.

From that day onwards the term "black swan" has acquired the meaning of some highly unexpected event, especially with reference to Nassim Nicholas Taleb's book *The Black Swan – the Impact of the Highly Improbable* (Random House: 2007). According to him black swan events are marked by three characteristics: rarity outside the context of historical knowledge or expectations; consequences that cannot be calculated in advance owing to the low probability of the events; and the tendency to rationalise the event in retrospect as if it could have been predicted.

Typical black swan events of the recent past are the 9/11 attacks on various targets in the USA and the so-called Arab Spring which began on 17 December 2010 when a fruit seller in Tunisia set himself alight after a police officer had confiscated his fruit. This was the fuse that started a wildfire in the Arab world and led, among other things, to the fall of governments and of dictators who had ruled for decades, such as Hosni Mubarak in Egypt and Gaddafi in Libya. The wildfire in that part of the world is in fact still burning.

The black swan day for nuclear power was 11 March 2011, when the Tohoku earthquake struck Japan. Four nuclear reactors at Fukushima Daiichi were destroyed – not by the earthquake but by the aftermath of gigantic tsunamis.

The Fukushima disaster

Early in March 2011 there were 19 nuclear power plants in various parts of Japan, with 63 nuclear reactors. Two reactors were no longer in operation and four new ones were under construction. Five of the nuclear power plants were situated on the north-east coast of Japan's largest island, Honchu: Fukushima Daiichi (6 reactors); Fukushima Daini (4 reactors); Higashidori (1 reactor); Onagawa (3 reactors); and Tokai Daini (1 reactor).

The Fukushima Daiichi reactors were commissioned between 1971 and 1979. Units 1 to 5 were first-generation boiling water reactors of American design – therefore using mainly late-1960s technology – while unit 6 was built according to an improved design. These reactors gave good service for between 30 and 40 years and even survived unscathed after the Miyagi earthquake in 1978 (7.7 on the Richter scale).

But at 14:46 on 11 March 2011 Japan was hit by the biggest earthquake it had ever suffered. The epicentre was just over 100 km east of Fukushima in the Pacific Ocean and the quake lasted a full three minutes. Later measurements place the Tohoku earthquake at a monstrous reading of 9 on the Richter scale, one of the 16 biggest earthquakes in the world since 1900.

As a result of the earthquake, the five reactors in the five nuclear power plants in the area shut down automatically, as they were designed to do. Even if the chain reaction in the nuclear fuel comes to a halt, the nuclear fuel rods are still physically very hot and must be cooled by continuously circulating cooling water. The earthquake cut off the electricity supply to the reactors from outside, but to make provision for such an event each reactor has diesel generators to supply emergency power. The situation immediately after the earthquake was that the reactors in the area had shut down automatically and the reactor cores were being cooled with the aid of the available emergency power.

For about 40 minutes after the earthquake everything appeared to be under control, but a minute later the first tidal wave (tsunami) of seven struck the Fukushima Daiichi power plant. The tidal wave was about 4 metres high. Because of Japan's history of earthquakes, the design made provision for the plant to withstand tidal waves of 5.7 metres. Eight minutes later a tidal wave of unknown height washed over the plant. Marks left on buildings showed afterwards that at least one of the tidal waves must have been 14 to 15 metres high – almost three times the design value. The buildings and the emergency generators in the basements flooded, the intake points for coolant water from the sea were blocked by debris and 51 minutes after the earthquake there was a complete loss of power to the cooling pumps of units 1 to 5 (units 5 and 6 had been switched off for maintenance and refuelling, but cooling was still required for the spent fuel in the storage pools).

Temperatures in the reactor cores were very high and in time the lack of coolant caused the zirconium casings of the fuel rods to react with the available water at the high temperature and produce hydrogen gas. Despite heroic efforts to cool the reactors from the outside and as a result of a complex chain of circumstances, the pressure in the reactors rose until it was decided to open the safety valves to relieve the pressure. Hydrogen gas collected in the upper sections of the reactor buildings and between 12 and 15 March hydrogen explosions destroyed most of the buildings of units 1 to 4. On 20 March units 5 and 6 were declared to have been safely shut down.

The decompression of the reactors and the explosions also caused the release of radioactivity into the air. Residents within 20 km of the nuclear power plant were evacuated and those between 20 and 30 km away were told to remain indoors. The immense disruption caused by the events is still vividly remembered by most people, thanks to the dramatic media coverage.

The 1906 earthquake in San Francisco, which registered about 8 on the Richter scale, is remembered as "The Great Fire" on account of the huge fires that broke out following damage to gas pipes. Few people who lived through those events remembered them as a destructive earthquake. Despite the fact that the Tohoku earthquake and tidal waves of 2011 destroyed 500 000 dwellings; left four million people without power for weeks; caused the death of 16 000 people (90% by drowning); left 4 000 people unaccounted for; and did immeasurable damage to roads, bridges and railway lines, it will be remembered mainly for the damage to the Fukushima Daiichi nuclear power plant and the accompanying release of radioactivity.

Emergency workers were inevitably exposed to radiation, but it was strictly controlled. Residents in the area were also exposed to radioactivity, but not a single person died as a result of radiologic damage. Naturally, long-term genetic damage has to be taken into account. Richard

> Garwin, a well-known nuclear expert in the USA, has estimated conservatively that over a period of 70 years there could be an additional 1 500 cancer cases in the area as a result of radiation. Professor Richard Muller of the University of California, Berkeley, illustrates in his book, Energy for Future Presidents: The Science Behind the Headlines, *that if Garwin's methodology is applied to a high-altitude city like Denver in the USA – known for its relatively high level of natural radiation – there would be an additional 5 000 cancer cases in that city, three times as high as the number Garwin calculates for Fukushima. Even if Garwin's assumptions are correct, the radiation consequences would be less than one-tenth of the immediate deaths as a result of the tidal waves – and furthermore they would be spread over a period of 70 years.*
>
> An interesting sidelight is provided by the famous British environmental activist, George Monbiot, who wrote the following in The Guardian:
>
>> You will not be surprised to hear that the events in Japan have changed my view of nuclear power. You will be surprised to hear how they have changed it. As a result of the disaster at Fukushima, I am no longer nuclear-neutral. I now support the technology. A crappy old plant with inadequate safety features was hit by a monster earthquake and a vast tsunami. The electricity supply failed, knocking out the cooling system. The reactors began to explode and melt down. The disaster exposed a familiar legacy of poor design and corner-cutting. Yet, as far as we know, no one has yet received a lethal dose of radiation.

Before the Fukushima Daiichi nuclear accident there were the Windscale accident in Britain (1957), the Three Mile Island accident in the USA (1979) and the biggest of all, namely the accident at Chernobyl in the Soviet Union (1986). The Windscale reactor was designed to produce plutonium and is therefore in a different class from Three Mile Island and Chernobyl, since those two facilities were built for generating electricity. Can these accidents also be seen as black swan events?

The accident at Three Mile Island (TMI) happened when a coolant water pump malfunctioned. The reactor shut off automatically according to plan but it still had to be cooled. Because there was too little coolant water the reactor overheated and the pressure began to build up. To prevent the pressure from building up too high, a safety valve opened. This valve was designed to close as soon as the pressure was relieved, but it did not do so. There was no alarm in the control room to warn the operators. The reactor operators began activating the special system which was designed to let emergency coolant water into the reactor, but steam and water sprayed out of the open safety valve. The water level in the reactor core began to drop, which exposed the fuel rods and caused about half the fuel to melt. The operators did not realise this and were under the impression that there was too much water in the reactor. As in the later Fukushima accident, hydrogen was also produced in the reaction between the zirconium alloy in the fuel rods and water, but it was contained in the reactor vessel where, in the absence of oxygen, it did not explode. The operators were eventually able to cool the overheated core. Radioactive water nevertheless reached the river nearby and radioactive gases were released. Fortunately this was confined by built-in filter systems. The reactor could not be used again, which was a big financial loss, but the radiation to which the public was exposed was very slight, less than one-sixth of the radiation produced by a chest X-ray and only about one-hundredth of the annual natural environmental radiation.

TMI was not a black swan event. After all, special systems are designed for reactors to counteract any loss of coolant water. It was therefore not unexpected. The molten core did not pass right through the earth until it got to China, as implied in the popular movie *The China Syndrome*. The accident did lead to improved instrumentation and procedures to give operators a better understanding of situations so that they can operate reactors safely. All it was, really, was a very expensive accident.

The Chernobyl accident was not a black swan event either. Without being flippant, this incident can be compared to what happens when a naughty little boy playing on his grandfather's farm prods a sleeping stud bull with a hay fork.

The fourth reactor at the Chernobyl nuclear power plant in the Ukraine had only been in service for two years. The RBMK reactors at that power plant were quite different from the Western designs. They were originally intended for plutonium production but had been adapted to generate electricity. The moderator was not water, but water-cooled graphite. Furthermore, the reactor was not protected by a Western-type containment building. Certain design features made the reactor unstable and unsafe. There was another problem as well …

As in all other reactors, the core still had to be cooled after the reactor had been shut down. An interruption in the circulation of the coolant water, as in the case of TMI and Fukushima, leads to overheating and damage to the core and therefore provision is always made for emergency cooling. At the Chernobyl reactor there was over a minute's difference between the power interruption and the provision of emergency power by diesel generators to keep the cooling pumps going. Several tests to determine what would happen to the reactor during this minute proved inconclusive and a further test was planned for 26 April 1986. For various reasons this test took place in the middle of the night when only junior staff were on duty. The experiment began at 01:23. Because of the unique features of the reactor and certain concurrent events that the operators did not understand, the core overheated and a few minutes later the reactor exploded – not a nuclear explosion but an ordinary steam explosion. It was so violent that the 2 000-ton steel plate over the reactor, to which the whole assembly was coupled, was blown into the air. The building was destroyed and because the glowing graphite was exposed to oxygen, it caught fire and the radioactivity that was released sent a spreading plume up to a kilometre into the atmosphere. Eyewitnesses described the explosion as similar to a kind of volcanic eruption. The burning graphite that shot up into the air fell onto rooftops and set buildings on fire.

The fire brigade was called in to put out an ordinary building fire. The firemen fought the fires in the midst of the radioactive rubble. By around 06:35 all the building fires had been put out. The reactor core of unit 4 continued to burn for several days, which naturally contributed to the emission of further radioactivity into the atmosphere.

In their customary manner, the Soviet authorities kept quiet about the accident, but they did send a commission headed by the internationally renowned Valery Legasov to investigate. The members of the commission arrived on the evening of 26 April and immediately realised the nature and extent of the accident. On Legasov's orders the residents of the nearby village of Pripyat were evacuated "for three days". In their haste they left their possessions behind – and they are still there today, because no one has ever been permitted live to in Pripyat again.

The outside world knew nothing about the accident until radiation alarms went off when an engineer tried to enter the Forsmark reactor in Sweden – about 1 000 km from Chernobyl. It was soon found that the radiation was coming from the soles of his shoes. It was thought at first that a nuclear bomb must have been tested somewhere and that this was the source of the contamination. Radiation levels were swiftly measured in other European countries and the radioactive cloud was even found to have spread as far as Japan and the USA. President Mikhail Gorbachev was forced to admit openly that a serious accident had taken place at Chernobyl.

During attempts to limit the further release of radioactivity, the army was called in to help cover the smouldering reactor with sand and lead and clear up the rubble. In all, 237 people contracted acute radiation sickness and 31 of them died within three months – mainly firemen and military personnel – the so-called "liquidators".

On 3 July the Politburo, consisting of Communist Party leaders, and the commission headed by Valery Legasov discussed the accident. The talks took place at the Kremlin. *Der Spiegel* subsequently got wind of some of the matters discussed and reported on 24 March 2011 that the deputy minister of energy, Shasharin by name, had admitted that they had always had doubts about the safety of the RBMK reactors. Because of strong opposition, however, these reservations were never documented. The opinion of the minister of energy, Anatoli Majorets, was that this type of reactor should not be used and that there had been a similar incident – fortunately without the same consequences – at an RBMK reactor in Leningrad back in 1975. Gorbachev labelled this "criminal negligence" and also referred to a "shocking lack of responsibility".

Despite this inside knowledge the blame was outwardly placed on the shoulders of the reactor operators. No finger could apparently be pointed at Soviet technology.

Legasov only spoke once at this meeting. He said that he had been preaching about the unsafe RBMK reactors for years but that his words had fallen on deaf ears. He was vehemently opposed to allowing the reactor operators to take all the blame, as the party leadership wanted to do.

Four months after the accident Legasov appeared before a meeting of the IAEA. He presented an in-depth and surprisingly frank report on the most serious nuclear accident that had ever occurred. The Soviet leaders found this candour unacceptable. On the second anniversary of the accident a conference was held in the Soviet Union on the causes and results of the Chernobyl disaster. Various experts were invited to participate in the debate. Legasov was not among them. On the following day, 27 April 1988, the day before he was to present his final report to the Politburo, he hanged himself. The world was informed that he might possibly have been a victim of the radiation that followed the accident …

Legasov's contribution to the investigation into the real causes of the accident and consequently to the improvement of the RBMK reactors was only acknowledged eight years later, by President Boris Yeltsin after the fall of the Soviet Union. Legasov was posthumously honoured as a "Hero of the Russian Federation".

Nuclear energy, green energy and the German experiment

From 1955 onwards, when the first nuclear reactor started delivering electricity, to around 1970, an average of about six new reactors were commissioned annually in the whole world. The number of reactors under construction grew at more or less the same rate. After 1970, however, there was a sudden spurt for the next 15 years, with about 20 new reactors coming on stream annually. The number of facilities under construction exceeded this figure. The Three Mile Island incident of 1979 changed this situation dramatically, however. The number of reactors under construction began to decline rapidly after this and in the USA especially no new construction of reactors was undertaken.

However, the number of reactors in operation continued to grow at the previous slow rate until the Chernobyl disaster of 1986. After this there was almost no growth. As of June 2015 there were 437 reactors in operation. This figure was established by the World Nuclear Association (WNA). According to the WNA there are another 66 new reactors under construction at present. Almost half these reactors are in China, 16% are in the Russian Federation and 11% are in India. Nuclear reactors are even being built in the USA again for the first time in three decades.

The accidents at Three Mile Island and Chernobyl therefore had a drastic influence on the growth of nuclear energy production throughout the world. Apart from all the repercussions in Japan, the problems at Fukushima also had an impact on the industrial giant Germany.

The history of nuclear power in Germany has followed a long and complex route during which three obstacles have had to be overcome. Two of the three have already been successfully surmounted but the third still lies ahead. The postwar period up to the end of the 1980s is referred to as a period of reconstruction, and sometimes as the "economic miracle". The Germans were able to get back on their feet during this period, thanks to hard work. This was followed by the difficult and costly reunification of West and

East Germany. Today the *Energiewende* or energy transition lies ahead for them. This involves the elimination of nuclear energy and its replacement with sustainable "green" energy (in theory at least).

Like many other industrial countries, Germany at first viewed nuclear energy in a positive light. But then, strangely enough, resistance was encountered not from the population but from the utility companies. To overcome this resistance, the government built two extensive nuclear research stations, at Jülich and Karlsruhe. Research was soon carried out on uranium enrichment and the reprocessing of nuclear fuel, essential for a country aiming to manufacture nuclear weapons as well. These activities, along with Chancellor Konrad Adenauer's open declaration in 1957 that Germany was pursuing the production of nuclear weapons, caused a general sensation. The Second World War was still vividly remembered in Germany and the fear of a Third World War – with nuclear weapons this time – in which Germany would be the first victim, caused extreme anxiety. Germany's communist neighbours were also especially worried. As in many other countries, left-wing parties, under pressure from their communist masters, did all they could to arouse the population's suspicion of anything to do with nuclear energy. The result was that a generation of Germans developed a deep anti-nuclear psychological scar, which is mockingly referred to by others as "German Angst". Nuclear energy became an emotional, almost an ideological issue. People were simply not open to reason on this subject.

In the early 1970s plans were announced to erect a nuclear power plant at Wyhl. Local inhabitants occupied the area, not really because they were opposed to nuclear power but because they were angry about the clouds of steam released by the cooling towers. They believed that these would affect their wine production. Ultimately nothing came of the project. To prevent a similar protest action at another project, the Brokdorf nuclear power plant, the police fenced the area with barbed wire in October 1976 before it could be occupied. On the same night the police came to blows with activists and four weeks later the demonstrators numbered 30 000. When construction was resumed in February 1981, 100 000 people took part in a vehement protest and tens of thousands of policemen – the highest number ever deployed in Germany – had their work cut out to quell the demonstration. Some people described this as a kind of civil war. The anti-nuclear seeds of internal discord were sown at this time and lay dormant until the radioactive rain from Fukushima caused them to germinate 30 years later.

In 2010 a coalition government under the leadership of Angela Merkel agreed to extend the operational life of existing German nuclear power plants by twelve years to allow a convenient period for the development of alternative energy sources – read "green energy". This was considered a big political victory. However, one year later, within 48 hours after the explosion at reactor 1 at Fukushima, that decision was summarily reversed. Merkel, who holds a doctorate in physics, is said to have discussed the situation overnight, over a bottle of red wine, with her husband, Professor Joachim Sauer (also a physicist). But physics didn't win that round. About 100 000 demonstrators had taken part in a rally against nuclear power in 400 German cities the previous day and three important elections in federal states lay ahead. As a politician it was clear to Merkel what the decision should be, but it was a drastic one. The eight oldest nuclear power plants were immediately shut down and legislation was prepared in terms of which the last nine remaining reactors would be shut down in by 2022. Experts were aghast at this turnabout. The well-known American business journal *Forbes* asked bluntly: "Germany: insane or just plain stupid?"

Consequently Germany is under great pressure at present to develop alternative energy sources rapidly, in the context of the "biggest experiment" ever undertaken by a renowned industrial country. With the decommissioning of the eight oldest reactors electricity suddenly had to be imported from France and the Czech Republic – ironically this was electricity generated by nuclear power plants. Germany's coal imports were doubled to supply the needs of German coal-fired power stations and electricity was even imported from Polish coal-fired power stations. Austria also had to come to their rescue with some of their pumped storage schemes.

The intention was to harness wind energy and solar power to fill the gap. But alas the sun does not shine in the night and there is little sunlight to be enjoyed in the European winter. The wind does not always blow and to complicate matters there has been vigorous resistance to the installation of wind turbines in the forests that cover much of the land area of Germany. The turbines are therefore installed offshore, mainly in the North Sea, far from the coast. This means that the electricity generated has to be fed by undersea cable to land and then carried by transmission lines mounted on tall power masts to the south of Germany where it is needed. A power distribution grid covering almost 4 000 km has to be built for this purpose and serious objections have been raised by the environmental activists – the same people who are opposed to nuclear energy. Wind energy and solar power are erratic and can only be effectively used if the energy generated can be efficiently stored.

To date there is only one way of doing this, a pumped storage scheme – and the environmental activists don't find this acceptable either.

Electricity consumption in every country varies considerably throughout the day (and night). When factories, businesses, transport networks and households get going in the morning the consumption easily rises to double the level required during the night. Throughout the day there are times when additional electricity is suddenly required. An effective energy system has a so-called constant baseload which provides the bulk of the daily demand for electricity and cannot be changed much in the short term. Such a baseload is typically provided by large hydro, coal-fired or nuclear power stations. Gas turbines, pump storage schemes and hydro power are able to deliver the necessary supplementary energy at short notice and in a predictable and reliable manner as required during the day. When a large part of the baseload is removed, as in the case of Germany, and there are no pumped storage schemes or hydro power (or they are not desirable) a serious problem with energy supply arises. In February 2012 a total power collapse in Germany was avoided by a hair's breadth.

The world is waiting anxiously to see how the Germans are going to solve the problem. A future without nuclear energy is going to cost billions. Rises in the cost of electricity are already pricing it beyond the means of many households. For an ordinary household the price per kilowatt-hour has gone up by a factor of 10 over the last decade. According to the consulting firm McKinsey, electricity was 45% more expensive on average in Germany in 2013 than in other EU states. Big German industrial consumers are paying €1 million more for 50 GWh than industrial consumers in the rest of Europe. The picture is even worse when compared to the USA. The additional costs are €3 million higher.

According to various critics, Germany is spending the most money on subsidies for "green" technology, which is currently the most expensive option, but makes the lowest contribution to the overall energy supply.

The third obstacle, the so-called energy transition, will have to be successfully overcome during the next 10 years if Germany wants to retain its reputation as a competitive industrial country.

And South Africa?

The government approved a nuclear energy policy in 2008. This policy provided a framework for prospecting and mining as well as for the use of nuclear materials and energy for peaceful purposes.

In May 2011, two months after the Fukushima disaster, the South African Minister of Energy announced in parliament that South Africa was nonetheless going ahead with plans to raise the share of nuclear power in the national system to 20%. This will require an additional 9 600 MW (about five to six times the equivalent of the output of the existing Koeberg power station). The minister said that the lessons of Fukushima would be taken into account when building the new nuclear power plants.

In accordance with the government's master plan, the so-called Integrated Resource Plan (IRP2010-30), the additional nuclear energy should become available between 2023 and 2030 and provide 23% of the energy mix, which will include wind and solar energy. In terms of the plan these energy sources will contribute 9% to the total and the contribution of coal-fired power stations will drop from 90% to 65%.

In February 2012 the minister announced that provision would be made not only for new nuclear power plants but also for uranium conversion (to uranium hexafluoride), uranium enrichment and fuel fabrication – all of which are functions that used to exist but have since been dismantled. The idea appears to be that South Africa should be independent of political pressure and events elsewhere in the world. Local plans have suddenly grown into one of the most ambitious projects in the world as regards the nuclear fuel cycle. The estimated costs could overshadow even those of the controversial arms purchases of the late 1990s. In Trevor Manuel's National Development Plan 2030, which was announced in August 2012 while he was responsible for planning in the presidency, reservations were expressed as follows about the nuclear programme:

> South Africa needed a thorough investigation of the implications of nuclear energy, including its costs, financing options, institutional arrangements, safety, environmental costs and benefits, localisation and employment opportunities, and uranium-enrichment and fuel fabrication possibilities. While some of these issues were investigated in the IRP, a potential nuclear fleet will involve a level of investment unprecedented in South Africa. An in-depth investigation into the financial viability of nuclear energy is thus vital.

The National Nuclear and Energy Executive Coordination Committee (NNEECC) was established in 2011 to manage the nuclear part of the programme. The executive head of the National Nuclear Regulator (NNR) complained to the parliamentary energy committee in March 2012 that South Africa was in danger of having a "Mickey Mouse" regulator that would be unable to cope with such a comprehensive programme. He also complained that neither the NNR nor the Nuclear Energy Corporation of South Africa (Necsa) had been included in any discussions on the proposed programme and that it might possibly already be too late for proper regulation.

The first meeting of the NNEECC only took place in August 2012. The IAEA was asked to assist in an advisory capacity and a three-day workshop was held in October 2012 to discuss the IAEA's nineteen milestones for a nuclear programme of this nature. These milestones include a comprehensive set of infrastructure requirements such as safety, financing, legislation, safeguards, regulation, radiation protection, purchases, personnel development, environmental protection, emergency planning, security and physical protection, the handling of radioactive waste etc. A provisional self-evaluation in respect of some of the requirements was discussed with the IAEA and it appeared that two of the outstanding gaps were funding and a lack of expertise.

The IAEA's first visit was followed by a Integrated Nuclear Infrastructure Review (INIR) in February 2013. An IAEA delegation, headed by the director-general of the organisation, Yukiya Amano, visited South Africa between 30 January and 8 February 2013. On the last day of their visit the members handed a preliminary report to the South African government. This report lists the strengths and weaknesses of the country, and makes recommendations for future nuclear power expansion. According to Amano, South Africa is the first African country to have undergone this survey and the first country with an existing nuclear capacity to have consented to such an investigation. On the last day of the delegation's visit the director-general of the Department of Energy announced that the minister would publish important guidelines on the nuclear programme in March 2013 and that a construction programme would be decided on by June 2013. The department undertook to reveal the contents of the report as soon as the final IAEA document was available. The report was received in May 2013 but by the middle of 2015 it has still not been made public.

The buzzword these days is "localisation", which means that as many components as possible must be manufactured locally. This makes sense, as long as the technological expertise and the means are available. Rob Davies, the Minister of Trade and Industry, has a solution for this which boils down to killing two birds with one stone. According to him a nuclear power plant of this kind consists of two parts, namely the core section and the balance of the plant. In his opinion South Africa already has sufficient expertise for the second half. If all the reactors are ordered at the same time, but with different completion dates, so much expertise can be built up through technical transfer that in time it will also be possible to take over the nuclear core. He did acknowledge that the biggest problem lies in the lack of the necessary expertise.

South Africa is not unique in this respect. There is a worldwide shortage of nuclear experts at the moment. Few people are interested in entering a profession that appears to be doomed after Fukushima and the German decision to eliminate all nuclear power. Even in France, where about 78% of the electricity is generated by nuclear power plants, there is a serious lack of interest. The French estimate that 500 new engineers will have to be trained in this field annually. At present they can hardly come up with 350. Even if all the nuclear power plants in a country are switched off, nuclear experts will be required for decades to decommission the reactors and dismantle them safely, as well as to handle and store nuclear waste safely. Many countries are faced with the problem of finding a way to train and motivate nuclear funeral undertakers.

It came as a big surprise when the Russian Rosatom International Network, a subsidiary set up in 2014 to oversee foreign marketing offices, announced in September 2014 that an agreement had been signed with the South African Minister of Energy in Vienna which would lay the foundation for the procurement and development of a nuclear power capacity based on up to eight Russian VVER reactors with a total installed capacity of 9,6 GW. The minister stated: "This agreement opens up the door for South Africa to access Russian technologies, funding, infrastructure, and provides a proper and solid platform for future extensive collaboration."

The announcement was greeted by a public outcry because it appeared that the Russians had been awarded the contract without an open and transparent tendering process, which is a constitutional requirement. The Rosatom agreement was headline news for a day. Then a spokesman for Necsa explained that there had been a misunderstanding and that the government had not awarded the contract to Rosatom; the agreement in question was simply a standard framework agreement and the minister planned to sign similar agreements with France and China, and possibly other countries that had expressed interest in bidding for the contract.

In a press briefing on 14 July 2015 the Department of Energy announced that intergovernmental agreements had already been signed with China, France, Russia, the USA and South Korea and that negotiations were also under way to conclude IGAs with Canada and Japan. In terms of the agreements more than 500 South African students will be trained in Russia, China, South Korea and France.

Prospective vendors have already participated in workshops with interested South African government officials and experts to exchange views and answer technical questions.

The procurement process and the selection of strategic partners are expected to be completed by the end of the 2015 financial year. It is interesting to note that the only current operator of a nuclear power plant in South Africa, namely Eskom, which operates Koeberg, has been sidelined and that the Department of Energy has been officially designated as the procuring agency. As to the all-important question of the funding required for the enormous project – some estimate it to be as much as R1 trillion – the department has stated that the funding model cannot be discussed because of "strategic reasons".

It would seem, therefore, that the government's plans for starting the project are on track. The objective is to have the first power unit on line in 2023, as required by the IRP.

As to the preferred bidder or bidders, the 300 students in training in China and the 200 in Russia appear to indicate that these two countries are the forerunners.

One can only commiserate with the National Nuclear Regulator, who will have the unenviable task of regulating the large fleet of reactors with three different designs. Currently they only have experience of the Framatome/Westinghouse design (Koeberg); they have no experience of the new Russian VVER or the Chinese Hualong One reactors.

The press briefing of 14 July 2015 provided no information on plans for enrichment, fuel fabrication and reprocessing except for the reference to the approved Nuclear Energy Policy of 2008, which requires "self-sufficiency in the nuclear energy sector in the long term".

Apart from the technical and funding hurdles, this is a high political hurdle to overcome. When a country talks about uranium enrichment and reprocessing of spent fuel from which plutonium can be reclaimed, the world sits up straight – as the recent, decade-long negotiations with Iran can attest. Enormous international political pressure will probably be exercised to eliminate these two aspects of the fuel cycle. Outside the nuclear-weapon states this has only been permitted on a significant scale in one NPT state party, namely Japan – for complex historical reasons.

The renowned American nuclear expert Prof. Frank von Hippel reported in *The New York Times* in November 2012 that a South African official had confided to him that: "Reprocessing is the currency of power in the modern world."

If the nuclear programme is going to be seen as a means of acquiring status and power and not as a way of providing expensive but essential energy in a poor country, there could be big political problems ahead.

Furthermore, South Africa is still storing highly enriched uranium inherited from the abandoned weapons programme. It is enough to make several nuclear bombs. The reason given has always been that it is required for medical isotope manufacture by the Safari reactor, but Safari has already been converted to operate on low-enriched uranium feedstock.

A country with nuclear weapons material in storage and plans to enrich uranium and reclaim plutonium is something of a rarity.

Interesting times await South Africa.

GLOSSARY

Advena – This plant was built close to the Kentron Circle facility to the east of Pelindaba. The aim was to use Advena to supplement the limited facilities at the Circle facility and to develop implosion technology there in order to build new, smaller nuclear weapons for use in missiles. Advena was not yet fully operational when South Africa's nuclear programme was officially closed down in 1989.

Armaments Corporation of South Africa (Armscor) – Armscor is a state institution which was established in 1968 for the purpose of supplying South Africa's armaments requirements. This was in response to the international sanctions campaign launched against the apartheid government by the United Nations from 1963 onwards and formalised in 1977.

Atom – An atom is the smallest particle of an element which has all the characteristics of that element and is capable of taking part in a chemical reaction. An atom consists of a nucleus containing protons and neutrons. Electrons orbit the nucleus at a relatively large distance. The electron configuration is responsible for the chemical behaviour of the atom. The word atom is derived from the Greek word *atomos*, which means indivisible.

Atomic bomb – This is an archaic term for a nuclear bomb.

Atomic Energy Board (AEB) – The South African Atomic Energy Board, which was established in 1948.

Atomic Energy Corporation (AEC) – The AEC was established in 1982 with the subsidiaries Ucor and Nucor. The AEC was an amalgamation of the nuclear activities at Valindaba and Pelindaba outside Pretoria.

Atoms for Peace – "Atoms for Peace" is the title the press gave to a speech delivered by President Dwight D. Eisenhower at the United Nations Security Council (UNSC) on 8 December 1953. This speech was followed by a programme to promote the peaceful application of nuclear power, both in the USA and internationally.

Beva – Beva was the fuel element fabrication plant of the Atomic Energy Corporation (AEC) responsible for manufacturing fuel elements for the Koeberg nuclear reactors.

Cascade – Little enrichment is achieved by a single isotope separation element. The slightly enriched uranium therefore flows to the following separation element where it is again slightly enriched. The process is repeated many times in a so-called cascade chain in order to achieve the desired degree of enrichment.

Chain reaction – When a uranium-235 or a plutonium-239 nucleus absorbs an incoming neutron, it may break up (split or fission) into two smaller nuclei with the release of energy and two to three additional neutrons. These neutrons may cause successive fissions – so that a chain reaction follows. This can be technically controlled at the level of a self-sustaining reaction as in a nuclear reactor, or it may be uncontrolled and release large amounts of energy within a short time, as in a nuclear weapon.

Circle facility – Kentron, which was part of Armscor at the time, built the so-called Circle facility next to the Gerotek vehicle testing track near Pelindaba and began using it in 1981. South Africa's nuclear weapons were built and stored there.

Critical mass – The minimum quantity of fissionable material required to cause a self-sustaining chain reaction under given conditions. The precise mass depends, among other things, on the type of fissionable material (U-235 or Pu-239), its density, chemical composition, geometrical shape, concentration and the presence of neutron reflectors.

Criticality – The conditions required for a self-sustaining chain reaction. This happens when the neutrons released during the fission process are precisely balanced by the number of neutrons that are absorbed and those that escape from the material. The condition is subcritical when the chain reaction cannot be sustained and supercritical when the chain reaction proceeds at a rate that cannot be controlled.

GLOSSARY

Depleted uranium – Uranium which contains less than the natural concentration (0.71%) of U-235 (usually between 0.2 and 0.4%) and which is a by-product of the uranium enrichment process. Depleted uranium metal is often used in armour-piercing ammunition.

Deterrent – This is the military means, such as a nuclear bomb, by which a state could deter a potential opponent from launching an attack or initiating conflict.

Deuterium – This hydrogen isotope has one proton and one neutron in its nucleus. When deuterium combines with oxygen the result is heavy water.

Disarmament – Article VI of the Nuclear Non-Proliferation Treaty (NPT) refers in vague terms to the necessity to stop the nuclear arms race "at an early date" and to a treaty, to be drafted some time in the future, in terms of which general and complete disarmament (not only nuclear disarmament) should take place under international control.

Dual-use items – The term refers to items that have both ordinary industrial and also military applications. For example, certain lathes, valves and pipes which are used in industry can also be used in the manufacturing process leading to nuclear weapons. Certain chemicals and materials used in nuclear weapons also have everyday applications.

EMIS uranium enrichment process – "EMIS" stands for electromagnetic isotope separation. This method was abandoned in America soon after the Second World War because of the high electricity consumption required but was later used again in Iraq. Large magnets are used in this process to separate ionised isotopes.

Enriched uranium – Enriched uranium contains a higher concentration of the isotope uranium-235 than is found in nature. Natural uranium contains only 0.71% of U-235. Uranium with a U-235 content of up to 90% or more is required for nuclear weapons. On the other hand, nuclear power plants run on uranium containing between 3 and 5% U-235.

Fissile material (fissionable material) – Material that can be fissioned by neutrons with the release of energy and additional neutrons.

Fission bomb – A nuclear bomb which is based on the concept of energy release through the fission of heavy elements such as uranium-235 or plutonium-239 by neutrons.

Gas centrifuge uranium enrichment process – Uranium hexafluoride (UF$_6$) is fed into a cylindrical tube which rotates in a vacuum at very high speed. The heavier molecules containing U-238 move outwards towards the wall of the rotating tube while the lighter molecules containing U-235 are concentrated towards the centre of the tube. The lighter and heavier molecules can then be drawn off separately. This uranium enrichment process is operated on a large scale by Urenco (a firm established by Germany, the Netherlands and Britain). The modern gas centrifuge was developed after the Second World War by the Austrian, Gernot Zippe, while in Russian captivity. It is currently the most energy-efficient isotope separation process.

Gaseous diffusion uranium enrichment process – A process of enriching uranium by forcing uranium hexafluoride (UF$_6$) in gaseous form through a porous barrier. The lighter molecules containing U-235 move through the barrier slightly more easily than those containing U-238. The separation achieved is very slight and the process has to be repeated numerous times. The electricity consumption is high and this is the most expensive of all the uranium enrichment processes. This method is still used in France.

Gun-type weapon – A nuclear weapon in which two subcritical pieces of fissile material are united at high speed to form a supercritical mass which causes a nuclear explosion. This design cannot be used in plutonium weapons.

Highly enriched uranium (HEU) – In highly enriched uranium the natural uranium-235 isotopes are enriched from 0.71 to 20% or higher. In the case of nuclear weapons the U-235 isotopes must be enriched to 90% or higher.

Implosion-type weapon – A spherical assembly of high explosives which is so designed that the explosive yield is concentrated towards the centre to compress a subcritical mass of fissile material into a critical form and thereby cause a nuclear explosion.

International Atomic Energy Agency (IAEA) – The International Atomic Energy Agency has been seated in Vienna, Austria, since 1957. It is an au-

GLOSSARY

tonomous agency of the United Nations. The two principal aims of the IAEA are the promotion of the peaceful use of nuclear energy and the application of safeguards to prevent the further proliferation of nuclear weapons.

Isotope – Isotopes are forms of an element in which the nuclei have the same atomic number (in other words, number of protons in the nucleus) but different atomic masses because they contain different numbers of neutrons. Isotopes of the same element therefore have different atomic masses. The word isotope comes from the Greek words *iso* = equal and *topos* = place. This is a reference to the fact that all isotopes of an element appear at the same position on the periodic table of elements because they are chemically similar.

Kiloton – The energy from a nuclear explosion that is equivalent to the explosive force of 1 000 tons of trinitrotoluene (TNT).

Lithium-6 – A compound of the lithium-6 isotope with deuterium (lithium deuteride) is used to create a more powerful or boosted nuclear weapon by means of nuclear fusion.

Low-enriched uranium (LEU) – In low-enriched uranium the uranium-235 isotope is enriched to below 20% – usually only to between 3 and 5%. This uranium is then used for nuclear fuel in nuclear reactors.

Megaton – The energy of a nuclear explosion which is equivalent to the explosive force of a million tons of trinitrotoluene (TNT).

National Institute for Defence Research (Somchem) – This institute in Somerset West was originally part of the National Institute of Defence Research of the Council for Scientific and Industrial Research (CSIR), but is currently a division of Denel.

Natural uranium – Uranium with the isotope ratio of U-238 (99.284%), U-235 (0.711%) and U-234 (0.0053%) as it occurs in nature.

Necsa (South African Nuclear Energy Corporation) – Formerly the Atomic Energy Corporation (AEC), Necsa was established in 1999.

Non-nuclear-weapon states (NNWS)– All states which signed and/or ratified the Nuclear Non-Proliferation Treaty (NPT) but did not build and test a nuclear explosive device before 1 January 1967.

Non-proliferation – Actions aimed at preventing the proliferation of weapons of mass destruction.

Nuclear explosive device – Generally speaking, a nuclear explosive device is an experimental device, often a first prototype, which is tested to determine whether the theoretical calculations and execution of the design have produced the desired result, or to demonstrate a nuclear capability by means of an underground test.

Nuclear fuel cycle – The process which starts with the mining of uranium and the production of yellowcake, the conversion of yellowcake into uranium hexafluoride, the enrichment of the uranium, the fabrication of fuel elements and the production of electricity by nuclear reactors. If the spent fuel is simply stored as waste, this is referred to as an open cycle. When the spent fuel is reprocessed, the reclaimed uranium and plutonium are used to fabricate new nuclear fuel and the cycle is described as closed.

Nuclear fusion – The process by means of which the nuclei of light elements (especially the isotopes of hydrogen, namely deuterium and tritium) fuse under high pressure and temperature conditions with an accompanying release of large amounts of energy and neutrons.

Nuclear material – Source material (natural uranium) or fissionable material (U-235, Pu-239).

Nuclear Suppliers Group (NSG) – This organisation was established in 1975 after India detonated a nuclear bomb, thereby demonstrating that transferred nuclear technology and equipment are not always used for peaceful purposes. The NSG, which consists of a group of almost 50 nuclear supplier countries, draws up guidelines and lists of controlled items for the exporting of nuclear materials, equipment and technology, as well as for nuclear-related dual-use items. The NSG has made additions to the Zangger Committee's guidelines on the transfer of technology, the control of re-exports and the physical security of nuclear materials. Special attention is also given to the transfer of so-called sensitive technology, namely enrichment and reprocessing.

Nuclear weapon – A nuclear weapon is a militarily qualified item which is purpose-made to be delivered by aircraft, missile or glide bomb in order to cause a nuclear explosion. A nuclear weapon has to be able to withstand the rigours of military life and must be ready for offensive deployment. A distinction is drawn between strategic weapons (used for attacks on enemy territory) and tactical weapons (used to support a specific military or naval operation).

Nuclear-weapon states (NWS) – A nuclear-weapon state is defined by Article IX.3 of the Nuclear Non-Proliferation Treaty (NPT) as a state which has manufactured or exploded a nuclear weapon or other nuclear explosive device before 1 January 1967. The only recognised nuclear-weapon states are the USA, Russia (formerly the Soviet Union), Britain, France and China. Other countries, such as India and Pakistan, which do possess and have tested nuclear weapons, are not formally recognised as nuclear-weapon states because of the cut-off date.

Operation Plowshare – This term was used by the United States of America (USA) to refer to the development of techniques for using nuclear devices for peaceful purposes. The phrase was coined in 1961 and comes from the Old Testament (Isaiah and Micah) where the reference is to swords being beaten into plowshares.

Partial Test Ban Treaty (PTBT) – This treaty entered into force in October 1963. The nuclear-weapon states agreed to stop all nuclear tests in the atmosphere, in outer space and under water and decided to monitor any possible tests of this nature in future by means of satellites and seismic methods.

Peaceful Nuclear Explosion (PNE) – This description refers to the peaceful use of nuclear explosions, for example in the excavation of harbours or canals. The Nuclear Non-Proliferation Treaty (NPT) makes provision for peaceful nuclear explosions, although they have never taken place in practice in terms of the treaty.

Pebble-bed modular reactor (PBMR) – This is a gas-cooled reactor which uses spherical fuel elements – a composition of silicon carbide-coated, enriched uranium granules – in a graphite ball. With the aid of foreign investors, South Africa further developed the original concept, which was designed and built in Germany. In view of escalating costs the project was abandoned in 2010. Pebble-bed modular reactors are nevertheless still undergoing development, especially in China.

Pelinduna – Pelinduna was an indigenous reactor which South Africa intended to develop using natural uranium and heavy water as the moderator. The project was abandoned in 1969, however. Owing to funding limitations it was decided to focus instead on uranium enrichment by means of the vortex tube technique.

Plutonium – Unlike uranium, plutonium is a man-made element that is not found in nature. It is formed in nuclear reactors during nuclear reactions by the bombardment of fuel elements with neutrons. Various plutonium isotopes, including Pu-239, Pu-240 and Pu-241, are produced in this way. The American Glenn Seaborg created this element in December 1940 and named it plutonium. Less plutonium (Pu-239) than enriched uranium is required for a nuclear weapon, but the technology is more advanced than that required for a gun-type enriched uranium weapon.

Pressurised water reactor (PWR) – The reactor core consists of fuel elements in water which serves as both the moderator for the nuclear chain reaction and the coolant. The water is under high pressure, which causes the temperature to rise to about 450 °C.

Proliferation – The spread of weapons of mass destruction (chemical, biological and nuclear weapons) and their delivery systems.

Radioactivity – The spontaneous emission of radiation, usually alpha or beta particles, often accompanied by gamma rays, by the nuclei of unstable isotopes.

Reprocessing – The recovery of unused uranium and produced plutonium from spent nuclear reactor fuel.

GLOSSARY

Safari-1 – A research reactor of American manufacture which has been in service at the Necsa site outside Pretoria since 1965 and is now used to manufacture isotopes for medical purposes.

Safeguards – The inspection and verification system used by the International Atomic Energy Agency (IAEA) to establish whether declared nuclear material is being used only for peaceful purposes and not being diverted to covert nuclear weapons programmes and to detect undeclared nuclear material and activities.

Safeguards agreement – A bilateral agreement between a state and the International Atomic Energy Agency (IAEA) which depends on a prescribed model agreement in terms of which certain obligations are imposed on the state in respect of nuclear material. The IAEA obtains the right to verify the declared nuclear material through inspections. There are several kinds of agreements: those required by the Nuclear Non-Proliferation Treaty (NPT); those in which only certain facilities are covered (states that did not sign the NPT); and voluntary safeguards agreements on some facilities in nuclear-weapon states.

Separation element – A basic component of an enrichment plant, such as a vortex tube, centrifuge, etc. It divides an incoming feed stream into two components, namely an enriched component and a depleted component.

Stage – The size of the enriched stream leaving a separation element is relatively small. Various separation elements are therefore arranged in parallel to form a stage in order to increase the flow of enriched uranium (for instance in grams per hour). Stages are then linked successively to form a cascade, not only to achieve the required degree of enrichment but also to attain a satisfactory production rate (for example in kilograms per hour).

Thermonuclear bomb – A nuclear bomb in which high temperature and pressure cause light hydrogen isotopes, namely deuterium and tritium, to fuse, with the release of large amounts of energy and neutrons. The conditions for nuclear fusion are created in the primary section of the bomb, namely by a plutonium implosion, which ignites the secondary, fusion section. This type of bomb used to be known as a hydrogen bomb.

Treaty of Pelindaba – This treaty, the African Nuclear-Weapon-Free Zone Treaty, bans the production, testing, presence and use of nuclear weapons in Africa. The treaty also bans the storage in African countries of radioactive waste that originated elsewhere in the world.

Treaty on the Non-Proliferation of Nuclear Weapons (NPT) – The NPT (also called the Nuclear Non-Proliferation Treaty) entered into force in March 1970 for a period of 25 years. It was extended indefinitely in 1995. The treaty distinguishes between nuclear-weapon states (NWS) and non-nuclear-weapon states (NNWS). The former undertake not to assist the latter to build or acquire nuclear weapons and in addition to promote access to the peaceful uses of nuclear energy. The NNWS in turn undertake not to build or acquire nuclear weapons and to place their nuclear activities under the safeguards verification system of the IAEA.

Tritium – A hydrogen isotope with one proton and two neutrons in the nucleus. It is made in reactors and is radioactive. It has a half-life of 12 years.

Uranium – A silvery-white metal which is slightly radioactive and denser than lead. The nucleus contains 92 protons and between 141 and 146 neutrons. Uranium is the element with the highest atomic mass found in nature.

Uranium Enrichment Corporation (Ucor) – Ucor was established in 1970 and was later incorporated as one of the two branches of the Atomic Energy Corporation (AEC). The other branch was Nucor.

Uranium hexafluoride (UF$_6$) is a toxic and corrosive substance which is a solid at room temperature and pressure and forms the essential feed material for uranium enrichment plants because it can be converted into a gas by heating.

Uranium-235 – Uranium-235, unlike uranium-238, is a fissile material for so-called thermal or low-energy neutrons, which makes it ideal for use in a nuclear reactor. It is also fissionable by high-energy neutrons and for this reason it is used in nuclear weapons. U-235 only occurs in low concentrations (0.71%) in natural uranium and the uranium must be enriched to increase the amount of U-235 to 4% for reactors and 90% for nuclear weapons.

GLOSSARY

Uranium-236 – This isotope is not found in nature. It is formed in the nuclear fuel of reactors and is therefore present in spent nuclear fuel. When this fuel is reprocessed to recover the unused uranium and the plutonium that has been produced, U-236 will be found along with the other uranium isotopes, which will provide an indication of the reprocessing history.

Uranium-238 – Over 99% of natural uranium consists of U-238, which is not fissionable by thermal (low-energy) neutrons. Therefore it cannot be used as nuclear fuel in a typical pressurised water reactor. However, U-238 in nuclear fuel absorbs some of the fission neutrons to form plutonium-239, which plays an important part in the release of energy in the reactor core. U-238 is fissionable by high-energy neutrons and therefore contributes to the explosive force of advanced thermonuclear bombs. U-238 can also serve as fuel in reactors where graphite or heavy water is used as the moderator.

Urenco – The Urenco group is a European nuclear fuel company which operates various uranium enrichment plants in Germany, the Netherlands, Britain and the USA. Urenco supplies enriched uranium to about 15 countries and uses the gas centrifuge uranium enrichment method.

Vastrap – The site near Upington in the Northern Cape where two test shafts were dug for the possible demonstration of a South African nuclear capability.

Vortex tube process – Also known as the Ucor separation process. This is a unique, aerodynamic method of separating isotopes which was developed in South Africa by Dr Wally Grant and his collaborators. The modern gas centrifuge and the German Becker process are also aerodynamic separation processes. Aerodynamic processes depend on the fact that in gases rotating at high speed the heavier isotopes are separated from the lighter ones by centrifugal forces, just as milk and cream are separated in a cream separator.

Weapons grade – Only certain concentrations of U-235 and Pu-239 are suitable for making nuclear weapons. Weapons-grade uranium typically contains 90% U-235 and weapons-grade plutonium contains less than 7% Pu-240, which is an undesirable isotope, because it can cause predetonation in plutonium weapons.

Yellowcake – A uranium concentrate as received from the mines. The concentrate is converted in a conversion plant into uranium hexafluoride, which is required in the uranium enrichment process.

Yield – The total amount of effective energy released in a nuclear explosion. It is usually expressed as the equivalent amount (measured in kilotons or megatons) of trinitrotoluene (TNT) required to produce the same amount of energy.

Y-plant – Also known as the pilot enrichment plant. This plant was built by Ucor at the former Valindaba site to test the Ucor process of isotope separation and to gain experience with the operation of the enrichment cascades. In time, the plant produced highly enriched uranium (HEU) for the weapons programme, as well as low-enriched uranium (LEU) for Koeberg fuel. The whole cascade was fully operational in March 1977 and the first small quantities of highly enriched uranium were extracted on 30 January 1978. The plant was decommissioned at the end of 1989.

Zangger Committee – This committee came into being in 1971 with 15 countries as members. Its official name is the Nuclear Exporters Committee, but since it was set up under the aegis of Prof. Claude Zangger of Switzerland it is usually referred to as the Zangger Committee. Article II.2 of the Nuclear Non-Proliferation Treaty (NPT) calls for export control on "equipment or material especially designed or prepared for the processing, use or production of special fissionable material". The aim of this committee was to provide technical definitions for the undefined items in the NPT and lay down guidelines for exports.

Z-plant – This semi-commercial uranium enrichment plant of the Atomic Energy Corporation (AEC) for the production of low-enriched uranium (LEU) for Koeberg fuel was commissioned in 1987. The plant was shut down in 1991, because enriched uranium could be obtained more cheaply on the open market after South Africa became a signatory to the Nuclear Non-Proliferation Treaty (NPT).

BIBLIOGRAPHY

Books

Alvarez, L.W. (1987). *Adventures of a physicist*. New York: Basic Books.

Blix, H. (2004). *Disarming Iraq: the search for weapons of mass destruction.* London: Bloomsbury.

Charlton, M. (1986). *The Star Wars history – from deterrence to defence: the American strategic debate*. BBC Publications.

Crocker, Chester A. (1993). *High noon in southern Africa: making peace in a rough neighborhood*. New York: Norton.

Delpech, T. (2012). *Nuclear deterrence in the 21st century*: Lessons from the Cold War for a new era of strategic piracy. Rand Corporation.

Fisher, D. (1997). *History of the International Atomic Energy Agency: the first forty years*. Vienna: IAEA Publications.

Frantz, D. & Collins, C. (2007). *The nuclear jihadist*: The true story of the man who sold the world's most dangerous secrets. New York: Twelve.

Heald, G.R. (2010). "South Africa's voluntary relinquishment of its nuclear arsenal and accession to the treaty on the non-proliferation of nuclear weapons in terms of international law". Master's dissertation. University of the Witwatersrand, Johannesburg.

Hounam, P. & McQuillan, S. (1995). *The mini-nuke conspiracy: how Mandela inherited a nuclear nightmare*. Viking Adult.

International Atomic Energy Agency. (1997). *Personal reflections. A 40th anniversary publication*. Vienna: IAEA Publications.

Kernenergieterme/Nuclear energy terms. (1976). Pretoria: South African Academy for Science and Arts.

Levy, A. & Scott-Clark, C. (2007). *Deception: Pakistan, the United States and the secret trading in nuclear weapons*. New York: Walker Publishing.

Markram, T. (2004). *A decade of disarmament, transformation and progress*. Pretoria: SaferAfrica.

Meyer, C.M. (2011). *Is Chernobyl dead? Essays on energy – renewable and nuclear*. Muldersdrift: EE Publishers.

Muller, R. (2012). *Energy for future presidents: the science behind the headlines*. New York: W.W. Norton & Company.

Newby-Fraser, A.R. (1979). *Chain reaction: Twenty years of nuclear research and development*. Pretoria: Atomic Energy Board.

Papenfus, T. (2010). *Pik Botha and His times*. Pretoria: Litera.

Polakow-Suransky, S. (2010). *The unholy alliance: Israel's secret relationship with apartheid South Africa*. New York: Pantheon Books.

Potter, W.C. ed. (1990). *International nuclear trade and nonproliferation: the challenges of the emerging suppliers*. Toronto: Lexington Books.

Purkitt, H.E. & Burgess, S.F. (2005). *South Africa's weapons of mass destruction*. Bloomington: Indiana University Press.

Reiss, M. (1995). *Bridled ambition: why countries constrain their nuclear capabilities*. Washington, DC: Woodrow Wilson Center.

Rhodes, R. (1986). *The making of the atomic bomb*. New York: Touchstone, Simon & Schuster Inc.

Rhodes, R. (1995). *Dark sun: the making of the hydrogen bomb*. New York: Touchstone, Simon & Schuster Inc.

Steyn, H., Van der Walt, R. & Van Loggerenberg, J. (2003). *Armament and disarmament: South Africa's nuclear weapons experience*. Pretoria: Network Publishers.

Newspaper and journal articles

Agence France Presse. (2004, February 14). "US investigators in South Africa probe nuclear technology ring". AFP.

Agence France Presse. (2014, January 16). "White House to release Iran implementation agreement". AFP.

Broad, W.J. & Sanger, D.E. (2008, August 24). "In nuclear net's undoing, a web of shadowy deals". *The New York Times*.

Coll, S. (2006, August 7). "The atomic emporium": Abdul Qadeer Khan and Iran's Race to Build the Bomb *The New Yorker*.

Cook, E. (1999, March 29). "Interview: Janet Coggin – The spy who lied to me". *The Independent*.

De Villiers, J.W., Jardine, R. & Reiss, M. (1993, November–December). "Why South Africa gave up the bomb". *Foreign Affairs*.

Gupta, V. & Pabian, F. (1997). "Investigating the allegations of Indian nuclear test preparations in the Rajasthan desert". *Science & Global Security*, vol. 6 no. 2.

Harris, V., Hatang, S. & Liberman, P. (2004, September). "Unveiling South Africa's nuclear past". *Journal of Southern African Studies*, vol. 30, no. 3.

Harvard University. (2008, November). "Securing the bomb 2008".

Henderson, S. (2009, September 20). "Simon Henderson: Investigation: nuclear scandal – Dr Abdul Qadeer Khan". *The Sunday Times*.

Hibbs, M. (1992, October 21). "Washington wants to purchase South Africa HEU inventory". *Nuclear Fuel*.

Masiza, Z. (1993). "A chronology of South Africa's nuclear program". *The Nonproliferation Review*.

Meek, J. (2012, September 13). "How we happened to sell off our electricity". *London Review of Books*, vol. 34 no. 17.

Norris, R.S. & Kristensen, H.M. (2012, October 19). "The Cuban missile crisis: a nuclear order of battle, October and November 1962". *Bulletin of Atomic Scientists*.

Reuters (1988, August 14). "Pretoria says it can build A-arms". *New York Times*.

Scholtz, L. (2010, May 28). "G'n teken van Israelse aanbod aan Pretoria". *Beeld*.

Sokolski, H. (1993, August 31). "Ending South Africa's rocket program: A non-proliferation success". Non-proliferation Policy Education Centre.

Traynor, I. (2005, June): "UN alert as nuclear plans go missing". *The Guardian*.

07PRETORIA3091: WikiLeaks
08PRETORIA234 : WikiLeaks
07BERLIN2239: WikiLeaks

Internet
AEC vs Armscor arguments regarding nuclear weapons (1989, November 17). South African Foreign Affairs Archives, NPT-IAEA Agreement/Negotiations on full-scope safeguards. Obtained and contributed by Anna-Mart van Wyk, Monash South Africa. http://legacy.wilsoncenter.org/va2/index.cfm?topic_id=1409&fuseaction=HOME.document&identifier=4B499425-5056-9700-0357B89399938034&sort=Collection&item=South African Nuclear Development

Africa Report. (1989, December 8). CIA. http://www.nti.org/media/pdfs/south_africa_missile.pdf?_=1316466791

Albright, D., Brannan P., Laporte Z., Tajer K., & Walrond, C. (2011, November 30). "Rendering useless South Africa's nuclear test shafts in the Kalahari desert." ISIS Report. http://isis-online.org/uploads/isis-reports/documents Vastrap_30 November2011.pdf

Albright, D. Hibbs, M. (1993, April). "South Africa: The ANC and the atom bomb", *Bulletin of the Atomic Scientists*. http://www.bullatomsci.org/issues/1993/a93/a93AlbrightHibbs.html

Buys, A. (2011, April). "Tracking nuclear capable individuals" (address delivered in Washington). http://nautilus.org/wp-content/uploads/2011/12/Andre-Buys-TRACKING-NUCLEAR-CAPABLE-INDIVIDUALS.pdf

Carter's press conference (1977, November 23). South African Foreign Affairs Archives, Brand Fourie, Atomic Energy, File 2/5/2/1, vol 1, vol 2. Obtained by A.M. van Wyk, Monash, South Africa. http://legacy.wilsoncenter.org/va2/index.cfm?topic_id=1409&fuseaction=HOME.document&identifier=4A2CAB96-5056-9700-03B1B27C01416A56&sort=Collection&item=South African Nuclear Development

CBS News (2010, June 21). "Nuke facility raid an inside job?" http://www.cbsnews.com/stories/2008/11/20/60minutes/main4621623.shtmlvisit

Chapter 5: "South Africa's nuclear weapon programme" – R. van Vuuren (2003) http://uir.unisa.ac.za/bitstream/handle/10500/1379/05chapter5.pdf

CIA. (2003, December). Unclassified report to Congress on the acquisition of technology relating to weapons of mass destruction and advanced conventional munitions, 1 July through 31 December 2003. https://www.cia.gov/library/reports/archived-reports-1/july_dec2003.htm

Creamer, T. (2013, February 8). "SA to reach nuclear 'point of no return' by June." *Engineering News*. http://www.engineeringnews.co.za/print-version/iaea-2013-02-08

Daily Telegraph. "F.W. de Klerk says Nelson Mandela was brutal and unfair" (2012, April 11). http://www.telegraph.co.uk/news/worldnews/nelson-mandela/ 9194297/FW-de-Klerk-says-Nelson-Mandela-was-brutal-and-unfair.html

Der Spiegel (17/1992). Operation Anadyr von Anatolij Gribkow; "Im Dienste der Sowjetunion. Erinnerungen eines Armeegenerals." http://www.spiegel.de/spiegel/print/d-13679831.html

Graham, T. (1995, June 12-18). *Defense News*. http://www.carlisle.army.mil/library/bibs/infowar.htm

Highlights of the IAEA General Conference: 32nd regular session. http://www.iaea.org/Publications/Magazines/Bulletin/Bull304/30401182637.pdf

Herman Stadler (2009, August 31). Radio interview conducted by De Wet Potgieter. Oudio-l.er AL3283_PTA_STADLERHERMAN-20090831_2 INFCIRC/314. http://www.iaea.org/Publications/Documents/Infcircs/Others/infcirc314.pdf

Iklé, F.C. (1973, January). Can nuclear deterrence last out the century? http:/www.foreignaffairs.com/articles/24394/fred-charles-ikl%C3%83%C2%A9/can-nuclear-deterrence-last-out-the-century

Israel-South-Africa agreement (1975, April 3). South Africa History Archive, The Freedom of Information Programme Collection, Nuclear Weapons History, Department of Defence. Obtained by A.M. van Wyk, Monash South Africa. http://legacy.wilsoncenter.org/va2/index.cfm?topic_id=1409&fuseaction=HOME.document&identifier=49CBC4C9-5056-9700-03BA475BF449650C&sort=Collection&item=South African Nuclear Development

Israel South Africa meeting (1975, June 7). South Africa History Archive, The Freedom of Information Programme Collection, Nuclear Weapons History, Department of Defence. Obtained by A.M. van Wyk, Monash South Africa. http://legacy.wilsoncenter.org/va2/index.cfm?topic_id=1409&fuseaction=HOME.document&identifier=49D8CD04-5056-9700-038100514D673111&sort=Collection&item=South African Nuclear Development

A.Q. Khan website: http://www.draqkhan.com.pk

Kepon, M. (2012, Augustus 12). ArmscontrolWonk

Letter – Vance to Pik Botha (1977, August 19). South African Foreign Affairs Archives, Brand Fourie, Atomic Energy, File 2/5/2/1, vol 1, vol 2. Obtained by A.M. van Wyk, Monash, South Africa. http://legacy.wilsoncenter. org/va2/index.cfm?topic_id=1409&fuseaction=HOME.document&identifier=4A24105A-5056-9700-03E0C91C259DF383&sort=Collection&item=South African Nuclear Development

Message to Botha by ambassador Bowdler (1977, August 18). South African Foreign Affairs Archives, Brand Fourie, Atomic Energy, File 2/5/2/1, Vol 1, Vol 2. Obtained by A.M. van Wyk, Monash, South Africa. http://legacy.wilsoncenter.org/va2/index.cfm?topic_id=1409&fuseaction=HOME.document&identifier=49E64C29-5056-9700-03ADAC396216F98E&sort=Collection&item=South African Nuclear Development

Mossad and the Khan network. (1981). http://www.historycommons.org/context.jsp?item=a051881markdorfbomb

Pabian, F.V. (Fall 1995). "South Africa's nuclear weapon program: lessons for U.S. nonproliferation policy." James Martin Center for Nonproliferation-Studies. http://cns.miis.edu/npr/pdfs/31pabian.pdf

"Programme for promoting nuclear non-proliferation (1988, November)." Newsbrief number 3. http://www.mcis.soton.ac.uk/PPNN/news-briefs/nb03.pdf

"Programme for promoting nuclear non-proliferation (Autumn 1990)." Newsbrief number 11. http://www.mcis.soton.ac.uk/PPNN/news-briefs/nb11.pdf

SA's nuclear-tipped ballistic missile capability / UN A/45/571) (1991). http://www.un.org/disarmament/HomePage/ODAPublications/DisarmamentStudySeries/PDF/SS-23.pdf

Simpson, J. (2012). CSSS JMCNS NPT Briefing Book. http://www.kcl.ac.uk/sspp/departments/warstudies/research/groups/csss/2012nptbook.pdf

Slijper, F. (2007, September 12). "Project Butter Factory: Henk Slebos and the A.Q. Khan nuclear network". http://www.tni.org/archives/know/200

Sokolski, H. "Ending South Africa's rocket program: a nonproliferation success" (1993, Augustus). Nonproliferation Policy Education Centre. http://www.npolicy.org/article.php?aid=458&rtid=2

Wellerstein, A. (2012, August 6) "Hiroshima at 67: The line we crossed". Restricted Data: http://www.timesonline.co.uk/tol/news/world/asia/article 6839044. ece

Yengst, W.C., Lukasik, S.J.& Jensen, M.A. (1996, October). "Nuclear weapons that went to war". http://www.nuclearfiles.org/menu/key-issues/nuclear-weapons/ issues/weapons-in-war/index.htm

Interviews
Prof. Johan Slabber: 25 April 2013
Prof. Waldo Stumpf: 7 March 2013
Mr Daan van Beek: 2 May 2013

APPENDIX

1. Minutes of first ISSA meeting held at 09:30 on Monday, 30 June 1975, in the government guest house, Pretoria [Pages 460–461]
2. South African-Israeli agreement (3 April 1975) [Pages 462–464]
3. Letter from Cyrus Vance to Pik Botha (19 August 1977) [Pages 465–466]
4. Press statement by Jimmy Carter (23 August 1977). http://digitalarchive.wilsoncenter.org/document 16600 [Pages 467–470]
5. SA and the bomb (31 August 1977). http://digitalarchive.wilsoncen-ter.org/document 114181 [Pages 471–474]
6. Draft speech for the opening of Kentron Circle by the Prime Minister (4 May 1981) [Pages 475–479]
7. Meeting of ad hoc cabinet committee under the chairmanship of The Honourable the State President on Tuesday 3 September 1985 at 15:00 [Pages 480–483]
8. Programme Olympic: Corroborative notes following an information session for the Minister of Defence in Cape Town 27 July 1987 [Pages 484–485]
9. Submission to the Witvlei Control Committee (3 September 1987) [Pages 486–496]
10. Programme Dunhill: Development of a nuclear capability for the SADF – decision of ad hoc cabinet committee (16 April 1988) [Pages 497–498]
11. Memo: Main points arriving from luncheon on 14 November 1989 – Richard Carter [Pages 499–501]
12. Programme for weapons dismantling – South African Air Force (31 January 1990) [Pages 502–505]
13. Phasing out of the RSA's nuclear weapons capability – AEC (15 February 1990) [Pages 506–511]
14. Dismantling of nuclear weapons – State President (26 February 1990) [Page 512]

Every reasonable effort has been made to enhance the print quality of this section. The original documents are just as difficult to read, but in view of their historical importance the English documents have been reproduced in facsimile and the Afrikaans documents in translation.

TOP SECRET   Copy No. 3 of 25

MINUTES OF THIRD ISSA MEETING
HELD AT 09h30 ON MONDAY, 30TH
JUNE 1975, IN THE GOVERNMENT
GUEST HOUSE, PRETORIA

PRESENT:

Prof H J Samuels : President of the Armaments Board : Chairman

REPUBLIC OF SOUTH AFRICA

S A Defence Force	Armaments Board
Lt Gen E Pienaar	Mr J F H Jagoe
Lt Gen M A de M Malan	Mr T D Zeederberg
Lt Gen R F Armstrong	Mr J P J de Jager
Lt Gen H de V Du Toit	Mr F J Bell
Lt Gen R H D Rogers	Mr S F Engelbrecht
Rear Adm S C Biermann	Mr P F Dillen
Maj Gen I Lemmer	Mr P C H Frylinck) Secre-
Brig D Bielich	Mr T G Grobler) tariat

---oooOooo---

WELCOME

The Chairman extended a most cordial welcome to the Israeli representatives attending the meeting, to which ▓▓▓▓ suitably replied.

The Chairman also extended a welcome to members of the S A Defence Force and Armaments Board present at the meeting.

DEFENCE INTELLIG.
DECLASSIFIE
1 3 JUL 2006
F / SMIT
68484963PE WO?

APPENDIX

Copy 2 of 10.

TOP SECRET

- 2 -

8.2.3 Total in one or other country.

9 Minister Botha said that he insisted on being able to withdraw from the project - i.e. being able to proceed in phases.

Minister Peres took note. His staff will make proposals on how this can be achieved.

10 Minister Botha expressed interest in a limited number of units of Chalet provided the correct payload could be provided. Minister Peres said that the correct payload was available in three sizes. Minister Botha expressed his appreciation and said that he would ask for advice.

11 Minister Botha said that we have no aggressive intentions and hence Burglar is for us a low priority, even the 3 000 km model. It was stated that the 6 000 km model proposal had been made at the request of R.S.A.

12 Minister Peres asked that R.S.A. should declare their interest in BlueBat and Olive. Minister Botha undertook to do this.

13 Minister Peres asked that R.S.A. should declare their interest in Night Vision equipment. Minister Botha undertook to do so.

14 Minister Peres offered half of their production of 10 units per month of the new tank to R.S.A. Production to commence in June 1976, although mention was also made of December 1976.

The cost of the tank was stated to be $ .810 000 including development charges and based on an order for 1 000 units.

461

THE BOMB

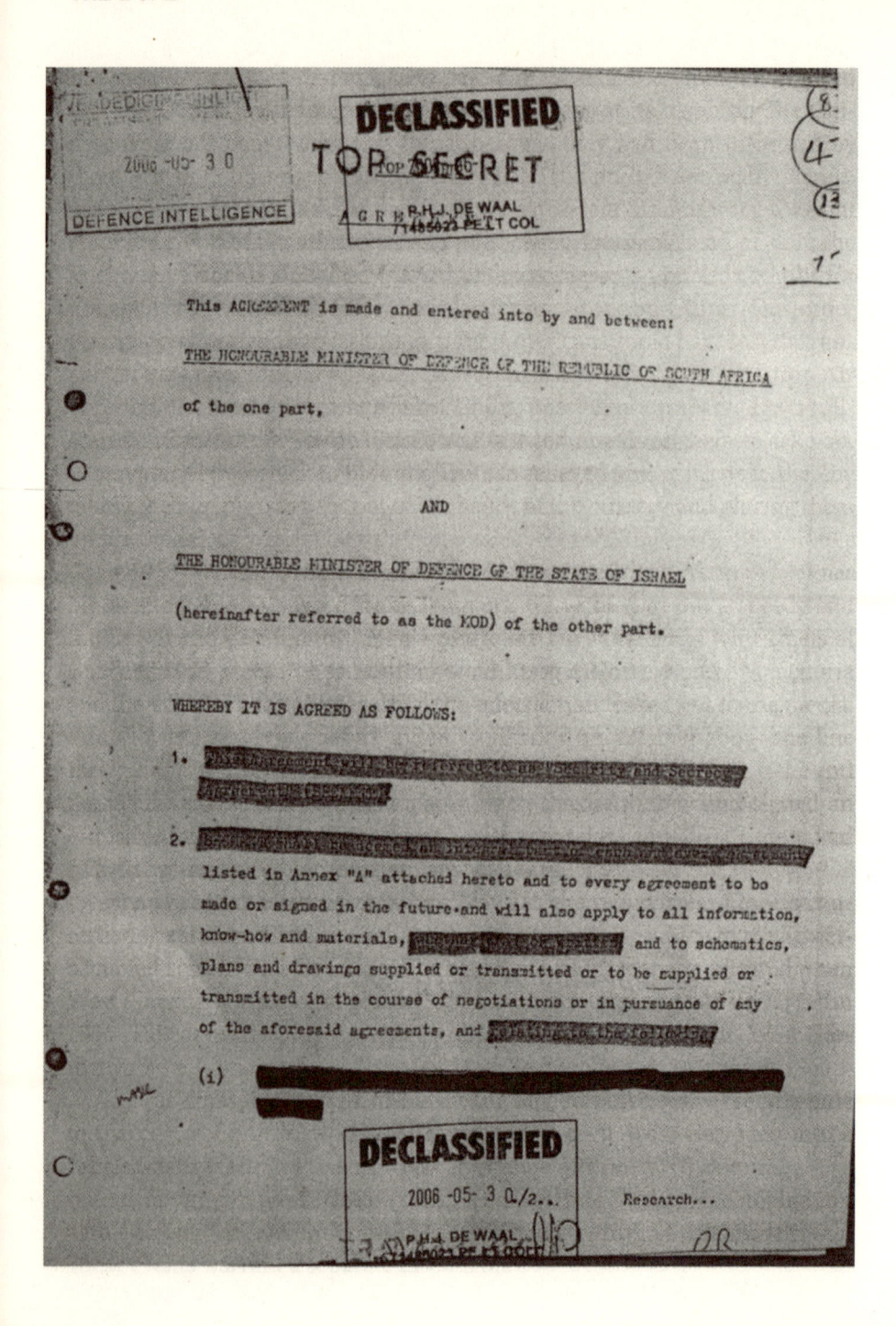

DECLASSIFIED
TOP SECRET
P.H.J. DE WAAL
71485021 LT COL

This AGREEMENT is made and entered into by and between:

THE HONOURABLE MINISTER OF DEFENCE OF THE REPUBLIC OF SOUTH AFRICA

of the one part,

AND

THE HONOURABLE MINISTER OF DEFENCE OF THE STATE OF ISRAEL

(hereinafter referred to as the MOD) of the other part.

WHEREBY IT IS AGREED AS FOLLOWS:

1. ▓▓▓▓▓▓▓▓▓▓▓▓▓▓▓▓▓▓▓▓▓▓▓▓▓▓▓▓▓▓▓▓

2. ▓▓▓▓▓▓▓▓▓▓▓▓▓▓▓▓▓▓▓▓▓▓▓▓▓▓▓▓▓▓▓▓ listed in Annex "A" attached hereto and to every agreement to be made or signed in the future and will also apply to all information, know-how and materials, ▓▓▓▓▓▓▓▓▓▓▓ and to schematics, plans and drawings supplied or transmitted or to be supplied or transmitted in the course of negotiations or in pursuance of any of the aforesaid agreements, and ▓▓▓▓▓▓▓▓▓▓▓▓

   (i) ▓▓▓▓▓▓▓▓▓▓▓▓▓▓▓▓▓▓▓▓▓▓▓▓▓▓▓▓

DECLASSIFIED
2006-05-30/2
P.H.J. DE WAAL

462

APPENDIX

DECLASSIFIED
P.H.J. DE WAAL
27T485023 PE LT COL

(ii) ████████████████████
████████████████████

(iii) ████████████████████

(iv) ████████████████████

(hereinafter referred to as "secret information").

3. It is hereby expressely agreed that the very existence of this Agreement as well as any other agreement relating to the activities defined in Clause 2 hereof, including information about the terms or contents of any such agreement, shall be secret and shall not be disclosed by either party, except as hereinafter provided. The foregoing shall apply notwithstanding the fact that any particular subject of an agreement may carry a lesser classification but for this clause.

Should any subject of an agreement be accorded a higher classification than "secret" by mutual consent of both parties then the highest of such classifications shall apply.

4. The parties will agree on mutually acceptable security procedures which will be reduced to writing, signed by the appropriate agencies and such security procedures will define and determine the proper means and methods for transmittal, distribution, use and storage of secret information which may be required by either party in order to perform effectively any Agreement between them. Pending signature

DECLASSIFIED
./3.. of such procedures...
P.H.J. DE WAAL
71485023 PE LT COL

463

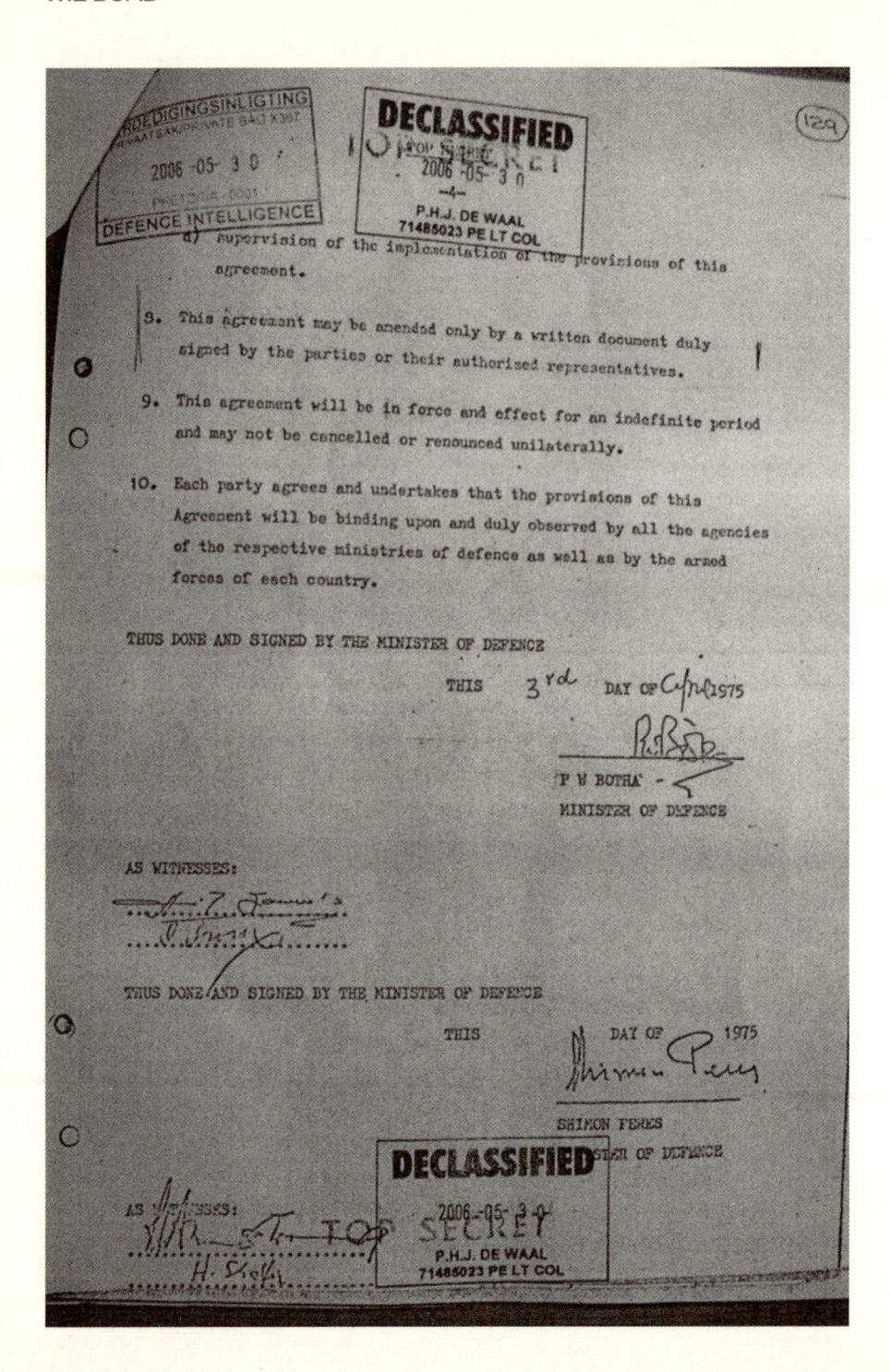

THE BOMB

    d) supervision of the implementation of the provisions of this agreement.

8. This agreement may be amended only by a written document duly signed by the parties or their authorized representatives.

9. This agreement will be in force and effect for an indefinite period and may not be cancelled or renounced unilaterally.

10. Each party agrees and undertakes that the provisions of this Agreement will be binding upon and duly observed by all the agencies of the respective ministries of defence as well as by the armed forces of each country.

THUS DONE AND SIGNED BY THE MINISTER OF DEFENCE

THIS 3rd DAY OF April 1975

P W BOTHA
MINISTER OF DEFENCE

AS WITNESSES:

THUS DONE AND SIGNED BY THE MINISTER OF DEFENCE

THIS   DAY OF   1975

SHIMON PERES
MINISTER OF DEFENCE

AS WITNESSES:

APPENDIX

SECRET

August 19, 1977

The Honorable
R. F. Botha
Minister of Foreign Affairs
Pretoria

Dear Mr. Minister:

President Carter and I have been closely following the dialogue between our governments concerning allegations of a nuclear weapons program in South Africa. Ambassador Bowdler has already conveyed to you the nature of our concerns.

In your conversation with him, you asked to be provided with the evidence that had led us to express doubts about the purposes of the Kalahari facility. Our experts have concluded, on the basis of experience with analogous installations, that the most likely purpose of a facility-- like the one in the Kalahari--is to conduct underground tests of nuclear explosive devices.

The facility that concerns us is located in the southern part of the Kalahari Desert, about 100 km. south of Botswana and 145 km. east of Namibia at approximately 27-45 S, 21-27 E. It consists of:

(a) A drill rig and associated facilities;

(b) A square lattice tower in a cleared area enclosed by a wall, about 1 km. from the drill rig;

(c) An area, about 3 km. from the square tower, containing a pad; this area is connected to the tower area by power or communications lines;

SECRET

SECRET

(d) A secured housing area 15 km. from the tower area, containing approximately ten buildings;

(e) A hard-surface airstrip approximately 1,600 meters long and 3 km. from the housing area. In addition, the entire area is surrounded by an outer patrol road.

We are prepared to show you photographs from which this data is derived.

I believe the only way to resolve existing doubts is to permit a prompt visit by a small U. S. technical team to inspect the location in the Kalahari Desert, which we have identified as a possible nuclear test site. I believe that it is in both of our governments' interest that this visit take place no later than Sunday, August 21, before the start of the Lagos conference, where some will seek to exploit politically, to our mutual disadvantage, the uncertainties raised publicly by South Africa's nuclear activities. Our experts are prepared to leave for South Africa at a very short notice.

I hope that with your government's cooperation we can quickly put this matter to rest.

Sincerely,

Cyrus Vance

SECRET

APPENDIX

IMMEDIATE

DESPATCHED, 24/8/77 (0925)

NO 262.

MY NO 259.

FOLLOWING IS RELEVANT TEXT OF PRESIDENT CARTER'S OPENING STATEMENT AT HIS PRESS CONFERENCE OF 23 AUGUST.

"FIRST OF ALL, IN RESPONSE TO OUR OWN DIRECT INQUIRY AND THAT OF OTHER NATIONS, SOUTH AFRICA HAS INFORMED US THAT THEY DO NOT HAVE AND DO NOT INTEND TO DEVELOP NUCLEAR EXPLOSIVE DEVICES FOR ANY PURPOSE, EITHER PEACEFUL OR AS A WEAPON, THAT THE KALAHARI TEST SITE WHICH HAS BEEN IN QUESTION IS NOT DESIGNED FOR USE TO TEST NUCLEAR EXPLOSIVES AND THAT NO NUCLEAR EXPLOSIVE TESTS WILL BE TAKEN IN SOUTH AFRICA NOW OR IN THE FUTURE.

WE APPRECIATE THIS COMMITMENT FROM SOUTH AFRICA AND ITS INFORMATION. WE WILL, OF COURSE, CONTINUE TO MONITOR THE SITUATION VERY CLOSELY. WE WILL ALSO RENEW OUR EFFORT TO ENCOURAGE SOUTH AFRICA TO PLACE ALL THEIR NUCLEAR POWER PRODUCTION CAPABILITIES UNDER INTERNATIONAL SAFEGUARDS AND INSTRUCTIONS AND ENCOURAGE THEM, ALONG WITH OTHER NATIONS, TO SIGN A NUCLEAR NONPROLIFERATION TREATY."

STATEMENT PROVOKED NO FURTHER QUESTIONS. SAFDEL HAS ALREADY CABLED TEXT OF POSITIVE EDITORIAL IN NEW YORK TIMES. WASHINGTON POST TAKES SOMEWHAT DIFFERENT VIEW IMPLYING THAT THERE WAS "STRONG REASON TO SUSPECT SOUTH AFRICA" THUS CREATING IMPRESSION THAT GOVERNMENT HAS YIELDED TO STRONG INTERNATIONAL PRESSURE.

THE BOMB

IN VIEW OF PRIME MINISTER'S SPEECH TONIGHT, TEXT IS QUOTED BELOW:

"SOMETHING OF ENORMOUS POTENTIAL CONSEQUENCE — AND EQUAL DELICACY — HAS BEEN GOING ON IN THE PAST SEVERAL DAYS CONCERNING THE SOUTH AFRICAN GOVERNMENT'S NUCLEAR INTENTIONS. IT WAS AN INTERNATIONAL BOMB SCARE OF THE FIRST ORDER, AND PRESIDENT CARTER'S CAREFULLY MEASURED ANNOUNCEMENT YESTERDAY SEEMED TO REFLECT BOTH THE INITIAL RELIEF AND THE CONTINUING WARINESS THAT HIS ADMINISTRATION FEELS ABOUT THE OUTCOME. SOUTH AFRICA, THE PRESIDENT SAID, ''HAS INFORMED US THAT THEY DO NOT HAVE AND DO NOT INTEND TO DEVELOP NUCLEAR EXPLOSIVE DEVICES FOR ANY PURPOSE, EITHER PEACEFUL OR AS A WEAPON ... THAT NO NUCLEAR EXPLOSIVE TEST WILL BE TAKEN IN SOUTH AFRICA NOW OR IN THE FUTURE.'' HE ADDED HIS APPRECIATION OF THIS ''COMMITMENT'' AND MADE A POINT OF NOTING ''WE WILL, OF COURSE, CONTINUE TO MONITOR THE SITUATION THERE VERY CLOSELY.''

WHAT HAS BEEN GOING ON IS THIS: THE U.S. GOVERNMENT — IN CONCERT WITH THE BRITISH, FRENCH, WEST GERMANS AND RUSSIANS — HAS BEEN PUTTING TERRIFIC HEAT ON THE SOUTH AFRICAN GOVERNMENT BECAUSE THERE WAS STRONG REASON TO SUSPECT THAT THE SOUTH AFRICANS WERE IN FACT PREPARING A NUCLEAR EXPLOSION FOR SOMETIME SOON, AN EXPLOSION OF UNIMAGINABLE POLITICAL IMPACT, WHATEVER ITS ACTUAL NUCLEAR TONNAGE. THE FRENCH FOREIGN MINISTER, LOUIS DE GUIRINGAUD, WHOSE HARSH WARNING TO THE SOUTH AFRICANS MADE NEWS EARLIER IN THE WEEK, LED THE OPEN, PUBLIC PROTEST. THE OTHER COUNTRIES, ALONG WITH FRANCE, PUSHED VERY HARD IN PRIVATE. THE UPSHOT HAS BEEN THE SOUTH AFRICAN GOVERNMENT'S STATEMENT CITED BY MR CARTER. EITHER THEY NEVER WERE GOING TO DEVELOP A NUCLEAR EXPLOSIVE DEVICE OR THEY ARE NOT GOING TO DO SO NOW. WHICHEVER IS THE CASE, IT IS WELCOME NEWS — THOUGH HARDLY ENOUGH TO WARRANT A RELAXED RETURN TO OTHER BUSINESS.

APPENDIX

THERE WERE TWO VERY POSITIVE, <u>UPBEAT ASPECTS TO THE DRAMA THAT LED TO THE SOUTH AFRICAN ASSURANCES. ONE IS THAT A GROUP OF NATIONS WHO OTHERWISE COMPETE ON A WIDE RANGE OF MATTERS, INCLUDING NUCLEAR ONES, WERE ABLE TO GET TOGETHER AND ACT FORCEFULLY AND FAST TO INDICATE TO A PROSPECTIVE NEW NUCLEAR POWER WHAT THE CONSEQUENCES WOULD BE IF IT WENT AHEAD.</u> NOTHING LIKE THAT, YOU WILL RECALL, OCCURRED AT THE TIME OF INDIA'S NUCLEAR EXPLOSION IN 1974. THE OTHER PROMISING SIGN IS THAT SO-CALLED PEACEFUL NUCLEAR EXPLOSIONS SEEM FINALLY AND APPROPRIATELY TO BE LOSING THEIR MYSTIQUE. MR GUIRINGAUD HAD IT JUST RIGHT. HE DECLARED THAT ''NO DISTINCTION COULD BE MADE BETWEEN AN ATOMIC EXPLOSION FOR PACIFIC PURPOSES AND ONE FOR MILITARY NUCLEAR EXPERIMENTATION.'' THAT IS THE CASE AND THE ''PEACEFUL EXPLOSION'' DODGE HAS LONG SINCE DESERVED THE CONTEMPT IN WHICH IT IS INCREASINGLY WIDELY HELD.

WHY WOULD SOUTH AFRICA WANT NUCLEAR WEAPONS? PRESUMABLY, IF IT DID, FOR THE SAME SCARE AND SYMBOLISM REASONS THAT MANY OTHER NON-NUCLEAR NATIONS WITH BIG TROUBLES WANT THEM. THE GRIM FACT IS THAT OVER THE LONG HAUL SOUTH AFRICA COULD PROBABLY ACQUIRE NUCLEAR INDEPENDENCE. IT HAS GREAT SUPPLIES OF URANIUM AND COULD IN TIME DEVELOP THE TECHNOLOGY TO DO WITH IT AS IT PLEASED. FOR THE PRESENT, HOWEVER, THE SOUTH AFRICANS DEPEND ON OTHER COUNTRIES SUCH AS THE UNITED STATES AND FRANCE TO PROVIDE IT ENRICHED URANIUM FUEL. THAT MEANS WE STILL HAVE SOME LEVERAGE AND SOME TIME TO ACT.

MR CARTER WAS RIGHT IN TAKING THE INCIDENT AS CAUSE TO ''RENEW OUR EFFORTS TO ENCOURAGE SOUTH AFRICA TO PLACE ALL THEIR NUCLEAR POWER PRODUCTION CAPABILITIES UNDER INTERNATIONAL SAFEGUARDS AND INSPECTIONS'' AND TO SIGN THE NUCLEAR NONPROLIFERATION TREATY. BUT THE CASE IS BIGGER THAN THE SOUTH AFRICAN EPISODE--BLOODCHILLING AS

THAT HAS BEEN. IT ILLUSTRATES AGAIN, THE URGENCY OF TRYING TO WORK OUT SOME INTERNATIONAL DISCIPLINE IN THE FIELD OF NUCLEAR-WEAPONS AND ENERGY DEVELOPMENT. PARTIAL AND AD HOC AS IT WAS, THE INTERNATIONAL EFFORT OF THOSE WHO LEANED ON SOUTH AFRICA SHOWS THAT IT CAN BE DONE.

SALES

RECEIVED OK?

S

7-693 SA

24836A SALE UPM

APPENDIX

Received Office : 1/7/1977

TELEGRAM

FROM : S.A. EMBASSY WASHINGTON
TO : Secretary for Foreign Affairs. PRETORIA
DESPATCHED : 31/8/1977

==

NO. 273.   TOP SECRET.

SOUTH AFRICA AND THE BOMB.

1(1. WE ARE SENDING YOU BY BAG DETAILED PRESS REPORTS ON THE ABOVE COVERING ALSO THE FLURRY OCCASIONED BY SENATOR HORWOOD'S STATEMENT BUT WOULD DRAW SPECIAL ATTENTION TO FULL TEXT OF ARTICLE IN SUNDAY'S WASHINGTON POST (WHICH WILL HAVE BEEN SUMMARISED IN SOUTH AFRICAN PRESS) SINCE IT FLOWS FROM A DIRECT WHITE HOUSE/STATE DEPARTMENT BRIEFING.

2(2. WHETHER OR NOT SOUTH AFRICA DOES IN FACT HAVE THE BOMB THE OVERALL EFFECT OF THE CARTER ANNOUNCEMENT AS ELUCIDATED IN THE WASHINGTON POST ARTICLE HAS BEEN TO MAKE THE INTERNATIONAL COMMUNITY BELIEVE THAT SOUTH AFRICA HAS MANUFACTURED A NUCLEAR DEVICE, WHICH REMAINS UNTESTED. THIS UNDOUBTEDLY IMPLIES A NEW WATERSHED IN SOUTH AFRICA'S INTERNATIONAL RELATIONS. NOTHING CAN BE THE SAME AGAIN, SOUTH AFRICA HAS BECOME THE SEVENTH NUCLEAR POWER EVEN THOUGH IT WILL NOT BE RECOGNISED AS SUCH. CARTER'S STATEMENT IS REGARDED AS TACIT CONFIRMATION OF THIS. ALTHOUGH ISRAEL HAS LONG BEEN SUSPECTED OF HAVING THE BOMB AT NO TIME HAS THERE BEEN ANY CONFIRMATION OF THIS FROM WESTERN SOURCES COMPARABLE TO THE EFFECT OF CARTER'S STATEMENT IN THE CASE OF SOUTH AFRICA. MOREOVER, THE COMMENT BY MINISTER HORWOOD, IN SPITE OF THE

SUBSEQUENT DEMENTI, IS VIEWED AS CONFIRMATION OF SOUTH AFRICA'S NUCLEAR CAPACITY FROM THE HIGHEST POSSIBLE FINANCIAL SOURCE WHICH WOULD HAVE BEEN CONCERNED WITH THE FUNDING OF THE PROJECT.

3(3. IT IS TOO SOON TO ASSESS ALL THE IMPLICATIONS OF THIS WATERSHED IN OUR FOREIGN RELATIONS BUT AS SEEN FROM WASINGTON OUR INITIAL COMMENTS ARE AS FOLLOWS -

A(A THE THESIS THAT SOUTH AFRICA POSES A THREAT TO WORLD PEACE IS IMMENSELY RE-INFORCED AND WILL BE EXPLOITED TO THE FULL IN THE U.N. AND ELSEWHERE BY OUR OPPONENTS WHO CAN BE EXPECTED TO MAKE EVERY USE OF THE EMOTIONAL FACTORS INVOLVED IN THE ALLEGED POSSESSION OF THE BOMB BY A GOVERNMENT WHOSE POLICIES ARE THE SUBJECT OF WORLD WIDE CONDEMNATION. THE PROSPECT OF A CHAPTER VII SANCTIONS RESOLUTION IS THUS BROUGHT MEASURABLE NEARER.

B(B. SINCE THE BOMB CAN BE USED TO DEAL NEITHER WITH GUERILLA ATTACKS FROM OUTSIDE THE COUNTRY NOR TERRORISM WITHIN THE COUNTRY POSSESSION OF THE BOMB IS SEEN TO BE NO DETERRENT WHATSOEVER IN DEALING WITH PRESSURES TO SUBORN OR OVERTHROW WHITE RULE - ON THE CONTRARY IT IS SEEN AS AN INCENTIVE TO STEP UP THOSE PRESSURES -

C(C. THE RESPONSE OF THE SOUTH AFRICAN GOVERNMENT TO THE REPRESENTATIONS FROM THE WESTERN POWERS, AND FROM THE U.S. IN PARTICULAR, NOT TO PROCEED WITH THE TESTING OF A NUCLEAR DEVICE IS ONCE MORE BEING INTERPRETED AS FURTHER SUBSTANTIATION OF THE THESIS OF THE CARTER ADMINISTRATION THAT PRESSURE ON SOUTH AFRICA IS MORE

APPENDIX

—3—

PRODUCTIVE OF RESULTS THAN THE KISSINGER POLICY OF ATTEMPTING TO WORK WITH SOUTH AFRICA. THIS AGAIN IS AN INCENTIVE TO STEP UP THE PRESSURES —

D(D. THE EVIDENCE THAT THE U.S.S.R. AND U.S.A. WITH SUPPORT FROM WESTERN EUROPE CAN SUCCESSFULLY WORK IN CONCERT TO PRESSURISE SOUTH AFRICA IS VIEWED AS FURTHER PROOF OF THE EXTENT OF SOUTH AFRICA'S ISOLATION, FROM WHICH THE CONCLUSION CAN BE DRAWN THAT SOUTH AFRICA'S FRIENDS AND SUPPORTERS (IN WESTERN EUROPE FOR EXAMPLE) WILL BE ABLE IN FUTURE TO OFFER LESS EFFECTIVE RESISTENCE TO PROPOSALS FOR ECONOMIC SANCTIONS —

E(E. UNITED STATES POLICY VIS-A-VIS BLACK AFRICA IN GENERAL AND VIS-A-VIS WHITE RULED SOUTHERN AFRICA IN PARTICULAR HAS DEVELOPED A MOMENTUM OF ITS OWN TO WHICH IT WOULD NOW BE DIFFICULT TO APPLY A BRAKE, EVEN IN THE UNLIKELY EVENT OF THE CARTER ADMINISTRATION UNDERGOING A CHANGE OF HEART —

F(F. THE WHOLE PATTERN OF DEVELOPMENTS HAS THUS PRODUCED A SITUATION WHERE SOUTH AFRICA IS FAR MORE EXPOSED THAN EVER BEFORE IN HER HISTORY TO POLITICAL PSYCHOLOGICAL AND ECONOMIC PRESSURES —

G(G. THE CIRCUMSTANCE THAT THESE PRESSURES ARE BEING EXERCISED, IN PARTICULAR BY THE WESTERN POWERS, WITHOUT ANY PROPER APPRECIATION OF WHAT COULD BE THEIR END-RESULT AND WHAT HARM THIS COULD DO TO THEIR OWN INTERESTS IS A FACT OF LIFE WHICH WE HAVE TO FACE UP TO, HOWEVER MUCH WE MAY DEPLORE OR CONDEMN IT —

H(H. WE SHOULD ACCELERATE TO THE EXTENT NECESSARY THE TEMPO OF OUR CONTINGENCY PLANNING AGAINST THE POSSIBILITY OF SANCTIONS —

THE BOMB

—4—

(1). THE SITUATION COULD CONCEIVABLY BE DEFUSED TO A CERTAIN EXTENT IF WE COULD SHOW TO THE WORLD THAT THE FACILITY NEAR UPINGTON REPORTEDLY IDENTIFIED AS A NUCLEAR DEVICE TESTING GROUND IS NOT IN FACT ANYTHING OF THE KIND. HOWEVER, WE ARE OBVIOUSLY IN NO POSITION TO OFFER COMMENT ON THE PROS AND CONS OF SUCH A COURSE

APPENDIX

TOP SECRET
DRAFT

Notes partly used

File No: 13/2/8/C
Date : 1981-05-04

DRAFT SPEECH FOR THE OPENING OF KENTRON CIRCLE BY THE PRIME MINISTER

1. It is my pleasant duty to be here with you this evening on this historic occasion – the opening of the Kentron Circle Facility, called after the code word under which this facility was erected on portion III van Elandsfontcin 352-JR.
2. ~~To put it differently, ladies and gentlemen,~~ [it is your privilege tonight to attend the opening of South Africa's own nuclear weapons research, development and manufacturing plant. This Plant [deleted: ladies gentlemen] can be seen as the **equivalent** of the USA's Los Alamos and Lawrence Livermore Laboratory and Britain's Atomic Weapon Research Establishment!
3. One of the Government's policy baselines has always been to ensure the peoples of South Africa a free and safe existence. To achieve this goal, the Government has exploited resources to put its chosen policy into practice. This is why the goal of the research and development programme with the establishment of the AEB has been a comprehensive nuclear energy programme that will make the RSA independent as far as possible of foreign assistance as regards its needs in the area of nuclear energy.
4. The AEB [deleted: ladies and gentlemen] has set out to ascertain, as part of this task, what the USA has done in respect of the peaceful uses of nuclear explosives, the so-called "Plowshare Program". You may be interested to know that the name of this Program is derived from a Biblical text, where the reference is to beating swords into ploughshares after the battle.
5. In view of the fact that the RSA is pre-eminently a mining country, the possible applications of nuclear explosives in this area, as well as others, are obvious. Although it is theoretically possible that a non-nuclear power could be assisted by a nuclear power under an international treaty

TOP SECRET

475

TOP SECRET

to carry out civil projects with the aid of nuclear explosives supplied by the latter, there are very serious doubts about whether this would be practicable, especially in view of SA's position in world politics. Therefore, ladies and gentlemen, if SA wants to enjoy the benefits of a nuclear explosives programme, it must be self-sufficient in respect of the supply of explosive devices.

6. In view of what I have just presented to you, an <u>internal committee was appointed by the AEB in 1969</u> to investigate the economic and technical requirements of nuclear explosives. This Committee found that SA does have the capacity to carry out a development programme successfully. The former President of the AEB consequently launched a comprehensive research programme in the course of 1970, which was to be carried out in parallel with a development programme and include test explosions. A site for such tests was acquired in 1974 and developed for this purpose.

7. In order to ensure terminal explosive yield, accommodate the necessary measuring instrumentation and provide sufficient advance protection for the instruments, the first peaceful device prepared for test detonation was very large and very heavy. Its physical properties, ladies and gentlemen, were as follows:
    a. Length : 4 metres
    b. Diameter : 600 milimetres
    c. Mass : Approximately 4 tons

8. Because the RSA had often been accused over the years of being engaged in making nuclear weapons, with certain ulterior motives, this development programme was run in the utmost secrecy right from the start. The need to keep this programme secret for a further number of years prompted the <u>decision in 1977 to postpone a test detonation indefinitely</u> and continue with the refinement, miniaturisation and improvement of the handling aspects of the existing device design.

TOP SECRET

APPENDIX

TOP SECRET

9. ~~Ladies and gentlemen, so much progress has been made with this that the present device is far smaller and lighter, but with the retention of its explosive capability.~~
10. ~~But ladies and gentlemen~~ Owing to the nuclear capability of the RSA, the USA and Russia have become aware that it cannot be taken for granted that the realisation of their political goal, the abdication of the whites, is practical politics. This awareness has led to an increasing indirect onslaught which, if the RSA allows this, will impair the credibility and restrict the freedom of trade of the RSA on the road to their [the USA's and the USSR's] ultimate objective of the abdication of the whites. The time has therefore come for the South African "Plowshare" to be forged into a sword for the battle that lies ahead! In this way the RSA can regain the initiative to force Russia and the USA to a conference table to negotiate. This will enable the RSA to handle the conflict from a power base of nuclear strategy instead of from a power base of black politics. This provides a key to the peaceful solution of the conflict situation in Southern Africa and it must be utilised as such.
11. As far back as 1975 I, as Minister of Defence, initiated discussions in respect of the possibility of creating nuclear weapons for the RSA. This capability of South Africa's was established even then and further discussions followed in 1976 in the course of which the need for tactical weapons emerged.
12. In July 1977 I also gave orders, from a strategic perspective, that national strategic guidelines should be laid down for nuclear weapons; this was accordingly done and was approved by me on 1978-04-04. One of the guidelines which I approved was the development of a military nuclear capability. On 1978-10-31 I, as Prime Minister, requested that an action committee be formed and tasked with determining the way forward in the transition to the manufacture of suitable nuclear weapons for SA – taking into account the development already accomplished by the AEB with the peaceful uses of nuclear explosives – and, after approval of the proposals, implementing them in earnest. This Committee set about their task with great zeal, enthusiasm and competence, so that by 1979-07-04 I was already able to approve draft proposals on the proposed weapon and construction of certain facilities, the so-called Project Festival.

TOP SECRET

TOP SECRET

13. This, ~~ladies and gentlemen,~~ was how Project Festival came to be established. A board of management, organisation and responsibilities in respect of the project were created. Kentron accordingly accepted the responsibility of supplying a qualified and cleared nuclear weapon to the SADF, and establishing and running the necessary facilities to supply a qualified warhead. The AEB in turn accepted responsibility for supplying certain qualified warheads.
14. Ladies and gentlemen, my colleagues and I have learned with gratitude tonight of the progress that has already been made and the establishment of the Facility, the Environmental Testing Facility and the Magazine is evidence of this.
15. The creation of a strategic nuclear power base is already at an advanced stage. The RSA's option in respect of its national security is to gain the cooperation of the Black States of Southern Africa by applying a total strategy aimed at promoting their common anti-communist interests in order to achieve the ultimate goal, the establishment of a survival-oriented bloc of states.
16. Cooperation with the USA, ~~ladies and gentlemen,~~ gives us the option of obtaining the support of the West to join the Black States in Southern Africa in promoting joint anti-communist interests. However, Black Africa is forcing us back to the first option I presented to you.
17. The fact, ~~ladies and gentlemen,~~ that the RSA possesses a nuclear weapons capability, is known only to a limited number of members of the Cabinet and a dedicated group of scientists and officials. Thanks to you, the group I am addressing tonight, the RSA is on the eve of developing a national weapons system – a nuclear weapons system.
18. After the attack on Hiroshima the world realised that the atom bomb is not a conventional bomb with an enormously high explosive yield – a bomb that belongs solely in the arsenals of a Defence Force – but that in the hands of world leaders it is an instrument of inducement, persuasion and coercion.

TOP SECRET

APPENDIX

TOP SECRET

19. Nuclear is primarily a political weapons system and not a military system. When the national strategic guidelines for nuclear weapons were adopted on 1978-04-04 this was accordingly the first principle we laid down. This political weapons system leaves a further option open to the RSA – an option to negotiate the birthright of the RSA at the negotiating table of the Superpowers; with a nuclear deterrent strategy as the basis. The basis of the present conflict between the West and the East lies in a nuclear deterrent strategy with its accompanying détente policy.
20. This birthright of the RSA's, ladies and gentlemen, is the prime target of the onslaught of West and East at this stage. The key to depriving the RSA of this right is the signature of the Nuclear Non-Proliferation Treaty. The RSA is currently being placed under increasing pressure by the West to sign the Treaty. As you know, this would take away the RSA's nuclear capability. This would deprive the RSA of its primary means of inducement, persuasion and coercion. As far as possible the RSA and the Cabinet will not give in to this pressure.
21. The RSA, ladies and gentlemen, has the right to decide on its own future just as any other state does, and refuses to follow a road that would lead to its downfall.
22. In conclusion I should like to express my thanks to all persons and bodies that have been and are involved in Project Festival and congratulate them on their achievements up to the present and wish them well in their endeavours and their share in ensuring a free and safe future for all the peoples of SA.
23. It is now my privilege to unveil a plaque and declare the Kentron Plant officially open.

(translation)

TOP SECRET

TOP SECRET

MEETING OF AD HOC CABINET COMMITTEE UNDER THE CHAIRMANSHIP OF THE HONOURABLE THE STATE PRESIDENT ON TUESDAY 3 SEPTEMBER 1985 AT 15H00

Present: The Honourable the State President (Chairman)
The Ministers of : Foreign Affairs
: Defence
: Finance
: Mineral and Energy Affairs
Dr L Alberts (Director-General : Mineral and Energy Affairs)
Cmdt. P G Marais (Chairman : ARMSCOR)
Dr J W L de Villiers (Chairman : AEC)

SUMMARY OF DECISIONS TAKEN:
1. Future BIBO Strategy
   After discussing the report of the Chairman of the Witvlei Council the following decisions were taken:
   (a) Manufacture a maximum number of 7 A-type warheads. (Gun- type, yield 5-20 KT TNT equivalent);
   (b) Do engineering development of implosion type;
   (c) Do limited research and development on the A* warheads (booster-type with yield in the order of 100 KT TNT equivalent);
   (d) The production of plutonium warheads to be discontinued, but expertise developed with the aid of laboratory-scale plant must be retained, with the emphasis on fission element and transuranium element research. Only a limited programme is envisaged;
   (e) Integration of payload with long-range delivery system to be continued;
   (f) The production of lithium-6 to be continued until sufficient material (about 40 kg) has been produced, which must be stored for future use;

TOP SECRET

TOP SECRET

2

- (g) Continue with theoretical work on all types of warheads(A-, A-*, implosion and B-types);
- (h) The Gouriqua project to be continued for the development of pressurised water reactor technology and for the testing of Koeberg fuel, and to retain the option of manufacturing tritium or plutonium in future if necessary;
- (i) Expertise must be preserved so that the option of continuing with advanced systems at a later stage, if necessary, can be retained;
- (j) With a view to cost-saving, the operating strategy for the pilot enrichment plant must be adapted to meet the needs outlined above, together with a prudent stockpile.

The nuclear weapons strategy, as originally approved in 1978, and as set out in paragraph 2 of the Memorandum of 19 March of the Chairman of the Witvlei Council is confirmed, namely:

"At that stage the nuclear strategy was essentially restricted to the following:

- (a) A number of 5 to 6 A weapons will be "kept on the shelf" (Current Resolution 7);
- (b) If the RSA were to find itself in a "back to the wall" situation,
  - (i) the existence of the RSA's nuclear capability should be made known to the Western countries (especially the USA) in a covert manner and if this does not alleviate matters,
  - (ii) an underground test must be carried out to demonstrate the RSA's capability (overt disclosure), and
  - (iii) finally, an above-ground test if the threat persists.

  Any decision in the above regard will be authorised solely by the State President."

TOP SECRET

The strategy specifically excludes the operational application of nuclear weapons.

2. International nuclear safeguards at the AEC enrichment plant
The decision that in the final instance nuclear safeguards at the semi-commercial enrichment plant will not be accepted is confirmed.
This means that the current negotiations between the AEC and the IAEA on nuclear safeguards will have to be discontinued at a convenient time or indefinitely suspended. A decision on the discontinuation of negotiations will be taken after the General Conference of the IAEA which will take place in the last week of September 1985, by which time there will also be greater clarity on possible sanctions or boycotts against the RSA, especially by the USA.

3. Payment of the RSA's membership fees to the IAEA
Resolved that arrear membership fees should be paid so that the RSA will not be more than 2 years in arrears, and will therefore not be in default in terms of the Statute of the IAEA.

4. Marketing of armaments containing uranium
Resolved that the anti-tank weapon may be marketed to South Korea and Australia but not to Iraq.
The Minister of Defence, in consultation with the Minister of Foreign Affairs, will decide on an ad hoc basis which countries it may (or may not) be marketed to.

5. AEC budget
The Minister of Finance expressed concern about the size of the AEC budget and the way in which it is being funded (through loans).

TOP SECRET

4

After some discussion it was decided that alternative funding possibilities should be investigated and that, by re-evaluating its priorities, the AEC should try to curtail its expenditure.

It was mentioned that the full effect of the current rationalisation of the AEC will only materialise in 2 to 3 years' time. The guideline laid down was that a real reduction of 10 percent per annum over the following 3 years should be accepted as the target. However, the biggest saving can only be achieved by retrenching staff. It would not, however, be appropriate in the present economic climate to retrench staff who have made extraordinary efforts to deal with the crisis which arose in 1978 in respect of fuel for the Koeberg Nuclear Power Station.

The State President fully agrees with the last point.

Cmdt. P G Marais
CHAIRMAN ARMSCOR

DATE: 9-9-1985

COUNTERSIGNED

Gen. M A Malan
MINISTER OF DEFENCE

DATE: 9 Sept 85

TOP SECRET

TOP SECRET

Dr JL Steyn

Telephone : 291-2395
Enquiries: Maj.-Gen. M.C. Botha

Copy no. I of 1 copies

HS/PLAN/302/6/DUNHILL

Chief of the SA Defence Force
(Planning Division) Private Bag X161
Pretoria
0001

30 July 1987

PROGRAMME OLYMPIC : CORROBORATIVE NOTES FOLLOWING THE BRIEFING OF THE MINISTER OF DEFENCE IN CAPE TOWN ON 27 JULY 1987

Present:
Gen. M.A. de M. Malan	Minister
Mr W.N. Breytenbach	Deputy Minister
Gen. J.J. Geldenhuys	CSADF
Cmdt. P.G. Marais	Chairman Armscor
Brig G.N. Opperman	Military Secretary

Briefing team
Lt-Gen. F.E.C. van den Berg	CS Plan
Maj.-Gen. A.J.S. van der Lith	CAF
Maj.-Gen. M.C. Botha	CDLP

1. The main points of the briefing to the Minister were:
   a. A status report on Programme Olympic
   b. Certain recommendations which were accepted by the Reduced WCC on 25 June 1987.

2. Recommendations accepted by the Reduced WCC. The following are the most important recommendations as accepted by the reduced WCC and as presented to the Minister:
   a. Number of Missile Weapon Systems. Six.
   b. Number of Payloads

TOP SECRET

APPENDIX

TOP SECRET

      i. Seven primarily for aircraft (Type A, gun-assembled)
      ii. Six primarily for missiles of which three will be A* boosted gun-assembled type
        (AK Type)
      iii. Payloads must be operationally interchangeable between air craft and missiles.
  c. Demonstrator. One (Modulus) AK Type
  d. Implosion technology. The study to acquire this technology must continue.
  e. Investigation/negotiations must continue in order to allow the Reduced WCC to fulfil the role of the WCC as well. In this regard Cmdt. P.G. Marais will take the lead.

3. The Minister accepted the figures in respect of the number of missile systems and the number of payloads and made the following remarks:
  a. The basis in respect of the above-mentioned figures must now be regarded as firm and from now on this must be the basis that is used. Every new team that takes over this matter cannot be permitted to produce new figures.
  b. It should not be forgotten that the development of space technology in the RSA will have a big and beneficial influence on industrial development and therefore also on the creation of employment. This has already proved to be the case in countries that have advanced with the introduction of technology of this kind.

4. The Minister accepted that the demonstrator should only be Modulus (clean test). It was confirmed that the previous underground "dirty test" should not be prepared again.

[signature]
RECORDING OFFICER MAJ.-GEN.

30 July 1987

REMARKS

[signature]
MINISTER OF DEFENCE

Date: 27 AUG 87

TOP SECRET

THE BOMB

TOP SECRET

Copy no 1 of 2 copies

CS PLAN/302/6/DUNHILL]

Telephone : 291-2395
Enquiries : Maj.-Gen.M.C. Botha

Chief of the SA Defence Force
(Planning Division)
Private Bag X161
Pretoria
0001
3 September 1987

The Secretary
Witvlei Control Committee

SUBMISSION TO THE WITVLEI CONTROL COMMITTEE (WBK)

1. The attached submission as recommended by the Coordinating Subcommittee (CSC) viz KRAMAT CAPABILITY: CURRENT STATUS AND FURTHER DEVELOPMENT is hereby sent to you to serve at the following Witvlei Control Committee meeting, please.
2. Since the various code words in terms of security usage have changed with effect from 1 Sep 87, the meanings of the code words are given below for the convenience of the WCC members:
a.	KRAMAT	Nuclear
b.	MODULUS	"Clean" underground test device
c.	GARDENIA	System of placement shafts and "dirty" underground test device
d.	MELBA	"Dirty" underground test device
e.	CABOT	Formerly Hobo (Dumb weapon)
f.	HAMERKOP	Formerly Bakker (Smart weapon)
g.	HUSKY	Medium-range ballistic missile system
h.	OSTRA	Payload on Husky
3. Thank you for your attention.

n/s *[signature]* Botha Genl mag

pp CHIEF OF THE SA DEFENCE FORCE: GENERAL

(translation)

TOP SECRET

APPENDIX

TOP SECRET

Copy No 1 of 2 copies

KRAMAT CAPABILITY: CURRENT STATUS AND FURTHER DEVELOPMENT

BACKGROUND

1. Following a submission on the inspection of the placement shafts and development of MODULUS (Test device for a backfilled test) the Witvlei Control Committee requested at its meeting held on 14 April 1987 that a status report containing proposals for further development should be submitted to the committee. The WSWG (Weapons System Working Group) was instructed to determine the number of missiles and KRAMAT payloads from a strategic and operational point of view. This report deals with both aspects.

STRATEGIC REQUIREMENTS

2. The approved strategy for the use of the KRAMAT capability as approved by the Minister of Defence on 24 November 1986 may be summed up as follows:

   a. During the stage of strategic uncertainty the existence of a KRAMAT capability will be denied.

   b. During the stage of covert negotiation the KRAMAT capability will be revealed as a means of inducement, persuasion and coercion.

   c. During the overt deterrent stage the following actions will be considered:

1

TOP SECRET

THE BOMB

TOP SECRET

    i. Overt announcement.

    ii. Display of force.

    iii. Demonstration (underground or atmospheric test detonation).

    iv. Threaten to use.

    v. Use on battlefield as DETERRENT against conventional assault forces.

    vi. No strategic application foreseen, merely the threat of use.

3. In order to carry out this strategy with credibility, the following weapon systems are required:

    a) Explosive device for underground demonstration test.

    b) Air-launched weapon for atmospheric demonstration test and use in battle.

    c) Long-range ballistic missile for threat of strategic use.

CURRENT STATUS

4. GARDENIA/MELBA

    a. The GARDENIA system (MELBA device with placement and control systems) is in working order and regular

TOP SECRET

TOP SECRET

maintenance is carried out on it. The MELBA device is designed to produce an explosion of 6 kilotons of TNT equivalent. The system is 8 years old and is technologically obsolete. The reliability of the system is no longer satisfactory either. The estimated time required to prepare the system is 21 days.

   b. The Vastrap test site is available for a demonstration test. Two placement shafts exist, namely;

      i. PH 1 - 390 metres deep (It is possible that there is an obstruction in the shaft);

      ii. PH 2 - 216 metres deep.

   c. Both shafts were sealed in 1977 and have not been inspected since. The GARDENIA system was designed for an OPEN underground test explosion. This means that a considerable amount of radioactivity will be discharged into the atmosphere during a test of this kind.

5. CABOT/HAMERKOP

   a. CABOT is a ballistic bomb designed to produce an explosion of 6 kilotons of TNT equivalent. The weapon is six years old and is technologically obsolete. There is only one weapon of this kind and it has never been subjected to flight tests. Its reliability is therefore uncertain. The weapon will be withdrawn from service shortly and replaced by HAMERKOP weapons.

TOP SECRET

TOP SECRET

b. The HAMERKOP weapons system is a fair weather guided glide bomb with a 20 kiloton TNT equivalent warhead. One preproduction model is currently available for use. The first production model of a series of five will be available by October 1987. The completion date for the production series is December 1989. At present the weapons can only be employed from a Buccaneer aircraft. Clearance on Mirage Fl and Cheetah aircraft is contemplated. For radiological safety reasons, atmospheric demonstration tests can only be carried out at remote testing sites at sea.

6. HUSKY

  a. HUSKY is an all-weather medium-range ballistic missile system which is currently under development. Successful flight tests with single-stage missiles have already been carried out overseas. Scale-model rocket motors were locally manufactured and tested. The preparation of the Overberg test range and Houwteq (systems supplier) company is progressing satisfactorily. Commencement of production of the weapons system has been planned for 1996. The development of a KRAMAT payload (Project OSTRA) has already started and will be completed by 1996.

FURTHER DEVELOPMENT

7. The current approval in respect of the number and type of KRAMAT payloads is that of the Ad Hoc Cabinet Committee of 3 September 1985 and is as follows:

TOP SECRET

APPENDIX

TOP SECRET

    a.   Manufacture a maximum number of 7 A gun-type payloads.

    b.   Do engineering development of implosion-type payloads.

    c.   Do limited research and development of the A* payloads.

    d.   Discontinue the development of plutonium payloads.

    e.   Develop a payload for HUSKY.

    f.   Produce 40 kg of Lithium-6.

    g.   Continue theoretical work on all types of payloads.

    h.   Retain expertise in order to continue with advanced systems later on.

    i.   With a view to cost reduction, the operating strategy for the pilot enrichment plant must be adapted to meet the needs outlined above, together with prudent stockpiling.

8.   The above-mentioned approval predates the latest approved strategy. The WSWG therefore appointed a subworking group to determine the type and number of KRAMAT payloads and weapons systems that will be required to carry out the strategy. This also addressed the aspect of "prudent stockpiling" of KRAMAT material. The WSWG accepted the recommendations of the subworking group on 23 June and submitted them to the "VBR" for consideration. The "VBR" accepted the proposals for submission to the bodies responsible for approving them. [Note: The abbreviation "VBR" is currently unknown. It is worth bearing in mind that in a few places in these documents "W" was incorrectly reflected as "V", apparently a typographical error.]

TOP SECRET

TOP SECRET

The proposals in respect of the number and type of missile systems were submitted to the WCC on 25 June and approved. The proposals in respect of the type and number of KRAMAT payloads will now be submitted to the KRAMAT approval body for approval.

RECOMMENDATIONS

9. The following recommendations are submitted for consideration and approval.

    a. <u>GARDENIA/MELBA/MODULUS</u>. In view of the present shortcomings of the GARDENIA/MELBA system, namely;

        i. Obsolete MELBA device;

        ii. Possible obstruction in placement shaft;

        iii. Back-filling of placement shaft not possible,

    it is suggested that a new test device (MODULUS) with accompanying placement and control equipment should be developed and manufactured to replace MELBA. (MELBA will be kept operational until it is replaced in 1991. In the meanwhile only a "dirty" test is possible.) It must be possible to use the MODULUS device for a back-filled "clean" underground demonstration test. In addition, an inspection of the placement shafts must be carried out to determine their condition, in a manner that will not attract international attention to the test site. If this is not possible, an alternative test site must be sought.

TOP SECRET

APPENDIX

TOP SECRET

b. <u>KRAMAT PAYLOADS</u>. The current approval is for 7 A gun-type payloads plus a feasibility study in respect of implosion-type payloads (which could possibly double the number to 14) and a "prudent stockpile" of KRAMAT material. Taking into account the strategic and operational requirements and financial constraints, it is the view of the SADF that a minimum of 14 KRAMAT payloads will be required, as follows:

   i. One warhead for MODULUS.

   ii. 10 A gun-type payloads which are operationally interchangeable between air-launched weapons and medium-range ballistic missiles. The payloads will initially be allocated as follows: 3 for missiles and 7 for aircraft weapons.

   iii. 3 A* gun-type payloads for the same kind of missiles, for the threat of strategic point targets. This results in a better balance between circular error probabilities of ballistic missiles and payload yield.

c. <u>TECHNOLOGICAL DEVELOPMENT</u>. It is proposed that a feasibility study in respect of implosion technology and theoretical studies of other types should be continued but that the first generation of KRAMAT weapons should be equipped with gun-type payloads. The reasons for this recommendation are as follows:

   i. The gun-type technology has proved itself and is available

7

TOP SECRET

whereas implosion technology is still at an early stage of development. The switch to the implosion-type payloads has additional financial implications and will only be possible after the year 2000, if the user were to decide to update.

ii. The AEC pilot plant will be kept in operation for longer. The need for stockpiling therefore falls away. If the need for more payloads were to arise in future, implosion technology could probably be used to double the numbers with the aid of existing material. This is regarded as sufficient for the long term.

iii. Implosion and other types of payloads may be better suited to new generation lighter and smaller weapons systems which may become available in future.

10. The estimated financial implications of the above recommendations are shown in the following Table. The procurement costs indicate only the development and production costs of KRAMAT payloads for the period 1981-2006.

APPENDIX

TOP SECRET

FINANCIAL IMPLICATIONS (1987 RAND VALUES) ONLY FOR PAYLOAD PORTION OF SYSTEMS

SERIES NO	DESCRIPTION a	PROCUREMENT COSTS (1981-2006) b	ALREADY SPENT (1981-1987) c
1	KRAMAT PAYLOADS		
	i. MODULUS	R20m	0
	ii. HAMERKOP[1] (factory interchangeable)	R30m	R15m
	iii. A.K. OSTRA (Operational interchangeable HUSKY 1/v)	R243	R4.9m
	iv. HAMERKOP[2] (Operationally interchangeable 1/v between HAMERKOP and HUSKY)	R60m	0
	v. A*-OSTRA	R10m	0
2	TECHNOLOGY DEV.		
	i. IMPLOSION	R43M	R6m
TOTAL. (Dept. Defence):		R406m	R25.9m

TOP SECRET

9

THE BOMB

TOP SECRET

NOTE: The financial implications of user systems, for which payloads are subsystems, are contained in user budgets. The HUSKY user budget will be updated in November 1987, as an integral part of the DUNHILL Baseline document.

3	BIBO MATERIALS		
	i RXVH	R355m	R233m
	ii A* MATERIALS	R17m	R2m
4	THEORETICAL STUDIES	R30m	R5m
TOTAL (Dept. Economic Affairs):l		R402m	R240m

[Note: BIBO is a code word for the weapons project/ RXVH = highly enriched uranium/ A* materials are for boosted weapons.]

REQUEST
11. The KRAMAT approval body is requested to TAKE NOTE of the current status of the KRAMAT capability and the view of the SADF, as confirmed by the "VBR", on the type and number of KRAMAT payloads required and to APPROVE the recommendations. [VBR currently unknown]

Lieut.-Gen. F.E.C.v den Berg
Chairman: Co-ordinating Subcommittee

Date: 2 September 1987

10

(translation)

TOP SECRET

APPENDIX

TOP SECRET

Copy No. 1 of 2

PLAN/UG/306/4/16/2

Telephone : 291-2395
Enquiries: Maj.-Gen.M.C. Botha

Chief of the SA Defence Force
(Planning Division)
Private Bag X161
Pretoria
0001
18 April 1988

Dealt with at meeting in the office (Illegible) *4 Aug. 88.*
(Illegible) *notes copy 1 of 1 handed to Dr Steyn of (illegible).*
(Initialled by two people, initials illegible.)

PROGRAMME DUNHILL: DEVELOPMENT OF A NUCLEAR
CAPABILITY FOR THE SADF
DECISION OF AD HOC CABINET COMMITTEE

1. Approved by Ad-Hoc Cabinet Committee on 3 Sep 85
   a. Manufacture a maximum number of <u>seven</u> gun-type warheads. ✓
   b. Do engineering development on implosion type. ✓
   c. Do limited research and development of the A star warheads. ✓
   d. Discontinue development of Plutonium warheads. ✓
   e. Develop a warhead for the missile systems. ✓
   f. Produce 40 kg Lithium - 6.
   g. Continue theoretical work on all types of warheads.
   h. Retain expertise in order to proceed with advanced systems later. ✓
   i. Adapt the operating strategy of the pilot enrichment plant to meet the needs as outlined above, together with prudent stockpiling. ✓

USER ACTIONS

2. <u>Introduction</u>. The SA Air Force was appointed on 21 Apr 86 as user of the Nuclear and missile programme and went through several processes in the course of 86/87 to determine the needs of the SADF.
3. <u>SADF Needs</u>. The following have been determined as the SADF needs:
   a. Manufacture a total of 14 Nuclear warheads for the following possible applications:
      i. One for a <u>clean</u> underground demonstration (Code name Modulus).
      ii. Ten Gun-type warheads that will be operationally interchangeable between aircraft-deliverable and missile-deliverable weapons.
      iii. 3 A star gun-type warheads deliverable by long-range missiles.

Why, (illegible)? *AEC* (illegible) *How fast? Period: finance: raw materials available*

TOP SECRET

TOP SECRET

   b. Continue with the development of the implosion technology and do theoretical studies on the other nuclear technologies.

4. Approval Received by User

   a. "VBR" on 23 Jun 87.

   b. WCC on 25 Jun 87.

   c. The Minister of Defence. Verbally on 27 Jul 87 and in writing on 27 Aug 87.

PROBLEM

5. Dr W.L. de Villiers of the Atomic Energy Corporation (AEC) requests that the instruction to him to manufacture the Nuclear material, as requested now by the SADF should be given to him by his Minister, viz the Minister of Economic Affairs and Technology.

REQUEST

6. It is requested that the Minister of Defence give the necessary leadership in solving the problem outlined in paragraph 5 above.

CHIEF OF THE SA DEFENCE FORCE: GENERAL
MCB/ab
DISTR
Deputy Minister of Defence
File PLAN/UG/306/4/16/2

	Copy no
Deputy Minister of Defence	1
File PLAN/UG/306/4/16/2	2

(translation)

TOP SECRET

APPENDIX

Ministerie van Verdediging **Ministry of Defence**

Dawie,
This is very sensitive. Please read it and we will discuss the contents after this meeting.

Magnus 11/5/88

THE BOMB

89111504u10

TOP SECRET

TO   :   HERBERT BEUKES

FROM   :   RICHARD CARTER

DATE   :   17 NOVEMBER 1989

MAIN POINTS ARISING FROM LUNCHEON ON 14 NOVEMBER 1989

1. AEC's two main arguments are -
   - ANC takeover - therefore pressure on SA to accede NOW
   - We get no quid pro quo for accession

2. Enrichment package produced by AEC is 50% more expensive than international markets. (Not more expensive than SPOT market, but no power generating utility buys on the spot market because a package is sought - ie. uranium, enrichment, fuel rod manufacture, delivery, loading and end of use removal, dumping and/or reprocessing).

3. AEC should be attempting to penetrate international enrichment markets - it can provide the package mentioned above. WdeV is in principle against trying for political reasons. Stumpf easier. Initial enquiries have shown some interest - Taiwan.

4. ARMSCOR no longer committed to a weapons program. Feel that a satellite and/or conventional delivery system program is worth focusing on. Considerable financial saving.

5. Decontamination is a major problem. Even a major, 3 year decontamination program will be unlikely to completely eradicate all traces of highly enriched (95%)

APPENDIX

TOP SECRET

2

product. Leaks from cooling tower, complex machinery etc aggravate this problem. IAEA inspectors using sensitive equipment will be able to detect the prior existence of 95% enriched product.

6. Existing items could be degraded within about a year without trace ie. reduced to highly enriched gas. Some records would have to be destroyed. Highly enriched product thus created could be further degraded over time but para 5 remains still applicable.

7. Suggestion : That 6 be implemented as an accession strategy. That SA "come clean" and admit that it has enriched uranium to weapons grade, but that it has not made weapons. Doing this does away with the lengthy, expensive, dubious decontamination program. The process could be completed in 12-18 months, after which accession could take place followed by ± 18 months safeguards negotiations.

8. If we came clean on the 95% enriched product, we would have to do very little arguing over safeguards. The "secret" would be out. Manufacture of weapons however need never be admitted. Only 2/4 of the Y-facility's units would have to be shut down and dismantled or "transformed". This could probably be achieved within the 18 months period before accession.

8. AEC probably does not have the manpower - or inclination - to embark on the time consuming decontamination program. It is considered to be "non-productive" and bad for morale.

10. WdeV is "yesterday's man" using yesterday's arguments. A more pragmatic approach may be expected from Stumpf - although he remains at this time "under Wynand's influence".

THE BOMB

TOP SECRET

Suid-Afrikaanse Lugmag • South African Air Force

Telephone : 312-2743
Enquiries : Maj.-Gen. Van der Lith

Air Force Headquarters
Private Bag X 199
Pretoria
0001
31 January 1990

Dr J. L. Steyn
Private Bag X337
Pretoria
0001

L.A.
31.1.90.

Brig Anton van Graan
1. *Submitted to CAF in the absence of CSADF.*
2. *Would you please submit this to the Minister as agreed?*
3. *Please phone me if clarity is needed.*

Hannes Steyn
1 Feb 90]

PROGRAMME FOR WEAPONS DISMANTLING

1. Your letter (number illegible) dated 31 January 1990 refers.

2. In the absence of CAF and the urgency of your request I have studied your letter in consultation with CDLP, CLS Ops and the Director of the Dunnhill Programme, with reference to the Command and Control Procedures to which you refer. From an operational point of view I am in agreement with the content of your submission.

(Maj.-Gen. A.J.S. VAN DER LITH)
pp   CHIEF OF THE AIR FORCE : LT-GEN.

(translation)

TOP SECRET

APPENDIX

TOP SECRET

KRYGKOR ARMSCOR

Chief of the SA Air Force
Private Bag X199 PRETORIA
0001

Privaatsak X337
0001 Pretoria
Reoubliek van Suid-Afrika

Telegramme ARMSCOR

Private Bag X337
0001 Pretoria
Republic of South Africa

Telegrams ARMSCOR 320217

Tel. (012) 428-1911
Datum/Date 31 JANUARY 1990
Enquiries DR J L STEYN
Tel: (012) 428 4516
Ons verw/Our ret NO/120/030/4

PROGRAMME FOR DISMANTLING OF WEAPONS
1. Attached please find a letter to Gen. M A de M Malan concerning the above matter for signature by CSADF.
2. I invite your comments with a view to direct submission to the Minister.

With kind regards
Yours sincerely

[signature]

pp ACTING EXECUTIVE CHAIRMAN

(translation)

TOP SECRET

THE BOMB

TOP SECRET

DATE : 31 JANUARY 1990
FILE NUMBER : NO/120/030/4

Gen. M A de M Malan
Minister of Defence CAPE TOWN
8000

PROGRAMME FOR DISMANTLING OF WEAPONS

1. I refer to the discussion you had with Dr J L Steyn of Armscor on Friday, 26 January 1990 in connection with certain Cabinet decisions regarding the RSA's nuclear weapons programme.

2. As Dr Steyn has pointed out to you, there are formal Command and Control Procedures for removal of weapons from weapon vaults. The order to put the dismantlement plan into operation must also be given in terms of this procedure. For the record a copy of the Command and Control Procedures is attached as Annexure A.

3. I shall summarise this for you briefly:
For the sake of Safety, Security and Responsibility double locking is used throughout (down to the lowest tactical and technical level). The safes can never be opened by a single person, for example. The warhead is also divided into two parts and the front
warhead (the Controlled Unit) cannot be removed from the safe without a command from the State President through two separate Channels of Command.

2/

TOP SECRET

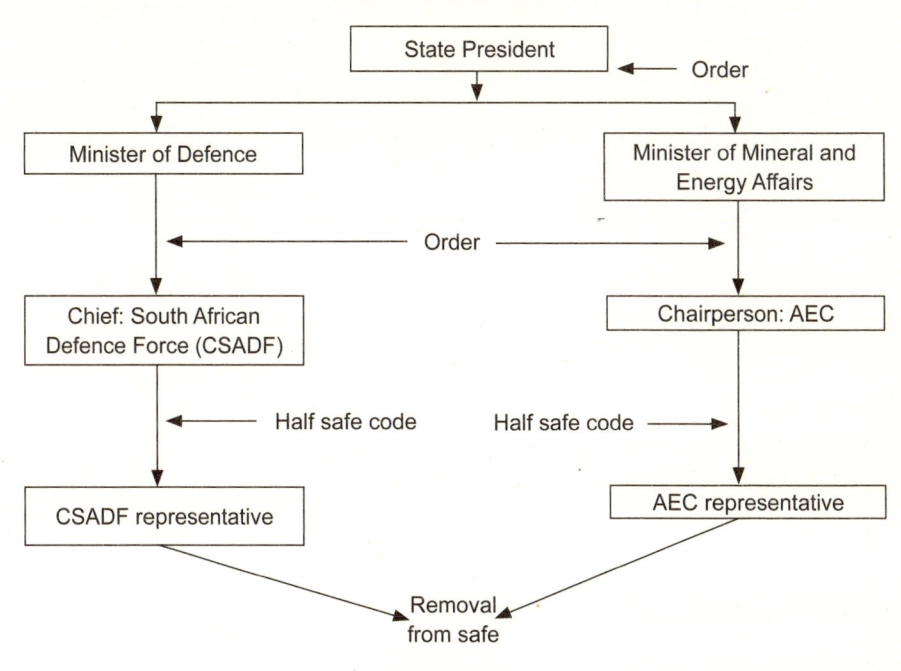

APPENDIX

TOP SECRET

```
                         State President ──── Order
                         ┌──────┴──────┐
                         ▼             ▼
              Minister of Defence    Minister of Mineral and
                                      Energy Affairs
                    │ ◄──── Order ────► │
                    ▼                   ▼
              Chief: South African    Chairperson: AEC
              Defence Force (CSADF)
                    │                   │
                ◄── Half safe code   Half safe code ──►
                    ▼                   ▼
              CSADF representative    AEC representative
                         \             /
                          Removal
                         from safe
```

4. I propose that you suggest to the State President that he should formulate his command in such a way that:

   (a) A separate command <u>does not have to be issued for every removal of the warheads from the safe</u>.

   (b) The <u>command will apply to both the Controlled Units (front warhead) and the Weapon System Units (rear warhead)</u>.

   (c) An independent <u>auditing authority should be appointed to monitor the whole process</u>.

   proposed by Dr Mouton

5. It is essential now (perhaps especially now) that the RSA act with the highest degree of responsibility regarding its nuclear capability.

   Heading dismantlement process begins.

Respectfully yours

(GEN. J J GELDENHUYS)
CHIEF OF THE SA DEFENCE FORCE

TOP SECRET

THE BOMB

TOP SECRET

Page 1 of 1
Copy 2 of 3

P.O. BOX 582
PRETORIA 0001
Tel.: 31 6--4222
ISOTOPE
321047 SA
Telefax 79 1515

ATOMIC ENERGY CORPORATION OF SOUTH AFRICA LTD

ENQUIRIES
OUR REF HUB900/01/02
YOUR REF
DATE 15 February 1990

The Minister
Mineral and Energy Affairs and Public Enterprises
Private Bag X9079
CAPE TOWN
8000

ATTENTION: Minister D J de Villiers

Dear Minister De Villiers

PHASING OUT OF THE RSA'S NUCLEAR WEAPONS CAPABILITY

Following the meeting of the ad hoc Cabinet Committee in De Tuynhuys under the chairmanship of the State President held on 22 January 1990, Drs W E Stumpf of the AEC and J L Steyn of ARMSCOR held discussions to define a procedure for phasing out the RSA's nuclear capability.

I attach two copies of the proposed procedure for your consideration and for submission to the State President for final approval. A decision on which of the three alternative communication channels should be followed, as proposed in paragraph 6.2, would be appreciated.

With kind regards

Yours sincerely

J W L de Villiers
<u>CHAIRMAN</u>

TOP SECRET

APPENDIX

TOP SECRET

PAGE 1 OF 4
COPY 3 OF 4

HUB 901/50
8 FEBRUARY 1990

THE "MANTEL" PROJECT

This document defines the main objective, the general working procedure as well as the control and communication channels for the "Mantel" project.

1. MAIN OBJECTIVE
   To dismantle the present 5 nuclear weapons devices together with half-completed devices, components and material in an orderly and controlled manner, melt down the highly enriched uranium they contain and store it safely and perform the necessary cleaning operations to attach credibility to the statement that the RSA did manufacture highly enriched uranium but did not undertake the final step of manufacturing nuclear weapons.

2. SECURITY CLASSIFICATION
   The project will bear the classification TOP SECRET at all times.

3. PARTIES INVOLVED
   Only the SADF, ARMSCOR and the ATOMIC ENERGY CORPORATION are involved.

4. TIME SCALE
   The final objective must be achieved within 20 months, that is, before 30 September 1991.

TOP SECRET

TOP SECRET

5. **CONTROL STRUCTURE**

   The following control structure is proposed for the project:

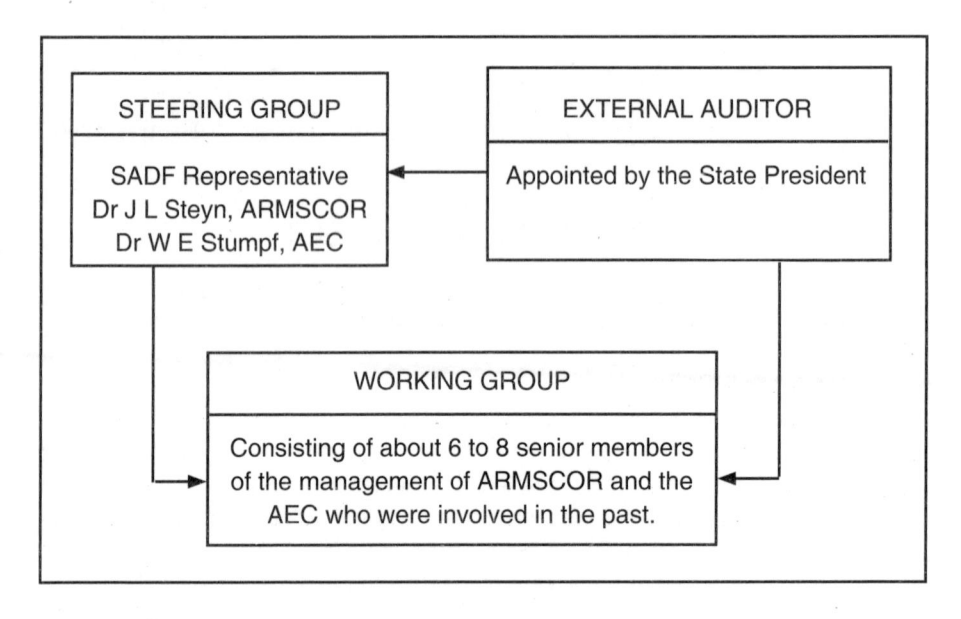

```
┌─────────────────────────────┐      ┌─────────────────────────────┐
│      STEERING GROUP         │      │      EXTERNAL AUDITOR       │
│                             │◄─────│                             │
│   SADF Representative       │      │ Appointed by the State      │
│   Dr J L Steyn, ARMSCOR     │      │ President                   │
│   Dr W E Stumpf, AEC        │      │                             │
└──────────────┬──────────────┘      └─────────────────────────────┘
               │
               ▼
        ┌─────────────────────────────┐
        │      WORKING GROUP          │
        │                             │
        │ Consisting of about 6 to 8  │◄──
        │ senior members of the       │
        │ management of ARMSCOR and   │
        │ the AEC who were involved   │
        │ in the past.                │
        └─────────────────────────────┘
```

The <u>STEERING GROUP</u>'s duties consist in the planning and overall control of the project and the formulation of policy for submission to the Government. The <u>WORKING GROUP</u>'s duties consist in carrying out the detailed planning and control and ensuring that the various actions are carried out.

The <u>EXTERNAL AUDITOR</u>'s duties consist in providing independent assurance to the Government regarding the orderly progress and final completion of the project.

6. **COMMUNICATION CHANNELS**

   The following communication channels were proposed to the Government:

TOP SECRET

TOP SECRET

PAGE 3 OF 4
COPY 3 OF 4

6.1 The <u>EXTERNAL AUDITOR</u> reports directly to the State President and also receives his orders directly from the State President.

6.2 The <u>STEERING GROUP</u> could report to the Government in one of three ways. The three alternatives are presented here for a final decision by the State President:

    6.2.1 Alternative 1

    The representative of the AEC on the steering group (W E Stumpf) will act as convenor of the steering group and, after consensus has been reached by all three members of the steering group, official reporting to the State President will take place via the Chairman of the AEC and the Minister of Mineral and Energy Affairs and Public Enterprises.

    6.2.2 Alternative 2

    The representative of ARMSCOR on the steering group (J L Steyn) will act as convenor of the steering group and, after consensus has been reached by all three members of the steering group, official reporting to the State President will take place via the Chairman of ARMSCOR and the Minister of Defence.

    6.2.3 Alternative 3

    The steering group will not have a single convenor and, after consensus has been reached by all three members of the steering group, official reporting to the State President will take place via the respective heads to the respective Ministers.

TOP SECRET

TOP SECRET

PAGE 4 OF 4
COPY 3 OF 4

All three members of the proposed steering group would find any of the three alternatives acceptable although the third alternative might possibly result in divided accountability which could complicate any auditing action.

7. **FREQUENCY OF REPORTING**

    7.1 Policy matters that require a decision at a higher level will be submitted on an ad hoc basis.

    7.2 Progress with the project will initially be reported every three months but this could initially be reduced to every six months as operations begin to run smoothly.

_____
90-02-13
W E STUMPF
CHIEF EXECUTIVE OFFICER
A E C

_____
13.2.90
J L STEYN
SENIOR GENERAL MANAGER : R&D
ARMSCOR

TOP SECRET

APPENDIX

TOP SECRET

CANDIDATES FOR EXTERNAL AUDITOR	PROF W L MOUTON	DR L D BARNARD	DR J B CLARK
INFORMATION	M	M	M
EXPERTISE	H	M	M
AVAILABILITY	M	L	L
INDEPENDENCE	H	H	H

TOP SECRET

THE BOMB

TOP SECRET

The Minister of Defence
HF Verwoerd Building
CAPE TOWN
8000

DISMANTLING OF NUCLEAR WEAPONS

1 Authorisation is hereby given, in terms of the Command Order and Control Procedures (LMH/UG/306/4) and subject to the conditions in paragraphs 2 and 3 below, to:

   1.1 Remove the following from the vaults: The Controlled Units as well as the Weapons System Units of all existing nuclear weapons, together with material and material components of incomplete weapons.

   1.2 Dismantle the above-mentioned weapons and incomplete weapons and hand the highly enriched material to the Atomic Energy Corporation, under safe and secure procedures, for storage.

2 The dismantling and cleaning-up process must take place under the supervision of a steering group consisting of senior managers of the SADF, AEC and Armscor. This steering group, whose duties and working procedure are described elsewhere, must:

   2.1 Approve the plan for dismantlement and cleaning up.

   2.2 Authorise the dismantlement and cleaning-up process step by step.

   2.3 Report regularly on the process.

3. To ensure that the weapons dismantlement and cleaning-up process takes place with the highest degree of responsibility, safety and security, I hereby nominate Prof. W L Mouton as independent auditor to monitor the dismantlement and cleaning-up process and report to me on the matter on a continuous basis.

[signature]
STATE PRESIDENT
REPUBLIC OF SOUTH AFRICA
1990-02-26

(translation)

TOP SECRET

APPENDIX

"Author Nic von Wielligh obtained the original documents (mostly in Afrikaans) from the AEC and Advena at the time of the IAEA's investigation of South Africa's nuclear weapons programme. In accordance with President de Klerk's requirement of total transparency, the documents were shown to the IAEA and their authenticity was verified. The author then made copies for the purpose of compiling the report on South Africa's nuclear weapons history for the IAEA and for back-up reference purposes. The original documents were returned to the AEC and Advena. Von Wielligh's copies were reproduced and published in the Afrikaans edition of this book, Die Bom – Suid-Afrika se kernwapenprogram in 2014."

THE BOMB

INDEX

(P = black-and-white photograph section; CP = colour photograph section)

A

Abdera 3, 4
Academic Assistance Council (AAC) 68
Accabo (*see also* Project Festival) 165, 168
accidents (*see also* disasters) 105, 129, 135, 149, 210, 256, 309, 403, 404, 426-430
accounting, nuclear material (*see also* Initial Report) 87, 88, 224, 232, 233, 236, 242, 253, 258
Acheson, Dean 73, 78
Acheson-Lilienthal plan 74
ad hoc cabinet committee 176, 180-183, 189, 191, 216, 218, 480-483
Adam, Rob xv
Adams, Lytle 24
Additional Protocol (*see* IAEA)
Adenauer, Konrad 285, 431
Advena facility 187, 189, 267-270, 310, 311, 439
Advisory Committee on Uranium 24
Aeolus 305-306
Afghanistan 210, 353, 354, 406, 412, 415
Africa iv, v, 86, 105, 124, 131, 132, 196, 205, 213, 231, 240, 253, 277, 278-280, 292, 305, 306, 320, 322, 334
African National Congress (ANC) iv, 144, 197, 198, 213, 230, 257, 259, 266, 271, 276-278, 280, 281, 301, 310, 311, 334, 335
African Nuclear-Weapon-Free Zone Treaty (*see also* Treaty of Pelindaba) 280, 448
Afrikaner 142, 177, 204, 265, 291
  Volksfront 264
  Volkswag 271
  Vryheidstigting 271
AFTAC (*see* Air Force ...)
Agnew, Harold 48
agreement
  bilateral 76, 77, 81, 84, 109, 131, 194, 295, 321, 322, 359, 421
  comprehensive safeguards (*see* IAEA)
  cooperation 292, 293, 309, 357, 364
  model 83, 87, 109
Agreements
  INFCIRC (*see* INFCIRC)
  Quebec 57
  Safeguards (*see* IAEA)
  Security and Secrecy (Secment) 293
  Simonstown 131
  US-UK Mutual Defence 308, 309
agriculture 71, 98, 101, 104, 106, 292
Agu, Benson 280
Ahmadinejad, Mahmoud 415, 416
Air Force Technical Applications Center (AFTAC) 151, 152, 154, 249
aircraft 46, 131, 153, 160, 164, 194, 206, 288, 298, 400, 401, 408
  bomb delivery/bombers 24, 37, 41, 43, 44, 55, 58, 60, 135, 149, 165, 172, 176, 185, 188-191, 290, 307, 322, 329, 353, 357, 396, 400, 401, 403, 404, 407, 411, 413, CP4
  carriers 25, 44, 404, 413
  observation/sampling 58, 137-139, 148, 154, 160, 254, 263
  spy 148, 287, 400, 401

515

aircraft
    B-29   37, 41, 43, 44
    B-52   135
    Beechcraft   148
    Bock's Car   41, 58
    Boeing B-29 Superfortress   37
    Buccaneers   185, 190
    C-130 (*see* Hercules *below*)
    Cheetah   190, 298
    Enola Gay   41
    F-15 and F-16   290, 353
    Hercules C-130   149, 352, 355, 357
    Ilyushin-28   400, 401
    MiG   164, 185
    Mirage   185, 190, 194, 288
    Su-22   185
    U-2   287, 400
Akram, Zamir   422
Alamogordo   37
Alaska   71
Alberts, Johan   339
Alberts, Louw   180
Albright, David   244, 265, 313
Algeria   60, 62, 64, 159, 286, 288, 412
Alguadis, Selim   362, 364, 367, 368, 390
Alkantpan   270
Allied nations/Allies   38, 40, 42, 44, 393, 398, 411, 413
Alliluyeva, Svetlana   52
Allis-Chalmers   29, 106
alloys   233
    Monel   384
    uranium-aluminium   104, 107-109
    zirconium   196, 203, 427
al-Qaeda   405, 406, 408
Al-Shamli, Ali   385
Alsos Mission   44, 45, 47
aluminium   104, 105, 107-109, 114, 185, 307, 308, 364, 373, 382
Alvarez, Luis   155, 156
Amano, Yukiya   335, 435
amber   4
America (*see also* United States of America)   xvi, 17, 18, 21-30, 32, 33, 37-53, 55-64, 68-70, 73-80, 86, 90-92, 97, 100, 101, 104-110, 112, 119, 121, 124, 127, 130-133, 135, 138-151, 153-163, 168, 169, 171, 177-183, 185, 187, 189, 192, 194-196, 203, 204, 206, 210-216, 219, 224, 226-228, 230-232, 235, 238, 239, 244, 245, 247-249, 251, 254-257, 261-263, 265-268, 272-275, 277, 286-289, 298, 299, 301, 307, 309, 313, 314, 318-323, 325-330, 338-340, 344, 347, 352-354, 356, 358, 360, 362, 364, 365, 367-372, 376-379, 385, 387-390, 393, 394-418, 420-424, 426, 429, 430, 433, 437, 438
amimut strategy   188, 288
ammonium nitrate   408
ammonium perchlorate   185
ammunition (*see also* arms; nuclear stockpiles)   120, 161, 211, 292, 356
    depots   170, 264, 270
    testing grounds   270
Ammunition Defects Museum   CP15
Anderson, John   58, 97
Angola   iii, 131, 133, 164, 165, 177, 181, 185, 186, 211, 258, 259, 273, 281, 282, 291
Anti-Apartheid Act   179, 299
Anti-Apartheid Movement (AAM)   334
anti-apartheid organisations   213
anti-landmine vehicles   164
anti-nuclear power group   198
anti-Semitism (*see also* Jews)   67, 68
apartheid   vi, 121, 123, 141, 145, 184, 197, 224, 279, 280, 291-293, 299, 301, 335, 336
Arab Spring   423
Arab states   123, 163, 194, 273, 288, 291, 324, 326, 330, 332, 333, 355, 390, 406, 414, 415, 417, 418, 423
Ardenne, Manfred von   46, 47, 111

INDEX

Ardennes 38
Areva 204
argon 114
Argonne, National Laboratory 101, 109, 181
Arkhipov, Vasili 402
Armaments Corporation of South Africa (Armscor) 143, 146, 164-167, 171, 172, 174-176, 178, 180, 181, 182, 185-187, 191, 192, 201, 216-218, 220-222, 224, 243, 247, 255, 257, 259, 260, 263, 264, 266-268, 270, 274, 297, 312, 316-319, 339, 439, CP10
arms (*see also* guns; weapons)
    control/exports/trade 123, 163, 263, 274, 301, 331
    embargoes (*see* sanctions)
    industry (*see also* Armscor) 164, 165, 178, 263
    race 40, 56, 85, 394
Arms Control and Disarmament Agency (USA) 156
Armstrong, R.F. 293
Arniston 299
Ashton, Catherine 416
Assam 90
Atlantic Ocean 131, 143, 151, 257
atmosphere 55, 59, 62, 86, 139, 150, 151, 152, 154, 156, 159, 209, 428
atmospheric pressure 114, 127, 152, 209
atom ii, 3, 4, 6, 8-15, 21, 67, 104, 439
    radioactive (*see also* radioactivity) 9
    splitting of the nucleus 17-19, 25, 27, 36, 59
    uranium (*see also* uranium) 19, 20, 27, 59, 129
atomic
    bazaar 343-390, CP12
    bombs (*see also* bombs) 439
    energy (*see also* nuclear energy) 80, 104
    mass 8, 10, 12, 20
    nucleus/nuclei 9-15, 17-20, 28, 30, 31, 34, 36, 250
    number 12
    particles (*see* particles)
    weapons (*see also* bombs; weapons) 78
Atomic Energy
    Act (USA) 44, 58, 59, 76, 99, 130
    Authority (UK) 106
    Board (AEB) 58, 97-102, 104, 110, 111, 113, 114, 117, 118, 121, 122, 124, 134, 136-138, 142, 148-150, 165, 166, 168, 170, 174, 175, 180, 181, 439
    Commission (AEC) (USA) 44, 74, 80, 90, 106, 294
    Corporation of South Africa (AEC) i, 101, 107, 109, 124, 159, 160, 163, 167, 168, 173, 180-183, 187, 190-192, 201, 203-205, 214-216, 218-220, 222-224, 232-234, 236, 237, 240, 241, 243, 244, 246-248, 251-255, 257, 259-261, 264-271, 274, 276, 277, 439
    Research Establishment (AERE) 49
Atomic Weapons Establishment (AWE) 309
Atomic Weapons Research Establishment (AWRE) 59, 168
Atoms for Peace iii, 75-79, 90, 92, 100, 104, 106, 130-132, 181, 194, 262, 286, 358, 439
Attlee, Clement 59, 307
Auergesellschaft 46
Auger, Pierre 60
autoclaves 127, 200, 350, 351, 377, 378, 384, CP2
Australia 59, 79, 106, 154, 156, 289, 331, 413, 423
Austria 17, 25, 70-72, 81, 82, 211, 234,

517

332, 369, 419, 421, 432
Austrian Pledge 332
AVE firm 350, 373
axial flow compressors 202, P6

B
Baader-Meinhof group 198
backfilling 190, 191, 275, 321, CP15
Bain, G.W. 58
Balkan states 71, 72
ballistic missiles (*see* missiles)
ballistics 134
ballpoint pens 246, 247
Bangladesh 90, 346
Barak, Ehud 417
barium 17
Barnaby, Charles Frank 138
Barnard, Niel 277, 278
Baruch, Bernard 74
Baruch plan 74, 75
Barwich, Heinz 47
baseload, constant 433
Batista, Fulgençio 399
Battle of the Bulge 38
Bawa, Ahmed 277
Bay of Pigs 399
BBC China 364, 365, 367, 369, 370, 373, 386, 389, CP12
Beams, Jesse 344
Becker nozzle 125
Becker, E.W. 125
Becquerel, Henri 11, 59
Bedell, Jeff 377
Begin, Menachem 294
Belgian Congo (*see also* Congo) 23, 27
Belgium 48, 79, 111, 195, 346
Benghazi 363
Ben-Gurion, David 285, 287, 292
Bentov, Cheryl ("Cindy") 289
Bergmann, Ernst David 285
Beria, Lavrenti 51-53
Berlin 7, 16, 17, 22, 23, 40, 46, 47, 345, 388, 398

Berlin Wall 211
Bernadotte, Folke 298
beryllium 11, 34
Bethe, Hans 21, 26, 49, 53, 221
Beukes, Herbert 217
Beva (*see* plants)
Beveridge, William 67
Bhabha Atomic Research Centre (BARC) 91
Bhabha, Homi 80
Bhagavad Gita 37
Bhagwati, P.N. 258
bhangmeter 151-154, 156
Bharatiya Janata Party (BJP) 358, 359
Bhopal 345
Bhutto, Zulfikar Ali 92, 347-349, 354, 357, 360
Bikini Atoll 44, 55
Bin Abdulaziz, Abdullah 418
Bin Laden, Osama 405-407
Biological Weapons Convention (BWC) 333
Birch, Douglas 197
"biscuit" card 219
Blaauw, Jan 297
black
    Africans 124, 170, 176, 177, 200, 213, 259, 300, 310
    chamber 419
    majority government/regime 142, 213, 276, 277, 309
    market xvi, 372, 379
    swan events 423, 426, 427
blackmail 266
blackouts, electricity 199, 200
blast yield (*see* yield)
Blitzkrieg 48
Blix, Hans ii, 212, 216, 225, 227, 228, 231, 238, 240, 261, 270, 282, 316, CP14, CP16
Board of Governors (*see* IAEA)
boats (*see also* ships) 21, 22, 288
Bohr, Niels 17-19, 21, 33, 57

INDEX

Boeing 37, 202
Boeremag 199
Boettcher, Alfred 106
Boipatong 258
Bolsheviks 51
bomb (*see also* bombs)
    atomic (*see also* nuclear bombs) 43, 45, 61, 64, 77, 78, 279
    ballistic design 190
    bat 24
    boosted 34, 55
    dirty/radiological 109, 408
    dumb 190
    fission 26, 53, 54, 55, 122, 442
    fusion 53, 55, 69, 175, 273
    glide 135, 165, 172, 190, 192, 263
    gravity 190, 401
    gun-assembled/gun-type 34, 35, 41, 116, 172, 219, 297, 358, 442
    hydrogen (*see* thermonuclear)
    implosion 34, 53, 297, 358, 442, CP4
    incendiary 39, 43
    plutonium (*see also* plutonium) 34, 35, 37, 41, 44, 46, 52, 62, 347, CP4, P2, P3
    smart 190
    snoops 154, 156
    thermonuclear/hydrogen 26, 48, 53, 54, 62, 63, 69, 71, 80, 104, 122, 135, 155, 175, 269, 272, 273, 290, 307-309, 394, 447, CP4, P3
    uranium (*see also* uranium) 35, 41, 297, 347, 358, P2
bombers (*see* aircraft)
bombing, precision 397
bombs (*see also* devices; explosives; missiles; nuclear bombs)
    Able 44
    "African" 278-280, 312
    "Arab" 390
    B-38 CP4
    Baker 44

Bakker 190
Fat Man 41, 42, 59, CP4, P3
First Lightning 52
Gadget 37, P2
Hamerkop 190
"Islam" 112, 159
Joe-1 52, 53, 394, CP4
Joe-4 55
letter 352, 353
Little Boy 41, 42, 155, P2
"Muslim" 353, 356, 390
"Pakistani" 371, 389
RDS-1 52, CP4
RDS-37 55
"Super" 26, 53
Tsar Bomba 55
Border War (*see* wars)
Born, Max 21, 28, 49
Bosnia 72
bosons 13
Botha, Fanie 180, 294-297
Botha, R.F. (Pik) 123, 124, 140, 141, 146, 169, 177, 180, 192, 193, 195, 211, 212, 226, 230, 231, 257, 260, 276, 278, 279, 281, 316, 319, 320, 339, 465, 466, CP16
Botha, P.W. iii, 122, 131, 132, 144, 147, 148, 157, 165, 166, 168, 169, 172, 177, 180, 181, 192, 193, 212, 213, 261, 263, 265, 277, 282, 293, 300
Bothe, Walther 11
Bowdler, William 140
boycotts (*see* sanctions)
Bradbury, Norris 42, P2
Brazil 80, 86, 125, 328
Brazzaville Protocol 211, 212
Bredell, Piet 203
Bretscher, Egon 33, 57
Britain/British 18, 20, 21, 24, 25, 34, 40, 45, 46, 49-51, 56-63, 67-69, 73, 74, 76, 80, 90, 97, 99, 104, 106, 111, 117, 121, 124, 131, 143, 145, 150, 168, 204, 212, 224, 226, 227, 230,

519

261, 267, 268, 273, 286, 298, 305-310, 326, 327, 329, 334, 338, 343, 345, 364, 365, 367-370, 376, 377, 379, 387, 388, 398, 404, 412, 413, 419, 420, 426
British East India Company 63
British Nuclear Fuels (BNFL) 206
Brodie, Bernard 396
Broederstroom Commando 216, 223, 254
"broken arrows" accident 404
Broodryk, Alta 311
Buddha Purnima 359
buildings, Pelindaba
    C, D, E, H, J 126, 127, 246
    Complex 5000 134, 149, 254-257, CP5, CP6
    Hall A-D 134, 255, 256
    X 251
Bukit Aman 367
Bulganin, Nikolai 52
bulk analysis 249
bulk facilities 233
Bundesrat 371
Bunn, Matthew xv, xvi
Burgess, Stephen 146
Burr, William 288
Bush, George H.W. (1989–1993) 299, 318
Bush, George W. (2001–2009) 288, 327, 370, 405, 406
Bush, Vannevar 26, 27
Butler, Lee 403
butter factory 352
butterfly effect 209, 210
Buys, André 274, 275, 312

C

calibration 256, 257, 376
calutrons 30, 52, 238, 250
Canada 9, 23, 57, 71, 73, 76, 77, 79, 91, 131, 333, 437

cancer cases 426
carbon 205
carbon dioxide 308
carbon-nitrogen cycle 26
Carey, Michael 404
Carter, Jimmy 141, 147, 148, 155, 156, 183, 219, 467-470
Carter, Richard 217, 218, 499-501
Cartwright, James 420, 421
cascades 47, 126, 127, 129, 200, 202, 217, 246, 247, 253, 350, 376, 377, 440, CP2, CP3
    C1 and C2 378
    HC01, HC02 and HC03 378
casings 135, 149, 373, 425, CP15
castings 223, 321, 373
Castro, Fidel 281, 310, 323, 399
Castro, Raúl 281
Cavendish Laboratory 6-8, 10, 11, 15, 27, 56, 57
Central Intelligence Agency (CIA) 60, 61, 64, 127, 130, 156, 157, 161-163, 215, 244, 257, 299, 320, 346, 352, 353, 356, 362, 365, 367, 369-371, 377, 380, 394, 399, 400
centrifuge (*see* gas centrifuges)
cesium 251, 272, 409
Cetec firm 362, 384
Chadwick, James 11, 33, 56, 57, 59
chain reaction 18-24, 28, 32-36, 47, 69, 77, 102, 105, 110, 129, 196, 199, 205, 256, 307, 424, 440
chaos theory 209
Charlton, Michael 395
Che Guevara 281, 399
Chemical Weapons Convention (CWC) 331, 333
Cheney, Dick 219
Chernobyl 210, 309, 426
China xvi, xvii, 40, 50, 62-64, 77, 78, 85, 90, 150, 224, 252, 253, 268, 287, 310, 320, 321, 330, 353, 356, 357, 358, 389, 396-398, 410, 411, 413,

INDEX

414, 416, 419, 420, 422, 427, 430, 437
Chitumbo, Kaluba 240, 245
Chotek, Sophie 71, 72
Choudree, Anand 375, 376
Churchill, Winston 40, 57-59, 80, 307, 394, 403
Circle facility (*see also* Kentron) 166-171, 187-191, 201, 222, 223, 230, 264, 267, 268, 270, 297, 440, CP6, CP7, CP8
Cire, Günes (Jireh, Gunas) 345, 362, 364, 367, 368
Ciskei 259, 309
civil plutonium 33
Clark Amendment 131
Clinton, Bill 153, 219, 327
coal 15, 70, 170, 193, 196, 199, 200, 204, 270, 432-434
cobalt 251, 272, 409
Cochran, Thomas 244
Cockcroft, John 307-309
Codesa talks 310
Coertse, Mimi 234
Coggin, Janet 145
Cohen, Avner 288
Cohen, Herman (Hank) 230, 278
Colborn, Rod 203
cold tests (*see* tests)
cold traps 115, 126
Cold War (*see* wars)
Colex separation process 274
Coll, Steve 349
Collins, Catherine 369
colonialism 292, 324
Comitato Nazionale della Energia Nucleare 106
Commissariat á l'Énergie Atomique (CEA) 60, 106
Committee on the Social and Political Implications of the Atomic Bomb 40

Commonwealth Observer Mission to South Africa (Comsa) 259
communism/communists 28, 49, 51, 59-61, 130, 142-145, 169, 210, 211, 253, 272, 282, 291, 310, 399, 403, 429, 431
Comprehensive Anti-Apartheid Act 299
Comprehensive Nuclear-Test-Ban Treaty (CTBT) 326, 330, 421, 422
Comprehensive Nuclear-Test-Ban Treaty Organization (CTBTO) 327
Comprehensive Safeguards Agreement (CSA) (*see* IAEA)
compressors 113, 115, 126, 175, 200-202, 246, 314, 351, CP2, P5, P6
Compton, Arthur 26
computers 127, 156, 179, 286
   AX-1 program 101
   hard drives 369, 375, 377, 379
   PELX-1 program 101, 102
   programs 77, 101, 102, 134, 256
   supercomputer 318
conferences
   consensus document 325, 329, 330, 333, 422
   Disarmament 333, 336
   Geneva 80
   IAEA (*see* IAEA, General …)
   NPT Revcon/review 89, 323-333, 335-337
   Peaceful Uses of Atomic Energy 80
   Potsdam 40, 45, 75
   Yalta 45
Congo 23, 27, 281
Conservative Party 264
contamination (*see also* decontamination; radioactive) 55, 62, 114, 128, 223, 237, 274, 314, 415
controlled unit (CU) 219
conversion process 31, 108, 114, 166, 168, 203, 217

521

coolant 100, 106, 110, 111, 196, 205, 424
copper 30, 109
Cora Engineering 352, 353
correctness and completeness investigation (CCI) ii, 237-239, 243, 244, 262, 267
corrosion 113-115, 171, 202
corruption 278
costs 24, 29, 48, 110, 114, 116, 121, 176, 189, 191, 200, 204, 237, 244, 260, 321, 357, 382, 387, 388, 434, 437
Couchepin, Pascal 371
Council for Scientific and Industrial Research (CSIR) 97
Cressey, Roger 407
Crimea 330, 405, 410
Criminal Procedure Act 375
criminality (*see also* exports, illegal; scams; smuggling; terrorism) xv, xvi, 272, 278, 382, 385, 387, 388
critical assembly 255, 256
critical mass 19, 24, 32-37, 59, 60, 129, 440
critical/subcritical/supercritical system or test 36, 422, 440
criticality 28, 34-36, 52, 105, 106, 110, 129, 222, 223, 256, 440
Crocker, Chester 177, 211, 258
Crocodile River 102, 105, 150
Cuba 131, 133, 142, 164, 177, 211, 212, 259, 281, 282, 291, 310, 312
Cuban-American Treaty 399
Cuban Missile Crisis 394, 397, 399, 404
Curie, Irène 14, 17
Curie, Marie 14, 59, 61
Curie, Pierre 59
cyber war 420
Czechoslovakia 23, 47, 48, 71, 80, 81, 403, 432

D
Dair Alzour 329
Dar es Salaam 197, 408
Dargan, B. 106
Davies, Rob 436
Dayan, Moshe 292
Davy, Humphrey 6
De Gaulle, Charles 60-62, 286, 288
De Guiringaud, Louis 140
De Hevesy, George 21
De Klerk, F.W. i, iii, 97, 144, 160, 189, 213, 216, 218, 220-222, 230, 234, 240, 255, 257-261, 263-267, 270, 271, 275-277, 309-311, 318, 339, 411
De Klerk, Jan 97
De Villiers, Dawie 216, 264
De Villiers, J.W.L. (Wynand) 77, 100, 101, 121, 137, 159, 160, 163, 181, 183, 191, 214, 218, 231, 256, 257, 261, 266, 297, 313, P4, P8
De Villiers, W. van Zyl 311
De Vlamingh, Willem 423
De Waal, Tielman 260
De Wet, Carl 122
De Wit, Chris 311
decontamination 217, 218, 223, 233, 409
Defense Intelligence Agency (DIA) 156
Defense Support Program (DSP) 156
democracy iv, vi, 263, 272, 278, 279, 310, 311
Democritus 4, 67
demolition, facilities and technology (*see also* documentation) 320, 321
Dempster, Arthur 19
Denmark 21, 48, 408
Denn flow forming machine 376, 384-386
Denner, Lou 254
depleted uranium (*see* uranium)
depositary states 212, 226, 230

INDEX

deterrent 63, 133, 169, 170, 185, 188, 261, 265, 288, 393, 395, 403, 410, 411, 413-415, 441
detonation 32, 34, 37, 44, 52, 55, 62, 70, 91, 122, 131, 136, 141, 149, 151, 153, 156, 225, 327, 347, 357, 359, 360, 363
deuterium 12, 26, 32-34, 54, 122, 175, 273, 441
deuterium-tritium gas CP5
device
    boosted 122, 175, 188, 191
    containment and surveillance 236
    fission 26, 53, 54, 55, 122, 442, CP
    fusion 54, CP5
    gun-type 122, 134, 167, 171, 174, 175, 191, 442, CP1
    nuclear iii, 77, 91, 108, 109, 122, 135, 140, 141, 143, 149, 156, 159, 171, 175, 251, 257, 282, 327, 346, 353, 357, 380, 393, 394, 397
    nuclear explosive vii, 91, 94, 131, 133, 170, 255, 257, 326, 408, 444, CP1
    type A 122, 174
    type A* 122, 175, 188, 191
    type B 122
devices (*see also* bombs; missiles; weapons)
    Cabot 172, 174, 190
    Gardenia 190
    Hobo 172, 174, 190
    Melba 171, 173, 174, 190, 191, 201, 270
    Mike 54, 273
    Modulus 191
    Video 149, 170, 171, 174, 190
Dhanapala, Jayantha 326
diamonds 297, 301
Diebner, Kurt 45, 48
Diederichs, Nic 119
Diên Biên Phú 61, 78

diffusion
    gas/gaseous 25, 29, 47, 52, 63, 111, 112, 116-118, 214, 261, 344, 442
    thermal/thermodynamic 29, 125
Dillon, Garry 239
Dimona (*see* reactors)
disarmament v, vi, 84, 85, 94, 228, 323, 325-334, 336, 393, 394, 412, 421, 422, 441
disasters (*see also* accidents; terrorism) 307-309, 345, 424, 426, 429, 430, 434
dismantlement i, iv, v, vi, 56, 85, 128, 173, 175, 216-218, 220, 222, 224, 225, 253, 255, 258, 259, 262, 264-266, 268, 269, 272, 275-277, 282, 296, 306, 309, 321, 334, 337-339, 385, 411, 424-426, 434, 436, 502-505, 506-511, 512
documentation, destruction of 224, 225, 258, 260, 296, 320, 371, 386
Donner, Reg 301
Dornberger, Walter 46
double flash 151-153
Dragon experiment 35
drones 322
drum scanners 237
Du Plessis, Barend 180, 183
Du Plessis, Pietie 180
DuPont USA 29
Du Preez, Helgard 311
Du Preez, Jean 325, 327
Du Toit, S.J. 100, 209, P8
dual-use items 93, 94, 153, 274, 313, 315, 322, 362, 441
Dubai 343, 351, 360, 361, 364, 366, 368, 369, 380, 382-386, 389
Dulles, John Foster 78
Duynefontein farm 194
Dynamic Engineering firm 377, 384
dynamite 18, 38

523

E

Earle, Ralph II 156
East/Far East 29, 39, 42, 343
Eden, Anthony 307
Edmondson, William 148
Egypt 67, 132, 225, 231, 280, 286, 287, 289, 292, 315, 323, 328, 329, 332-334, 353, 422, 423
Eichenwald, Kurt 405
Einstein, Albert 3, (14), 15, 16, 18, 21-23, 47, 419, P1
Eisenhower, Dwight David (Ike) iii, 38, 67, 74-79, 90, 100, 104, 130, 181, 189, 194, 263, 395, 398, 399, 405
Eitan, Raful 290, 291
ElBaradei, Mohamed 225, 335, 343
Électricité de France (EDF) 197, 198
electricity 4, 6, 29, 117, 199, 201, 202, 204, 247, 339
   generation xvii, 19, 25, 32, 33, 69, 70, 76, 106, 205, 206, 426, 427, 432, 436
   static 5
Electricity Supply Commission (Eskom) 97, 177, 194, 195, 197-201, 204-206, 437
electromagnetic isotope separation (EMIS) (*see also* isotopes) 441
electromagnetism 6, 11, 13, 30, 52, 152, 153, 238, 250
electronics 152, 164, 263, 356, 362, 364, 371, 376-379, 383, 390
electrons 8-14
elements, chemical 4, 6, 8, 11, 12, 14, 17-19, 22, 26, 32
Elprod 201
Els, General 121
Elugelab 155
embargoes (*see* sanctions)
Emergency Committee for Israel (ECI) 161
emissions, uranium (*see* uranium)
Energiewende 431

energy (*see also* nuclear energy) 10, 11, 14-16, 18-20, 22, 26, 28, 31, 33, 287, 308, 430
energy transition 433
Engineering Research Laboratories (ERL) (Pakistan) 349
England/English (*see also* Britain) 7, 15, 33, 42, 60, 69, 71, 82, 196
enriched uranium (*see* uranium)
environment (*see also* contamination) 36, 309, 427
   monitoring 150, 249, 250, 421, 422
   testing facility 166
environmental activists 426, 432, 433
Erwin, Alec 199
Eskom (*see* Electricity Supply Commission)
especially designed or prepared (EDP) materials and equipment 86, 87, 89
espionage (moles/spying) 49-51, 64, 83, 119, 138, 139, 143-145, 148, 149, 158, 161-163, 186, 247, 262, 289, 290, 307, 348, 352, 393, 400
EU-3 415
Euratom 344
Europe 17, 29, 38, 42, 62, 72, 78, 112, 130, 195, 198, 251, 257, 273, 292, 300, 301, 305, 319, 343-346, 352, 361, 368, 372, 393, 397, 400, 410, 411, 423, 429, 432, 433
European Union (EU) 323, 409, 410, 415, 416
europium 251
exchange, of information (*see also* transfer) 7, 57, 58, 80, 86, 124, 162, 294, 309, 321
Exelon 206
expenditure (*see* costs)
explosions (*see* nuclear explosions)
explosive yield (*see* yield)
explosives
   chemical/conventional 34, 37, 43, 55, 122, 166, 167, 270, 272, 408

INDEX

high- 166, 219, 222, 256, 415
HMX 166
nuclear (*see also* nuclear explosions) 74, 102, 122, 134, 139, 141, 168, 272, CP1
exports (*see also* arms; exchange)
  among countries 64, 77, 107, 110, 120, 164, 176, 194, 286, 313, 320, 322
  control 93, 94, 274, 312, 313, 315, 316, 321, 351, 383
  embargoes/restrictions (*see* sanctions)
  guidelines/safeguards for 82, 86, 89, 92-94, 97, 229, 253, 274, 312, 315, 321
  illegal 63, 146, 322, 343, 351, 352, 360, 362, 369, 383, 385, 386, 390
expulsion, of members of embassy/mission 148, 255

F

Fabian, F. 359
facilities (*see* nuclear facilities)
Facility Attachments 87, 88
fallout (*see* radioactive)
Faraday, Michael 6
Farewell Dossier 144
Farm Hall 45
Farouk, S.M. (Mohamed) 361
FDO research laboratory 346, 347
Federal Bureau of Investigation (FBI) 28, 144, 420
Federal Register 318
feed-and-withdrawal system 350-352, 364, 383
feedstock 116, 134, 253
Feklisov, Alexander 50
Fermi, Enrico 14, 15, 17, 19, 21, 22, 28, 30, 53
Feynman, Richard 4, 5, 68
filters i, 114, 126, 128, 129, 233, 237, 242, 308, 314

candles 246, 314
chambers 307-309
vessels 129, P5
firebombing 43
firestorms 39
First World War (*see* wars)
fissile material 75, 76, 79, 81-85, 176, 406, 419, 421, 422, 441
Fissile Material Cut-off Treaty (FMCT) 422
fission 19, 20, 26, 32, 33, 54, 55, 129, 256, 273, CP1
  devices/weapons (*see also* bombs) 53, 122, 442
  products 31, 36, 59, 109, 154, 196, 248, 251, 309
fissionable material 85-87, 89, 362, 441, CP1
flow meters 364, 377, 383, 390
fluorine gas 202, 352
force de frappe 59, 62
Fordow 415
forensics 249, 250, 265
Fourie, Brand 169
fracking 70
Framatome-Framateg 194, 196, 198, 204, 437
France/French 14, 17, 20, 22, 40, 45, 48, 51, 59-63, 72, 74, 76, 77, 79, 80, 84, 106, 112, 117, 118, 121, 124, 140, 144, 150, 159, 164, 170, 176, 186, 194-199, 203, 204, 221, 224, 230, 239, 240, 253, 268, 272, 285, 286, 288, 290, 297, 320, 329, 346, 355, 369, 412, 413, 415, 432, 436, 437
Franck, James 40
Franklin, Benjamin 5
Franz Ferdinand, Archduke 71, 72
Franz Josef, Emperor 71, 72
Freedom Front 271
Freedom of Information Act 257
French Indochina 60, 61, 78
French Polynesia 62

Freon gas 351
Frisch, Otto 17-19, 21, 24, 25, 56, 57
Frisch-Peierls memorandum 24
Frisch, Robert 33, 35, 57
Fuchs Electronics 146
Fuchs, Klaus 21, 33, 49, 50, 53, 57, 63, 307, 393, P6
fuel (*see also* Koeberg; Safari)
   cycle 203, 204, 229, 311, 358, 434, 438, 444
   elements 106-109, 130, 194, 196, 201, 203-205, 233, 307, 308
   fabrication 434, 437
   hydrazine 186
   mixed oxide (MOX) 196
   reprocessing of (*see* reprocessing)
   rods 203, 205, 424, 425
   spent 33, 83, 91, 250, 419, 425, 437
   uranium-silicide 108
Fukushima Daiichi 423-428, 430, 431, 432, 434, 436
fusion (*see also* bombs) 26, 34, 54, 55, 80, 175, 273, 444, CP5

G

Gaddafi, Muammar 278, 310, 360, 362, 363, 365-367, 370, 377, 379, 386, 388-390, 423
Gaddafi, Saif 370
gamma rays 11
Gandhi, Indira 91, 356
Garwin, Richard 155, 425
gas centrifuges 47, 52, 111, 112, 113, 116, 214, 251, 253, 261, 290, 344, 350, 357, 365, 373, 415, 416, 420, 442, CP2, CP12
   CNOR/SNOR 346
   G-1 and G-2 346, 349
   L-1 363
   P-1 and P-2 349, 355, 363, 376, 379
gaseous diffusion (*see* diffusion)
Gauvenet, André 106

Geiger, Hans 9
Geiger-Müller counter 9, 11
Geiges, Daniel 372, 373, 375, 376, 382, 383, 385-388
General Conference (*see* IAEA)
Gerber, Anton xiv, xv
Gerboise Bleue (*see* tests)
Gerhardt, Dieter Felix 143-145, 158, P6
Gerhardt, Ruth 143, 144, P6
Germany 7, 11, 14-18, 20-23, 25, 28, 38-40, 44-53, 56, 63, 67, 71, 72, 75, 86, 111, 112, 124, 125, 144, 145, 202, 205, 206, 211, 215, 239, 261, 285, 286, 292, 307, 339, 343, 344, 346, 347, 349, 350, 352, 353, 364, 367-369, 372, 380, 383, 384, 387, 388, 393, 398, 404, 410, 415, 416, 430-433
Gerotek site 166, 167, 171
Ghana 323
Gilbert, William 4
Gimbel, John 46
glasnost 210
Gleeson, I.R. 298
global community (*see* international community)
Global Positioning System (GPS) 153, 247
Global Zero 337, 410, 411
globalisation 410
gluons 13
Goiâna incident 409
gold 6, 9, 57, 58, 97, 112, 275
Gold, Harry 49
Goldschmidt, Bertrand 61, 76
Goldstone Commission 258
golem 68
Goosen, Peter 325, 327, 373
Gorbachev, Mikhail 210, 211, 429
Gore, Al 146, 325
Goudsmit, Samuel 45
Gouriqua 174, 175, 182, 270

INDEX

government bonds 410
Government Communications Headquarters (GCHQ) 420
GPU (State Political Directorate, Russia) 51
gradient 126, 128, 246
Graham, Thomas 326
Grant, W.L. (Wally) 99, 100, 110, 112, 113, 115, 118, 119, 121, 216, 256, 271, P4, P8
graphite 28, 30, 31, 205, 307-309, 427, 428
gravity 5, 184, 190, 205
Greece 4, 316
green energy 430-433
Green Paper on the future of nuclear energy 340
Greenglass, David 49
Greenland 404
Gribkov, Anatoly 401
Griffin, Paul 367
Griffin, Peter 361, 367, 368, 384
Group J-7 153
Group of Eight 79
Group of Twelve 80
Group of 77 132
Groves, Leslie 27-30, 35, 39-41, 44, 45, 52, 57, 58, P1, P8
GRU (Main Intelligence Directorate, Russia) 49, 50, 143
Guam 399
Guantanamo Bay (Gitmo) 399
guidelines (*see* exports; IAEA)
Gulf Technical Industries 361, 384
Gulf War (*see* wars)
gun-assembled/gun-type bombs/devices/weapons 34, 35, 41, 116, 122, 134, 165, 167, 171, 172, 174, 175, 181, 191, 219, 297, 358, 442, CP1
gun barrels 122, 143, CP1
gunpowder 62
guns (*see also* arms; weapons) 122, 147
  anti-aircraft 164, 185

assault rifles 164
G5 and G6 272, 281
gas 256
Gupta, V. 359

H

Haak, Jan 118
Haarhoff, Pierre 201
Habsburgs 71, 72
hackers 420
Hagel, Chuck 161, 163
Hahn, Otto 14, 17, 19, 22, 45, 59, P7
Haig, Alexander 169, 170
Haigerloch 45-47
half-life 9
Halls A-D, Pelindaba (*see* buildings)
Hanford 28, 31, 34, 35, 39, 50
Hangklip 321
Hani, Chris 310
Haqqani 406
Harencak, Garrett 412
Harvey, Leonard Jack 377, 382, 383, 390
Hasegawa, Tsuyoshi 42, 43
Havana Declaration 323
Heald, G.R. 140, 148, 276-278, 338
heat exchangers 126, 200, 202
heavy water 47, 57, 60, 77, 91, 98, 100, 110, 111, 113, 285, 286
Hecateus 67
Hechingen 45, 46
Hecker, Siegfried 414
Heinonen, Olli 389
Heisenberg, Werner 22, 45, 48, 53
Helikon technique 202
helium 9, 115, 175, 205, 206
Henderson, Simon 389
Herrington, John 195
Hersh, Seymour 158
Hertz, Gustav 46, 47
Heyns, Johan 310
Heyser, Richard 400
Hibbs, Mark 244, 255, 313

527

Higgs boson 13
Higgs, Peter 13
highly enriched uranium (HEU) (*see* uranium)
Hilsch, Rudolf 112
Hindu people 345, 355, 358
Hiroshima 16, 30, 41-43, 45, 58, 61, 69, 77, 78, 155, 171, 221, 337, 393, 397, 419, P2
Hitler, Adolf 20, 21, 26, 38, 39, 60, 62, 67, 68, 72, 74, 215, 403
Hohenzollern Castle 45
Hooper, Richard 239, 245, 246
Horten, Roy 130
Horthy, Miklós 67
Hot Cell Complex 107, 203, 233
Hounam, Peter 271, 272
Houwhoek 316
Houwteq 186, 320
Hugo, J.P. 100
Human Intelligence (HUMINT) 162
Humanitarian Impact of Nuclear Weapons (HINW) 331-333
Hungary 17, 18, 21, 26, 53, 67, 71, 81, 211
Hurwitz, Harry 294
Hussein, Saddam 150, 226-228, 238, 246, 255, 327
Huyser, Bossie 133
hydro-acoustic signals 154, 421
hydrodynamics 134
hydrofluoric acid 114, 202
hydrogen (H) 8, 12, 26, 113, 114, 126-128, 185, 215, 246, 273, 425, 427
  bombs (*see* bombs)
  fluoride 129
  gas 114, 246, 425
  H:U-235 ratio 129
hydrophones 154
hydropower 433

I

ideology 145, 282, 292, 301, 406, 414, 431
Iklé, Charles 405
Imaq'iq, Al-Karim 385
implosion 54, 167, 175, 188, 191
  bombs 34, 53, 297, 358, CP4
  devices 37, 122, 182, 183
  lenses 34, 35, 37
  weapons 37, 41, 63, 182, 442
independence, countries 60, 90, 131, 145, 148, 164, 169, 282, 292, 305, 306, 324, 354, 355
India vi, xvi, 77, 80, 82, 84, 90-92, 112, 130-133, 157, 194, 213, 224, 225, 258, 288, 300, 313, 320, 321, 323, 324, 327, 339, 343, 345-347, 353, 355-361, 373, 383, 389, 390, 406, 414, 422, 430
Indian Ocean 143, 151, 154, 268
Indochina 60, 61, 78
Indonesia 323
Industrial Development Corporation (IDC) 118, 206
INFCIRC Safeguards Agreements 83-85, 87, 89, 93, 110, 229, 313
Information Scandal 296
Initial Report of Nuclear Materials and Facilities i, ii, 232-237, 239, 241, 243
Inkatha Freedom Party (IFP) 310
inspection (*see also* IAEA) 73, 74, 137, 150, 191, 192, 204, 226, 287, 288, 295, 306, 318, 321, 379, 381, 382, 385, 417, CP6
Institut für Transuranelemente 47
Integrated Nuclear Infrastructure Review (INIR) 435
Integrated Operational Nuclear Detection System (IONDS) 153
Integrated Resource Plan (IRP) 434, 437
intellectual reparations 46

INDEX

interconnectivity   420, 421
intercontinental ballistic missiles (ICBM) (*see also* missiles)   184, 185, 318, 320, 404
international
  authority/organisation (*see also* IAEA)   72-75, 82, 84, 90, 94
  community   i, 120, 121, 123, 165, 176, 179, 216, 257, 266, 276, 289, 291, 301, 312, 336, 343, 360, 375
  isolation   iii, 123, 130, 131, 291
  market (*see also* black market)   205, 252, 295
  pressure (*see also* sanctions)   i, 130, 134, 140-142, 160, 161, 176, 177, 213, 214, 230, 233, 237, 251, 257, 265, 276, 314, 338, 415, 434, 438
  prestige/standing   58, 60, 130, 266, 280, 311, 335
  treaties (*see also* NPT; treaty)   84, 88, 93, 94, 316, 328
International Atomic Energy Agency (IAEA)   vi, xvi, 76, 80, 102, 106, 119, 133, 149-151, 160, 163, 216, 226, 241-249, 257, 266, 267, 269, 271, 274-275, 281, 282, 295, 297, 312, 313, 316, 339, 340, 358, 376, 380, 385, 408, 409, 417, 429, 435, 442
  Additional Protocol   229, 236, 239, 335, 336
  Board of Governors   61, 81, 87, 132, 176, 225, 228, 253, 254, 270, 280, 315, 334, 374, 376, 416
  Comprehensive Safeguards Agreement (CSA) (*see also* INFCIRC)   i, ii, vi, 87, 92, 94, 232, 236, 270, 315, 326, 415
  General Conference   ii, 81, 132, 157, 177, 183, 193, 212, 213, 230, 231, 237, 335, 356
  guidelines   71, 89, 93, 236
  inspections   i, 77, 82, 83, 85, 88, 94, 110, 120, 132, 141, 177, 213, 214, 217, 224, 227-230, 232-236, 238-240, 250-252, 254, 255, 260-262, 265, 268, 270, 277, 287, 306, 311, 329, 336-338, 371, 374, 377, 389, 415, 416, CP6, CP8
  legal powers/rights   229, 236, 239, 260
  safeguards   i, ii, 81-89, 92, 94, 120, 132-134, 183, 193-195, 212-215, 218, 227-229, 232, 234-241, 253, 260, 270, 271, 313, 326, 335, 336, 344, 351, 435, 447
  Safeguards Agreements   i, ii, vi, 83, 85, 109, 157, 193, 194, 228, 229-232, 234, 237, 239, 244, 250, 295, 416, 447
  Safeguards Department   227, 236-239
  statute   79, 81, 82, 89, 225
  Symposium on International Safeguards   311
International Business Machines Corporation (IBM)   155
International Convention on the Suppression and Punishment of the Crime of Apartheid   123
International Monetary Fund (IMF)   319
International Olympic Committee (IOC)   334
International Signal and Control (ISC) (USA)   146, 318
Inter-Services Intelligence (ISI)   389, 406
inventories
  book   242
  nuclear materials and facilities   i, ii, 88, 232, 233, 237, 239, 242
iodine   154
Ioffe, Abram Fedorovich   59
ionisation/ions   30, 32, 33
Iran   64, 86, 94, 119, 164, 244, 272, 298,

529

310, 312, 313, 316, 319, 321, 324, 328-330, 333, 336, 343, 355, 360, 367, 389, 414, 415-418, 420, 422, 438
Iraq i, 119, 176, 225-229, 237-239, 250, 265-268, 272, 290, 319, 324, 327, 328, 337, 338, 343, 355, 370, 406, 412, 415
Iraq Liberation Act   327
Ireland   328
Iron Curtain   81, 82, 211
Islam (*see also* Muslims)   112, 159, 336, 354, 406
Islamic State (IS)   64, 406
Islamic terrorism (*see also* terrorism)   64, 406
isotopes   8, 12, 101, 104, 105, 107, 201, 249, 308, 443
   high-mass   115, 125
   low-mass   115
   medical   260, 266, 267, 438
   radioactive   71, 98, 106, 408
   separation of   20, 25-27, 29, 30, 47, 113-115, 117, 120, 125-127, 246, 251, 273, 290, 344, 418, 441
   uranium (U-233; U-235; U-238; U-239)   19, 20, 24, 25, 29-37, 89, 108, 116, 129, 130, 233, 243, 244, 245, 249, 250, 252-254, CP1
Israel (*see also* Jews)   vi, 62, 77, 83, 84, 154-164, 176, 184-188, 214, 225, 257, 272, 274, 285-301, 310, 313, 317-319, 321, 324, 326, 329, 332, 333, 339, 343, 353-257, 390, 414, 415, 417, 418, 420, 422
Istanbul   408
Italy   14, 15, 17, 21, 67, 106, 275, 364, 404
Ivy, Robert Clyde   146, 147, 318

J

Japan (*see also* Hiroshima)   24, 26, 29, 39-44, 51, 63, 69, 75, 86, 104, 176, 196, 320, 335, 360, 396, 404, 419, 423, 426, 429, 430, 437, 438
Jardine, Roger   340
Jews (*see also* Israel)   16-18, 21, 26, 27, 40, 48, 49, 53, 56, 67, 68, 155, 161, 163, 230, 285, 289, 291, 292, 294, 300, 356, 362, 369, 390
Jireh, Gunas (Cire, Günes)   345, 362, 364, 367, 368
Johnson, Lyndon   395
Johnson, Samuel   375
Joliot-Curie, Frédéric   19, 22, 59-61
Joliot-Curie, Irène   14, 17, 59
Jordan   292, 385
Jugashvili, Ioseb B.D.   51
Jülich Research Centre   106, 431

K

Kaiser Wilhelm Institute   7, 15-17, 22, 23, 38, 46, 47
Kaiseraugst   195
Kalahari Desert/test site (*see* Vastrap)
Kamra Air Base   407
Karachi Steel Mills   385
Karlsch, Rainer   48
Karlsruhe   124, 347, 431
Karni, Asher   390
Kaufmann, William (Bill)   396, 397
Kay, David ("Ramrod")   228
Kayani, Ashfaq Parvez   407
Kazakhstan   52, 55, 393
Kelley, Bob   268
Kellogg   29
Kennedy, John F.   287, 399-402
Kentron   146, 147, 166, 167, 187, 270, 320, 475-479
Kentron Circle facility (*see* Circle facility)
Kenya   306
kerosene   185
KGB (Committee for State Security, Russia)   50, 51, 144, 210, 272
Khamenei, Ayatolla Ali   416
Khan, Abdul Qadeer (A.Q.)   92, 111,

112, 345-350, 352-370, 372, 377, 379, 380, 383, 387, 388-390, 415, CP12
Khan, Feroz   365
Khan, Hendrina   112, 345, 346, 348, 355, 389
Khan, Munir Ahmad   347, 348, 356, 358
Khan Research Laboratories (KRL)   349, 357, 360, 361, 366, 377, 389
Kharan Desert   360
Khrushchev, Nikita   52, 210, 398, 400-403
Kidger, Alan   274
Kim Jong-un   420
Kissinger, Henry   92
Klydon   100
Knesset   292
Kobe   39
Koeberg
  fuel for   124, 128, 132, 134, 170, 183, 191, 194-196, 200, 201, 203, 205, 252, 253, 260, 350
  power plant/reactors   28, 32, 36, 84, 106, 116, 117, 132, 133, 140, 169, 170, 175, 177, 193-199, 205, 206, 214, 233, 434, 437
  sabotage of   197-199
Koevoet   258
Kokura   41
Koornhof, Piet   295
Korea (*see* North Korea; South Korea)
Korean Airlines Flight 007   153
Kosygin, Alexei   395
Koussa, Moussa   370
Kremlin   410, 429
Kriel, Hernus   258
Krisch Engineering   64, 202, 251, 350, 372-374, 377, 382, 385, 386, 390, CP12
Krosney, Herbert   159
Kruger, Paul   171

Kruger rands   179
Kurchatov, Igor   52
Kuwait   226, 227, 338

L

Labour Party (Israel)   292, 294
Labuschagne, Joop   386, 387
Lagattu, André   239, 240, 254, 267
Lamprecht, Jan   265
Langenhoven, C.J.   235
Langevin, Paul   60
Large Hadron Collider (LHC)   13
laser-guided weapons   298
laser isotope separation (*see also* isotopes)   250, 251, 290
Lashkar-e-Taiba   406
Lawrence Livermore Laboratory   54, 168
Le Roux, L.   P8
lead   9, 429
League of Nations   72, 73
leftist/left-wing   28, 61, 213, 299, 431
Legasov, Valery   428-430
LeMay, Curtis   39, 40, 43
Lenin, Vladimir   51
leptons   13
Lerch, Gotthard   349-352, 362, 364, 367, 368, 372, 373, 375, 376, 381-383, 385, 387, 388, 390
Lesotho   292
Levy, Adrian   356
Leybold-Heräus   349, 350, 376
liberation movements   131, 132, 276, 301, 336
Libya   64, 94, 272, 310, 312, 313, 319, 320, 343, 355, 360, 363, 365, 367, 370, 372, 373, 379-382, 385, 387, 389, 390, CP11, CP12
Liel, Alon   300, 301
light intensity   152, 153
light-water reactor   20
Likud Party (Israel)   294
Lilienthal, David   73, 74

lithium (Li)   54, 122, 175, 182, 273, 274, 290, 443
load-shedding   199, 200
localisation   435
Loew ben Bezalel, Rabbi Judah   68
Logichem   377, 383
London Club   92
Lop Nor   63
Lorenz, Edward   209
Los Alamos   28, 33, 38, 40, 44, 49, 50, 53, 54, 73, 156, 160, 168, 221, 377
Los Alamos Primer   33
loss rate, neutrons   36, 37
Loubser, Anton   300
low-enriched uranium (*see* uranium)
Lubbers, Ruud   346, 347
Luther, Martin   419

M
MacArthur, Douglas   398
Machine Shop 1001   362, 368
Machon 2 facility   289, 290
MacMahon Act   307
Macmillan, Harold   305-309
MAD (mutually assured destruction)   56, 79, 394, 395
Mad Dog   369
Maduna, Penuell   339
magnesium   43
magnetism (*see also* electromagnetism)   6, 8, 11-13, 30, 52, 152, 153, 238, 250
magnets, ring   373, 390
Maharaj, Mac   197, 198
Majorets, Anatoli   429
Malan, Magnus   160, 180, 189, 193, 216, 264, 290, 291, 297, 298
Malawi   292
Malaysia   306, 343, 361, 362, 364, 367-369, 389, CP12
Malenkov, Georgy   52
Mahmood, Bashir-ud-Din   347
Manchuria   40, 43, 398
Mandela, Nelson   iv, 204, 213, 216, 230, 258, 276, 278, 281, 310, 311
Manhattan Engineer District   27
Manhattan Project (*see* Projects)
Manuel, Trevor   434
maraging steel   352, 364, 384, 385
Marais, Eugène   103
Marais, John   203
Marais, Piet   181
Markram, Thomas   325, 327
Marsden, Ernest   9
Marshall Islands   55
Marshall, James   27
Martin Marietta   214
Marx, Karl   51
mass (*see also* critical mass)   10-12, 15, 16, 18-20, 30, 36, 113, 115, 233, 243
mass spectrometer   19
Massachusetts Institute of Technology (MIT)   155
material balance area (MBA)   235, 242, 253
material, nuclear (*see* nuclear)
material unaccounted for (MUF)   242, 244
Matoug, Matoug Mohamed   362, 363
Matsu Island   78
Maud Committee   25, 57
Mau-Mau rebellion   306
Mauth, G.H.   156
Maverick test assembly   246
Maxwell, James Clerk   6, 7
May, Allan Nunn   307
Mbeki, Thabo   146, 274, 309-311, 324, 325, 337-339
McNamara, Robert   395, 396, 402, 403
McRae, Ian   197, 198
Mebus, Heinz   345, 352, 353, 367
medical field/medicine   71, 76, 98, 104, 106, 107, 260, 266, 267
Mediterranean Sea   298
Medvedev, Dmitry   411
Meir, Golda   288, 289, 292
Meiring, Ria   xiv, xv

Meitner, Lise 14, 17-19, 24, 59
Melkbosstrand 196
Mennega, Willem 377, 384
mercury 272-274
Merkel, Angela 431
Metternich, Klemens 419, 420
Mexico 328, 331
Meyer, C.M. 160, 171, 181, 275
Meyer, Johannes Andries Muller (J.A.M.) 350, 351, 373-377, 381-387, CP11
MI5 49
MI6 365, 367, 370, 377
microstations 378
Middle East 157, 158, 273, 274, 287, 289, 298, 326, 329, 330, 332, 333, 343, 418
Migule, Albrecht 353
Military Application of Uranium Detonation Committee (Maud Committee) 25, 57
military cooperation 158, 159, 294, 334
military-industrial complex 79, 189, 263
military threat 130, 165, 188
mining industry 58, 97, 98, 122, 295
ministations 378
Mintek (Council for Mineral Technology; previously National Institute for Metallurgy) 180
Minty, Abdul Samad xvi, 325, 331, 334-337, 374-376, 388
Miskell, Ron 377
missile 34, 46, 63, 131, 133, 135, 146, 147, 164, 165, 167, 172, 175, 188, 189, 194, 219, 227, 256, 263, 264, 268-270, 288, 324, 330, 348, 355, 357, 370, 394, 396, 397, 399-401, 403, 404, 413, 414, 415
   ballistic 158, 182-187, 190, 191, 297, 298, 316, 318-322, 358, 359, 396, 400, 401, 404, 411, 413, 418, 421, CP5, CP10
   cruise 184, 322, 400, 407
   ground-to-air 185
   intercontinental ballistic (ICBM) 184, 185, 318, 320, 404, 412
   long-range 184, 185, 187, 299
   medium-range 185, 187, 190, 191
   surface-to-surface 400
missiles (*see also* bombs; nuclear bombs; weapons)
   FKR-1 401
   Frog 400
   Ghauri 358, 359
   Hatf 357
   Husky 190
   Jericho I and II 185-187, 293, 298, 317, CP10
   Jupiter 401
   Luna 400
   M-11 ballistic 358
   Minuteman III 404
   Nodong 358
   RSA series 184, 186, CP10
   Shavit SLT 186
   SS-4 and SS-5 401
   Trident 413
Missile Technology Control Regime (MTCR) 298, 316, 370
mixed oxide (MOX) fuel 196
Mlambo-Ngcuka, Phumzile 340
moderator 47, 60, 77, 91, 100, 106, 110, 111, 129, 196, 205
Modise, Joe 277, 278
molecular laser isotope separation (MLIS) 251, 253
moles (*see* espionage)
Mollet, Guy 285
molybdenum-99 (Mo-99) 107
Monbiot, George 426
Monsanto 29
Montgomery, Bernard Law (Monty) 75

533

Morgan, Allen 339
Mossad 176, 274, 289, 290, 353
Mouton, W.L. (Wynand) 220, 222, 226
Mozambique 131, 133, 177
MPLA (Movement for the Liberation of Angola) 131, 177
Mubarak, Hosni 423
Müller, Erwin 9
Muller, Richard 426
Multiple Independently Targetable Re-entry Vehicle (MIRV) CP5
multiplication factor k 36, 293
Musharraf, Pervez 365, 366, 389, 390
Muslims (*see also* Islam) 111, 345, 353, 355-357, 361, 362, 390, 406
Mussolini, Benito 67
mutually assured destruction (MAD) 56, 79
MVD (Ministry of Internal Affairs, Russia) 51
Myanmar 244

N

Nagasaki 31, 41, 43, 45, 54, 58, 77, 337, 393, 397, 419, P3
Nagoya 39
Nairobi 408
Namibia (*see also* South-West Africa) 58, 148, 177, 211, 212, 281, 282
napalm 24, 43
Naschem 270
Nash equilibrium 394, 395
National Development Plan 2030 434
National Industrial Safety Libya 383
National Institute for Defence Research (NIDR) 122, 134, 137, 146, 147
National Institute for Metallurgy 180
National Intelligence Service (NIS) 277, 377
National Nuclear Energy Executive Co-ordination Committee (NNEECC) 435

National Nuclear Regulator (NNR) 109, 435, 437
National Party (NP) 157, 310
National Prosecuting Authority of South Africa (NPA) 372, 377-379, 388
National Security Management System 263
National Socialists (*see also* Nazi ...) 17
nationalism 73, 294, 305
naval blockade 400-402
Naval Ocean Surveillance Information Center (NOSIC) 162
Naval Research Laboratory (NRL) 154
Nazi Germany 17, 38, 39, 49, 289
Nazi sympathisers, South Africa 144, 145, 215
Necsa (*see* Nuclear Energy Corporation of South Africa)
Negev Desert 285, 288, 295
Negev Nuclear Research Centre 286
negotiations 57, 86, 90, 142, 193, 212, 214, 218, 229, 232, 259, 265, 279, 280, 282, 287, 294, 326, 328, 333, 336, 340, 365, 370
Nel, Ben 373
neptunium (Np) 32
Netanyahu, Benjamin 301, 417
Netherlands/Dutch 48, 92, 111, 112, 171, 194, 240, 344-348, 350, 352, 368, 404
Neustadt-Glewe 46
neutronics 134
neutrons 10-14, 17-20, 25, 31-37, 55-57, 59, 106-108, 129, 175, 199, 205, 250, 256, 272, 273, 308
New Agenda Coalition (NAC) 327, 328
New National Party (NNP) 310
New Mexico 28, 33, 37, 44
New START 411

INDEX

New York 27, 144, 322
New Zealand 8, 328
Newby-Fraser, A.R. 102, 105
Newton, Isaac 5, 6
Nicholls, Dave 204
nickel 114
Nier, Alfred 19
Niigata 41
nitromethane 408
Nixon, Richard 288
NKVD (People's Commissariat for Internal Affairs, Russia) 51, 52
Nobel, Alfred 38, 393
Nobel prize 4, 7-9, 11, 15, 21, 26, 28, 33, 40, 46, 48, 56, 67, 68, 155, 262, 307, 310
Non-Aligned Movement (NAM) 322-324, 329, 334
non-nuclear-weapon states (NNWS) iv, xvi, 85, 86, 88, 90-92, 94, 225, 230, 235, 260, 324, 326, 413, 419, 421, 444
non-proliferation of nuclear weapons (*see also* Nuclear Non-Proliferation Treaty [NPT]) v, vi, 94, 155, 195, 224, 306, 311, 321-326, 334, 343, 375, 444
Non-Proliferation of Weapons of Mass Destruction Act 315, 374, 384, 386
Norris, Chuck 223, 224
Norris, Robert 64
North Atlantic Treaty Organization (NATO) 60, 143, 316, 398, 400, 404, 405, 411, 413
North Korea i, vi, 64, 77, 86, 94, 224, 225, 231, 244, 321, 324, 329, 343, 358, 365, 389, 414, 420
North Sea 432
Northern Tyres and Accessories 112, 113
Norway 48, 286, 288, 334
Novotný, Antonín 403

nuclear
  accidents (*see* accidents)
  arsenals (*see also* nuclear stockpiles) iv, vi, 44, 56, 69, 75, 90, 140, 276, 277, 279, 289, 328-330, 362, 397, 400, 405, 407, 410, 412-414, 421
  bombs (*see also* bombs) xvi, 20, 21, 24-26, 32-34, 36, 38-43, 45, 47, 48, 53-57, 61-64, 69, 71, 77, 78, 92, 104, 112, 116, 146, 152, 157, 181, 216, 265, 269, 271-274, 276, 279-281, 289, 295, 307, 309, 347, 348, 364, 371, 373, 379, 393, 398, 400, 404, 407, 408, 410, 428, 438
  capacity ii, vi, 133, 148, 157, 182, 436
  devices (*see* devices)
  disarmament (*see* disarmament)
  energy (*see also* peaceful applications) 25, 28, 32, 33, 54, 60, 61, 73, 74, 80, 81, 98, 99, 116, 152, 159, 193, 196, 285, 286, 340, 430
  explosions (*see also* detonation; peaceful explosions) 19, 34, 35, 37, 44, 54, 55, 62, 63, 77, 86, 109, 114, 150-158, 166, 172, 190, 191, 194, 197, 198, 215, 251, 273, 360, 394, 409, 414, 422, 425, 428, 432, CP9
  explosive devices (*see* devices)
  exports (*see* exports)
  facilities i, ii, 28, 29, 31, 50, 52, 69, 71, 74, 76, 80, 82-85, 87, 88, 92, 104, 112, 114, 118, 125, 131, 134, 141, 148, 165, 168, 171, 174, 177, 180, 186-189, 194, 201, 205, 213, 214, 216, 223, 228, 232, 233, 236, 237, 242, 245, 250, 251, 255, 256, 260, 262, 267-270, 287, 290, 311, 320, 327, 331, 336, 355, 370
  "football" 219
  forensics 249, 250

fuel (*see* fuel)
fission (*see* fission)
fusion (*see* fusion)
industry   73, 93, 110, 164, 214, 272, 358
material (*see also* fissile; fissionable; source material)   i, ii, xvi, 33, 34, 79, 87, 88, 92, 94, 182, 191, 195, 197, 220, 222, 224, 228, 229, 232-237, 241, 251, 253, 258, 260, 267, 269, 270-272, 282, 315, 335, 336, 343, 434, 444
materials and facilities, accounting (*see* Initial Report; inventory)
medicine (*see* medical …)
missiles (*see* missiles)
power (country)   62, 64, 76, 86, 141, 154, 159, 259, 260, 286, 423-426, 430-437
power plants/stations (*see* plants)
reactors (*see* reactors)
research (*see* reactors, research)
stock/stockpiles   xvii, 55, 69, 75, 84, 85, 182, 191, 235, 260, 269, 295, 331, 411, 414, 417
technology   71, 84, 85, 89, 90, 92, 93, 112, 132, 179, 194, 285, 312, 313, 326, 336, 355, 367, 372
tests (*see* tests)
triad   396
"Walmart"   343
waste (*see also* radioactive)   34, 205, 233, 237, 243, 246, 314, 378, 408, 436
weapons (*see* missiles; weapons)
weapons programme (*see* weapons)
Nuclear Energy Act   315, 351, 374, 386
Nuclear Energy Corporation of South Africa (Necsa)   xv, xvi, 311, 340, 435, 436, 443
Nuclear Exporters Committee (*see also* Zangger Committee)   89, 312
Nuclear Non-Proliferation Treaty (NPT)   iii, iv, vi, 83, 84, 87, 88, 90, 92, 94, 109, 120, 132, 194, 195, 228, 253, 320, 327, 338, 414, 415, 417, 419, 422, 438, 448
   accession by South Africa   i, ii, iv, x, 133, 157, 169, 188, 193, 204, 212-214, 216, 217, 224-226, 229-232, 234, 237, 260, 271, 277, 279, 280, 313, 324, 351
   Articles   85, 86, 93, 225, 323, 328, 333
   conferences   89, 323-333, 335-337
   extension   323, 325, 326, 328, 421
   Revcon (NPT Review Conference 2015)   330, 332, 333, 337
Nuclear Safety Council (NSC)   109
Nuclear Suppliers Group (NSG)   93, 94, 274, 312-315, 320-322, 324, 335, 444
nuclear-weapon states (NWS)   vi, 64, 73, 85, 90, 94, 108, 119, 150, 193, 204, 224, 225, 239, 323-326, 328-330, 359, 412, 421, 422, 438, 445
nucleus, atom   9-15, 17-20, 28, 30, 31, 34, 36, 250
Nucor   101
Nuremberg laws   67
Nyerere, Julius   278-280
Nzo, Alfred   325, 326

O

Oak Ridge National Laboratory   106, 377, 385
Oak Ridge Research Reactor (ORR) (*see* reactors)
Obama, Barack   160, 329, 330, 408, 411, 412, 418
observation satellites (*see* satellites)
oceans   86, 131, 143, 150, 151, 154, 157, 257, 268
October Revolution   51
Office of Scientific Research and Development (OSRD)   26, 27
OGPU (Joint State Political Directorate,

INDEX

Russia) 51
oil industry 70, 71, 123, 194, 316, 362, 416
Oliphant, Mark 24-26
O'Malley, Padraig 211
Onslow, Sue 230, 278
Operation (*see also* Project)
    Alsos 44, 45, 47
    Anadyr 400
    Chagai 327, 360
    Chalet 293
    Chariot 71
    Crossroads 44
    Gasbuggy 70
    Paperclip 46
    Phoenix 158
    Plowshare 70, 169, 445
    Pokhran 91, 92, 131, 327, 359
    Shakti (Pokhran-II) 327, 359, 360
    Smiling Buddha (Pokhran-I) 90-92
    Tea Leaves 294
opium 63, 103
Oppenheimer, J. Robert 26-28, 33, 37, 38, 42, 52, 53, 68, 73, 221, P1, P2, P8
Opperman, Rooi-Gert 223
organ pipes 115
Organisation for the Prohibition of Chemical Weapons (OPCW) 327
Organisation of African Unity (OAU) 276, 279
Osaka 39
Overberg test range 186, 187, 298, 316, 317
oxygen 114, 126, 185, 308, 427, 428

P

P5 group 331-333, 337
P5+1 group 86, 416, 417
Pabian, Frank 244
Pacific Ocean 43, 44, 54, 140, 155, 404, 424
packing lists 374, CP13
Pahad, Aziz 159, 160, 277

Pakistan vi, xvi, 64, 77, 83, 84, 90-92, 111, 112, 163, 224, 321, 324, 327, 339, 343, 345-348, 350-367, 371, 376, 387, 389, 390, 406-408, 414, 415, 418, 422
    Atomic Energy Commission (PAEC) 347, 348, 358, 360
    Pipeline 352
Palestine 161, 285, 289, 310
Palestine Liberation Organization (PLO) 132, 163, 301
Pan Africanist Congress (PAC) 213
Pan American flight 103 363
Panofsky, Wolfgang 155
Papenfus, Theresa 169, 177, 211, 278
"paper tiger" 64, 397, 398
Paris Group 56
Partial Test Ban Treaty (PTBT) 150, 151, 157, 445
particle analysis 249
particles
    alpha 9, 11, 34
    beta 9
    subatomic 8, 13
Pash, Boris 45
PBMR (*see* reactors)
peace, international/world iv, 11, 67, 73, 90, 147, 329, 331, 393, 411
peaceful
    applications/purposes/uses 69, 70, 71, 73, 75-77, 79, 80, 81, 85, 86, 91, 93, 94, 98, 101, 104, 110, 117, 118, 120, 122, 131, 133, 141, 153, 165, 168, 172, 181, 225, 262, 263, 267, 286, 287, 295, 312, 318, 323, 325, 326, 335, 336, 346, 393, 434
    explosions/tests 70, 77, 86, 91, 101, 117, 121, 131, 132, 134, 137, 141, 153, 313, 347
    nuclear explosion (PNE) 70, 117, 445
Pearl Harbor 26, 41, 155, 396
Peenemünde 46

537

Peierls, Rudolf   21, 24, 25, 33, 49, 56, 57
Pelindaba   i, iii, xiv, xvi, 77, 91, 101-105, 121, 122, 124, 136, 149, 150, 166, 168, 175, 200, 203, 233, 254, 255, 266, 313, 335, 340, 350, 374, 376, 377
   Building Complex 5000   134, 149, 254-257, CP5, CP6
   Treaty of   iv, 86, 280, 448
Pelinduna (*see* reactors)
Pelsakon cycle   127
Penney, William   33, 57, 58, 106
Pentagon   27, 29, 154
Peres, Shimon   285, 286, 292-294, 297
perestroika   210
Perricos, Dimitri   238-241, 245, 247, 248, 265, 268, 316, CP14
Perrin, Francis   59, 60
Philippines   399
phosphate mining   295
photodiodes   152
photographs, aerial/satellite   139-141, 148, 254, 255, 287
photons   13
Pickering, Thomas   299
Pienaar, Noel   203
plant   27, 31, 84, 110, 150, 194, 236, 238, 311, 335, 353, 364, 372, 377
   conversion   200, 202, 233
   demonstration   111, 206
   desalination   206, 286
   enrichment   25, 29, 30, 35, 86, 112, 113, 116, 118, 124-126, 134, 197, 200, 214, 224, 344, 346, 350-352, 356, 360, 362, 363, 367, 373, 374, 381, 382, 387, 390, 414, 419, 420
   gas diffusion   63, 117, 214
   manganese   287
   pesticide   345
   pilot   30, 58, 114, 117, 119, 120, 125, 128, 175
   power   69, 196, 198, 424, 425, 427, 431, 432, 434, 436, 437
   reprocessing (*see* reprocessing)
   textile   287
   waste treatment   105
   water purification/treatment   105, 382, 385
plants (*see also* reactors)
   Advena   187, 189, 267-270, 310, 311
   Almelo   111
   Beva   124, 193, 200, 201, 203, 204, 233, 440
   Brokdorf   431
   Calder Hall   69
   Chernobyl   210, 309, 426
   Dimona (*see* reactor)
   Fessenheim   198
   Gouriqua   174, 175, 182, 270
   K-25   29, 30, 35
   Kahuta   349, 351, 352, 354-358
   Koeberg (*see* Koeberg)
   Marcoule   62
   Oak Ridge   27, 29-31, 39, 50
   Obninsk   69
   Pantex   56
   Rokkasho   419
   S-50   29, 30, 35
   Safari (*see* Safari)
   Shippingport   69
   Tricastin   117
   U-   200-204, 233
   UP1   62
   West Rand Consolidated   58
   Wyhl   431
   Y-   107, 126-128, 134, 137, 138, 149, 182, 191, 201, 204, 214-217, 224, 233, 245-247, 250, 253, 265, 314, 450, P4, P5
   Y-12   30, 35, 407
   Z-   134, 183, 191, 193, 200-204, 214, 215, 224, 233, 252, 253, 350, 374, 450
Pliyev, Issa   401
plutonium (Pu)   26, 27, 30-37, 41, 44, 46, 47, 52, 54, 57, 60-63, 74, 77, 80,

INDEX

89, 91, 117, 130, 150, 151, 159, 174, 175, 182, 183, 196, 233, 249-251, 261, 286, 288-290, 295, 297, 307, 309, 347, 348, 355, 358, 373, 408, 417, 419, 426, 427, 437, 438, 446
Pokhran   91, 92, 131, 327, 359
Polakow-Suransky, Sasha   184, 293, 295, 297, 301
Poland   20-22, 48, 59, 71, 74, 80
Politburo   429
Pollard, Jonathan Jay   161-164
pollution (*see also* contamination)   150
polonium   34, 59, 308
Polyani, Michael   7, 21
Pope, the   71, 332
Portugal/Portuguese   79, 131
Potgieter, Schalk   311
Power, Thomas   395-397
power, nuclear (*see* nuclear)
Prague   68, 329
Prague Statement   337
predetonation   32, 34
Preller, Gustav   103
pre-production models   135, 171-173
pressure vessels   110, 126, 373
Prevention of an Arms Race in Outer Space Treaty (PAROS)   422
Prince Edward Island   151, 154, 159, 187, 317
Princip, Gavrilo   72
Principles and Objectives for Nuclear Non-Proliferation and Disarmament   326, 328, 421
Pripyat   428
process gas   113, 115, 126, -129, 200, 246
production models   172-174
Programme
    Dunhill   497-498
    for Promoting Nuclear Non-Proliferation (PPNN)   267, 271
    Olympic   484, 485
Project (*see also* Operation)
    596 (China)   63
    Alsos   44, 45, 47
    Church Steeple/Tower   266, 317
    Festival   165, 168, 187
    Gas Cooling   113
    Gouriqua   174, 175, 182, 270
    Manhattan   28, 38, 39, 44, 47-50, 52, 53, 56-58, 61, 68, 122, 125, 155, 221, 238, 260, 261, 307, 344, 345, 393, P1, P3
    Manhattan Engineer District   27
    "Mantel"   216, 218, 220
    Ostra   190
projectiles   33, 122, 134, 135, 149, 175, CP1
proliferation (*see also* non-proliferation)   73, 84, 92, 94, 163, 225, 258, 260, 267, 274, 276, 278, 313, 321, 344, 349, 366, 371, 446
Proliferation Security Initiative (PSI)   364
protons   10-14, 17, 19
Puerto Rico   399
Purkitt, Helen   146
Putin, Vladimir   50, 412, 413

Q

quarks   13
Quemoy Island   78

R

Rabi, Isidor Isaac   14, 287
Rabin, Yitzhak   292, 293, 295, 301
Rabinowitz, Or   192
radiation   9, 11, 15, 41, 50, 54, 55, 59, 61, 98, 105, 109, 129, 152, 167, 224, 256, 309, 408, 409, 425-427, 428, 429, 435
Radiation Hill (Thabana)   167, 233, 314
radioactive
    contamination/fallout (*see also* decontamination)   55, 78, 150,

154, 156, 222, 223, 237, 309, 314, 396, 408, 409, 427-429
decay 9, 10, 13, 15, 32, 107, 175, 273
isotopes 71, 98, 106, 408, 435
material/products/substance xvi, 9, 11, 13, 33, 58, 70, 86, 109, 129, 154, 190, 272, 273, 309, 357, 408, 409
waste 31, 105, 109, 167, 237, 313, 314, 336, 428, 435
radioactivity 9, 11, 31, 55, 59, 109, 307, 308, 409, 421, 425, 428, 429, 446
radium 22, 59
Rafsanjani, Ayatollah Akbar Hashemi 310
Rajastan Desert 131
Ramanna, Raja 91, 356
Rand Corporation 318
Ranque, Georges 112
Ranque-Hilsch tube 112
rate of loss, neutrons 36, 37
Rautjaervi, Juha 234, 235, 239
Rawalpindi 407
reactor
    core 70, 108, 176, 196, 290, 308, 417, 424, 425, 427, 428, 436
    heavy-water reactor 416, 417
    high-temperature gas-cooled reactor (HTGR) 205
    light-water reactor (LWR) 20
    pebble-bed modular reactor (PBMR) xvii, 205, 206, 446
    plutonium production 27, 31, 32, 34, 46, 47, 52, 61, 62, 74, 91, 286, 307
    pressurised water reactor (PWR) 175, 196, 205, 446
    research 76, 77, 83, 104, 106-108, 286
    safety 31, 77, 101, 109, 111, 135, 203, 222, 223, 308
reactors (*see also* plants)
    A 52
    Arak 416
    Chernobyl 210, 309, 426
    Cirus 77, 91
    Dimona 77, 159, 286-289, 290, 295
    Forsmark 428
    Fukushima Daiichi 424
    G1 62
    Gouriqua 174, 175, 182, 270
    Hualong One 437
    Koeberg (*see* Koeberg)
    Marcoule 61, 62
    Oak Ridge Research (ORR) 104, 106
    Osirak 176, 290, 355
    Pelindaba (*see* Pelindaba)
    Pelinduna 100, 101, 110, 111, 117, 446
    RBMK (high-power channel-type) 427, 429, 430
    Safari (*see* Safari)
    Soreq 286
    Tammuz 176
    VVER 436, 437
    Windscale Pile 1 and 2 307-309, 426
    X-10 30, 31
Reagan, Ronald 132, 153, 169, 170, 192, 195, 211
recipient countries/states 82-84, 86, 89, 214, 351
reclamation (*see also* reprocessing) 33, 60, 61, 83, 91, 109, 233, 242, 250, 257, 273, 288
red mercury 272-274
Reduced Enrichment for Research and Test Reactors (RERTR) 108
Rees, Mervyn 296
reflux 127
Reichmann, Reinhold 47
Reines, Fred 153
relativity, theory of 15, 48

INDEX

Rens, Brian 311
report, nuclear materials and facilities (*see* Initial Report)
reprocessing (*see also* reclamation) 31, 62, 80, 83, 94, 196, 229, 250, 252, 295, 307, 358, 419, 431, 437, 438, 446
resolutions
    IAEA ii, 183, 193, 213
    NPT 326, 329
    UN 133, 164
    UNGA 121, 123, 176, 281, 293
    UNSC 120, 121, 147, 176-179, 211, 226, 227, 416, 418
Reterink, Hendrina 345
Retief, Willem 148
Rhodesia 123, 145
Rhoodie, Eschel 296, 297
Rice, Megan 407
Riehl, Nikolaus 46, 47
right-wing groups 199, 213, 215, 264, 265, 266, 271, 272, 309
ring magnets 373, 390
Risquet, Jorge Valdés 281, 282
Robbins, Lionel 67
Roberts Construction 104, 119
Roberts, J.D. 104
Robinson, Richard 128, 129
rockets 46, 63, 137, 184, 185-187, 318, 321, 322
Roedtan ammunition depot 264, 270
rogue states 343
Rokkasho 419
Röntgen, Wilhelm 11
Rooiels 187, 321
Roosevelt, Franklin D. 21, 22, 24, 26, 39, 47, 57, P1
Rosatom International Network 436
Rosenberg, Julius and Ethel 49, 50
Ross, Dennis 418
Rotblat, Joseph 21
rotors 199, 344, 350, 362, 364, 376-378, rotor tubes 352, 384

Rouhani, Hassan 416
Roux, Abraham J.A. (Ampie) 97-104, 112, 114, 117, 121, 124, 130, 181, 295, P7
Roux, Jannie 261, 266
Roxound Engineering Works 351
Ruina, Jack 155, 156
Rumsfeld, Donald 288
Russia (*see also* Soviet Union; USSR) 28, 40, 42, 45-47, 49-51, 5355, 56, 59, 60, 63, 69, 71, 72, 79, 111, 138, 143-145, 150, 169, 205, 211, 224, 230, 235, 247, 268, 269, 272, 273, 287, 310, 326, 330, 356, 396, 403-406, 408, 410-413, 416, 421, 422, 430, 436, 437
Rutherford, Ernest 8-11, 14, 15, 17, 24, 56, P7

S

sabotage 197-199, 290, 399
Sachs, Alexander 24
Safari research reactor 77, 214, 311, 438
    fuel for 128, 130, 132, 178, 201, 203, 233, 260, 267
    Safari-1 84, 101, 105-107, 109, 110, 119, 130, 133, 201, 233, 266, 447
Safeguards Agreements (*see* IAEA; INFCIRC)
Sahara Desert 62
Sakharov, Andrei 55
Salehi, Ali Akbar 416
Salvetti, Carlo 106
sampling 9, 58, 88, 150, 154, 160, 236, 237, 244, 248, 249, 252, 297
Samson option 288
San Francisco 425
sanctions (boycotts/embargoes)
    against Iran 418
    against Iraq 338
    against Israel 155, 318
    against Libya 363

541

against Pakistan   354, 360
against Rhodesia   123
against South Africa   94, 107, 123, 132, 133, 142, 147, 158, 164, 176, 178, 179, 181, 183, 185, 194, 195, 200, 204, 237, 252, 253, 263, 268, 269, 281, 299-301, 314, 318, 319, 334, 338
Sandia base   44
Sandia National Laboratories   156
Sänger, Eugen   46
Sarajevo   72
Sarkozy, Nicolas   199, 413
Sasharin, G.A.   429
Satellite Data Systems (SDS)   156
satellite launch vehicles (SLVs)   184, 318-320, 322
   RSA-3   186, CP10
   Shavit   185
satellites   33, 80, 83, 143, 146, 147, 150, 184, 185, 187, 217, 247, 299, 319, 320, 322, 356, 359
   Big Bird 1977-56A   139, 140
   Cosmos 922   138
   Cosmos 932   139
   GPS military   153
   KH-9 Hexagon series   139
   Kosmos 2019   317
   Navstar 5 and 6   153
   Ofeq   186
   Vela 6911   151-156
Saudi Arabia   406, 415, 418
Sauer, Joachim   432
Savimbi, Jonas   177
Savitsky, Valentin   402, 404
scams   272-274
Schell, Jonathan   403
Schmidt, Cecile   ii, 231
Schumann, T.E.W.   104, 114, 130
Schütze, Werner   47
Schwarz, Harry   230, 318
Scomi   362, 364, 367
Scope firm   367-369

Scotland   363, 413
Scott-Clark, Catherine   356
Seaborg, Glenn   32, 40, 61
Second World War (*see* wars)
Segrè, Emilio   21, 34
Sella, Aviem (Avi)   162
Semark, Paul   196
Semipalatinsk test site   52, 55, 394
Sensitive Compartmented Information (SCI)   162
separation elements   113, 126-129, 200-202, 246, 447, CP3
separative work units (SWU)   116, 117, 127, 128, 201
September 11 (9/11)   364, 396, 405, 406, 408, 423
Serber, Robert (Bob)   33
Serbia   72
Shabangu, Susan   339
Shah of Iran   298
Shahi, Agha   354
Shamir, Yitzhak   298-300, 318
Shapin, Stephen   221
Sharif, Nawaz   360, 365
Sharon, Ariel   291
Shavit missiles   186
Shavit satellite launch vehicles   185
Shearer, Jeremy   261, 266
sheep thyroids   154, 156
ships (*see also* boats)   44, 69, 158, 159, 164, 178, 364, 400-402, 408, 413, 423
   Aleksandrovsk   400, 401
   BBC China   364, 365, 367, 369, 370, 373, 386, 389, CP12
   Indigirka   400
   Mary Celeste   252
   Ridderschap van Holland   423
   USS Beale   402
   USS Randolf   402
Shlykov, Vitaly   143, 144
shock wave   37, 152
silicon   108
silicon carbide   205

INDEX

silos   396, 403, 404, 421
silver   30, 57, 63
Simon, Franz   25, 56
Simonstown Naval Base   143, 158
Simpson, John   326
Single Integrated Operational Plan (SIOP)   78, 395
SIPRI (*see* Stockholm ...)
Site X (*see also* Oak Ridge)   27
Sklodowska, Maria   50
Slabber, Johan   256, 268, 277, 311, CP14
Slebos, Henk   345, 348, 352, 361, 368
SMB Computers (Dubai)   361
Smit, André   377, 383
Smith, Ian   123
smuggling   112, 273, 274, 344, 354, 360, 361, 364, 376, 382, 389
Smuts, Jan   57, 58, 72, 73, 97
Smyth report   69
snap-back sanctions (*see also* sanctions)   418
Snowden, Edward   420
Soccer World Cup   409
Socialist Party (France)   297
sodium, liquid   100, 110, 111
Sokolski, Henry   318-320
solar energy   432, 434
Sole, Donald   61
Somchem   122, 134, 149, 186, 270, 320, 321, 443
Sony Pictures   420
Soreq Nuclear Research Centre   286, 294
source material   57, 87, 89
South Africa   100, 131, 184, 189, 311, 316, 343, 434, 471-474
  accession to the NPT (*see* Nuclear Non-Proliferation Treaty)
  Board of Governors, IAEA   xvi, 280, 315, 334, 335, 374
  Constitution   279, 280
  cooperation with Israel   285-301, 462-464
  delegation to Iraq   337, 338
  Initial report (*see* Initial Report)
  nuclear energy policy   434-438
  Referendum   255, 310
  sanctions (*see* sanctions)
  state of emergency   132, 179, 181
  strategy, nuclear   133, 134, 182, 188, 259, 434, 506-511
South African
  Air Force (SAAF)   136, 185, 186, 188, 189, 248, 264
  Council for the Non-Proliferation of Weapons of Mass Destruction   334, 374
  Defence Force (SADF)   133, 136, 137, 165, 173, 180, 189-192, 197, 216, 219, 220, 247, 259, 263, 264, 298
  Institute of International Affairs (SAIIA)   327
  Nuclear Energy Corporation (Necsa)   xv, xvi, 311, 340, 435, 436, 443
  Olympic Committee   334
  Police Service (SAPS)   148, 176, 198, 258, 259, 264, 372-378
South Korea   320, 397, 414, 437
South-West Africa (*see also* Namibia)   58, 131, 146, 169, 281
Southern Africa   123, 133, 169, 170, 177, 211, 226, 279, 291
Soviet Union (*see also* Russia; USSR)   xvi, 42, 43, 49, 51, 55, 56, 63, 69, 70, 74, 78, 79, 81-83, 86, 90, 104, 131, 138, 140, 143-146, 170, 209, 210, 212, 259, 307, 344, 353, 354, 356, 393, 394, 397-401, 406, 426, 429, 430
Soweto riots   132
space programmes   320
Spain   135, 383, 384, 399, 404

543

Sparks, Allister Haddon 296, 297
Spector, Leonard 244
spectrometer, mass 19
Speer, Albert 48
splitting of the nucleus (*see* atom; nucleus)
spy satellites (*see* satellites)
spying (*see* espionage)
Stadler, Herman 145
stages, enrichment 114, 126, 127, 246, 253, 447
stages, rockets 184, 186
Stalin, Joseph 40, 42, 48, 51-53, 79, 210, 393, 394, 398
Stalin organ 137, 147
Stalin prize 47
Standing Advisory Group
    on Nuclear Energy (SAGNE) 312
    on Safeguards Implementation (SAGSI) 312
    on Technical Assistance and Cooperation (SAGTAC) 312
Stanley, Robert 405
Stassfurt 45
State Security Agency (SSA) (South Africa) xvii
State Security Council (South Africa) 263
Staten Island 27
Steinkohlen-Elektrizität AG (Steag) 125
steel, maraging 352, 364, 384, 385
Steenbeck, Max 46, 47, 111
Steyn, J.L. (Hannes) 146, 218
Stimson, Henry 39, 42, 75
St Lucia testing range 316
Stockholm International Peace Research Institute (SIPRI) 138, 139
Stone & Webster 29
storage
    facilities 233, 236, 252, 264, 266, 270
    lockers CP8, CP9

scheme, pumped 432, 433
vaults 172, 173
Stott, Noel vii
Strassmann, Fritz 14, 17, 19
Strategic Air Command (SAC) 395, 396
Strategic Arms Reduction Treaties (START) 411
strategic points, inspection 88
stratosphere (*see also* atmosphere) 150
Strauss, Franz-Josef 124
Strauss, Lewis 80
stripper section 126, 127
Stumpf, Waldo E. iv, 124, 160, 171, 181, 203, 216, 218, 220, 241, 260, 261, 265-267, 274-277, 281, 296, 311, 312, 316, 334, 335, 338-340, 390, CP14
Stuxnet 420
submarines 25, 135, 156, 164, 178, 194, 204, 396, 397, 401-404, 413
    B-59 402, 404
    Nautilus 69
Subsidiary Arrangements 87
Suez Crisis 78, 285, 412
superpowers 235, 394, 395, 418
supplier countries/groups (*see also* Nuclear Suppliers Group) 79, 82-85, 104, 110, 200, 322-324, 352, 369
Swaziland 292
Sweden 328
Sweeney, Charles 41
Switzerland 14, 143, 144, 195, 332, 343, 350-353, 362, 367, 368, 371-373, 382-384, 387
Synatom 195
Syria 163, 244, 289, 292, 329, 355, 406
Szilard, Leo 18-22, 40, P1

T
Tabor, W.H. P8
tactical warheads (*see also* warheads) 411

INDEX

Tahir, Buhary Seyed Abu   361-364, 367, 368, 372, 380, 381, 383, 385, 387, 388
tails, depleted (*see also* uranium, depleted)   116, 128, CP3
Taiwan   78, 154, 310, 320
Taleb, Nassim Nicholas   423
Taliban   406
tamper (neutron reflector)   36
Tanzania   278, 279
Taranto   364, 365
Target Committee   40
Tasmania   154
Taylor, Geoffrey   34
technetium   107
Teflon   115, 237, 246, 314, 315
Tehrik-e-Taliban Pakistan   406
Teller, Edward   21, 26, 53-55, 71, 221, P3
Teller-Ulam configuration/device   54, 55
terror bombing   43
terrorism   xv, xvi, 64, 108, 109, 161, 251, 291, 294, 309, 363, 364, 371, 394, 399, 403, 406-409, 414, 418
Tessier, Georges   60
test   35, 38, 48, 50, 56, 63, 69, 70, 74, 90, 92, 104, 105, 109, 112, 117, 119, 122, 125, 130, 139, 141-143, 155, 158-160, 163, 164, 166, 167, 169-172, 186, 187, 203, 204, 214, 251, 255, 256, 286-288, 298, 299, 316-318, 321, 360, 361, 372, 394, 397, 415, 421, 422, 428
   atmospheric/above-ground   55, 59, 86, 150, 151, 156, 182
   ballistics   134
   cold   136-138, 140, 145, 147, 149, 168, 358
   dirty   190
   oceanic/underwater   44, 54, 86, 150, 151, 154, 157, 257, 268

   peaceful (*see* peaceful ...)
   shafts   91, 136, 190-192, 247, 270, 275, 359, CP15
   underground   55, 59, 62, 133, 135, 150, 165, 182, 327
tests (*see also* bombs; missiles; operations)
   Castle Bravo   55
   Chicago Pile-1   28
   Gerboise Bleue   62
   Ivy-Mike   135
   Jerboa, Blue/Green/Red/White   62
   Stalin organ   137, 147
   Trinity   37, 39, 40, 48, 49, 69, 75, P2, P3, P8
Thabana (Radiation Hill)   167, 233, 314
Thales   4
Thar Desert   91
thermite   43
thermodynamics   100, 125, 134
thermonuclear bombs (*see* bombs)
Thiessen, Peter Adolf   46, 47
Thin Man   35
Thobejane, (Mr) Lord Senti   340
Thomson, Joseph John (J.J.)   8, 14
Thor Chemicals   274
thorium   89, 98
Thorne, Carl   215
Thorstensen, Svein   239, 240, 248
Three Mile Island, accident   426, 428, 430
Tibbets, Paul   41
Tinian Island   41
Tinner, Friedrich, Urs and Marco   345, 362, 364, 367-369, 371, 384
Tobey, William   377
Togo, Shigenori   42
Tohoku earthquake   423-425
Tokyo   39, 41, 43
Traco firm   362
Tradefin Engineering   64, 372-374, 376-378, 381-385, 390, CP11, CP13

transfer, of knowledge, materials and technology 76, 92, 94, 132, 144, 194, 225
Treaty
   African Nuclear-Weapon-Free Zone 280, 448
   Almelo 111
   Comprehensive Nuclear-Test-Ban 326, 330
   Fissile Material Cut-off 326, 422
   Non-Proliferation of Nuclear Weapons (*see* Nuclear Non-Proliferation Treaty)
   of Pelindaba iv, 86, 280, 448
   Partial Test Ban 150, 151, 157, 445
   Prevention of an Arms Race in Outer Space (PAROS) 422
   Tlatelolco 86
   Versailles 72
trigger 34, 175, 296, 308, CP5
trigger list 89, 93, 94
trinitrotoluene (TNT) 37, 41, 44, 54, 55, 62, 63, 91, 131, 181, 190, 396, 404
Trinity test (*see* tests)
Tripoli 363, 365, 379
tritium 12, 26, 34, 54, 122, 175, 273, 290, 296, 297, 308, 448
Trombay 357
Truman, Harry 39-42, 48, 53, 54, 394, 397, 398
Truth and Reconciliation Commission (TRC) 145, 197
tsunami 423, 424, 426
Tube Alloys programme 25, 40, 57, 307
Tuck, James 33, 34, 57, 221
tungsten 37, 134
Tunisia 423
Tuohy, Tom 308, 309
Turkey 76, 362-364, 367, 368, 377383, 390, 401, 415
Tutu, Desmond 411

U
Ucor (*see* Uranium Enrichment Corporation ...)
UF_6 (*see* uranium hexafluoride)
Ukraine 330, 405, 406, 410, 413, 427
Ulam, Stanislaf 54, 55
ultraviolet rays 11, 152
Umkhonto we Sizwe (MK) 197, 198, 310
Union Carbide Corporation 29, 345
UNITA (National Union for the Total Independence of Angola) 177
United Kingdom (UK) (*see also* Britain) 79, 118, 286, 288, 333, 370, 415, 416
United Nations (UN) (*see also* resolutions; sanctions) 76, 80, 81, 90, 101, 122, 141, 148, 164, 180, 185, 194, 212, 254, 255, 291, 299, 317, 324, 326, 332, 338, 379
   Atomic Energy Commission (UN-AEC) 74
   Charter 73, 123
   Conference on Disarmament 333, 336, 421, 422
   General Assembly (UNGA) ii, iii, 67, 73, 75, 79, 84, 104, 121, 123, 147, 157, 176, 281, 292, 293
   inspectors 379, 417
   Office for Disarmament Affairs (UNODA) 327
   Security Council (UNSC) 120, 121, 123, 124, 147, 176, 179, 204, 211, 213, 225-227, 237, 239, 258, 270, 281, 334, 343, 363, 416, 418
   Special Commission (Unscom) 226, 227, 266, 338
United States of America (US/USA) (*see also* America)
   Air Force (*see also* AFTAC) 39, 154, 400, 404, 407, 412
   Congress 39, 132, 194, 219, 369, 395, 402, 418
   Department of Energy (USDOE)

INDEX

153, 194, 214, 274, 377
Department of State 214, 265, 275, 287, 352
National Security Agency (NSA) 420
Universal Declaration of Human Rights 123
uranium (U) 9, 12, 14, 17, 18, 22, 26, 27, 38, 41, 46, 47, 52, 54, 57-61, 69, 73, 79, 80, 90, 91, 97-99, 101, 102, 119, 120, 131, 132, 136, 141, 159, 175, 184, 187, 193, 194, 219, 223, 229, 234, 235, 237, 238, 242, 248, 251, 256, 267, 285, 295, 297, 307, 309, 313, 347, 349, 379, 407, 408, 441, 448, CP2, CP3
   aluminium alloy 104, 107-109
   anthropogenic 250
   cylinders 105, 127, 243, 244, 252, 297, 307, 351, 363, 364, 378
   depleted 89, 116, 126-128, 200, 233, 243, 244, 252, 270, 272, 377, 378, 441, CP2
   dioxide 196, 205, 308
   enrichment 20, 100, 110, 111, 113, 114, 121, 125, 169, 228, 239, 249, 250, 261, 262, 290, 344, 348, 357, 360, 362, 373, 378, 382, 387, 390, 415, 416, 431, 434, 437, 441, 442, CP2, CP3
   enrichment plants (*see also* plants) 25, 29, 30, 35, 86, 112, 113, 116, 118, 124-126, 134, 197, 200, 214, 224, 344, 346, 350-352, 356, 360, 362, 363, 367, 373, 374, 381, 382, 387, 390, 414, 419
   hexafluoride (UF$_6$) 29, 30, 35, 113-116, 126-128, 166, 168, 195, 200, 201-203, 217, 233, 244, 246, 249, 250, 252, 253, 260, 350-353, 357, 363, 364, 377, 383, 384, 434, 448
   highly enriched (HEU) i, xvi, 30, 35, 63, 104, 106-108, 116, 117, 121, 126, 128, 129, 134, 135, 137, 145, 149, 157, 159, 163, 165, 167, 168, 170-174, 183, 191, 214, 217, 218, 220, 222, 230, 233, 241, 243, 250, 253, 257, 260, 261, 266, 267, 271, 275, 312, 314, 315, 358, 415, 438, 442
   irradiated (*see* irradiation)
   low-enriched 108, 109, 128, 134, 191, 195, 204, 252, 253, 260, 417, 438, 443
   natural 20, 28, 47, 60, 91, 100, 110, 116, 125, 128, 134, 135, 149, 217, 243, 250, 253, 272, 307, 377, 378, 443
   oxide 28, 45, 46, 196, 203, 233
   tetrachloride (UCl$_4$) 30
   U-233; U-235; U-236; U-238; U-239 (*see also* isotopes) 19, 20, 24, 25, 29-37, 89, 108, 116, 129, 130, 233, 243, 244, 245, 249, 250, 252-254, 448, 449, CP1
Uranium Committee 24, 25
Uranium Enrichment Act 121
Uranium Enrichment Corporation of South Africa Ltd (Ucor) 99-101, 116, 121, 124, 125, 128, 165, 166, 200, 201, 209, 246, 250, 251, 350, 351, 448
uranium-silicide fuel 108
Uranmaschine 47, 48
Uranverein 48
Urenco 111, 251, 344, 346, 347, 349, 350, 363, 377, 380, 449
USSR (*see also* Russia; Soviet Union) 42, 46, 49-53, 55, 56, 60, 62, 63, 69, 70, 78, 138, 140, 141, 143, 145, 150, 153, 209-212, 261, 394, 395, 397, 401, 403, 404, 410, 412
US-UK Mutual Defence Agreement 308

547

V

vacuum pumps 237, 349, 350, 373, 383
vacuum valves 362, 384
Vajpayee, Atal Bihari 358, 359
Valindaba 101, 121, 126, 134, 148, 168, 214, 275, 297, P4
valves 115, 127, 200, 202, 274, 350, 351, 362, 364, 383, 384, 425, P5
Van de Graaff particle accelerator 105
Van den Bergh, Hendrik 295, 296
Van der Walt, Richardt 137, 138, 170, 256
Van Doornse Transmissie (VDT) 352
Van Eck Committee 117-119
Van Eck, Hendrik 118, 119
Van Heerden, Niel 211
Van Middlesworth, Lester 154
Van Vuuren, Fires 187
Vance, Cyrus 141, 148, 258, 259, 465, 466
Vanderbijlpark 351, 368, 372-376, CP11
Vanunu, Mordechai 289, 290
Vastrap 136-147, 149, 168, 183, 191, 192, 247, 248, 270, 275, 449, CP15, P5
Veerman, Frits 346, 347
Vela Incident 747 151-156
Vela satellite (see satellites)
Venda 309
ventilation grilles 166, CP8
ventilation towers 114, 125-127, P4
Verwoerd, Hendrik F. 106, 114, 115
Vetrov, Vladimir 144
Victoria (Australia) 154
Vienna International Centre (VIC) 82
Vietnam 412
Viljoen, Constand 264
Volkseenheidskomitee 271
Volkstaatraad 271
Volmer, Max 46
Von Ardenne, Manfred 46, 47, 111

Von Baeckmann, Adolf 239, 241, 252, 267
Von Braun, Wernher 46
Von Hippel, Frank 438
Von Hirschberg, Carl 169
Von Kármán, Theodor 21
Von Neumann, John 21
Von Weizsäcker, Carl Friedrich 45
Von Wielligh, Nic i, iv, v, 234, 311, 312, 314, 325, 372, 375, 378, 379, CP9
Von Wielligh-Steyn, Lydia iv, v, CP15
Vorster, John 119, 120, 142, 169, 292, 295-297
vortex tube 100, 112-115, 117-119, 125-128, 250, 449
VVERs (Water-Water Energetic Reactors) 436, 437

W

Waddington, P.A.J. 258
Waldheim, Kurt 87
Wannenburg, Jannie 201, 241, P6
warheads 135-137, 145, 149, 166, 170-172, 174, 181-183, 187, 188-191, 218-220, 223, 224, 250, 293, 297, 299, 309, 317, 318, 329, 330, 379, 380, 400-402, 404, 406, 407, 411, 413, 415, 419, 421, CP5
wars (see also Hiroshima)
    Anglo-Boer 102, 103
    Arab-Israeli 292, 299
    Border 164, 176, 185, 281, 282
    "Bush-Blair" 370
    Cold iii, 31, 55, 74, 81, 133, 136, 138, 143, 235, 323, 324, 328, 330, 353, 394, 402, 404, 410, 413, 414
    First World 11, 17, 72, 98
    Great 72
    Gulf 93, 238, 313, 327, 338
    Indochina 60
    Indo-Pakistani 356
    Korean 75, 78, 146, 297, 397
    Opium 63

INDEX

Second World iii, 7, 21, 32, 38, 39, 45, 47, 49, 53, 55, 56, 59, 60, 67, 72, 73, 99, 111, 145, 261, 279, 289, 344, 396, 412, 431
Six-Day 159, 292
Spanish-American 399
Third World 431
Yom Kippur War 159, 288, 289, 292
Warsaw Treaty countries 133
water, heavy (*see* heavy water)
weapon systems unit (WSU) 219
weapons (*see also* bombs; devices; missiles; tests)
   biological 226, 227, 315, 321, 331, 337, 370
   boosted 182, 290
   chemical 226, 227, 293, 315, 321, 331, 337, 363, 365, 370
   conventional 41, 109, 132, 159, 164, 165, 287, 289, 290, 293, 294, 317, 359
   design 33-35, 52-56, 64, 135, 149, 165, 171, 175, 176, 184, 190, 224, 268, 286, 309, 317, 358, 371, 380, 382, 412, 415
   dismantlement (*see* dismantlement)
   gun-assembled/gun-type 34, 165, 172, 175, 181, 191, 219, 442, CP1
   laser-guided 298
   non-strategic 411
   nuclear (*see also* bombs) 33, 94, 100, 135, 174, 218, 445
   programme v, vi, 25, 26, 45, 47-50, 69, 97, 102, 112, 133, 138, 140, 142, 144, 147, 154, 158, 159, 160, 176, 180, 181, 183, 187, 189, 193, 214, 216, 217, 220, 222, 224, 228, 238, 255, 259, 263, 264, 269, 275-277, 285, 286, 311, 312, 335, 336, 338, 343, 354, 355, 365, 394, 419
   stockpiles (*see* nuclear arsenals; nuclear stockpiles)
   strategic 400, 401, 411, 421, 422
   upgrading/modernising of 298, 330, 331, 337, 356, 405, 412, 413
weapons-grade material xvi, 167, 169, 217, 234, 235, 241, 243, 246, 261, 270, 344, 357, 407, 419, 449
weapons of mass destruction v, vi, 311, 315, 321, 325-327, 329, 331, 332, 334, 337, 345, 364, 370, 374, 388
Weinberg, Alvin 106
Weissman, Steve 159
Welgegund farm 102
Wellerstein, Alex 43
West German Federal Nuclear Research Centre (GfK) 124, 125
Westinghouse Corporation 29, 195, 196, 206, 437
Wheeler, Thomas (Tom) 325, 327
whistle meter 115
Whiting, Neville 311
Wigner effect 308
Wigner, Eugene Paul 21, 287
WikiLeaks 387, 388
Wilhelm II, Emperor 71
Wilkinson, Rodney Lawrence and Heather 197
wind energy 432, 434
Winkler, Bert 109
Wisser, Erika 375
Wisser, Gerhard 202, 251, 350, 351, 364, 372, 373, 375, 376, 380-388, 390, CP12
Wittle, Frank 99
Witvlei Council 181, 182, 189, 190, 486-496
Wohlstetter, Albert 396
World Bank 360
world market (*see* international market)
World Nuclear Association (WNA) 430
World Trade Center 408

549

X

X-rays 11, 54, 152, 153, 321, 427

Y

Yadlin, Amos 418
yellowcake 450
Yeltsin, Boris 144, 210, 272, 430
yield 37, 41, 44, 54, 55, 62, 63, 91, 175, 181, 190, 273, 394, 396, 404, 450
Y-plant (*see* plants)
Yugoslavia 323

Z

Zangger, Claude 89
Zangger Committee 89, 92-94, 274, 312, 313, 315, 322, 324, 450
Zedong, Mao 63, 64, 397
Zeeberg, Amos 394
Zia ul-Haq, Muhammad 349, 353, 354, 356
Zifferero, Maurizzio 227
Zinn, Walter 19
Zionism 293
Zippe, Gernot 46, 47, 111, 344
zirconium 196, 203, 425, 427
Z-plant (*see* plants)
Zuma, Jacob 197
Zwartkop Air Force Museum 186, 298, CP10